Residential Conveyancing

Residential Conveyancing

Lorraine Richardson M.A. (Cantab)

CILEX | Education

Disclaimer

ISBN: 978-1-911698-35-7
E-ISBN: 978-1-911698-36-4

First paperback edition 2023
Second paperback edition 2025

Layout by codemantra U.S. LLC

British Library Cataloguing in Publications Data
A catalogue record for this book is available from the British Library

Printed by CILEX Education in the United Kingdom.
CILEX Education
Kempston Manor,
Kempston,
Bedford,
MK42 7AB

www.cilex.org.uk

Cover image: AzmanJaka/iStock

CILEX titles are printed by Mimeo, who are very proud to be a part of the Woodland Trust's Woodland Carbon Capture Scheme via Premier Paper. Mimeo partner with Woodland Carbon because 100% of the money they give is spent on planting deciduous trees in the UK. Papers are from sustainable sources and waste is recycled. Mimeo continue to use only Forest Stewardship Council accredited paper in their printed items.

About Lorraine Richardson

Lorraine is an experienced property solicitor and trainer who is a popular conference and CPD speaker. Lorraine is now freelance, but when in practice, she ran a branch office and was a partner and the compliance officer for legal practice for her firm.

She also designs and delivers property and legal skills-related courses. Lorraine has developed a skill for writing and delivering webinars and aims to produce work that is both interesting and accessible for the viewer. Lorraine is the major writer for the monthly update journal for practitioners, the '*Practical Lawyer*' and her books *A Practical Guide to Document Signing and Electronic Signatures for Conveyancers* and *A Practical Guide to Residential Freehold Conveyancing* have been published.

Lorraine has set up her own company, Adapt Law Limited, and offers property-related courses and webinars.

Summary of Changes

General

This course book has had some additional content included, as well as various updating changes, including in relation to forms.

Chapter 1

The Law Society's "Code for signing and exchanging property contracts 2024" is referred to, although, at the date of writing, it has not yet been introduced.

The 5th edition of the Law Society's Property Information Form (TA6) is introduced and has been added to the Appendix. The current position in relation to the controversy about its introduction is outlined. The Completion Information and Undertakings Form (TA13) has also been added to the Appendix.

Chapter 2

Changes to stamp duty land tax have been made (as at April 2025) together with links to current rates for land transaction tax in Wales.

New case:

***Waller-Edwards v One Savings Bank Plc* [2024] EWCA Civ 30**

Chapter 4

The removal of the right to send certified copies of unregistered title deeds in first registration applications to the Land Registry is explained.

Chapter 6

A new section dealing with the required mental capacity to buy and sell land has been included at **6.11**.

Chapter 7

Changes to the time limits for enforcement action for breaches of planning control and building regulations are set out.

Chapter 8

The Law Society's practice note on the impact of climate change is referred to.

Chapter 9

More information on the Law Society's "Code for signing and exchanging property contracts 2024" is included.

Chapter 10

The New Homes Quality Board, set up under the **Building Safety Act 2022**, is described.

Future changes to new build warranties under the **Building Safety Act 2022** are outlined.

Chapter 11

The **Renters' Rights Bill** is referred to.

Chapter 12

Changes to "historic" rentcharges under the **Leasehold and Freehold Reform Act 2024** are described.

Chapter 13

Changes to ground rents in residential houses and flats introduced by the **Leasehold Reform (Ground Rent) Act 2022** are set out.

The impact of future changes to enfranchisement rights of long leaseholders under the the **Leasehold and Freehold Reform Act 2024** is set out.

The key provisions of the **Renters' Rights Bill** are outlined.

Guide to the Book

This course book contains a range of features which have been developed to help support your learning and reinforce your understanding. The guided tour below explains how to use these features to get the most from your study.

Activity

Follow the link below to the Law Society's wesbite and download the Protocol

https://www.lawsociety.org.uk/topics/property/conveyancing-protocol

Keep it for reference throughout this course book.

Activities

In each chapter you are presented with activities which engage you with the content and help you to develop research skills, explore topics in more depth and consolidate your knowledge.

1.12 Chapter summary

(1) Conveyancing is the process of transferring estates or interests by document.

(2) Generally legal estates and legal interests can be created or transferred only by deed.

(3) The Crown owns all land in England and Wales.

Chapter Summaries

At the end of each chapter the key points are summarised, allowing you to reinforce your understanding before moving on to study the next topic. The summaries can also be used for quick revision.

INLAND REVENUE PRODUCED | £750

THIS CONVEYANCE is made the 15th day of November 1958 BETWEEN Frank Jennings of 15 The Chase, Harcourt Newton, Cambridgeshire (the Vendor) of the one part and Lillian Stebbings of Little Timbers, Lakeview Road, Harcourt Newton, Cambridgeshire (the Purchaser) of the other part

Figures

Figures have been designed to help define complex issues and clearly illustrate key concepts.

Example

Usually (e.g. in a situation where a husband and wife buy a house jointly), the trustees are also the beneficiaries. So, if, for example, Jenna and Sam bought a house together, they would be the trustees holding the legal estate. At the same time, they would also be the beneficiaries in equity holding the land on behalf of each other. They would therefore hold a beneficial or equitable interest in the property as well as being the legal owners.

Examples

Examples provide you with an opportunity to contextualise what you have learnt and explore legal concepts in a real world setting.

Link to practice

Read the CILEX Regulation Risk Management: Property Fraud factsheet at https://cilexregulation.org.uk/wp-content/uploads/2018/11/Cilex-doc-3-Property-fraud.pdf.

Link to practice

Short explanations or scenarios, designed to help you relate what you are learning to the work of a conveyancer or private client practitioner.

Examples of items which HMRC will normally regard as chattels	Examples of items which HMRC will normally regard as fixtures
Carpets (fitted or otherwise)	Fitted kitchen units and sinks
Curtains and blinds	Wall mounted ovens and agas
Freestanding furniture	Central heating systems
Kitchen white goods (unless fully integrated)	Fitted bathroom sanitary ware
Light shades and fittings (unless recessed)	Intruder alarm systems

Tables

Tables have been designed to present information clearly.

News

In the news...

Unmarried father has half share in house cut to 10%

A controversial ruling which awarded an absent father half the value of the family home he left 18 years ago was yesterday overturned by judges – who awarded him just 10 per cent

. . . Supreme Court judges . . . said . . . it was the duty of the courts to decide what the intentions of a couple were during the course of their relationship and afterwards . . . They decided a "'fair" split of assets in the case of Mr Kernott – whose name was on the deeds along with Miss Jones – would be for him to receive just 10 per cent . . .

Daily Mail*, *10 November 2011

News

News items link the material to real world concepts.

Contents

Table of Cases

Abbey National Building Society v Cann [1990] 1 All ER 1085

Aston Cantlow and Wilmcote with Billesley Parochial Church Council v Wallbank [2003] 3 All ER 1213

Ayannuga v Swindells [2012] EWCA Civ 1789

Bakewell Management Ltd v Brandwood [2004] 2 All ER 305

Barclays Bank plc v O'Brien [1993] 4 All ER 417

Barclays Bank v Weeks [1998] 3 All ER 213

Becker v Partridge [1966] 2 All ER 266

Birdlip Limited v Hunter [2015] EWHC 808 (HC)

Birmingham Midshires Mortgage Services Ltd v Sabherwal [1999] 80 P & CR 256

Circular Facilities (London) Ltd v Sevenoaks District Council [2005] Env LR 35

Citadel Management v Thompson [1999] 1 FLR 21

Clarke v Ramuz [1891] 2 QB 456

Cottingham v Attey, Bower & Jones (a Firm) [2000] EGCS 48

Cuckmere Brick Co Ltd v Mutual Finance Ltd [1971] 2 All ER 633

Cumberland Court v Taylor [1963] 2 All ER 536

Davies v Jones [2009] EWCA Civ 1164

Domb v Isoz [1980] 1 All ER 942

E Surv Ltd v Goldsmith Williams Solicitors [2015] EWCA Civ 1147

Elliston v Reacher [1908] 2 Ch 374

Federated Homes v Mill Lodge Properties [1980] 1 WLR 594

Ferrishurst v Wallcite [1999] 1 All ER 977

Fidler v Secretary of State for Communities and Local Government [2010] EWHC 143 (Admin)

First National Bank plc v Achampong 147 SJLB 419

First National Commercial Bank v Loxleys [1996} 141 SJLB 6

Freeguard v Rogers [1999] 1 WLR 375

Goodman v Elwood [2013] EWCA Civ 1103

Grindal v Hooper [1999] EGCS 150

Halsall v Brizell [1957] Ch 169

Harcus Sinclair v Your Lawyers [2021] UKSC 32

Harris v Wyre Forest Borough Council [1989] 2 All ER 514

Hart v Burbidge; Samways v Burbidge [2014] EWCA Civ 992

Hole & Pugsley v Sumption [2001] LSG 32

In the Estate of Crippen [1911] All ER Rep 207

In the Estate of Hall [1914] P.1

In the Estate of Jones [1927] 43 TLR 324

Janmohamed v Hassam [1976] 241 EG 609

Jones v Kernott [2011] UKSC 53

Khan v Crossland [2012] WTLR 841

Lee-Parker v Izzet (No. 2) [1972] 2 All ER 800

Link Lending Ltd v Bustard [2010] EWCA Civ 424

Liverpool City Council v Irwin [1977] AC 239

Midland Bank Trust Co v Green [1981] 1 All ER 153

Morrells of Oxford v Oxford United Football Club [2000] 04 EG 147

Mortgage Corporation v Shaire [2000] 80 P & CR 280

Mortgage Express v Bowerman [1996] 2 All ER 836

Nickerson v Barraclough [1981] Ch 426

North Eastern Properties Ltd v Coleman & Quinn Conveyancing [2010] EWCA Civ 277

Pankhania v Chandegra [2012] EWCA Civ 1438

Patel v Daybells [2001] 32 EG 87

Penn v Bristol & West [1997] 3 All ER 470

P&P Property Ltd v Owen White & Catlin LLP and Dreamvar (UK) Ltd v Mishcon de Reya [2018] (Dreamvar) EWCA Civ 1082

Re Duce and Boots Cash Chemist (Southern) Ltd's Contract [1937] 3 All ER 788

Re King's Will Trusts [1964] 1 All ER 833

Re North East Property Buyers' Litigation [2012] EWCA Civ 17

Rhone v Stephens [1994] 1 WLR 765

Roberts v Lawton [2016] UKUT 395 (TCC)

Royal Bank of Scotland v Etridge (No. 2) [2001] 4 All ER 449

Santander v RA Legal Solicitors [2014] EWCA Civ 183

Saunders v Vautier [1841] Cr & Ph 240

Scarfe v Adams [1981] 1 All ER 843

Selby District Council v Samuel Smith Old Brewery (Tadcaster) Ltd [2001] 80 P & CR 466

Smith v Eric S Bush (a Firm) [1989] 2 All ER 514

Spiro v Glencrown Properties [1991] 2 WLR 931

Stack v Dowden [2007] UKHL 17

Introduction

Welcome to this Professional Stage – Residential Conveyancing course book. This is the part of your conveyancing studies which overlays more detailed content on the introduction to conveyancing and "black letter law" which you have encountered on the Foundation and Advanced courses.

There will be some areas of practice in this course book which we recap and which you have come across before. However, the objective of this course book is to add further detail and explanation to key aspects of the conveyancing process to enable a conveyancer working at the level of the Professional Stage to deal effectively with the more complex areas that they will encounter in practice.

The Professional Stage – Residential Conveyancing syllabus focuses heavily on subject areas which practitioners are likely to encounter in their everyday work. HM Land Registry (HMLR) features heavily, including consideration of the importance of title plans and property extent, and common restrictions encountered in conveyancing and how to deal with them.

This course book will also consider a range of more complex residential conveyancing transactions to assist practitioners to evaluate how best to advance the transaction and protect the client's interests. These include acting on a sale of part and a new build transaction, acting in a probate transaction and dealing with a deed of easement.

In addition, the course book will consider in detail standard aspects of the conveyancing transaction such as drafting the contract, pre-contract searches and enquiries and problems between exchange and completion such as the death of a contracting party. Throughout the course book we will consider key risks and steps required to mitigate those risks.

Where we talk in this course book about a particular regulator and their requirements, we will refer specifically to the lawyers whom they regulate (for example, CILEX Regulation and chartered legal executives). However, many different lawyers can carry out conveyancing work, so when we talk about the conveyancing process more generally, we will refer to "conveyancers" to include all who carry out this work.

Activities and links to practice

Your course book will contain activities to enhance your learning. Where there is an opportunity for you to widen your knowledge and engage with the material, an activity will be set. It might ask you to go to a website or read a document – in all cases, there are no "answers" or other information provided for these activities. They do not form part of your assessment – they are just for your own reference and to help you locate more information about the points discussed in the course book.

In addition, we will give you "links to practice" – which are short explanations or scenarios, designed to help you relate what you are learning to the work of a conveyancer. If you work in a conveyancing firm, you can ask how your firm handles particular aspects of the conveyancing transaction as you come across them in your course book.

By the end of this course book you will be able to:

(1) Identify appropriate steps and advise the client accordingly in relation to a residential conveyancing transaction.

(2) Investigate a registered and an unregistered title and explain the steps required to remedy any title defects.

(3) Determine the appropriate action to take to deal with commonly encountered HMLR issues.

(4) Consider a range of more complex residential conveyancing transactions and evaluate how best to advance the transaction and protect the client's interests.

(5) Draft a range of undertakings, a more complex contract, a straightforward transfer of part (TP1), or a straightforward declaration of trust.

(6) Identify situations that potentially give rise to conflicts of interest, issues of professional ethics or other issues under the applicable Codes of Conduct.

CHAPTER 1

Overview of the conveyancing transaction

1.1 Introduction

When considering more complex conveyancing issues and transactions, it is essential to remember the underlying legal principles and the basic conveyancing process which will be followed for all transactions, whether freehold or leasehold. A seller does not "own" land; as we know, they hold an estate in land which is either the freehold estate or the leasehold estate. However, it is a convenient shorthand to refer to land "ownership" and we will continue to do that in this course book.

This chapter will cover:

- what is conveyancing?
- the nature of rights in land;
- key stages of the conveyancing process – a recap;
- the use of checklists;
- software solutions.

1.2 What is conveyancing?

Conveyancing is the process of transferring estates or interests by document. In general, legal estates and legal interests can be created or transferred only by deed. We will encounter various deeds in this course book including, a transfer of whole (TR1), a transfer of part (TP1) and a deed of easement.

Because conveyancing is concerned with the transfer of abstract rights, rather than of a tangible object such as a TV or a car, there are different procedures and different considerations for the parties involved.

(1) **When acting for a seller**

It is necessary to prove the ownership of the estate or interest being sold. The method by which a seller does this will vary as there are two conveyancing systems in existence:

(a) the older **unregistered** system, where a seller proves ownership or title by producing the deeds and documents tracing the ownership of the relevant estate being sold over a period of time, usually at least 15 years.

(b) the newer **registered** system, where proof of ownership is by the production of an official copy of the register held at HMLR. This is the more common system and is more straightforward.

(2) **When acting for a buyer**

In addition to being satisfied that the seller is entitled to sell the property, further investigations are necessary. The extent of the property being sold should be checked. We will look at the importance of HMLR plans later in the course book. It is also necessary to ensure that any rights of way or other rights the buyer wishes to acquire are included. We will look at the creation of new rights via a transfer of part (TP1) and a deed of easement later in the course book.

A buyer will also want to know whether there are any restrictions on their intended use of the property, in particular whether any third parties have rights over the land they wish to buy or whether there are any public matters, such as planning control, affecting it.

1.3 The nature of rights in land

Let's briefly recap on rights in land, estates and interests as they are central to the understanding of the conveyancing process.

Although it is common to talk of buying and owning land, it is not the land itself which is being acquired but specific rights relating to the land. It may sound surprising but, technically speaking, the Crown owns all land in England and Wales.

Individual landowners hold their land ultimately from the Crown. Historically, the land would have been held in return for services such as bringing in the harvest or providing soldiers, but this is of little importance nowadays. However, because all land is technically owned by the Crown, it is only the estates and interests, which exist separately from the land, which can be owned and transferred.

Activity

The organisation that deals with land belonging to the Crown is called The Crown Estate.

"Crown land" includes land belonging to the King as monarch, the King's private property, property of the duchies and government land.

Who owns The Crown Estate?

The Crown Estate belongs to the reigning monarch "in right of The Crown", that is, it is owned by the monarch for the duration of their reign, by virtue of their accession to the throne. But it is not the private property of the monarch – it cannot be sold by the monarch, nor do revenues from it belong to the monarch.

The Government also does not own The Crown Estate. It is managed by an independent organisation – established by statute – headed by a Board (also known as The Crown Estate Commissioners), and the surplus revenue from the estate is paid each year to the Treasury for the benefit of the nation's finances.

Does The Crown Estate assume management of unclaimed land?

Freehold land can sometimes effectively become ownerless. When this happens, title to the land may, in certain circumstances, revert to the Crown as the ultimate owner of all the land in England, Wales or Northern Ireland. This process is called "escheat". It can happen in a variety of situations.

The most common is where a registered company is wound up and dissolved without all its property being accounted for in the liquidation.

The Crown Estate deals with escheat where the land falls within England, Wales or Northern Ireland and outside Cornwall and the County Palatine of Lancaster – where escheat is dealt with by the Duchy of Cornwall and the Duchy of Lancaster respectively.

Escheat should not to be confused with what in common parlance might be called "unclaimed land". Land can often have no apparent owner, but The

Crown Estate will not generally be involved with such land unless it is in fact ownerless in circumstances where escheat applies.

Land comprised in the estates of persons who died without making a will and without known family is administered by the Treasury Solicitor.

Follow the link below to The Crown Estate website:

www.thecrownestate.co.uk

Look for the FAQs under the "Resources" tab and look up the answers to the following interesting questions:

How did The Crown Estate come into being?
What is the Crown Estate's relationship with the Treasury?
How are properties and land subject to escheat sold back into private ownership?

Look at the remaining FAQs and under the "What we do" tab, click on the Asset map. You will see the assets currently held by The Crown Estate. You will note how much of the land is actually part of the foreshore and seabed. You will also note the extent of their activities on the seabed and coast much of which revolves around energy, windfarms and marine planning. The Crown Estate is therefore very much an active organisation.

These estates and interests are classified as legal estates, legal interests or equitable interests.

(1) **s1(1) Law of Property Act 1925** (**LPA 1925**) states that there are only two **legal estates**:

   (a) the "fee simple absolute in possession" – more commonly known as the **freehold** estate;

   (b) the "term of years absolute" – more commonly known as the **leasehold** estate.

The word "estate" relates to the duration of the land ownership, as land must be held of the Crown for a certain duration. The freehold estate is the best type of estate in terms of duration. It indicates a grant of land from the Crown that lasts forever, whereas a leasehold estate lasts for a defined period of time which is determined by the length of the lease (e.g. 99 years).

(2) **s1(2) LPA 1925** lists the five **legal interests**. These include legal easements (e.g. rights of way) and legal mortgages.

These interests are rights that other people have over the land; for example, a neighbour might have a right of way over the garden (an easement) and a mortgage lender would have an interest in the home over which the mortgage was created, enabling the lender to sell the land if the mortgage was not paid.

(3) **s1(3) LPA 1925** provides that all other estates or interests in land are **equitable interests**, for example, restrictive covenants, rights of beneficiaries under a trust of land and equitable mortgages.

The main significance of the classification into legal and equitable interests lies in determining whether an interest will be enforceable against future owners of the land, that is, whether the interest will "bind" later owners. This will be of great relevance to someone buying a house as the buyer will want to know about any rights which will affect their property ownership, for example whether they will have to comply with a covenant not to use the house for business purposes. In general terms, the rules differ according to whether the interest is legal or equitable and whether the land has registered or unregistered title.

In addition, it is now possible to register an estate in commonhold under the **Commonhold and Leasehold Reform Act 2002**. Commonhold is a form of freehold title which is rarely used and will not be covered further in this course book. However, it is possible that commonhold may be reinvigorated as means of owning land, so conveyancing practitioners may have to become familiar with it in the future.

In practice, of course, most buyers do not think about the theory behind estates and interests, but this knowledge will be necessary for a conveyancer handling the legal work.

1.4 Key stages of the conveyancing process – a recap

A seller will sell the "estate" that they hold in the land in question which the buyer will acquire by way of a deed. The seller will sell either a freehold or leasehold estate and you will recall that a conveyancing transaction follows broadly the same process whether it is freehold or leasehold.The stages of a standard conveyancing transaction are based on two events:

- **exchange of contracts** – when the parties become legally bound;
- **completion** – when the purchase money is handed over in return for the title documents. In residential transactions, this is usually the day when the seller moves out of the house and the buyer moves in.

The entire conveyancing process revolves around these pivotal points, with the conveyancer ensuring that all relevant steps have been taken and all relevant enquiries made.

This section mentions the key stage in the conveyancing process of exchange of contracts. Note that in November 2023 the Law Society released the 'Code for signing and exchanging property contracts 2024'. There was a short consultation but, as yet, no further information is available as to whether the new Code will be introduced and, if so, when.

If the Code is introduced, it will replace the long-standing Formulae for Exchanging Contracts and will represent a significant change in the methods and practice of exchanging contracts.

For more information go to: https://www.lawsociety.org.uk/topics/property/code-for-signing-and-exchanging-property-contracts.

In most cases, a seller will instruct an estate agent to assist with the sale of a property. The seller must provide an Energy Performance Certificate to a buyer which is an energy efficiency report on the property; this is often commissioned by the estate agent. The estate agent will market the property and will negotiate the sale price once a buyer is found. It is generally at this point that the estate agent will produce a "memorandum of sale" which will include details of the seller and buyer, the property, the agreed price and the details of the conveyancers acting for the parties. This is usually the first time that the conveyancers become involved and the process below is followed.

Occasionally, a seller and buyer will come to an arrangement regarding the sale and purchase of a property without the assistance of an estate agent. This is called a "private sale".

Let's look at the conveyancing stages and process in the table below.

The stages of the conveyancing process	Description
1 Pre-contract	This is the stage of the transaction which involves most work for the conveyancers and takes the longest time. As well as file opening, anti-money laundering (AML) work, client identification and due diligence, the seller's conveyancer will send the contract package to the buyer's conveyancer who will submit searches, check the title, raise enquiries and resolve their clients financing. It is only once all of these aspects are concluded that the parties can move on to the next crucial stage of the transaction.

2	Exchange	This is the stage of the transaction where the contract between the seller and the buyer becomes legally binding. The conveyancers acting for both parties will generally exchange contracts on the telephone and there is a procedure to follow in this regard. In most cases, the buyer will pay a deposit on exchange of 10% of the purchase price. Once exchange of contracts has taken place, the seller and buyer are contractually bound to proceed and neither party can withdraw from the transaction without financial consequences.
3	Pre-completion	This is the part of the transaction between exchange of contracts and completion where the seller and buyer are likely to be doing very practical things such as booking removals and packing their belongings whilst their conveyancers will be preparing for the completion day. The seller's conveyancer will arrange for the seller to sign the transfer document which is prepared by the buyer's conveyancer and will obtain up-to-date redemption figures on any mortgages that the seller has over the property being sold. In parallel, the buyer's conveyancer will carry out some pre-completion searches and will obtain the buyers funding to purchase the property (very often by requesting drawdown of the mortgage advance from a lender).
4	Completion	This is the moving date. This is the day which the seller and buyer have been waiting for. The seller will move out of the property being sold and the buyer will move in. However, before this can happen, the buyer's conveyancer must pay the completion money to the seller's conveyancer. Upon receipt of these funds, the seller's conveyancer will contact the estate agent to confirm that the keys can be released to the buyer, so that the buyer can move in.

However even the most straightforward research on this subject will reveal that there is a wide-range of options, some of which streamline the entire conveyancing process, others only part of it. Choose one of the providers and look in more detail at the tasks that the system covers such as:

- Completing standard forms
- Submitting forms to HMLR
- Digital signing features for clients
- Recording key milestones in the transaction
- Submission of SDLT return on line
- Standard reports
- Automated production of completion statements and bills
- Automated email updates
- Case tracker.

There are electronic checks which enable conveyancing firms to search against other firms as a means of reducing fraud in addition to a wide-range of products enabling firms to carry out AML and due diligence checks against their clients.

HMLR is increasingly moving towards digitisation of the land registration process and as a response to the Covid-19 disruption in summer 2020, decided to accept deeds signed using both the Mercury signature process and witnessed electronic signatures. HMLR is liaising with around 30 software providers regarding the development of software packages which incorporate HMLR's specific requirements for the electronic signature of deeds.

Some case management systems have been designed for use via an app on mobile phones to ensure that automated updates and prompts are sent to the client at all stages of the transaction.

There is no doubt that these software solutions are helping conveyancing firms streamline the conveyancing process. However, it is important to remember that a case management system is only as good as the people who use it and the data that is fed in.

Link to practice

One of the main purposes of a case management system is risk management. The idea is that at any given time, any conveyancer should be able to access a file and know exactly what stage the transaction has reached. For example, the system should display things such as whether:

- a transaction is high risk because for example, it is a cash transaction or a client that is not known to the firm;
- any undertakings have been given on the file and, if so, to whom and the terms of the undertaking;
- exchange of contracts has taken place;
- the expiry of the priority period of an official HMLR search with priority;
- completion has taken place;
- the SDLT has been paid;
- the HMLR application has been submitted.

If you work in a firm that has a department wide case management system, consider whether all of its features are being used. Is the information on the system up to date and accurate?

Electronic identification

The Legal Sector Affinity Group (LSAG) issued AML guidance in January 2021. The guidance refers to electronic identification and verification (EID&V) tools which professionals subject to the Money Laundering Regulations are permitted to use to assist with fulfilling obligations under the regulations. The LSAG made a point about these EID&V tools which is equally applicable to any electronic product used to support the conveyancing system. They said (our emphasis added):

"In an increasingly digital age, it is clear that non face-to-face customer onboarding can no longer be viewed as always high risk (although it remains a key risk factor to be assessed in the context of the wider relationship) – a more nuanced approach should therefore be adopted to these types of relationships.

The use of EID&V is increasingly viewed as being as robust as traditional verification methods (physical documentary evidence such as passports, driving licences etc.). Electronic verification methods are becoming increasingly more secure and sophisticated and may in fact be lower risk than traditional means in some circumstances.

CHAPTER 2

Regulatory matters and taxation

2.1 Introduction

Conveyancing is a risky business. Conveyancers face frequent threats from fraudsters whether posing as sellers of property, committing mortgage fraud or cybercrime. The ever-increasing amount of due diligence in relation to issues such as money laundering and sanctions add to the mix and the potential for a negligence claim. This chapter will consider all of these issues together with the importance of undertakings and a recent Supreme Court case which considered undertakings in conveyancing. We will consider risky advice to be given in "***Etridge***" situations and will conclude by considering key taxation issues in conveyancing transactions.

This chapter will cover:

- fraud in conveyancing including mortgage fraud, bogus law firms and identity theft;
- the ***Dreamvar*** case and the impact on the Code for Completion by Post;
- money laundering risks in conveyancing;
- Legal Sector Affinity Group AML guidance;
- cybercrime risks;

- professional negligence and the risks of "***Etridge***" advice;
- undertakings;
- taxation issues: capital gains tax (CGT), SDLT and LTT.

2.2 Fraud in conveyancing

Throughout the transaction, the firm of solicitors (or licensed conveyancers where applicable) must be aware of the possibility of fraud. Various measures will be taken as safeguards, including checking a client's identity. There is an increasing body of case law on fraud in conveyancing.

In ***Penn v Bristol & West* [1997]** the seller's solicitor did not know that the signature of the seller on the transfer deed was a fake. The buyer's mortgage lender successfully sued the seller's solicitor.

This situation is now unlikely to occur as the **Money Laundering Regulations 2017** and the **Proceeds of Crime Act 2002** require all conveyancers to verify their clients' identity. HMLR has also introduced fraud prevention measures regarding identities which apply to conveyancers when dealing with an unrepresented party such as a buyer or seller who does not have a conveyancer acting for them but who is doing their own conveyancing.

The UK Finance Mortgage Lenders' Handbook contains various requirements which must be followed by firms acting for lenders in order to combat fraud. Some of the steps to be taken by firms are contained in section 3 of the Handbook ("Safeguards") and include the requirement for the firm to:

- follow the rules and guidance of the firm' professional body relating to money laundering;
- comply with the current money-laundering regulations and the **Proceeds of Crime Act 2002**;
- follow other guidance as relevant (for example, Law Society Practice Notes);
- verify that the sellers regulated legal representatives are currently on record with the SRA, Council for Licensed Conveyancers (CLC) or other legal regulatory body as practising at the address provided, if the sellers legal representative is not familiar to the firm;
- check directly with the lender if the seller does not have legal representation. Note that the lender might not be prepared to proceed in this circumstance;
- obtain identification documents in accordance with the lists in the Handbook, unless the signatory of a document is personally known to the conveyancer;

- check that any document used to verify a signatory identity appears to be authentic and current and signed in the relevant place. The firm should take a copy of the document and retain it on file. Importantly, the firm should also check that the signatory's signature on any document being used to verify identity matches the signatory's signature on the lender's document.

We will look at these in more detail below.

Activity

The Law Society and HMLR published a joint Practice Note to help conveyancers spot and avoid fraud. It focuses on the risks relating to property and registration fraud and supplements existing advice from both organisations about combatting fraud and scams. It was updated in 2020.

Follow the link and download the Practice Note. Read it carefully.

https://www.lawsociety.org.uk/topics/property/property-and-registration-fraud

Retain the Practice Note for your file as it contains important advice for conveyancing firms. Focus in particular on the fraud threats for property transactions which include impersonation of anyone in a conveyancing transaction including buyers, sellers and conveyancers.

Clients at particular risk of fraud include:

- a sole owner;
- elderly owners who are in hospital or have moved into a care home;
- owners living abroad;
- owners no longer living in the property as the result of an acrimonious break up with a partner;
- owners whose property is empty;
- owners whose property is let;
- an owner who has already been the victim of identity fraud;
- deceased owners and/or personal representatives responsible for a property where the property is to be sold.

HMLR has identified certain types of property which are vulnerable to transactional and registered title frauds including:

- unoccupied properties;
- tenanted properties;
- high value properties without a legal charge;
- high value properties with a legal charge in favour of an individual living overseas;
- properties undergoing redevelopment.

The following have been identified as fraud risk factors:

- properties owned by vulnerable owners;
- vulnerable properties;
- when you're pressed about the urgency of transaction;
- where there's a possible undervaluation of the property;
- there exist some other reasonable grounds for suspecting there is property fraud within your transaction;
- where you have limited or conflicting client contact details.

If you have a red flag or fraud checklist in your firm, compare it to all of the risks and threats contained in this Practice Note. How comprehensive is your firm's checklist?

If you do not currently work in practice, prepare your own red flag checklist.

2.2.1 Fraudulent sellers

Conveyancers are at risk from fraudulent activity, which can come in a huge number of guises. A significant risk in recent years has been fraudsters pretending to be the seller of a property. The fraudster poses as the owner of a property. If the conveyancing firm who the fraudster instructs does not have sufficiently robust identification and due diligence processes in place, it is possible for fraud to be committed in that the buyer's conveyancer will send the purchase money on completion to the seller's conveyancer who then pays it away to the fraudster. Obviously, there has been no completion of a conveyancing transaction as there has been no transaction at all.

It is often the case that the fraud does not come to light until after the purported completion when the fraudster has long since disappeared with the money. The courts have had to decide where liability lies in this situation. The matter becomes more complex if the defrauded buyer has a mortgage because the buyer's conveyancer holds the mortgage advance on trust for the lender pending completion. If there has been no actual completion due to the fraud, the buyer's conveyancer is also in breach of trust to the lender.

This issue was considered by the Court of Appeal in ***P&P Property Ltd v Owen White & Catlin LLP and Dreamvar (UK) Ltd v Mishcon de Reya* [2018] *(Dreamvar)*.**

The Court of Appeal heard two cases together with startlingly similar facts relating to the liability of solicitors and estate agents in cases involving identity fraud. In both cases, the fraudster posed as the owner of a registered property in London. He instructed solicitors and agents to act for him on the sale of the property and genuine buyers were found. The buyers instructed their own solicitors and proceeded to exchange of contracts and completion in accordance with the Law Society Code for Completion by Post (2011 edition). Following completion, but before registration of title, the fraud was discovered but, unsurprisingly, the fraudster and the purchase money had disappeared.

There were several threads to the appeal including issues relating to breach of warranty of authority, breach of undertaking, negligence and breach of trust. The main finding of direct relevance to conveyancing firms is that the conveyancing firm acting for the fraudulent seller was giving a warranty to the buyer's conveyancer that it acted on behalf of the genuine owner of the property.

Activity

Read the ***Dreamvar*** judgment at:

https://www.bailii.org/ew/cases/EWCA/Civ/2018/1082.html

Why did the anti-money laundering checks at Owen White & Catlin LLP fail to prevent the fraud?

2.2.2 Impact of *Dreamvar* on completion procedures

Prior to ***Dreamvar***, conveyancers did not give much day to day thought to completion processes – but the result of the case has led to some importance changes and to the significance of this part of the transaction being placed in the spotlight.

Between exchange of contracts and completion, the seller's conveyancer will usually send a completed protocol form TA13 to the buyer's conveyancer – Completion Information and Undertakings (see **Document 8** of the **Appendix**). This form enquires about the arrangements for completion and it is important to ensure that the arrangements are made in advance if, as is most common, the buyer's solicitors are not going to attend the completion of the transaction in person.

Traditionally, completion takes place at the offices of the seller's conveyancer as the deeds are likely to be retained there pending the transaction. Standard Condition (SC) 6 follows tradition: it provides for completion to take place either at the seller's conveyancers' office or at some other place as the seller reasonably requires.

Very occasionally, completion will be at the premises of the seller's mortgage lender where, for example, the lender is unwilling to release the deeds to the seller's conveyancer because they are not on the lender's approved panel of conveyancers.

Methods of completion

The following different methods of completion exist.

(1) **By personal attendance**, that is, the buyer's conveyancer attends the seller's conveyancers' offices in person. This is uncommon.

(2) **By agent**, that is, the buyer's conveyancer employ a firm local to the seller's conveyancer to go along (for a fee) and complete on their behalf. It is necessary for the buyer's conveyancer to give full instructions to their agents (who will obviously be unaware of any previous arrangements or negotiations); they should receive a list of all the necessary steps to be taken upon completion, together with a list of what they are to hand over and the documents they are to receive. This is also uncommon.

(3) **By post**, that is, the seller's conveyancer acts as the buyer's agents upon completion and post all the necessary documentation to them immediately afterwards. This is the most commonly used method where completion is routine. Provided those full instructions are given by the buyer's conveyancer as to exactly what they require to be done upon completion, there should be no conflict in the seller's conveyancer acting for both parties. To avoid uncertainty, the Law Society established the **Code for Completion by Post** (the Code), which may be adopted where specifically agreed between the conveyancers, with the agreement preferably in writing. Form TA13 asks the seller's s conveyancer to confirm whether they agree to complete through the post and, if so, to confirm that they undertake to adopt the Code. Other forms of pre-completion requisitions deal with similar points.

The Law Society Code for Completion by Post 2019 incorporates case law developments concerning fraudulent sellers following ***Dreamvar***.

Essentially, the Code has been tightened to clarify and confirm that the seller's conveyancer is acting in a genuine sale with a genuine seller and using the funds received for a genuine completion. This is intended to provide innocent buyers with greater protection from fraudsters. The changes also include undertakings that the seller's conveyancer has authority from the true owner of the property named in the contract to receive the purchase money and, that, at the point of completion, such person is entitled to convey the title the contract says will be conveyed. Further, the seller's conveyancer holds the purchase money received on trust for the buyer and is under a duty not to deal with that money other than in accordance with the Code.

Firms which are members of the CQS (which obliges member firms to use the Protocol), and other Protocol users, must use the Code when completing by post. The Protocol requires use of the Code without variation unless the parties to the transaction give specific instructions which make some variation necessary. The Protocol states that general exclusions of liability for obligations within the Code will be viewed as a breach of the Protocol. It is normal for non-Protocol users to adopt the Code as well.

The Code embodies professional undertakings and a prominent warning to this effect is included at the start of the Code.

The Code divides the steps to be taken into those applicable before completion, on completion and after completion. The main provisions of the Code can be summarised as follows (the Code itself should be consulted in practice).

General

The Code provides that, if the seller's conveyancer has to withdraw from using the Code, they should notify the buyer's conveyancer of this by 4.00 pm on the working day before completion at the latest.

The seller's conveyancer agrees under the Code that they act as the buyer's conveyancer's agent on completion without a fee.

When the seller's conveyancer receives and/or holds the completion money, they receive and hold this on trust for the person or persons providing it and must use it only for a completion in which the seller executes and delivers a valid conveyance or transfer (i.e. a genuine completion) or it must be repaid if completion does not take place.

(1) Before completion

The Code provides that the seller's conveyancer will provide the replies to form TA13 at least five working days before the completion date (unless replies have already been provided in a form sent by the buyer).

Various advance arrangements need to be made, including:

- a clear agreement (preferably in writing) that the Code for Completion by Post will apply. Adoption of the Protocol however automatically implies use of the Code unless otherwise stated in writing by either conveyancer;
- identification in writing, from the seller's conveyancer, of the mortgages to be redeemed and by what method;
- a statement from the buyer's conveyancer of any copy/abstract documents to be marked up (usually, only for unregistered land), any memoranda to be endorsed, any undertakings to be given, any deeds and documents to be sent following completion and any other relevant matters.

The Code provides that the buyer's conveyancer will use all reasonable endeavours to ensure that sufficient funds are obtained from the buyer and mortgage lender in good time to be able to transmit them to the seller's conveyancer on or before the agreed completion date. The seller's conveyancer undertakes that they will have the seller's authority to receive the purchase money on completion, that they are agent of any mortgage lender whose mortgage over the property should be discharged, with authority to receive the redemption money and that they will not complete without the buyer's conveyancer's instructions. The Law Society states that undertaking in this manner to have the seller's authority means that the seller's conveyancer is undertaking they have the authority from the true owner of the title to the property named in the contract to receive the purchase money and that the seller is entitled to convey the title as promised by the contract. This ties in with the points above about protection from fraudulent sellers.

The buyer's conveyancer will send the money needed to complete to the seller's conveyancer (usually by telegraphic transfer, the money being held to order pending formal completion). The seller's conveyancer must report to the buyer's conveyancer that the funds have been received.

(2) On completion

The seller's conveyancer will complete once the funds have been received, unless the parties have agreed otherwise, or have agreed that completion will take place at a later time.

When completing, the seller's conveyancer undertakes to comply with any agreed completion arrangements and instructions given by the buyer's conveyancers before completion (see above). They also undertake to redeem or obtain discharges for the mortgages which have been specified (again see above) unless they have already been redeemed or discharged. They further undertake that each specified lender has been identified by the seller's conveyancer to the extent necessary for the purposes of the buyer's conveyancer's registration application at HMLR.

(3) After completion

The seller's conveyancer undertakes to hold the documents to the order of the buyer's conveyancer and as soon as possible after completion to confirm to the buyer's conveyancer by phone, fax or email the date and time that completion has taken place The seller's conveyancer also undertakes to send written confirmation to the buyer's conveyancer, as soon as possible after completion but in any event by the end of the working day after completion, that completion has taken place and to notify the estate agent or key holder that completion has taken place and to authorise them to release the keys to the buyer immediately. The seller's conveyancer further undertakes, as soon as possible after completion, and in any event by the end of the working day following completion, to send the deeds and documents to the buyer's conveyancer by first class post or DX. Such deeds and documents are sent at the risk of the buyer's conveyancer. Finally, the seller's conveyancer undertakes to notify the buyer's conveyancer of the mortgage discharge.

Points to note about the Code include the following:

(1) As can be seen from the above summary of the duties under the Code, it relies upon undertakings, and all the points made later in this chapter should be borne in mind. The Law Society stresses in the 2019 Code that, as it embodies professional undertakings, it is only recommended for adoption between solicitors and licensed conveyancers.

(2) The seller's conveyancer should restrict their undertaking to discharge mortgages over the property to mortgages which they have specified in writing and should also consider using the Law Society form of undertaking.

(3) Following completion and once the documents have been posted by the seller's conveyancer, those documents are at the risk of the buyer.

(4) Fundamentally, the Code is for adoption only where there is no conflict of interest between the two parties – otherwise, it is not possible for the seller's conveyancer to act for both upon completion.

(5) Where there is to be synchronisation of two or more transactions, the buyer's conveyancer should include with their instructions specific provisions about the time for completion to ensure that the purchase is not completed before the sale has been completed. Otherwise, should the latter fall through or be delayed, they are going to be exposed to great problems.

A reminder about the importance of the nature of an undertaking was given in ***Thames Valley Housing Association and Others v Elegant Homes (Guernsey) Limited and Others* [2009]**. An undertaking in completion of the Completion Information and Requisitions on Title Form (as it was then called – now TA13) to redeem any outstanding mortgage was given (a common practice). However, it subsequently became apparent that the mortgage owed was far more than what the solicitor considered. The High Court confirmed that a buyer must be able to rely upon an undertaking absolutely regardless of the situation. This reiterates the need for obtaining an accurate redemption figure from every relevant lender before providing any undertaking.

Activity

As the Code is the most common method of completion, its terms are important. Follow the link and read the Code and the Law Society's guidance notes on the 2019 version and the changes made as a result of ***Dreamvar***:

https://www.lawsociety.org.uk/en/topics/property/code-for-completion-by-post

Link to practice

When acting on a purchase, many conveyancing firms now insist upon receiving the Completion Information and Undertakings (TA13) duly completed and signed by the seller's conveyancer prior to exchange of contracts. What they are keen to ensure is that the seller's conveyancer agrees to adopt the Code unamended. You will see that the point of this is to ensure that the buyer's conveyancer can rely on the warranty contained in the 2019 version of the Code that the seller's conveyancer is acting for the true owner of the property.

Such a request will sometimes be resisted by the seller's conveyancer. They will not want to give the undertaking in section 5 of the TA13 until they have obtained an up to date redemption figure from the seller's lender after exchange of contracts.

Both of these are valid points – the conveyancers must negotiate and deal with these issues to ensure that seller and buyer are adequately protected as the transaction progresses.

What types of property are particularly vulnerable to registered title fraud?

Link to practice

Read the CILEX Regulation Risk Management: Property Fraud factsheet at https://cilexregulation.org.uk/wp-content/uploads/2023/04/03-Property-Fraud-2024.pdf

2.2.3 Bogus law firms and identity theft

Another type of fraud faced by conveyancers is a fraudster pretending to be a law firm or a branch office of an existing law firm. All of the legal regulators have notes and advice to support the firms that they regulate to assist them to identify possible fraud and to mitigate the risk of it happening to the firm. The SRA has produced a non-exhaustive list of factors that might raise suspicions about a firm including:

- errors in letterheading — for example misspelling the name of the town in which a firm or office is supposedly based;
- no landline telephone number — note that numbers beginning with 07 are mobile telephone numbers;
- inconsistent telephone or fax numbers with those usually used by the firm;
- telephone calls being diverted to a call-back service;
- a firm apparently based in serviced offices;
- email addresses using generic email accounts, e.g. gmail — most law firms have addresses incorporating the name of their firm. If in doubt, check the genuine law firm's website to identify its contact email address. You may well notice a difference;
- sudden appearance in your locality of a firm with no obvious connection to the area, probably not interacting with other local firms at all;
- a firm appearing to open a branch office a considerable distance from its head office for no obvious reason;

- a firm based in one part of the country supposedly having a bank account in another part of the country — this is a strong indicator and has been seen several times;
- a client account apparently overseas — this is a major red flag;
- a firm's website which does not display the SRA's clickable logo—all firms regulated by the SRA must display the SRA's clickable logo on their website (see rule 1 of the Transparency Rules);
- a strange or suspicious bank account name — such as the account not being in the name of the law firm you are supposedly dealing with either at all or by some variation.

Activity

Read the CILEX Regulation Risk Management: Bogus Law Firms factsheet at:

https://cilexregulation.org.uk/fraudulent-law-firms/

What steps should your firm take to ensure that its name is not being used by a fraudster?

Link to practice

If a conveyancer has any sort of suspicion about a firm or a client, they should immediately report the matter to the firm's money laundering reporting officer (MLRO) or senior person in the firm. It might be necessary to report suspicions to a regulator – but this would always be by the appropriate officer in the firm and not the individual conveyancer.

2.2.4 Mortgage fraud

The Law Society states that:

"Mortgage fraud occurs where individuals defraud a financial institution or private lender through the mortgage process.

The definition of fraud in the Fraud Act 2006 covers fraud by false representation and by failure to disclose information where there is a legal duty to disclose. False representations can be made explicitly or implicitly and may occur even where you know only that the representation might be misleading or untrue.

The money obtained through fraud will be the proceeds of crime. Under the Proceeds of Crime Act 2002 as amended, you risk committing a money laundering offence if you:

- acquire, use, have possession of, enter into an arrangement with respect to, or transfer this criminal property
- fail to report suspected money laundering."

Mortgage fraud is a serious problem for institutional lenders. It takes many different forms, such as:

(1) a fraudulent survey enabling a buyer to borrow more than the lender would otherwise permit;

(2) stating a misleading price on documentation. This could occur where an additional amount is being paid for contents without the lender's knowledge;

(3) sham transactions. These are transactions set up for the sole purpose of defrauding the lender. A particularly notorious form involves repeated sub-sales of the property to an imaginary buyer.

Where mortgage fraud has occurred, suspicion may well fall upon the conveyancers or their staff. Remember that the conveyancer owes fiduciary duties to their client-lender as well as to their client-borrower. The Law Society has issued guidance to protect practitioners from implications of fraud. Any unusual instructions received from a borrower should be queried, especially instructions relating to a variation in the price or to sub-sales. Consent should then be obtained from the borrower to notify the lender of the position. Only when the lender has received full information and has agreed to proceed (in writing) can the conveyancer proceed with the transaction.

This issue is important in practice as conveyancers can be found criminally liable if clients commit mortgage fraud, because of the extension of the definition of fraud in the relevant legislation and the UK anti-money laundering regime. The **Law Society Code for Completion by Post 2019** contains provisions designed to reduce the risk of fraudulent sellers. The provisions of the Code are intended to clarify and confirm that the seller is genuine and that the purchase funds being paid on completion are being used for a genuine transaction and a genuine completion.

Activity

The Law Society has issued a mortgage fraud practice note, which highlights the warning signs of mortgage fraud and outlines how lawyers can protect themselves and their firms from being used to commit fraud.

Follow the link to the Practice Note and download it:

https://www.lawsociety.org.uk/topics/property/mortgage-fraud

Read it carefully – note that it states that: "Solicitors responsible for supervising others doing conveyancing work should ensure those staff have read this practice note."

Note in particular the warning signs for mortgage fraud contained in section 3 of the Practice Note.

2.2.5 UK Finance Mortgage Lender's Handbook

Conveyancers are required to comply with anti-fraud and anti-money laundering rules and regulations. Lender's Handbook 3.1.2, for example, requires solicitors and those working in practices regulated by the SRA to follow the rules and guidance of their professional body relating to money laundering and to comply with the current money laundering regulations and the **Proceeds of Crime Act 2002** to the extent they apply. Firms are further required to follow other relevant guidance such as the Law Society's mortgage fraud practice note. Lender's Handbook 3.2.2 contains similar requirements for licensed conveyancers' practices, requiring them to follow the professional guidance of the Council for Licensed Conveyancers (CLC) relating to money laundering, to comply with the current money laundering regulations and **Proceeds of Crime Act 2002** to the extent that they apply and to follow all other relevant guidance issued by the CLC.

In addition to the checks against fraud and money laundering, the conveyancer should check the following.

(1) **Signatures**

Lenders' Handbook 3.1 and 3.2 state that the signatures must be checked. Two lists of acceptable evidence are provided in 3.1. A single item from List A (e.g. passport or UK photocard driving licence) will suffice; alternatively, two items from List B must be checked (e.g. cheque guarantee card and receipted utility bill which is less than three months old). The evidence should be photocopied and retained on file. There were a number of requests to allow electronic identification. This is now permitted for licensed conveyancers only. The Handbook does not actually make specific mention of electronic checks nor does the **SRA Standards and Regulations 2019** but they do state that a solicitor must identify who they act for in relation to any matter. Licensed conveyancers are, however, permitted by the CLC's guidance in its own Handbook, to verify identity electronically.

Before signing, the terms and conditions of the mortgage need to be explained to the borrower. The Handbook (at 11.2.1) states that the signature of a document that needs to be witnessed must be witnessed by an independent person, and that all documents required at completion must be dated with the date of completion of the loan.

(2) **The other side's legal representative**

The name and address of the seller's solicitor or licensed conveyancer, if the firm is not familiar, should be checked against legal directories and/or the appropriate professional body (Lenders' Handbook 3.1 and 3.2).

(3) **Details of the valuation**

The description of the property in the valuation report should be checked against the deeds. Furthermore, if the valuer has mentioned any assumptions regarding the title (e.g. the tenure of the property or any restrictions on its use), then these assumptions should be checked. If there are any concerns on this point, they need to be referred back to the lender, who will raise them with the valuer. The requirements set out in the Lenders' Handbook apply equally to a valuation report and a home condition report (Lenders' Handbook 4; see also Lenders' Handbook 6.2 regarding checking that boundaries match).

The Handbook makes it clear (at 4.1) that conveyancers are not expected to advise on any discrepancies between the valuation report they receive and what the lender has, if the lender does not supply the report directly to them.

Discrepancies in the mortgage offer need to be notified to the lender (Lenders' Handbook 6.1.2).

(4) **How long the seller has owned the property**

If this is less than six months, the lender will generally need to know this so that it can carry out various fraud prevention checks.

Lenders' Handbook 5.1 requires the conveyancer to report this immediately. The conveyancer must therefore check this with the register (which will show the date when the registered proprietor became the owner) or the deeds.

Lenders may accept the situation in some limited circumstances but this will depend on their individual instructions in Part 2.

Some lenders may put the mortgage application on hold pending receipt of further information on this issue.

(5) **Where the seller is not the owner or registered proprietor**

The lender must be notified if the person selling to the borrower is not the owner or registered proprietor (Lenders' Handbook 5.2), unless the seller is (Lenders' Handbook 5.2.1):

- a personal representative (PR) of the registered proprietor;
- an institutional mortgagee exercising its power of sale;
- a receiver, trustee in bankruptcy or liquidator;
- a developer or builder selling a property acquired under a part exchange scheme; or
- a housing association exercising a power of sale.

(6) **Not acting for the lender if the solicitor or a partner in the firm are related to the borrower**

The Lenders' Handbook prevents sole practitioners from acting for the lender if they are related to the borrower. In partnerships, some lenders allow a different fee-earner (not the relative) to act for the lender (Lenders' Handbook 1.13 and 1.14).

(7) **How the buyer will fund the purchase**

The mortgage will not normally cover the entire purchase price. If the buyer is obtaining a second mortgage or receiving funds from a third party, this must be notified to the lender (Lenders' Handbook 5.13). The buyer should be asked to consent to this disclosure – if they refuse, the conveyancer cannot act as there will be a conflict of interests.

(8) **Whether the price is as instructed/disclosure of incentives**

Lenders' Handbook 6.3 requires any discrepancies in the price to be notified to the lender.

The lender should also be notified if the purchase price (or part) is not being paid via the conveyancer in the usual way, for instance if it is proposed that the borrower/buyer is to pay part of the purchase money direct to the seller.

Conveyancers also have an obligation to disclose any incentives provided by developers of new-build properties to buyers using the UK Finance Disclosure Form. This is dealt with at 6.4 of the Lenders' Handbook 6.4 (incentives). The reason for this is that lenders have become increasingly concerned that valuations of new property can be distorted if various incentives are included in the package. Examples of such incentives are deposits paid by the seller, payment of SDLT by the seller, cashback schemes, inclusion of white goods and kitchen appliances, free holidays or cars, or free garden landscaping (these examples are not exhaustive). All of these types of incentives mean that the headline purchase price may not be a completely accurate reflection of the property's value.

One effect is that the borrower might then borrow a sum effectively in excess of the true property value, thus creating a situation of negative equity from the beginning. In 2008, the CML (as it was then called) introduced a Disclosure of Incentives Form, to be completed by the developer. As mentioned above, this is now called the **UK Finance Disclosure Form**, and the current version was introduced in February 2018. The form captures information about incentives, as well as a wider range of information about the new-build property which might affect a lending decision. Examples of such information in the new form are discounts from the developer's list price, the method of construction of the property, and luxury or non-standard shared facilities on site such as communal gyms or swimming pools.

The form is required for all newly built property including renovations and conversions, where mortgage finance is required. The seller (e.g. developer) must complete the form and it will be given to the valuer and the lender's conveyancer. The lender's conveyancer should be sent the form as early as possible in the conveyancing process, but no later than seven working days before exchange of contracts. The lender's conveyancer (who will frequently be acting for the lender and the buyer) will confirm with the borrower/buyer that the information on the form concerning incentives offered and the agreed sale price is correct. The conveyancer will only be required to report information to the lender where required by the provisions of the Lenders' Handbook; for example some lenders only want to know about incentives where they are in excess of five per cent of the purchase price.

Completion of the form should reassure lenders that they have sufficient security for the money secured against the property. The Lenders' Handbook states that the form must be supplied by the developer's conveyancer in relation to any property which is to be occupied for the first time (i.e. new build) or for the first time in its current form (e.g. a renovation or conversion). The Handbook further says that the certificate of title cannot be submitted to the lender unless the form has been received.

Activity

Follow the link to the UK Finance Disclosure Form Version 1:

https://lendershandbook.ukfinance.org.uk/lenders-handbook/disclosure-form/

Download the form and keep it for future reference. We will mention it again when we look at acting for a buyer on a new build purchase.

Download and read the FAQs about the Form – note that:

(1) The purpose of the form is to draw all the relevant financial and other key information about the sale of newly built, converted and renovated property transactions into a single form.

It is the responsibility of the seller to complete the form.

(2) The form must be provided to the lender's solicitor/conveyancer as a standard part of the process and to the valuer when requested.

2.3 Money laundering risks in conveyancing

Money laundering is the practice of passing illegal money (proceeds of criminal activity) through a series of seemingly legitimate business or personal dealings so that it is difficult for the law enforcement agencies to identify the source of the funds.

There is a particular difficulty here regarding professional ethics. Usually, solicitors are subject to a duty of confidentiality which protects clients. Under the **EC Money Laundering Directive** and the **Criminal Justice Act 1993**, it became a criminal offence to assist with money laundering, and it became obligatory to notify the Serious Organised Crime Agency (SOCA) (the National Crime Agency (NCA) from October 2013) should it be suspected. The **Proceeds of Crime Act 2002** widened the circumstances in which a solicitor or other person acting should report suspected money laundering activities to the authorities. Assisting a money launderer or failing to report a client where there is a suspicion of money laundering could render the solicitor liable to prosecution under the **Proceeds of Crime Act 2002**.

The current legal requirements relating to anti-money laundering (AML) obligations are found in:

- the **Proceeds of Crime Act 2002**; and
- **the Money Laundering and Terrorist Financing (Amendment) Regulations 2019** (which amend the **Money Laundering, Terrorist Financing and Transfer of Funds (Information on the Payer) Regulations 2017** and implement the EU's **5th Money Laundering Directive**) referred to in practice as the **Money Laundering Regulations 2017** (**MLR 2017**).

Some of the key requirements under **MLR 2017** are that firms must:

- carry out a firm-wide written risk assessment to identify and assess the risk of money laundering and terrorist financing which the firm potentially faces;
- develop and maintain written policies and procedures to manage and mitigate money laundering risks identified in the firm's risk assessment. Such policies and procedures must be proportionate to the size and nature of the firm and should be risk-based;
- comply with various internal rules such as keeping records and appointing a person (known as a money laundering compliance officer) at senior level to be responsible for ensuring compliance with the regulations;
- train staff to recognise potential money laundering situations (e.g. suspicious circumstances such as where a client offers a large sum in cash as payment for a deposit or where a client is unusually secretive about the source of funds);
- report suspicious money laundering activities to the authorities (the National Crime Agency (NCA));
- appoint a money laundering reporting officer (MLRO) (also referred to as a nominated officer) within the firm to whom members of staff can report suspicious transactions and who can then report to the NCA if necessary (the MLRO can be the same person as the money laundering compliance officer if wished).

One major obligation under **MLR 2017** is the duty to carry out customer due diligence (CDD) in relation to clients. This CDD must be carried out at the beginning of the business relationship and monitored on an ongoing basis.

An important aspect of CDD is that the identity of clients must be checked. Identity checks will often be dealt with in the initial letter, in the firm's terms of business and/or at the initial interview. For example, conveyancers will ask to see evidence of identity such as:

- a current signed passport;
- a photo-card driving licence;
- a birth certificate; or
- a recent utility bill (in this context, "recent" normally means that the bill must not be more than three months old).

Two items of evidence are usually required (e.g. a passport for proof of identity and a recent utility bill for proof of address).

Some firms also make electronic identity checks with companies offering this service, in which case a small fee will usually be charged to the client.

The SRA is responsible for monitoring and enforcing solicitors' compliance with their anti-money laundering obligations. It exercises this function independently on behalf of the Law Society.

Activity

CILEX Regulation has produced some useful resources for the firms that it regulates.

Follow the link to the CILEX Regulation Resource Library and read the "Sectoral risk assessment":

https://cilexregulation.org.uk/resource-library/?child_category=6

Make a note of the key areas of risk identified by CILEX Regulation.

2.3.1 Legal Sector Affinity Group (LSAG) AML Guidance

All practitioners must be aware of the law and what they must do to comply with AML obligations. The LSAG comprises the AML supervisors for the legal sector and includes the Law Society, SRA, CLC and CILEX. In January 2021 it produced guidance on and good practice for compliance with **MLR 2017**. The guidance has now been approved by HM Treasury.

Note that the LSAG guidance was updated in 2022 and 2023, although there are no changes that are significant for conveyancing. The LSAG did issue an advisory note in March 2023 on Chinese underground banking and funds from China. Here is the link:

https://www.lawsociety.org.uk/topics/anti-money-laundering/chinese-underground-banking-and-funds-from-china

Activity

The LSAG guidance is extensive and conveyancing fee earners will not generally need to read all of it – it is the responsibility of a firm's MLRO and compliance officers to ensure that the firm's policies and procedures are reviewed and amended to incorporate relevant areas of the guidance.

However, it is important to know what the guidance contains, so follow the link to the SRA website and click on the PDF of the guidance:

https://www.sra.org.uk/solicitors/resources/money-laundering/guidance-support/

Read section 3 – the High-Level Compliance Principles that underpin the guidance.

CILEX Regulation has also produced a summary of the key changes introduced by the 2017 Regulations. Follow the link to the "Resource library" and click on "Key changes (January 2020)":

https://cilexregulation.org.uk/resource-library/?child_category=6

Link to practice

Although money laundering is a scary prospect, as a fee-earner you should remember that your duty is to recognise potential money laundering and report it to your MLRO. You then follow their instructions. The responsibility is then with the MLRO, not you!

If suspicions are aroused, a report should be sent to the NCA. If the NCA is informed, no offence will be committed, unless lawful directions given by the NCA are ignored. Detailed rules exist which govern the procedure to be followed if money laundering is suspected.

Activity

Follow the link to the CILEX Regulation website and download and save the document under the "Resource Library" tab – "Your anti-money laundering obligations"

https://cilexregulation.org.uk/resource-library/?child_category=6

Anti-money laundering obligations are also relevant in the context of acting for a lender. Where the firm is acting for the buyer and the mortgage lender, the UK Finance Mortgage Lenders' Handbook requires the conveyancer to comply with

MLR 2017 and the **Proceeds of Crime Act 2002**, to the extent that they apply. It also requires conveyancers to follow other relevant guidance such as that issued by the Law Society.

Anti-money laundering obligations are also important to ensure compliance with the Protocol when it is being used. The Protocol contains the following requirement in its section on general solicitor obligations in a conveyancing transaction:

- Ensure you comply with the **Money Laundering, Terrorist Financing and Transfer of Funds (Information on the Payer) Regulations 2017** and client identification requirements.
- Step 3 of the Protocol contains requirements for sellers' and buyers' conveyancers in relation to client identity and verification and reminds them that this issue must be kept under review during the transaction.

Activity

CILEX Regulation has issued a conveyancing AML red flag checklist – follow the link below to download it:

https://cilexregulation.org.uk/wp-content/uploads/2018/12/AML-Red-Flag-Indicators.pdf

Link to practice

Employees in conveyancing firms should therefore consider money laundering implications very carefully where there are suspicious circumstances, as the obligation to report rests with the individual concerned and not simply the employer, and penalties for failing to comply are potentially severe. Suspicious circumstances, some of which have been highlighted above, might for instance include a client wanting to make a large payment with cash, a client who is unusually secretive, or an unusual purchase price.

Another suspicious circumstance might occur where a client paid a deposit, withdrew from the transaction for no good reason and required the deposit to be repaid to them (although there might, of course, be a perfectly innocent explanation). As indicated above, firms should apply customer due diligence (CDD) measures and monitor client activity using a risk-based approach. This means that more stringent procedures should be followed in high-risk situations and less stringent measures in low-risk situations. Staff should have regular training, which should cover terrorist financing issues.

Sanctions

Linked to AML responsibilities is the issue of sanctions. These are restrictive measures that can be put in place to fulfil a range of purposes. In the UK, these include complying with UN and other international obligations, supporting foreign policy and national security objectives, as well as maintaining international peace and security, and preventing terrorism.

The UK implements a range of sanctions regimes through regulations made under the **Sanctions and Anti-Money Laundering Act 2018** (**SA-MLA 2018**). **SA-MLA 2018** provides the main legal basis for the UK to impose, update and lift sanctions. UK sanctions regulations made under **SA-MLA 2018** apply in the whole of the UK, including in Northern Ireland. The prohibitions and requirements in these Regulations apply to conduct by UK persons. This includes anyone in the UK (including its territorial waters), UK nationals outside of the UK, and bodies incorporated or constituted under the law of any part of the UK. It is government policy for UK sanctions measures to be given effect in the British Overseas Territories and Crown Dependencies to make sanctions as effective as possible.

The UK may impose the following types of sanctions measures:

- trade sanctions, including arms embargoes and other trade restrictions;
- financial sanctions, including asset freezes;
- immigration sanctions, known as travel bans;
- aircraft and shipping sanctions, including de-registering or controlling the movement of aircraft and ships.

Some sanctions measures (such as asset freezes and travel bans) apply only to persons or ships which have been designated or specified by the UK Government. This is publicised through the UK Sanctions List, which contains designations or specifications made using legislation under **SA-MLA 2018**.

Activity

Conveyancing firms must ensure that they have policies and procedures in place to ensure that the sanctions list is checked when a prospective client comes to the firm. This is likely to be done in many cases by using an electronic verification tool. It is unlikely that an individual conveyancer would have to go through the sanctions list, but follow the link below to the list:

https://www.gov.uk/government/publications/the-uk-sanctions-list

It is important for you to have an understanding of the extent of the list and the frequency with which it is updated by the government.

The Office of Financial Sanctions Implementation (OFSI) in HM Treasury also maintain a Consolidated List of Asset Freeze Targets, which contains details of designations specifically for financial sanctions, where asset freeze measures apply. OFSI helps to ensure that financial sanctions are properly understood, implemented and enforced in the UK.

Financial sanctions include restrictions on designated persons, such as freezing their financial assets, as well as wider restrictions on investment and financial services.

OFSI helps companies understand their financial sanctions obligations, monitors compliance and assesses suspected breaches. OFSI can also issue licences to allow for an activity that would otherwise be prohibited by financial sanctions regulations, under certain circumstances.

The Russian invasion of Ukraine in February 2022 has brought sanctions back to the forefront of concerns for all lawyers, not least conveyancers because it is necessary to check that clients of the firm are not on the sanctions list. It is likely that most firms will check whether a client is on the sanctions list by doing an electronic search as part of the file opening due diligence. All of the regulators have issued comment and guidance on the matter.

Activity

If you work in a law firm, go to the website of your regulator and see what the regulator is saying about compliance with the sanctions requirements.

Follow the link below to the CILEX Regulation website:

https://cilexregulation.org.uk/entity/anti-money-laundering/

You will see that it contains very useful resources relating to sanctions and wider AML duties.

Reads and make notes in particular on the section "how to spot risks" and think about how you would put this into practice.

Note that the financial sanctions regime prevents law firms from doing business or acting for listed individuals, entities or ships (without a licence). Firms should check the financial sanctions lists before offering services or undertaking transactions for clients. If an individual is on the sanctions list and subject to an asset freeze, firms may not deal with those funds or make resources available to that person. There are some exemptions for which firms can seek a licence from OFSI. These include applying for a licence in order to receive reasonable fees for the provision of legal advice. OFSI will judge whether the fees are reasonable. Failing to follow the financial sanctions requirements could result in criminal prosecution or a large public fine.

Link to practice

Note that a relevant firm (which includes law firms) is legally obliged to report to OFSI if it knows or suspects that a breach of financial sanctions has occurred, that a person is a designated person, or it holds frozen assets and that knowledge or suspicion came whilst conducting its business. The firm must contact OFSI at the earliest opportunity.

Regulations require individuals, entities and bodies to supply OFSI as soon as practicable with any information that would "facilitate compliance" with the regulations. Any information provided will only be used for the purposes for which it was provided or received. This requirement applies to natural and legal persons, entities and bodies in the UK or under UK jurisdiction.

Note that OFSI requires a breach to be reported on a "Compliance Reporting Form" but this will not be done by a conveyancer or fee earner.

If your due diligence produces and questions, suspicions or positive matches, you should contact your MLRO or someone senior in the team without delay.

2.4 Cybercrime risks

The SRA reports that cyberattacks make up 75 per cent of all reported crime in the UK and law firms are particularly at risk due to the amount of money that they hold and the sensitive information that they hold about their clients. The SRA also reports that cyberattacks also increased by 400 per cent in the first few weeks of lockdown in March 2020 as criminals took advantage of people having to work at home.

Activity

Follow the link below and download and keep the "Risk Management: Cyber Security" factsheet produced by CILEX Regulation:

01-Cyber-Security-2022-1.docx (live.com)

The National Crime Agency (NCA) states that:

"Cyber criminals seek to exploit human or security vulnerabilities in order to steal passwords, data or money directly. The most common cyber threats include:

- Hacking – including of social media and email passwords
- Phishing – bogus emails asking for security information and personal details
- Malicious software – including ransomware through which criminals hijack files and hold them to ransom
- Distributed denial of service (DDOS) attacks against websites – often accompanied by extortion

The scale and complexity of cyber attacks is wide ranging. 'Off the shelf' tools mean that less technically proficient criminals are now able to commit cyber crime, and do so as awareness of the potential profits becomes more widespread. The evolving technical capabilities of malware means evolving harm as well as facilitating new crimes, such as the cryptomining malware which attacks digital currencies like Bitcoin.

Cyber attacks are financially devastating and disrupting and upsetting to people and businesses. We know that there is significant under-reporting, although the new General Data Protection Regulation is likely to prompt a better picture of scale. Currently the level of sentencing at court is not commensurate with the seriousness of attacks, and this is an area which is ripe for consideration.

Most cyber attacks could be prevented by taking these basic security steps:

- Choose strong passwords and don't reuse them for multiple logins
- Install security software such as anti-virus and two-factor authentication. This kind of software is often available for free.
- Keep all security software and operating systems updated (this can be set to update automatically)"

The CILEX Regulation Sectoral Risk Assessment unsurprisingly identifies cybercrime as a continuing risk to law firms. It states:

"Technology

The increased use of technology will mean opportunities for criminals to exploit any weaknesses in their design or application. For any new technology you use, you should assess the risks that they may introduce and understand effective mitigation of these risks where possible (e.g. two level passwords, firewalls etc).

We are all seeing the importance of cyber security in protecting our data and systems, so preventing cyber security breaches will help combat criminal activity. Preventing cyber-crime should be a feature of your firm's routine programme of training."

Activity

Follow the link below and read the CILEX Sectoral Risk Assessment – you will recognise a number of common themes and threats. Prepare a summary of the various threats identified by CILEX Regulation:

https://cilexregulation.org.uk/resource-library/?child_category=6

Activity

Social media is a fact of everyone's life now – but using our own devices or home wifi for work purposes presents risks for us and our employers

Follows the link below and download and read the fact sheet and advice note from CILEX Regulation on the risks of social media, texting and websites:

https://cilexregulation.org.uk/entity/social-media-and-other-communications/

Think about what steps you can take to mitigate the risks that they identify.

What changes to your behaviour can you make?

2.5 Riskier advice and negligence

We will now move on to think about negligence claims against conveyancers and some of the riskier advice that we can give to our clients.

2.5.1 Professional negligence

Conveyancers owe a duty of care to their clients, and must give all advice relevant to the transaction. If this duty is breached, and the clients sustain damage, then they are entitled to sue the solicitor in negligence. All conveyancers are required to obtain indemnity insurance to cover such errors.

Negligence claims are clearly most undesirable, so the highest standards of professional practice should always be followed. Appropriate and full attendance notes should be kept of interviews with clients so that the advice given can be established in a court if necessary.

Clients sometimes request a departure from a standard procedure. For example, to save time, client-buyers may request that the local search is not undertaken. In such cases, the clients must be advised as to the dangers of the proposed action (what could the search reveal?) and any alternative methods (e.g. a personal search or insurance cover). If they still wish to proceed, they must give the conveyancer written and signed confirmation of their instructions and that they understand the relevant points. If the conveyancer acts for the lender, a co-buyer or any other relevant party to the transaction, that other party must be advised of the same points and sign written confirmation in the same way.

If the conveyancer acts for the buyer's proposed lender, the bank or building society must be advised fully and give consent accordingly. In ***Mortgage Express v Bowerman*** **[1996]** the solicitors acting for both the buyer and the lender became aware of the fact that the property had recently been sold for considerably less than the mortgage valuation. The solicitors failed to notify the lenders and so were liable in negligence.

E Surv Ltd v Goldsmith Williams Solicitors **[2015]** confirms that the duty to report matters relevant to the lender's valuation still stands, despite the introduction of the CML Lenders' Handbook (now UK Finance Mortgage Lenders' Handbook) which contains standard instructions to solicitors acting for lenders and borrowers. The court held that, if during searches and enquiries which the solicitor is obliged to carry out under the terms of the CML Lenders' Handbook, the solicitor comes across information which a reasonably skilled and competent solicitor would consider might have a material bearing on the value of the lender's security, the solicitor is obliged to tell the lender client, subject to duties of confidentiality. In this case, the solicitors failed to report that the sellers had been the registered proprietors for less than six months and had paid substantially less for the property when they bought it. Judgment was given against the firm of solicitors who were found to be in breach of the duty to report. The main impact of this case is that the CML Lender's Handbook (now UK Finance Mortgage Lenders' Handbook) instructions do not negate a solicitor's duties of reasonable skill and care owed to lenders and borrowers. Solicitors must therefore continue to advise lender clients of any information which might cast doubt on the valuation or any other aspect of the decision to lend the money.

Santander v RA Legal Solicitors **[2014]** illustrates the fact that an action may be brought against a firm for breach of trust (rather than negligence) when the firm has acted incompetently, even where it has been caught out by a fraudster. It appears that the fact the losses incurred may have happened in any event, irrespective of the firm's actions, does not provide a complete excuse. In this case, the buyer's solicitors sent the purchase money to a firm which was genuine, but which turned out to be fraudulent. Following completion, it was discovered that the sale had taken place without the owner's knowledge and that the purchase money had been withdrawn from the seller's solicitor's bank account. The lender sued the buyer's solicitors for breach of trust. The Court of Appeal held that the firm was in breach of trust as it had parted with the mortgage advance other than at a "proper completion". The court refused to grant relief for breach of trust (a court can relieve a trustee of liability in certain circumstances) as there were failings by the firm which were sufficiently connected with the loss – for instance, it had transferred the completion money without confirmation of adoption of the Law Society's Code for Completion by Post, it had failed to obtain an undertaking to discharge the existing mortgage on the property, it had failed to address certain requisitions on title, it had made mistakes in relation to the lender's certificate of title, sending it when the investigation of title had not fully taken place, and it had failed to recognise that completion had not taken place properly when no mortgage discharge evidence was received. The court stated that the failings formed part of a larger picture of shoddy performance of a conveyancing transaction which meant that it would not be fair to excuse the firm from liability.

2.5.2 Riskier advice – cases involving the possibility of undue influence

Sometimes, a conveyancer is involved in a situation where undue influence might be involved. This is the equitable doctrine under which the court may set aside, or decline to enforce, any bargain, including a mortgage, reached by means of undue influence.

In ***Royal Bank of Scotland v Etridge (No. 2)* [2001]** (see **2.5.3**) "undue influence" was described as follows:

"6. Undue influence is one of the grounds of relief developed by the courts of equity as a court of conscience. The objective is to ensure that the influence of one person over another is not abused. In everyday life people constantly seek to influence the decisions of others. They seek to persuade those with whom they are dealing to enter into transactions, whether great or small. The law has set limits to the means properly employable for this purpose. To this end the common law developed a principle of duress. Originally this was narrow in its scope, restricted to the more blatant forms of physical coercion, such as personal violence.

7. Here, as elsewhere in the law, equity supplemented the common law. Equity extended the reach of the law to other unacceptable forms of persuasion. The law will investigate the manner in which the intention to enter into the transaction was secured: 'how the intention was produced', in the oft repeated words of Lord Eldon LC, from as long ago as 1807 (*Huguenin v Baseley* 14 Ves 273, 300). If the intention was produced by an unacceptable means, the law will not permit the transaction to stand. The means used is regarded as an exercise of improper or 'undue' influence, and hence unacceptable, whenever the consent thus procured ought not fairly to be treated as the expression of a person's free will. It is impossible to be more precise or definitive. The circumstances in which one person acquires influence over another, and the manner in which influence may be exercised, vary too widely to permit of any more specific criterion.

8. Equity identified broadly two forms of unacceptable conduct. The first comprises overt acts of improper pressure or coercion such as unlawful threats. Today there is much overlap with the principle of duress as this principle has subsequently developed. The second form arises out of a relationship between two persons where one has acquired over another a measure of influence, or ascendancy, of which the ascendant person then takes unfair advantage."

Examples include the following:

(1) The conveyancer acts for the seller. The conveyancer is asked to obtain the consent of an occupier to the sale.

(2) The conveyancer acts for a husband and wife who are jointly mortgaging their home to a bank. The mortgage is for the benefit of the husband's business and the wife will gain no direct benefit.

(3) The conveyancer acts for an elderly client who is selling her house. The client is in hospital and the conveyancer has never met her. All advice is given to the client's adult son or handled through the post, and the son gives all instructions.

In each of the above situations, there is a danger that undue influence could have been exerted on the occupier, wife or client.

In (3), fraud could even be taking place. In (3), the conveyancer actually acts for the client who may be under undue influence. The conveyancer must ensure that the client is fully informed and understands the position and the legal implications of the sale. It is not satisfactory to advise the son and expect them to convey the information to the client. It would be strongly desirable for the conveyancer to meet the client to discuss the case and ensure that the client's wishes are followed. In view of the client's illness, a doctor should confirm that the client understands what is happening. If the client does not understand the position, then an application to the Court of Protection may be required. The Court of Protection is a specialist court which makes decisions, and appoints other people to make decisions, for people who lack mental capacity to make those decisions themselves. Further information about the role of the Court of Protection can be found at www.gov.uk/courts-tribunals/court-of-protection.

A good example which illustrates the potential problems where a client is elderly and matters are being handled by relatives is ***Hart v Burbidge; Samways v Burbidge* [2014]**.

This case concerned an elderly woman who had made three related lifetime transfers totalling £700,000 to her daughter and the daughter's husband, who used the money to buy a property shortly before her death. The property was put into the ownership of the daughter and husband. The mother was to live in the property with them but died soon after moving in. The effect of the transfer of money was to cause others to lose gifts from the estate and to take a smaller share of the residue.

They therefore claimed that the daughter's undue influence had caused them to lose these gifts.

The court found that the mother relied on the daughter, placing trust and confidence in her, and there was a relationship of dependence. There was no evidence that the daughter had poisoned her mother's affections or that the mother was coerced by the daughter so as to justify a finding of actual undue influence, but the transaction did call for an explanation. The mother had not received independent legal advice as to whether it was sensible to transfer over 90 per cent of her estate to the daughter and husband, or how her future interests would be protected. It was not clear why the mother's name was not on the title and it was not certain that the mother had understood the various letters that went out with her signature or whether she intended to deprive others of legacies.

The court stated that the burden of rebutting the presumption of undue influence in this case shifted to the daughter and her husband. In all the circumstances, the court was not satisfied that the mother was acting fully independently of undue influence. It ordered the couple to restore the deceased's estate to what it would have been had the transaction not taken place.

On appeal, it was argued that the judge had erred in finding that any presumption of undue influence arose. The daughter and her husband contended that there was a reasonable explanation for the mother's actions in giving them the money. The Court of Appeal disagreed and dismissed the appeal, holding that the three transactions overall called for an explanation. They were not readily explicable by the relationship of the parties and the judge had properly found that the presumption of undue influence had not been rebutted.

2.5.3 The *Etridge* situation

Conveyancers must be particularly wary of the situation where a spouse wants to mortgage the matrimonial home for business purposes. The point is that undue influence causes someone to be pressurised into entering into a transaction such that it is against their own free will and not in their best interests. In the context of mortgages this could be being pressurised into accepting very unfavourable terms in the mortgage.

Undue influence in the context of mortgages could also arise for instance where a husband and wife co-own property. The husband persuades his wife to sign the mortgage agreement under false pretences. If the wife can prove her case, the mortgagee cannot enforce the mortgage against her.

Undue influence can be either actual or presumed. Presumed undue influence arises when there is a relationship of trust and confidence combined with circumstances justifying the presumption that the relationship was abused in order to achieve the bargain. Two House of Lords decisions have clarified the doctrine in the context of mortgages. The issues are:

- Is there undue influence?
- Is the mortgagee tarnished with the undue influence?
- Has the mortgagee taken steps to ensure that its mortgage is not void because of the undue influence?

In ***Barclays Bank plc v O'Brien* [1993]** the husband owned a manufacturing company. The company had a large overdraft with the bank and, in order to secure overdraft facilities, both the husband and wife signed a second charge over their house in favour of the bank. The wife was a surety for her husband. A surety is a person who acts as a guarantor for another's debts. The wife did not read the charge and when the bank sought to enforce the charge, she argued that her husband had pressurised her into signing it, that she thought that it would only be for three weeks and that her husband had led her to believe that the charge was limited to £60,000 (as opposed to the total debt of £135,000).

The House of Lords held that there was no undue influence but there was misrepresentation. The bank would have constructive notice of any right of the surety (the wife) to have the charge set aside, here the misrepresentation, unless the bank had taken reasonable steps to satisfy itself that there was no such right. In order to avoid liability, the bank should have warned the surety of the potential liability, the risks involved and advised her to take independent advice. As this was not done, it was held that the bank could not enforce the charge against the wife.

The different forms of undue influence were set out in ***Barclays Bank plc v O'Brien***. Class 1 was actual undue influence. In Class 2(A) undue influence was presumed because of the relationship of the parties, for example, doctor and patient. Class 2(B) was where the claimant had to prove that confidence and trust were placed in the wrongdoer, for example, husband and wife. In Class 2 the claimant would have to show that they were disadvantaged by the transaction, called a manifest disadvantage. In Class 2 the burden of proof changed and was on the wrongdoer.

In ***Royal Bank of Scotland v Etridge (No. 2)* [2001]** the House of Lords moved away from ***O'Brien*** and provided authoritative and detailed guidance on the obligations of solicitors and lenders. The case applies wherever a property is jointly owned, and the owners have a non-commercial relationship (e.g. marriage, cohabitees, family, etc.). One of the owners then obtains a mortgage to finance, for example, their business affairs, from which the other does not directly benefit.

What has happened in the past is that, after financial problems, the mortgage lender has endeavoured to repossess. The other owner (who signed the mortgage but did not directly benefit) has alleged that they did so under undue influence or misrepresentation. The question then arises: Did the lender know of this undue influence? In reality the lender has passed the obligation on to a solicitor (usually the same solicitor acting for both owners). Accordingly, whether or not the claimant can establish undue influence will depend on the advice given by the solicitor at the outset of the mortgage.

Accordingly, the House of Lords has provided the following guidance:

(1) The bank does not have to have a meeting with the surety but should ensure that the surety receives legal advice and that the bank receives confirmation from the solicitor confirming that the nature and implications of the mortgage have been explained to the surety.

(2) The solicitor should advise the surety of any potential liability at a face-to-face meeting in the absence of the mortgagor.

(3) The role of the solicitor is to explain the nature of the documents, their practical consequences and the seriousness of the risks involved.

(4) The bank should provide the solicitor with the necessary financial information to enable the solicitor to advise.

(5) It is not for the solicitor to veto the transaction, although if it is glaringly obvious the surety is being grievously wronged, the solicitor should decline to act further.

(6) The solicitor may also act for the mortgagor or the bank provided that they are satisfied it is in the surety's best interests and there is no conflict of interest.

(7) Normally, the bank will be able to rely upon the solicitor's certificate confirming the discussions without question, but it will not be protected if it knows, or ought to have known, that the solicitor's advice was either not given or was inadequate.

The House of Lords judgment sets out the core minimum requirements for advice and confirms that the giving of such advice is an important role and not a mere formality.

The solicitor does not need to establish conclusively that there is no undue influence. They do need to provide the co-owner with the full facts of the case (e.g. the amounts which can be borrowed, the potential consequences, the extent of risks such as earlier borrowings). This should be done at a face-to-face interview, and only if they are happy to go ahead without further negotiations with the lender, should the matter proceed. Advice given should also be confirmed in writing.

The House of Lords indicated that the solicitor concerned could be the same for both owners, except where the case has a special feature. Most firms, however, would be keen to avoid the possibility of a conflict of interest arising and insist that one party was separately advised on this matter. The Law Society has issued guidance stating that the risk of a conflict arising in these circumstances is extreme, so that in most cases the other owner will need to be separately advised. The UK Finance Mortgage Lenders' Handbook makes clear that any borrower who does not personally benefit from the loan must normally be separately advised.

Note that the Court of Appeal had to consider ***Etridge*** issues in ***Waller-Edwards v One Savings Bank Plc* [2024]**. The case involved the extent to which a lender is put on enquiry as to the possibility of undue influence where a secured loan is made to joint borrowers who are romantically linked. ***Etridge*** involved a wife claiming that she had charged her interest in the matrimonial home as a result of the undue influence of her husband and the court held that the bank is put on inquiry to watch out for undue influence or misrepresentation in such cases. Banks are obliged to make sure that the party who is not directly benefitting from the loan (often the wife) obtains independent legal advice where the security is the matrimonial home.

In ***Waller-Edwards***, the Court of Appeal considered whether to extend the ***Etridge*** principles to a new category. There are currently two scenarios to consider:

1. **"Surety" cases**: where (i) one borrower guarantees the debts of the other or a company or (ii) security is taken over jointly owned property to finance debts of only one borrower. In this case, ***Etridge*** applies; and

2. **"Joint borrowing" cases:** where a joint loan is taken out for joint, non-business purposes. In these cases lenders are not on enquiry for undue influence and ***Etridge*** does not apply.

In the present case, Ms Waller-Edwards tried to argue that a third "hybrid" category should exist to cover the situation where some, but not all, of the loan benefits one party. The Court of Appeal rejected this view, presumably to the lender's relief. Sir Geoffrey Vos MR said:

*"This is a sad case. In my judgment, however, we must apply **Etridge** to the facts as found by the trial judge. **Etridge** does not demand that, in a hybrid case, a lender is put on inquiry unless the element of the transaction that is for the sole benefit of one of the borrowers is trivial. Instead, it requires the court to look at a non-commercial hybrid transaction as a whole and to decide, as a matter of fact and degree, whether the loan was being made for the purposes of the borrower with the debts,*

as distinct from their joint purposes. In this case, the judges below decided, and I would agree (though there is no appeal on the point), that the loan was, looked at as a whole and from the point of view of what the bank knew, a joint borrowing made for their joint purposes [38]."

Activity

Follow the link below and read the Law Society's guidance on "Undue influence – solicitors' duties post Etridge":

https://www.lawsociety.org.uk/Topics/Property/Tools/model-letter-post-etridge

Download and read the "Model letter to wife where charging home to secure loan to husband or his business".

Part 1 of the UK Finance Mortgage Lenders' Handbook (at Clause 8) states that, unless permitted by the individual lender in Part 2, the solicitor must not advise the following categories of people, and must arrange for them to seek independent legal advice:

- any borrower who does not personally benefit from the loan;
- any guarantor;
- any person intending to occupy the property who is to execute a consent to the mortgage.

Individual lenders may vary this requirement, but there are often conditions attached. Each individual lender's position can be checked in Part 2 of the UK Finance Mortgage Lenders' Handbook, which sets out whether the lender allows the solicitor to advise any of the people listed above, and, if so, under what circumstances.

Even where the lender does allow the solicitor to advise these people, it states that they must only do so after recommending independent legal advice in the absence of any other person interested in the transaction. Any advice given must also be in the absence of any other person interested in the transaction. The Handbook states that the solicitor should be particularly careful if the matrimonial home or family home is being charged to secure a business debt, and that any consent should be signed by the person concerned. A power of attorney is not acceptable for this purpose.

2.6 Mitigating risk

We have seen that there are a significant number of risks relating to conveyancing transactions. A firm must have appropriate policies, controls and procedures (PCPs) in place to help mitigate these risks. However, there are also steps which conveyancers can suggest that their clients take to diminish the risk of property fraud. Remember a property is more at risk if:

- the registered proprietor's identity has been stolen;
- the property is rented out;
- the registered proprietor lives overseas;
- the property is empty;
- the property is not mortgaged;
- the title to the property is unregistered.

Property Alert service

Property Alert is a free property monitoring service provided by HMLR for anyone who thinks that a registered property could be at risk of fraud. It is necessary to create an account to use the service. It is possible to monitor up to 10 title numbers and the property to be monitored must be situated in England or Wales and registered at HMLR. Email alerts will be sent when official searches and applications are received against a monitored property. This means that if an alert is received about activity which appears suspicious, the recipient of the email should take swift action.

Not all alert emails will mean that there is fraudulent activity and signing up to Property Alert will not automatically stop fraud from happening. The recipient of the email will need to decide if the activity on the property is potentially fraudulent and the alert email will tell them whom to contact. The point is that if an email is received alerting the recipient that an Official Search with Priority has been submitted against a title, for example, this could mean that the property is about to be mortgaged or sold. If the property owner is not carrying out those transactions, this could alert them to fraudulent activity.

Conveyancers should consider notifying all clients who purchase a property of the Property Alert service. However, it will be particularly useful for registered proprietors who do not live at a property, such as owners of investment/buy to let property. Property Alert is mentioned at para 34 of the Protocol.

Example

A homeowner recently hit the headlines for all the wrong reasons:

Luton man left shocked as his house is 'stolen'

(1 November 2021)

The BBC and many other news outlets reported on the story of the man who was shocked at returning to his home to find it stripped of all furnishings after it had been stolen without his knowledge. A BBC investigation found that the man's identity had been stolen and used to sell the house and bank the proceeds. The man did not live at the property at the time and it is possible that had the property been registered with the Property Alert service, the man would have received notification in sufficient time to enable him to take steps to thwart the fraud.

Follow the link below for the full story:

https://www.bbc.co.uk/news/uk-england-essex-59069662

The interesting postscript is that some four years after the initial incident, the owner has finally secured an order for possession in his favour. Here is the link to the new story:

https://www.bbc.co.uk/news/articles/cwygv79n8x1o

Register a restriction

A registered proprietor can prevent HMLR from registering a sale or mortgage over their property unless a conveyancer certifies that the disposition was made by the registered proprietor by putting a Form LL restriction on the register of title. The restriction is designed to help prevent forgery by requiring that a conveyancer certifies that they are satisfied that the person transferring or mortgaging the property is the same person as the owner.

A restriction can be added to the title by an owner who does not live at the property using form RQ – see https://www.gov.uk/government/publications/restriction-by-owner-not-living-at-property-request-registration-rq. The Form LL restriction can be added to the proprietorship register for free. The restriction is in the following terms:

> "No disposition of the registered estate by the proprietor of the registered estate is to be registered without a certificate signed by a conveyancer that that conveyancer is satisfied that the person who executed the document submitted for registration as disponor is the same person as the proprietor."

Activity

Follow the link below and download the CILEX Regulation document: "Risk Management: Resources"

https://cilexregulation.org.uk/resource-library/?child_category=19

Retain this information and use it to help you keep up-to-date with risk management issues.

2.7 Undertakings

We will now move on to consider undertakings. The SRA Glossary defines an undertaking as:

"A statement, given orally or in writing, whether or not it includes the word 'undertake' or 'undertaking', to someone who reasonably places reliance on it, that you or a third party will do something or cause something to be done, or refrain from doing something."

The conveyancing process relies on professional undertakings. Without them, transactions could not proceed. For example:

(1) If a conveyancer has to obtain a set of unregistered title deeds that are deposited with a lender as security for a loan, the conveyancer will need to give the lender a professionally binding undertaking that they will not release the unregistered deeds to any other party until the loan is repaid.

(2) The Law Society's formulae for exchange of contracts contain implied undertakings including that the buyer's conveyancer will send their clients signed part of the contract and the agreed deposit to the seller's conveyancer on the day of exchange of contracts.

(3) Completion will not take place unless the seller's conveyancer provides an undertaking to the buyer's conveyancer on the Completion Information and Undertakings Form that the seller's mortgage(s) will be discharged out of the sale proceeds on completion.

Accordingly, the giving and receiving of undertakings is of central importance to the conveyancing process. When a solicitor gives an undertaking, they are professionally and personally bound to carry out that undertaking. A solicitor must undertake to do only what is strictly within their control. To undertake to do something which they might not be able to do would be folly or, at least, unprofessional.

This is clearly illustrated by ***Hole & Pugsley v Sumption* [2001]**, where a solicitor gave an undertaking to repay a mortgage on completion of a transaction. It subsequently transpired that there was considerably more to pay to discharge the mortgage than the solicitor had previously thought, and the firm concerned argued before the court that the undertaking could not be relied on as there had been a change of circumstances. The court rejected this argument and ordered the firm concerned to pay the shortfall. The case clearly illustrates that the court will construe and enforce undertakings strictly.

The SRA states that undertakings should be specific, measurable, agreed, realistic and timed (SMART).

(1) **Wording**

The precise wording used in an undertaking is of vital importance for both the person receiving the undertaking and the person giving it. For example, in ***Barclays Bank v Weeks* [1998]** an undertaking not to effect completion unless a "good marketable title" was obtained was not breached, even though the property was subject to a right of way, because the title was nevertheless "good" and "marketable".

If ambiguous, the undertaking will be construed strictly against the person who gave it.

Consider the wording of the following examples of undertakings.

(a) ***To obtain deeds on loan from a building society or other lender at the outset of the case***

The letter to the lender would begin by stating the borrower, account number and address. It would confirm that the solicitor was acting in the sale of the property and request the deeds and documents of title in order to progress the legal formalities. The solicitor would then give an undertaking in the letter so that the deeds could be released to the firm. The undertaking would typically be worded along the following lines:

> "We undertake to hold the deeds to your order [i.e. to the order of the mortgagee] pending redemption of the mortgage and either return them to you on demand or redeem the mortgage."

The lender will be prepared to release the deeds to the solicitor on receipt of such an undertaking, as undertakings are binding.

(b) ***To discharge a mortgage***

A discharge undertaking may be given before completion in response to the Completion Information and Undertakings Form.

Activity

By way of reminder, look again at the Completion Information and Undertakings Form (TA 13) - see **Document 8** of the **Appendix**.

Look in particular at question 5 where the seller's conveyancer will confirm that they will list the mortgages or charges secured on the property which they undertake to redeem on completion.

A discharge undertaking may also be given by the seller's solicitor to the buyer on completion of the transaction. The Law Society's recommended form of wording is:

> "In consideration of you today completing the purchase of [property] WE HEREBY UNDERTAKE forthwith to pay over to the [name] Building Society the money required to redeem the mortgage/legal charge dated [date] and to forward the receipted mortgage/legal charge to you as soon as it is received by us from the [name] Building Society."

Note that this undertaking is very specific as to which mortgage will be redeemed. Before it is given, enquiries will have to be made of the building society (and any other lenders if there is more than one mortgage on the property) to ensure that the solicitor has sufficient funds to discharge the mortgage on completion. The evidence of discharge will be forwarded only "when received" – therefore, the seller's solicitor is protected if the documents are delayed or lost in the post.

It would be necessary to adapt the wording in some cases. One example would be where the land was registered (when a form DS1 is handed over, not the receipted mortgage, or mortgages of registered land can be discharged electronically). Another example would be in relation to a second mortgage (where, in unregistered land, the land charges cancellation certificate must also be handed over).

The following provides an example of a discharge undertaking in registered land where form DS1 is being used:

> "In consideration of your today completing the purchase of [address] we hereby undertake forthwith to pay over to [name of lender] the money required to discharge the mortgage dated [date] and to forward a copy of the lender's letter confirming successful redemption of their charge and lodgement of an electronic discharge at the Land Registry as soon as we receive it from the lender."

The following provides an example of a discharge undertaking in registered land where the mortgage is to be discharged electronically:

> "In consideration of your today completing the purchase of the above property on behalf of your clients, we hereby undertake on behalf of our clients forthwith to pay over to [name of lender] the money required to redeem the mortgage dated [date] and to forward the sealed form DS1 to you as soon as it is received by us from [name of lender]."

The Court of Appeal confirmed in ***Patel v Daybells* [2001]** that it is acceptable for a buyer's solicitor to rely on a seller's solicitor's undertaking in the form explained above, unless there are exceptional circumstances, such as where the amount owed exceeds the minimum level of solicitors' indemnity insurance, or the lender concerned is not a member of UK Finance. The Law Society has produced guidance for practitioners detailing steps to be taken when these exceptional circumstances apply.

Activity

Follow the link below and note the Law Society's answer to the question: *"Do I need confirmation from the mortgagee that I can receive redemption funds?"*

https://www.lawsociety.org.uk/Contact-or-visit-us/Helplines/Practice-advice-service/Q-and-As/Do-I-need-confirmation-from-the-mortgagee-that-I-can-receive-redemption-funds

(c) ***To repay a bridging loan***

A bridging loan is typically given to assist a buyer with short-term financing problems between buying a property and selling the buyer's existing property. The bank usually requires the solicitor to undertake that the bank will receive the net proceeds of sale.

As the solicitor must undertake only what is within their personal power to perform:

(i) the solicitor must undertake to pay over only the net proceeds of sale (i.e. after paying off any mortgages, legal costs and other prior matters);

(ii) the solicitor must undertake to pay the money only if they actually receive it. Completion could fail to take place, or some of the completion money could be paid to the estate agent, or funds could be paid directly from the buyer to the seller, or the client could withdraw instructions from the solicitor. The solicitor needs to ensure that if any of these events happens, they will not be obliged to pay over the funds;

(iii) owing to the nature of this undertaking, the solicitor will require the client to give a written irrevocable authority to the solicitor, authorising the solicitor to pay over the proceeds of sale to the bank.

An example of an undertaking to a bank which has provided bridging finance to a client:

> "In the event that you provide my client [name] with bridging finance as set out below, I undertake to pay to you the net proceeds of sale, being the sale price of [amount] less [amount] (mortgages, legal fees and expenses). This undertaking shall only be binding on me to the extent of the net proceeds of sale actually received by me and which are available for credit to the account."

(2) Undertakings and the SRA Standards and Regulations 2019

The **SRA Standards and Regulations 2019** state that you must "perform all undertakings given by you, and do so within an agreed timescale or if no timescale has been agreed then within a reasonable time".

(3) Verbal undertakings

Usually, an undertaking is given in writing by a partner in the firm. Sometimes it is necessary, however, to give a verbal undertaking, in which case both sides should keep written memoranda of the conversation including the specific wording of the undertaking, and then confirm the details in writing, as soon as possible. It is important to maintain effective systems for recording when undertakings have been given and discharged.

(4) Authority to give undertakings

With authority from the firm, a solicitor's employee can give an undertaking in the name of the firm. The firm is bound to the same extent as if a partner had given the undertaking.

(5) **Breach**

If an undertaking is given, every partner in the firm is responsible for ensuring compliance. If the undertaking is breached, the partners can be:

(a) ordered by the court to make good the breach (note that this may involve the solicitors in paying off a mortgage from their own personal resources);

(b) disciplined by the SRA (this may involve having to pay a financial penalty or being suspended or removed from the roll of solicitors);

(c) in extreme cases, imprisoned for contempt. As solicitors are officers of the court, a solicitor who breaches an undertaking given to the court could be imprisoned for contempt of court. In ***Citadel Management v Thompson*** **[1999]** a solicitor breached an undertaking. When they were ordered by the court to comply and did not do so, they received a six-month prison sentence.

It is possible for all the above to apply.

If an employed solicitor had given the breached undertaking, they could face disciplinary action by the SRA. The firm would still be bound, and the partners would face the above courses of action.

(6) **Telephonic exchange and postal completion**

Formulas A, B and C for exchange of contracts involve the giving of undertakings. The Law Society Code for Completion by Post is also based on reliance on undertakings. These would be used only in dealings with other solicitors or licensed conveyancers; they could not be used if the other party to the transaction was unrepresented.

(7) **Chartered legal executives**

Chartered legal executives may give undertakings provided that they are authorised to do so by their firm. The undertaking is given on behalf of the firm, not the individual. Further information is available at: https://www.cilex.org.uk/membership/practice_advice/undertakings/undertakings_on_behalf_of_firm.

(8) **Licensed conveyancers**

Licensed conveyancers' undertakings are as acceptable as undertakings given by solicitors. Licensed conveyancers are subject to professional rules which are similar in content to those relating to solicitors. Similar methods of enforcement to those available against solicitors (disciplinary proceedings taken by the CLC) exist against licensed conveyancers. If in doubt, it is possible to check that a conveyancer is, indeed, licensed by enquiry of the CLC.

It is prudent to make an undertaking by a solicitor or licensed conveyancer contractual so that there is the additional remedy of enforcement in contract law. Therefore, the standard wording of an undertaking on completion might state, "**in consideration of** you today completing the above transaction I hereby undertake . . .".

Link to practice

Undertakings must not be accepted from unqualified persons as there is no method of enforcing them. This essentially means that undertakings in conveyancing matters can only be accepted from solicitors, licensed conveyancers or notaries who are qualified to undertake conveyancing work (notaries are qualified lawyers and are regulated by rules which are broadly similar to those affecting solicitors).

Summary of Facts

2.1 In 2018 the Firm acted for a property developer on the sale of a new build residential property.

2.2 On 7 March 2018 the Firm gave an undertaking to the buyers' solicitor to provide a Building Regulation Certificate and a structural defects insurance policy (the Policy) on or before completion.

2.3 Completion took place on 23 April 2018.

2.4 The Firm provided the buyers' solicitor with the Building Regulation Certificate on 10 January 2019. It did not provide the Policy. Instead, it provided a certificate of completion from an architect. The architect certificate gave less protection than the Policy would have.

3. Admissions

3.1 The Firm admits, and the SRA accepts, that by failing to provide the buyers' solicitor the Building Regulation Certificate until 10 January 2019 and failing to provide the Policy at all:

a. it failed to perform all undertakings given by it within an agreed timescale or within a reasonable amount of time and in doing so, did not achieve Outcome 11.2 of the SRA Code of Conduct 2011, and

b. it failed to behave in a way that maintains the trust the public places in you and in the provision of legal services and therefore, breached Principle 6 of the SRA Principles 2011.

4. Why a written rebuke is an appropriate outcome

4.1 The SRA's Enforcement Strategy sets out its approach to the use of its enforcement powers where there has been a failure to meet its standards or requirements.

4.2 When considering the appropriate sanctions in this matter, the SRA has taken into account the admissions made by the Firm and the following mitigation which it has put forward:

a. the Firm has shown insight of the situation and understands the important role undertakings play in the delivery of legal services

b. this is an isolated incident

c. the Firm has cooperated fully with the SRA's investigation.

4.3 The SRA considers that a written rebuke is the appropriate outcome because:

a. by failing to comply with the undertaking the Firm was reckless as to the risk of harm to the purchasers

b. by providing the architect's certificate the Firm took some remedial action to lessen the harm to the buyers, but some harm persists

c. a public sanction is required in order to uphold public confidence in the delivery of legal services.

5. Publication

5.1 The SRA considers it appropriate that this agreement is published in the interests of transparency in the regulatory and disciplinary process. The Firm agrees to the publication of this agreement.

6. Acting in a way which is inconsistent with this agreement

6.1 The Firm agrees that it will not deny the admissions made in this agreement or act in any way which is inconsistent with it.

6.2 If the Firm denies the admissions or acts in a way which is inconsistent with this agreement, the conduct which is subject to this agreement may be considered further by the SRA. That may result in a disciplinary outcome or a referral to the Solicitors Disciplinary Tribunal on the original facts and allegations.

6.3 Acting in a way which is inconsistent with this agreement may also constitute a separate breach of principles 2 and 5 of the Principles and paragraph 3.2 of the Code of Conduct for Firms.

2.7.1 Undertaking breach – a practical example

Conveyancers are faced with the risk of undertakings every day. Below is the outline of an investigation by the SRA against a firm that gave an undertaking in a conveyancing transaction with which it was ultimately unable to comply. The firm was rebuked, had the agreement published and had to pay £300 towards the costs of the investigation. The publicity was no doubt of far more concern to the firm than the financial penalty.

2.7.2 Drafting an undertaking – checklist

You can see that giving undertakings is risky. Accordingly, if you have to draft an undertaking, consider the following:

- Can I deal with this issue without giving an undertaking?
- Is the undertaking which I am giving within my power to perform? If not, I must limit the undertaking accordingly.
- Are the terms of the undertaking which I am giving specific?
- Are the terms of the undertaking which I am giving measurable?
- Am I authorised to give the undertaking on behalf of my firm?
- What is my firm's policy regarding giving an undertaking?
- Should a partner sign my undertaking?

2.7.3 Undertakings from solicitors and licensed conveyancers

The Supreme Court considered the issue of undertakings in ***Harcus Sinclair v Your Lawyers* [2021]**. The case involved a dispute between two law firms and whether a non-compete undertaking given by one law firm to another in relation to contemplated group litigation was unenforceable as an unreasonable restraint of trade. The Supreme Court held that the non-compete undertaking was not a solicitor's undertaking because it had nothing to do with the provision of legal advice. However, the decision on the facts is perhaps of less interest to conveyancers than some of the issues which the Supreme Court considered. The judgment contains an interesting historical summary of the development of undertakings and of central relevance is the fact that if a solicitor gives an undertaking, the court's supervisory jurisdiction to enforce such an undertaking is an aspect of its inherent jurisdiction over solicitors as officers of the court. This is significant because this method of enforcement is swift and effective and in many cases can be said to be what gives an undertaking from a solicitor it's "teeth". The court's jurisdiction may be invoked on an application to the court without the need to commence a separate action and as such, the inherent supervisory jurisdiction continues to play an important role in relation to solicitor's undertakings.

The Supreme Court drew a distinction between undertakings given by a solicitor and the status of an undertaking given by somebody working for an LLP or a licensed conveyancer. The latter are not "officers of the court" and therefore are not subject to the inherent jurisdiction of the court in the same way that solicitors are. This led commentators to consider whether an undertaking from a licensed conveyancer in a conveyancing transaction is in some way worth less than that given by a solicitor. The reality is that undertakings given by licensed conveyancers have been relied upon since the qualification of licensed conveyancer was created and breach of an undertaking given by a licensed conveyancer is still professional misconduct.

The Supreme Court gave some interesting comments and examples in relation to undertakings and made the point that not every statement given by a solicitor is capable of being an undertaking. The Supreme Court observed as follows:

(1) Undertakings are the bedrock of our system of conveyancing. The recipient of an undertaking must be able to assume that once given it will be scrupulously performed. If property purchasers and mortgage lenders cannot have complete confidence in the safety of the money they put into the hands of a solicitor in the course of a property transaction, our system of conveyancing would soon break down. The breach of an undertaking given by a solicitor damages public confidence in the profession and in the system of undertakings upon which property transactions depend.

(2) A solicitor's undertaking involves a promise to do or refrain from doing a certain act. It will often be contractual, but it need not be and there is no requirement of consideration or of legal enforceability.

(3) The mere fact that the undertaking is given by a solicitor does not make it a solicitor's undertaking. The generally accepted test is that the undertaking must be given by the solicitor in his or her "capacity as a solicitor". It is the fact that the undertaking is given professionally that engages the court's supervisory jurisdiction. The court is concerned with undertakings given by solicitors in their professional capacity rather than in some other capacity, such as their private capacity.

The Supreme Court went on to give some helpful examples in relation to undertakings:

"An example of an undertaking given by solicitors in their capacity as solicitors would be an undertaking to hold money or deeds to another's order in relation to a property transaction in respect of which they were engaged by a client. An example falling on the other side of the line would be an undertaking to hold or pay money in relation to the lease of a solicitor's office space. Another such example, falling outside what counts as a solicitor's undertaking, and closer to the facts of this case, would be an undertaking given under a covenant by a solicitor on leaving a firm not to work for any client of the firm for a period of time. It has never been suggested that such covenants are or should be summarily enforceable as solicitors' undertakings."

Examples of undertakings held to be **given by solicitors acting in their capacity as solicitors** include the following:

(1) An undertaking by a solicitor to repay money to a third party in the event that negotiations for an agreement between the third party and the solicitor's client did not result in agreement by a certain date.

(2) An undertaking by a solicitor given to his client's former solicitors not to release moneys in his possession belonging to the client until a dispute between them over unpaid fees had been sorted out.

(3) An undertaking, provided in the context of proceedings brought for the recovery of moneys due, given by the defendant's solicitor to the claimant's solicitor that the directors of the defendant would provide security for its liabilities to the claimant by creating second charges in the claimant's favour on their personal properties.

Examples of undertakings held **not to be given by solicitors acting in their capacity as solicitors** include the following:

(1) An undertaking given by an assistant solicitor on behalf of his firm that an advance of money obtained for a client of the firm from another firm of solicitors would be repaid by a certain date with interest at 2 per cent a month.

(2) An undertaking by a solicitor to repay moneys due or to become due to the claimant from a third party and a guarantee of a third party's obligation to repay a loan to the claimant with interest.

The Supreme Court went on to consider the central importance of undertakings to day to day conveyancing work. Although they declined to extend the ambit of the enforcement of an undertaking to licensed conveyancers and LLPs, their comments are still of great interest:

"126. A typical residential conveyancing transaction affords a good illustration of what is at stake. Most residential conveyancing adopts the Law Society's Code for

Completion by Post. This enables the parties' solicitors to avoid the time, expense and inconvenience of an old-style completion where the solicitors all attend in person and transact face to face. Numerous undertakings are given and received. They include: following the provisions of the Code, the redemption or discharge of mortgages out of the purchase moneys, undertakings to have the authority of seller and mortgagee to receive moneys, to deliver specified documents to the purchaser, to notify that completion has taken place to the parties and their agents and to authorise the seller's agents to release the keys to the purchaser. This efficient and economical scheme could only be prudently used by participating solicitors as part of their service to their clients if the solicitor could be sure that the various undertakings were all going to be complied with without question by all the other solicitors concerned. Where there is a chain of transactions all completing at the same time, the interlocking undertakings would be forthcoming from a significant number of different firms.

127. There can be no doubt that the underpinning of those undertakings by the availability of rapid summary enforcement under the court's supervisory jurisdiction has been a significant buttress for their reliability, and for the propriety of accepting them as part of the every-day machinery for modern conveyancing. This is not because there is a history of frequent non-compliance followed by court enforcement. Rather, the mere existence of that ready and swift means of enforcement made it inherently unlikely that a solicitor would fail to comply. The undertaking did not depend for its enforcement upon it being given contractually, supported by consideration. Thus, a solicitor's undertaking has a value greater than that of the client for whom the solicitor acts.

136. Prior to the coming into force of the relevant provisions in the AJA 1985 [**Administration of Justice Act 1985**] *there was nothing inconvenient in defining the extent of this jurisdiction by reference to status, because solicitors were, with minimal exceptions, the only persons authorised to provide solicitor services, including conveyancing, probate and the conduct of litigation in court. Thus a status-based supervisory jurisdiction covered almost all the relevant functional ground.*

137. But this fundamentally changed in and after 1985. Licensed conveyancers became authorised to conduct conveyancing. Solicitor LLPs eventually became authorised to conduct the whole range of legal services formerly conducted by solicitors, whether as sole practitioners or, more importantly, in partnership. At this point a status-based delineation of the ambit of the court's supervisory jurisdiction began to distinguish between different classes of persons (collectively referred to in this judgment as 'law firms') providing the same legal services in competition with each other. Furthermore, a solicitor's undertaking given by (say) Smith & Jones LLP on a Friday would not be buttressed by the court's power of summary enforcement, whereas an identical undertaking given by the Smith & Jones partnership on the previous Monday, before its members incorporated as an LLP on the Wednesday, would be. In that example exactly the same solicitors who had constituted the former partnership would be the members (ie owners and managers) of the LLP which succeeded to the same practice. But the LLP would not itself be a solicitor, or an unincorporated association of solicitors. It is a separate legal person, distinct from the solicitors who own and manage it.

138. A debate whether the court should extend its supervisory jurisdiction in this way presupposes that it is at liberty to do so. A main argument advanced by the respondents in this court is that there is no such liberty. It is said that by section 50 of the Solicitors Act 1974 Parliament confined the jurisdiction to solicitors as officers of the court, and that the absence of any conferral of that status on the newly authorised incorporated law firms in the AJA 1985 or the LSA 2007 [**Legal Services Act 2007**], *or by amendment of section 50 of the Solicitors Act 1974, means that the jurisdiction cannot be extended to them.*

139. We are not persuaded that this is an insuperable objection. Section 50 repeats the substance of a provision originally appearing in section 87 of the Supreme Court of Judicature Act 1873 which created the Supreme Court of Judicature and the High Court. Its effect is not to replace a previously inherent jurisdiction with a new statutory jurisdiction, set in stone unless altered by Parliament, but rather to recognise a continuing inherent jurisdiction as residing in the newly created courts in the same way as it had in the old courts which were being replaced. A similar technique was deployed in relation to the power to grant injunctions, in section 25(8) of the 1873 Act. This did not replace the previously inherent equitable jurisdiction, and it has continued to develop and extend into new fields, such as the freezing order, the search order, the Norwich Pharmacal and Bankers Trust orders, anti-suit injunctions and, most recently, the website blocking order.

140. Nor can section 50 of the Solicitors Act 1974 be read as containing some kind of Parliamentary prohibition. While it recognised that the inherent supervisory jurisdiction over solicitors had indeed been based until then on their status as officers of the court, it was silent as to whether it might become appropriate to extend it, and the circumstances which call that question now into sharp focus did not then exist. In our view, it is therefore open to us as a matter of developing the inherent jurisdiction of the court (or, perhaps, as a purposive interpretation of section 50) to treat a solicitor's undertaking as extending to an undertaking given by an incorporated law firm.

141. The question whether the inherent jurisdiction might be extended to incorporated law firms as providers of legal services formerly only provided by solicitors does not appear to have been the subject of judicial consideration in the Assaubayev case, although Christopher Clarke LJ was well aware of what (at para 62) he called 'curial creativity' in relation to inherent jurisdiction. As in this case, it was not necessary to do so. So we do not regard that case as a binding precedent against doing so.

142. We recognise that there are powerful arguments both ways on this question, with different force in relation to different types of incorporated law firms. The strongest argument in favour seems to us to be that the court's buttressing of professional undertakings within the provision of 'solicitor services' ought fairly to be equally available across all types of provider: ie that the jurisdiction should now be applied along functional lines, to all authorised providers of solicitor services, rather than continue to be status-based. There is in that respect an analogy with the way in which, for certain purposes, the Civil Procedure Rules treat as a solicitor any person (individual or incorporated) authorised to conduct litigation under the LSA 2007: see CPR 6.2(d) and 42.1. This functional approach is of particular force in relation to a solicitors' LLP which, although a separate legal person from the solicitors who own and manage it, is the vehicle by which they provide solicitor services, and on behalf of which they continue to give solicitors' undertakings. The strongest argument against is that, from 2007, incorporated law firms need no longer be owned, controlled or even managed by solicitors, and that conveyancing services have been available from 1985 from licensed conveyancers, who have apparently been able to provide satisfactory undertakings without the court's backing in terms of summary enforcement.

143. However, with considerable reluctance, we do not consider that this case is an appropriate occasion for making a decision whether, and if so how far, to extend that inherent jurisdiction. This is for three main reasons. First, our views would only have the force of obiter dicta, for the reasons already explained. This is not, as it turns out, a case about a solicitor's undertaking at all. It would not therefore bind lower courts. Secondly, we consider that a properly informed decision would much better be made with the assistance of submissions from the Law Society, and from any other professional or regulatory body with a legitimate interest such as, for example, the Council of Licensed Conveyancers or the Solicitors' Regulation Authority. Thirdly, although this continues to be an inherent jurisdiction, this question is probably better dealt with by legislation than by the courts, because of the availability of procedures for consultation which the court lacks. In the context of this case, we have not been provided with much of the evidence and information about the operation and structure of today's law firms that we would need to develop the law properly in this area.

148. In the meantime, we share the judge's concern about whether those dealing with incorporated law firms, and with solicitors' LLPs in particular, are sufficiently aware that undertakings given by them are not currently buttressed by the court's supervisory jurisdiction. We note, however, that the following passage appears in the latest online version of Cordery on Legal Services*, at para 319:*

'Given that most solicitors now practise through some form of entity, the practical effect of the decision [of the Court of Appeal] in Harcus Sinclair *is that most undertakings can now only be enforced by a breach of contract claim. Alternatively, an aggrieved party can hope that the risk of being reported to the SRA will encourage compliance. This clearly falls well short of the protections that made undertakings such a powerful tool, and clients and law firms alike may want to review their reliance upon them.'*

It may be that, as the judge suggested, the lacuna may be addressed by ensuring that a relevant undertaking is given personally by a solicitor, as well as, or in the alternative to, the incorporated law firm for which he or she acts. But that may not always be a satisfactory solution where summary enforcement is sought, if the individual solicitor lacks the power within his or her incorporated law firm to ensure that compliance occurs. We take the view that this is at best a partial and temporary solution. We therefore express the hope that Parliament will consider the lacuna that this judgment has confirmed in relation to undertakings given by solicitors working for incorporated law firms, particularly LLPs."

Activity

Follow the link below and note the Law Society's view on issues to consider following the above case:

https://www.lawsociety.org.uk/topics/regulation/professional-undertakings

Link to practice

You will note from the Law Society's comments above that they suggest exploring the option of personal undertakings that is, the situation where a solicitor is asked to give an undertaking in their personal capacity, rather than on behalf of their firm.

Whilst this might be attractive for the firm requesting the undertaking, it is suggested that an individual solicitor should never give a personal undertaking to try to ensure that their personal position is protected.

Accordingly, always take care to establish the basis upon which a firm might be requesting an undertaking and, the basis upon which you are giving it.

If in doubt, decline to give an undertaking and confirm the position in writing.

2.8 Taxation in conveyancing transactions

We will conclude this chapter by looking at the key taxation matters which conveyancers are likely to come across. A very important point to appreciate from the outset is that you are conveyancing practitioners, not accountants. You must, therefore, understand the extent of the taxation advice which your firm will permit you to give. There are, of course, some lawyers who have a very detailed knowledge of taxation matters and can advise accordingly. However, most conveyancers do not profess to have expertise in taxation matters and will generally highlight key principles to their clients but will also advise them to take specialist accountancy advice as appropriate. It is very important that you limit or qualify the taxation advice which you give to your clients as appropriate.

2.8.1 Capital gains tax (CGT)

At the initial interview the seller of property should be advised on the situation with regard to CGT liability. Where the sale is of the seller's dwelling-house together with garden or grounds of up to 5,000 square metres (just over an acre, roughly the size of a football pitch) it will be exempt providing it was the client's only or main residence throughout the period of ownership. This is known as the **private residence relief**.

Obviously, this means that there may be a liability for CGT when the client is selling more than 5,000 square metres of land with the house. There may also be a liability where the client has been absent from the property for a significant period, although the seller may be absent for up to 18 months before the sale, as long as it was their only or main home for some of the time they have owned it. Periods of absence when working outside the UK are also allowable, as is absence incurred by an employer's requirement to live elsewhere in the UK, up to a prescribed limit. There may be liability where the client has another home and where the property has been used partly for business purposes. CGT liability may also arise if the property was a buy-to-let property.

Activity

The government has produced useful non-technical CGT guidance about selling a home. Follow the link below and read the advice and note all key points:

www.gov.uk/tax-sell-home

In essence, a seller will not have to pay CGT when selling the home if all of the following apply:

- the seller has one home and has lived in it as their main home for all the time they have owned it;
- the seller has not let part of it out (this does not include having a single lodger);
- the seller has not used part of it for business only;
- the grounds, including all buildings, are less than 5,000 square metres in total;
- the seller did not buy the property just to make a gain.

Once the conveyancer has checked the statutory provisions to be sure whether there will be any CGT liability, they must then be able to explain to the client how the tax will be calculated. In general terms, CGT is payable only in respect of any **gain** made on the sale or gift of the property. The gain is calculated by taking the sale price or market value; from that is deducted the value of the property at either acquisition, or the 1982 value if it was owned by the client in 1982. Legal and related costs and expenses and costs of improvement can also be deducted. An individual's annual CGT exemption can be set against the gain; any balance thereafter is taxed at the current rate. The rates currently in force for individuals in relation to residential property are 18 per cent and 24 per cent. The tax rate used depends on the total amount of the individual's taxable income so this needs to be worked out first. It is often prudent to refer the client for specialist tax advice to an accountant.

It may also be necessary to discuss future potential CGT liability with a buyer if they are not proposing to purchase the property as their main residence.

2.8.2 Stamp duty land tax (SDLT)

This is a tax on land transactions with a legal obligation on the buyer to declare the transaction. There is therefore little opportunity to avoid paying the tax. SDLT must be paid when a buyer purchases a property over a certain price in England or Northern Ireland. SDLT is not payable on properties purchased in Wales as Land Transaction Tax (LTT) is payable instead.

The SDLT return and any tax must be paid to HMRC within **14 days of completion**.

Link to practice

Generally, the conveyancer will ask their buyer client to sign a completed SDLT return in advance of completion. The conveyancer will request the amount of SDLT payable from the buyer prior to completion on their statement. The conveyancer will usually file the return online and pay the tax on behalf of their client. Note that this is a **self-assessment tax** and it is therefore up to the buyer to ensure that they declare all appropriate information to their conveyancer to enable the SDLT return to be completed accurately.

Submission within 14 days of completion is a tight timeframe although most conveyancers will do this on the day of completion itself. Note that this is 14 straight days, including weekends and bank holidays, and not "working days".

If the SDLT return is completed late, penalties and interest are payable. There is an automatic penalty of £100.

SDLT is payable when someone:

- buys a freehold property;
- buys a new or existing leasehold property;
- buys a property through a shared ownership scheme;
- has land or property transferred to them in exchange for payment, for example buying a share in a house. Note that taking on part of a mortgage debt on a property transfer could give rise to SDLT liability even if no money actually changes hands – it is the assumption of the debt which is relevant for SDLT.

The SDLT threshold for residential properties as at April 2025 is £125,000. There are different SDLT rates according to whether a property is residential, non-residential or mixed use. There are also higher rates for additional properties such as second homes.

SDLT on residential property is charged at different rates depending on the portion of the purchase price that falls within each rate band.

Value bands	Rate of SDLT
Up to £125,000	0%
Over £125,000 to £250,000	2%
Over £250,000 to £925,000	5%
Over £925,000 to £1.5 m	10%
Over £1.5 m	12%

It is therefore necessary to take the purchase price and see which bands apply to each slice of it.

The following example is from the HMRC website:

In April 2025 you buy a house for £295,000. The SDLT you owe will be calculated as follows:

0% on the first £125,000 = £0

2% on the second £125,000 = £2,500

5% on the final £45,000 = £2,250

Total SDLT = £4,750

Activity

To assist with the correct calculation of SDLT due on a particular transaction, there are online calculators available on several websites. HMRC, for instance, has an online calculator which can be accessed via the link at:

https://www.tax.service.gov.uk/calculate-stamp-duty-land-tax/#/intro

Go to the calculator and work out the SDLT on a purchase of a main residence for £950,000.

Different SDLT rates for specific cases

In certain specific cases, the standard SDLT rates are varied. Some examples are as follows (the details of these examples are outside the scope of this course book but may be relevant in practice).

There is a special higher SDLT rate of 17 per cent for some dwellings costing over £500,000 where they are purchased by certain corporate bodies. There are specified reliefs which apply in defined cases (e.g. for property developers who meet certain conditions and for property rental businesses).

Additionally, certain corporate bodies which own interests in dwellings valued above a certain amount are liable to pay an annual tax on enveloped dwellings (ATED). This is an annual tax and requires annual returns and payments. The amount of tax depends on which fixed band a dwelling falls within. There are a number of reliefs available.

There are a number of other reliefs which can reduce or negate the SDLT payable. Note that multiple dwelling relief was abolished from 1 June 2024.

An additional 2 per cent stamp duty tax is now payable on all non-UK residents buying residential property in England and Northern Ireland. This will be in addition to any duty already payable.

SDLT relief for first-time buyers

There is a specific SDLT relief for first-time buyers. This relief applies where buyers are purchasing their first home and the purchase price is £300,000 or less. No SDLT will be payable on the purchase price up to £300,000 and 5 per cent will be payable on any portion between £300,001 and £500,000. If the purchase price is more than

£500,000, the relief does not apply and the buyers must pay the standard SDLT rates on the total purchase price. In order for the relief to be claimed:

- the purchase must be completed on or after 22 November 2017;
- the purchase price must be £300,000 or less;
- the purchaser, and anyone else they are buying with, must be first-time buyers; and
- the purchasers must intend to occupy the property as their only or main residence.

The relief is claimed by entering a specific code in the land transaction return (LTR).

It is relevant to note that first-time buyers can be any age and that the relief does not affect the amount of any SDLT which may be payable on the rental element of a new lease.

The SDLT calculator mentioned above can be used to work out the amount of SDLT payable where the purchaser is a first-time buyer. The calculator asks whether the purchaser has ever owned another property.

SDLT rates on additional properties

From 1 April 2016, higher rates of SDLT have been charged where a person is buying an additional residential property such as a second home or a buy-to-let property. The buyer will have to pay 5 per cent on top of the normal SDLT rates if buying a residential property results in them owning more than one property. Properties purchased for under £40,000 are excluded from the higher rates but of course most properties cost a lot more than £40,000.

The SDLT rates for additional properties are therefore as follows – it can be seen that there is an additional 5 per cent on each value band when contrasted with the table of normal residential rates.

A buyer will also need to pay the higher rates if they do not own a residential property and buy at least two residential properties at the same time.

There is a limited exception in relation to main residences, so a buyer may replace their main residence without paying the higher rates of SDLT. This is so they can sell their main residence and replace it with a new one. A buyer won't have to pay the higher rates if they sell their main home on the same day as they buy their new home. The basic question to ask is how many properties the client will own at the end of the day of completion of their purchase transaction. The sale and purchase of the main residence does not have to take place at the same time however. The higher rates will not be payable if the property being purchased is replacing the buyer's main residence and the main residence has already been sold. If the buyer has not yet sold their existing main residence on the day of completion of the new purchase then the higher rates will be payable as the buyer will own two properties, but the buyer can claim a refund of the amount paid over and above the "normal" SDLT rates if they sell their previous main residence within 36 months. If a person already has two or more properties and sells their main residence, they will not have to pay the higher rates if they buy a new main residence within 36 months.

The rules can be quite complex. For instance, where there are joint buyers and one of them already owns one or more properties, the higher rates may be payable. The solicitor must assess the precise circumstances, check the exact rules and rates which will apply, and advise accordingly.

The SDLT calculator mentioned above can also be used for working out the SDLT due on an additional property. The calculator asks at the appropriate point as to whether the purchase will result in the buyer owning two properties and will adjust the calculation accordingly.

As an example to illustrate how the SDLT can vary, consider the following case of a client.

Novak already owns his main home in Manchester but is now buying a second home for weekend use in the Lake District where he likes to go hill walking. The purchase price of the second home is £250,000. Under the normal SDLT rates, Novak would have had to pay SDLT of £2,500. Under the rules for additional properties, Novak will now have an SDLT bill of £10,000 on his second home.

This is something clients will have to budget for, and be advised upon, in appropriate cases. Most transactions will not of course be affected by the additional rates.

SDLT on leasehold properties

There are additional rules for leasehold property. As well as paying duty on any premium (purchase price) for a new lease, SDLT on new leases is also calculated on the net present value (NPV) of the rent payable. This is based on the value of the total rent over the life of the lease. There is a complicated formula to calculate this.

SDLT can now be paid online. This is very quick and easy. The details on the SDLT1 form are submitted and the receipt (SDLT5) issued immediately. The SDLT5 is then submitted with the HMLR application to register the transfer of ownership.

SDLT rates are subject to fairly regular change. Always use this link to find out the most up-to-date thresholds:

https://www.gov.uk/stamp-duty-land-tax/residential-property-rates

Circumstances where no SDLT return is needed

It is not necessary to pay SDLT or file a return if:

- no money or other property changes hands for a land or property transfer;
- property is left to someone in a will;
- property is transferred due to divorce or dissolution of a civil partnership;
- a freehold property is purchased for less than £40,000;
- a new or assigned lease is purchased of 7 years or more, where the premium is less than £40,000 and the annual rent is less than £1,000;
- a new or assigned lease is purchased for less than 7 years and the amount paid is less than the residential threshold (or non-residential threshold) for SDLT;
- alternative property financial arrangements were used for example, to comply with Sharia law.

2.8.3 Land transaction tax (LTT)

Land Transaction Tax (LTT) has replaced SDLT in relation to property purchased in Wales with effect from 1 April 2018. LTT is broadly consistent with the SDLT regime but there are some notable differences in relation to the rates and some of the available reliefs, as well as the administration and forms.

LTT is payable when someone:

- buys a freehold property;
- buys a new or existing leasehold;
- takes a transfer of land or property in exchange for payment for example, taking on part of a mortgage debt or buying a share in a house.

LTT is also a self-assessment tax and it is the responsibility of the taxpayer to complete and submit an accurate tax return and pay any tax due. It is necessary to submit a LTT return even if there is nothing to pay except for the following transactions that do not need a return:

- property that is left in a will (and no payment is made for the transfer of);
- property is transferred due to divorce or dissolution of a civil partnership;
- a freehold property purchased for less than £40,000;
- a new or assigned lease of 7 years or more is purchased and the premium is less than £40,000 and the annual rent is less than £1,000;
- a new or assigned lease of less than 7 years is purchased, provided that the amount paid is less than the residential (or non-residential) LTT zero rate threshold.

The LTT regime will affect the advice and financial calculations, as well as the actual payment of tax, where clients are buying a property situated in Wales after 1 April 2018.

LTT applies to the purchase of land situated in Wales and the location of the buyer is not relevant (e.g. the buyer could be living in England but buying a house in Wales).

Link to practice

Use the postcode checker to establish if a property is situated in Wales for LTT:

https://gov.wales/find-out-if-postcode-wales-land-transaction-tax

Where properties are situated partly in Wales and partly in England (cross-border cases such as a large property or a farm which straddles the English and Welsh borders), then basically SDLT is payable on the part of the property situated in England and LTT is payable on the part of the property situated in Wales. An apportionment of the purchase price will be necessary in such cases, perhaps with the help of a surveyor, and two returns will be filed, one with HMRC for the SDLT element and one with the Welsh Revenue Authority (WRA) for the LTT element.

The following rates and bands apply in relation to LTT for residential property. The rates apply to the portion of the price paid in each band.

Find the updated rates at:

https://www.gov.wales/land-transaction-tax-rates-and-bands

In this section there is a table showing the main differences between LTT and SDLT. Refer to the updated table at the following link:

https://www.gov.wales/land-transaction-tax-differences-stamp-duty-land-tax

First-time buyer relief does not apply to LTT. However, purchases of additional residential property in Wales are subject to higher rates of LTT of 3 per cent on each band. There are special rules where a buyer is replacing a main residence.

LTT is payable on the premium element of a new residential lease, using the rates in the table above, but there is no LTT payable on the rental element of a new lease for residential property.

Link to practice

The Welsh Revenue Authority (Awdurdod Cyllid Cymru) (WRA), which has responsibility for the LTT regime, has produced a LTT calculator which can be viewed at:

https://www.gov.wales/land-transaction-tax-calculator

LTT returns must be filed with the WRA and most will be filed electronically via an online system using a "WRA online tax account". Paper returns must be sent by post to the WRA in Pontypridd. Returns must be made within a 30-day period beginning on the day after the effective date of the transaction (this is normally the completion date).

LTT must also be paid within 30 days from the day after the effective date of the transaction. The WRA will issue a certificate (a Land Transaction Tax certificate) to show that the LTT has been paid, which must be sent to HMLR with the registration application.

The WRA website provides guidance notes for practitioners. There are interest charges and penalties for late payment of LTT.

The main differences between LTT and SDLT
https://gov.wales/land-transaction-tax-differences-stamp-duty-land-tax

	LTT	SDLT
Rates and bands	The Welsh Government sets the **rates and bands for LTT**. To calculate how much LTT to pay use their **tax calculator**.	The UK government sets the rates and bands for SDLT. To calculate how much SDLT to pay use **HMRC's tax calculator**.
Higher rates: intermediate transaction rule	The purchase of a new main residence will not be chargeable to LTT at the higher rate if a previous main residence was disposed of.	SDLT does not apply an interim transaction rule.

	However, if the seller purchases another property (for example, buy-to-let) before completion of the purchase of a new main residence, the seller may be required to "look back" to that **intermediate transaction** and pay the higher rates.	
Meaning of residential and non-residential	LTT has its own **specific interpretation guidance**.	SDLT also has its own specific interpretation guidance, found on the HMRC website.
Residential leases	LTT is only payable on any premium (or other consideration) that does not consist of rent. Rent figures are not required when completing a return for a new **residential lease**.	SDLT is charged on both rent and any premium (or other consideration) for a new residential lease.
Non-residential leases: relevant rent rule	The 0% band for premiums (and other non-rent consideration) extends to £150,000. This band can increase to 1% where the "relevant rent" exceeds £13,500. **Relevant rent** is usually the highest rent payable in any year across the entire term of the lease.	SDLT does not apply a relevant rent rule.
Reliefs	First-time buyer relief is not available. The 0% band currently applies to purchases up to £180,000.	First-time buyer relief is available. The 0% band currently applies to purchases up to £125,000.
Avoidance and compliance	There's an anti-avoidance rule that applies to all LTT reliefs.	There are rules that target specific aspects of particular reliefs.

	The general anti-avoidance rule allows the WRA to counter any artificial tax avoidance arrangement.	**ss 75A-C Finance Act 2003** anti-avoidance rules apply.
Deferral of tax	A taxpayer must supply an expected end date of the **deferral** and where one cannot be predicted use the fifth anniversary of the transaction.	The taxpayer need not supply an expected end date of a deferral period.

2.8.4 Lender's requirements – SDLT and LTT

The Lender's Handbook contains the following provision:

"**10.4** You are only authorised to release the loan when you hold sufficient funds to complete the purchase of the property and pay all stamp duty land tax and registration fees to perfect the security as a first legal mortgage or, if you do not have them, you accept responsibility to pay them yourself."

The Building Societies Association Mortgage Instructions: England and Wales contains the following provision:

"**B.5.** Your charges and disbursements are payable by the borrower and should be collected from the borrower on or before completion. You must not allow non-payment of fees or disbursements to delay the payment of stamp duty land tax, the lodging of any stamp duty land tax return and the registration of our mortgage at the Land Registry. For solicitors, the Law Society recommends that your costs for acting on our behalf in connection with the mortgage should, in the interests of transparency, be separately identified to the borrower."

This means that the conveyancer must have the SDLT funds in hand from the buyer prior to releasing the mortgage advance on completion. The conveyancer will have to pay the SDLT from their own funds if the money is not held on completion. The conveyancer will add the amount of the SDLT to the sum due from the client on the completion statement. This will also apply to LTT.

2.8.5 Law Society's Protocol and Core Practice Management Standards (CPMS)

The Law Society has recognised that solicitors have been giving weak or inconsistent advice in relation to SDLT to their buyer clients. Accordingly the Law Society has introduced additional requirements in the Protocol and the Core Practice Management Standards (which CQS accredited firms must comply with).

At various intervals throughout the Protocol the solicitor is obliged to give appropriate SDLT or LTT advice to their buyer client. This reinforces the importance of keeping the amount of SDLT or LTT that may be payable under review as more is discovered about the client's circumstances as the transaction progresses.

The CPMS contains the following obligation:

"**5.15** Practices must have a policy in relation to Stamp Duty Land Tax (SDLT), which must include:

a. A procedure for giving clients clear and timely advice and information on SDLT including the meaning for SDLT purposes of 'First time buyer' and 'Major interest in a dwelling'.

b. A procedure for ensuring that the practice provides a clear written SDLT calculation to the client at the outset.

c. A procedure for verifying the amount of SDLT payable, where applicable, before exchange.

d. A procedure setting out how and when the practice makes checks between the consideration stated in the:

    i. sale contract

    ii. transfer deed

    iii. SDLT Return and

    iv. the payments on the solicitors' client account ledger for the transaction."

The CPMS guidance states:

"**5.15**

The client should be asked to sign an appropriate declaration that will enable practices to accurately calculate the SDLT payable and make it easier for the calculation to be checked later. The client should be reminded to inform the practice of any change of circumstance which may affect that calculation.

Practices must ensure there is a procedure for verifying the amount of SDLT payable, before exchange of contracts. Where possible, this should involve another experienced individual, other than the fee earner, and the verification should be recorded on the file.

Requirement 5.16.c. might not be applicable if the calculation is outsourced. (Note – It is assumed that the Law Society means 5.15.c in this part of their guidance).

Sole practitioners and smaller practices should consider what steps they could put in place if no other experienced individual is available: this could simply involve re-checking the SDLT payment at a later date and noting the file.

The amount of SDLT should be documented in a cash statement, readily accessible to supervisors, and be supported by evidence of payments into and out of client account."

2.9 Chapter summary

(1) The **Money Laundering Regulations 2017** and **Proceeds of Crime Act 2002** require all conveyancers to verify their client's identity.

(2) The ***Dreamvar*** case involved a fraudulent seller and the loss of the buyer's purchase money. The Court of Appeal held that in a conveyancing transaction, the seller's conveyancer is warranting that they act for the true owner of the property. The Law Society Code for Completion by Post 2019 reinforces this point.

(3) Conveyancers must make appropriate checks to ensure that the law firm on the other side of the transaction is legitimate.

(4) Mortgage fraud is a serious problem for institutional lenders and there are a number of requirements imposed on conveyancers in the Lenders Handbook to try to minimise the possibility of mortgage fraud including the requirement for conveyancers to:

- check identification documents and signatures;
- check the other side's legal representative;
- check the valuation of the property;
- check how long the seller has owned the property;
- notify the lender if the seller is not the registered proprietor;
- ask how the buyer will fund the purchase;
- submit the UK Finance Disclosure Form on a new build transaction.

(5) Conveyancing firms must have appropriate firmwide policies, controls and procedures (PCPs) in place to mitigate the risk of money-laundering.

(6) The Legal Sector Affinity Group issued detailed guidance in January 2021 to assist firms to comply with their AML responsibilities.

(7) Law firms must also ensure that they have appropriate policies and procedures in place to check the sanctions list which has become particularly relevant following the invasion of Ukraine by Russia.

(8) Firms must have appropriate policies and procedures in place to mitigate the risk of cybercrime.

(9) Conveyancers owe a duty of care to their clients which, if breached, could lead to a negligence claim against the firm if the client suffers loss.

(10) Conveyancers must be wary of cases involving undue influence – this is the equitable doctrine under which a court may set aside, or decline to enforce, any bargain, including a mortgage, reached by means of undue influence.

(11) Examples of undue influence include:

- The solicitor acts for the seller. The solicitor is asked to obtain the consent of an occupier to the sale.
- The solicitor acts for a husband and wife who are jointly mortgaging their home to a bank. The mortgage is for the benefit of the husband's business and the wife will gain no direct benefit – this was considered in ***Royal Bank of Scotland v Etridge (No. 2)* [2001]**.
- The solicitor acts for an elderly client who is selling her house. The client is in hospital and the solicitor has never met her. All advice is given to the client's adult son or handled through the post, and the son gives all instructions.

(12) To assist clients to mitigate the risk of property fraud, conveyancers should consider advising their clients to subscribe to HMLR's Property Alert service and/or register a Form LL restriction against the proprietorship register, particularly if the registered proprietor does not live at the property (for example, because it is an investment/buy to let property).

(13) An undertaking is defined as:

"A statement, given orally or in writing, whether or not it includes the word 'undertake' or 'undertaking', to someone who reasonably places reliance on it, that you or a third party will do something or cause something to be done, or refrain from doing something."

(14) The conveyancing process relies on professional undertakings. Without them, transactions could not proceed. For example:

- If a solicitor has to obtain a set of unregistered title deeds that are deposited with a lender as security for a loan, the solicitor will need to give the lender a professionally binding undertaking that they will not release the unregistered deeds to any other party until the loan is repaid.

- The Law Society's formulae for exchange of contracts contain implied undertakings including that the buyer's conveyancer will send their clients signed part of the contract and the agreed deposit to the seller's conveyancer on the day of exchange of contracts.
- completion will not take place unless the seller's conveyancer provides an undertaking to the buyer's conveyancer on the Completion Information and Undertakings Form that the seller's mortgage /s will be discharged out of the sale proceeds on completion.

(15) In ***Harcus Sinclair v Your Lawyers*** **[2021]** the Supreme Court drew a distinction between an undertaking given by a solicitor and one given by an LLP or licensed conveyancer. An undertaking given by a solicitor is subject to the court's inherent jurisdiction in relation to enforcement. The Supreme Court declined to extend the ambit of the enforcement of an undertaking to licensed conveyancers and LLPs.

(16) Capital gains tax (CGT) is payable if a gain is made when an asset is sold by a taxpayer. However most property sales do not attract GGT when sold due to the private residence relief.

(17) A seller will not have to pay CGT when selling the home if all of the following apply:

- the seller has one home and has lived in it as their main home for all the time they have owned it;
- the seller has not let part of it out (this does not include having a single lodger);
- the seller has not used part of it for business only;
- the grounds, including all buildings, are less than 5,000 square metres in total;
- the seller did not buy the property just to make a gain.

(18) SDLT must be paid when a buyer purchases a property over a certain price in England or Northern Ireland.

(19) The SDLT return and any tax must be paid to HMRC within 14 days of completion.

(20) Land Transaction Tax (LTT) has replaced SDLT in relation to property purchased in Wales with effect from 1 April 2018.

(21) LTT must be paid within 30 days from the day after the effective date of the transaction.

CHAPTER 3

The contract for sale

3.1 Introduction

If we are acting for a seller, we will be responsible for drafting the contract in accordance with our client's instructions and based upon our investigation of the title.

In drafting a contract for sale, the seller's conveyancer must investigate the seller client's title. If that title is registered, the conveyancer must consider the contents of the official copy entries of the register and title plan together with the standard form of contract, usually, the Law Society's form, and consider how to start the drafting. Many firms will use their own contract precedents.

This chapter will cover:

- formation of the contract and signature;
- conditional contracts;
- drafting the contract;
- conditions of sale;
- open contract position;
- Standard Conditions of Sale (Fifth edition – 2018 revision);
- Seller's duty of disclosure;

- **Contracts (Rights of Third Parties) Act 1999**;
- void conditions;
- examples of common special conditions;
- time limits for raising requisitions.

3.2 Formation of the contract of sale

First it is necessary to revisit some basic contract law and, in particular, the requirements for a valid contract in conveyancing.

In order for a contract of sale to be valid, two conditions must be satisfied.

(1) The normal requirements for any valid contract must be present. There must be offer and acceptance, certainty as to terms, and the parties must have the necessary capacity, have given consideration and intended to create legal relations.

(2) The correct legal formalities must have been used. The formalities are contained in **s2 Law of Property (Miscellaneous Provisions) Act 1989** (**LP(MP)A 1989**): a contract for the sale of land or an interest in land must be in writing, incorporate all the terms agreed between the parties, and be signed by or on behalf of each party to the contract. The traditional method of conveyancing, whereby the seller signed one copy of the contract and the buyer signed an identical copy, is preserved by **s2**. It will therefore be acceptable if the contract is in two identical parts, providing one part is signed by or on behalf of the seller and the other is signed by or on behalf of the buyer.

3.2.1 Who should sign the contract?

The seller's signature to the contract does not need to be witnessed (as it does with a deed) but it is still important to consider who should sign the contract.

If the contract is being signed on behalf of someone, then that person should authorise this in writing. Verbal authority would not suffice for **s2**.

A conveyancer must obtain express authority from the client if they are to sign the contract on the client's behalf. Unless the conveyancer holds a power of attorney, the authority should be obtained in writing. This is to protect the conveyancer in case of any problems.

Where the seller is a company, the contract will be signed by an authorised officer of the company, normally a director or company secretary.

It is also important that the correct people enter into the contract. It is always necessary therefore to consider the identity of the sellers when drafting the contract. Usually this will be obvious, but conveyancers must always consider the issue and cater for any variations. The seller's conveyancer must produce evidence of the seller's entitlement to sell the property when submitting the contract package.

For sales by personal representatives (PRs) of the estate of a deceased person, **s16 Law of Property (Miscellaneous Provisions) Act 1994** (**LP(MP)A 1994**) requires the concurrence of all the PRs in respect of the contract. If there is only one PR, they can contract to sell the land on their own. The contract will reflect the fact that the sellers are the PRs of the deceased owner. A grant of representation must be produced to demonstrate the PR's authority to sell the property and sign the contract. For instance, where the sellers are executors, they will be named in the contract and the contract will explain the capacity in which they are selling, for example:

> Daisy Muller and Pauletta Lianne Smith of 56 High Street, Bedminster, Bristol, BS3 5RS (as executors in the estate of Jason Robert Conran deceased).

It could be, for instance, that a company is selling land. Take the example of a developer who is selling new homes on an estate. An authorised officer of the company would sign the contract on behalf of the company. The seller in the contract would be the company itself, for example:

> Smart Homes (Northern) Limited whose registered office is at 12 Plymouth Grove, Ivybridge, Hartshire, HG12 YXR

A different example would be where one joint owner has died and a survivor is selling the property. It may be necessary for an additional trustee to be appointed in these circumstances. If so, this issue must be dealt with in the contract. The second trustee could be appointed (by a deed of appointment) prior to the contract being entered into. If this is done, the second trustee will be named as a seller in the contract, together with the survivor, so that they are a party to the contract, and will be bound by its provisions. In this case, both trustees would sign the contract.

Alternatively, the contract could be entered into by the survivor alone but contain a special condition to require the appointment of the second trustee as a party to the purchase deed to receive the money. In this case, the sole surviving owner would sign the contract (see further below).

Link to practice

In the event that a second trustee is appointed, the buyer's conveyancer must raise an enquiry to seek confirmation that the seller's conveyancer has properly identified the new trustee and has carried out appropriate due diligence. This is because the buyer's conveyancer will be confirming in the application to HMLR that the identity of all parties has been obtained and HMLR will place reliance on this statement by the buyer's conveyancer (see "confirmation of identity" on the HMLR forms – boxes 12 and 13 of the AP1 Change the register (AP1) - GOV.UK (www.gov.uk) and boxes 14 and 15 of the FR1 First registration: application (FR1) - GOV.UK (www.gov.uk)).

If a person has lost mental capacity, their property may be dealt with by an authorised person, called a deputy, appointed by the Court of Protection under the **Mental Capacity Act 2005**. A deputy is usually a close friend or relative, but can also be a professional such as an accountant or solicitor. The deputy would sign the contract. The seller would need to produce a certified copy of the order which provides the deputy's authority to act. the order will be made by the Court of Protection under the **Mental Capacity Act 2005**.

Alternatively, if an attorney has been appointed to deal with the affairs of the property owner, the seller would still be shown as the owner, but the contract (and transfer) would be signed on their behalf by the attorney. A certified copy of the power of attorney appointing the attorney must be provided.

Link to practice

Where someone is signing the contract (and transfer) on the owner's behalf as an attorney, the buyer's conveyancer will need to see the power of attorney document but in addition, the buyer's conveyancer must raise an enquiry to seek confirmation that the seller's conveyancer has properly identified the attorney and has carried out appropriate due diligence. This is because the buyer's conveyancer will be confirming in the application to HMLR that the identity of all parties has been obtained and HMLR will place reliance on this statement by the buyer's conveyancer (see "confirmation of identity" on the HMLR forms – boxes 12 and 13 of the AP1 and boxes 14 and 15 of the FR1).

Note that the attorney is not named as the seller in the contract (or transferor in the transfer).

Refer to HMLR's Practice guide 67: Evidence of identity for conveyancers for information as to identification requirements:

https://www.gov.uk/government/publications/evidence-of-identity-conveyancers/practice-guide-67-evidence-of-identity-conveyancers

Activity

Follow the link below to HMLR's Practice Guide 9: Powers of attorney and registered land:

https://www.gov.uk/government/publications/powers-of-attorney-and-registered-land/practice-guide-9-powers-of-attorney-and-registered-land#evidence-of-the-power

Read it to ensure that you understand HMLR's requirements when a power of attorney is produced to them as part of a registration application. Take particular care to note the provisions of section 8 – the checklists.

There could also, for example, be a sale by a lender under its power of sale. The lender might be exercising its power of sale because the borrower had failed to make the required mortgage repayments or had broken a term of the mortgage agreement. The lender would be the seller and the contract would be signed on behalf of the lender.

3.2.2 s2 Law of Property (Miscellaneous Provisions) Act 1989

This section provides that a contract is valid only if it is:

- signed by or on behalf of each party;
- is in writing; and
- incorporates all the terms the parties have agreed.

It is therefore important that, when advising a buyer, you ensure that anything of importance is incorporated into the contract, or it will not be binding.

(1) s2 and variation of a contract

In ***McCausland v Duncan Lawrie Ltd* [1996]** it was held that a variation of an existing and enforceable contract had to comply with **s2**.

Link to practice

This is important. If the completion date is missed, it may be because the buyer could not draw down their mortgage advance in time, but their conveyancer is confident that it will happen in a day or two. The parties might therefore informally agree to a new completion date and not serve a notice to complete under Standard Condition 6.8.

In this case, the conveyancers cannot rely on the informal agreement to vary the contract and should take steps to ensure that the contract is varied to ensure compliance with s2.

Follow the link below to read the Law Society Gazette's summary of the case:

https://www.lawgazette.co.uk/news/property-law-/20430.article

(2) Rectification of a contract

If there is an oral agreement and some of the terms agreed orally are, by mistake, not incorporated in the written contract, it may be possible to rectify the written contract so as to incorporate the terms originally omitted. **s2(4) LP(MP) A 1989** expressly refers to the possibility of rectification. In ***Wright v Robert Leonard (Developments)*** **[1994]** rectification of the contract was granted. ***Oun v Ahmad*** **[2008]** is a case where rectification of a contract was not ordered. Not all of the express terms of the contract had been included in the contract, but, as the parties had expressly agreed to leave them out, there was no mistake requiring rectification. In ***North Eastern Properties Ltd v Coleman & Quinn Conveyancing*** **[2010]** the buyer of the land argued that a contract for the sale of land was void because it did not include all the express terms. The buyer had expressly asked that the term was not included so the court thought this was an "unattractive submission". It was held that the excluded term formed no part of the land contract.

(3) s2 and an option to purchase

Spiro v Glencrown Properties **[1991]** concerned the formalities necessary to create and execute an option to purchase a particular estate in land for a particular sum within a particular period. An option to purchase is an estate contract. It was anticipated that such interests would be a source of potential difficulty under **s2** in that the options take effect in two stages: first, the grantor grants the option to the grantee; second, the grantee (at any time within the agreed period that they choose) calls for the sale to them by the grantor of the estate at the agreed price. (Options to renew, which commonly appear in leases, share this characteristic.) It was held that, whilst the agreement itself must be signed by, or on behalf of, all the parties, a letter exercising the option need not. On the facts, a letter signed by the option holder only was valid. The **only contract for the sale or other disposition of an interest in land** for the purposes of **s2** is the grant of the option.

3.2.3 Conditional contracts

It is possible to enter into a contract which is expressed to be subject to some condition. Conveyancers are understandably wary of conditional contracts. There is a considerable risk of disputes between the parties, which may result in expensive court action. Furthermore, the conveyancer needs to take great care in drafting or approving the clause, at the risk of a negligence claim. As the cases mentioned below illustrate, the choice of wording is not at all straightforward. You will need to use precedent books and to ask colleagues to comment on drafts produced.

Conditional contracts are sometimes used to save time (e.g. a contract conditional upon obtaining a mortgage or local search satisfactory to the buyer). They are also used in development situations (e.g. a contract conditional upon the grant of planning permission on terms satisfactory to the buyer).

(1) There are two types of conditions.

   (a) **Conditions precedent to a contract**. In this case no agreement exists between the parties unless and until the condition is fulfilled. Either party is free to withdraw for any reason until the condition is performed and the contract comes into existence.

   (b) **Conditions precedent to performance**. Alternatively, and more frequently, the condition is held not to prevent the formation of a binding contract, but its non-fulfilment renders the contract unenforceable by either party until the condition has been fulfilled. The effect is that either party can withdraw from the contract only on the ground of non-fulfilment of that particular condition.

(2) If no date is fixed for fulfilment of a condition, the condition must be satisfied within a reasonable time. Non-fulfilment discharges the parties from their obligations under the contract and the buyer can recover their deposit. Where fulfilment of this condition requires action on the part of one of the parties, however, that party cannot rely on the non-performance unless they have taken reasonable steps to secure its fulfilment. A condition which is for the sole benefit of one of the parties may be waived by that party, who can then enforce the contract without that term.

(3) A condition that is so vague or imprecise that no definite or practical meaning can be given to it voids the entire contract. The courts are reluctant to declare the contract void on the ground of uncertainty. In ***Lee-Parker v Izzet (No. 2)* [1972]** it was held that a contract for sale subject to *"the purchaser obtaining a satisfactory mortgage"* was void for uncertainty because the amount of the loan and the terms of repayment were

unspecified. By contrast, it was held in ***Janmohamed v Hassam* [1976]** that a contract subject to the buyer obtaining a mortgage satisfactory to him was not void for uncertainty. The reason the latter contract was upheld was that Slade J felt it possible to imply a term that such satisfaction should not be unreasonably withheld.

3.3 Drafting the contract

When drafting a contract, it is important to identify the conveyancer's objective. The contract is drafted by the seller's conveyancers. Their objective is to commit their client to selling all that they want, and are able, to sell. The contract needs to be in clear, straightforward terms, which will enable the recipient (the buyer's conveyancers) to identify what is being sold and on what terms.

Link to practice

It is imperative that the seller's conveyancer does not make any assumptions as to what their seller client is selling.

For example, the seller might not want to sell all of the land within their title. If there is a big garden, the seller might want to retain part of the land for development. The seller's conveyancer cannot rely on the estate agent to give them this information and although it is hoped that the conveyancer would obtain the correct information when taking instructions, it is always prudent to check the extent of the land being sold at the time the contract is drafted.

Accordingly, as a risk management precaution, the seller's conveyancer should forward a property plan to the seller and ask the seller to confirm that the (usually) red edging represents the full extent of the property being sold. This will often be straightforward exercise and will simply involve the conveyancer emailing a copy of the title plan to their seller client/s.

A separate, but linked point relates to professional conduct. The seller's conveyancer should obtain confirmation from all of the sellers, if more than one, as to the extent of the land being sold.

It is not hard to imagine the negligence claim which would follow if the seller's conveyancer drafts the contract on the basis that all of the land within the seller's title was being sold whereas in actual fact the seller only wanted to sell part of the land, but this was only discovered after exchange of contracts or completion.

3.3.1 Devolution of title of joint tenants and tenants in common

We have seen that it is part of the duty of the seller's conveyancer to ensure that they accurately identify the party entitled to sell the property at the time the contract is drafted. This issue is important at the contract drafting stage as the conveyancer must consider who has the right to sell, and whether any additional trustee needs to be appointed.

Where two or more people own property as co-owners, a trust of land automatically arises. The legal estate in the property will be held by those to whom it is conveyed as trustees. The legal estate can only be held by the trustees under a joint tenancy. At law, all co-owners are joint tenants. This means that the legal estate in the land will always pass, on the death of a co-owner, to the surviving trustees under the doctrine of survivorship.

The beneficial interests can be held in equity in one of two ways, as a beneficial joint tenancy or as a beneficial tenancy in common. There is therefore a choice as to how the beneficial interests will be held.

The key difference is that on the death of one joint tenant, the deceased's interest passes under the doctrine of survivorship to the surviving joint tenants, whereas on the death of a tenant in common, the deceased's interest passes according to their will or on intestacy (the intestacy rules govern the position where there is no valid will).

(1) Joint tenants

If the property was conveyed to two joint tenants and one of them dies, the survivor is entitled to the whole property, provided that severance has not occurred.

The buyer's conveyancer checks an official copy death certificate to prove the death has occurred.

Then, to prove that severance has not taken place:

(a) in registered land, the buyer's conveyancer simply checks whether there is a restriction on the register relating to severance

(b) in unregistered land, the buyer must obtain the protection of **s1 Law of Property (Joint Tenants) Act 1964** by the conveyancer checking that:

  (i) the survivor of the joint tenants is described as solely and beneficially interested in the conveyance by which the survivor sells (or, before the **Law of Property (Miscellaneous Provisions) Act 1994**, the survivor could convey as beneficial owner);

(ii) there is no memorandum of severance endorsed on the conveyance to the joint tenants;

(iii) there is no bankruptcy registration against either joint tenant as bankruptcy automatically severs the joint tenancy.

If any of the three requirements cannot be satisfied, the buyer's conveyancer must insist on the appointment of a second trustee.

When preparing requisitions on title in unregistered land, the conveyancer must check each sale by a survivor of joint tenants since the root of title, to ensure that the above steps have been complied with.

(2) Tenants in common

On a sale by the survivor of tenants in common, the buyer's conveyancer checks the official copy death certificate to prove death. Whether or not the land is registered, the buyer has two options.

(1) The best method is to have the surviving co-trustee appoint a second trustee. The PR or a beneficiary of the deceased co-owner does **not** appoint the new trustee. The PR's only interest is in receiving the appropriate share of the purchase money after completion. The two trustees then sign the purchase deed, which includes the receipt for purchase money. As purchase money has now been paid to two trustees, the beneficial interests of the deceased co-owner (and any other beneficial interests) are overreached.

(2) Another method is sometimes used where the surviving co-trustee has inherited the property and thus become the sole owner. The equitable title could be deduced to the buyer. This is not as good a method as (1), however, as it may not be acceptable to HMLR, and the buyer can still insist on having a second trustee.

Link to practice

Although the requirement for a second trustee should be addressed by the seller's conveyancer at the contract drafting stage, often the issue does not come to light until the buyer's conveyancer has received the contract pack and investigated the seller's title.

Appointment of a second trustee in a deed of appointment will require an application to HMLR so in most cases, the way that the issue is addressed is to ensure that an appropriate provision is included in the contract of sale by the addition of an additional Special Condition. A suitable clause is below.

It is essential for the buyer's conveyancer to review the contract when they draft the transfer to ensure that any such provision is included in panel 11 of the TR1 – see https://www.gov.uk/government/publications/registered-titles-whole-transfer-tr1.

In most cases where one of two registered proprietors has died, the legal estate will be transferred to the surviving co-owner using HMLR form DJP (death of joint proprietor) – see https://www.gov.uk/government/publications/deceased-joint-proprietor-djp. The seller's conveyancer should be required to submit this form to HMLR together with a certified copy of the death certificate. This will result in the legal estate being held by one trustee. Accordingly, the appropriate provision for the transfer will involve the appointment of an additional trustee as opposed to the appointment of a replacement trustee.

Suggested additional Special Condition (where the title is registered):

"The transfer to the buyer shall contain the following provision:

For the purpose of giving a valid receipt for the purchase price, [insert full name of sole registered proprietor] in exercise of the power under section 36(6) of the Trustee Act 1925 appoints [insert full name of additional trustee] to be a trustee of the Property with the said [insert full name of sole registered proprietor]"

HMLR Practice Guide 21: Using transfer forms for complex transactions contains more information. Follow the link and read section 6 "Transactions involving trustees":

https://www.gov.uk/government/publications/using-transfer-forms-for-less-straightforward-transactions/practice-guide-21-using-transfer-forms-for-complex-transactions

3.3.2 Open contracts and standard conditions

(1) Open contracts

An open contract arises where the seller and the buyer have simply agreed on the essential terms in the written contract. Remember that in order for the contract to be valid it must incorporate all the terms **agreed** between the parties. Some matters, though, may simply not have been discussed at all and do not therefore appear in the contract. For example, the parties may have signed an agreement which adequately describes the property, states the consideration (price) and all the other agreed terms but the matter of a completion date was never actually discussed. The contract would be said to be "open" with regard to the completion date and the common law or open contract rule would be applied.

The following is an example of an open contract. It is valid under **s2 LP(MP)A 1989** as it sets out all the terms agreed by the parties. Thus, the parties have not agreed anything regarding insurance, completion dates, completion procedure, time limits, etc.

> "CONTRACT made 15 May 2022 between JAMES WHITE of 5 Chapel Street Newtown Powys and KERRY BROWN of 18 Chapel Street Newtown Powys. James White agrees to sell to Kerry Brown the property known as 5 Chapel Street Newtown aforesaid for £300,000.
>
> [signed by both parties]"

A conveyancer would not advise a client to sign an open contract due to the uncertainty and risks it involves. If clients did sign an open contract before taking legal advice, however, it would be necessary for the conveyancer to use the open contract rules to try to rescue the situation.

Example of a partly open contract:

> "CONTRACT made 15 May 2022 between JAMES WHITE of 5 Chapel Street Newtown Powys and KERRY BROWN of 18 Chapel Street Newtown Powys. James White agrees to sell to Kerry Brown the property known as 5 Chapel Street Newtown aforesaid for £300,000. Standard Conditions of Sale (Fifth Edition – 2018 Revision) apply except for Standard Conditions 6.8 and 7 which are deleted.
>
> [signed by both parties]"

This contract is partly open because Standard Conditions 6.8 (completion notices) and 7 (remedies for breach of contract) do not apply. This does **not** mean, however, that completion notices cannot be served and there are no remedies for breach. Rather, completion notices can be served and remedies are available – but they are the open contract rules and remedies rather than the ones under the Standard Conditions. Sometimes, a contract could be partly open because (as here) the contract excludes certain Standard Conditions but does not provide replacement clauses.

Link to practice

Dealing with a contract for the sale of a residential property under the open contract provisions is a rare situation and is included only for completeness. It is unlikely that you will encounter this in practice as contracts are usually based on the standard conditions of sale (SCs) (explained below).

(2) Standard Conditions (SCs)

In most contracts, the procedural matters are dealt with by express conditions. It is usual for conveyancing firms to adopt general printed conditions which cover the procedural matters. The general conditions incorporated into most contracts, and to which reference is made throughout this coursebook, are the **Standard Conditions of Sale** (Fifth Edition – 2018 Revision): see **Document 1** of the **Appendix**. The explanatory notes are available at **Document 2** of the **Appendix**.

The Protocol requires use of the SCs. Amendments and additions are permitted, but the Protocol states that the addition of further clauses is discouraged. It states that they should not be included unless it is necessary to accord with the current law or specific instructions from the seller. Furthermore, any additional clauses should be necessary and required for the transaction.

(3) Special Conditions

Special Conditions are those conditions included in the contract to deal with a matter specific to that particular property, that particular transaction or those particular parties. Wherever the parties agree a matter that is not adequately covered by the provisions of the SCs, they should include a Special Condition in the contract. In so far as the Special Conditions are inconsistent with the SCs, the Special Conditions will prevail.

In order to draft the contract, the seller's conveyancers need to have the title deeds in their possession, if the title is unregistered. They need to have official copies of the register entries and title plan if the title is registered. If the land is unregistered, it would be prudent to check that all necessary documents have been included.

There may be deeds and documents that are required which are in the possession of a mortgage lender though, in fact, fewer lenders now store their borrowers' deeds. If the mortgage lender is a building society (or similar institutional lender), it will normally release them to the seller's conveyancer if they are on the panel of the society. The conveyancer will be required to give an undertaking to hold the deeds to the order of the lender, to return them on demand, and only to part with them to a third party on payment of all outstanding money due to the lender.

3.3.3 The parts of a formal contract

As indicated above, where a conveyancer is instructed to act for a seller client, a formal written contract will be used. The most common form is that incorporating the Standard Conditions of Sale (see **Document 1** of the **Appendix**).

The date of the contract is not filled in at the drafting stage. It is left blank when the contract is drafted and inserted on exchange. This is because there is no binding contract in existence before exchange.

The full names and addresses of the sellers and buyers must also be filled in, including postcodes. As explained above, the sale might not be made by individual owners. The sellers could, for instance, be executors, a company or a lender under its power of sale.

The contract will therefore be drafted accordingly. We will now look at the rest of the contract provisions.

Traditionally, a formal contract comprised two parts:

- the particulars of sale – these provide a legal and physical description of the property and may include incumbrances;
- the conditions of sale – these contain the terms on which the property is to be sold and are the subject of negotiation between the parties. They will comprise general conditions (now usually the SCs) and any Special Conditions agreed between the parties.

Particulars of sale

The particulars of sale on the standard form contract have been reduced to a simple property description. The requirements for an adequate description of the land that is being sold are still important. Where the land is registered, the description is simpler than it is where the land is unregistered. With unregistered land, the root of title is the starting point of the description.

Whether the land is registered or unregistered, the contract will state whether the property being sold is freehold or leasehold property. The relevant option (freehold/leasehold) on the contract form will be chosen and the other option deleted.

(1) Unregistered title – property description/root of title/specified incumbrances

The property description is more complex for unregistered land because the description will be based on the title deeds rather than the address in the register. The particulars should contain the following.

(a) An accurate physical description of the land to be sold – by reference to a plan where necessary. A previously prepared plan drawn to a good-sized scale is considered essential when the seller is only selling part of their land (***Scarfe v Adams*** **[1981]**). Usually, in unregistered land, the contract description is based on a description in a previous conveyance – though, obviously, you need to bear in mind that transactions since that conveyance may have necessitated adjustments.

A typical description might be:

"All that freehold land known as 57 Allington Street, Trowbridge, Wiltshire, BA14 6JF as is more particularly described in a Conveyance dated 15 November 1969 and made between Norman James (1) and Marion Slater (2) and edged in red on the plan attached thereto."

It is important that the description is accurate as there may otherwise be disputes about the extent of the land sold.

Freeguard v Rogers **[1999]** involved a dispute regarding the extent of a property described as "the property known as No. 9 Graffham Close". The documentation did not state whether this included merely the house at 9 Graffham Close, or the house and its garage, and this was disputed between buyer and seller. This case reinforces the need for a carefully prepared description in a contract selling unregistered land (or a sale of part in registered land); a professionally drawn-up plan by a surveyor should be obtained.

(b) An adequate legal description with three components.

(i) **The tenure** – that is, the exact estate or interest to be sold should be stated. On the standard form contract this is achieved simply by striking through either leasehold or freehold on the front page.

(ii) **The benefits** – mention may be made of the existing benefit of covenants and easements attaching to the property. The benefit of existing easements would, in fact, pass anyway under **s62 LPA 1925**, but the object is to make your client's property appear as attractive as you are able and to set the position out clearly for the buyer.

(iii) **The burdens** – existing incumbrances (e.g. covenants affecting the property) must be disclosed. In the current standard form contract they appear under the heading "Specified Incumbrances" so this part of the contract form must be completed accordingly.

The burdens can either be expressly repeated in the contract or referred to by implication, for example:

> *"Subject to the covenants, conditions and all other matters contained in a conveyance dated 4 April 1982 and made between S Thyme (1) and P Dillon (2)".*

If this latter method is used then, obviously, the buyers must be provided with copies of the documents referred to, otherwise the contract will not make sense.

A contract for the sale of unregistered land, whether freehold or leasehold, must also state the root of title. This is a reference to a document such as a conveyance which is to form the starting point of the chain of unregistered title.

(2) Registered title – property description/title number/ specified incumbrances

The particulars of sale/property description has always been much shorter than in unregistered title. The seller's conveyancer will rely for an adequate description on the one in the property register of the title, and then state that the property is that which is comprised under the particular title number.

Official copies of the register and title plan will usually have been obtained online via the HMLR portal. The seller's conveyancer will supply up-to-date official copies with the draft contract.

If the Protocol is being used, the official copies supplied with the contract should be less than six months old and any information which needs to be updated (e.g. a change of name) should have been rectified by the seller's conveyancer in advance.

The property description will normally be the full address taken from the property register.

In registered land transactions, the specified incumbrances are normally referenced to the register of title, for example:

> "The matters contained in the register of the above title save for financial charges."

The phrase "save for financial charges" is designed to exclude the seller's current mortgages, which would be paid off on completion.

Alternatively, the contract could refer more specifically to numbered entries, for example (this example is on the basis that the numbered, excluded entries are the entries recording the seller's current mortgage):

"The matters contained or referred to in the register of the above title save for entries 2 and 3 of the charges register."

Each case must of course be considered on its facts to see which incumbrances will apply and which will not apply on sale. Similarly, the actual numberings of the register entries will have to be checked against the official copies for the particular property so that the correct ones are stated in the contract.

The title number will also be stated in the contract and reference to root of title deleted. The title number will be taken from the official copies.

3.3.4 Errors in the contract particulars

We will be continuing our look at the standard form contract shortly, but this section explains why it is important to draft the contract accurately. Inaccurate drafting may result in such court action as:

- a **misrepresentation** inducing the contract;
- a **misdescription** in the particulars themselves;
- **non-disclosure** – where the seller omits to disclose some matter which they are obliged to reveal.

An overlap can exist between misrepresentation and misdescription – what starts out as a misrepresentation inducing the contract can later constitute a misdescription if it is incorporated into the contract. The distinction between the two remains important, as different remedies are available.

3.3.5 The seller's duty of disclosure

The duty of disclosure is linked to the issue of accurate contract drafting and the requirement to disclose incumbrances. The extent of the seller's duty of disclosure depends on whether the open contract rule or the SCs are being used.

(1) The open contract rule

The seller is duty bound to disclose **latent defects in title**, that is, third party rights which prevent them selling free from incumbrances and which are not apparent on a reasonable inspection by the buyer – for example, restrictive covenants and easements of which there is no physical evidence on the property. Note the following points.

(a) The seller's duty does not extend to physical defects and defects in the quality of the land unless they are also defects in title.

(b) The seller does not have to disclose a latent incumbrance which will not remain binding on a buyer after completion (e.g. a mortgage to be discharged on or before completion but this should be evident from the title).

(c) The seller does not have to disclose a third party right statutorily void against the seller due to non-registration as a land charge.

(d) Given that there may be some difficulty in determining whether a particular incumbrance is patent or latent, it may be advisable for the seller to disclose all defects in the title in the contract. For example, an easement may be patent if there is found to be physical evidence of it which is reasonably discoverable on inspection; if not, it will be latent and required to be disclosed under the open contract rule.

(e) In registered title the open contract rule means that the seller must disclose all latent overriding interests – again, if in doubt as to latent/patent, the seller should disclose the interest.

(2) The Standard Conditions of Sale (see **Document 1** of the **Appendix**)

SC 3 provides that a seller is in roughly the same position as they would be in an open contract, with the following important differences.

(a) Any adverse rights which the seller is required to disclose must be set out, or referred to, in the contract itself. Generally, these are listed under "Specified Incumbrances" on the front page.

(b) The seller does not have to disclose any adverse rights that could be discovered by inspecting the property (i.e. any patent rights).

(c) The seller does not have to disclose any adverse rights which fall into the following categories.

   (i) Any adverse rights that the seller did not know about and could not have found had the seller tried to investigate the position. (This seems reasonable as, of course, the seller had no way of discovering the problem. It does, however, leave the buyer unable to sue the seller if the buyer later discovers any such matters.)

   (ii) Those rights, other than mortgages, which the buyer knows about. This was added as a new provision by the Fifth Edition of the Standard Conditions. The Law Society states that it was not considered fair for a buyer to be able to take action against a seller in respect of a matter which they knew about but which was not expressly included as a matter subject to which the property was sold. The buyer may gain knowledge of these rights from a variety of sources, for example, from the seller, from searches and enquiries, inspection, survey, neighbours and so on.

(iii) Any adverse rights in public registers. The public registers to which this refers include the Register of Local Land Charges, which is one of the reasons why the local land charges search (often called "local search") is made before exchange of contracts.

As an exception to this rule, however, any adverse matters set out in the HMLR, Land Charges Registry or at Companies House must be disclosed by the seller before exchange.

(iv) Public requirements: notices, orders and similar given on statutory authority. (This may not be satisfactory to a buyer as the seller will know if they have received notices and there may be no other way of knowing the contents of these notices. Thus, the buyer will normally ask about this at the preliminary enquiries stage.)

(3) Effect of the duty of disclosure

The seller is required to disclose relevant matters before exchange of contracts. If the seller fails to do this, the buyer could sue the seller for breach of contract. The duty of disclosure only relates to the relationship between the seller and the buyer. It does not affect the enforceability of third-party rights against the buyer.

Examples of defects include the following

(a) A mortgage

A mortgage does not need to be disclosed if it will be redeemed on or before completion and so the buyer will not be bound by it. However, in registered land, any mortgage will appear in the charges register of the title and the buyer will check to ensure it will be discharged on or before completion.

If (in a very exceptional situation) the buyer is buying subject to the mortgage and the buyer will repay it, then, under the open contract, this is a latent defect in title so the seller must disclose the defect before exchange. Under the SCs, the mortgage must be mentioned in the contract (SC 3.1.2(a)) as it does not fall within any of the other clauses of SC 3.1.2.

(b) A right of way (easement)

If there is an obvious path leading over the property to neighbouring land, it could be argued that the easement is a patent defect and so does not need to be disclosed under an open contract or under SC 3.1.2(b). This may be open to dispute, however, so it would be safer for the seller to disclose the easement.

If there are no signs on the ground of a right of way, this is a latent defect in title and so must be disclosed under both the open contract and the SCs.

(c) An adverse right not known to the seller

Under the open contract, this matter must be disclosed if it is a latent defect in title. As, however, the seller does not know of the defect, they obviously cannot disclose it. Accordingly, if the buyer discovers the defect after exchange, the buyer can sue the seller for damages for loss suffered and pursue the other applicable remedies.

Under the SCs, this falls within SC 3.1.2(c). The seller need not disclose it – if the buyer discovers the defect after exchange, the buyer is obliged to continue the contract and will suffer the loss.

(d) A restrictive covenant

Restrictive covenants are latent defects in title and should be disclosed both under the SCs and under an open contract.

---

(4) Another type of defect in title

Also, within the duty to disclose latent defects in title is the need to disclose any flaw in the documentary title which might affect the seller's ownership of the property and, therefore, their right to deal with it. How should the seller (or the seller's conveyancer) deal with such a defect? Some contract provision possibilities are considered below. These would normally, if relevant, be added as special conditions on the back page of the contract form.

(a) *"The buyer shall assume . . ."* The buyer may be required to assume the truth of something which the seller is not in a position to establish by legal proof. Such a condition could be included where, for example, the seller cannot prove that an old mortgage has been discharged.Such a condition is valid, even though it is intended to cover a flaw which is fundamental to the title. But the seller cannot require the buyer to assume that which they know to be false.

(b) *"The buyer shall accept the seller's title and raise no objection or requisition thereon"* – such a condition does not absolve the seller from their obligation to disclose defects of which they know or ought to know (e.g. ***Becker v Partridge* [1966]**, where the seller failed to disclose breaches of covenant of which his solicitor ought to have known). Similarly, the seller cannot conceal a defect in title by stipulating that the title to be deduced shall commence after the defect. If the seller knows of, or ought to know, about the defect they must disclose it.

(c) The correct procedure is for the seller's conveyancer to include in the contract a condition fully disclosing the position and then to provide that the buyer shall buy with full notice of the defect and shall raise no objection or requisition in respect thereof. The buyer can still raise preliminary enquiries on the problem and evaluate the risk. If necessary, they could try to arrange insurance cover in respect of it before deciding whether to proceed.

Similarly, where the seller has lost or mislaid a document of title, they should provide for this by way of Special Condition which will disclose the problem and set out what secondary evidence (if any), such as copies or a statutory declaration, is to be provided.

3.3.6 Title guarantee

(1) The background

When a property is sold, the seller may give various implied covenants, the purpose of which is to ensure that the buyer can sue the seller if, for some reason, the buyer discovers after completion that they received an unexpectedly defective title. Obviously, the chances of this happening are rare – especially if the title is registered so that the HMLR state guarantee of title also applies.

It is important to appreciate that these implied covenants are not the same thing as the HMLR class of title in registered land, such as title absolute or good leasehold title. These implied covenants, which apply to both registered and unregistered land, relate to implied promises which give a potential remedy if a defective title is given.

The implied covenants given by the seller are termed the "title guarantee". A seller could refuse to give any implied covenants at all, or could give a limited range of covenants, or the full list set out in **LP(MP)A 1994**. It is also possible that the buyer and seller could agree various adaptations of the covenants in **LP(MP)A 1994**.

The type of title guarantee is stated on the front page of the contract. If using the standard form contract, the appropriate alternative (full/limited) will be used and the non-applicable alternative deleted. The type of guarantee will also be written into the contract at the relevant place, e.g. "full title guarantee" or as appropriate.

The covenants are implied into the transfer or other purchase deed. The purchase deed, however, will merely state whatever title guarantee was agreed in the contract. Thus, the appropriate time to negotiate the implied covenants is when drafting or approving the draft contract.

Students often query which covenants for title should be offered by a seller or negotiated by a buyer. The key points to realise are:

(a) a buyer would prefer full title guarantee as it gives the greater protection. By contrast, the seller would prefer to give no guarantee at all as, by giving title guarantee, the seller incurs an ongoing liability for the property (and the seller will be liable for a considerable time into the future);

(b) although a buyer benefits from full or limited guarantee, the guarantee is only as good as the person giving it. If the seller cannot be traced or has no money, the guarantee will be worthless;

(c) as a compromise, some conveyancers may offer and accept limited guarantee, irrespective of whether the seller is a sole owner, trustee, or whatever. The usual and most acceptable approach, however, is for a beneficial owner to offer full title guarantee, but for fiduciary owners (e.g. trustees) or PRs (e.g. executors) to offer limited title guarantee. Many lenders will insist on giving no title guarantee if selling the property under the power of sale.

Sometimes, it may be considered desirable to vary the standard wording of covenants for title. In such cases, the buyer ought to retain a copy of the transfer (preferably certified) with the title documentation. This will enable the transfer to be used in evidence should the alterations to the implied covenants be relevant to any future legal action.

Link to practice

Ultimately, the title guarantee given by the seller is a matter of negotiation between the conveyancers. However, their use is generally uncontroversial and the following are typically given without a problem:

Full title guarantee – given by a seller who has owned a property and lived in it. Note that if a property is being sold by an attorney on behalf of the legal owner, it is expected that the seller will still give a full title guarantee.

Limited title guarantee – given by a seller who is a Personal Representative who will have no personal knowledge of the property.

No title guarantee – given by a mortgagee in possession or by someone who is gifting a property.

Note that the guarantee to be given **must** be indicated on the front of the contract in the appropriate section in the particulars of sale. Do not leave this section blank otherwise the Standard Conditions of Sale will provide a backup position and will specify that a full title guarantee is being given (SC 4.6.2)

(2) Law of Property (Miscellaneous Provisions) Act 1994 (LP(MP)A 1994)

LP(MP)A 1994 sets out the covenants implied where the sellers convey either **with full title guarantee** or **with limited title guarantee**, under the terms of the contract.

The following covenants by the seller are implied on any sale with full or limited guarantee.

(a) That the seller has the **right to dispose** of the property (**s2(1)(a)**); for example, a seller who does not, in fact, own the whole of the property sold could be sued after completion for breach of this covenant.

(b) For **further assurance** (**s2(1)(b)** and **s2(2)**); for example, if the purchase deed is technically defective in some way, the seller is obliged to correct this at their own expense.

(c) For **freedom from charges, incumbrances and third-party rights** (**s3**); on a sale with limited guarantee, the covenant relates only to the period since the last sale for value (usually, when the seller bought the property). For example, a seller who failed to disclose that they had created an easement over the property in favour of a neighbour could be sued by the buyer on this ground.

(d) If the land is leasehold, that the **lease is valid** and the tenant has not breached conditions, or breached covenants which might result in forfeiture (**s4**). If there had been such breaches, the landlord could still forfeit the lease (subject, of course, to the rules regarding forfeiture), so the buyer would lose the property. The buyer would, however, be able to sue the seller.

(3) Exceptions

LP(MP)A 1994 provides that the covenants for title cannot be sued on where:

(a) matters arise between exchange and completion, as these are breaches of contract, not breaches of covenant;

(b) the sale is made expressly subject to defects which would otherwise constitute a breach of the seller's implied covenants (**s6(1)**);

(c) the buyer already knew of such defects before completion (or if they ought to have realised the position from the facts that they knew) **s6(2)**);

It is common practice to add a modification to **s6(2)** in the contract, to state:

> "For the purposes of s6(2) Law of Property (Miscellaneous Provisions) Act 1994, all matters now recorded in registers open to public inspection are to be considered within the actual knowledge of the buyer."

If this modification is to be made, it is usually done by adding a special condition on the back page of the contract form. In a standard form contract incorporating the SCs this would be special condition 2, and the phrase above would be added underneath the existing pre-printed wording:

> "2. Subject to the terms of this contract and to the Standard Conditions of Sale, the seller is to transfer the property with either full title guarantee or limited title guarantee as specified on the front page."

(d) the covenants for title entitle the buyer (or the buyer's successors in title under **s7**) only to sue the seller. They do not entitle the buyer to have any defect in title removed (unless the seller can do this without the need for any other person to consent).

As a practical point, if the seller cannot be traced after completion or has no money, the buyer would be unable to sue them. The guarantee (whether limited or full) is only of value if the seller can be successfully sued and any damages paid.

Where the contract makes no reference to the title guarantee, SC 4.6.2 provides that the seller will sell with full title guarantee. If a seller does not wish to sell with full title guarantee, they should therefore ensure that the alternative is clearly stated.

3.3.7 Completion date

The completion date will normally be left blank when the contract is drafted, since the exact date will not usually be known at that early stage. It will then be inserted on exchange of contracts.

Under the open contract rule, it is an implied term that completion will take place within a reasonable time. What is reasonable is to be determined by the facts of a particular case (***Dean v Upton* [1990]**). Practitioners, however, will not wish to rely on this and a standard contract invariably specifies the date which will be a mutually convenient one to the parties, bearing in mind the need for synchronisation where parties are buying and selling. If no provision is made on the front of the contract form and the SCs apply, SC 6.1.1 provides for completion to be the 20th working day after exchange of contracts. In practice, the completion date will have been the subject of much discussion and a specified date agreed.

3.3.8 Contract rate of interest

The contract will provide for the rate of interest payable under the contract. The principal use of the interest rate is in calculating the amount payable if completion is delayed beyond the contractual date. When using the SCs the full and precise method of calculation is dealt with in SC 7.

The seller will be keen to ensure that the rate is reflective of current interest rates – often 3–5 per cent above the base lending rate of one of the major clearing banks is used. For instance, the contract could state:

"4% above the base rate of HSBC Bank plc from time to time in force".

Alternatively, the front page of the contract can state:

"The Law Society's interest rate from time to time in force" (or similar wording).

In addition, the seller's conveyancer should ensure that it is not less than the rate provided for in the contract for any linked purchase by the seller to ensure that the seller who delays completion because of the fault of their own buyer is not significantly out of pocket in respect of the interest they would receive from their buyer and that which they would have to pay on their own purchase.

If no rate of interest is specifically included on the front of the form, the SCs provide for the use of the Law Society interest rate mentioned in SC 1.1.1(e). The Law Society's rate is 4.75 per cent above the base rate of Barclays Bank plc.

Activity

The Law Society's interest rate was first published in 1990. It might be necessary to establish what the interest rate was at some point in the past, for example, to calculate the penalty interest due in the event of late completion on a transaction.

Follow the link below to the Law Society's interest rate and click on the link for "historic rates". You will see that in July 2007 for example, the rate was 9.75 per cent. This reflects the higher bank base rates that were in effect at that time. Retain this link for future reference.

https://www.lawsociety.org.uk/en/topics/property/law-society-interest-rate

3.3.9 Root of title/title number

Where the title to the property is unregistered, the contract should state the date and nature of the instrument with which the abstract or epitome of title shall begin. In other words, the document which is to be the starting point of the chain of unregistered title must be stated in the contract. This document is called the "root of title". A good root of title is usually defined as a document which is at least 15 years old, clearly describes the land in question, deals with the whole legal and equitable estate and interest in the property and contains nothing to cast doubt on the title. There is no need to state a good root for a registered title.

An example of what would be included under root of title on the contract form would be:

> "A conveyance dated 15 November 1978 between (1) James Higgins and (2) John Brown."

Best practice is to choose the latest root possible as long as it meets all the criteria for a good root. Therefore, for instance, if there was a choice between using a 1970 conveyance as the root, or a 1984 conveyance as the root, best practice (as long as the deed met all the specified criteria) would be to select the 1984 conveyance as the root of title.

Where the description of the property and the specified incumbrances are cross-referenced to the root deed, it can avoid duplication in the contract to set it out in the following way (obviously the exact wording will depend on what is in the deeds).

Assume that the root is a conveyance on sale dated 15 November 1981.

The description of the property might read:

> "The freehold land known as 66 River View, Bath, Somerset, BA17 3YR as is more particularly described in a conveyance dated 15 November 1981 and made between Lucy Rice (1) and Franz and Joanna Schmidt (2) (the Conveyance)"

The root of title could then read:

> "The Conveyance"

The specified incumbrances could then read (according to the deed):

> "The covenants conditions and provisions contained mentioned or referred to in the Conveyance"

In registered land, the requirement as to title will be satisfied by stating the title number and possibly other brief details such as the class of title.

3.3.10 Deposit

Under the open contract rule, no deposit is payable; in practice, however, a deposit is invariably stipulated. SC 2.2.1 requires that a 10 per cent deposit is payable. The SCs will, of course, apply only if there is no Special Condition varying the amount. If a reduced deposit has been agreed, this should be shown clearly in the contract. It would normally be sufficient to state the amount clearly on the front page of the contract along with the amounts payable for purchase price, contents price (if separate) and balance.

It is important to consider not only how much deposit is paid but what the seller will be entitled to do with it when they receive it. This depends on the capacity in which the deposit is held by the seller's conveyancer. Traditionally, there were two options.

(1) Arrange that the deposit will be held by the seller's conveyancer as **agent** for the seller. This means that the seller's conveyancer can release the money to the seller, who can use it for any purpose they wish (e.g. for a deposit on a related purchase). This may cause problems where the seller defaults on completion, as the buyer may have difficulty in recovering the money (e.g. where the seller is missing or insolvent). The advantage of this method from the seller's point of view is that it allows them to use the deposit as they wish.

(2) Arrange that the deposit will be held by the seller's conveyancer as **stakeholder**. This means that the seller's conveyancer hold the deposit money in a neutral position pending completion and must not part with it. It cannot therefore be used by the seller for the deposit on any related purchase or for any other reason. The deposit is therefore held by the seller's conveyancer until one party becomes entitled to it. This will normally be the seller on completion but if something goes wrong that makes the deposit refundable, it will be returned to the buyer's conveyancer without question. This capacity is usually viewed as being disadvantageous to the seller (because they cannot access the money immediately) but advantageous to the buyer who knows that the money is safely held in the conveyancer's bank account and is recoverable in the event that the sale goes off due to the seller's default.

There is a compromise provided by the SCs. SC 2.2.5 allows the deposit to be held by the seller's conveyancer as agent insofar as it is needed for any related residential purchase in England and Wales. This means that all or part of the deposit can be used by the seller for such a related purchase provided that in such a purchase the deposit will be held on the same terms as SC 2.2.5 and SC 2.2.6. Any sums not so required must be held by the seller's conveyancer as stakeholder in accordance with SC 2.2.6. So even if a deposit is passed along a chain of related purchase transactions, it will ultimately be held by a firm of conveyancers as stakeholder. Due to these provisions in the SCs, sale deposits are routinely used in practice for related purchase deposits.

For this SC to be used properly and effectively, all the parties in a chain transaction must adopt SC 2 or similar provisions.

3.3.11 Riskier advice – accepting a reduced deposit on a sale

We have seen that, typically, the buyer pays a deposit of 10 per cent of the purchase price on exchange of contracts and this is the expectation under the SCs. However, the buyer may offer the seller less than 10 per cent on exchange and the question is whether the seller should accept a reduced deposit.

If the seller's conveyancer receives a request for a reduced deposit, they should first inquire as to why a reduced deposit is being offered. If the buyer is funding the balance of the purchase price with a 95 per cent mortgage, then a reduced deposit is a "Hobson's choice" in that there is no choice at all because the buyer will not have more than 5 per cent of the purchase price to offer.

However, if the answer is that the buyer has to give notice to get some funds off deposit or is relying on a reduced deposit on their related sale, the seller's conveyancer should advise their seller client to carefully consider whether the seller wants to accept a reduced deposit. It might be preferable to wait until the buyer has taken their funds off deposit, for example, and receive a full 10 per cent deposit.

The risk to the seller of accepting a reduced deposit must be explained to them. The risk will arise in the event that the buyer fails to complete the purchase. If the buyer does not complete on the contractually agreed completion date, the seller's conveyancer will liaise with their client to establish whether a notice to complete under SC 6.8 should be served. Once the notice is served, under SC 6.8.3, if the buyer has paid a deposit of less than 10 per cent on exchange of contracts, they are forthwith to pay a further deposit equal to the balance of that 10 per cent.

Once a notice to complete is served, the buyer then has 10 working days (excluding the date of service of the notice) within which to complete the transaction. The risk to the seller is that the buyer does not in fact have the additional money to make the deposit up to the full 10 per cent. The seller will have a contractual right under the SCs to sue the buyer in the event of default. However, this contractual right is worth very little if the buyer does not, in fact, have the funds because they will probably not be worth suing. This risk must be explained to the seller in writing. Ultimately, it is up to the seller to decide whether they are prepared to take the risk and accept less than 10 per cent of the purchase price as a deposit on exchange of contracts.

Link to practice

Despite the fact that it is good practice for the buyer's conveyancer to inform the seller's conveyancer of the amount of deposit on offer early in a conveyancing transaction, in practice, it is often the case that the amount of deposit is not clear until the point of exchange of contracts itself. Quite often, the buyer's conveyancer will offer the seller's conveyancer a deposit of less than 10 per cent to exchange because this is what they are receiving on their related transaction.

Despite the fact that it is tempting to proceed to exchange of contracts, in this situation, the seller's conveyancer should refuse to exchange contracts and should check with their seller client that the seller is prepared to accept a deposit of less than 10 per cent on exchange of contracts.

3.3.12 Chattels

These are referred to as "contents" under the SCs.

Under the general law, the buyer would be entitled to all fixtures along with the property, but not mere chattels. It is, to say the least, uncertain under the general law as to whether, and under what circumstances, many items are fixtures or chattels. It is highly desirable to specify exactly which fixtures are to be removed and which chattels are included in the sale. Doing this will minimise the risk that the buyer finds that items they had expected to get on completion have been removed shortly before they move in. Disputes about contents can be difficult to sort out after completion and can cost a disproportionate amount in legal fees to resolve.

This is why the Fittings and Contents form (TA10 or equivalent) is important – see https://www.lawsociety.org.uk/topics/property/transaction-forms.

To provide certainty in the contract, the Fifth Edition of the Standard Conditions of Sale provides (see Special Condition 3) for a list of any contents to be included to be set out and attached to the contract. Any separate amount payable for these can be stated on the front page of the contract as the contents price. Form TA10 (Fittings and Contents Form) may be attached to the contract itself under Special Condition 3.

The Condition also provides that a list of excluded fixtures may be attached.

Under SC 9, ownership in contents is to pass at completion. Furthermore, whether or not a separate price is paid for the contents, the contract takes effect as a contract for the sale of goods, with the effect that the seller warrants that they have the right to sell the contents.

Contents may of course be included for no additional charge (e.g. the carpets and curtains are included in the sale). In this case there will be no contents price to insert in the contract. It can be stated as Nil or left blank.

Sometimes the seller wants an additional payment for contents.

With regards to the contents price, this may be agreed as being a figure which is additional to the purchase price (i.e. it may be agreed that an additional price is to be paid over and above the purchase price for the contents). For example, the purchase price is £400,000 and the buyer is to pay an additional contents price of £1,000 on top of this for an antique table, bedroom curtains and leather armchair.

Sometimes the purchase price is said to be "apportioned" partly to contents. For instance, the purchase price may be £200,000 but there is to be an apportionment from this of £2,000 for a designer sofa and living room carpet. In this case the contract would show the purchase price as being £198,000 with a contents price of £2,000. There are several points to note about apportionment.

(1) Sometimes this can reduce the amount of SDLT payable, as it can move the purchase price into lower rate bandings. SDLT is payable on the land (purchase price) but not on contents (chattels).

(2) Care must be taken as the apportionment must be a realistic one. It is not possible to invent a higher figure for the contents than can be genuinely supported, as this may constitute a fraud against HMRC. Similarly, the items which are subject to the apportionment must genuinely be chattels. HMRC has issued guidance on apportionment, stressing that it will not be acceptable simply because the parties have agreed the figures in the contract. Any apportionment must be just and reasonable and HMRC has the power to make enquiries if it thinks that it is not genuine. HMRC has also given some guidance as to the items it regards as chattels and the items it regards as fixtures for the purposes of apportionment, although it stresses that the lists are not definitive and each case would be considered on its own merits. The following table provides some examples.

Examples of items which HMRC will normally regard as chattels	Examples of items which HMRC will normally regard as fixtures
Carpets (fitted or otherwise)	Fitted kitchen units and sinks
Curtains and blinds	Wall mounted ovens and agas
Freestanding furniture	Central heating systems
Kitchen white goods (unless fully integrated)	Fitted bathroom sanitary ware
Light shades and fittings (unless recessed)	Intruder alarm systems

(3) If there is a reduction in the purchase price due to an apportionment for contents, it will be necessary to tell the lender about this, if the purchase price now differs from the information the lender has previously been given. This change may affect the decision on how much the lender is prepared to advance. Further, the conveyancer owes a duty in the UK Finance Mortgage Lenders' Handbook to tell the lender about any discrepancies in the purchase price.

3.3.13 Vacant possession

Under the open contract rules, it is an implied condition that vacant possession will be given on completion. (Exceptionally, this might be rebutted if the property was obviously not vacant when visited by the buyer.) Vacant possession essentially means free of any physical or legal impediment to the buyer taking possession.

The SCs deal with this by allowing the deletion of one of the two alternatives in Special Condition 4. The relevant alternative must be selected and the other deleted. Where the property is being sold with vacant possession (the usual case as opposed, for example, to a sale with existing tenants in the property), then the first alternative (the property is sold with vacant possession) should be left intact and the second alternative deleted.

A non-owning spouse's or civil partner's **statutory right of occupation** under the **Family Law Act 1996** is also relevant here. Where, under the contract, the seller is to give vacant possession on completion there is an implied term in the contract that any charge protecting the spouse or civil partner's right of occupation will be discharged. The interest would be protected as a Class F land charge in unregistered title and an agreed notice in registered title. This condition would be satisfied by the seller handing over, on completion, an application for discharge of the entry signed by the person whose right is protected.

In registered land, for instance, this would be a completed form HR4 – cancellation of a home rights notice – see https://www.gov.uk/government/publications/cancel-home-rights-registration-hr4 . If the property is in the name of one party alone, the seller's conveyancer should ensure that this problem is sorted out before exchange of contracts. If the spouse or civil partner agrees to the sale, their agreement to remove the land charge or notice can be sought. They can be asked to join in the contract to agree to discharge the interest. Special Condition 7 on the contract form is a pre-printed occupier's consent clause.

Link to practice

The presence of a Home Rights notice or a class F land charge affecting the title can be used by the non-owning spouse or civil partner as a "bargaining chip" in divorce proceedings. It is therefore essential for the buyer's conveyancer to ensure that they have received an undertaking from the seller's conveyancer to provide a duly signed HR4 (if the land is registered) from the non-owning spouse or civil partner on completion. Preferably, the buyer's conveyancer would require sight of the signed form prior to exchange of contracts.

On the other side of the equation, the seller's conveyancer should ensure that they have a buyer's signed application for discharge on the file before exchange of contracts. If the spouse or civil partner is not happy about the sale, negotiations for the removal of the discharge of the charge should be commenced (with the spouse or civil partner being asked to take independent advice). It will be a great deal easier to negotiate before exchange of contracts than to attempt to do so afterwards with a spouse or civil partner who knows their partner is up against the ropes and liable to pay substantial damages to the buyers if agreement cannot be reached. (For damages, note ***Wroth v Tyler*** **[1973]**.)

Remember also that the seller's conveyancer should not advise the non-owning spouse or civil partner due to the significant risk of a conflict of interest arising. If there is a divorce or separation, it is likely that the non-owning spouse or civil partner will instruct their own family lawyer. This is likely to delay the transaction and the conveyancers for seller and buyer should review the file and consider whether their costs will increase as a result. Any increase of costs should be notified to the client in advance of the costs being incurred.

Non-owning occupiers will also be asked to sign a consent clause to release any other rights or interests they may have in the property, and to promise to vacate on completion. Again, Special Condition 7 is an occupier's consent clause.

By signing the clause at Special Condition 7, the occupier is confirming all of the following:

- that they concur in the sale of the property on the terms of the contract;
- that they undertake to vacate the property on or before the completion date; and
- that they release the property and any included fixtures and contents from any right or interest that they may have.

Link to practice

An example of a non-owning occupier could be a parent living with their family or an adult child living with their parents.

The situation regarding a non-owning spouse or civil partner mentioned above is specific because they have the right to register the Home Rights notice to protect their occupation of the matrimonial home. No such protection is available to a cohabiting partner or an adult who is simply living with the owner of the property.

However, in all cases, whether it is a non-owning occupier, they should be required to sign Special Condition 7 of the contract as evidence of their intention to vacate the property on completion.

Remember that the seller should disclose who lives at the property on the Property Information Form (question 11).

The seller's conveyancer will usually send the contract to the non-owning occupier to request that they signed Special Condition 7 and return the contract prior to exchange. It is important not to give the non-owning occupier any advice due to the significant risk of conflict of interest. The non-owning occupier should be informed in writing that they should obtain their own independent legal advice.

3.3.14 Insurance

Under the open contract rules, the risk in the property passes to the buyer on exchange of contracts. The seller is, however, well advised to maintain their insurance cover until completion, in case, for instance, the buyer should become entitled to rescind. It is, however, the buyer's responsibility to insure the property and if any accident should befall the property before completion the buyer may still be required to purchase the property at the full contract price (even if the property is merely a burned-out shell). The doctrine of frustration of contracts does not usually apply to contracts for the sale of land but the court has jurisdiction to order repayment of the deposit to the buyer depending on a number of factors including the size of the deposit (***Universal Corporation v Five Ways Properties*** **[1979]**). **s47 LPA 1925** provides for the possibility of recovery being made from the seller if the seller actually had a policy of insurance. **s47**, however, is fraught with problems, which means that the ability of the buyer to recover in the event of an accident is, to say the least, uncertain.

The Fifth Edition of the Standard Conditions (2018 Revision) provides that the risk passes to the buyer on exchange. SC 5.1.1 states that the property is at the risk of the buyer from the date of the contract.

SC 5.1.2 states that the seller is under no obligation to the buyer to insure the property unless the contract provides otherwise, or the property is let on terms under which the seller (whether as landlord or tenant) is obliged to insure.

Even when the seller is not obliged to insure, this does not mean that they are not entitled to do so. Many sellers will continue to insure, and will indeed be required to do so by their mortgage lenders.

This means that there may well be double insurance (two policies in effect at the same time), each covering the same risks.

To cater for this possibility, SC 5 states that where the property is damaged, and a payment under a policy taken out by the buyer is reduced because of insurance held by the seller, the purchase price is to be reduced (abated) by the amount of the reduction.

Where the seller is obliged to insure (e.g. as a tenant under a lease), SC 5 requires the seller to maintain the policy and, if the property is damaged, to pay the buyer the amount of the policy proceeds which the seller has received (so far as not used in repairing the property), or to assign the claim to the buyer.

3.3.15 Existing covenants

SC 4.6.4 provides that the purchase deed shall include a covenant by the buyer to indemnify the seller in respect of a breach of any covenant for which the seller will remain liable provided that the covenant was disclosed to the buyer before exchange.

Despite this SC, many practitioners prefer to deal with this issue expressly, by including a special condition in the contract. By dealing with this issue in a Special Condition, the parties can agree the exact wording of the indemnity covenant and this also draws the matter to the attention of the buyer's conveyancer.

Link to practice

Look out in the proprietorship register for the following entry:

"The transfer to the proprietor contains a covenant to observe and perform the covenants referred to in the Charges Register and of indemnity in respect thereof".

This denotes that the seller gave an indemnity in respect of the restrictive covenants contained in the charges register. This means that the sellers agreed to cover any costs incurred by their seller for their breaching the covenants. If there is an established chain of covenants from seller to seller, the contract will need to make provision for the buyer to give an indemnity covenant upon completion. Such a clause will form a special condition in the contract and will need to be incorporated into the transfer deed.

3.3.16 Latest time for completion

SC 6.1.2 provides that completion must take place by 2.00 pm on the completion date. If completion is later than this time, it is treated (for compensation for late completion: SC 7.2) as if it had happened on the following working day.

The aim of this provision is to ensure that the transaction and related transfers of funds have passed through the banking system in time for the close of banking on the completion date.

This can create difficulties in chain transactions. The problem is that a number of delays can occur between the sale being completed and the purchase. These delays can be prolonged if a number of properties are in the same chain, each purchase dependent on its related sale.

SC 6.7 provides that the completion money is to be sent by a direct transfer of cleared funds. This is an automatic system of transferring funds through the banking system, and although this can occur quite quickly, there can be delays in giving instructions to the bank and in waiting for the bank to process the payment.

Accordingly, a Special Condition is often added to the contract to provide an earlier time on the client's sale than on the purchase. The times stated should allow sufficient time following the completion of the sale to complete the purchase. Preprinted Special Condition 5 can be used for this purpose. This allows the 2.00 pm time limit in SC 6.1.2 and SC 6.1.3 to be varied. The Law Society states that this is designed to be useful in the case of a chain, for example, the seller under the first contract in the chain might require payment by 1.30 pm to allow time to receive funds and transmit them on their own purchase by 2.00 pm. In practice an even earlier time would be better in order to allow for delays, for example, 11.30 am.

3.3.17 Contracts (Rights of Third Parties) Act 1999

Previously, the doctrine of privity of contract has meant that only the parties to a contract can sue under that contract. Thus, someone who is not party to the original contract has no right to sue under it.

Under the **Contracts (Rights of Third Parties) Act 1999** (**C(RTP)A 1999**), a contract can provide for court-actionable benefits to be given to someone who is not party to that contract. The wording "third party" in the name of **C(RTP)A 1999** is perhaps misleading because we are considering the rights of someone who is not a party to the original contract.

The rights are given to the third party by their being named or referred to by description in the original contract. For example, a contract between a builder and an architect for the design of a new property might refer to the "future occupiers" of the property. It would appear that this description might give the future occupiers specific actionable rights under the contract between the builder and architect. Similar considerations could give rights to a future sub-tenant on the grant of a head lease, or to neighbours on a building estate (making covenants mutually enforceable), or in a wide variety of other conveyancing situations.

Unless the contract expressly allows, rights of third parties cannot be altered by the parties to the original contract after such rights have crystallised. This occurs if the third party notifies its assent to the contract, or if the appropriate party to the relevant contract knows or ought to know that the third party has relied on the relevant term of the contract. In some situations, it will be desirable for those acquiring such rights to serve formal notices on the original parties to the contract in order to preserve their rights.

Unless it is intended to grant third party rights, it is prudent to include in the contract an express declaration that the parties do not intend to create any rights in favour of third parties and exclude the effect of **C(RTP)A 1999**. If the Standard Conditions of Sale (Fifth Edition – 2018 Revision) are used, this is catered for by SC 1.6.

3.3.18 Void conditions

There are some conditions which, even if included in the contract by way of Special Condition, will have no effect because they are made void by statutory provision. Examples of such conditions include the following.

(1) A stipulation requiring the buyer to accept a title made with the concurrence of a person entitled to an equitable interest if, in fact, the title could be made free from the interest by overreaching.

Example

X is selling High Trees. X is the sole legal owner but the equitable owners are X and Y. There are two ways in which the buyer can take the property free of the interest of Y. The first is for Y to join in the conveyance to release their interest. The second is for X to appoint a second trustee (either Y or anyone else) to overreach Y's equitable interest. If the contract states that the buyer will be given good title using the first method, the buyer could not, even after exchange of contracts, be held to this condition but could, if they wished, insist on the second method (**s42 LPA 1925**).

(2) A provision requiring the buyer to pay or contribute towards the costs of any document necessary to cause overreaching (e.g. a condition in the situation above requiring the buyer to pay for the cost of appointing a second trustee).

(3) Any stipulation restricting the buyer in the selection of a conveyancer or requiring the conveyance to be prepared at the buyer's expense by the seller's conveyancer.

(4) Any condition which attempts to preclude the buyer from examining any power of attorney under which a document in the title is executed.

(5) Any condition which prevents the buyer from objecting to the inadequacy of stamping on any document of title.

(6) Any clause which attempts to penalise a party who defaults in performing contractual obligations. Clauses such as those requiring interest to be paid on late completion are acceptable if they represent liquidated damages (a means of calculating the damages payable for loss suffered, based on a reasonable advance assessment of the likely amounts), but would not be acceptable if they imposed a penalty.

(7) A clause which attempts to bar or restrict remedies for misrepresentation is valid only if it passes the reasonableness test in the **Unfair Contract Terms Act 1977** or the **Consumer Rights Act 2015** (depending on which legislation applies – this will depend on whether the parties are individuals or businesses).

3.3.19 Options to purchase

Options are relevant at this stage as an option to purchase is essentially a type of contract whereby one person (the owner of the land) gives another person (the grantee of the option) the right to buy certain defined land within a certain period of time.

Example

Saima could give Lee the option of purchasing a specific piece of land, Green Field, for five years.

The option will allow the grantee to serve notice on the grantor to exercise the option to purchase within the stipulated time period of the option.

This does not mean that Lee must buy the land. They are given the option to do so, and they can then decide whether to exercise the option or not. If they do so, then Saima is obliged to sell it to them.

The original option agreement must comply with **s2 Law of Property (Miscellaneous Provisions) Act 1989** as it is a (conditional) contract for the sale of land (i.e. it must be in writing, contain all the agreed terms and be signed by or on behalf of both parties).

The option agreement must therefore contain all the terms agreed between the parties. Examples of typical terms are:

- for the grantee to pay a fee to the owner for giving them the option;
- the time limit within which the option must be exercised (e.g. 10 years). There used to be a maximum period of 21 years under the **Perpetuities and Accumulations Act 1964**, but this has not applied since 6 April 2010 (**Perpetuities and Accumulations Act 2009**);
- provisions for the service of notice to exercise the option by the grantee (e.g. that it must be in writing and sent in a particular way);
- how the purchase price is to be calculated once the option has been exercised (e.g. a fixed price or some other method of valuation);
- the provisions of the sale contract on the assumption that the option is exercised (e.g. that the SCS Fifth Edition (2018 Revision) will apply);
- for a completion date upon serving of notice (e.g. that completion will be 14 days after service of the notice).

When the option is exercised, a binding contract for sale and purchase of the land comes into existence.

The option is an estate contract and should be protected by the grantee in order to bind future buyers of the land from the owner (i.e. future owners). In unregistered land, it is protected as a class C(iv) land charge, whereas in registered land it is protected by way of notice on the register.

The material above describes the most common type of option.

As is the case with other complex conveyancing documentation, conveyancer may use precedents to help with the drafting. Any precedents should of course be adapted to suit the transaction in hand.

3.3.20 A general approach to drafting and approving the contract

In drafting a contract, remember not to lose sight of the facts and of common sense. Conveyancers want the contract to sell exactly what the client wants to sell and no more. They want the sale to be on terms that are acceptable to the client. Remember:

- to consider the client's particular circumstances and wishes as well as the law;
- that in any controversial issue there will be two sides to the matter. Conveyancers need to know what is the best contractual provision from the client's point of view.

Conveyancers also need to know what the buyer is likely to regard as most desirable and what form a compromise contractual provision might take. Remember that, if the buyer does not like the terms which have been included in the draft contract, they will negotiate and might ultimately decide not to enter into the contract. Conveyancers should consider whether, if they received a draft contract like this, they would be able to ascertain exactly what they were buying and on what terms.

Draft contracts may be sent electronically as a Word document or may be sent in a paper format. Any conveyancer will use their own precedent for drafting the contract. There are many practitioner works which can assist with drafting.

Link to practice

A draft contract package usually comprises:

- draft contract in duplicate;
- Property Information Form;
- Fittings and Contents Form;
- evidence of title – usually, official copies of register entries and title plan or an epitome of title if unregistered land;
- any supporting documents such as guarantees for work completed on the property, for example, damp-proof course;
- any copy of planning permissions or building regulation approvals;
- the EPC.

The contract package will also contain any additional documents which are relevant in the circumstances of the individual case and will contain additional items where the property is leasehold.

Activity

Follow the link below to the Law Society's website and click on the link for the Protocol:

https://www.lawsociety.org.uk/en/topics/property/conveyancing-protocol

Look at section 13.

You will see that the Protocol contains detailed requirements regarding the content of a Protocol package.

The Protocol also contains provisions inviting the seller's conveyancer to consider preparing a draft transfer to attach to the contract or to submit with the contract. This is not mandatory, but does reflect the practice of some firms, irrespective of whether the Protocol is adopted or not.

If the buyer's conveyancer does not agree with any of the clauses in the contract, or if there is a typographical error anywhere, they will mark the contract with their proposed changes. If dealing with a paper copy of the contract, this will usually be done in red pen on the contract. The front of the contract would usually also be marked, in red, along the lines of "Amended in red on 17 April 2022". The buyer's conveyancer then sends it back to the seller's conveyancer for amendment to be agreed. Further amendments (if any) should be made in a different colour. If the amendments are substantial, another clean copy of the contract may be produced; if not, the handwritten amendments can be agreed as manuscript amendments.

If the draft contract has been sent electronically, use can be made of the word-processing options to mark up and track any changes so as to make them evident to the seller's conveyancer, who can then email them back approved.

A contract which passes between the parties for amendments to be made is often called a "travelling draft".

It is important that you are familiar with the elements of a contract, the sources of information, the terms of the standard conditions and how to amend them.

3.4 Examples of Common Special Conditions

We have seen that if the seller and the buyer agree something between themselves that is relevant to the transaction, this must be included in the contract for it to be legally binding on both parties. We have also seen that the contract incorporating the Standard Conditions of Sale (Fifth edition – 2018 revision) contains seven pre-Special Conditions on the reverse of the contract. If any other Special Conditions are going to be added to the contract to reflect an agreement between the seller and buyer, the conveyancers will simply agree the wording between themselves and will add the additional Special Conditions to the contract, often by stapling an additional sheet to the contract. Any new Special Conditions will start at number 8.

The content of these specific Special Conditions are limitless in that anything that is agreed between the parties should be included in the contract. It is therefore often the case that there are no standard precedents for these provisions and the conveyancers must use their common sense to draft the additional provisions.

When thinking about additional provisions for the contract, keep in mind the following:

(1) Specify exactly what has been agreed between the parties.

(2) If additional money is payable, make it clear how much and include the figure in words and figures.

(3) If anything is to be removed from the property, or work done, ensure that there is a provision on the party carrying out the work to "make good any damage caused".

(4) Ensure that any relevant time limits are included in the drafting; for example, is a document to be produced "on or before completion" or within a specified time after completion?

(5) Should a long stop date be included?

(6) Ensure that the provision is written in plain English.

(7) Ensure that the provision is approved by the seller or buyer client prior to being incorporated into the contract.

Let's look at some common examples

The seller agrees to carry out specified works to the property between exchange of contracts and completion

The special condition might read as follows:

"Between the date of this agreement and completion, the seller will carry out the following work to the property [insert schedule of work] (the Work). The Work will be carried out at the seller's expense in a good and workmanlike manner and to the reasonable satisfaction of the buyer."

The above is only a simple clause to deal with something fairly straightforward. If the seller agrees to carry out extensive or expensive work to the property between exchange of contracts and completion, a more detailed contract provision would be needed to cover issues such as the right for the buyer to inspect the property with a surveyor or suitably qualified professional. The contract may also need to include the right for the buyer to withhold a specified portion of the purchase price on completion if the work is not carried out to a reasonable standard.

The seller agrees to provide a statutory declaration or statement of truth on completion

There are a number of situations where the buyer's conveyancer may want the seller to provide a statutory declaration or statement of truth. For example, to deal with the fact that a document of title has been lost or evidence the fact that a right of access or right to use pipes have been exercised during the seller's ownership. This would be required because the title documents do not contain the appropriate rights.

Best practice demands that the conveyancers agree the form of the statutory declaration or statement of truth prior to exchange of contracts. The document can then be attached to the contract on exchange for clarity.

The special condition might read as follows:

"On or before completion, the seller will provide to the buyer a duly sworn and dated [statutory declaration or statement of truth – insert as appropriate] in the form annexed hereto."

Seller to provide indemnity insurance policy on completion

Linked to the above point, where a statutory declaration or statement of truth is required to explain the circumstances relating to a defect in title or lack of rights, the buyer's conveyancer will also want an indemnity insurance policy to protect their buyer client (and lender, if any). Whether the seller is prepared to provide and pay for an indemnity insurance policy is a matter for negotiation between the parties. We will look at indemnity insurance in more detail in Chapter 8. However, if the seller agrees to provide an indemnity insurance policy, best practice demands that a draft of the insurance policy is attached to the contract on exchange of contracts.

The special condition might read as follows:

"On or before completion the Seller will at their own expense, provide to the buyer an indemnity insurance policy in the form annexed hereto."

Buyer agrees to purchase additional fittings and contents

The Fittings and Contents Form is fairly extensive and will be completed by the seller and appended to the contract on exchange. Accordingly, there should be little room for dispute between the buyer and seller as to what is and is not included in the sale price. However, the seller and buyer often agree to the sale and purchase of additional items. Best practice demands that this is included in the contract rather than let the parties deal direct. Both conveyancers should obtain a list of items to be purchased by the buyer from their respective clients and this should be added to the contract for clarity. The particulars of sale includes a section for a separate contents price on the front page, but it is good practice to include an additional Special Condition for the sake of clarity.

The special condition might read as follows:

"In addition to the purchase price, on completion the buyer will pay [insert agreed sum in words and figures] for the following items: [list the agreed items]"

Where the parties agree to a retention

Very often in a leasehold transaction, the seller and buyer will agree that one of the conveyancers holds back part of the purchase price as a retention pending production of the audited service charge accounts. Generally, the amount of service charge that a seller pays in advance is based on a budgeted figure calculated in the year of payment. The actual sums paid can only be accurately calculated retrospectively at the end of the service charge year. Most leases include a clause requiring the landlord or management company to produce audited service charge accounts. If these reveal a shortfall for the previous accounting year, the tenant will be required to make up the shortfall. Obviously, this is an issue for an incoming buyer if the shortfall relates to a period of time during which the seller owns the property. Accordingly, this is often dealt with by way of a retention. This is a sum of money held back on completion which the buyer can then use to pay any shortfall attributable to the period of the seller's ownership. Many firms have their own standard precedent to include in the contract and each precedent will need to be amended to suit the circumstances of the particular transaction. However, it is very important to ensure that the contract provision contains a long stop date by which the retained sum is either kept by the buyer or paid to the seller to ensure that the parties are not subject to an open-ended contract provision.

The special condition will depend on the circumstances but should deal with the following:

- define the amount of the retention;
- agree which conveyancer will hold the retention;
- agree whether any interest will be payable on the retention;
- define what evidence is required for payment of the balance of service charge due under the lease (for example, audited service charge accounts for a particular service charge year);
- specify the timeframe within which the balancing sum required must be paid;
- specify to whom any surplus of the retention sum will be paid;
- a long stop date.

Where the parties agree to an allowance from the purchase price

There are many reasons why the seller and buyer might agree to an allowance from the purchase price. For example, the buyer's survey may reveal that work needs to be carried out to the property. Rather than delay the transaction by requiring the seller to carry out work, the parties might agree a price reduction. In this case, the purchase price of the property will decrease and any mortgage offer must be amended accordingly.

However, reducing the purchase price generally does not leave the buyer with any money in hand to carry out the specified works once their purchase completes. Accordingly, the parties often negotiate an "allowance" meaning that the purchase price remains as originally agreed, but the seller agrees to accept a reduced sum on completion. This will then leave the buyer with the agreed allowance sum in hand on completion to carry out work.

The fact that an allowance is being made must be reflected in the contract and this is usually by a fairly simple special condition which might read as follows:

"On completion, the seller will make an allowance to the buyer of [insert agreed sum in words and figures] for the purpose of carrying out the following work to the property after completion [insert purpose for allowance]."

It is essential that the buyer's conveyancer reports any allowance, however modest, to the buyer's lender if any. The buyer must consent to this being done but the buyer's conveyancer must do so to comply with the Lender's Handbook (para 6.4.4).

Link to practice

Clients often indicate that something has been agreed with the other party in a telephone call or email. It is imperative that you review your file prior to exchange of contracts to ensure that all matters that are agreed between the parties are included in the contract. Remember that the issue will not be binding if it is not included in the contract.

Buyers are particularly sensitive about the fittings and contents which are to be left at a property. When you are taking your client's authority to exchange, it is good practice to ask your client whether the buyer has agreed to pay anything extra for any fittings and contents and ensure that this is included in the contract. This will help you to pick up these points which you might have missed during the transaction.

3.5 Time limits for raising requisitions

We will move on to look at how to deduce and investigate unregistered and registered title in the next chapters. First, we should briefly consider a matter which is covered in the Standard Conditions of Sale, but which is rarely relevant in practice.

When investigating the documentary evidence of title, it may be important to remember the time limits. If title is being investigated before exchange of contracts, contractual time limits are of no importance – the contract has not yet been entered into and the time limits in it are therefore meaningless. If, however, there is a provision in the contract barring requisitions after exchange, the buyer must regard this as their deadline and be sure, before exchange, that there are no outstanding matters about which they are unhappy. SC 4.2.1 provides that, if title is deduced before exchange, any requisitions in respect of that title must be raised before exchange, other than requisitions about matters coming to the buyer's attention for the first time after the contract has been entered into.

Given that the buyer is bound by exchange of contracts, it is probably negligent to raise requisitions after exchange when there is little you can do about the answers. The importance of the time limits essentially arises only when title is being investigated after exchange of contracts which of course is rare.

SC 4.3.1 contains the timetable. Briefly (where the completion date is at least 15 working days after exchange):

- the seller must provide evidence of title immediately after exchange, if not already provided;
- the buyer must raise requisitions within six working days of exchange of contracts or delivery of the evidence of title, whichever is the later;
- the seller must reply to requisitions within four working days after receiving the requisitions.

There is also provision for additional requisitions to be raised after this, however, where the first requisition amounted to a request to see a missing document, in which case the buyer is allowed additional time to raise requisitions arising out of that document. There are also certain other situations where requisitions may be raised out of time.

The time limits are important in two ways:

- if the buyer misses the time limit for raising requisitions there is then no obligation at all on the seller to answer requisitions which are made late (except possibly for requisitions on fundamental title defects, and final searches);
- a failure to observe these time limits may result in the delaying party being liable for damages in the event of delayed completion.

3.6 Example of a completed contract

Below is an example of a drafted contract of sale.

CONTRACT

Incorporating the Standard Conditions of Sale (Fifth Edition - 2018 Revision)

For conveyancer's use only

Buyer's conveyancer: ....

Seller's conveyancer: ....

Law Society Formula: [A / B / C / Personal exchange]

The information above does not form part of the Contract

Date :	
Seller :	Marilyn Tennant and Edward Alan Tennant of 2 Hazel Grove, East Corner, Shropshire, SY6 5TA
Buyer :	Daljit Johal of Flat 5B, 12 High Street, Neston, Shropshire, SY2 7JU
Property (freehold/~~leasehold~~) :	2 Hazel Grove, East Corner, Shropshire, SY6 5TA
Title number / ~~root of title~~ :	SF604950
Specified incumbrances :	The matters contained or referred to in the register of the above title (save for financial charges)
Title guarantee (full/~~limited~~) :	Full title guarantee
Completion date :	
Contract rate :	The Law Society's interest rate
Purchase price :	£155,000
Deposit :	£15,500
Contents price (if separate) :	Nil
Balance :	£139,500

The seller will sell and the buyer will buy the property for the purchase price.

WARNING	**Signed**
This is a formal document, designed to create legal rights and legal obligations. Take advice before using it.	Seller/Buyer

SCS1_2/1

SPECIAL CONDITIONS

1 (a) This contract incorporates the Standard Conditions of Sale (Fifth Edition - 2018 Revision).
(b) The terms used in this contract have the same meaning when used in the Conditions.

2 Subject to the terms of this contract and to the Standard Conditions of Sale, the seller is to transfer the property with either full title guarantee or limited title guarantee, as specified on the front page.

3 (a) The sale includes those contents which are indicated on the attached list as included in the sale and the buyer is to pay the contents price for them.

~~(b) The sale excludes those fixtures which are at the property and are indicated on the attached list as excluded~~ from ~~the~~ sale

4 The property is sold with vacant possession.

~~(or)~~

~~4 The property is sold subject to the following leases or tenancies:~~

5. The transfer shall contain a covenant by the buyer that the buyer will (by way of indemnity only) observe and perform the covenants referred to in entry no. 2 of the charges register and will indemnify and keep the seller and his estate indemnified against all actions, proceedings, costs, damages or expenses incurred or suffered by the seller or his estate in respect of future breach, non-observance or non-performance of those covenants.

~~5 Conditions 6.1.2 and 6.1.3 shall take effect as if the time specified in them were rather than 2.00 p.m.~~

6 **Representations**
Neither party can rely on any representation made by the other, unless made in writing by the other or his conveyancer, but this does not exclude liability for fraud or recklessness.

~~7 **Occupier's consent**~~
~~Each occupier identified below agrees with the seller and the buyer, in consideration of their entering into this contract, that the occupier concurs in the sale of the property on the terms of this contract, undertakes to vacate the property on or before the completion date and releases the property and any included fixtures and contents from any right or interest that the occupier may have.~~
~~**Note:** this condition does not apply to occupiers under leases or tenancies subject to which the property is sold.~~

~~Name(s) and signature(s) of the occupier(s) (if any):~~

~~Name~~

~~Signature~~

Notices may be sent to:
Seller's conveyancer's name: [Details of seller's firm]

E-mail address:*

Buyer's conveyancer's name: [Details of Sue's firm]

E-mail address:*

*Adding an e-mail address authorises service by e-mail see condition 1.3.3(b)

3.7 Chapter summary

(1) A contract for the sale of land must comply with **s2 LP(MP)A 1989**. It must:

- be in writing;
- incorporate all terms;
- be signed by or on behalf of both parties.

(2) **s2** can be satisfied by exchanging identical contracts signed on behalf of all parties.

(3) Contracts may be conditional upon certain events.

(4) The contract is normally drafted by the seller's conveyancer.

(5) If terms are not expressly included, the common law implies certain conditions by way of rules called the "open contract rules".

(6) Instead of using the open contract rules, most contracts for residential transactions adopt the Law Society's Standard Conditions of Sale (Fifth Edition – 2018 Revision).

(7) Contracts for the sale of land will contain terms which:

- describe the land and the estate sold;
- determine the seller's duty of disclosure and obligation to deduce title;
- provide for the title guarantee to be given;
- determine the completion date;
- provide for remedies if completion is delayed or a misrepresentation/ misdescription occurs;
- describe any contents to be sold;
- deal with insurance between exchange and completion;
- provide for any rights to be granted or reserved (e.g. covenants or easements).

(8) Notwithstanding the express terms of the contract, the law may render certain terms void.

(9) An option to purchase land at a future date may be given.

(10) The draft contract will be sent to the buyer's conveyancer as part of the pre-contract package.

(11) It may be necessary to amend the contract.

(12) Time limits for raising requisitions are set out in SC 4.3.1.

CHAPTER **4**

Deducing and investigating title – unregistered land

4.1 Introduction

Now we have started the process of contract drafting by the seller's conveyancer, the seller will deduce title to the buyer which the buyer's conveyancer has to investigate. The terminology is important:

Seller's conveyancer	**Deduces** title
Buyer's conveyancer	**Investigates** title

The process of deducing title is where the seller, having shown in the contract what they are proposing to sell, actually proves that they can do it. They do this by providing the buyer with documentary proof that the situation is as they have said it is in the contract. There are two systems by which the seller can prove that they have good title to land: the unregistered and registered systems. This chapter will consider the unregistered system which is the traditional method, based on producing documentary evidence of title to land. It will be necessary for the seller's conveyancer to obtain the unregistered title deeds. These may be held by the seller, or another firm of solicitors. If the property is in mortgage, the unregistered title deeds will be held by the lender as security for the loan and the seller's solicitor will have to give an undertaking to the lender for their release.

This chapter will cover:

- the obligation on the seller to show good title;
- the root of title;
- chain of ownership;
- the abstract and epitome of title;
- the methodology for investigating title;
- an example of investigating an unregistered title with an epitome;
- an example of investigating and unregistered title with an abstract;
- how to make the application for first registration;
- voluntary and compulsory registration;
- first registration if deeds are lost or destroyed.

4.2 Recap

The process of investigating title consists of the buyer's conveyancer checking the documents and raising requisitions (written queries on the title) about any document, or part of any document, which is either unacceptable or missing.

Modern practice is to deduce and investigate title before exchange of contracts – the Fifth Edition (2018 Revision) of the Standard Conditions assumes this. In practice, this is required in most residential transactions as evidence of title is required before a buyer can safely proceed (see **Chapter 3**). If the Protocol is being used, the seller's conveyancer is required to submit the title at the pre-contract stage in all cases.

If there is a Special Condition in the contract barring requisitions on title, then the buyer must ensure that the seller deduces title and that it is properly investigated and any requisitions are raised before exchange. After that it will be too late.

Obligation on the seller to show good title

In order to show good title, the seller must demonstrate that the legal title is vested in them, or in some person whom they can compel to convey. The seller must also show by the documentation that they can convey the property free from incumbrances, except those disclosed in the contract. If the defect is a "matter of conveyance" (i.e. some defect which the seller can remove without requiring the cooperation of another, for example, the discharge of a mortgage), this is not a defect of title provided that the seller removes the defect on completion.

In practice, with the obligation upon the seller to deduce title, any defects should be apparent before exchange.

Most problems concerning the showing of good title will be quite clear where there is an undisclosed incumbrance or a defect in the seller's documentation. It is therefore essential for conveyancers acting for a seller to check their own client's title carefully. If there is any problem, it is essential for it to be corrected (if possible) or otherwise for the conveyancer to offer the property to the buyer on the basis that, at exchange of contracts, they accept it subject to identified defects or not at all.

4.3 Deducing and investigating title in unregistered land

4.3.1 The root of title

In unregistered land title is proved using title deeds, as there is of course no register of title. A good title must start from a good root of title. A **good root** is usually defined as a document being:

(a) at least 15 years old;

(b) clearly describing the land in question;

(c) dealing with the whole legal and equitable interest in the property; and

(d) containing nothing to cast doubt on the title.

The buyer's conveyancer should always check, before exchange of contracts, that the contract does not provide for the root to be a document which would not satisfy the statutory requirement. If the buyer's conveyancer does accept an inadequate root, there are likely to be problems. For example, by **s44(8) Law of Property Act 1925** (**LPA 1925**), the buyer is deemed not to have notice of any matter of which they might have had notice had they investigated the title before the period of commencement fixed by statute (unless they actually did investigate that earlier title). They are thereby protected against certain matters discoverable in the prior title. If the buyer accepts a short root (less than 15 years old at the date of the contract), they will be bound by any interest which they would have discovered had they investigated title for the full statutory period (***Re Nisbet and Potts' Contract* [1906]**).

Although the requirement, in practice, is for a good root, those documents which actually satisfy the requirement are of differing quality. The best root is a conveyance on sale which satisfies the requirements for a good root. The reason for this is the reasonable assumption that the buyer named in the root would, at the time they bought the property, have investigated the title fully. There is therefore less likelihood of a pre-root problem existing than in the case of a deed of gift where one might reasonably assume that the recipient would not turn down a gift. The equivalent of a conveyance for unregistered leasehold land is called an assignment.

Other documents capable of satisfying the requirement for a good root are:

- a deed of gift;
- a post-1925 assent;
- a legal mortgage.

Each of these must, of course, be checked individually to see whether it does, in fact, satisfy the requirements. It is best practice to choose the latest root document possible, so if there was a choice between using a 1970 conveyance and a 1984 conveyance, best practice would be to choose the 1984 conveyance (provided it met all the requirements of a good root of course).

Once conveyancers have established the root of title (either by applying the statutory provisions or under the contractual provisions), they should note that the buyer is not able to require the production, or any other evidence, of any document dated before the root. They are also precluded from raising any requisition, objection or enquiry with regard to the earlier title (**s45(1) LPA 1925**).

There are certain exceptions to this rule. The buyer can require production of the following pre-root documents:

(1) A power of attorney under which any abstracted document is executed. For example, it does not matter that the root is dated 1972 if there is a conveyance after 1972 which is executed using a power of attorney made before 1972; the buyer can require to see the power even though it pre-dates the root. This is because the buyer will need to check that the power was of the correct type and actually authorised the transaction.

(2) A document creating or disposing of an interest, power or obligation, which is not shown to have ceased or expired and subject to which any part of the property is disposed of by an abstracted document. For example, the root or a post-root document may refer to covenants contained in a pre-root document. The buyer would be entitled to production of that one pre-root document but not any others in between. Another example would be where the property is described by reference to a plan in a pre-root document. The buyer would be entitled to see the plan.

(3) A document creating any limitation or trust by reference to which any part of the property is disposed of by an abstracted document. The buyer is not, of course, affected by any trust the interests in which will be overreached on completion.

4.3.2 Chain of ownership

After fixing the root of title the seller's conveyancer must usually trace all the links in the chain of title from the root document to the document or event by which the ownership became vested in the seller (or in some person whom they can compel to convey). This is illustrated by the diagram below.

Deducing title: unregistered land

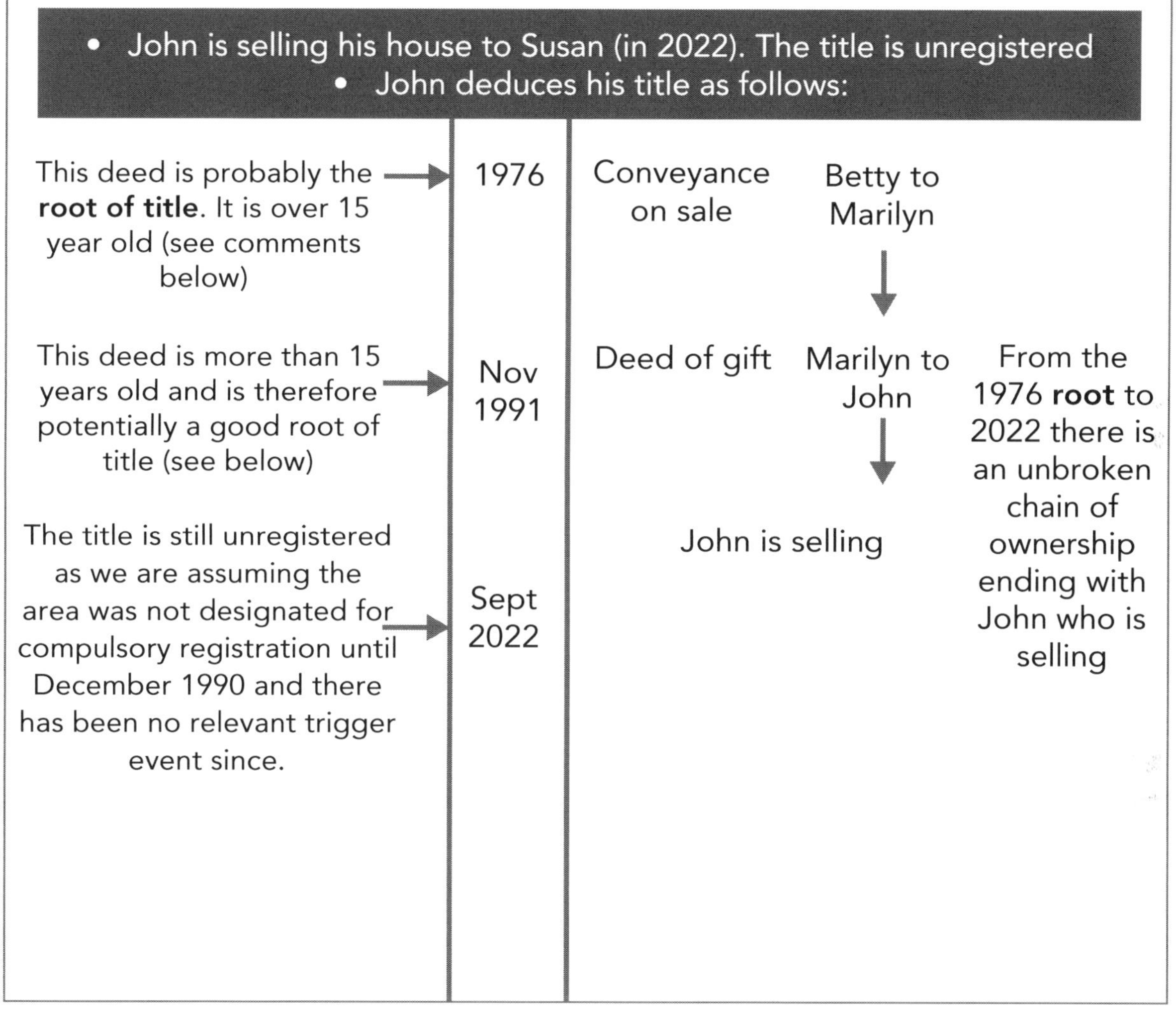

Note that even though the deed of gift here may potentially constitute a good root of title as it is more than 15 years old, a buyer is likely to insist that the 1976 conveyance forms the root as the recipient of the gift is unlikely to have investigated title. In addition, such deeds often do not contain an adequate description of the property and therefore do not satisfy the requirements of a good root, or the requirements of the Lenders' Handbook.

4.3.3 Abstract or epitome of title

It is the seller's conveyancer's duty to deliver to the buyer an abstract or epitome of title. In the past, abstracts followed a stereotyped pattern. The abstract was a typed summary of the main contents of each document or event, written in an abbreviated shorthand. The usual practice now is for the seller's conveyancer to provide the buyer with an epitome of title. This comprises a list of the deeds and documents with photocopies attached. The list will be in the form of a front sheet, listing all the documents in the epitome in chronological order.

It is possible for the unregistered title evidence to consist of part abstract and part epitome. However, it is usual for an epitome only to be used nowadays.

If the title deeds are to be handed over on completion, the buyer's conveyancer simply needs to check that they are happy with the copies, and then, on completion, check the copies against the originals (verification of title). If the title deeds are not to be handed over on completion (e.g. on a sale of part) the buyer's conveyancer must ensure that, at completion, they check the copies against the originals and mark them as having been examined against the originals. Those marked copies, which bear the signature of the conveyancer on behalf of the firm which examined them, are thereafter described as certified or examined copies and are generally accepted by other conveyancer and HMLR as virtually as good as the originals.

The abstract or epitome must contain all the relevant documents and events affecting the ownership of the land from the root to the present. Not only must all conveyances, etc. of the property be included but also both subsisting and discharged mortgages. If the mortgage has been discharged, the buyer will wish, and will be entitled, to see proof that the mortgage has been properly discharged.

There is no obligation to supply search certificates although it is common practice, and courteous, to do so. There is no obligation in the case of matters of public record, such as deaths and marriages, to provide the buyer with anything other than sufficient information to enable them to obtain a copy of the document for themself. Again, if the seller has the document in their possession, it is usual and helpful to provide a copy of it. Matters which do not need to be abstracted include wills (the grant of probate or administration will provide evidence of death and the proof of ownership of the legal estate by the PRs). Interests which will be or have been overreached also do not need to be abstracted.

Note that if the Protocol is being used, the following must also be included if the title is unregistered (section 13):

"(a) a land charges search against the seller and any other appropriate names;

(b) an official search of the index map;

(c) an epitome of title;

(d) those documents on which the buyer can reasonably be expected to rely in order to deduce title (e.g. a certified copy of a grant of probate, a power of attorney, etc.).

Note: check all plans on copied documents are accurately coloured."

Any seller or seller's conveyancer who, with intent to defraud, conceals from the buyer any instrument or incumbrance material to the title is guilty of a criminal offence.

In summary, documents in the title must be abstracted in the abstract or epitome as follows:

(1) **Conveyances** – both on sale and voluntary (by gift).

(2) **Mortgages** – both subsisting and discharged. In the case of the former, they must be included even if they are to be discharged out of the proceeds of sale at completion. In relation to the latter, the buyer is entitled to see the vacating receipt.

(3) **Leases** – subsisting leases and tenancies must be disclosed. Leases which have expired by effluxion of time (i.e. run out) need not be abstracted, but those which have come to an end by surrender should be.

(4) **Grants of representation** – if the grant is relevant in vesting the legal title in the deceased's PRs it must be abstracted – in other words, whenever a **sole** legal owner dies. Remember that, if the deceased is not the sole legal owner, the legal estate will not pass to their PRs but by survivorship to the remaining legal owners.

(5) **Death certificates** – if the grant of representation is being deduced it is not strictly necessary to deal with the death itself. The grant will be sufficient evidence (in the absence of any contrary evidence) of the death itself. If, however, one of the legal owners has died, the death will be an essential event in the title. The death of that owner shows how it is that the surviving legal owners can deal with the property without the deceased's signature. All that is strictly necessary is to provide sufficient evidence for the buyer to obtain their own official copy death certificate; alternatively, the seller's conveyancer can confirm in writing the full name of the deceased, date and place of death, and date of birth or age at death. HMLR will accept this written confirmation from a conveyancer in place of a death certificate – conveyancer s' certified copy death certificates should not be used.

(6) **Assents** – these must be included, as an assent is the means by which the PRs transfer the legal estate to the person entitled to it under a will or intestacy.

(7) **Search certificates** – usual as a matter of courtesy but not essential.

Where the Protocol is being used, the seller must provide:

- land charges searches against the seller and all relevant names;
- an official search of the index map (SIM);
- an epitome or abstract and all other relevant documents (e.g. copies of pre-root deeds containing covenants which affect the property).

4.3.4 Checking each document

In addition to checking that there is a good root and that the links in the title are intact, the form of the documents also needs to be checked. Each document must be checked to ensure that it is in the proper form. For example, if the document is a conveyance on sale, it must be in the form of a deed. It should be checked that the formalities required for a deed have been complied with.

Before 31 July 1990 it was required to be "signed, sealed and delivered". After that date the requirements for a valid deed are contained in **s1 Law of Property (Miscellaneous Provisions) Act 1989** (**LP(MP)A 1989**).

s1 LP(MP)A 1989 provides that a deed must:

- be in writing;
- make it clear on its face that it is intended to be a deed (e.g. by expressing it to be executed as a deed);
- be validly executed by the parties to it; and
- delivered.

Valid execution by an individual requires the deed to be signed by the individual in the presence of a witness who attests (i.e. signs to confirm they have witnessed) the signature. Alternatively, the deed may be signed at the direction of, and in the presence of, the individual if attested by two witnesses who are present.

Other documents may also need to be in the form of a deed – for instance, it is important to remember that a legal mortgage must be created by deed.

4.3.5 Stamp duty and Particulars Delivered

Until 1 December 2003, transactions were subject to stamp duty. Each document before this date must be stamped correctly. The seller cannot prevent the buyer from requisitioning that any stamping defects are corrected, under **s117 Stamp Act 1891**. Furthermore, incorrectly stamped documents cannot be produced in evidence in civil cases, and will not be accepted by HMLR. A financial penalty may have to be paid on late stamping. Where a document in the title has been incorrectly stamped, the seller's conveyancer will therefore have to arrange to correctly stamp the document and bear the cost of late stamping.

Stamps will be seen on the relevant deed, normally at the top of the document. The following provides an example of how a Particulars Delivered Stamp (PD Stamp) and an *ad valorem* stamp (see below for an explanation of these) would be represented when looking at a deed:

INLAND REVENUE PRODUCED

£750

THIS CONVEYANCE is made the 15th day of November 1958 BETWEEN Frank Jennings of 15 The Chase, Harcourt Newton, Cambridgeshire (the Vendor) of the one part and Lillian Stebbings of Little Timbers, Lakeview Road, Harcourt Newton, Cambridgeshire (the Purchaser) of the other part

Particulars Delivered Stamp

The PD Stamp confirms that particulars of the transaction were delivered to the Inland Revenue (now HM Revenue and Customs). A PD Stamp was required for:

- all freehold conveyances and transfers;
- leases for seven or more years;
- assignments of the above leases.

Ad valorem stamp duty

This duty varies according to the amount of the consideration (price). Different rates have applied at different times. To work out the correct stamp duty on old transactions (when investigating title), it is necessary to refer to the rates in force at the relevant time.

When looking at pre-2003 conveyances, you may come across a certificate of value within the deed. This will start with the words "It is hereby certified that" and will state that the transaction does not exceed a certain value. This certificate was required to claim a reduced rate of duty or a nil rate of duty which applied to transactions below specified amounts. It follows from this that a conveyance on sale which does not bear *ad valorem* stamps and which does not contain a certificate of value has not been properly stamped.

Mortgages since 1 August 1971 do not require stamping. Before this date, they are required to be stamped at the rates then in force.

Before 1 August 1971 vacating receipts were stamped if they did not relate to building society mortgages.

Leases, exchanges of property and voluntary conveyances can be subject to quite complex rules, so the correct stamping should be carefully checked. The duty on leases depends, for example, on the premium, the term and the rent applicable.

Deeds of gift and assents executed after 30 April 1987 are exempt from stamp duty as long as they contain a certificate, the form of which is specified in regulations. The certificates are divided into different categories (e.g. A, B and so on) depending on the nature of the transaction.

Here is an example of a certificate to illustrate generally what this would look like in a deed:

> "It is hereby certified that this Deed falls within category . . . in the Schedule to the Stamp Duty (Exempt Instruments) Regulations 1987."

If a document has been stamped incorrectly, similar consequences to those outlined above apply. The presence of an adjudication stamp, however, confirms that a document has been correctly stamped.

Link to practice

Details of historic stamp duty land tax and stamp duty rates are available at:

- https://www.gov.uk/government/publications/rates-and-allowances-stamp-duty-land-tax
- https://www.gov.uk/guidance/stamp-duty-rates-on-land-transfers-before-december-2003

If your firm carries out transactions involving unregistered land, check the stamps on one of the past conveyances to see whether the correct stamp duty was paid.

Fixed rate stamp duty

Assents under seal, appointments of new trustees and powers of attorney, if dated before 25 March 1985, should all bear fixed rate duty.

A blue denoting stamp was placed on certain documents, for example, duplicate conveyances, to indicate that duty had been paid on the original.

Note that documents executed after 1 December 2003 no longer have either PD or *ad valorem* stamps affixed. SDLT is paid on the transaction rather than the document. There are still financial penalties for late payment or non-payment, and HMLR will not register the title without evidence of payment. This is provided by HMRC in the form of a land transaction return certificate (SDLT5).

From 1 April 2018, SDLT has been replaced in relation to properties purchased in Wales by land transaction tax (LTT). This works in a broadly similar way to SDLT. A land transaction tax certificate is issued to evidence payment of LTT and this must be sent to HMLR with the registration application in the same way as SDLT5 must be sent for SDLT purposes.

4.3.6 Particular issues in deducing/investigating title

In unregistered title, conveyancers will need to check all the different transactions in the documents forming the chain of title. They may be buying from a sole owner but there may in the past have been a sale by, say, PRs. Conveyancers need to consider not only whether the conveyance to the current seller was in order but also whether there is anything earlier in the title which might mean that the seller cannot pass a good title to the property.

In registered title, the task is much simpler. Conveyancers do not need to consider earlier transactions. If the title is registered with absolute title, they can presume that the registered proprietor is the owner and that their ownership is not subject to some defect in the earlier documentation. Sometimes, conveyancers will find that the registered proprietor is not the same person as the seller; for example, the registered proprietor might be John Smith, but John Smith has died and the property is now being sold by PRs. In this case, additional documentation would be required to explain how the PRs can sell. If they were executors, for instance, the Grant of Probate would be required.

Strict settlements

Strict settlements exist where land is shared between two or more people in succession (e.g. "to A for life, remainder to B"), and no trust for sale applied. They are regulated by the **Settled Land Act 1925** (**SLA 1925**). Since 1997, no new strict settlements can be created. Any attempt to create one results in a trust of land, where the trustees hold the legal title and have power to sell.

Existing pre-1997 strict settlements, however, continue to be governed by the old law in **SLA 1925**. In summary, the tenant for life will appear as the seller in the conveyance; the trustees must also join in the conveyance to receive the sale money and therefore effect overreaching. Settled land is not routinely encountered in conveyancing practice and transactions involving settled land would usually be dealt with by an experienced practitioner.

Trusts of land

(1) Pre-1997 position

Until January 1997, co-owned land was held under either a strict settlement or a trust for sale.

The latter was by far more common. The legal owners (trustees) held the land with a duty to sell it, but a power to postpone sale. Usually, the trustees were also the beneficiaries of the land (e.g. a husband and wife buying a property jointly) – however, sometimes, a more complex arrangement applied and the beneficiaries and trustees were different people. Although it was important for the seller to know who was beneficially entitled (and therefore entitled to receive the proceeds on sale), the buyer did not normally investigate this because, provided that sale was by the trustees (at least two in number or a trust corporation), the beneficial interests were overreached. After overreaching, the beneficiaries can pursue the trustees only for their share of the sale proceeds – they cannot pursue the buyer.

The old law, with its dual system of strict settlements and trusts for sale became complex and outdated. Therefore, a new regime was introduced in 1997.

(2) Trusts of Land and Appointment of Trustees Act 1996

The **Trusts of Land and Appointment of Trustees Act 1996** (**TLATA 1996**) came into force on 1 January 1997. It introduced a completely new trust called a trust of land, abolished trusts for sale, and prevented the formation of new strict settlements. Existing trusts for sale became trusts of land automatically. All situations of co-ownership of land created after **TLATA 1996** are subject to a trust of land (**s1 TLATA 1996**).

Therefore, with the exception of strict settlements created before 1 January 1997, all trusts relating to land now operate as trusts of land. Trusts of land include many types of trusts including expressly created trusts, implied trusts and trusts imposed by statute as in cases of co-ownership.

The legal estate in property subject to a trust of land is held by the trustees. The overreaching rule still applies, that is, the sale deed must be receipted by all the trustees, who must be two or more in number, or a trust corporation.

Under **s6 TLATA 1996**, the trustees have the same powers as an absolute owner would have. These powers may be restricted by the trust instrument when the trust is created. The trustees have the power to postpone sale of the land (and thus to retain the land) and the power to sell the land. They may exercise either at their discretion if all trustees agree.

As under the old law, buyers are protected on sale so long as they effect overreaching by purchasing from the trustees (at least two in number) or a trust corporation (and inspect two **s10** consents where relevant – see below). There is no provision for the protection of a buyer who does not overreach (In this case, there is a sole legal owner, but also equitable owners who occupy and are protected by **para 2 Sch 3 LRA 2002** in registered land or by the doctrine of notice in unregistered land). Such a buyer needs to take appropriate steps to ensure that there are no other equitable owners and, if in doubt, to insist on the appointment of a second trustee to overreach.

ss19–21 TLATA 1996 relate both to trusts of land and trusts of personalty. These provisions apply only where the beneficiaries are all of full age and fully entitled, and the trust instrument does not provide another procedure for the appointment of new trustees. Under the rule in ***Saunders v Vautier* [1841]**, the beneficiaries are entitled in such situations to bring the trust to an end. **s19 TLATA 1996** allows the beneficiaries (acting together) to direct existing trustees to retire and/or to appoint new trustees. In relation to trusts of land, it is possible that the legal owners (trustees) are different people from the beneficiaries. Applying **TLATA 1996**, the beneficiaries will be able, by simple direction, to insist on their retirement from the trust and replacement.

From this outline of **TLATA 1996** it will be seen that the obligations binding the seller are wider than those affecting the buyer.

4.3.7 The technique in raising requisitions on title

Practice Point

There are various mistakes which are commonly made both by students and by practitioners.

(1) Many offices use a standard form of requisitions (see https://www.lawsociety.org.uk/support-services/advice/articles/transaction-forms/). A common mistake is to think that this is bound to cover any problems in the title. It will not. Not only does this form contain a number of matters which are merely procedural, it is by no means exhaustive as to requisitions. It is really a questionnaire about arrangements for completion. It is best to think of form TA13 as relating to pre-completion procedural requisitions. A failure to consider, and raise if appropriate, all necessary title requisitions could be a source of professional negligence.

(2) There is a tendency, particularly among students, to say things such as "I didn't think you needed to raise requisitions in registered title".

It is true that most registered transactions are a great deal more straightforward than unregistered, but the fact remains that solicitors must consider whether there are any documents which they have not been shown which they think they should have been shown, and whether there is anything which they have been shown with which they are not satisfied. For example, if there was a pre-LRA 2002 caution entry in the register, the buyer's solicitors would want to raise a requisition asking the seller's solicitors to provide further details of what the caution related to, and to confirm that it would be cancelled.

(3) Ineffectual requisitions are often raised. There is no prescribed wording for requisitions but their purpose should be borne in mind. Solicitors use them to require the seller to show good title to the property or to draw the seller's attention to what they require to be remedied. A requisition which says "We note that the copy conveyance dated 1.4.63 and made between R Ross (1) and P Rose (2) has no plan attached to it" may well receive the reply "We note _ that you note it". While impolite, the reply is not incorrect. The requisition has not even asked for a reply. A better requisition would be "The plan annexed to the conveyance dated 1.4.63 and made between R Ross (1) and P Rose (2) appears to have been omitted from the epitome. Please provide a copy."

The following provides an example of how to approach the issue of raising requisitions on title in respect of an epitome of title in unregistered land.

(1) If raising requisitions on the documents supplied in the epitome, these would not be a repetition of all the questions covered in form TA13. Most of the questions in TA13 cover practical completion arrangements and not requisitions on the title.

(2) All documents in the epitome should be carefully examined and a list of requisitions compiled. Here are some examples of requisitions and the reasons for them - the actual requisitions will of course vary from case to case depending on the contents of the documents in the epitome and the issues which they raise:

(a) Please supply details of stamp duty and PD stamp on [specify relevant documents].

The stamp duty should comply with the rates then in force (in practice, conveyancers would be able to check this with tables of historical rates).

(a) Please supply an earlier document to act as the root of title, as [the first document supplied] is not a good root.

To ascertain whether a document is or is not a good root, it is essential to remember the definition: a good root of title is usually defined as a document which is at least 15 years old, clearly describes the land in question, deals with the whole legal and equitable estate and interest in the property and contains nothing to cast doubt on the title.

(b) Please supply land charges searches in respect of [state names and dates].

The seller is not generally obliged to supply these, but may do so if he has copies with the epitome. The correct search dates, search periods and names of the estate owners will be relevant to any specific request for land charges searches

(c) Please note that first registration of title should have been effected following [first appropriate document after introduction of compulsory first registration] and kindly rectify the position.

(1) Starting with the root of title, check each document in turn and check that the progression from each document to the next is in order. For example, the following types of requisitions may be necessary.

(a) [Document] was a sale by a survivor of tenants in common. Please arrange for the position to be rectified, so that a second trustee is appointed to overreach the equitable interests.

(b) Please supply [marriage certificates/death certificates] [specify whose].

As these are matters of public record, the seller is not required to deduce these documents, but must give sufficient information for the buyer to obtain them. In practice, most sellers will provide copy documentation. A good conveyancers will have anticipated the question and have enclosed the additional documents in the contract package. If a woman's name has changed, for instance, an official copy marriage certificate may well be applicable. Where a coowner has died, the official copy death certificate is required to establish that the legal title has passed to the survivors.

If a sole owner has died, a grant of representation is required to establish the identity of the PR. If the grant is missing, this must be requested.

Conveyancers are normally unable to raise requisitions on pre-root documents (**s45 LPA 1925**). There are certain exceptions, however – particularly important are pre-root plans and covenants which are referred to in post-root documents.

Having checked every document supplied, the conveyancer should read through the wording again and make sure that there are no defects there.

4.4 Example of deducing an unregistered title using an epitome of title

You act for Sean and Alice Groves who are buying Drovers Cottage, Dunston Heath from Jayne Birch. You have been sent an epitome of title (below) with photocopies of the documents listed in support. You need to approach this like a jigsaw starting by identifying your Root of Title and then working down to the seller, Jayne Birch, to check that she is entitled to sell Drovers Cottage.

EPITOME OF TITLE Drovers Cottage, Dunston Heath, Stafford, Staffordshire			
Date	**Details**	**Parties**	**Original**
15.2.1978	Conveyance	Julian Nelson (1) Agatha Birch (2)	Yes
15.2.1978	Mortgage (with vacating receipt)	Agatha Birch (1) Midland Bank (2)	Yes
6.12.1980	Deed of Gift	Agatha Birch (1) Jayne Birch (2)	Yes
6.12.1980	Land Charges Search results	Julian Nelson Agatha Birch	Yes

(1) The seller's conveyancer will have prepared the epitome of title from the title deeds in their possession. The epitome will be supplied to the buyers' conveyancers in order to deduce title and the buyers' conveyancers will then investigate the title on behalf of the buyer clients.

(2) The seller's conveyancers will have to check the title to ensure that the client can sell what she purports to sell, and to ensure that there are no other problems which need to be catered for in the contract or otherwise.

(3) The seller's conveyancer will first identify which document should be specified as the root of title in the contract. The root should be at least 15 years old.

This means that the deed of gift in the schedule is potentially a good root of title. However, as the title may not have been fully investigated when the gift was made, it will probably not satisfy the buyers' conveyancer. This means that the document which best satisfies the definition of good root is the 1978 conveyance. The seller's conveyancer would have to check that the conveyance satisfies the other requirements of a good root – for example, the conveyance may not have an adequate description, or its description may refer back to a document which cannot be produced. If the latter, the seller's conveyancer should include a Special Condition in the contract barring out requisitions on this point.

(4) There is a mortgage listed in favour of Midland Bank, granted by Agatha Birch at the time of her purchase. There is also an entry stating that a vacating receipt is included. This is the evidence that the mortgage was repaid. The vacating receipt would usually be endorsed on the original mortgage deed.

(5) The deed of gift was dated 1980, which is before the date when compulsory first registration of title was extended across all of England and Wales. As a deed of gift, it would not have required registration (deeds of gift became compulsorily registrable if made on or after 1 April 1998).

(6) Many areas of the country, however, were subject to compulsory first registration at earlier dates – so, if Stafford was in a compulsory first registration area at the date of the 1978 conveyance, the title should have been registered when the property was sold in 1978.

(7) The buyer cannot require the seller to produce land charges searches, although these should be produced as a matter of courtesy where available. Searches are needed against the correct names of all owners revealed by the title for the period in which they owned the property. This includes the names of estate owners revealed in any pre-root documents supplied. Where it is not clear when a person acquired or disposed of a property, the search must cover all possibilities (e.g. if it was clear that a person sold the property in 1970 but it was not clear when they acquired it, the search should be made from 1926 to 1970 to cover all eventualities). If any problems are revealed by searches supplied (e.g. the transaction took place outside the priority period conferred by the search, the search was for the wrong period or the names were incorrectly stated) then the search must be repeated. Otherwise, where satisfactory searches have been supplied with the epitome, the buyer need not repeat these (except for the seller who must be searched against again). The form of search is a K15 (https://www.gov.uk/government/publications/land-charges-official-search-application-k15). This should include any PRs and attorneys for dates they held the property.

(8) Where the Protocol applies, the seller's conveyancer should carry out all necessary land charges searches at the outset of the transaction, and should obtain an Index Map search. The Protocol provides for a land charges search against the seller, land charges searches against any other appropriate names and an Index Map search to be sent out as part of the contract package.

(9) Agatha Birch's gift of the property to Jayne Birch in 1980 was a transaction at an undervalue. It is therefore possible that, if Agatha became bankrupt within five years of the date of the gift, her trustee in bankruptcy could have applied to court to have the disposition set aside. To ensure that she was not made bankrupt within five years of the gift, a bankruptcy search for the period 1980 to 1985 should therefore be carried out against Agatha Birch.

(10) Correct stamping and PD stamps on all relevant documents should be checked. Also, all documents should be executed as appropriate.

(11) By checking through and preparing the title in this way at an early stage, the seller's conveyancer aims to ensure that all problems are resolved (or barred out by Special Conditions in the contract). Having done so, there is every prospect that any relevant requisitions can be resolved satisfactorily.

(12) Once the epitome has been supplied to the buyers' conveyancer (e.g. as part of the contract package) the buyer's conveyancer will investigate the title and raise any requisitions.

4.5 Example of investigating unregistered title using an abstract of title

When the buyer's conveyancer investigates title, the aim is to identify and resolve any defects in the title. Any problems are raised in the form of requisitions. Nowadays, it is normal practice for title to be deduced before exchange of contracts and so requisitions on title would be raised before the parties commit themselves to the purchase. Although an epitome of title is usually used in unregistered land transactions, it is also possible to deduce unregistered title by providing an abstract of title. This section of the coursebook therefore looks at an abstract of title and investigation of title by the conveyancer.

You are acting for Harry Ash in his purchase of 8 Occidental Road. The abstract of title printed below has been supplied by the seller's solicitor. The title is unregistered. The seller is Sam Oak, who acquired the property in 1989. The description of the property in the contract reads: "All that freehold land dwelling house and outbuildings (if any) known as 8 Occidental Road Weston more particularly described in a conveyance dated 17.6.1980 and made between Richard Box (1) and Sarah Chestnut (2) (hereinafter called 'the Conveyance') and edged in red on the plan attached thereto".

ABSTRACT OF THE TITLE
- of -
SAMUEL WILLIAM OAK
to 8 Occidental Road Weston

17 June 1980

PD Stamp

BY CONVEYANCE of this date between RICHARD BOX of 8 Occidental Road Weston (thereinafter called "the Vendor") of the one part and SARAH CHESTNUT of 7 Newtown Road Weston (thereinafter called "the Purchaser") of the other part

RECITING seisin of the Vendor and agreement for sale

WITNESSED that in pursuance of the said agreement and in consideration of £5,000 paid by the Purchaser to the Vendor (the receipt acknowledged) the Vendor as BENEFICIAL OWNER conveyed unto the Purchaser

ALL THAT freehold land dwelling house and outbuildings (if any) as was more particularly delineated on the plan annexed thereto and edged in red

TO HOLD the same unto the Purchaser in fee simple

EXECUTED by all parties and attested

The plan referred to on the Conveyance of 17.6.1980

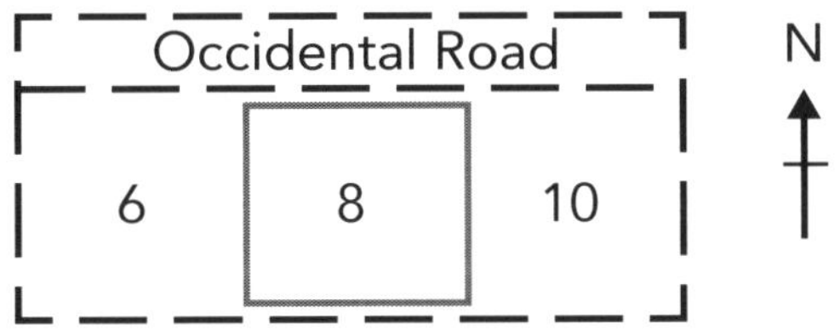

17 June 1980

BY MORTGAGE of this date made between the said SARAH CHESTNUT ("the borrower") of the one part and WESTON BANK PLC whose registered office is situate at Occidental Terrace Weston ("the lender") of the other part being a charge expressed to be by way of legal mortgage of the before abstracted property to secure a loan of £2,000 and interest and any further advances as therein mentioned. Other usual mortgage clauses.

EXECUTED by the borrower and attested

22 July 1989

The said SARAH CHESTNUT died in Weston

20 November 1990

BY ASSENT of this date between HENRY WHITE of 19 Occidental Road Weston (being PR of SARAH CHESTNUT aforesaid) (thereinafter called "the Executor") of the one part and SAMUEL WILLIAM OAK of 18 Chester Road Weston (thereinafter called "the Beneficiary") of the other part

RECITING the Will, Death and Probate of Sarah Chestnut

The Executor assented as personal representative of the said Sarah Chestnut deceased to the vesting in the Beneficiary of ALL THAT freehold land dwellinghouse and outbuildings (if any) as was for the purposes of identification only delineated on the plan annexed thereto and edged in red

TO HOLD the same unto the Beneficiary in fee simple

SIGNED by the Executor

The plan referred to on the Assent of 20.11.1990

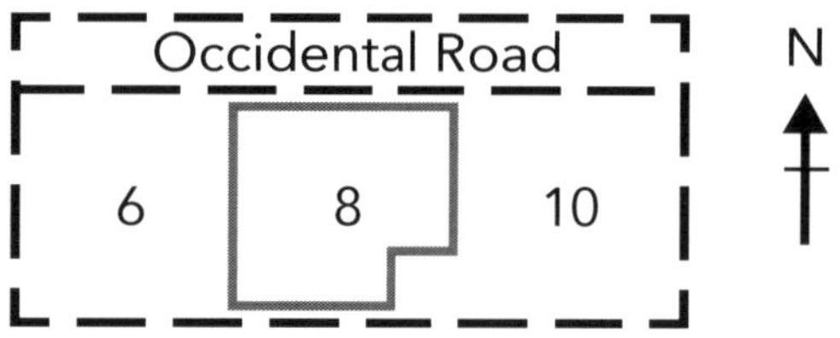

Example of the requisitions raised by the buyer's conveyancer in this case:

(1) The conveyance dated 17.6.1980 appears not to be stamped, but has no certificate of value. Please correct this, and confirm what action is being taken.

Explanation: the buyer's conveyancer needs to check that all documents are correctly stamped.

(2) There is no vacating receipt on the 17.6.1980 mortgage. Please confirm that this mortgage will be discharged on or before completion, or supply a copy of the vacating receipt.

Explanation: presumably, this mortgage was, in fact, discharged before the assent in 1990. If it was not discharged, however, it continues to bind the property. If the discharge is not effected now, then the buyer will be obliged to repay the mortgage after completion, which is clearly unsatisfactory. It will also be necessary to check in this case that the vacating receipt names the owner as the person paying off the mortgage, assuming the seller is able to produce the receipted mortgage.

(3) Please supply a certified copy of grant of probate of Sarah Chestnut, together with certified copies of any endorsements thereon.

Explanation: the grant evidences the PR's title to the property. There should be an endorsement relating to the assent of this property, and one would expect no other endorsements relating to this property. The grant should be in favour of Henry White.

(4) There appears to be a discrepancy in the plans in the conveyance of 17.6.1980 and the assent of 20.11.1990. The contract obliges the seller to convey all the land described in the 1980 conveyance. Please supply title to the missing area in the south-east corner of the rear of the property.

Explanation: the buyer is entitled to all the land in the 1980 conveyance, because the contract states this. Clearly, the 1990 assent does not include an area of land which was included in the 1980 conveyance. If this area has been sold, or claimed by a neighbour through adverse possession, there may be no way in which the extra area of land can be sold by the seller.

The buyer's surveyor should check the plans against the site. It is possible that the 1990 assent shows a simplified plan – the plan is referred to "for identification"; unlike the 1980 conveyance where the property is "more particularly delineated" on the plan.

(5) The 1990 assent should include an acknowledgment for the production of the original grant. Please rectify this and supply evidence of rectification.

Explanation: these seem to have been omitted from the assent (or perhaps from the abstract) in error. A document correcting these matters could be executed at this stage if the PR can be traced.

There is also a problem with the assent in that it has not been dealt with correctly for stamp duty purposes – there should be a certificate within the assent that this is an "exempt instrument". This then means that no stamp duty was payable. After 30 April 1987 (this assent is dated 1990) a conveyance by way of gift is exempt from stamp duty, provided that the instrument (assent here) is correctly certified. This assent does not have the correct certificate and is therefore lacking evidential value.

(6) Please supply land charges searches against all known estate owners since 1925.

Explanation: it is customary for the seller's conveyancer to provide these but, if not available, the buyer's conveyancer will carry out these searches. You need to check that there are not any adverse entries which affect the property.

It would be necessary to check when the area became a compulsory first registration area and, if before 17 June 1980, you would require the seller to effect registration (note that the assent would not have given rise to an obligation to register as the law stood in 1990). Failure to register would have caused the legal title to revert to the seller after two months, and this should be corrected by late registration of title.

Key principles – recap

(1) In unregistered land, the seller must show:

- a good root of title, which is usually a conveyance on sale of the property which is not less than 15 years' old;
- all links in the chain of title to the current seller from that root;
- other documents such as mortgages (whether or not discharged), death certificates, grants of probate and current leases.

It is also good practice for the seller's conveyancer to include land charges certificates previously obtained.

(2) The following title issues may need to be considered by the buyer's conveyancer:

- stamping and execution of documents;
- strict settlements;
- trusts of land, co-ownership and sales by sole surviving trustees;
- sales by PRs;
- sales by mortgagees;
- discharge of existing mortgages;
- voluntary dispositions;
- dispositions by attorneys or deputies;
- dispositions by bankrupt owners;
- dispositions by companies in liquidation or administration;
- dispositions by charities.

A check should also be made as to when the land became compulsorily registrable. All of England and Wales became subject to a requirement to register on a conveyance on sale on 1 December 1990. Almost all dispositions of freehold land are now registrable under **LRA 2002**.

(3) Unregistered title can be deduced by epitome or abstract. An epitome is usually used as it is easier to draft.

4.6 Application for first registration of unregistered land

On completing the conveyance of unregistered property, the legal estate will immediately pass to the buyer. Where first registration is required, an application for first registration must be made within two months of completion, otherwise, the legal estate will automatically revert to the seller (**s7 LRA 2002**).

The whole of England and Wales is now a compulsory first registration area so that a conveyance on sale of freehold property will always give rise to the requirement for first registration.

Activity

Follow the link below to HMLR Practice Guide 1: First registrations:

https://www.gov.uk/government/publications/first-registrations/practice-guide-1-first-registrations

Read all of it but focus on section 4.4 – "Documents that must accompany form FR1" to ensure that you are clear as to what you must submit to HMLR on an application for first registration.

The application for first registration must be made on form FR1 https://www.gov.uk/government/publications/first-application-registration-fr1 and accompanied by all the documents relating to the property listed in form DL https://www.gov.uk/government/publications/documents-list-dl .

The buyer is obliged to disclose interests which override first registration (**Sch 1** and **s71 LRA 2002** using form DI). It is necessary for HMLR to see all documents relating to the property so that it can investigate the title for itself (e.g. this includes documents such as the contract, pre-contract searches, all relevant title documentation and pre-completion searches). Remember that, once it has investigated the title, the former deeds will usually become irrelevant and the strength of the title will be the class of title awarded by HMLR.

Note particularly the following clauses in form FR1.

Clause 3 relates to the extent of the property. Usually, a plan, which should be signed by the parties, will need to be referred to (e.g. in the transfer inducing registration), unless an earlier plan from, for example, the root of title is used.

Clause 4 states the class of title sought, for example, absolute freehold. The clause lists absolute and possessory freeholds and leaseholds, and good leaseholds.

In **Clause 5** the applications must be set out in order.

In **Clause 11** the conveyancer must either confirm that there are no disclosable overriding interests or submit form DI detailing such interests. **s71 LRA 2002** and the **Land Registration Rules 2003** oblige the buyer to disclose to the Registrar any interests that override first registration within the actual knowledge of the buyer. This is to enable HMLR to enter the interests on the charges register of the title, which then cease to be overriding.

Clause 12 confirms to HMLR that all matters affecting the property are disclosed in the documents supplied, or, alternatively, gives the conveyancer the opportunity to list known matters that are not actually set out in the supplied documents. This clause and **Clause 13** (confirmation of examination of title) need to be treated with caution because HMLR's guarantee of title is given in reliance on the conveyancer's confirmation and could be the subject of legal liability, for example, in negligence. The logical conclusion of this is that, even for transactions where in the past (i.e. before the **Land Registration Act 1997** extended the compulsory first registration requirement), a conveyancer would not have needed to make a full title investigation and searches (e.g. in the case of many assents or deeds of gift), this may now have to be done in order to satisfy HMLR on the application for first registration.

Clauses 14, **15** and **16** relate to HMLR's identity requirements. To protect HMLR and its customers from identity fraud, HMLR requires completion of these panels when registering a transfer, lease or charge. If these are not completed, then HMLR may reject the application.

In panel 14 the applicant should put a cross in the appropriate box depending on whether they are a conveyancer or not. Depending on the answer, complete panel 15 or 16 by listing the parties to the deeds and who acted for them. Evidence of identity for an unrepresented party must be supplied.

Activity

Follow the link below to HMLR Practice Guide 67: Evidence of identity:

https://www.gov.uk/government/publications/evidence-of-identity-conveyancers/practice-guide-67-evidence-of-identity-conveyancers

Read it all but in particular focus on what **'Rule 17' evidence** means. You will see that it gives HMLR wide scope to request further evidence of identity for parties referred to in a registration application.

r17 Land Registration Rules 2003 allows HMLR to ask for more documents or evidence to help it complete an application. HMLR may cancel an application if a firm does not provide what they need.

The application must be accompanied by the correct fee.

Once HMLR has examined the title documentation, a new register and title plan will be generated for the title and this register will reflect the matters carried on to the title from the examination of the documents lodged (e.g. restrictive covenant entries will be made where applicable).

From November 2016 to September 2024, HMLR allowed practitioners to submit applications for first registration using certified copies of the unregistered title deeds. However, this facility was withdrawn from 1 October 2024. After this date, it is necessary to submit original title deeds for first registration.

4.6.1 Discharge of a charge in unregistered land

r114(4) Land Registration Rules 2003 allows the registrar discretion to accept any other proof of satisfaction of a charge that the registrar may regard as sufficient. For charges secured against unregistered land, HMLR will accept a receipt endorsed on the charge itself as proof of discharge.

4.7 Compulsory vs voluntary registration

4.7.1 Compulsory registration

The registered system has been phased in over a number of years. Over more than 50 years, various areas of England and Wales have gradually been designated as areas of compulsory registration, meaning that unregistered land has had to be registered when a designated trigger event, such as a sale, has taken place. It was not until December 1990 that the last area of the country was designated as one of compulsory registration, making the whole of England and Wales a compulsory registration area. Since that date, it has been compulsory to register all previously unregistered land on sale, and upon other specified trigger events, such as the grant of certain leases. It has only been compulsory to register changes of ownership following death or gifts of land since April 1998.

Compulsory first registration only had to be carried out following one of the trigger events where the land was situated in an area of compulsory registration. The areas were phased in over a number of years, with some areas of the country being designated as compulsory registration areas much earlier than others. For instance, parts of Surrey were designated as far back as 1937, Derby was designated in 1968, Exeter in 1974 and parts of Suffolk not until 1990. The whole of England and Wales became an area of compulsory registration in December 1990, meaning that those areas not previously so designated came within the compulsory registration scheme from that date. First registration would then have to be applied for upon the happening of a trigger event.

Example

A simple example will illustrate the effect of this. Imagine that John bought a house with unregistered title in Exeter in 1977. Upon the sale to John (a trigger event) the house would have been registered for the first time (first registration) as Exeter was an area of compulsory registration at the time.

If John bought a house with unregistered title in 1991, it would have triggered first registration irrespective of where it was located in England and Wales, as the whole country was an area of compulsory registration from December 1990 onwards.

As first registration depended (and still depends) on there being a trigger event, we must now look at what events triggered first registration before **LRA 2002**.

Under **LRAs 1925–1997** the following events triggered first registration:

- a conveyance on sale of freehold land;
- a grant of a new lease for more than 21 years;
- the assignment of a lease (i.e. sale of an existing lease) having more than 21 years left to run at the date of assignment;
- as from 1 April 1998, all gifts, assents, conveyances arising from court orders and first legal mortgages.

LRA 2002 extended the requirement for compulsory registration and this was, from 6 April 2009, extended further in respect of land held in trust.

s4 LRA 2002 stipulates that in unregistered land, compulsory registration is required for:

- a transfer of the freehold, whether for valuable consideration (e.g. a conveyance on sale), or by way of gift (e.g. an assent on death or a gift of land during lifetime) or in pursuance of a court order;
- the grant of a lease for more than seven years;
- the assignment of a lease which at the time of assignment has more than seven years unexpired;
- the grant of a lease where the right to possession is discontinuous provided that the periods of possession when added together total more than seven years;

- the grant of a lease (for any term) to take effect in possession after the end of the period of three months beginning with the date of the grant (e.g. a student signs a lease in June but the lease starts in October);
- the creation of a first legal mortgage;
- the partitioning of unregistered land amongst the beneficiaries of the trust;
- the appointment of new trustees of unregistered land if the land vests in the new trustee by deed or by vesting order of the court.

Example

Although most applications for first registration are made following a sale of unregistered land, it is important to appreciate that other trigger events will also require the conveyancer to apply for first registration.

For instance, imagine that Petra owns Church Farm, a freehold property comprising 100 acres, which is still unregistered. Petra does not want to sell her farm but she wants to raise some capital to improve her farm buildings and convert her stables into holiday cottages. She therefore borrows £100,000 from Lloyds Bank plc which is secured by way of a first legal mortgage against the 100 acres comprising Church Farm. The grant of this first legal mortgage will trigger first registration of the entire 100 acres of Church Farm.

Petra's conveyancer will have to make the first registration application to HMLR within two months of completion of the new mortgage.

Link to practice

If in the example above, Petra decided to create a first legal charge over only 40 of the 100 acres that she owns, then she would be obliged to register the 40 acres subject to the charge and could choose to leave the remaining 60 acres unregistered.

In some cases, the grant of a discontinuous lease will trigger compulsory registration. A discontinuous lease is a lease whereby the tenant has the right to occupy a property for a set period each year (e.g. a timeshare lease). The grant of a discontinuous lease with a term of more than seven years triggers first registration. To calculate the length of the term to see whether it exceeds seven years, you have to multiply the number of complete weeks each year by the number of years granted. If the total is more than seven years (i.e. more than 364 complete weeks) the lease will trigger compulsory first registration.

Example

If, for instance, Suki had a timeshare lease allowing her to occupy a flat for two weeks per year for 10 years, the total would be 20 weeks, which would not exceed seven years. Therefore, although these types of lease may last for many years, they are unlikely to trigger compulsory first registration, though they can be voluntarily registered.

4.7.2 Voluntary registration

Voluntary registration is encouraged by HMLR to accelerate the process of registration of title. HMLR offers reduced fees for voluntary registration applications.

The most likely circumstance where a voluntary first registration is likely to happen is if the unregistered title documents are in some way incomplete or, as is often the case, the plan of the land falling within the title is very poor. The conveyancer acting for the seller might advise the seller to apply for a voluntary first registration to make the eventual sale of the property run more smoothly. A buyer's conveyancer might be disinclined to accept an unregistered title if it appears defective or the plans are of poor quality. A typical circumstance where this might happen is in the event of a probate sale where the legal owner has died and the personal representatives want to sell the property.

HMLR PG1 states:

"3.1 Registration in advance of a dealing

Voluntary application for first registration may be particularly useful where a prospective purchaser or mortgagee may have doubts about accepting the title. This may happen where, for example, the title deeds have been lost or destroyed, or are for some reason unavailable to the estate owner. Although we may not grant an absolute title, the title may still be acceptable to purchasers and mortgagees, particularly if supported by a title indemnity insurance policy.

You must apply in form FR1 in the usual way"

Activity

Read the following Land Registry blogpost about comprehensive registration:

https://hmlandregistry.blog.gov.uk/2018/04/27/why-hm-land-registry-wants-to-achieve-comprehensive-registration/ .

Why does the Land Registry believe it is important to achieve comprehensive registration throughout England and Wales?

Link to practice

A common misconception is that an unregistered title is unacceptable per se. This is not the case. Conveyancers tend to dislike dealing with an unregistered title because it is uncommon but an unregistered title with all of the relevant title documents and decent plans should be perfectly acceptable to any conveyancer acting for a buyer.

4.7.3 First registration if deeds are lost or destroyed

A voluntary registration referred to above describes the situation where the party entitled to sell the property holds the unregistered title deeds but due to a possible defect in title, decides to voluntarily submit the title deeds to HMLR for registration even though there is no triggering event.

Contrast this with the situation where the unregistered title deeds have been lost. This is one of the key drawbacks of the system of unregistered conveyancing. If the unregistered title deeds are lost, the holder of the legal estate has no evidence of their title.

The seller's conveyancer will have to address the situation if the holder of the legal estate or party entitled to sell the property wants to sell but it transpires that the unregistered title deeds have been lost. Typically, this arises on a probate sale where the last legal owner has died. An elderly person may have lived in the property for many years and, after their death, their personal representatives cannot locate the deeds.

HMLR has special requirements in relation to first registration of land if the title deeds have been lost or destroyed.

Activity

Follow the link below to HML "Practice guide 2: First registration of title where deeds have been lost or destroyed":

https://www.gov.uk/government/publications/first-registration-of-title-where-deeds-have-been-lost-or-destroyed/practice-guide-2-first-registration-of-title-if-deeds-are-lost-or-destroyed

Read the practice guide and note what information HMLR will require to explain the events leading to the loss or destruction of the title deeds.

The conveyancer acting for the applicant must advise their client to make an extensive search for the lost title deeds including contacting former solicitors of the landowner, banks or building societies that may have held the title deeds and any other organisation or party which may have held the deeds. Any evidence of these enquiries, such as correspondence and emails, should be included with the application for first registration – the applicant is effectively telling the story regarding the loss of the title deeds and the attempt to find them in their own words. This is significant from a drafting point of view. It is not necessary to use complex or overly legalistic language. The conveyancer must simply take instructions from the applicant as to the circumstances of the loss of the title deeds and describe that loss and the attempts to locate the deeds in plain English. The applicant should always be required to read the document prepared by the conveyancer because it is necessary that all information contained within the document is from the applicant's own knowledge.

Traditionally, the conveyancer would have prepared a statutory declaration on behalf of their client. This is a formal document which would be sworn in front of a solicitor or Notary Public. However, HMLR has now produced a statement of truth to be used for an application for first registration based on loss of title deeds. The significance of a statement of truth is that all of the information required by HMLR is already set out in the framework of the document and it does not need to be sworn in front of a solicitor. The signature of the applicant will suffice. Accordingly, in most cases, the statement of truth will be used these days although it is still possible to use a statutory declaration if the particular conveyancer prefers.

Activity

Follow the link below to HMLR "Practice guide 73: Statements of truth":

https://www.gov.uk/government/publications/statements-of-truth/practice-guide-73-statements-of-truth

> Read the Practice Guide as this will give helpful information about the different types of statement of truth, their purpose and how they must be completed.

The appropriate statement of truth is ST3: Statement of truth in support of an application for registration of land based upon lost or destroyed title deeds – https://www.gov.uk/government/publications/lost-or-destroyed-deeds-statement-of-truth-st3 .

You will see from the form that the ST3 is straightforward to complete. However, the more detailed the information provided, the more likely that HMLR is to register the title based upon the information provided.

Let's look at the boxes required to complete the ST3:

Box 1 – this is the name and address of the applicant.

Box 2 – this is the status of the person making the statement. A personal representative might make the statement on behalf of somebody who has died.

Box 3 – the description of the land should include the address and it should be clearly identified on a plan. It will be necessary to carry out a Search of the Index Map to verify that the title is currently unregistered and this should accompany the application.

Box 4 – indicate whether this is a first registration of freehold land, leasehold land or some other application.

Box 5 – the period of ownership of the estate is inserted in this box. This is likely to be the period from the date of purchase of the property to the date of the application.

Box 6 – insert details of the person or body who had possession of the title deeds and where they were held when lost or destroyed. This section could include details of a bank or solicitor's firm which had custody of the deeds. Any correspondence with the organisation should be appended to the application.

Box 7 – insert details of why the party mentioned in box 6 had custody of the deeds. This might be, for example, that a firm of solicitors were holding the deeds for safekeeping or that a lender was holding them as security for a loan.

Box 8 – insert details of where, when and how the loss or destruction occurred. In this section the "story" of the loss of the title deeds can be told. For example, the facts surrounding the attempt to find the deeds, together with any relevant correspondence or communications (note the public domain/confidentiality point mentioned below).

Box 9 – insert details of what steps have been taken to recover the deeds. As much detail as possible should be inserted including details of organisations contacted (for example, solicitors and banks and building societies), regulators if a firm of solicitors known to be holding the deeds has closed or been taken over, extensive searches of the office or home of the estate holder.

Box 10 – insert details of any mortgages or charges over the property if known.

Box 11(a) – insert details of the evidence of possession of the applicant. For example, if the property has been owned for many years by someone who has recently died, any correspondence with their papers evidencing their ownership and occupation of the property could be included, for example, letters from their solicitors confirming that the solicitor holds the title deeds, utility bills, council tax bills, details of repairs carried out – anything to "paint the picture" of ownership and occupation of the property.

Box 11(b) – insert details of any rights exercised by the legal owner. For example, any right of way accessed over neighbouring property.

Box 12 – if photocopies of any of the title deeds are available this section should be completed.

Box 13 – this is confirmation from the applicant that they are entitled to apply for registration.

Box 14 – this is the evidence of identity section.

Box 15 – if the applicant or their conveyancer holds any other information which might be relevant, it can be referred to here If the applicant is a personal representative applying on behalf of an estate, a certified copy of the grant of representation should be included.

Box 16 – this is the statement of truth by the applicant who must sign and print their full name and date that the ST3 was signed.

Note in particular from HMLR Practice guide 2: first registration of title if deeds are lost or destroyed (www.gov.uk/government/publications/first-registration-of-title-where-deeds-have-been-lost-or-destroyed/practice-guide-2-first-registration-of-title-if-deeds-are-lost-or-destroyed) the documents which must be sent to HMLR, including land charges searches. It is also necessary to declare any overriding interests if known (section 2).

The following is a helpful checklist produced by HMLR for first registration of title if deeds are lost or destroyed:

"Before submitting your application, make sure:

- we can identify the land on the Ordnance Survey map
- the account of events in the statutory declarations, form ST3 or certificates adequately accounts for the loss or destruction of the deeds
- the applicant's title to the land has been established
- you have included evidence of possession
- the title has been reconstructed as far as possible
- any disclosable overriding interests that you or your client are aware of and that are not apparent from the reconstructed title have been disclosed using form DI
- you have enclosed an undertaking to send to HM Land Registry any lost deeds that are subsequently found
- to properly complete form ID1 (or form ID2) and enclose for each applicant
- you have enclosed the correct fee
- you have signed form FR1
- you have checked clerical details in all forms and deeds (especially charges and mortgages) and have paid particular attention to all dates, property descriptions and full names of parties, especially where they appear in more than one deed"

What class of title is HMLR likely to grant?

HMLR is likely to grant a possessory title. HMLR is also likely to make a protective entry in the charges register of the newly created title because missing deeds may contain or refer to restrictive covenants which, of course, will not be apparent from the application. The entry will state that the land is "subject to such restrictive covenants as may have been imposed thereon before the date of first registration, so far as such covenants are subsisting and capable of being enforced".

As the class of title is likely to be possessory and there may be a protective entry on the charges register, the registered proprietor is likely to be asked to supply defective title indemnity insurance upon a sale of the property.

Link to practice

If you have to make an application for a client using form ST3, you should point out that there is no guarantee that HMLR will grant any form of title at all. If the information provided regarding the holding of the title deeds and the circumstances of the loss is scant and vague, HMLR might not feel able to grant even a possessory title. Accordingly, the more information that can be provided in the application the better.

However, a word of warning – remember that any application to HMLR puts all of the documents accompanying the application into the public domain. This means that anyone can apply for copies of the documents submitted. Accordingly, always carefully check the content of the documents accompanying your application. For example, you might not want to include bank statements or bank account details or anything which might make it easy for a fraudster to steal the identity of the applicant.

Do not confuse an application for first registration based upon lost or destroyed title deeds with an application for adverse possession. The latter is based on the situation where the applicant has only ever possessed the land and has done so for a period of time such that they may have dispossessed the holder of the paper title. The present application is on the basis that it is known that the applicant has held the title deeds at some point, but they have been lost.

4.8 Chapter summary

(1) It is essential to differentiate registered and unregistered title.

(2) Title is usually deduced by the seller's conveyancer supplying official copies (registered land) or an epitome of title (unregistered land) with the contract package. It is necessary to deduce title to show that the seller is capable of selling the property and it is not subject to onerous or inappropriate incumbrances.

(3) For a complete investigation of the title the buyer's conveyancer in **unregistered title** must peruse the epitome or abstract of title and raise requisitions. This will ensure that:

- there is a good root under the contract;
- there are no breaks from the root through the chain to the seller as shown in the contract;

- if the person selling the property is not, or was not at any stage in the chain of title, the person to whom it was previously conveyed, there is sufficient evidence in the form of other documentation (e.g. powers of attorney, grants of probate/letters of administration or, possibly, a mortgage) that gives that person the power to sell;
- there is no defect in the title which might result in the buyer failing to acquire or losing the legal estate (e.g. a sale by trustees to one of their own number without the necessary authority);
- there are no outstanding incumbrances save those which have been disclosed in the contract;
- the documents are properly stamped;
- each document is properly executed – including the proper receipting of any mortgages;
- no abstracted disposition has given rise to the requirement for compulsory first registration.

(4) The buyer's conveyancer in unregistered title must also verify the abstract. If the originals are being handed over, the copies simply need to be checked against them. If the originals are being retained (e.g. on a sale of part), examined copies should be made of any document the original of which is not to be handed over.

(5) The buyer's conveyancer must check the land for evidence of third-party rights – in particular the rights of occupiers.

(6) The buyer's conveyancer must make final pre-completion searches, in particular those at the Land Charges Department against the seller (and all previous estate owners save in so far as the satisfactory searches have been provided).

(7) First registration applications can now be made using certified copies of the title documents.

(8) It is compulsory to make an application for first registration of unregistered land in the occurrence of a triggering event; but it is possible to make a voluntary application for first registration.

(9) Form ST3 can be used to make an application for first registration if deeds are lost or destroyed.

CHAPTER 5

Deducing and investigating title – registered land

5.1 Introduction

Now we have started the process of contract drafting by the seller's conveyancer, the seller will deduce title to the buyer which the buyer's conveyancer has to investigate. The terminology is important:

Seller's conveyancer	**Deduces** title
Buyer's conveyancer	**Investigates** title

As we have seen, the process of deducing title is where the seller, having shown in the contract what they are proposing to sell, actually proves that they can do it. They do this by providing the buyer with documentary proof that the situation is as they have said it is in the contract. There are two systems by which the seller can prove that they have good title to land: the unregistered and registered systems. This chapter will consider the registered system which is the modern method, based on producing a register of title, created and maintained by the government agency, HM Land Registry (HMLR).

This chapter will cover:

- registration and overriding interests;
- classes of registered title;
- upgrading of titles under the **Land Registration Act 2002** (**LRA 2002**);
- form of the register;
- interests which must be protected by an entry on the register;
- electronic conveyancing and the move to digitisation;
- deducing and investigating title in registered land;
- dispositions of registered land and registration;
- rectification and indemnity under the **LRA 2002**;
- **s77 LRA 2002.**

5.2 Recap

We have seen that in order to convert unregistered land to registered land an application has to be made to HMLR providing the title with documents in support. HMLR staff will examine the unregistered title and create a new register to reflect the registered ownership. A new title plan will also be prepared.

The registered system is now governed by **LRA 2002**, which came into force in October 2003. **LRA 2002** is supplemented by the procedures contained in the **Land Registration Rules 2003** (**LRR 2003**). These replaced the former law and procedures found in the **Land Registration Acts 1925–1997** and the **Land Registration Rules 1925**.

The Public Register under the Land Registration Act 2002

One key feature of the register is that it is open to public inspection (**s66 LRA 2002**). To find out whether land is registered, you can carry out an Index Map search, which discloses any relevant freehold or leasehold title numbers. If the title is registered, then anyone can apply for an official copy of the register and a title plan using form OC1 – see https://www.gov.uk/government/publications/official-copies-of-register-or-plan-registration-oc1) or through HMLR's Portal if they are a business user.

From April 2000, the price paid for a property has been entered on the register, allowing anyone who obtains an official copy to find out the price paid for the property at the last transaction. As members of the public may access HMLR website, you can therefore find out how much your neighbours paid for their house.

LRA 2002 also allows inspection of any document kept by the Registrar, which means that leases and mortgages, as well as registered titles, are open to public inspection. Under **LRR 2003** a person may apply to exempt a document if the document contains prejudicial information (e.g. information that is commercially sensitive). An application must be made on forms EX1 and EX1A and include a copy of the relevant document excluding the prejudicial information.

5.3 Registration and overriding interests

The system of land registration was introduced in the 1920s with the aim of eventually replacing the older, unregistered system of conveyancing, which requires the title deeds to be produced and checked on the occasion of each successive dealing with the land. Under the system of land registration, the register is proof of the seller's title and records a description of the property, the nature of the estate held by the seller and many third parties' rights over the land.

Under the registered system, the register itself is proof of ownership and so it becomes an owner's proof of the title to a property. Once a title is registered, there is no longer a need for title deeds as evidence of ownership. The names of any buyer must be entered on the register. Upon a sale of registered land, the legal estate does not pass upon completion of the transaction (as it does in unregistered conveyancing) but upon registration – that is, when the seller's name has been deleted from the register and the buyer's name is inserted as the registered proprietor (registered owner).

The register is a register of titles, not of land: each estate is registered with a separate title, which is given a unique title number, so that there may be several registers relating to one piece of land – for example, one for the freehold estate and one for each registrable leasehold estate.

The system was intended to provide a complete and up-to-date record of the estate owner's title so that, when they sold, any buyer would be able to rely upon the register as conclusive evidence of all matters affecting the seller's title. This aim has not been fully achieved, as certain third-party rights are binding upon the estate owner and buyer even if they do not appear on the register. These are known as interests which are overriding (more commonly referred to in practice as **overriding interests**).

Details of beneficial interests arising under trusts of land are kept off the register as private arrangements. Those interests were (and still are) protected by an entry on the register notifying any buyer that the property is trust property and that to buy the property free from those interests they must comply with the required formalities.

Link to practice

We have made this point before – but it is important. Due to the fact that the register is public and beneficial interests are kept off the register, you should not send documents dealing with the beneficial interest to HMLR, for example, a declaration of trust. This is because someone else could request a copy of it.

If HMLR asks for a copy of a declaration of trust in a requisition on a registration, revert to them and ask for written confirmation as to the exact reason that they want it. If sending it to HMLR to complete your registration is unavoidable, seek the authority of all parties to the document to send it to HMLR.

You might even need to consider the exempt information procedures – but this would be rare in residential conveyancing.

Activity

Follow the link below to HMLR "Practice guide 57: Exempting documents from the general right to inspect and copy":

https://www.gov.uk/government/publications/exempting-documents-from-the-general-right-to-inspect-and-copy/practice-guide-57-exempting-documents-from-the-general-right-to-inspect-and-copy

Look at section 2.3 "Which provisions may justify exemption".

What does section 2.3.2 say? Do you think that an application to exclude some of the information in a declaration of trust would be successful?

The registered system was set up with District Land Registries, which dealt with the registration of titles to land within their allocated districts. Land registration means that the state guarantees title to land and, subject to specific rules, compensates those who suffered loss through error or fraud.

5.3.1 Interests which are overriding ("overriding interests")

Overriding interests are a "gap" in the registered system as they do not appear on the register of title but they are still binding on a buyer of the land. They can be dangerous in that there is no entry on the register to warn a buyer of their existence but, if the buyer goes ahead and purchases the land, they will be bound by the overriding interest. Conveyancers therefore make extensive enquiries during the pre-contract stage of the conveyancing process, to find out whether there are any overriding interests affecting the land. If there are any, the conveyancer would have to warn the buyer of their existence and the buyer could then assess whether they had any impact on their decision to purchase the property. In some cases it is possible for the conveyancer to take steps, during the conveyancing process, so that the buyer does not buy the land subject to the overriding interest. This is not possible in all cases however.

LRA 1925 listed 12 types of **overriding interest** in **s70(1) LRA 1925**. This Act was repealed by **LRA 2002**, but some categories of overriding interest were retained.

LRA 2002 lists:

- types of unregistered interests which override first registration (**Sch 1**);
- types of unregistered interests which override registered dispositions (**Sch 3**).

The types of rights that are the most important are:

- legal easements and profits *à prendre*;
- rights of those in actual occupation of the land;
- leases.

The pre-**LRA 2002** law is still of some limited relevance in relation to rights created before 2003, in relation to understanding the current law and in relation to some of the pre-**LRA 2002** case law.

We will therefore consider:

- overriding interests under **LRAs 1925–1997** (but only briefly as this would only really be significant in practical terms where rights were created before 2003);
- overriding interests under **LRA 2002.** We will be looking at overriding interests in relation to registered dispositions (**Sch 3**) and in relation to land when it is first registered (**Sch 1**).

5.3.2 Easements and profits

Easements are property rights which one person has over another person's land. Examples of common easements are rights of way, rights of drainage and rights to run cables or pipes under another person's land. Profits are rights to enter on to the land of another person and take something from the land. Examples are fishing rights or grazing rights for animals.

Link to practice

When a client buys a property, he will want to know whether he is bound by any easements. If, for instance, the property was subject to the right for a neighbour to use a driveway on the property the client was proposing to buy, this would be highly relevant to the client. The conveyancer must check the register to see whether there are any easements affecting the property, but he must also check whether there are any easements which would be overriding interests, since these would be binding even though there was no register entry. Conveyancers will make various enquiries to try to find out whether any overriding easements exist.

For instance, Question 9 of the Property Information Form (See **Document 8** of the **Appendix**) contains queries about rights such as shared accessways, rights for other people to take things from the land, and services such as pipes, drains or wires which may cross the property.

(1) **Easements as overriding interests pre-LRA 2002**

Under **LRA 1925**, all legal easements and profits, and some equitable easements, were capable of being overriding interests. Any rights which satisfied these provisions before **LRA 2002** came into force and which were created before 13 October 2003 **continue** to affect the land they burden, and retain their overriding status, under transitional provisions in **LRA 2002**.

(2) **Easements as overriding interests under LRA 2002 – para 3 Sch 3 LRA 2002**

para 3 Sch 3 specifies the easements and profits which, under **LRA 2002**, will override a registered disposition. **LRA 2002** attempts to reduce the easements which are capable of being overriding and therefore not obvious from inspection of the register of title.

The provisions under **LRA 2002** apply only to legal easements and profits, and therefore exclude equitable easements created after 13 October 2003. In addition, under **s27 LRA 2002**, any express easement created after 13 October 2003 must be protected by registration, so the only easements which are protected under **para 3** are legal easements which:

- arise from implied grant or reservation (e.g. easements which are not created expressly but which arise by way of necessity or common intention);
- arise by prescription (through long use of the right, normally 20 years or more); or
- arise under **s62 LPA 1925**.

So, easements which are created expressly or which are equitable easements created after 13 October 2003 have to be registered against the title to which they apply or they will not bind subsequent owners.

Legal easements which arise by implication, prescription or under **s62 LPA 1925** will be overriding, subject to additional conditions applicable from October 2006 which are set out below.

Example

When considering whether an easement can be an overriding interest under **LRA 2002**, it is necessary to look at **how the easement was created**.

Imagine, for instance, that Marko is the owner of 24 Bridge Yard.

He grants an easement to his neighbour Harry who lives at 25 Bridge Yard. This easement is expressly granted in the form of a deed entered into on 13 November 2018 which allows the owner of 25 Bridge Yard (currently Harry) to use the driveway passing over 24 Bridge Yard "with or without vehicles at any time and for ever". This is a legal easement which has been expressly created. Under **LRA 2002** this must be registered. The easement will be binding on a future buyer of Marko's land as it will appear in the charges register of his title. If it had not been registered, it would not be an overriding interest under **LRA 2002** because expressly granted easements have to be registered.

Another neighbour, William, who lives at 23 Bridge Yard has used a right of way over a path on Marko's land since 1990. William may have acquired an easement by prescription (long use) as he has used the path for more than 20 years. If this is the case (there are certain conditions for prescription to be claimed but these are beyond the scope of this course book) then this easement will potentially bind a buyer of Marko's land without any entry on the register since a prescriptive easement can be an overriding interest under **LRA 2002**.

There are some additional conditions which now apply for easements to be overriding interests. From 13 October 2006 any easement created after 13 October 2003 that is a legal easement **not** expressly granted, will take effect as an interest which is overriding unless, at the time the land was disposed of, it:

- was not within the actual knowledge of the person to whom the disposition was made; and
- would not have been obvious on a reasonably careful inspection of the land.

LRA 2002, however, provides that if a person who is entitled to such an interest can show that the interest has been exercised in the year before the disposition, the interest will bind the purchaser as an interest which is overriding. The purpose of this provision is to ensure that implied rights which are unused and difficult to discover will not bind a purchaser.

(3) **Easements under LRA 2002 – para 3 Sch 1 LRA 2002**

para 3 Sch 1 specifies what easements will **override first registration** under **LRA 2002**. **para 3** states that legal easements and profits will override first registration. Equitable easements will not take effect as interests which are overriding. These will still need to be registered as a Class D(iii) land charge to bind the owner of unregistered land and affect a purchaser of unregistered land on first registration.

5.3.3 Rights of persons in occupation

Link to practice

We have come across this issue before, but it is of great significance in practice, so we will revisit the point.

Non-owning adult occupiers can cause problems if they have an interest in the land, as their interest may be overriding and bind a buyer of the land despite the fact there is no record of the interest on the register of title.

Example

If a client, Salma, was buying a house which was registered in the sole name of Harry, but the house had been purchased partly with money provided by Harry's mother, Nikita, there could be a problem. Nikita may have an interest in the property due to her contribution towards the purchase price (this would be an interest under a trust of land). If Nikita was in actual occupation of the property at the time of sale, her interest may be overriding, which means it would bind Salma if she bought the property.

Nikita might refuse to leave the property on completion. Salma would own the property subject to Nikita's interest and Nikita might then go to court to require the property to be sold and part of the proceeds to be paid to her. This would clearly be most unsatisfactory!

Buyers' conveyancers will therefore make extensive enquiries about occupiers as part of the conveyancing process. For instance, following Question 21 of the Property Information Form any non-owning adult occupiers would be expected to sign a clause in the sale contract to release any rights, so that they did not remain attached to the house on completion and to promise to vacate (leave) on completion (see **Document 9** of the **Appendix**).

(1) **Pre-LRA 2002**

Under **LRA 1925**, the rights of persons in actual occupation of the land, or in receipt of rents or profits, were overriding unless certain specified exceptions applied.

We will not consider the details of the pre-**LRA 2002** law as it is most unlikely that you would need to apply this in practice. The old law would only be relevant where the transaction concerned (e.g. sale) was one which was completed before 13 October 2003.

However, the case law which related to **LRA 1925** will be relevant when considering the similar provision contained in **LRA 2002**.

(2) **LRA 2002 – para 2 Sch 3 (registered dispositions)**

This provision makes any interest belonging to a person in actual occupation overriding so far as it relates to registered land of which that person is in occupation. A person claiming a right on the basis of their occupation will need to show both that they have an interest in the property and that they are or were in occupation at the time of the disposition. There are two elements (occupation **and** interest) – mere **occupation** on its own is of no effect.

Interest + occupation = overriding interest

(a) **Actual occupation**

This is given its common-sense meaning and will vary on the facts of each case. The case law has established that, in most usual domestic dwelling cases, it means living on the premises. At the very least it is likely to mean some physical presence on the land. Although occupation usually has to be personal, it could be possible for an individual to establish their occupation by means of an agent (perhaps a housekeeper or, where the property is empty, builders).

Under **LRA 1925**, "actual occupation" did not have to be occupation of the whole of the land in the title. In ***Ferrishurst v Wallcite* [1999]** it was held that occupation of part of a property could give rise to an overriding interest over parts of the property which were not being occupied. However, under **LRA 2002**, the occupier is able to assert their rights only over the part that they occupy, rather than the whole estate.

What constitutes occupation under **LRA 2002** will be determined to some extent by the case law relating to **LRA 1925**. In addition, the courts will consider similar case law when determining what is capable of constituting an interest under **Sch 3 LRA 2002**.

The Court of Appeal considered the meaning of *"actual occupation"* in ***Link Lending Ltd v Bustard* [2010]**. The court held that the defendant, Ms Bustard, was *"a person in actual occupation"* for the purposes of entitlement to an overriding interest under **Sch 3 LRA 2002**. This was despite her enforced residence in a care home due to being sectioned under the **Mental Health Act 1983**. The court found that there was a sufficient degree of permanence and continuity of occupation coupled with a persistent intention to return home when possible. Her furniture and possessions were still at the house, and she returned home for weekly supervised visits in order to collect her mail.

The court said that there was no single test for determining "actual occupation", but that the following factors were all relevant:

- the degree of permanence and continuity of presence;
- the intentions and wishes of the person concerned;
- the length of absence from the property and the reasons for it;
- the nature of the property;
- the personal circumstances of the person concerned.

In this case, the lender was not entitled to dispossess Ms Bustard on the ground that she was not in actual occupation of her home. Mummery LJ said that earlier (pre-**LRA 2002**) cases on actual occupation by the House of Lords were binding on the court, and assisted in clarifying the principles to be applied. The special feature of this case was that she remained in actual occupation despite her enforced removal to the care home – he distinguished cases such as ***Abbey National Building Society v Cann* [1990]**, where acts were only preparatory to actual occupation.

In relation to the date of actual occupation, ***Abbey National Building Society v Cann* [1990]** has been confirmed and applied in ***Re North East Property Buyers' Litigation* [2012]**. The issue in that case concerned the date of occupation in relation to actual occupation under **para 2 Sch 3 LRA 2002**. It was confirmed that the relevant date when the claimant has to be in actual occupation is the date of the transfer.

(b) **Interests/rights in the land**

Examples of types of rights which are sufficient are the rights of beneficiaries under a bare trust, an option to purchase the freehold, an equitable lease and (probably most significantly) the rights of a beneficiary under a trust for sale (now a trust of land) (***Williams & Glyn's Bank Ltd v Boland* [1980]**).

Certain rights are not capable of being overriding interests, including:

- rights of a beneficiary in a strict settlement created before 1997 under the **Settled Land Act 1925;**
- a spouse's or civil partner's statutory home rights to occupy the home. The spouse or civil partner must register their right of occupation if it is to bind a buyer. It is registrable as a notice, under the **Family Law Act 1996** (**FLA 1996**). A civil partner's right to occupy is protected following the **Civil Partnership Act 2004** (**CPA 2004**).

(c) **Interests excluded from being overriding under Sch 3 LRA 2002**.

Interests that **Sch 3 LRA 2002** excludes from being overriding are:

- the interests of those of whom enquiry was made and who failed to disclose such right when they could reasonably have been expected to do so; and
- the interests of those whose occupation would not have been obvious on a reasonably careful inspection of the land at the time of the disposition and of which the person to whom the disposition is made does not have actual knowledge.

A buyer will not therefore be bound if the occupation by the person claiming the interest was not reasonably obvious on inspection. This will cut down the number of rights which can be overriding, under the aim of the legislation to reduce the number of interests which are unregistered.

(3) **LRA 2002 – para 2 Sch 1 (first registration)**

This provision determines what interests of those in occupation will be overriding on first registration under **LRA 2002**. An interest belonging to a person in actual occupation at the time of registration so far as it relates to the land which the person is occupying will be overriding. As with **Sch 3 LRA 2002** rights, the interest will take effect only against the land occupied. Rights under strict settlements or home rights will similarly not be protected under **Sch 1 LRA 2002**, and those concerned will need to protect their rights by registration. Note that there are no exclusions of rights not disclosed or which were not known and would not have been obvious on a reasonably careful inspection.

As with **Sch 3 LRA 2002**, the case law relating to **LRA 1925** will be of relevance in determining what constitutes occupation and what interests are capable of being overriding.

5.3.4 Leases

(1) **Pre-LRA 2002**

Leases for any term not exceeding 21 years were overriding interests against any registered title. Equitable leases were not included under this head. Of course, an equitable lease could be protected under the occupiers' provisions in **LRA 1925** if the person with the benefit of the equitable lease was in actual occupation of the property.

Link to practice

It will be relevant, if acting for a buyer, to find out about any leases which may affect the property being purchased.

Example

Imagine that you are acting for a client Bertrand who is buying a property from Toby. Bertrand finds out that Toby has leased the property to Charmaine for six months. Bertrand will want to know whether Charmaine's lease will be binding on him, in which case he will have to let her stay there for the remainder of the six-month period, or whether it will not bind him, in which case he can ask Charmaine to leave. Certain short leases will qualify as overriding interests.

Again, the Property Information Form asks the seller to state whether the property is subject to any short leases of less than seven years.

(2) **LRA 2002 – para 1 Sch 3 (registered dispositions)**

To reflect the rule that grants and assignments of leases with more than seven years unexpired at the date of grant or assignment will need to be registered, **LRA 2002** restricts leases having overriding status to those not exceeding seven years at the date of grant. There are some exceptions to this: certain other leases, such as time-share leases and certain future leases, which must be registered in their own right, will not be overriding. Subject to those exceptions, however, only leases granted after 13 October 2003, which are of seven years or less, are capable of being overriding.

Note that any leases that were overriding under **LRA 1925** at the time **LRA 2002** came into force continue to be overriding under **LRA 2002**.

(3) **LRA 2002 – para 1 Sch 1 (first registration)**

Very similar provisions to those in **Sch 3 LRA 2002** are set out in **para 1 Sch 1 LRA 2002** for determining which leases override first registration.

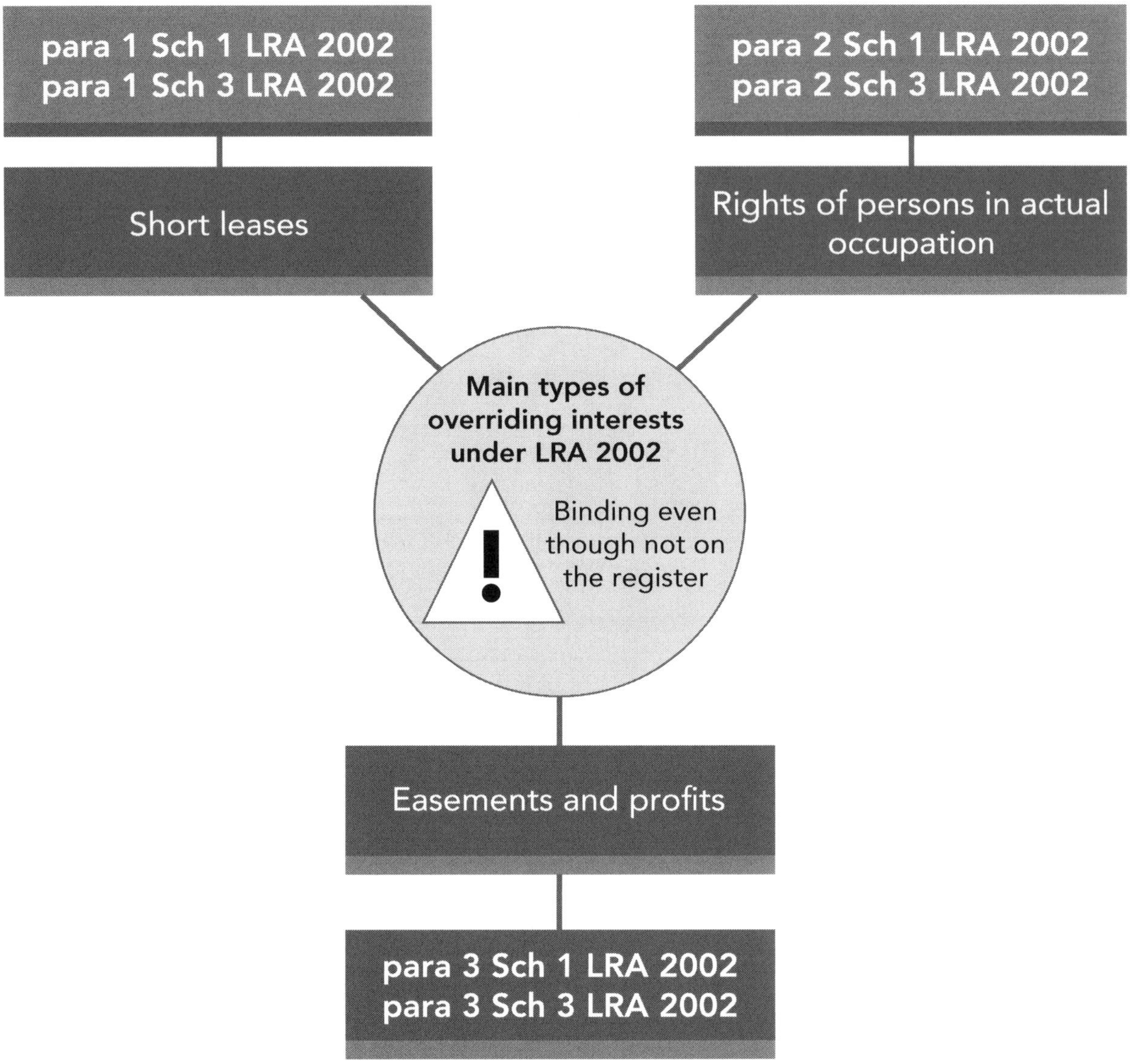

5.3.5 Additional points about overriding interests

Some interests can be protected on the register even though they are technically overriding interests – for example, a lease of between three and seven years can be protected by notice against the landlord's title even though it would be an overriding interest. The same would apply with a prescriptive easement, which could be protected by notice on the register even though it would be an overriding interest. If an entry on the register is made, the interest ceases to be overriding as it does not need to be – it is protected by virtue of the fact there is a register entry.

Link to practice

In practice, it is normally preferable for interests to be entered on the register rather than placing reliance on the law relating to overriding interests. A register entry can be clearer and more certain.

Example

Imagine that in 2021 Liam, the freehold registered proprietor of 44 Channel View, granted a five-year legal lease of a workshop in his garden to Tom. Liam is now selling 44 Channel View to Arun. Arun will want to know whether the five-year lease will be binding on him as this will determine whether he has to allow Tom to use the workshop until the lease runs out.

The five-year legal lease is not substantively registrable with its own title/title number as it does not exceed seven years. However, it can be protected by way of a register entry (notice) on Liam's title register. Arun's conveyancer would clearly be able to see the register entry about Tom's lease when examining Liam's title register. If there was no register entry, Tom's lease would, alternatively, bind Arun under para **1 Sch 3 LRA 2002** as an overriding interest but this would not be on the register and would not therefore be so immediately obvious.

There is an obligation to disclose overriding interests when making registration applications so that, where possible, HMLR can make register entries. This is in line with the aim of **LRA 2002** to make the register as complete a record of the title as is possible.

5.4 Classes of registered title

It is necessary to be aware of the classes of title awarded on first registration under **LRAs 1925–1997** as many registers which conveyancers may come across today were created before October 2003 when **LRA 2002** came into force (e.g. if Samir bought his house in 1992 when it was registered for the first time, his register would have been created in 1992 and the appropriate class of title awarded at the time).

When considering an application for first registration of an estate under **LRAs 1925–1997**, the Land Registrar registered it with one of a number of alternative classes of title. The class of title granted determined the extent of the state guarantee of title. Absolute title was, and still is, the best class. The other classes were, and still are, inferior. The possible classes were as follows:

Class of title	Availability
Absolute title	Available for both freehold and leasehold titles
Good leasehold	Available for leasehold titles only
Possessory title	Available for both freehold and leasehold titles
Qualified title	Available for both freehold and leasehold titles

Classes of title under the Land Registration Act 2002 and the effects of registration

The classes of title described above – absolute freehold and leasehold, good leasehold, qualified and possessory freehold and leasehold – continue to be available largely unchanged under **LRA 2002**. **LRA 2002**, however, also sets out the effect of first registration. It specifies the matters to which certain classes of title remain subject, notwithstanding registration.

We will now look at each class of title in turn, to see when it may be awarded by HMLR and its effect under **LRA 2002**.

(1) Absolute title

This class of title is available to both freehold and leasehold estates. Absolute title is the best class and is the most commonly awarded in practice. It is the class of title a conveyancer would hope to find when acting for a buyer!

Absolute freehold title means that the buyer holds the freehold estate in the land together with all related benefits such as the benefit of covenants and easements.

LRA 2002 states that absolute freehold title will, on first registration, be subject to:

- interests which are subject to an entry in the register relating to the estate;
- unregistered interests which fall within **Sch 1 LRA 2002** (overriding interests);
- interests acquired under the **Limitation Act 1980** of which the proprietor has notice (e.g. squatters' rights);
- the interests of any beneficiary of which the proprietor has notice, if the proprietor is a trustee.

Absolute leasehold title is the best class of leasehold title. It guarantees not only that the registered proprietor is the holder of the lease, but also that the lease was validly granted. An applicant cannot be registered with absolute leasehold title unless HMLR has examined and approved not only the title to the lease on first registration, but also the freehold title out of which it has been granted and any intermediate leases there might be.

LRA 2002 states that absolute leasehold title will, on first registration, be subject to the same matters as absolute freehold title, with the addition that the estate is also subject to the duties imposed on the tenant by the terms of their lease and which affect the freehold title.

(2) Good leasehold title

This class of title would be awarded by HMLR where it is satisfied that the leasehold title is satisfactory, but it had no access to the freehold title when it was registering the title on first registration.

This class of title is inferior to absolute leasehold title. HMLR has not checked the freehold title, so it cannot guarantee that the landlord was entitled to grant the lease. If the landlord was not entitled to do so, the tenant would lose the property. The tenant has no HMLR guarantee in respect of this, so would not be entitled to compensation from HMLR. Further, this class of title does not provide evidence of freehold incumbrances, such as restrictive covenants, on the leasehold title.

Good leasehold title will not apply in cases where the freehold (and all intervening leaseholds if the applicant is a sub-leaseholder) is already registered with absolute title at HMLR. As HMLR has already checked the title, an absolute title would be available.

Marketability of good leasehold titles varies from region to region. In some areas of the country, they are acceptable and common. In other areas, a title indemnity insurance policy may have to be obtained before the property can be sold. Many lenders are reluctant to accept good leasehold title as security for a mortgage. A lender could lose its security if the landlord's right to grant the lease was shown to be without basis. The UK Finance Mortgage Lenders' Handbook contains requirements about the acceptability of good leasehold title at clause 5.6.2 of Part 1. It states that good leasehold title will be acceptable if:

- a marked abstract of the freehold (and any intermediate leasehold title) for the statutory period of 15 years (see **Chapter 4**) before the grant of the lease is provided; or
- the conveyancer is prepared to certify that the title is good and marketable when sending the certificate of title to request the mortgage funds (because, for example, the landlord's title is generally accepted in the area); or
- the conveyancer arranges indemnity insurance which complies with the requirements set out in the UK Finance Mortgage Lenders' Handbook.

LRA 2002 states that good leasehold will, on first registration, in addition to being subject to the same matters as absolute titles, be subject to the incumbrances which led the Registrar to award the lesser class of title.

(3) Possessory title

This class of title is available to freeholds and leaseholds. Possessory title is not common but is awarded where an applicant's title is based solely on possession of the property as opposed to documentary evidence. Examples are where title has been acquired by adverse possession (by a squatter) or where an applicant has been unable to produce title deeds to HMLR on first registration, perhaps because they have been lost.

LRA 2002 provides that possessory title will be awarded where the Registrar is of the opinion that:

- the person is in actual occupation of the land, or in receipt of the rents and profits of the land;
- there is no other class of title with which they may be registered.

LRA 2002 states that possessory titles (both freehold and leasehold) will, on first registration, in addition to being subject to the same matters as absolute titles, be subject to the incumbrances which led the Registrar to award the lesser class of title.

(4) Qualified title

This class of title is available to freeholds and leaseholds but it is quite rare.

The effect of this title is the same as for absolute title, but the title is subject to some specified defect or qualification, for example, where there has been a breach of trust in the past (e.g. a sale by trustees to themselves leaving it open for the beneficiaries to have the sale set aside) or where the title produced on first registration does not cover the minimum required period of 15 years starting with a good root (see **Chapter 4**).

Unless the qualification relates to a very minor matter, the title will not normally be acceptable to a future buyer or mortgage lender. Defective title indemnity insurance would have to be obtained.

LRA 2002 states that qualified titles will, on first registration, in addition to being subject to the same matters as absolute titles, be subject to the incumbrances which led the Registrar to award the lesser class of title.

(5) General points

LRA 2002 specifies rules for the Registrar to apply when considering what class of title to grant on an application for first registration or for upgrading a title.

(1) Absolute freehold title and good leasehold title may be registered where the title obtained is *such as a willing buyer could properly be advised by a competent professional adviser to accept.*

(2) Absolute leasehold title may be registered if, in addition to the above, the Registrar is able to inspect and approve the lessor's title to grant the lease.

In deciding to register an applicant with absolute freehold or leasehold or good leasehold title, the Registrar may disregard defects if they would not cause the holding under the title to be disturbed. In other words, it may be possible for HMLR to ignore very minor or technical defects when examining and approving title.

5.5 Upgrading of titles under the Land Registration Act 2002

We have seen that some classes of title are better than others. It is possible for the class of title to be upgraded in certain circumstances on application to HMLR.

s62 LRA 2002 gives the Registrar power to upgrade possessory title to either absolute freehold or good leasehold after at least 12 years if they are satisfied that the proprietor is in possession of the land. They may also upgrade possessory title where they are now satisfied as to the title (e.g. where possessory title was granted because the title deeds were missing but they have now turned up and establish a good title).

The Registrar can also upgrade other titles after they have been registered using the same standards that apply when deciding on which class of title to award on first registration. The Registrar may therefore decide to upgrade a good leasehold to absolute leasehold if the applicant produces evidence of the lessor's freehold title (e.g. perhaps because the freehold title has been registered for the first time), or to upgrade a qualified to an absolute title if the applicant produces evidence to resolve the title defect identified by the Registry.

Applications for upgrade are made on form UT1 (see https://www.gov.uk/government/publications/upgrading-of-title-application-ut1). A fee is normally payable. With the exception of applications to upgrade possessory to absolute freehold or good leasehold after at least 12 years from registration, the application must be accompanied by certified copies of all relevant supporting deeds and documents.

Form UT1 must be completed to show the upgraded class of title applied for (e.g. absolute title), the applicant's entitlement to make the application (e.g. that the applicant is the registered proprietor) and the basis upon which the application is being made.

Activity

Follow the link below to HMLR's "Practice guide 42: upgrading the class of title":

https://www.gov.uk/government/publications/upgrading-the-class-of-title/practice-guide-42-upgrading-the-class-of-title

Read section 2 to ensure you understand what the classes of title mean.

Look in particular at section 3.2 "When to apply" – you are most likely to come across upgrading a possessory title in practice – you will see that this can be done once a possessory title has been registered for 12 years.

Follow the link in the Practice Guide and look at form UT1.

5.6 Form of the register

The basic format of the register does not vary between pre-**LRA 2002** titles and post-**LRA 2002** titles.

Each title is given an individual title number. The register for each title number is split into three parts: the property register, the proprietorship register and the charges register. It is accompanied by a title plan.

The actual register is kept by HMLR. Under **LRAs 1925–1997** as evidence of their title, the registered proprietor was given a **land certificate**, a paper copy of the register bound in a special cover. If the title had been mortgaged or charged, then the land certificate was retained at the Registry and the mortgage lender/chargee was issued with a **charge certificate**, which was a paper copy of the register bound in a special cover together with a copy of the charge. If further charges were created, each chargee was issued with a separate charge certificate. When the loan was repaid and the mortgage was discharged, the charge certificate would be returned to the Registrar, who would then release the land certificate.

Under **LRA 2002**, with effect from 13 October 2003, HMLR ceased to issue any new land or charge certificates (referred to as "dematerialisation"), and they are now of very little significance in conveyancing. Conveyancers should, however, dispose of them carefully, which may require them to be sent to HMLR to be destroyed.

The contents of a register are now governed by **LRR 2003**. Let's look at the three parts.

(1) **Property register**

This describes the land with a brief description and a reference to the official plan (the title plan) based on a large-scale Ordnance Survey map. It will also state the estate held – freehold or leasehold. If it is leasehold, short details of the lease will be included; date, term, parties, rent and, where applicable, the lessor's title number.

The register may also include details of any easements or covenants which exist for the **benefit** of the land, although registration does mean that the proprietor gains these rights irrespective of whether they actually appear in this part of the register.

(2) **Proprietorship register**

This includes:

- the class of title, for example, absolute freehold title or good leasehold title;
- the name and address (or addresses) of the registered proprietor. The owner can list up to three addresses (addresses for service). One must be a postal address, but the others can be DX or email addresses;
- any limitations on the registered proprietor's powers to deal with the land; for example, if the registered proprietor cannot transfer the property without the consent of their mortgage lender. Such limitations are usually reflected by restrictions (see below);
- since April 2000 the price paid for the property is shown on the register.

The addresses for service will be used by HMLR if it needs to send any notices or communications to the registered proprietors at a later date, so it is important that addresses are accurate and kept up to date. From January 2013, HMLR has entered postal addresses for service under official Royal Mail address formats. HMLR states that this will record the address as accurately as possible, ensuring that the owner receives all HMLR notices and correspondence. The practical impact of this is that an address for service on the register may be very slightly different from that appearing on a deed or a HMLR application form.

Indemnity covenants are commonly noted in the proprietorship register. This is a covenant under which the buyer covenants to indemnify the seller against loss in certain circumstances.

It is also possible to find certain types of notices and possibly some positive covenants (e.g. a covenant to do something such as to repair a fence) entered in this part of the register (although also see below regarding positive covenants).

(3) **Charges register**

This contains details of incumbrances adversely affecting the title, for example, restrictive covenants, leases, easements and mortgages. Note:

- mortgages (registered charges) are usually shown by two numbered entries. The first entry records the existence of a registered charge; the second states its proprietor (i.e. the mortgage lender). The amount of the mortgage does not appear in the register;
- the burden of restrictive covenants (e.g. a covenant not to do something such as not to run a business from the property) is noted on the register – if a restrictive covenant is not noted, it will not bind a buyer;
- HMLR may note the burden of positive covenants on the register, and these might appear in the charges register, especially where they are mixed in with restrictive covenants. Deeds often contain a mixture of restrictive and positive covenants The fact that a positive covenant has been noted on the register does not, however, make it binding. The burden of a positive covenant does not run (pass) with the land even if it is on the register and other methods of enforcement must be used, but the existence of positive covenants (whether on the register or not) will warn the seller of the need to extract an indemnity covenant from the buyer.

Although the register entries will normally appear in the sections of the register as described above, HMLR has discretion to make entries in another part of the register where this would be more convenient, and this should be taken into account when reading register entries. This would not be common but, for instance, where a deed contained a mixture of beneficial and burdening easements and it would be unclear or complicated to divide them between the property and charges registers, they might be entered in the property register as one entry.

Link to practice

If there are no matters which will burden a title, such as a mortgage or covenants, the title will not have a charges register. You must always look for the words "end of register" when you look at a registered title as some titles will only comprise a property register and proprietorship register (and title plan, of course).

5.7 Interests which must be protected by an entry on the register

In deciding whether something is an interest requiring protection on the register, first consider whether the interest is a right which should appear on the register, either with its own title number or as a registered charge against an existing title. If the answer is that it is neither capable of registration with its own title nor a registered charge, then ask if it is an overriding interest. If it is not an overriding interest, it must be protected by an entry on the register.

Under **LRA 1925** these types of interests were called "minor interests" but the term is not used in **LRA 2002**. Under **LRA 1925**, minor interests could be protected on the register by the entry of a notice, caution, inhibition or restriction.

Under **LRA 2002**, though existing entries will continue to have effect, new rules have applied since 13 October 2003 to entries on the register from that date. Cautions and inhibitions can no longer be used to protect interests after 2003. Entries made under **LRA 2002** must be in the form of notices or restrictions.

Link to practice

Many registers were created before 2003, and many register entries were made before that date. When you are looking at a title register you may therefore come across a mixture of **LRA 1925** entries and **LRA 2002** entries. It is important to ensure that you do not ignore the old entries. They will need to be dealt with if they fetter the title or a buyer's interest.

Notice

This has always been the most common method of protecting third party rights and a notice will appear in the charges register of a title. Notices are used to protect a wide variety of interests such as estate contracts, restrictive covenants and matrimonial or civil partnership home rights of occupation.

The effect of a notice is that a disposition of registered land takes effect subject to the estate or interest protected by the notice, but only if, and so far as, such estate or interest is valid. In other words, the notice does not render enforceable an interest which could not be enforced under the general law.

Under **s32(1) LRA 2002** notices are therefore used to protect many types of interests in registered land. In fact, all interests which are not overriding will generally need to be protected by registration as a notice (other than interests under a trust or settlement and covenants between lessor and lessee which cannot be protected in this way).

Importantly, **s37 LRA 2002** provides that the Registrar may enter a notice in respect of any interest which would otherwise be overriding; this is to ensure that more overriding interests are recorded on the register. The interest ceases to be overriding once a notice of it is registered against the title as it does not need the overriding status anymore. Examples of interests which may be noted, even though they are technically overriding, are leases of between three and seven years, and prescriptive easements.

The registration of a notice under **LRA 2002** does not necessarily mean that the interest is valid but does give priority over subsequent interests. There are two kinds of notice under **LRA 2002**.

(a) **Agreed notice** – the Registrar will accept an application for an agreed notice only if:

- the applicant is the registered proprietor;
- the applicant is not the registered proprietor but the registered proprietor consents; or
- the applicant can satisfy the Registrar that the interest claimed is valid.

Note that the registered proprietor's consent is not required in relation to an application for an agreed notice of home rights under **FLA 1996** (as amended by **CPA 2004**).

In most cases, the application for an agreed notice must be made on form AN1 (see https://www.gov.uk/government/publications/agreed-notice-registration-an1) accompanied by sufficient details of the interest claimed to satisfy the Registrar of the nature of the applicant's claim. If the application is successful, HMLR will enter the notice in the charges register of the affected title.

Example

An example of an agreed notice entry would be:

(15.03.2022) Contract for sale dated 12.03.2022 in favour of Justin David Griffiths

NOTE: copy filed

There are separate forms for home rights notices. HMLR will only accept applications to register or cancel notices in respect of home rights if they are made using forms HR1 (application for registration of a notice of home rights - https://www.gov.uk/government/publications/notice-of-home-rights-registration-hr1) and HR4 (cancellation of a home rights notice) (see https://www.gov.uk/government/publications/notice-cancellation-cn1).

Link to practice

We have seen that the registration of a home rights notice can cause a difficulty on a sale. Go back to **Chapter 3** and reread the section on securing vacant possession. You will see that a home rights notice can sometimes act as a "bargaining chip" for a non-owning occupier and the conveyancer acting for a buyer will need to ensure that the seller's conveyancer will either attend to removal of the home rights notice prior to exchange of contracts or that a completed HR4 signed by the non-owning occupier will be handed over on completion.

(b) **Unilateral notice** – this does not require the registered proprietor's consent. Application must be made using form UN1 (see https://www.gov.uk/government/publications/unilateral-notice-application-to-enter-un1). The Registrar must give notice of the unilateral notice to the registered proprietor once the application has been completed.

Since 13 October 2003 unilateral notices have replaced cautions. Unlike a caution, the entry of a unilateral notice on the register will not entitle the beneficiary to notice from HMLR if an application is lodged for registration of a dealing with the property. The unilateral notice, however, will constitute notice to the purchaser.

Example

An example of a unilateral notice entry would be:

(15.02.2022) UNILATERAL NOTICE in respect of an agreement made on 10.02.2022 between (1) Kevin Myers and (2) Joe Kenton relating to the ownership of a fence on the southern boundary of the land in this title

(15.02.2022) BENEFICIARY: Joe Kenton of 88 City Road, Bristol, BS6 3HH

Removal of a notice

An application to cancel a notice (other than a unilateral notice) must be made in form CN 1 (see https://www.gov.uk/government/publications/notice-cancellation-cn1) and must be accompanied by appropriate evidence to satisfy the registrar that the protected interest has come to an end.

The registered proprietor of the estate or charge to which the notice relates may apply at any time to cancel the unilateral notice using form UN4 (see https://www.gov.uk/government/publications/unilateral-notice-cancellation-un4). The beneficiary of the notice (i.e. the person who entered it) then has 15 working days in which to object to the cancellation of the notice. This time limit can be extended by the Registrar. If the beneficiary objects, but fails to show an arguable case, the notice will be cancelled. If the beneficiary does not object, the Registrar must cancel the unilateral notice.

Contrast **cancellation** of a unilateral notice with **removal** of a unilateral notice. Removal is the term used to describe the procedure whereby a unilateral notice is withdrawn at the request of the beneficiary of the notice. Form UN2 (see https://www.gov.uk/government/publications/unilateral-notice-application-to-remove-un2) must be used for this purpose.

Activity

Follow the link below to HMLR's "Practice guide 19: notices, restrictions and the protection of third-party interests in the register":

https://www.gov.uk/government/publications/notices-restrictions-and-the-protection-of-third-party-interests-in-the-register/practice-guide-19-notices-restrictions-and-the-protection-of-third-party-interests-in-the-register

This Practice guide is important and one which you are likely to refer to fairly often in practice. However, it is rather large and you are unlikely to read it from cover to cover all one go!

It is also fair to say that HMLR updates this Practice guide fairly frequently, accordingly always check the latest version online as and when you need to refer to it.

Go to the Practice guide and to the section on "Notices" – read how to remove or cancel a notice.

Protection of a contract for sale

If a seller and buyer have exchanged contracts for the sale and purchase of land and completion is likely to be delayed for some time (for example, on new build transaction) the buyer's conveyancer will want to register an estate contract to protect their buyer's equitable interest in the property. The purpose of registering the estate contract is to put the world on notice of the fact that the registered proprietor has already entered into a contract to sell all or part of the land within the affected title.

Contract for sale may be protected by agreed notice or unilateral notice. If using an AN1 to apply for an agreed notice, a copy of the contract must accompany the application and the consent of the registered proprietor must be obtained. If applying for a unilateral notice using form UN1, the contract will not be sent to HMLR. Instead, the application will be accompanied by either a statement or conveyancer's certificate setting out the details of the contract including the date of the contract and the parties.

Link to practice

You can see that the contract of sale is not sent to HMLR when applying to register an estate contract using unilateral notice. Accordingly, if confidentiality is a concern, it may be preferable to register a unilateral notice. In this way, the contract itself will not be available for inspection.

You will see from the example above that the agreed notice shows that the contract is available for inspection because "copy filed" appears beneath the entry. Contrast this with the example of the unilateral notice where there is no such wording.

Go to Practice guide 19 and read section 2.4.2 "Points to consider when deciding which type of notice to apply for". You will see that confidentiality is one of the reasons that a unilateral notice might be chosen. However, note that the applicant should always be aware that the beneficiary of unilateral notice may be required at any time to prove the validity of their claim.

This is therefore of significance to a conveyancer acting for a buyer. Whilst there is no specific time limit requiring registration of an estate contract, where completion is likely to be more than a week or two after exchange of contracts, it is prudent to consider whether an estate contract should be registered against the seller's title.

On the other side of the coin, when acting for a buyer, we will see below that the buyer's conveyancer must investigate the seller's title. If it is clear that an estate contract is registered against the seller's title, the buyer's conveyancer should not exchange contracts until the estate contract has either been removed from the title or, the conveyancer is satisfied that the estate contract does not relate to the land within the title which their client is buying.

Caution

Under **LRA 1925** any person having an interest in any registered land, and whose interest was not registered or protected by a notice or restriction, was able to lodge a caution which was entered in the proprietorship register. The effect of a caution was that no dealing with the land was to be registered until notice had been served on the cautioner, thus giving them a chance to try and establish their claimed interest.

Under **LRA 2002**, cautions have not been registrable against titles since 13 October 2003 and those seeking to protect rights where the proprietor does not consent to the creation of an entry now have to use the **unilateral notice** procedure. Such a notice protects the interest, rather than merely giving a right to be informed of a proposed dealing, so is more effective at protecting the interest concerned than a caution. It should be noted that **existing** cautions against titles remain (so pre-**LRA 2002** caution entries may still be encountered when looking at registers) and are dealt with as before. It is also possible to apply to convert cautions to unilateral notices.

Link to practice

Do not confuse cautions with **cautions against first registration**. It is still possible to make an application for the latter.

A caution against first registration is a form of protection for interests affecting unregistered land – accordingly we could have discussed this in **Chapter 4**. Its effect is to require HMLR to give the person who has applied for the caution (the cautioner) notice of an application for first registration of the legal estate which the cautioner claims is affected by an interest to which they are entitled.

The application for a caution against first registration results in the creation of a caution register containing:

- a description of the legal estate which the caution relates;
- a description of the land affected land statement of the cautioner is claimed taken from either a statutory declaration or a conveyancer's certificate.

Only certain parties are entitled to make an application for a caution against first registration. The most frequently occurring will be a person who claims to be the owner of an estate in land or entitled to an interest affecting an estate in land.

Note, however that the owner of a freehold estate in land (including one acquired by adverse possession) or a leasehold estate in land granted for a term of more than 7 years cannot apply for a caution against first registration. This is because the correct form of protection for the owner of such an estate in land is to apply for first registration of their title.

The purpose of a caution against first registration is to alert the cautioner when an application for first registration is received against the affected land.

Follow the link below to HMLR "Practice guide 3: Cautions against first registration":

https://www.gov.uk/government/publications/caution-against-first-registration/practice-guide-3-cautions-against-first-registration.

Inhibition

An inhibition was a hostile act and could be entered in the proprietorship register on the application of a person interested and with the consent of the Registrar or the court. It was normally used only to protect rights arising out of the bankruptcy of a registered proprietor. The inhibition prevented the registration of any dealing with the land during a specified period or until the occurrence of a specified event.

Since 13 October 2003, no new inhibitions can be created. Existing inhibitions continue to affect titles, however, and are dealt with largely in the same manner as before. Matters previously protected by inhibitions are now protected by restrictions.

Restriction

Unless there is anything on the register to the contrary, anyone dealing with a registered proprietor can usually assume that the proprietor's powers of disposition are unlimited. If this is not the case, the appropriate way to record this is to enter a restriction on the proprietorship register. This is the method in which the equitable interests arising under a trust of land are normally protected.

In general terms, a restriction operates to prevent a disposition of the land taking effect without prior conformity to some specified requirement. The wording of the restriction will make it clear what has to be done to comply with it. For example, where there is a trust of land the restriction would require the payment of purchase money to be made to all the trustees and specify that there must be at least two of them, or if only one, then that one must be a trust corporation. This would ensure that the process of overreaching took place, meaning that the buyer would take the land free of the interests of any beneficiaries. The interests of the beneficiaries would no longer lie in the land itself, but would instead be interests in the proceeds of sale held by the trustees, who would be bound to pay them their share of the sale proceeds.

A restriction might also indicate that the consent of certain individuals or a lender is needed before any dealing can be registered.

Under **LRA 2002** restrictions are governed by **ss40–47** and **LRR 2003**. The Registrar has power to enter a restriction if it appears necessary or desirable to do so (**s42 LRA 2002**), and if there are two or more registered proprietors and the property is held by the owners as tenants in common in equity, the Registrar must enter the following restriction to ensure that overreaching can be effected (**s44 LRA 2002** and **LRR 2003**):

Example

Wording of the Form A restriction:

No disposition by a sole proprietor of the registered estate (except a trust corporation) under which capital money arises is to be registered unless authorised by an order of the court.

The registered proprietor's consent is not needed to enter a restriction provided that the applicant has sufficient interest in the making of the entry. **LRR 2003** contain a list of people regarded as having a sufficient interest and these include:

(a) any person who has an interest in a trust of land;

(b) a trustee in bankruptcy.

Any restriction must normally be in a standard form as set out in **Sch 4 LRR 2003**. The standard form restrictions cover the vast majority of cases. Non-standard restrictions must be specifically approved by HMLR.

An application to enter a restriction must be made on form RX1 (see https://www.gov.uk/government/publications/enter-a-restriction-registration-rx1), although an application for a standard form restriction can be made in a HMLR transfer, assent, or approved charge. An application for a standard form restriction may also be made in HMLR prescribed clauses of a lease.

Form RX1 must confirm the entitlement of the applicant to apply to enter the restriction and confirm whether the restriction is in a standard form or not. It will either state the type of standard form restriction applied for or state the wording of the restriction which is being requested. Any relevant documentary evidence must accompany the application form.

There are various ways in which restrictions can be removed. They can be voluntarily withdrawn on application by the persons interested in the restriction and they can be cancelled on application to HMLR where they are no longer required. HMLR itself has power to cancel a restriction where it is superfluous or no longer relevant (e.g. where it was entered in relation to a trust of land and HMLR is satisfied that the estate is no longer subject to the trust).

There are various standard HMLR application forms for removal or cancellation of restrictions which are used according to the circumstances.

It is also possible to apply to HMLR to modify the wording of an existing restriction.

Activity

Follow the link below to HMLR's "Practice guide 19: notices, restrictions and the protection of third-party interests in the register":

https://www.gov.uk/government/publications/notices-restrictions-and-the-protection-of-third-party-interests-in-the-register/practice-guide-19-notices-restrictions-and-the-protection-of-third-party-interests-in-the-register

This Practice guide is important and one which you are likely to refer to fairly often in practice. However, it is rather large and you are unlikely to read it from cover to cover all one go!

It is also fair to say that HMLR updates this Practice guide fairly frequently, accordingly always check the latest version online as and when you need to refer to.

Go to the Practice Guide and to the section on "Restrictions" – read how to remove or cancel a restriction and how to modify the wording of an existing restriction.

The effect of failing to protect an interest

The effect of failing to protect an interest, where necessary, is that it does not bind a purchaser. A purchaser of an absolute freehold estate will take it subject to registered charges, interests protected by notice and overriding interests, but free from other interests (**s29(1) LRA 2002**). Therefore, even though a purchaser or lender had **express** knowledge of such an interest, it would acquire the property free from that interest. In registered land, therefore, the doctrine of notice plays very little part, though the knowledge of the purchaser is relevant in limited cases, for example, two categories of overriding interests (easements and interests of those in occupation) within **Sch 3 LRA 2002** will bind only if obvious on a reasonably careful inspection or if the disponee had actual knowledge.

The following is an example of the register as a whole.

Title Number: SF604950 Edition Date: 01.01.1982

Official Copy of register of title

- This official copy shows the entries subsisting on the register on 10 April 2022 at 16:04:11
- This date must be quoted as the "search from date" in any official search application based on this copy
- The date at the beginning of the entry is the date on which the entry was made on the register
- Issued on 10 April 2022
- Under s.67 of the Land Registration Act 2002, this copy is admissible in evidence to the same extent as the original
- This title is dealt with by Land Registry Birkenhead Office

A: Property Register

This register describes the land and estate comprised in the title

SHROPSHIRE : EAST CORNER

1. (01.01.1982) The **freehold** land shown and edged with red on the plan of the above title filed at the Registry and being 2 Hazel Grove, East Corner, Shropshire SY6 5TA.

B: Proprietorship Register

This register specifies the class of title and identifies the owner. It contains any entries that affect the right of disposal

Title Absolute

1. (01.01.1982) **PROPRIETOR**: MARILYN TENNANT and EDWARD ALAN TENNANT of 2 Hazel Grove, East Corner, Shropshire SY6 5TA.
2. (01.01.1982) The transfer to the proprietors contains a covenant to observe and perform the covenants referred to in entry no. 2 of the Charges Register and of indemnity in respect thereof.

C: Charges Register

This register contains any charges and other matters that affect the land

1. (01.01.1982) – A conveyance dated 1 March 1921 made between (1) Alexander Parish (2) Hugo Landau contains restrictive covenants but neither the original conveyance nor a certified copy or examined abstract thereof was produced on first registration.
2. (01.01.1982) – A transfer of the land in this title dated 21 September 1971 made between (1) John Jones (Transferor) and (2) Emily Winston (Transferee) contains the following covenants:

"The Transferee to the intent and so as to bind the said land into whosesoever hands the same may come hereby covenants with the Transferor to observe and perform the covenants set out in the Third Schedule hereto."

THE THIRD SCHEDULE

1. Not to erect any buildings or structures or any additions or alterations to any buildings or structures on the said land except in accordance with plans previously submitted to and approved by the Transferor, such approval not to be unreasonably withheld.

2. No buildings or structures erected on the said land or any part thereof shall be used for any purposes whatsoever other than as a single private dwelling-house and outbuildings belonging thereto.

3. (01.01.1982) REGISTERED CHARGE dated 14.12.1981 to secure the moneys including the further advances therein mentioned.

4. (01.01.1982) PROPRIETOR: HABC BANK PLC of 1B The Strand, London, WC1 1TT.

****

End of register

5.8 Electronic conveyancing and the move to digitisation

LRA 2002 was intended to lay the foundations for the introduction of a system of electronic conveyancing to speed up the process of buying and selling land. A full system of electronic conveyancing has not yet been introduced however.

LRA 2002 aims to ensure that the register of title provides a complete and up-to-date record of the estate owner's title and all matters which affect that title, enabling land to be conveyed more easily than it had been under the old unregistered system. Though the existence of the register creates greater certainty for buyers, the aim has not been fully achieved as certain third-party rights, namely interests which are overriding (overriding interests) which do not appear on the register, continue to affect the title.

As part of the move towards electronic conveyancing, HMLR has been providing consistently increasing levels of electronic services over the past few years. HMLR Portal is a secure web-based facility, designed to support all current and future HMLR e-services, giving a faster turnaround time than paper-based applications and longer opening hours. There is also the ability to download material (e.g. register entries) and save it to the user's computer.

A range of electronic services has been developed for business users such as conveyancing firms and lenders, and these services are known collectively as "Business e-services". They are accessed through the Portal and paid for by variable direct debit. Once an organisation is registered as a Portal user, a named person within the firm controls access by individuals within the organisation, based on the services it has signed up for. Some firms can also access Business e-services through HMLR's Business Gateway, which enables them to access the facilities directly through the firm's own case management systems rather than going through the Portal. The main Business e-services are currently:

- information services – provides access to all pre-registration services such as requests for official copies of the register and HMLR searches;
- land charge services – provides access to land charges services such as bankruptcy only searches and full land charges searches;
- network services – enables certain electronic applications to be delivered to HMLR, for example, a notification of change of name or application to cancel a restriction;
- lender services – enables lenders to deal with mortgage business electronically (e.g. mortgage discharges);
- e-document registration service (e-DRS) – enables certain applications to be lodged electronically with scanned documentation.

Activity

HMLR is constantly updating the digital services that it offers. Follow the link below to read more about HMLR's Business e-services and make a note of any other services which are not mentioned in this section of your coursebook:

https://www.gov.uk/guidance/apply-for-hm-land-registry-business-e-services

Examples of types of applications which are available electronically are as follows:

AP1	Application to change the register affecting the whole of a registered title
AN1	Agreed notice
CCD	Application to cancel a caution against dealings
CN1	Cancellation of notice
HR1	Notice of home rights
HR4	Cancellation of home rights
RX1	Application to enter a restriction
TP1	Transfer of part
UN1	Unilateral notice

It should be noted that most applications for first registration are currently excluded from e-DRS, as HMLR needs to see paper title documentation. Further information about what has to be sent to HMLR with a first registration application is contained in **Chapter 4**.

HMLR launched the Digital Mortgage Service for remortgages in 2018 and, as of February 2020, has now completed over 7,000 digital mortgage deeds. The aim was to reduce paperwork and delays when applying for a remortgage and some clients can complete a remortgage in three days, which is 18 days less than a paper transaction.

This service is available to all people remortgaging their homes with the plan being to expand to all homeowners in the future.

5.9 Deducing and investigating title in registered land

When deducing title to registered land, the main reference is the official copy of the register held by HMLR. As we have seen, it is divided into three main parts: the property register, which outlines the extent of the property being sold (including any rights benefiting the land); the proprietorship register, which outlines the owner; and the charges register, which lists matters affecting the property.

The official copy of the register and title plan is the document which deduces title for registered land. When the contract package is sent to the buyer's conveyancer an up-to-date copy of the official copies of the register entries and title plan should be included. The buyers' conveyancers should therefore check the date of the official copies. Under the Protocol, the register entries should be less than six months old when the contract package is submitted.

The title plan for the property should also to be checked to verify that the extent of the land matches what the buyer client expects to buy.

The seller's conveyancers will usually obtain the official copies and title plan online via HMLR Portal, although they can be obtained from various search providers or by paper request from HMLR using form OC1 (see https://www.gov.uk/government/publications/official-copies-of-register-or-plan-registration-oc1).

Under SC 4.1.1, the seller is under an obligation to provide evidence of title and under SC 4.1.2 it states that the official copies are the required document, so a buyer may insist upon the seller providing them. Likewise, a document referred to in the official copies must be provided by the seller (and if missed out should be requested by the buyer). Most official copies will state if a copy of such a document is filed at HMLR (the register will usually say "copy filed"). Copies of filed documents can be obtained from HMLR for a small fee, using form OC2 (see https://www.gov.uk/government/publications/official-copies-of-documents-registration-oc2).

Link to practice

A common example of a filed document would be a past conveyance containing restrictive covenants where the covenants did not appear in full on the register.

Sometimes, when covenants are extensive, HMLR does not copy the full wording of the covenants into the register entries on first registration, but refers on the register to the deed containing them and states there is a copy filed. If this is the case the relevant deed must be obtained from HMLR so that the full wording of the covenants can be seen and the deed should be supplied with the title.

The following is an example extract from an entry in a charges register where covenants have not been extracted from the deed and entered on to the register but are contained in a transfer which is copy filed:

3. (19.12.90) A Transfer of the land in this title dated 14 August 1982 made between (1) Higgins Builders Limited and (2) Paul Townsend contains restrictive covenants.

NOTE: Copy filed

Alternatively, HMLR may have set out the covenants in full in the register when the register was created, extracting them from the relevant deed. Where the covenants are already set out in full, the deed itself will not need to be supplied (and should not be requisitioned as a missing document).

The seller's conveyancer deduces title by providing it as part of the contract package which, as previously explained, would usually consist of the following documents:

- draft contract in duplicate;
- official copies of the register, title plan and filed documents (if any);
- Property Information Form (TA6);
- Fittings and Contents Form (TA10);
- documents upon which the buyer can reasonably be expected to rely on;
- required consents (e.g. under restrictive covenants or restrictions);
- additional documents such as guarantees and planning permissions;

- any other documentation specifically relevant on the facts of the case (e.g. a marriage certificate to evidence a change of name);
- the EPC, if not supplied by the estate agent.

This list assumes the use of the Protocol. However, similar pre-contract packages are provided in most non-Protocol cases.

Note that there are additional documents where the land is leasehold, and that some firms may enclose a draft transfer at this stage to save time.

The buyer's conveyancer must check the title carefully and raise any problems in the form of written requisitions on title.

The buyer's conveyancer will carefully examine each section of the title register in turn and will check the title plan. They will be looking to spot any issues which arise and to determine what action will be required to resolve any problems. They can then decide which issues (if any) are to be the subject of requisitions and how any requisitions are to be drafted (e.g. to request a missing document, to request further clarity on an issue or to confirm that certain steps will be taken by the seller to resolve the issue). The conveyancer will also check whether there are any overriding interests since these will not appear on the register.

The following table provides some practical examples of basic matters which would be checked. This is not an exhaustive list but serves to highlight some of the main areas.

Property register	Are there any discrepancies in the property description? Are there any discrepancies in the title plan? Is the title number the same as the one stated in the contract? Is the estate consistent with that stated in the contract? Does the property have the benefit of any easements or other rights and, if so, are these sufficient for the client's needs? Do any rights carry an obligation to make payments towards them (e.g. a right of way subject to a maintenance obligation)? Do the boundaries on the title plan match the boundaries of the property on the ground? Are there any other entries which need to be taken into account (e.g. an entry showing that any land has been removed from the title or an entry stating that mines and minerals have been excepted from the registration)?

Proprietorship register	Is the class of title satisfactory? Do the names of the registered proprietors match the names of the sellers in the contract or is there a discrepancy? If so, why is there a discrepancy and what must be done to deal with this issue? Does the price paid entry (if any) look suspicious in any way? Are there any restrictions which affect the transaction and, if so, what is required by their wording? Are there any pre-**LRA 2002** caution entries? Are there any indemnity covenants?
	Link to practice Any inconsistencies with the names of the seller in the contract and the registered proprietor in the proprietorship register must be queried by the buyer's conveyancer, however minor. Practitioners should never assume that a typographical error does not matter – a discrepancy will be picked up by HMLR on registration. If it is evident that two registered proprietors have got married for example, the buyer's conveyancer should require the seller's conveyancer to update the register of title by submitting the marriage certificate to HMLR prior to exchange of contracts. Remember it is up to the seller's conveyancer to ensure that their seller client has good title. Any other name discrepancy should be properly investigated; a change of name by deed poll might be required, for example. In all cases where there is a name discrepancy, the buyer's conveyancer should seek specific confirmation from the seller's conveyancer that they have carried out appropriate identification and due diligence on their seller client.
Charges register	Are there any incumbrances (e.g. restrictive covenants, leases or easements) and, if so, are they problematic? Are there any mortgages (registered charges) affecting the property which must be redeemed on or before completion? Are there any other problematic entries which must be followed up (e.g. a notice protecting home rights)?
	Link to practice The buyer's conveyancer should always carefully note all legal charges that appear on the charges register. They will expect the seller's conveyancer to produce an undertaking to discharge all charges out of the sale proceeds on completion.

5.10 Dispositions of registered land and registration

Dispositions

Once title to a piece of land has been registered, it is important to appreciate that all future dealings with the land will be governed by the registered system. A disposition of land which is already registered will be governed by **s27 LRA 2002**.

Example

Marco owns a house with registered title which he is selling to Sam. Sam must register the change of ownership due to s27 LRA 2002 requirements. This is not the same as first registration where the land was previously unregistered.

---

s27 LRA 2002 makes clear that in registered land the legal estate passes to the buyer only once the transaction is registered. The following dispositions must be registered:

- a transfer;
- the grant of a lease for more than seven years;
- the grant of a lease (for any term) to take effect in possession after the end of the period of three months beginning with the date of the grant (e.g. a student signs a lease in June but the lease does not start until October);
- a discontinuous term (e.g. a holiday timeshare). This is the case even when it is for less than seven years;
- the express grant or reservation of a legal easement;
- the express grant or reservation of a rentcharge or right of entry;
- the grant of a legal charge.

The registered estate passes to the buyer only when the buyer is registered as proprietor.

Any disposition of a registered estate will be subject to:

- registered charges or other interests protected by notice in the register;
- an interest which is overriding as listed in **Sch 3** (which are similar to those in **Sch 1 LRA 2002** – see **2.6.2** for a fuller discussion);

- any interest which appears from the register to be excepted from the effect of first registration (e.g. where a title is qualified) and anything incident to the leasehold estate (most importantly, the covenants of landlord and tenant).

Registration

The registration formalities will vary according to whether the land is already registered, or whether it is currently unregistered. Where the client has purchased land which is already registered, the application will be to register the dealing with the registered land. If the land is currently unregistered, the sale to the client will trigger first registration (see **Chapter 4**).

The registration application must be sent to HMLR. In some cases, it can be sent electronically. In other cases, a paper application will be made, enclosing hard copies of forms and documents.

Link to practice

The majority of HMLR applications will be made electronically using the Portal. However, HMLR has published guidance about where to send paper land registration applications and correspondence. This can be viewed at:

www.gov.uk/guidance/hm-land-registry-address-for-applications

Business customers (e.g. conveyancer' firms) should send most paper applications and correspondence by Royal Mail or DX to a single standard HMLR address but will mark it with the name of their Customer Service team or their closest office.

The guidance contains a list of HMLR offices so that the closest one can be identified. Some firms deal with a dedicated HMLR Customer Service Team located at a particular office, and should direct correspondence and applications to their team.

Registering the transfer of a registered title

If the property is already registered, the buyer's conveyancer must apply for registration of the dealing after completion. **LRA 2002** provides that registered dispositions must be completed by registration to take effect. Until registration, the legal estate will not vest in the buyer; they will simply have an equitable interest in the property despite the fact that a deed of transfer has been executed. The buyer's mortgage must also be completed by registration in order to take effect as a legal charge.

Time limit and priority period

It is vital that the buyer applies for registration of the dealing within the period of priority conferred by their pre-completion form OS1 **or** OS2 search. The priority period is 30 working days from the date of the search. If completion takes place some time after the date of the search, the time available to the buyer after completion may be very limited. If the application for registration is not made within the period of priority conferred by the search, the buyer will take the property subject to any matter for which an application for registration has been made since the date of the search result.

Note that carrying out a second search after completion does not extend the period of priority conferred by the first search. It should not, therefore, be used as a method of obtaining further time in which to register the transaction after completion. A second search should usually be reserved for situations where, because of a later-than-anticipated completion, the priority period will have run out.

Early completion

The buyer's application for registration may, in fact, comprise more than a simple application for dealings. The buyer will often apply to register the transfer, register their new mortgage and discharge the seller's repaid mortgage (often referred to as a discharge/transfer charge).

The following contains a brief explanation of HMLR's early completion policy, which may apply where there are linked applications (e.g. discharge, transfer, charge), but where no evidence of mortgage discharge has been supplied with the registration application. This is a relevant consideration at the registration stage, and the Protocol reinforces the need for practitioners to take this policy into account.

Activity

Follow the link below to HMLR's "Practice guide 31: discharges of charges:

www.gov.uk/government/publications/discharge-of-charges/practice-guide-31-discharges-of-charges

It is all very relevant but look in particular at section 2.3 which mentions the early completion policy.

The early completion policy applies where there is an application to HMLR to remove entries relating to a registered charge from the register as part of a linked application, but where no evidence of discharge has been supplied to HMLR at the time of the application (e.g. with the form AP1). If HMLR has no evidence of discharge, it will no longer delay its registration of other linked applications lodged at the same time. It will proceed, where possible, to deal with the applications it is able to process (hence the term "early completion"). This means that, where the policy is applied, it will complete the registration of the new owner and any new charge, leaving the old charge on the register. This will then necessitate a further process to remove the old charge once the discharge evidence is available. This may raise issues of priority and possibly extra cost.

The policy will vary where the register contains existing lender restrictions. Where there is a restriction on the register preventing the disposal and the registration of a new charge without the existing lender's consent, the policy will not immediately be applied. HMLR will raise a requisition asking for evidence of discharge or evidence that the terms of the restriction have been met. If the requisition is not complied with, HMLR will cancel the applications for discharge, transfer and new charge.

If the restriction only prevents the registration of a charge, HMLR will complete the registration of the transfer but cancel the application to register the new charge.

Note that the early completion policy does not apply to applications relating to transfers of part.

Form AP1

The application for registration must be made in form AP1 (see https://www.gov.uk/government/publications/change-the-register-ap1). The following must to be submitted with the form AP1:

- form DS1 if the seller had a mortgage which has been discharged, unless an electronic method of discharge (ED) has been used. Where the mortgage is discharged by ED, the AP1 should be marked "charge discharged electronically" and where the mortgage is discharged by e-DS1, the AP1 should be marked "charge discharged by e-DS1". This explains to HMLR why there is no DS1 regarding the discharge application;
- a certified copy of the transfer;
- SDLT5 (LTT certificate if property is in Wales);
- certified copy of the mortgage deed (where there is a new mortgage);
- the appropriate HMLR fee (this will usually be taken by direct debit from the firm by HMLR);

- evidence of identity (only where necessary) – see below;
- form DI if there are disclosable overriding interests;
- any other documents which are relevant on the facts of the particular transaction, for example: a relevant death certificate, a certified copy of a general power of attorney, a certified copy marriage certificate to evidence a change of name, a certified copy of Grant of Probate where executors are selling or a form HR4 where there is a home rights notice to be cancelled.

Since June 2014, HMLR has no longer required original documents to be sent with an AP1 registration application. This brings the requirements for postal applications in line with those for electronic applications through the e-DRS service. Therefore, HMLR only requires certified copies of documents, not the originals. If originals are sent, they will be accepted but most documents will be scanned and destroyed.

So it is not necessary to send the original transfer or mortgage deed, for instance, only certified copies.

The Law Society and HMLR remind conveyancers that if they are acting for lenders, they may still have to keep original documents under individual lenders' requirements in Part 2 of the UK Finance Mortgage Lenders' Handbook.

Note particularly the following clauses in form AP1.

Clause 4 – the applications to be handled by HMLR must be listed in priority order. In a typical purchase this will be:

(a) discharge of the seller's mortgage by form DS1 or ED/e-DS1;

(b) the transfer to the buyer;

(c) the registration of the buyer's mortgage (if any).

Link to practice

The current edition of form AP1 makes the requirements clear in the note to panel 5:

"List the documents lodged with this form. We only need certified copies of deeds or documents you send to us with HM Land Registry application forms. Once we have made a copy of the documents you send to us, they will be destroyed, this applies to both originals and certified copies."

These will be entered in the boxes on the AP1 form as:

Discharge
Transfer
Charge

Note that where the seller's mortgage is being discharged by electronic methods (ED/e-DS1) and not by paper form DS1, it is not strictly necessary to list "discharge" on the form, but this is frequently done for clarity.

Clause 5 – this will list the documents enclosed with the application. They will obviously vary according to the individual transaction but a typical box 5 where there was a discharge using DS1, transfer and charge would be completed as follows:

Documents lodged with this form:

1. DS1
2. Certified Copy Transfer

Clause 9 – the buyer can include up to three addresses for service, one of which must be postal. It is possible to give an electronic address. Changes made by **LRA 2002**, particularly in relation to unilateral notices and rules relating to adverse possession, make it increasingly important to ensure that the buyer's address for service is kept up to date. These details are usually taken from the transfer deed.

Clause 11 – this reflects **s71 LRA 2002**. The buyer has a duty to inform the Registrar of any overriding interests affecting the property within their actual knowledge. This is to enable HMLR to enter details of such interests on the charges register of the title where appropriate. Such interests will then cease to be overriding. If there are disclosable overriding interests, form DI must be enclosed with the registration application.

The correct fee should accompany the application. It is important that the application is correctly submitted as HMLR has guidelines, which are strictly observed, on when it will reject applications which are not correct – if the application is rejected, it can jeopardise the priority obtained by HMLR search. The 2019 Protocol contains a paragraph at Stage F (Post Completion) to the effect that the contents of the application should be checked very carefully to avoid requisitions. It indicates to ensure that all the necessary documents are dated, properly executed and attached, and that any name discrepancies between documents and register are resolved or explained.

Form AP1 applications can be sent to HMLR using paper-based forms and enclosures, as described above. Alternatively, the AP1 registration application can be lodged electronically at HMLR, using the electronic document registration service (e-DRS).

Digital applications

HMLR is moving away from electronic applications, which are scanned copies currently uploaded and submitted using the HMLR portal e-DRS. Instead, customers should use the new portal **Digital Registration Service** or lodge a digital application using software connected to HMLR's Business Gateway Platform. Digital applications are quicker to create and process, and see fewer requisitions due to automatic error checking.

To create and submit a digital AP1 application, firms can use:

- the Digital Registration Service on the portal;
- a case management system connected to HMLR's Business Gateway platform.

A very important change for firms is that from November 2022 HMLR will no longer accept scanned or PDF copies of AP1s for changes to registered titles using the portal. HMLR states that:

"A digital application process, based on data rather than traditional paper-based methods, is fundamental to transforming the way we register land and ultimately will play a vital role in improving the end-to-end conveyancing journey. Not only does it offer the immediate benefits of quicker processing times and fewer errors, but it opens the opportunity for further innovation in the future."

Activity

Follow the link below and read the HMLR brochure on digital AP1s:

https://www.gov.uk/guidance/hm-land-registry-digital-applications

Identification

Boxes 12 and 13 of the AP1 deal with HMLR's identification requirements on registration.

When submitting registration applications, a conveyancer has to verify the identity of the party on the other side if they are unrepresented. This would be unusual in a standard conveyancing transaction but if this applies, form ID1 would be used where verification of an individual's identity was required. Form ID2 would be used for a corporate body. If forms ID1 or ID2 are required, since 7 April 2015 Chartered Legal Executives have been valid signatories for the purpose of these forms.

Note that these forms will not be required where conveyancing firms are acting for the parties, which is the usual case. The conveyancer acting for the buyer will indicate the conveyancers name address and reference for all parties to whom the buyer's conveyancer is not acting. HMLR will rely on the fact that conveyancing firms have carried out appropriate identification and due diligence checks on the parties to the transaction.

Activity

Follow the link below to HMLR's "Practice guide 67: Evidence of identity; conveyancers":

https://www.gov.uk/government/publications/evidence-of-identity-conveyancers

Go to section 8 and read how to complete forms ID1 and ID2.

Go to section 11 and look carefully at the examples of completed form AP1.

Use of e-DRS system

The e-DRS system is available through the HMLR Portal. To use the service firms must have a Portal account and a variable direct debit (VDD) agreement to pay the fees and the ability to scan documents so that they can be uploaded with applications.

The system allows conveyancers to submit the application to change the register electronically with scanned copies of supporting documents. Supporting documents are uploaded as separate files so that HMLR only retains the documents it is permitted to keep. Although most documents such as transfers and charges need to be scanned, certain application forms do not need to be. For instance, Form AP1 can be prepared in the conveyancer's system, signed with a typed signature and uploaded without the need for printing and scanning. Online versions of SDLT5 can be saved and uploaded without scanning. When HMLR receives the application, it processes it in the same way as a paper application and sends the completed documents electronically. The documents available to download will be the official copy of the register, the title information document (TID) and the registration completion sheet.

HMLR will send confirmation of successful submission with a reference, and a priority date and time. If HMLR has requisitions (e.g. regarding missing documents) they will be sent electronically and can be answered through the Portal. Missing documents can be attached. It is important that requisitions from HMLR are answered promptly and that they are not ignored as failure to deal with a requisition can not only delay the registration but can have serious implications, potentially even resulting in cancellation of the application.

Once the registration has been completed, HMLR will send the completed documents electronically, and they can be retrieved from the "pdf downloads" area. Conveyancers can also sign up to HMLR's e-notification service which means that they will receive alerts when documents have arrived in the downloads area.

5.11 Rectification and indemnity under the Land Registration Act 2002

It is possible for a register to be altered, where it is shown that there are errors or omissions. This must be handled in accordance with the provisions set out in **LRA 2002**.

Sch 4 LRA 2002 deals with alteration of the register. The process of changing the register is described under **LRA 2002** as **alteration**. An alteration can be made for a variety of reasons, for example, to correct a mistake.

Rectification is a specific type of alteration. It is an alteration which:

- involves the **correction of a mistake**; and
- **prejudicially affects the title** of a registered proprietor.

LRA 2002 goes on to state that such rectifications cannot be made without the consent of a proprietor in possession unless:

- they have caused or contributed to the mistake by fraud or lack of proper care; or
- it would for any other reason be unjust for the alteration not to be made.

Otherwise, for any other alteration not involving rectification, the Registrar or the court must make the alteration unless there are exceptional circumstances which justify not making it.

Sch 8 LRA 2002 makes provision for the payment of indemnity by the Registrar. This is a form of statutory compensation scheme. Indemnity is only available where the register is altered because of a rectification. A person is entitled to be indemnified by the Registrar if they suffer loss by reason of:

- rectification of the register; or
- a mistake whose correction would involve rectification of the register.

The right applies unless such loss has been caused by the claimant's fraud or lack of care.

Importantly, no indemnity is payable if the register is altered to give effect to an overriding interest, since the interest is binding in any event, despite not being on the register. The title will not be adversely affected by the register entry.

Activity

Follow the link below to HMLR's "Practice guide 39: rectification and indemnity":

https://www.gov.uk/government/publications/rectification-and-indemnity/practice-guide-39-rectification-and-indemnity

Read the Practice Guide.

5.12 s77 Land Registration Act 2002

s77 LRA 2002 must always be kept in mind when making any application to HMLR. This section imposes a duty to act reasonably when making an application. A person must not exercise the right to apply for an entry to be added to the register of someone else's title, or for the entry of a notice or object to someone else's application unreasonably and if they do so, they were duty to anyone who suffers damage. The existence of this duty entitles the person adversely affected to bring an action for damages.

Conveyancers should always keep this section in mind when applying to register a notice or restriction, for example or a caution against first registration or when advising the client whether they should object to an application which somebody is trying to make in relation to their title.

5.13 Chapter summary

(1) It is essential to differentiate registered and unregistered title.

(a) Title is usually deduced by the seller's conveyancer supplying official copies (registered land) or an epitome of title (unregistered land) with the contract package. It is necessary to deduce title to show that the seller is capable of selling the property and it is not subject to onerous or inappropriate incumbrances.

(b) In registered land, this is done by providing an official copy of the register and title plan in respect of the property together with any filed documents.

(2) On receipt of a first registration application HMLR will investigate the title and will create a new register and title plan.

(3) Once the register has been created, the unregistered title deeds no longer have any legal significance.

(4) The register is a register of title is, not land.

(5) A key feature of the register is that it is open to public inspection.

(6) The system of land registration was intended to provide a complete and up-to-date record of the estate owners title – this has not been fully achieved due to a class of interests called overriding interests.

(7) Some of the most important interests that are capable of being overriding interests are:

(a) easements;

(b) the person in actual occupation – there are two elements they must have actual occupation plus an interest in the land (very often having made a contribution towards the purchase price).

(8) Details of beneficial interests arising under a trust are kept off the register.

(9) There are various classes of title available on first registration:

(a) absolute title – available for freehold and leasehold titles; the best form of title available;

(b) good leasehold – available for leasehold titles only;

(c) possessory title – available for both freehold and leasehold titles;

(d) qualified title – available for both freehold and leasehold titles – rarely encountered in practice.

(10) Possessory title can be upgraded to either absolute freehold or good leasehold after at least 12 years if the Registrar is satisfied that the proprietor is in undisputed possession of the land.

(11) The register of title is divided into three parts:

(a) property register – describes the land with a brief description and a reference to the official plan (the title plan). It will indicate whether the estate is freehold or leasehold and will include details of any rights which benefit the land (for example, an easement);

(b) proprietorship register – includes the class of title and the name and address of the registered proprietor. The register proprietor can list up to three addresses for service including an email address;

(c) charges register – contains details of the encumbrances affecting the property for example, mortgages and covenants. If there are no encumbrances. There will be no charges register.

(12) protecting an interest on the register:

(a) a notice – protects a wide-ranging of interests including estate contracts, restrictive covenants and matrimonial home rights. A notice can be agreed or unilateral;

(b) a restriction – is the method of protecting equitable interests arising under a trust of land. In general, a restriction operates to prevent a disposition of the land taking effect without prior conformity to some specified requirement.

(13) After **LRA 2002**, no new caution is and inhibitions can be created but if any appear on a register, they must be dealt with.

(14) It is still possible to apply for a caution against first registration.

(15) Many applications to HMLR will be made electronically using the HMLR portal. Firms must enter into an agreement with HMLR to use Business e-services and HMLR fees must be paid by variable direct debit.

(16) From November 2002, HMLR are will require firms to submit straightforward registration applications via their Digital Registration Service.

(17) A seller deduces title to registered land by producing an official copy of the register and title plan (together with any documents indicated as available for download on the registers).

(18) The buyer's conveyancer will investigate the registered title and will require the seller's conveyancer to deal with any requisitions on title prior to exchange of contracts.

(19) Once title to a piece of land has been registered, all future dealings will be governed by the registered system.

(20) A registration application must be made on form AP1.

(21) HMLR can be liable if it has made errors with registration under the rectification and indemnity procedures.

(22) **s77 LRA 2002** imposes a duty to act reasonably on someone making an application to register an entry against someone else's title (or when making an objection). The existence of the duty entitles a person adversely affected to bring an action for damages.

CHAPTER 6
Capacity to sell

6.1 Introduction

Not all transactions involve a transfer of title by "ordinary" individuals. It is essential for the conveyancer acting for the seller and buyer to ensure that the title is vested in the seller or that the seller has the authority to sell the property. Another way of putting this is that the seller has "capacity" to sell. This is broader in this context than mental capacity. What we are talking about is that the seller has the authority to sell the property. At the end of this chapter we will also consider some key points relating to mental capacity.

There may be transactions involving a seller who is either not an individual or who is signing the documentation on behalf of the seller, for example:

- a transfer of title where the owner (or one of the joint owners) has died;
- a sale by a mortgage lender following repossession of the property;
- a transfer of title where the owner has lost mental capacity (e.g. by using a lasting or enduring power of attorney or by a deputy);

- a transfer of title where the owner is absent (e.g. where they have to go overseas on business and is not present to execute documents). They may wish to appoint an attorney to act for them (e.g. under a special or general power).

This chapter will cover:

- dispositions by co-owners;
- sale by a fiduciary owner;
- sale by personal representatives (PRs);
- sale by mortgagees;
- voluntary dispositions;
- disposition by an attorney;
- disposition by a deputy;
- capacity and covenants for title;
- execution by non-individuals.
- mental capacity

6.2 Dispositions by co-owners

6.2.1 Formalities when buying from trustees of land

From the buyer's point of view, there are comparatively few formalities to be observed. If the trust requires consents to be obtained then, unlike the trustees, the buyer needs only to ensure that evidence of the consent is produced to them (**s10 Trusts of Land and Appointment of Trustees Act 1996** (**TLATA 1996**)). Remember that the buyer is not concerned to see whether the beneficiaries should be or have been consulted about the sale. The buyer must ensure that the purchase money is paid to all the trustees (and that there are at least two of them) or to a trust corporation. This is vital for overreaching to operate and the buyer to take free of any equitable interests under the trust.

In registered title, although the beneficial interests are kept off the register, the register will tell the buyer what they must do in order to buy the property free of any interest under the trust. These instructions may be determined by looking at the restrictions on the proprietorship register. In the absence of any restrictions, a buyer may assume that the proprietors have full power to dispose of the land in the title.

6.2.2 Problems in co-ownership

Remember that whenever property is conveyed into the names of co-owners, the property will be subject to a trust of land.

Similarly, where property is conveyed into the name of a single individual but the purchase money is provided by two people, or someone other than the legal owner makes contributions to the property, there may, subject to the evidence, be a trust of land. It is a resulting or constructive trust of land (an implied trust) which is imposed by the courts, but it is still a trust of land. Consider the situation of the buyer from the sole owner. The fact is that the seller is a trustee of the legal estate holding it on trust for themself and X in equity. There is, however, nothing at all on the title deeds to suggest this, nor would there be on the register in registered title, as the Registrar, from the information they are given, would know nothing about the trust. Whether the buyer will take subject to the interests of X in this situation depends in unregistered title on whether the buyer has notice of X's interest and in registered title on whether X is protected under **para 2 Sch 3 LRA 2002**. In such cases, the buyer is entitled to insist on the appointment of a second trustee (**s42 LPA 1925**).

Case law

The following decisions have clarified and illustrated the situations where trusts of land differ from their predecessors, trusts for sale. These cases make reference to **s14 TLATA 1996**, which allows disputes about trust land to be taken to court. Any person who is a trustee or who has an interest in the land (this could include a mortgagee or a beneficiary) may apply to the court for an order (e.g. an order for sale or an order to prevent sale).

***Mortgage Corporation v Shaire* [2000]** drew an important distinction between the old trusts for sale and their replacement, trusts of land. An equitable mortgagee sought possession; the borrower pointed to **s14** and argued that rights of their family should come before those of the mortgagee. It was held that **TLATA 1996** gave the courts greater flexibility than under the trusts for sale regime, and that old precedents should be viewed with caution. Although a mortgagee's interests would usually come first, **s14** gave the court discretion to act differently in exceptional cases, such as the present case.

In ***First National Bank plc v Achampong* [2003]** the Court of Appeal accepted that it had discretion in exercising **s14** but ordered a sale despite the presence on the property of an abandoned wife, a daughter with mental health issues and a disabled grandchild. This was on the basis that unless an order for sale was made, the bank would be kept waiting indefinitely for payment.

In ***Birmingham Midshires Mortgage Services Ltd v Sabherwal*** **[1999]** a property was owned by two legal owners. There was, in addition, an equitable owner who was not a legal owner. The two legal owners mortgaged the property. The mortgagee sought repossession. This was challenged by the equitable owner. She argued that overreaching did not apply under the (then) new trusts of land regime – an argument rejected by the court, though in her case the events occurred before **TLATA 1996**.

Sale by a surviving co-owner

This situation is closely aligned to that of a trust of land. When property is conveyed to co-owners it is held, either expressly or impliedly, on a trust of land.

Assume that property is conveyed to A and B. A and B will hold the legal estate as trustees for themselves in equity. If A dies, B will be the sole owner of the legal estate. B may or may not be the sole equitable owner. If, at the time of A's death, A and B were joint tenants in equity, B will be the sole legal and equitable owner. If, however, they were tenants in common in equity, A's equitable interest will pass according to their will or the intestacy provisions. If B is not the sole equitable owner, they hold the legal estate as trustee and a second trustee would need to be appointed by B to ensure that the buyer took free of the other equitable interest.

The problem for the buyer is how to tell which situation we are dealing with. It is possible for the joint tenancy in equity to have been severed before A's death. It is even possible that B does not know of the severance and genuinely believes themself to be the sole equitable owner.

The way this issue is dealt with on sale varies according to whether the land is registered or not.

(1) Unregistered land

If the buyer finds evidence of severance then, obviously, they must insist that B appoints a second trustee to overreach the other equitable interest.

If there is no evidence of severance the buyer of **unregistered** land is offered protection by the **Law of Property (Joint Tenants) Act 1964** (**LP(JT)A 1964**), which provides that, in favour of a purchaser of the legal estate, a survivor of two or more joint tenants shall be deemed to be solely and beneficially interested if the conveyance by B includes a statement (typically in the Recitals) that the seller (B) is **solely and beneficially interested**. Before the **Law of Property (Miscellaneous Provisions) Act 1994** (**LP(MP)A 1994**), a sale **as beneficial owner** satisfied this requirement.

LP(JT)A 1964 will not, however, protect the buyer:

- if a memorandum of severance has been endorsed on or annexed to the conveyance to A and B; or
- if a bankruptcy order or petition has been registered under the **Land Charges Act 1972** against A or B.

In ***Grindal v Hooper*** **[1999]** it was held that a buyer under **LP(JT)A 1964** had to be a buyer in good faith and for value (applying **s205 LPA 1925**). The buyer in ***Grindal*** was the brother of the surviving co-owner, and had actual notice that the deceased co-owner had severed, so they could not obtain protection under **LP(JT)A 1964**.

(2) **Registered land**

LP(JT)A 1964 has no relevance in **registered title**. In the absence of a Form A restriction on the proprietorship register, the buyer is entitled to assume that the sole surviving registered proprietor is solely entitled to the property and that it is no longer the subject of a trust of land. Remember that the legal estate will be held as joint tenants and on the death of the first co-owner, it will be necessary to submit form DJP (death of joint proprietor) (see https://www.gov.uk/government/publications/deceased-joint-proprietor-djp) to HMLR with the death certificate to transfer the legal estate into the name of the surviving co-owner.

If there is a Form A restriction on the proprietorship register, this denotes a behind-the-scenes beneficial interest. The legal estate will be transferred into the name of the surviving co-owner by submission of form DJP, as above but this still leaves the Form A restriction on the register. As we have seen, a way to deal with this is for a second trustee to be appointed to overreach the beneficial interest.

However, if the surviving co-owner does not want to sell the property immediately but wants to deal with the removal of the Form A restriction, whether they are able to do so will depend on who has the behind-the-scenes beneficial interest. If the surviving co-owner holds the entire legal and beneficial interest, they will need to complete and sign a form ST5 (see https://www.gov.uk/government/publications/cancellation-of-restriction-statement-of-truth-st5) which is a statement of truth in support of an application to cancel a Form A restriction. The co-owner will need to produce sufficient evidence to HMLR to explain what has happened to the beneficial interest protected by the restriction. Often this might involve producing a copy of the will of the deceased to prove that they left their share in the property to their surviving co-owner.

Link to practice

Remember that any document which is submitted to HMLR is placed in the public domain. If a grant of representation has been obtained regarding the estate of the deceased, this will not be a problem as grants are publicly available. However, if it has not been necessary to obtain a grant of representation, submitting this to HMLR has the effect of putting the will into the public domain. It will not be referred to on the register of title but HMLR would have to provide a copy if someone applying for it.

The point of the ST5 is to explain what has happened to the beneficial interest in the property.

The ST5 explains to HMLR what has happened to the beneficial interest but it must be submitted to HMLR together with a form RX3 (see https://www.gov.uk/government/publications/cancel-a-restriction-registration-rx3) to cancel the Form A restriction.

Link to practice

If the surviving co-owner is not entitled to the entire legal and beneficial interest in the property, the Form A restriction must remain on the proprietorship register to protect the behind-the-scenes beneficial interest. An example of this situation is where the deceased co-owner left their share in the property to their child as opposed to their co-owner.

6.3 Sale by a fiduciary owner

There is a potential problem where property is owned by someone in a fiduciary capacity, for example a personal representative or trustees) and then immediately reacquired by way of purchase in their personal capacity.

An example would be a conveyance by PRs to one of themselves. The transaction must be authorised in the original will or trust instrument, consented to by the court by way of a court order, or the beneficiaries, all being *sui juris* (i.e. sane and adult), must consent. If none of these has happened, then the transaction could be set aside, at the request of the beneficiaries, for breach of trust. If a transaction like this appeared in the chain in an unregistered title, the title could be good apart from the particular defect. If anything came of it, though, the defect could be extremely serious. On an application for registration, such a title would, at best, be awarded a qualified title.

6.4 Sale by personal representatives (PRs)

On death, the deceased's real estate devolves upon their PRs. If the deceased was the **sole** or **sole surviving** legal owner, the title to the property will pass to their PRs.

If the deceased was one of a number of legal owners, the legal title will pass by survivorship to the surviving legal owners, and the PRs are unlikely to have any role in the sale of the legal estate; their only interest could be in the deceased's equitable interest in the property. The official copy death certificate will be required as evidence of death.

If the legal title passes through the PRs, evidence is needed of the PRs' entitlement. This takes the form of a grant of representation, usually either a grant of probate (where the PRs are appointed as executors under a will) or of grant of letters of administration (where the deceased died intestate).

PRs can sell the property (e.g. to pay the deceased's debts, and legacies made in their will). If they do so, the grant must be produced to the buyer.

Alternatively, the PRs may decide not to sell the property, but to pass it to a beneficiary under the will or intestacy, or to trustees (if a trust has been created). In these situations, an assent is drawn up in favour of the beneficiary or trustees as applicable.

Assents – unregistered land

By **s36(1) Administration of Estates Act 1925** (**AEA 1925**), a PR may assent to the vesting of the legal estate in a beneficiary. **s36(4)** requires the assent to be in writing, signed by the PR, and to name the person in whose favour it is given. An assent is therefore an exception to the rule in **s52 LPA 1925**, which requires a deed to convey a legal estate.

Note, however, that if the assent contains covenants by the beneficiary (e.g. an indemnity covenant) then the assent must be made in the form of a deed.

Link to practice

An important practice point was established in In ***Re King's Will Trusts* [1964]**. It was held that an assent in writing is necessary to pass a legal estate even where the legal estate was merely passing from one person in his capacity as PR to the same person in another capacity (e.g. trustee or legatee).

Example

If a deceased's will appointed Piers Trimble to be both the sole executor and the sole beneficiary, if Piers Trimble proves the will, he will continue to hold the property as executor until he executes an assent in writing from himself as executor to himself as beneficial owner.

Since 1925, a will no longer constitutes a document of title and the buyer is not concerned with the beneficial interests arising under it. If there is an assent in the title, then both the grant of representation and the assent will form part of the title. **s36(7) AEA 1925** provides that, in favour of a buyer, the assent shall be taken as sufficient evidence that the person in whose favour it is made is the person entitled to have the legal estate conveyed to them. It was held in ***Re Duce and Boots Cash Chemist (Southern) Ltd's Contract* [1937]** that, if a defect is, in fact, discovered, the word "sufficient" is not to be interpreted as "conclusive" and therefore an objection can be made to the title notwithstanding **s36(7)**. (In that case the recitals included in the assent actually made it clear that the assent had been incorrectly made.)

s36(5) allows a person to whom an assent or conveyance of a legal estate is made to require that notice thereof be endorsed on the grant. This is to prevent the land being disposed of twice by the PRs, perhaps even by mistake. For a buyer, this was a matter of good conveyancing practice. For an assentee, it was essential. If no endorsement were made and the PRs were later to purport to convey the property to a buyer, including in the conveyance to the buyer a statement that they had made no other assent or conveyance of the property (**s36(6)**), the assentee would lose the legal estate to the later buyer.

Nowadays, it is no longer strictly necessary to endorse a memorandum on the grant because the disposition of the land (on sale or assent) is subject to compulsory registration and will lead to an application for first registration. This means that any future buyer will be investigating a registered title and, as the title to the land has been registered it will prevent it being disposed of twice.

Assents – registered land

In registered land cases, the form of the assent is governed by the **Land Registration Rules 2003** (**LRR 2003**) and the forms used are:

- form AS1 (see https://www.gov.uk/government/publications/whole-of-registered-title-assent-as1 – where there is an assent of the whole of the registered title by PR(s);

- form AS3 (see https://www.gov.uk/government/publications/part-of-registered-title-assent-as3) – where there is an assent of part of the land in a registered title by PR(s).

In registered title, endorsements etc. lose their importance. The register is conclusive as to who is the registered proprietor. If an assentee is registered as the proprietor and the PRs then purport to resell the property, the assentee is protected by their status as the registered proprietor.

It is not essential for there to be two PRs as there must be in the case of trustees. A sale by the sole proving PR will be effective to overreach the interests of any beneficiaries under the will or intestacy.

In registered title, the PRs may make title to the property in one of two ways:

- using the grant, they could apply to HMLR to have themselves registered as the proprietors of the property in place of the deceased; or
- they could sell the property and provide the buyer with a certified copy of the grant to be sent to HMLR together with the transfer from the PRs to the buyer.

Activity

Follow the link below to HMLR "Practice guide 6: devolution on death of a registered proprietor":

https://www.gov.uk/government/publications/devolution-on-the-death-of-a-registered-proprietor/practice-guide-6-devolution-on-the-death-of-a-registered-proprietor

Read sections 2 and 3 carefully.

6.5 Sale by mortgagees

s101(1) LPA 1925 provides that every legal mortgagee (lender) has a statutory power of sale unless it is specifically excluded by the mortgage deed. The power of sale will arise when the legal redemption date has passed (this is traditionally six months after creation of the mortgage but the date will be in the mortgage deed). It will become exercisable under **s103 LPA 1925** when:

(a) there has been default for three months after written notice to repay the principal (capital) has been served on the mortgagor (borrower);

(b) interest under the mortgage is in arrears for at least two months; or

(c) there has been a breach by the mortgagor of some other implied or express provision in the mortgage (e.g. the borrower has granted a lease of the property to a tenant without permission).

If the seller is a mortgagee, it must ensure that it has the power of sale and that the power of sale has arisen and become exercisable. If it wishes to sell with vacant possession and the property is a dwelling-house, it must also ensure that it has possession of the property. If the mortgagor does not co-operate in leaving the dwelling, a court order is required.

A mortgagee is not a trustee of the power of sale for the mortgagor but has a duty to act in good faith and also to take all reasonable care to obtain whatever the property's true market value is (or, if the mortgagee is a building society, the best price reasonably obtainable) at the time. If, for example, the mortgagee when selling the property failed to tell a buyer that the property had the benefit of planning permission, the mortgagee could be liable to the mortgagor for the difference in price that could have been obtained if the additional information had been made known (***Cuckmere Brick Co Ltd v Mutual Finance Ltd* [1971]**).

A buyer in good faith from a mortgagee need not be concerned with any of the matters between the mortgagor and mortgagee. The only requirement for the **buyer** is to check that the power of sale has **arisen**. The mortgage deed should be checked to show that this has occurred. It is of no concern to the buyer whether or not it has become exercisable.

Link to practice

This is an important point.

A conveyance/transfer by a mortgagee in exercising its statutory power of sale operates to vest the mortgagor's fee simple estate in the buyer subject to any legal mortgage or other matter having priority to the selling mortgagee's charge, but **free from all subsequent mortgages**, the mortgagor's equity of redemption, and other matters over which the selling mortgagee's mortgage takes priority and evidence of discharge of the mortgage is, therefore, not required.

Thus, for example, on a sale by a second mortgagee, any third or subsequent mortgage would be overreached but the sale would be subject to the first mortgage. The buyer would therefore require the first mortgage to be paid off on or before completion and evidence produced of its discharge.

6.5.1 Receipted mortgages

Whenever there is a mortgage in the deduced title, it should be remembered that the property will be sold subject to that mortgage unless:

(1) the mortgage is adequately receipted; or

(2) the property is sold by the mortgagee; or

(3) the property is sold by a prior mortgagee, thus overreaching that mortgage.

(2) and (3) have been dealt with above, but the question of receipting needs some further consideration.

If there is a subsisting mortgage, the buyer should require confirmation by the seller that the mortgage will be redeemed on or before completion, and that either the receipted mortgage, if the title is unregistered, or the form DS1 (see https://www.gov.uk/government/publications/mortgage-cancellation-of-entries-for-lenders-ds1) or appropriate form of electronic discharge, if the title is registered, will be obtained on completion. If this confirmation is not forthcoming, the only acceptable alternative would be an undertaking by the seller's conveyancer to discharge the mortgage out of the sale proceeds on completion and to produce the evidence of discharge. This is usually addressed between exchange of contracts and completion on the Completion Information and Undertakings Form (TA13) (see **Document 8** of the **Appendix**).

Registered land

It is now more common in registered land for mortgages to be discharged electronically using an e-DS1 where the lender is one of the major banks or building societies than for the DS1 form to be provided. HMLR has developed the electronic system enabling lenders to discharge their registered charges electronically without having to use any paper application. The lender's computer sends the discharge directly to HMLR computer avoiding the delays in using a DS1.

Following redemption of a legal charge affecting registered land, an electronic instruction is sent by the lender to HMLR, authorising cancellation of the relevant entries. Provided that electronic validation is successful, the legal charge entries are removed automatically from the register. Once the instruction is received by HMLR, the electronic process takes only a matter of seconds to complete. If discharge is being done electronically, a revised form of undertaking should be given. This should state that, in consideration of the buyer completing the purchase, the seller's conveyancer will discharge the specified mortgage to enable the lender concerned to submit an ED to HMLR. The undertaking should then require the seller's conveyancer to forward a copy of the notification from the lender that an ED has been sent.

Link to practice

The following provides an example of a discharge undertaking in registered land where the mortgage is to be discharged electronically:

"In consideration of your today completing the purchase of [address] we hereby undertake forthwith to pay over to [name of lender] the money required to discharge the mortgage dated [date] and to forward a copy of the lender's letter confirming successful redemption of their charge and lodgement of an electronic discharge at the Land Registry as soon as we receive it from the lender."

Unregistered land

In unregistered land transactions, the mortgage deed itself must be receipted. Care should be taken to check the execution of the receipt and, in the case of non-building society mortgages, the identity of the payer. Receipts made under **s115 LPA 1925** require the receipt to name the person making the repayment. In the absence of any statement to the contrary and unless the payer is the person entitled to the equity of redemption (i.e. the owner of the legal estate at that date), the receipt will not operate to discharge the mortgage but to transfer it to the payer.

Example

Imagine that S is selling property which is subject to a mortgage to M Bank. The buyer, B, completes the purchase on 4 May. The mortgage to M Bank is repaid by S using the proceeds of sale on 5 May. The receipt names S as the payer, but on 5 May S is not the owner of the property. The receipt therefore operates not to discharge the mortgage but to put S into M Bank's position as mortgagee.

There are, of course, situations where this will not happen, for example, where the receipt expressly stipulates that the receipt is not so to operate.

Building society receipts using the form prescribed by the **Building Societies Act 1986** do not name the payer and so do not create the problem. In other cases, the transferee of the mortgage may be estopped from relying on the transfer (e.g. in ***Cumberland Court v Taylor* [1963]** where the conveyance stated that the seller/transferee of the mortgage sold the property "free from incumbrances"). The buyer's conveyancer must be able to recognise a possible transfer of mortgage and raise requisitions to ensure that the situation is acceptable to the buyer.

6.6 Voluntary dispositions

A voluntary disposition (e.g. a deed of gift) is a perfectly adequate link in a chain of unregistered title. In certain circumstances, however, such a disposition may be set aside and the buyer must check that the title is not, nor could be, so affected. In unregistered land, a voluntary disposition is readily discovered when investigating title.

In registered land, the proprietorship register will contain a "price paid" entry after 1 April 2000. It may be apparent from this register entry that the price paid by the proprietor was nil or an amount which was obviously an undervalue (well below market value). If this is the case, the provisions of the **Insolvency Act 1986** (**IA 1986**) must be borne in mind. The same would apply if there was an **Insolvency Act** entry on the proprietorship register. HMLR sometimes used to make such entries on first registration where such registration was based on a transaction at an undervalue. In such situations, the problems mentioned below need to be considered.

If a buyer in good faith is totally unaware of a voluntary disposition (perhaps because it took place in registered land and no note appears in the proprietorship register), the buyer is generally protected, as discussed below.

A voluntary disposition is one made by gift (e.g. by a deed of gift) or at an undervalue. In certain circumstances, the voluntary disposition can be set aside by a court on application by the donor's/seller's trustee in bankruptcy. This would mean that the trustee could reclaim the property from the current owner. It is therefore important to know whether there is a possibility of a voluntary disposition being set aside.

s339 IA 1986 gives the court power, on the application of the trustee in bankruptcy, to set aside a gift or an undervalue transaction should the donor or seller become bankrupt within **five years** after the date of the transaction.

If the seller is a company the time limit is **two years** and the transaction may be set aside by the liquidator on the company's insolvency under **s238 IA 1986**.

The **Insolvency (No. 2) Act 1994** (**I(No.2) A 1994**) amends **IA 1986** to provide protection to a subsequent buyer who buys in good faith and for value (previously only buyers without notice of the relevant circumstances were protected and there was considerable doubt as to what would constitute notice).

If the subsequent buyer, however, is **related to or associated with the person who became bankrupt** (or company which became insolvent) or if the buyer knew that insolvency proceedings would be taking place, the buyer is not protected.

In spite of the protection given by the **Insolvency (No. 2) Act 1994** (**I(No.2) A 1994**), the question still remains: knowledge of what specifically would cause the buyer to lose their protection? The Law Society has printed guidance (backed by counsel's opinion) to the effect that so long as the buyer really is acting in good faith, they will be protected. However, some conveyancers feel that they should not proceed with a purchase if they discover that there was a voluntary disposition by an individual within the last five years.

It is therefore advisable, when presented with a title which indicates that a voluntary disposition has been made within the last five years, to require, at the seller's expense:

- a statutory declaration from the donor to be provided stating that, at the time of the disposition, the donor was solvent and did not become insolvent as a result of making the disposition;
- an insurance policy indemnifying the buyer and their mortgagee from loss arising from the donor's insolvency;
- a clear bankruptcy search against the donor.

Dispositions made to defeat the other spouse's or civil partner's claim to financial relief under the **Matrimonial Causes Act 1973** or **CPA 2004** may be set aside unless made for valuable consideration to a purchaser in good faith without notice of such intention. A spouse's or civil partner's claim for a property adjustment order is registrable, and if registered this would be notice of the problem.

Some additional practical points to remember in connection with insolvency considerations are outlined below.

(1) It is important to appreciate that, once five years has elapsed (in the case of an individual), a voluntary disposition cannot be set aside.

Example

Therefore, if investigating an unregistered title where there was a deed of gift made more than five years ago, you would need to make a land charges search against the name of the donor. This would not only cover their period of ownership, but would also have to cover a period of five years after the gift was made. As long as there were no bankruptcy entries, it would be safe to proceed. If bankruptcy entries were revealed by the search, you would need to ensure that no application to set aside was going to be made, or had been made, by the trustee in bankruptcy.

(2) The UK Finance Mortgage Lenders' Handbook contains provisions which must be taken into account in practice where there is a mortgage lender. The Lenders' Handbook provides that if the title is subject to a deed of gift or transaction at an apparent undervalue completed within five years of the proposed mortgage then the conveyancer must be satisfied that the lender will acquire its interest in good faith and will be protected under the provisions of **I(No.2) A 1994** against the security being set aside. It further provides that where

the conveyancer is unable to give an unqualified certificate of title, they must arrange indemnity insurance.

Further, the conveyancer must obtain clear bankruptcy searches against **all** parties to any deed of gift or transaction at an apparent undervalue.

Activity

Follow the link below to the Lender's Handbook and check and make notes on 5.16 (Insolvency Considerations) to ensure that you fully understand the lender's requirements

https://lendershandbook.ukfinance.org.uk/lenders-handbook/

(3) As explained above, a gift could potentially be set aside should the donor become bankrupt within five years after the date of the transaction. It should be appreciated that since 1 April 1998, deeds of gift have triggered first registration of a previously unregistered title. Therefore, a current buyer's conveyancer looking at an epitome of unregistered title, should not come across a deed of gift dated within the last five years, since it would have triggered compulsory first registration of the title.

Activity

Just in case you were thinking that transactions at an undervalue and conflict-of-interest are only found in your coursebook, follow the link below to a Law Society *Gazette* article dated 15 April 2021, "Solicitor fined for undervalue property sale between couple".

https://www.lawgazette.co.uk/news/solicitor-fined-for-undervalued-property-sale-between-couple/5108128.article

6.7 Disposition by an attorney

Where there is a disposition in the title by an attorney, the buyer would have to check:

- that the power of attorney was validly executed;
- that the particular transaction came within the scope of the power; and
- that the power had not been revoked.

6.7.1 Types of power of attorney

A power of attorney is a legal document whereby one person (called the donor) gives others (their attorneys) the right to act on their behalf. Powers of attorney may be used for a variety of reasons. For instance, in relation to conveyancing, a client might want to appoint an attorney to execute documents on their behalf because they know they will be out of the country at the relevant times. A client might want to make a power of attorney so that others (e.g. their children) can deal with their affairs if they become mentally incapable in the future. As powers of attorney need to cater for different circumstances, there are different types. In order to make a power of attorney, the client must have mental capacity at the time they make it (i.e. they must be capable of making decisions for themself). Anyone can be an attorney as long as they are capable of making decisions and over 18, although in some cases someone who is bankrupt cannot be an attorney. Solicitors and trust corporations (such as banks) can act as attorneys, as can relatives or friends. A donor can appoint more than one attorney if they so wish.

Link to practice

A person appointed as an attorney can only do acts which the power authorises them to do.

Example

They could not sign the transfer for the sale of 66 The Paddocks if the power only authorised them to execute documents relating to the sale of 55 High Street.
Thus, it is very important to read the power of attorney document supplied to ensure that the transaction in front of you is actually authorised.

In relation to investigation of an unregistered title, there may be a past transaction involving a power of attorney within the chain of title.

Alternatively, powers of attorney may be relevant in a current transaction, in which case they must be taken into account during the conveyancing process. If the contract or transfer has been executed by an attorney acting on behalf of the seller, for instance, the buyer's conveyancer will require a certified copy of the power in order the check it and in order to send a copy to HMLR with the registration application.

A power of attorney may be:

- a **general** power, under which the attorney's power to act on behalf of the donor is unrestricted (except, of course, by the general law);
- a **special** power, which restricts the attorney, perhaps to executing deeds in respect of a specified property only;
- a **trustee** power, which ought to be used if a co-owner is executing by their attorney or in other situations where the land is held on trust;
- a **lasting** power, which is designed to cover the possibility of the donor becoming mentally incapable. Great care is needed when drafting this type of power to reduce the risk of fraud; the Law Society has issued detailed guidance regarding this.

Activity

Follow the link below to the Law Society's 'Private client' resources:

https://www.lawsociety.org.uk/topics/private-client/

Look through the resources and read and make notes on the guidance relating to mental capacity and vulnerable clients.

Link to practice

Lasting powers of attorney (LPAs) replaced **enduring** powers of attorney (EPA) from **1 October 2007**. However, enduring powers that were signed and witnessed before October 2007 can continue to be used.

Thus, if you are ever provided with an EPA, you must carefully check the date that it was signed. If it was signed after 1 October 2007, it is not valid and does not confer the appropriate authority on the attorney.

Under the **Mental Capacity Act 2005** (**MCA 2005**), LPAs were introduced and are the current means of granting a power of attorney which survives the donor's mental incapacity. It is necessary under such powers for a prescribed person (such as solicitor, social worker or doctor) to certify that, at the time of its execution, the donor had capacity to make the lasting power of attorney. Such a person is known as the "certificate provider". Note that CILEX have given guidance on the rights of CILEX Fellows to act as certificate providers – see https://www.cilex.org.uk/membership/practice_advice/certificate_provider_for_lpa/act_as_cp_for_lpa.

There are two types of lasting power that can be made:

- a health and welfare LPA; and/or
- a property and financial affairs LPA.

A donor can choose to make one type or both. It is therefore possible for donees each to be given specific powers for particular aspects of the donor's affairs (e.g. a professional solicitor or accountant could be appointed to deal with the donor's finances and a family member appointed for health and welfare decisions). The LPA can provide for replacement donees on the occurrence of a specific event, for instance, death of the donee, and thus save the power from lapsing if the donee dies.

Link to practice

Many people decide to appoint, say, adult children under the LPA so that they can assist them with their affairs if and when required in the future. Many people, especially younger people, may appoint their spouse or partner. This latter choice could potentially create a problem if they jointly own property with that same person, one party loses capacity and the property is to be sold. This issue arises because jointly owned property is held on trust and two signatures would be required to give a receipt for capital money for overreaching purposes. One practical way of overcoming this issue would be for each of them to appoint different attorneys or to appoint two attorneys with the power to act jointly and severally, for example the other spouse plus another person.

The old EPA would operate as a general power while the donor was still mentally capable. It had to be registered at the Court of Protection when the donor became incapable in order for it to continue to be effective. LPAs must be registered with the Office of the Public Guardian **before they can be used**, even if the donor still has mental capacity to provide instructions to their donee. It is therefore necessary to see **evidence of registration**. The Court of Protection has the power to revoke an LPA (once the donor has lost capacity) on specified grounds, such as the donee not acting in the best interests of the donor.

When acting for a buyer from an attorney under an LPA, the conveyancer should check that:

- the power is registered and is still in force. A register of lasting powers is maintained by the Public Guardian and can be searched to check that the power remains in force;

- the identity of the attorney is clear;
- the attorney is acting within the scope of their authority. In particular, the third party should check whether the authority is limited by any restrictions or conditions.

An office copy of the LPA is evidence of its contents and the fact that it has been registered. If it transpires that the power was not valid, the transaction between the attorney and the third party will still be valid unless the third party was aware that the power was invalid or was aware that there were circumstances that would have rendered the attorney unable to act.

A buyer from the third party (i.e. a subsequent buyer) in good faith for valuable consideration can presume that the transaction between the attorney and the third party was valid provided that **one** of the following conditions applies:

- the transaction between the attorney and the third party was completed within 12 months of the date on which the lasting power was registered; **or**
- the third party makes a statutory declaration, either before or within three months after completion of the purchase by the subsequent buyer, that they had no reason to doubt that the attorney had authority to dispose of the property at the time of the transaction.

6.7.2 Powers of attorney made by trustees

The **Trustee Delegation Act 1999** (**TDA 1999**) relates to where one or more trustees (e.g. co-owners of land) appoint someone else to act on their behalf by power of attorney. It makes the following provisions:

(1) **TDA 1999** provides that for dispositions dated after 29 February 2000, a receipt for capital money will overreach beneficial interests only if the attorney acts with at least one other person. This means that a receipt clause in a disposition (e.g. transfer) by joint proprietors is not acceptable for this purpose if the disposition is executed by only one person both as proprietor and as attorney for the other proprietor(s), or by one person as attorney for all the proprietors. There must be two signatures to effect overreaching. One co-owner should not therefore appoint the other to act as their attorney, nor should both co-owners appoint the same attorney.

(2) A trustee power, in the form specified in **TDA 1999**, should be used.

(3) General, special and LPAs can now be used for trustee purposes when the donor also has a beneficial interest in the land and if the attorney certifies that the donor has a beneficial interest in the land. Generally, this certificate would appear in the transfer deed. If the attorney cannot certify this, a trustee power must be used.

Link to practice

Where the statement as to beneficial ownership is made in the transfer deed, it will be along these lines:

(Name of attorney) confirms that (name of donor of the power) has a beneficial interest in the property at the date of this transfer

Alternatively, the attestation clause in the transfer could be adapted. It would read along these lines:

Signed as a deed by (name of donor of power) who has a beneficial interest in the property at the date of this transfer, acting by his attorney (name of attorney) in the presence of (witness)

Activity

Follow the link below to HMLR "Practice guide 9: powers of attorney and registered land":

https://www.gov.uk/government/publications/powers-of-attorney-and-registered-land/practice-guide-9-powers-of-attorney-and-registered-land

Read it to ensure that you understand the position in relation to powers of attorney and registered land in more detail.

6.7.3 Revocation of a power of attorney

The question of revocation can be problematic. The power can usually be revoked expressly. A power of attorney would also be revoked by the donor's death or bankruptcy. In the case of powers other than the LPA, it will also be revoked by the donor becoming mentally incapacitated. If the transaction is directly from the attorney, the buyer will be protected if the power has, in fact, been revoked providing they did not know of the revocation. A note of warning should be sounded, however, as knowledge of one of the matters giving rise to automatic revocation will amount to knowledge of revocation itself. All the buyer needs to do to be safe is to be sure of their own state of knowledge.

Example

If the buyer is one stage removed from the attorney – for example, the attorney (A) sold to X who is now selling to a buyer (B) – B's protection depends on the state of mind of X. B will be protected if A disposed of the property to X within 12 months of the date of the power or if, before or within three months of the sale by X to B, X makes a statutory declaration that they did not know of the revocation of the power or of any facts which would have given rise to the revocation (**s5(4) Powers of Attorney Act 1971**).

Where the land is to be registered, a buyer from an attorney may be required by HMLR to provide a statutory declaration or a statement of truth as to their lack of knowledge of revocation at completion when they apply for registration of the transaction, unless they bought within 12 months of the power being granted. There are other options which will be accepted by HMLR in place of a statutory declaration or statement of truth, such as a certificate from the conveyancer acting for the buyer that the buyer has no knowledge of revocation.

Where a conveyancer is applying to register a transaction made in exercise of a power of attorney, the conveyancer must supply HMLR with the original or a certified copy of the power and a certified copy should be certified as a true copy on each page.

6.8 Disposition by a deputy

Where someone has lost mental capacity, their affairs may be dealt with by someone else. This may be an attorney under an EPA or LPA.

But where there is no EPA or LPA in place, different considerations apply. Once a person has lost mental capacity, they can no longer make a power of attorney. It is possible to apply to the Court of Protection for a decision to be made about a specific matter (e.g. the sale of a specific property) but where there is a wider need to make continuing decisions, someone can be appointed as a deputy by the Court of Protection under **MCA 2005**. Prior to **MCA 2005**, a deputy was called a "receiver" and was appointed under previous legislation.

The deputy is usually a friend or a family member, although the Court of Protection has power to appoint a professional deputy if there is nobody else to act. The deputy can make decisions about such matters as property and financial affairs.

The deputy will deal with the person's affairs under the supervision of the Public Guardian and the court, which will give them defined powers in the Deputy Order, and can also require them to seek consent for certain acts.

Sometimes the deputy will be granted authority to deal with property and affairs with the powers of an absolute owner and this will extend to selling property. In this case, an application to the court will not generally be necessary before sale.

Link to practice

If the deputy is required to seek the authority of the court before sale of a property, this must be done as a first step where the property is to be sold. Having obtained the court's authority, where required, the deputy can then enter into the sale contract in the name of the seller *"acting by his deputy pursuant to an Order/Direction of the Court of Protection dated xxxxx"*. The address stated in the contract should be that of the deputy. The contract can be signed by the deputy followed by the words *"as deputy for xxxxx"*.

The contract should contain a special condition along the following lines:

"Copies of the said Order have been supplied to the buyer's solicitors and shall be deemed to be conclusive evidence of the seller's authority to sell. The buyer and his solicitors shall not be entitled to raise any requisitions or objections thereto."

The seller will appear in the transfer as:

xxxx [the name of the seller who has lost capacity] acting by xxxx [the name of the deputy] pursuant to an Order/Direction made by the Court of Protection dated xxxx.

The deputy must sign the transfer both in their own name and the name of the person who has lost capacity.

6.8.1 Replacement trustee

There are some variations where jointly owned property is involved. If one or more of the co-owners (trustees) becomes incapable of managing their property affairs, they will not be able to sign any transfer. If the property is to be sold, an application will have to be made for an order for a replacement trustee. A person appointed as deputy may be appointed as the replacement trustee but this requires a separate application since the deputy and trustee functions are separate roles. Where the incapable person is the only remaining trustee, an application needs to be made for two replacement trustees so that there are two trustees for the purposes, where required, of any sale. The application is made to the Court of Protection using a standard form (COP1) (see https://www.gov.uk/government/publications/apply-to-make-decisions-on-someones-behalf-form-cop1) with prescribed supporting evidence. Where the land is registered, this evidence includes an official copy of the register entries. If the land is unregistered, a copy of the conveyance or other trust deed must be included.

On a dealing by a deputy in registered land, HMLR will require a copy of the order authorising the sale and confirming the deputy's authority to act.

Note that a deputy is different from an attorney, who will have been appointed by the donor themself when they did have capacity. The deputy cannot trump the jurisdiction of the attorney.

6.9 Capacity and covenants for title

When checking through abstracts and epitomes of old deeds, reference to the capacity in which the seller sold the property and which were used before **LP(MP) A 1994** will often be found.

Terminology alert!

"Capacity" in this context relates to various covenants for title which would be implied into the conveyance. These are promises implied by statute and are similar to the covenants for title that relaced them (for example full and limited title guarantee).

Note however that here we are not talking about "capacity" as in "mental capacity".

These are mentioned here in case these phrases are encountered in old deeds.

Commonly met capacities included:

- **as beneficial owner**: this was used by a sole seller. Under **LP(JT)A 1964**, sale by a survivor of joint tenants should be in this capacity;
- **as trustees**: this was only acceptable for co-sellers, due to the need to effect overreaching. Sometimes, trustees conveyed "as beneficial owners", as this implied a greater number of covenants;

- **as personal representatives**: PRs who sell the property used this capacity. Suppose the PR does not sell, but becomes a beneficiary or trustee of estate property. In such situations, the PR should first assent to themself then sell "as beneficial owner" or "as trustees" (bearing in mind that at least two trustees are required to overreach). It is not acceptable for the PRs to sell "as beneficial owners" or "as trustees" if no assent was made (***Re King's Will Trusts* [1964]**);
- **as mortgagee**: this capacity was used by a mortgagee exercising its power of sale.

Example

The words of capacity were stated in the conveyance immediately before the operative words, for example:

The seller as beneficial owner hereby conveys to the buyer . . .

6.10 Execution by non-individuals

It is important for the buyer's conveyancer to check the format and execution of all deeds forming the root and chain of an unregistered title. More generally, the attestation clause of any transfer or deed should be checked carefully.

Where a deed is not executed by an individual, the format of the execution clause will vary, and the conveyancer must check that the correct formalities have been followed.

For instance, where a deed is executed by a company, it will need to comply with specified requirements relating to execution by companies. Normally the deed will be executed by the affixing of the company seal or by being signed by two specified officers of the company (a director and the company secretary or by two directors). Where the deed is executed by two officers it must be expressed to be executed by the company.

Where a deed is to be executed by a director and company secretary, they must be two separate people (i.e. the same person cannot sign in both capacities). From 6 April 2008, a deed can also be executed by a single director as long as the director's signature is witnessed (i.e. "executed as a deed by . . . Limited acting by a director" and then signed in the presence of a witness who adds their name and address).

There are also rules for other types of non-individuals such as charities. Note that in a disposition of land owned by a charity, the consent of the Charity Commissioners or a court order is sometimes required. For dispositions where the consent of the Charity Commissioners is not required, the deed should contain an appropriate certificate.

Where a deed is executed by an attorney, the attorney may execute the deed on behalf of the donor by signing their own signature. Alternatively, they can sign in the name of the donor of the power. In either case, the execution has to comply with **s1 LP(MP)A 1989**.

Activity

Follow the link below to HMLR "Practice guide 8: execution of deeds":

https://www.gov.uk/government/publications/execution-of-deeds

Check how a deed can be signed by a company after 6 April 2008. Always check this Practice guide when you have a document being signed by someone other than an individual.

6.11 Mental capacity

So far, this chapter has considered matters of legal capacity to own and deal in land. However, we do need to consider in outline an important topic for the property practitioner, that of mental capacity. We will give only an outline of some key considerations here.

There are a number of linked threads:

- whether the client has sufficient mental capacity to instruct their conveyancer;
- whether they are a vulnerable client;
- whether the client is being subject to undue influence.

All practitioners must ensure that their clients have sufficient mental capacity to instruct them and that the client is not being subject to any pressure from a third party, such as a family member or carer.

The Law Society summarises the legal test for capacity to make decisions as follows:

"A lack of capacity cannot be established merely because of a person's age, appearance, condition or an aspect of their behaviour. A diagnosis or condition does not mean the client lacks mental capacity to make the decision.

Section 2(1) of the Mental Capacity Act 2005 (MCA 2005) provides that a person lacks capacity to make a decision if:

1. they cannot:
    - understand information relevant to the decision or
    - retain that information or
    - use or weigh that information as part of the process of making the decision or
    - communicate the decision (by any means)

and

2. their inability to do so is because of an impairment or disturbance in the functioning in the person's mind or brain

Capacity is both decision specific and time specific. Capacity will vary depending on the decision being made, the time it is made, and the circumstances of the person being assessed.

An impairment or disturbance can be temporary, or fluctuate. The relevant time for establishing whether one exists is the time the decision needs to be made.

Information relevant to a decision will include:

- the nature of the decision
- the purpose for which it is needed
- the effect(s) of the decision
- the reasonably foreseeable consequences of deciding one way or another or of making no decision at all (MCA 2005 section 3(4)). This may include the available options, any alternatives and that the person has a choice

You must explain the relevant information in ways that are appropriate to the person's circumstances, using the most appropriate form of communication to help the person understand. Retaining information for even a short time may be enough for some decisions."

(from "Working with Clients Who May Lack Mental Capacity" – link available in Practice Box on the next page.)

A client may understand what they are doing (and thus have mental capacity), but the conveyancer still needs to be wary of whether the client is vulnerable for some other reason and/or is being subjected to some form of pressure (undue influence) to enter into the transaction. A common example in a conveyancing context might be a relative or carer trying to force a person to sell their home and possibly transfer all or part of the sale proceeds to the relative or carer. Conveyancers should therefore look out for this type of transaction and consider:

- Is the client moving into residential or another care setting?
- Who is giving instructions?
- Has the conveyancer met the client on their own?
- Is a family member or carer insisting on being present for all client meetings?

There are various circumstances which could make a client "vulnerable". These include clients who lack mental capacity to provide instructions, those who do have capacity but need extra support owing to mental and/or physical disabilities, and those who might be vulnerable to undue influence or pressure. Broadly, undue influence is the situation where a person has been put under pressure or coerced into taking a course of action which they did not want to take. A particular example of this is where a co-owing spouse may be pressured into charging the matrimonial home to secure their spouse's business debts. This is the classic ***Etridge*** situation (see **Chapter 2**).

Link to practice

The Law Society has released a number of resources in this area, which conveyancers should read:

"Meeting the Needs of Vulnerable Clients"

https://www.lawsociety.org.uk/Topics/Client-care/Guides/Meeting-the-needs-of-vulnerable-clients

"This guidance focuses on three broad categories of vulnerable clients:

- clients who have capacity to make decisions and give you instructions, but need extra support to do this because of mental and/or physical disabilities – see identifying vulnerable clients and enabling vulnerable clients to use your services
- clients who lack mental capacity to make decisions and provide you with instructions, for whom you must follow a range of statutory and other safeguards – see our guidance on working with clients who may lack mental capacity
- clients who are vulnerable to undue influence, undue pressure or duress and who may or may not have mental capacity to make decisions and provide you with instructions – see influence and undue influence."

"Working with Clients Who May Lack Mental Capacity"

https://www.lawsociety.org.uk/Topics/Client-care/Guides/Working-with-clients-who-may-lack-mental-capacity

"Mental capacity is the ability to make a particular decision. This includes both day-to-day decisions and more significant decisions that may have legal consequences, such as:

- buying, selling, mortgaging or charging a property
- entering into a contract
- making a will
- making a lasting power of attorney
- making a gift
- bringing or defending legal proceedings
- seeking a divorce

Capacity is decision-specific, so a client could have capacity to make a simple decision but not a complex one, or one that has significant consequences or carries significant risk.

The client may have capacity to make certain types of decisions, but not others. For example they may have capacity to make decisions about where they live and their care, but not have capacity to manage their finances to pay for the arrangements."

"Working with Vulnerable Clients Case Studies"

https://www.lawsociety.org.uk/Topics/Client-care/Guides/Working-with-vulnerable-clients-case-studies

Link to practice

Working out whether someone has the capacity to instruct a solicitor can be a complex task. It is very important if you are at the beginning of your legal career to ensure that you are not in a position where you are asked to see a client alone who might not be in a position to instruct you properly. Please ensure that you ask for support and assistance if you are placed in this position. If you are uncertain about whether a client is able to instruct you for any reason, always seek the assistance of a more experienced colleague and do not see the client alone.

Activity

This is an area of practice where making comprehensive attendance notes of meetings and discussions is essential.

For an example of the approach of the court to a case involving these issues, see the following case:

***Thorpe v Fellowes Solicitors LLP* [2011]**

In this case the court considered the attendance notes that a solicitor had taken during conversations about a property sale with an elderly client. Negligence was alleged but the court found in favour of the firm.

Read the judgment:

https://www.bailii.org/ew/cases/EWHC/QB/2011/61.html

The Court observed: *"A solicitor is generally only required to make inquiries as to a person's capacity to contract if there are circumstances such as to raise doubt as to this in the mind of a reasonably competent practitioner; see,* Jackson & Powell *at 11-221 and by analogy* Hall v Estate of Bruce Bennett [2003] WTLR 827. *This position is reflected in the guidance given to solicitors in* The Guide to the Professional Conduct of Solicitors *(8th edition, 1999) which was in force at the relevant time, where it is said that there is a presumption of capacity, and that only if this is called into question should a solicitor seek a doctor's report (with the client's consent) 'However, you should also make your own assessment and not rely solely upon the doctor's assessment' (at 24.04)."* [para 75]

What do you think of the attendance notes that the solicitor took?

As we have seen above, if someone has lost mental capacity, their attorney will instruct the firm if a power of attorney was entered into prior to capacity being lost. If someone has lost mental capacity and has not entered into a power of attorney, it will be necessary for a Deputy to be appointed to deal with their affairs.

Link to practice

It is important for a conveyancer to keep in mind their own competence levels when considering whether a Deputy might need to be appointed. This is typically work which would be done by the private client department. However, the conveyancer might be tempted to deal with it to ensure that a conveyancing transaction proceeds.

The process to appoint a Deputy takes time and money. For more information, follow this link:

https://www.gov.uk/become-deputy

Generally, it is not necessary for an attorney or a Deputy to apply to the Court of Protection for consent to sell a property if the Deputyship order authorises the Deputy to make decisions about the "property and affairs" or if the LPA or EPA authorises the attorney to deal with the property and affairs of the donor. The sale must be in the best interests of the person lacking capacity – this may well be the case if it is necessary to sell the property to fund care fees. However, if there is any doubt, the Deputy or attorney should apply to the Court of Protection for consent to the sale. The conveyancer acting on a sale should always be mindful of these issues.

6.12 Chapter summary

(1) If buying from trustees of land where a trust requires consent, the buyer needs only to ensure that evidence of the consent is produced to them and that the purchase money is paid to two trustees or a trust corporation to effect overreaching.

(2) Whenever property is conveyed into the name of co-owners, a trust of land arises automatically.

(3) Where property is conveyed into the name of a single individual but the purchase money is provided by two people, a trust of land will still arise. Details of the beneficial interest are kept off the register of title.

(4) Sale by co-owners:

- **unregistered land** – if there is evidence of severance of a beneficial joint tenancy, a buyer must insist that a second trustee is appointed. If there is no evidence of severance, a buyer is protected by the **Law of Property (Joint Tenants) Act 1964** which provides that if the conveyance by the seller includes a statement that the seller is solely and beneficially interested property, a survivor of two or more joint tenants shall be deemed to be so entitled;
- **registered land** – if there is no Form A restriction on the proprietorship register, a buyer is entitled to assume that the sole surviving registered proprietor is solely entitled to the property and no longer subject of a

trust of land. If there is a Form A restriction on the proprietorship register, a second trustee must be appointed to overreach the beneficial interest on sale. If the property is not being sold, if the co-owner holds the entire legal and beneficial interest, they can remove the Form A restriction upon submission to HMLR of a form ST5 and form RX3. The legal estate of a registered title will be transferred to the surviving co-owner(s) by submission of form DJP to HMLR.

(5) If a sale is by a fiduciary owner and they immediately reacquire the property in their personal capacity, consent must be provided by a court order or the beneficiaries otherwise the transaction could be set aside for breach of trust.

(6) On the death of a legal owner, if the legal title passes through their personal representatives, evidence is needed of their entitlement to sell which will typically either be a grant of probate (where they are appointed as executors under a will) or grant of letters of administration (where the deceased died intestate).

(7) If a personal representative is entitled to a property as a beneficiary, it is still necessary for the personal representative to assent property to themselves.

(8) If the seller is a mortgagee, it must ensure that it has the power of sale and that power of sale has arisen and become exerciseable. If it wishes to sell with vacant possession and the property is a dwelling-house, it must also ensure that it has possession of the property which must be acquired by court order if the mortgagor does not co-operate and leave the dwelling.

(9) A voluntary disposition (for example, deed of gift) is liable to be set aside by a trustee in bankruptcy under the **Insolvency Act 1986** if the donor or seller became bankrupt within five years after the date of the transaction (if the seller is a company the time limit is two years).

(10) If there is a disposition by a legal owner whose attorney signs on their behalf, the buyer must check:

- that the power of attorney is validly executed;
- that the particular transaction came within the scope of the power; and
- that power had not been revoked.

(11) Enduring powers of attorney are still valid if made before 1 October 2007. Following this date, a lasting power of attorney (LPA) is required.

When acting for a buyer from an attorney under an LPA, the conveyancer should check that:

- the power is registered and is still in force. A register of lasting powers is maintained by the Public Guardian and can be searched to check that the power remains in force;
- the identity of the attorney is clear;

- the attorney is acting within the scope of their authority. In particular, the third party should check whether the authority is limited by any restrictions or conditions.

(12) If someone loses mental capacity and has not appointed an attorney, it is necessary to apply to the Court of Protection for the appointment of a deputy if it becomes necessary to sell the person's property. The deputyship order specifies the power of the deputy which may or may not include sale of a property.

(13) It is important for the buyer's conveyancer to check the format and execution of all deeds forming the root and chain of an unregistered title.

(14) When handling a property transaction, the conveyancer must keep in mind:

- whether the client has sufficient mental capacity to instruct their conveyancer;
- whether they are a vulnerable client;
- whether the client is being subject to undue influence.

CHAPTER 7

Planning and building regulations

7.1 Introduction

Before we start looking at pre-contract searches and enquiries in detail in **Chapter 8**, we will now look at planning in more depth. You have to consider all the issues together as your results of the local searches may lead to planning issues, especially when compared with the Property Information Form (PIF) where the seller may have disclosed something relevant. Planning matters are relevant to a buyer, first because it is necessary to check that any changes made to a property have the appropriate planning consent. This is the retrospective aspect of the conveyancer's work. But in addition, a conveyancer acting for a buyer must understand what their buyer client intends to do with the property if the purchase completes and advise if there are likely to be any planning issues or concerns.

We will also look in this chapter at a separate, but related matter of building regulations.

As you will see in **Chapter 8**, the local search will reveal whether there are any planning permissions affecting the property or whether any enforcement notices have been served in respect of the property.

This chapter deals with the matters of planning control which relate specifically to the process of conveyancing. Planning is a complex area and we only discuss the key principles in this chapter.

This chapter will cover:

- planning overview;
- planning law in Wales (in outline);
- meaning of "development";
- obtaining planning permission:
    - permitted development;
    - express planning permission;
    - reserved matters;
    - planning conditions;
    - enforcement – planning;
- conservation area;
- listed buildings:
    - enforcement – breach of listing;
- building regulations:
    - enforcement – building regulations;
- other restrictions affecting development.

7.2 Planning overview

The main legislation affecting planning control is the **Town and Country Planning Act 1990** (**TCPA 1990**), which has been amended many times since that date. It is supplemented by a large number of statutory instruments. The **Planning Act 2008** introduced changes to try and streamline or speed up the system, especially in relation to planning consents for major infrastructure projects such as railways and airports.

The planning system as a whole was also overhauled as a result of the **Localism Act 2011** (**LA 2011**) and the introduction of a National Planning Policy Framework (NPPF) – which was designed to streamline and replace previous planning guidance – but many of the provisions do not directly affect the types of conveyancing transactions dealt with in this course.

In general terms, **LA 2011** was designed to give greater powers to communities, to improve certain aspects of the planning system and to tackle abuses. The provisions relating to the planning system were contained in **Part 6 LA 2011**.

In summary, the planning changes which have been implemented by **LA 2011** are:

(1) Developers have a duty to consult with local communities before submitting plans for certain types of major development (specified in regulations).

(2) Planning authorities are given power to refuse to determine retrospective planning applications where an enforcement notice has been served.

(3) Planning authorities are given increased powers to take enforcement action where a planning breach has been deliberately concealed.

(4) A system of neighbourhood planning has been introduced, involving communities in the planning process; and

(5) There are further changes to the planning regime for nationally significant infrastructure projects.

The government issued a new version of the NPPF in July 2021 and this replaced the earlier versions.

Activity

Follow the link below to the latest NPPF:

https://www.gov.uk/government/publications/national-planning-policy-framework--2

Read pages 1 to 7. What is the approach taken to sustainable development?

7.3 Planning law in Wales

There is one further important general point to make at this stage. If a property is being purchased in Wales, it will be necessary to check whether there are any differences from the planning law which applies in England, as planning is now included within the functions that have been devolved from the UK Parliament to the Welsh Assembly. This is likely to become even more significant in the future.

The Law Commission has been consulting on proposals to simplify and consolidate planning law in Wales and has sought views on the intention to introduce a Welsh

Planning Bill to replace more than 30 Acts and to incorporate secondary legislation and government guidance. The consultation closed at the end of March 2018 and the Law Commission produced its final report to the Welsh Government in November 2018. This work by the Law Commission will lead to the production of a new **Planning Code for Wales**. The Law Commission concluded that planning law in Wales needed to be simplified, consolidated and modernised as it had not been consolidated since 1990 and there had been numerous piecemeal changes since that time. The Welsh Government provided a response in November 2020.

The current divergence of planning law between England and Wales, together with the anticipated future changes, will be important to practitioners dealing with planning aspects of property transactions.

Planning (Wales) Act 2015

The detail of the **Planning (Wales) Act 2015** is outside the scope of this course book. The Act received Royal Assent on 6 July 2015 and is coming into force in stages. A residential conveyancer is unlikely to come across the Act in their day-to-day work as the key purposes of the Act are national and strategic in nature. It introduces a new legal framework for the Welsh Ministers to prepare a national land use plan (the National Development Framework for Wales) and to make provision for the production of Strategic Development Plans to tackle issues such as housing supply and areas for economic growth and regeneration. The Act will provide for planning applications for nationally significant projects to be made to Welsh Ministers.

The planning process will be streamlined and the enforcement and appeal procedures will be improved. In addition, changes will be made in relation to applications to register town and village greens.

7.4 Meaning of "development"

Under the planning legislation, certain activities upon land or changes to land can be carried out only with permission, and therefore a prospective buyer will want to know whether their intended use of the land will be permitted. Where a buyer intends to continue the present use of the property and does not propose to make any changes to it, they will merely wish to know that the present use of the property, and any alterations which were made in the past, are authorised. They can then be sure that the local planning authority will not take any enforcement action to remedy a previous breach of planning control. In practice, if the present use has been continuing for some years, and the property has not recently been altered, there are likely to be few problems. There are cases, however, where particular attention will need to be paid to the provisions of the planning legislation:

- where a buyer is buying an empty plot of land in order to build on it, for example, building a new house;

- where a buyer is buying an existing building but plans some alteration or change of use after completion, for example, to build an extension or to use an existing house as a doctor's surgery;
- where a buyer is buying a building which has recently been erected or altered.

In each of these cases, it is necessary to ascertain first which changes to land require permission. **TCPA 1990** states that permission is required for any development of land and **s55** defines development as being *the carrying out of building, engineering, mining or other operations in, on, over or under land, or the making of any material change in the use of any buildings or other land.*

Development can therefore be the carrying on of any physical **operations** or a **material change of use**.

(a) Operations

Operations include the erection of new buildings, structural alterations or additions to buildings except for those affecting only the interior and not materially affecting the external appearance. Works which increase space below ground level also require consent, as does work which adds mezzanine floors to certain commercial properties.

The definition of development also includes demolition works, but most types of demolition are classed as permitted development and do not therefore require express planning permission. Where demolition works are not covered by the permitted development rights, express planning consent will be required. One example is where the demolition works would be likely to have a significant effect on the environment. Further details are beyond the scope of this manual but would have to be checked if demolition was to be carried out.

(b) Material change of use

The question of what is "material" is one of fact and degree in each case, but would seem to include only relatively major changes.

Link to practice

The definition includes the change of use of a single dwelling-house to two or more separate dwellings (e.g. the conversion of a house into flats).

The use of a building within the curtilage of a dwelling-house for any purpose incidental to the enjoyment of the house (e.g. a shed or greenhouse) is not development.

7.4.1 Use classes

The **Town and Country Planning (Use Classes) Order 1987** (as amended) puts uses of land and buildings into various categories known as "Use Classes" which are detailed below. "Change of use" can occur within the same Use Class or from one Use Class to another.

A change of use within a Use Class category does not require formal planning permission.

The relevant building regulations (see below) also need to be considered for any proposed change of use. The current Use Classes were last updated on 1 September 2020.

A change of use within any single class of use set out in the **1987 Order** does not constitute "development".

Example

There are a number of Use Classes. Let's consider Class E – Commercial, Business and Service:

- **E(a)** Display or retail sale of goods, other than hot food
- **E(b**) Sale of food and drink for consumption (mostly) on the premises
- **E(c)** Provision of:
    - **E(c)(i)** Financial services,
    - **E(c)(ii)** Professional services (other than health or medical services), or
    - **E(c)(iii**) Other appropriate services in a commercial, business or service locality
- **E(d)** Indoor sport, recreation or fitness (not involving motorised vehicles or firearms or use as a swimming pool or skating rink)
- **E(e)** Provision of medical or health services (except the use of premises attached to the residence of the consultant or practitioner)
- **E(f)** Creche, day nursery or day centre (not including a residential use)

- **E(g)** Uses which can be carried out in a residential area without detriment to its amenity:
  - **E(g)(i)** Offices to carry out any operational or administrative functions
  - **E(g)(ii)** Research and development of products or processes
  - **E(g)(iii)** Industrial processes

The above means that it is possible to change premises from a retail shop (Use Class E(a)) to an accountancy firm (Use Class E(c)(ii) Professional services) without the need to apply for planning permission.

Dwelling houses fall within Use Class C. Generally, the Use Classes are not directly relevant to residential conveyancing, but are essential to commercial conveyancing. However, if a client is buying a residential property and wants to use part of it for commercial or business purposes, for example, the conveyancer should always check that the property can be used for its intended purpose from a planning point of view.

Note that a number of well-known Use Classes were revoked on 1 September 2020 including Class A (which included shops in Use Class A1) and B1 which included use of premises as offices.

Activity

Follow the link below to the Planning Portal website. Look at the content of the Use Classes. You will not need to know them in detail for residential conveyancing but you must be able to recognise them and their significance

https://www.planningportal.co.uk

7.5 Obtaining planning permission

If a developer's plans will involve development, either building operations or a change of use, they will have to seek planning permission. This can be given either by means of a deemed permission under a General Permitted Development Order or by express planning permission from the local planning authority.

7.5.1 Permitted development

Certain types of works can be done without the need to apply for express planning permission and these are called "permitted development rights". The relevant provisions governing permitted development rights in England are contained in the **Town and Country Planning (General Permitted Development) (England) Order 2015** (**TCP(GPD)O 2015**). Permitted development rights in Wales are set out in the **Town and Country Planning (General Permitted Development) Order 1995** (amended in relation to Wales on a number of occasions since 1995), which is similar in its provisions and effect.

From April 2012, it is also possible that permission might be given without the need for an express application, by means of a neighbourhood development order under **LA 2011**. These will be examined briefly below. There are also other types of development orders, such as local development orders, which can be issued by local planning authorities to permit certain specified development without express planning consent in their areas, but in practice the most important permitted development rights are under **TCP(GPD)O 2015**.

TCP(GPD)O 2015 contains a number of classes of permitted development, which may be undertaken without the need to obtain express permission of the local planning authority, providing the limitations within each class are observed.

Some examples of permitted development are:

- certain development within the curtilage of a dwelling-house such as the erection of extensions and porches;
- certain minor operations such as the erection of gates, walls and fences;
- certain changes of use between different Use Classes (see above).

Link to practice

If you are acting for a client who is purchasing a barn conversion, you will need to be aware of Class Q which is an order within the general permitted development rights.

The purpose of Class Q is to allow rural communities to convert agricultural buildings into family homes. In 2018, the rules were relaxed to increase the maximum number of new homes capable of being created from existing agricultural buildings from three to five. There are restrictions that apply which you would need to check if you are acting on such a transaction.

The following is a useful resource if you need more information:

https://www.planninginsight.co.uk/wp-content/uploads/2021/03/Class-Q-%E2%80%93-Agricultural-buildings-to-dwellinghouses-guidance-2021.pdf

There are conditions and restrictions set out in **TCP(GPD)O 2015** and these must be carefully checked to ensure that the permitted development rights actually apply in any particular case.

Link to practice

For instance, there are height limits in relation to fences and size limits in relation to home extensions.

Single-storey rear extensions must not extend beyond the rear of the original house by more than 3 metres for an attached house or by more than 4 metres for a detached house. The limit is increased to 6 metres if an attached house and 8 metres if a detached house, although the increased limits do not apply to land which is in certain designated areas such as conservation areas and national parks.

Extensions to be built under the increased limits (between 3 metres and 6 metres or between 4 metres and 8 metres) are subject to a neighbour consultation scheme. If objections are received, the proposed works might not be allowed. There are other limitations which apply to single storey extensions, such as restrictions on height and materials. Rear extensions of more than one storey must not extend beyond the rear wall of the original house by more than 3 metres or be within 7 metres of any boundary opposite the rear wall of the house. Again, there are additional limitations which apply. The limits and conditions on permitted development rights are numerous and must be checked in line with the individual case. All limitations need to be checked in line with the particular building proposals.

Go to the Planning Portal to check the detail:

https://www.planningportal.co.uk/permission/common-projects/extensions/planning-permission

7.5.2 Limitations on permitted development

Note that permitted development rights have been modified in some areas, such as National Parks and World Heritage sites. There may be further restrictions which do not allow the permitted change of use, for example if the property is within a conservation area (see below) or is a listed building (see below). In addition, some changes of use are subject to a prior approval procedure with the local planning authority which may typically include matters relating to parking, flooding and highways.

The local planning authority does not have to adopt **TCP(GPD)O 2015** throughout its district and can pass an **Art 4** direction that **TCP(GPD)O 2015** will be restricted in whole or in part in relation to its area. For example, it is common for an **Art 4** direction to exclude permitted development rights in conservation areas because the authority wishes to retain control over the development which would otherwise be permitted.

It is also possible for an **Art 4** direction to remove permitted development rights in relation to a change of use (or both operational development and change of use). The direction can cover an area of any geographical size from a specific site to the whole local authority area. It can remove the permitted development rights on a temporary or a permanent basis.

If an **Art 4** Direction has been passed and affects the proposed development, this does not necessarily mean that the development cannot take place. It only means that the development cannot be carried out under permitted development rights and therefore needs an express planning application. This enables the local planning authority to look at the proposal in more detail.

Local authorities can expand permitted development rights via local development orders or neighbourhood development orders (both of these types of orders are mentioned above).

Link to practice

Article 4 Directions are a good example of the significance of the local search when considering planning issues.

Practice Point

The existence of an **Art 4** direction can be discovered from the local search results. There may be an entry in the LLCI search result under Part 3 of the local land charges register which deals with planning charges. There may also be an entry in the CON 29 result. Question 3.9 on form CON 29 asks about notices, directions and orders under the **Planning Acts**. An example would be as follows.

3.9 Notices, orders, directions and proceedings under the Planning Acts: The property is within an area subject to an Article 4 Direction in respect of all building operations.

It is also possible for planning permission to be granted without express application through a **Neighbourhood Development Order (NDO)** introduced under **LA 2011**. The principle behind NDO's is that local communities should have the chance to be involved in the planning process. One potential benefit of this is that there should arguably be a less confrontational approach to planning applications. Communities are often focused on objecting to planning proposals for development in their areas, whereas where they have been involved in a development proposal from the start, they are more likely to "own" the project and less likely to have objections. It is also said that local people are the ones most likely to know what development is most needed, and most appropriate, for their own area.

The neighbourhood planning provisions allow a Parish Council or neighbourhood forum (a local body, such as a residents' association or community group, which meets specified criteria and has been designated as such) to initiate a process for making an NDO. Local authorities have a duty to make the order where a referendum has taken place and over 50 per cent of voters are in favour of the order. NDOs must be in line with local and national planning policy. They can be used to influence the type, location, design and mix of new development in the area.

NDOs can grant full or outline planning permission, with or without conditions, for development that complies with the order. This may be for specific sites or developments, or planning permission relating to specified types of development throughout all or part of the area. Some matters are excluded from neighbourhood planning, such as nationally significant infrastructure projects, mining-related development and waste development.

If development is not permitted development under **TCP(GPD)O 2015** or under a development order such as an NDO, the buyer will need to apply to the local planning authority for permission. This will be on a standard form together with such information as the authority requires, and will include a plan to identify the property. Applications can be made on a paper version of the form or online through the Planning Portal.

7.5.3 Express planning permission

We have seen that certain types of "development" are given deemed permission. However, in many cases, deemed permission will not be available and it will be necessary to apply to the local planning authority for express planning permission.

Application may be for either outline permission or detailed permission (the latter is also referred to as 'full planning permission'). The outline application is useful where a developer wants to see whether their proposals will be broadly acceptable before committing to the cost of drawing up detailed proposals.

Where a developer is unsure as to whether the proposed changes to the land constitute development, they can apply to the authority for a determination before going to the cost and trouble of applying for express permission.

Anyone interested in the land may apply for planning permission. So, for example, a builder may apply for planning permission before committing themself to purchase. When making an application, the applicant must certify either that they are the owner or that they have given notice of the application to the owner.

In reaching its decision, the authority must have regard to the development plan in force for that area (the plan in force will be indicated on the replies to standard enquiries of the local authority), and to any other material considerations which are those of a planning nature. The policies in the NPPF are material considerations.

Unless extended by agreement, the local authority must make a decision within eight weeks (13 weeks for major developments). If no decision is made within that time, the applicant may assume that the application has been refused. It is possible to appeal against a refusal of planning permission.

Any successful application will be revealed in the LLC1 and CON 29 search results (see **Chapter 8**). A full copy can then be requested from the local authority to check it refers to the correct building work.

Planning permission expires after a certain period of time. Generally, unless the planning permission states otherwise, there is a time limit of three years in which to commence the work. Note that planning permissions in Wales specify a time limit of five years within which to commence the work.

7.5.4 Reserved matters

Outline permission is granted subject to certain "reserved matters". These are specific details about the permission that can be confirmed later. Reserved matters can include:

- **Appearance** – aspects of a building or place which affect the way it looks, including the exterior of the development.
- **Means of access** – covers accessibility for all routes to and within the site, as well as the way they link up to other roads and pathways outside the site.
- **Landscaping** – the improvement or protection of the amenities of the site and the area and the surrounding area, this could include planting trees or hedges as a screen.

- **Layout** – includes buildings, routes and open spaces within the development and the way they are laid out in relation to buildings and spaces outside the development.
- **Scale** – includes information on the size of the development, including the height, width and length of each proposed building.

Outline planning permission does not act as consent for development to begin.

Once outline planning permission has been granted, a "reserved matters" application must be made within three years of the consent (or a lesser period if specified by a condition on the original outline approval). The details of the application must be consistent with the outline approval, including any conditions attached to the permission. Development must commence within two years from the latest reserved matters approval.

7.5.5 Planning conditions

Planning permission can be refused or granted with or without specific conditions. The main power to impose planning conditions are contained in **ss70, 72, 73, 73A** and **Sch 5 Town and Country Planning Act 1990**. In granting planning permission, the local planning authority can impose "such conditions as they think fit". This power needs to be interpreted in light of material considerations such as the NPPF, the government's supporting guidance on the use of conditions, and relevant case law.

Paragraph 56 of the NPPF makes clear that planning conditions should be kept to a minimum, and only used where they satisfy the following tests:

- necessary;
- relevant to planning;
- relevant to the development to be permitted;
- enforceable;
- precise; and
- reasonable in all other respects.

Planning conditions can include the obligation for a developer to landscape the communal areas of an estate in certain ways or may be required to submit further details of a specified aspect of the development before starting to build. Planning conditions can be used for issues such as contaminated land, noise and affordable housing.

The enquiries made of a local authority will reveal whether there are any planning applications in respect of the property and the result of them. A buyer should also see the decisions of any planning permissions upon which they rely to check that the conditions imposed have been complied with.

Local planning authorities are encouraged to use "model planning conditions" for the sake of ease and consistency. These are conditions containing standard wording.

Example

Examples of model planning conditions:

Time limit for commencement of development

1. The development hereby permitted shall be begun before the expiration of [three] years from the date of this permission.

Outline Permissions

2. Approval of the details of the siting, design and external appearance of the building[s], the means of access thereto and the landscaping of the site (hereinafter called "the reserved matters") shall be obtained from the local planning authority in writing before any development is commenced.

3. Plans and particulars of the reserved matters referred to in condition 2 above, relating to the siting, design and external appearance of any buildings to be erected, the means of access to the site and the landscaping of the site, shall be submitted in writing to the local planning authority and shall be carried out as approved.

Link to practice

Pre-commencement conditions

Look at the following conditions – what is the significance of the words in bold?

Transport

Development shall not commence until details of the proposed [bus/railway] station(s) or stop(s) have been approved in writing by the local planning authority; and the building(s) shall not be occupied until [that/those] station(s) or stop(s) have been constructed in accordance with the approved plans.

Landscape design proposals

No development shall take place until full details of both hard and soft landscape works have been submitted to and approved in writing by the local planning authority and these works shall be carried out as approved. These details shall include [proposed finished levels or contours; means of enclosure; car parking layouts; other vehicle and pedestrian access and circulation areas; hard surfacing materials; minor artefacts and structures (eg. furniture, play equipment, refuse or other storage units, signs, lighting etc.); proposed and existing functional services above and below ground (eg. drainage power, communications cables, pipelines etc. indicating lines, manholes, supports etc.); retained historic landscape features and proposals for restoration, where relevant.]

Sites of archaeological interest

No development shall take place until fencing has been erected, in a manner to be agreed with the local planning authority, about [insert name of monument]; and no works shall take place within the area inside that fencing without the consent of the local planning authority.

Contaminated land

Development shall not begin until a scheme to deal with contamination of the site has been submitted to and approved in writing by the local planning authority.

The above scheme shall include an investigation and assessment to identify the extent of contamination and the measures to be taken to avoid risk to the [public/buildings/environment] when the site is developed.

Development shall not commence until the measures approved in the scheme have been implemented.

All of the above are examples of **pre-commencement conditions** that is, planning conditions which must be complied with before the developer begins work on the site. It is very important when acting for a buyer to ensure that a developer provides evidence of compliance with the pre-commencement conditions. You will see that most of the conditions require the local planning authority to give consent in writing.

Link to practice

Restrictions on permitted development

We have seen above that some work to property has the benefit of deemed planning permission and the **General Permitted Development Order**. It is possible for a planning condition to disapply the **GPDO**. Accordingly, you should always consider the planning conditions carefully when acting for a buyer. Your client should be advised if the **GDPO** rights have been removed or restricted because this will mean that they will need to apply for formal planning permission for relatively minor changes to the property. Examples of planning conditions that restrict permitted development are as follows:

Notwithstanding the provisions of the Town and Country Planning (General Permitted Development) Order 1995 (or any order revoking and re-enacting that Order with or without modification), no garages shall be erected [other than those expressly authorised by this permission].

Notwithstanding the provisions of the Town and Country Planning (General Permitted Development) Order 1995 (or any order revoking and re-enacting that Order with or without modification), no fences, gates or walls shall be erected within the curtilage of any dwellinghouse forward of any wall of that dwellinghouse which fronts onto a road.

Notwithstanding the provisions of the Town and Country Planning (General Permitted Development) Order 1995 (or any order revoking and re--enacting that Order) (with or without modification), no windows/dormer windows [other than those expressly authorised by this permission] shall be constructed.

7.6 Enforcement action – breach of planning

A buyer who finds that there has been some previous development of the property which has taken place without permission will wish to know if the local authority can take any action. Control of development is within the discretion of the local planning authority.

The authority may issue an enforcement notice where there has been a breach of planning control, that is, development without permission or a breach of some condition. A copy of the enforcement notice will be served upon the owner and occupier and anyone else with an interest in the land who will be materially affected by the notice. The notice must be served at least 28 days before it is to take effect. In addition, the authority may issue a stop notice (see below) or a temporary stop notice if it considers that the activity giving rise to the breach should be stopped more quickly than this. A temporary stop notice would be relevant where the authority wants the activity to stop immediately. The temporary stop notice does not need to be accompanied by an enforcement notice but will only be effective for 28 days (or any shorter period specified in the notice). The temporary stop notice therefore differs from the stop notice described below because the authority does not have to wait for an enforcement notice to be prepared and served and the effect of the temporary stop notice is immediate.

In some cases, an enforcement notice cannot be served where the development was carried out more than four years ago. Thus, where a buyer knows that there was a wall built five years ago in the garden of the house they are buying, they can be sure that the authority cannot require it to be demolished.

Some people try to manipulate these time limits. In ***Fidler v Secretary of State for Communities and Local Government*** **[2010]** a Surrey farmer built a new home behind a wall of bales of straw. Four years later he removed the bales of straw to reveal the new structure believing that he was now outside the enforcement period for the **Town and Country Planning Act 1990**. The local authority challenged this view, asserting that the straw bales formed part of the building operations as it was always intended that they would be removed and that this was the final act in constructing his new home. Only when the bales were removed was the structure substantially complete. The High Court agreed.

LA 2011 contains provisions (by way of amendment to **TCPA 1990**) to tackle the problem of concealed development, but the concealment must be deliberate for the provisions to apply. It provides that enforcement action can be taken where the relevant time limits have expired where the breach has been concealed. The powers are exercised by way of a planning enforcement order, granted upon application by the local planning authority, by the Magistrates' Court. The order must be applied for within six months of the date the apparent breach came to the notice of the authority. The magistrates can only grant the order if satisfied that the breach was deliberately concealed. If an order is granted, the authority has 12 months (called the "enforcement year") in which to take enforcement action.

Also note that, where a person has deliberately concealed a breach, the courts have held that the normal enforcement time limits do not engage until the breach has been discovered. This means that in cases of deliberate concealment, the local planning authority may decide to serve an enforcement notice "out of time" or apply for a planning enforcement order. The local planning authority will need to decide which is most appropriate in the particular case.

An enforcement notice must state the breach of control alleged, the steps to be taken to remedy it and the date the notice takes effect. In order to prevent unauthorised development within the 28-day period before the notice takes effect, the local planning authority may serve a stop notice, which prohibits the activities alleged in the enforcement notice. The stop notice must specify when it is to take effect and the effective date must normally be no fewer than three days (or later than 28 days) after the date of service. Where there are special reasons, a stop notice may take effect before three days from service (e.g. where it is essential to protect a conservation area from imminent road building which would be especially harmful to the area) but a statement of reasons must be served with the stop notice. There are some activities which cannot be prevented by a stop notice and one such activity is the use of a building as a dwelling-house. If a stop notice has been served, the authority may be liable to pay compensation if the enforcement notice is subsequently quashed on appeal.

The time limit for taking enforcement action for breach of planning has been 4 years for a long time. Note that there has been an important update in this area. In many cases, the enforcement period has been increased to **10 years**. The key date is **25 April 2024**. The entire section of the coursebook on breach of planning must be read in the light of this change.

The time limits for taking enforcement action are set out in **s171B Town and Country Planning Act 1990** (see also **Planning Act 2008 (Commencement No. 8) and Levelling-up and Regeneration Act 2023 (Commencement No. 4 and Transitional Provisions) Regulations 2024** for transitional arrangements).

In most cases, development becomes immune from enforcement if no action is taken:

- within 10 years of substantial completion for a breach of planning control consisting of operational development where substantial completion took place on or after 25 April 2024;
- within 10 years for an unauthorised change of use to a single dwellinghouse where the change of use took place on or after 25 April 2024;
- within 4 years of substantial completion for a breach of planning control consisting of operational development where substantial completion took place before 25 April 2024;
- within 4 years for an unauthorised change of use to a single dwellinghouse where the change of use took place before 25 April 2024;
- within 10 years for any other breach of planning control (essentially other changes of use).

For more information, go to: https://www.gov.uk/guidance/ensuring-effective-enforcement#planning-enforcement--overview

The **Planning and Compensation Act 1991** also provided the local authority with extended powers of enforcement of planning control. Although the enforcement notice is the main method, other methods of enforcement include the planning contravention notice and the breach of condition notice.

Where there has been a breach of planning control (e.g. permission has not been obtained where required), the buyer's conveyancer should:

- identify the non-compliance;
- assess the risk of enforcement action being taken;
- advise on the solution.

The solution could be to require the seller to apply for retrospective planning permission. However, this would take time and would risk refusal or alerting the local authority, leading to the possible service of an enforcement notice or possibly the grant of planning consent subject to conditions. A common solution is therefore to obtain a lack of planning permission indemnity insurance policy.

This is often used, and a single premium will normally ensure cover for the buyers and successors in title. This insurance can usually be arranged online very quickly and is generally acceptable to mortgage lenders (although this must be checked with the individual lender). It is generally accepted that the seller will pay the premium although it is up to the parties to make their own arrangements. Where there is cover under such a policy, the client must not alert the local authority to the existence of the breach.

7.7 Conservation area

We have mentioned the potential impact of a property being in a conservation area on the planning process. Conservation areas exist to manage and protect the special architectural and historic interest of a place. Every local authority in England has at least one conservation area and according to Historic England, there are around 10,000 conservation areas in England. Most conservation areas are designated by the council as the local planning authority.

The designation as a conservation area is significant because it imposes extra planning controls and considerations to protect the historic and architectural elements of the area. They are most likely to have an impact on work to the outside of a building or trees on a property. As we have seen, a local authority can impose an **Article 4 Direction** which restricts work that can normally be done without planning permission. This can mean that relatively minor work such as replacing a door window or altering gutters and downpipes could require planning permission. Note that these controls are tailored to each locality by the local authority and are put in place when there are particular elements of local buildings that they want to protect.

If a property owner wants to cut down a tree in a conservation area, they must notify the local planning authority six weeks before the work begins. Note that this is different to a tree being protected by a **Tree Preservation Order** (TPO) (see **7.7.1**).

Permitted development rights are different in conservation areas. It is necessary to make planning applications for some forms of development which would not need such an application outside a conservation area. For example:

(1) Detailed residential changes like two-storey extensions, dormer windows and stone cladding.

(2) Extensions to retail premises (smaller floorspace increases; appearance should match the existing; limitations to click and collect facilities).

(3) Industrial and warehouse buildings (smaller floorspace increases).

(4) Controls on materials for buildings on the site of a school, college, university or hospital.

(5) Limitations on change of use such as retail or agricultural to dwelling house.

Whether or not a property falls within a conservation area will be revealed by the local search. The seller should also indicate whether the property is in a conservation area at Question 8.1 of the Property Information Form (TA6).

7.7.1 Tree Preservation Order (TPO)

A TPO is an order made by a local planning authority in England to protect specific trees, groups of trees or woodlands in the interests of amenity. An order prohibits the:

- cutting down;
- topping;
- lopping;
- uprooting;
- wilful damage; or
- wilful destruction,

of trees without the local planning authority's written consent. If consent is given, it can be subject to conditions which have to be followed. In the Secretary of State's view, cutting roots is also a prohibited activity and requires the authority's consent. Owners of protected trees must not carry out, or cause or permit the carrying out of, any of the prohibited activities without the written consent of the local authority. As with owners of unprotected trees, they are responsible for maintaining their trees, with no statutory rules setting out how often or to what standard. The local planning authority cannot require maintenance work to be done to a tree just because it is protected. However, the authority can encourage good tree management, particularly when determining applications for consent under a TPO. This will help to maintain and enhance the amenity provided by protected trees.

Arboricultural advice from competent contractors and consultants, or the authority, will help to inform tree owners of their responsibilities and options. It is important that trees are inspected regularly and necessary maintenance carried out to make sure they remain safe and healthy.

Whether will not a property is affected by a TPO will be revealed by the local search. The seller should also indicate whether the property is affected by a TPO at Question 8.5 of the Property Information Form (TA6).

7.8 Listed buildings

A listed building is a building that is of special architectural or historic interest. The detail is outside the scope of this course book, but it is important for a conveyancer to identify when they are dealing with a listed building because the enforcement provisions relating to contravention of the listing requirements are serious.

According to Historic England:

- Grade I buildings are of exceptional interest, only 2.5% of listed buildings are Grade I.
- Grade II* buildings are particularly important buildings of more than special interest; 5.8% of listed buildings are Grade II*.
- Grade II buildings are of special interest; 91.7% of all listed buildings are in this class and it is the most likely grade of listing for a home owner.

Buildings are listed to identify and protect the nation's architectural heritage. In a conveyancing context we tend to be thinking about large expensive houses, farmhouses or townhouses but listed buildings can include a wide range of structures such as windmills, bridges, walls and even letterboxes.

Listed buildings are protected by the **Planning (Listed Buildings and Conservation Areas) Act 1990** which is designed to ensure that such buildings are properly protected from neglect, inappropriate alteration, extension or demolition. All of a building is listed, including its interior and any object or structure fixed to the building or sited within its curtilage that is older than 1 July 1948.

The Secretary of State for Culture, Media and Sport is responsible for compiling the statutory list of buildings of special architectural or historic interest. Historic England is responsible for providing expert advice on which buildings meet the criteria for listing, and for administering the process.

Activity

Follow the link to the Historic England website at https://historicengland.org.uk/listing/the-list/ . Here you will find the search tool to enable you to establish whether a building is listed. You will see that you need to enter a keyword, postcode or the listing entry number. Search for CILEX's post code MK42 7AB – what can you find out about the listing of The Manor?

As with all other planning issues, whether a property is listed and any associated listed building consents will be revealed on the local search.

Note also that a seller should indicate whether the property that they are selling is listed by indicating as much at Question 8.2 on the Property Information Form (TA6).

In general terms, listed building consent is required for all works of demolition, alteration or extension to a listed building that affect its character as a building of special architectural or historic interest. The requirement applies to all types of work and all parts of those buildings covered by the listing protection. This includes buildings and other structures within the curtilage of the property.

The **curtilage** of a building (the principal building) is in general terms and area of land and the buildings that is around and associated with the principal building. Not all buildings have a curtilage and the facts of the case will need to be considered carefully.

An application for listed building consent is made to and determined by the local planning authority. Where works have an impact on the external appearance of the building, planning permission may also be required and if so, should also be applied for at the same time.

Link to practice

Another general point which ties in with planning issues, is where a buyer is planning to do works to a property or to change the use of the property, the mortgage lender (if there is one) must be informed to check that the lender is happy with the proposed changes. If the client refuses to allow the conveyancer to inform the lender of a relevant issue, this has professional conduct implications.

7.8.1 Enforcement action – breach of listing

Listed building consent is required for any work that affects the character of the building including alterations, extensions and demolition. **It is a criminal offence to carry out unauthorised work to a listed building**. Not knowing that a building is listed is not a defence to any criminal proceedings.

If unauthorised work has taken place to a listed building an enforcement notice can be served. This may require the work to be remedied or reversed.

Repairs that do not alter the character of a listed building do not require consent, such as splicing in a new section of timber to a window or replacing a section of guttering. The work should match the existing exactly in all respects. Replacing a window or other architectural feature and sandblasting finishes would, in most cases, require consent.

A significant difference between enforcement powers for breach of listing and breach of planning requirements is that an enforcement notice relating to breach of listing can be issued at any time; even many years after the unlawful works were carried out. It can be served on the current owner of a building irrespective of whether they, a previous owner or any other party was responsible for the works. This means that there is no time limit imposed in relation to breach of listing enforcement period.

Listed building enforcement notices enable an authority to require remediation of unauthorised works to bring a building either back to its former state or, where that is not practical or desirable, to alleviate the effect of the unauthorised works.

Link to practice

Planning permissions and the corresponding listed building consents will be revealed by the local search. You can see how essential the local search is to all issues relating to planning.

The local search will also reveal whether the local authority has taken or is taking any enforcement action for breach of planning control. It is essential that the conveyancer acting for a buyer is satisfied that any enforcement action is concluded prior to committing the buyer to exchange of contracts.

7.9 Building regulations

Building regulations and planning are often considered together and they are linked but building regulations is a distinct requirement which must be separately considered by the conveyancer when any work is carried out to a property. Not only must a developer seek planning permission for their proposed development, but any works carried out must also comply with the **Building Regulations** from time to time in force.

Building regulations used to be exclusively administer by local authorities. However, the **Building Act 1984** authorised other suitably qualified companies or individuals to carry out building control work in England and Wales under the 'Approved Inspector' scheme.

Most structural building work is subject to building regulations even when planning permission is not required. These **Building Regulations** relate to health and safety aspects of the work, and methods of construction and building materials. The current regulations are the **Building Regulations 2010** (**BR 2010**).

BR 2010 cover the construction and extension of buildings, together with many alteration projects such as installing a bathroom where this will involve plumbing work, changing electrics near a bath or shower, replacing windows or replacing a central heating system.

Therefore, when building works are planned, there are two separate issues to consider – planning permission and building regulations consent/approval.

An application in relation to building regulations approval will be made before the work is carried out. A building inspector will oversee the work as it progresses and, once it is finished, issue a certificate of compliance to confirm that the requirements of the building regulations have been met.

In some cases, works can be self-certified by a tradesperson under a competent person scheme. This allows approved individuals and companies (e.g. approved companies installing replacement windows) to self-certify that the work complies with the **Building Regulations** as an alternative to making an application for building regulations approval. There is a register of competent persons which can be checked by those wishing to undertake works and a separate register for electricians has been set up. The competent person will give the home-owner a certificate which can be used as evidence of compliance with the **Building Regulations**. The work carried out under the self-certification scheme should be notified to the local authority by the contractor. The fact that work has been carried out under the self-certification scheme will appear on the local search result. However, note that the local authority does not retain or issue copies of the certificates.

Link to practice

One of the most common types of work which conveyancers will come across when acting for a buyer is the installation of new windows and doors at the property. The seller should indicate that this work has been done at Question 17.1 of the Property Information Form (TA6).

Fensa is a government authorised scheme that monitors building regulation compliance for replacement windows and doors. Each Fensa approved installer is assessed regularly by Fensa to ensure its compliance with building regulations is continually maintained. Once the work is complete, the approved installer is permitted to produce the Fensa certificate which is proof that the window and door installations are building regulations compliant, energy-efficient and registered.

Generally, the seller should produce the Fensa certificate (and any guarantee or warranty) as part of the contract package when selling the property. However, the 2019 edition of the Protocol states as follows at para 13:

"Note: copies of competent person certificates are not always required if the existence of the certificate is clear as mentioned in the result of enquiries and noted on the relevant website (such as FENSA)."

This means that if the existence of the competent person certificates is revealed on the local search result, for example, the seller might not be obliged to produce the actual certificates. However, if the work was carried out by the seller or is very recent, the buyer's conveyancer may insist on the appropriate certificates being produced.

It is possible to check whether Fensa has issued a certificate for windows and doors by using the search facility on their website. The link is as follows:

https://forms.fensa.org.uk/fensa-certificate

BR 2010 are supplemented by detailed technical guidance called Approved Documents that explain how the **Building Regulations** requirements may be satisfied. This guidance is taken into account when building work is assessed.

The buyer of a property which has recently been erected or altered should not only check whether the requisite planning permission has been obtained and conditions complied with, but also ensure that **Building Regulations** approval has been obtained. It is important to remember that **Building Regulations** approval may be required even though the works do not amount to development for the purposes of planning permission.

In ***Cottingham v Attey, Bower & Jones (a Firm)* [2000]** a solicitor acted in the purchase of a property where various works had been carried out. In replies to preliminary enquiries, the seller stated that **Building Regulations** approval had been obtained, but did not produce copies. The solicitor proceeded on the assumption that all was in order. Problems arose after completion, when the buyer discovered that not only was the structure faulty, but also that the works had been carried out without Building Regulations approval. The buyer successfully sued the solicitor in negligence. The solicitor ought to have obtained copies of the **Building Regulations** approval and, in their absence, should have notified the buyer:

- that the work might not comply with the Regulations;
- that the survey might need to be revised; and
- that there was the danger of enforcement proceedings.

7.9.1 Enforcement – building regulations

Building Regulations are enforced by the local planning authority but are separate from planning control. Once planning permission has been granted or deemed, the building inspectors still have to check that the development was carried out under the current **Building Regulations** before issuing a certificate of compliance.

The time limit for taking enforcement proceedings for breach of building regulations has been one year for a long time. Note that there has also been an important update in this area. The **Building Safety Act 2022** has made a significant change to the enforcement for non-compliance with building regulations.

Where work is carried out which is not in compliance with building regulations, the local authority or building control authority can require the works to be removed or altered. From **1 October 2023** the one year enforcement period has been extended to 10 years after the works have been completed **(s39(3) Building Safety Act 2022)**.

In addition, stronger penalties have been introduced. Under the old regime, non-compliance was a summary-only offence with a fine of up to (plus a maximum fine of £50 per day of default after conviction). After **1 October 2023** the offence now carries an unlimited fine and/or imprisonment of up to two years plus a further fine day of default after conviction.

A local authority may be able to obtain an injunction at any time to require an owner to carry out works to bring a property up to the necessary standard (see ***Cottingham v Attey, Bower & Jones* [2000]**).

It may be possible to obtain an indemnity insurance policy for lack of building regulations, but these may be more expensive since the enforcement period has increased from one year to ten years.

Building Regulations have been revised and amended many times. Some relevant examples are as follows:

(1) From 1 April 2002, Building Regulations approval has been required for replacement doors and windows unless the contractor installing is a member of the Glass and Glazing Federation, and can provide a FENSA certificate (this is a self-certified certificate issued by the contractor on completion of the work).

(2) Fom 1 January 2005, Building Regulations approval has been required for certain electrical work in a domestic house unless the person carrying out the work is suitably qualified.

(3) From 6 April 2006, the Building Regulations promote safe construction and energy efficiency in buildings.

(4) If a property is not connected to mains drainage and a new septic tank or private treatment plant is installed, this installation also requires Building Regulations approval (in addition to consents to discharge if relevant).

Activity

Refer to **Document 9** of the **Appendix** - the Property Information Form (TA6):

Read through the form carefully and note:

- Question 12 – Notices and proposals – could provide information regarding planning applications relating to nearby land or properties; Question 17 – Alterations, planning and building work – you will see that in this section, the seller must give detailed information about work carried out to the property.

7.10 Other restrictions affecting development

The planning considerations above outline what **public** restrictions are placed upon development of land.

There may be **private** restrictions upon development, and any prospective buyer wishing to build or carry out alterations to the property will also need to know whether there are any rights of neighbouring landowners which could effectively restrict development. For example, there may be restrictive covenants against building on the land which a neighbour could enforce against the owner of the property, or perhaps a covenant restricting the use of any buildings erected (such as to use for dwelling-houses only).

The same applies to easements affecting the property; the buyer will need to know whether the proposed development will interfere with an easement benefiting adjoining land. For example, if the neighbouring property has the benefit of a right to light over the property, this could effectively prevent the erection of a building blocking the light.

In the case of both covenants and easements, the buyer's solicitors should check the terms of the contract, the register entries or title deeds and the results of the searches and enquiries to ensure that the proposed development is not unduly restricted.

Buildings may be subject to other restrictions (e.g. if it is a listed building), and separate steps are required if this is the case.

7.10.1 Restrictive covenants

Often, land which is the subject of proposed development is affected by a restrictive covenant. Usually, in such cases, consent to the development must be obtained from the person with the benefit of the covenant, the covenantee. There are other alternatives, however.

It may be that the covenant is void for non-registration as a Class D(ii) land charge in unregistered land. Such an unregistered but registrable covenant will not bind a buyer.

The covenant cannot be enforced against subsequent owners of the land unless the burden of the covenant runs with the land in equity – see the rule in ***Tulk v Moxhay* [1848]**. It may be, for example, that the original covenant was intended to be personal to the original covenantor and covenantee and so does not run (pass) with the land and bind successors in title. The covenant must have been registered as a Class D(ii) land charge in unregistered land or by way of a notice on the register of title in registered land.

Insurance – restrictive covenant indemnity cover may be obtained. This is the option preferred by most practitioners and usually required by the mortgage lender. It is normally the most practical and cost-effective way of dealing with problem covenants, as other methods, such as applying to the Upper Tribunal or trying to find the person with the benefit of the covenant, can be time-consuming, impractical or expensive to pursue.

Applications to the Lands Chamber of the Upper Tribunal, under **s84 LPA 1925** – this tribunal (formerly called the Lands Tribunal) has jurisdiction to modify or discharge a covenant if:

- there are changes to the character of the area (in ***Ward's Construction Application* [1994]**, this was applied to a covenant restricting housing density);
- the covenant impedes reasonable use of the land;
- the covenantees have consented to the modification/discharge; or
- the covenantees will not be injured by the modification/discharge.

It is important to realise that these considerations apply not only if a development is proposed, but also if it has occurred in the past and no consent from the covenantees is produced.

The person with the benefit of the covenant, such as a neighbour, may release the owner from the restriction.

7.10.2 Contaminated land

EPA 1990, as amended by the **Environment Act 1995** (**EA 1995**), makes provision regarding contaminated land.

Originally, it was intended that all land which had, in the past, been used for a suspected contaminated use should be registered with the local authority. Even though this was enacted, it was never brought into force due to the strength of opposition from industry, which was concerned that large areas of land might be blighted by their past use.

The provisions introduced by **EA 1995** are more restricted. They are aimed at identifying and remedying land which is **known** to have been contaminated (as opposed to registering land which **may** have been contaminated, as in the original proposals), and which is causing or likely to cause significant harm.

Since April 2000, local authorities have been under a duty to identify contaminated land.

When contaminated land has been identified, the local authority will begin negotiations with the person responsible for remediation. This person could be the original polluter, or someone who allowed the pollution to take place, or the current owner or occupier of the land. This means that a buyer of the land, who had no part in the original contamination of the site, could be required to rectify the problem – often at considerable expense.

In ***Circular Facilities (London) Ltd v Sevenoaks District Council*** **[2005]** it was held that the effect of **EPA 1990**, as amended by **EA 1995**, was potentially to make a later owner of a site liable for land contamination even though it had not itself deposited the material on the land. Though the owner concerned was successful on appeal in avoiding liability under the remediation notice, it would appear from the decision that those who are aware of contamination but who do not rectify it, or who later develop land which is contaminated and thereby cause possible harm to people or buildings, can be held liable to clean up the contamination. As was also illustrated, it does not matter whether the contamination is natural or artificial: in ***Circular Facilities*** the contamination was caused by rotting vegetation deposited in the ground which was subsequently developed.

If agreement can be reached on the appropriate course of action, a remediation statement is drawn up, but if not, the local authority serves a remediation notice, requiring appropriate steps to be taken. These statements and notices are set out in a public register, maintained by the local authority. A prospective buyer needs to check that there are no entries on the register relating to their property, by raising enquiries of the local authority with the local search. It is, however, important to bear in mind that the fact that the local search does not reveal contamination does not confirm that the land concerned is not contaminated.

In the first instance, the land will probably be identified from its past uses; such investigations remain the first course of action for a concerned buyer. The concern may arise for a variety of reasons, ranging from health worries to concern about the expense of putting the land in order. Many concerned buyers seek to obtain information from an investigation of old Ordnance Survey maps, trade directories and similar records.

Commercial search facilities exist to investigate past uses. More detailed investigations can be carried out by specialist surveyors and by scientific analysis if required. Insurance may also be considered (and is now provided for new properties if covered by NHBC, subject to detailed exclusions and terms in the NHBC policy documentation, but it must be remembered that the cover only lasts for 10 years).

The Law Society has issued guidance to the profession about contaminated land considerations and published its Practice Note on Contaminated Land. The emphasis is on considering whether contaminated land is an issue in a conveyancing transaction and on making all necessary searches and enquiries.

7.10.3 Party Wall etc. Act 1996

When new building work is to be carried out, it may be appropriate to consider the provisions of the **Party Wall etc. Act 1996** (as amended). This Act relates to the construction of new walls and construction works within the property boundaries which may affect the stability of adjacent property and give cause for disputes between neighbours regarding maintenance of boundary walls.

s1 contains provisions which apply where a new boundary wall is to be built. If both neighbours agree to the construction, the wall is built on the exact boundary, at shared expense, otherwise, the wall must be built on the side of the boundary within the land of the neighbour who is paying.

s2 gives rights to owners whose walls are on a boundary (whether the wall is a boundary wall or a wall of a building) – if works listed in the Act are to be carried out, the owner wishing to carry out repairs should serve a party structure notice (**s3**) on the neighbour and the neighbour may serve a counter-notice (**s4**) placing restrictions on the works. The purpose of this provision is to protect the neighbour, whose property might be damaged by works to a shared wall.

s6 deals with the situation where one owner proposes to carry out works (e.g. deep excavations or new constructions) which could affect the stability of neighbouring property. A notice of the intended work must first be served on the neighbour; and the owner who is carrying out the work is required, if necessary, to carry out structural improvements at their own expense to the neighbouring property in order to safeguard it.

s8 gives the person carrying out works the right to enter, if necessary, on to the neighbouring land to carry out various works as set out in the Act (having given notice, except in emergencies), but they must compensate the neighbour for any loss or damage caused. A procedure is provided for dispute resolution (**s10**).

7.11 Chapter summary

(1) It is important that the planning position is clarified when acquiring property for a client, as a local authority may take enforcement proceedings if there is, or has been, a breach of planning control.

(2) Planning permission is required for:

- operations, which generally include new building and changes to the exterior of property;
- a material change of use.

(3) Planning permission can be obtained either by:

- application; or
- under a permitted development order (e.g. **TCP(GPD)O 2015**).

An application can be made by someone who is not the owner of the land.

(4) Other restrictions on development which should be considered include:

- **Building Regulations** approvals;
- listed building controls;
- private restrictions, for example, by way of restrictive covenant;
- requirements under the contaminated land regime;
- requirements under the **Party Wall etc. Act 1996**.

CHAPTER 8

Pre-contract searches and enquiries

8.1 Introduction

A key part of the role of a conveyancer acting on a purchase is to gather information about the property and to advise their buyer client. Part of that process involves investigating the title and the other main aspect is to carry out the pre-contract searches and enquiries. This chapter will look at this aspect of the conveyancing transaction. When acting for a buyer you are checking more than just whether the seller may sell, but also any surrounding issues which may affect your client's use of the property. Problems are often revealed during this stage of the transaction; maybe a defect in title or an adverse search result. In these cases, it is often more expedient to obtain an indemnity insurance policy to enable the transaction to proceed. We will also look at some key points in relation to indemnity insurance in this chapter.

This chapter will cover:

- Why do searches and how?
  - standard searches;
  - local search;
  - environmental matters/search;
  - water and drainage search (CON 29DW);
  - enquiries of the seller;
  - inspection of the property.
- Non-standard searches:
  - bankruptcy search;
  - coal mining search;
  - other mining searches and Cheshire brine search;
  - flood search;
  - chancel repair liability search;
  - company search.
- Should searches be repeated?
- Indemnity insurance.

8.2 The seller's duty of disclosure

The seller's duty to disclose matters to the buyer is limited. The seller has to disclose defects in title, but nothing further. The conveyancer should, therefore, conduct a number of searches depending on the location of the property. It is always very important to look at the exact property location and address when deciding what searches will need to be made.

8.3 Why do searches and how?

Before entering into a legally binding agreement to buy the property, the buyer will want to know of any third-party rights or other matters affecting it. They will want to know whether there are any rights that will restrict their intended use of the property or will involve them in any expenditure. This, combined with the very limited scope of the seller's duty of disclosure means that the buyer's conveyancer will make a number of searches and enquiries on behalf of their buyer client (and lender, if any) in a residential conveyancing transaction.

The searches that a prudent buyer would make will vary according to the nature of the property, but most of the searches outlined in this chapter should be undertaken where indicated.

Searches can be carried out through the post or document exchange (DX), or electronically using the **National Land Information Service** (**NLIS**) or an alternative search provider.

NLIS became operational in 2001. It links a number of bodies together via the internet to facilitate the search process, including HMLR and local authorities. The central hub of the system is managed by Land Data, a community interest company. Various licensees provide the channels that make it possible to carry out searches electronically. The aim is to reduce the time-consuming and painstaking process of land and property searches to a simple on-screen routine. NLIS has also developed a system which allows much of the search information to be sent back directly into the conveyancer's case management system, saving time and avoiding the potential for error.

There are other electronic search providers available. Whichever method is used, the basic search is the same.

Activity

Follow the link below to the NLIS website; read more about it and find out which organisations are currently licensed:

https://www.nlis.org.uk/what-is-nlis

Many different search products are available. For example, searches can be sent to the following:

- all local authorities;
- Coal Authority (now known as the Mining Remediation Authority);
- Environment Agency;
- HMLR;
- Land Charges Department;
- drainage and water companies.

In addition, searches can be made in relation to such matters as companies, chancel repairs, geology, mining, telecommunications, transport and utilities.

There are some searches and enquiries that are carried out in virtually every residential conveyancing transaction. We will start with these and will then move on to the searches which are location or property-specific and which would not be carried out on every transaction.

Note that when we talk about "searches", we tend to think of completing a form and obtaining information from a search provider. However, a very important part of the pre-exchange information gathering process is the buyer physically inspecting the property and having a survey carried out and considering the pre-contract information provided by the seller, such as the Property Information Form (TA6).

"Raising enquiries" is simply the process whereby the buyer's conveyancer will ask written questions of the seller's conveyancer seeking further information or clarification of the search results and information gathered by the buyer prior to exchange of contracts.

The searches and enquiries which are carried out in every transaction are as follows:

- local search;
- environmental matters/search;
- water and drainage search;
- enquiries of the seller;
- inspection of the property.

We will deal with each in turn.

8.4 Local search

The local search comprises two forms – the LLC1 and CON 29. Together these forms provide a significant amount of information as to what is happening on a local level affecting a property.

8.4.1 Local land charges search (LLC1 form)

It is vital that the buyer discovers what local land charges affect the property they wish to buy, as they bind the owners of both registered and unregistered title. Local land charges are interests which are overriding for registered land and land when it is first registered under **para 6 Schs 1** and **3 LRA 2002**.

A local authority is bound by statute to keep a register of certain matters (but see below regarding the phased takeover of the local land charges register by HMLR). They are defined in **s1 Local Land Charges Act 1975** (**LLCA 1975**) and include:

- financial charges made by local authorities for making up roads;
- certain compulsory purchase orders;
- tree preservation orders which prevent specified protected trees being cut down, topped, lopped, uprooted, wilfully damaged or destroyed without written consent from the local planning authority (see **Chapter 7**);
- planning entries (see **Chapter 7**);
- entries relating to conservation areas and listing of buildings as being of special architectural or historical interest (see **Chapter 7**);
- a smoke control order which bans the use of non-smokeless fuel.

The local authority's register is kept in 12 parts and an official search of all the registers is made on a standard form (form LLC1) (see https://www.midsussex.gov.uk/media/2209/local-land-charge-llc1-form.pdf) giving a description of the land, together with a plan if the land cannot be clearly identified from its postal address. A fee is payable which varies between authorities. The result of a search is given in the form of a certificate as to all the registrations at the time of the certificate.

An important limitation is that the certificate is valid only at the time it is issued and offers the buyer no protection as to charges which are registered after its date, so care should be taken when relying upon a certificate which is not recent. Some insurers offer a search validation scheme which provides, for a small premium, insurance against any later entries being made between the date of the official certificate and exchange of contracts, up to a maximum period of six months. This scheme provides an indemnity against any difference in the market value of the property at the time of exchange of contracts caused by an adverse entry made between the date of the earlier search and the date of exchange. This is an example of indemnity insurance which we will look at below.

If a local land charge is not disclosed on the official search certificate, that charge is still binding because an interest registrable as a local land charge is valid even if not registered. If a buyer, however, later suffers loss due to the existence of a local land charge which was not revealed on an official certificate of search made before exchange of contracts (because it was not registered or due to an error in preparing the certificate), compensation is payable. Compensation is also payable when the buyer relies upon a certificate of search obtained by the seller or on behalf of their previous prospective buyer (**s10 LLCA 1975**).

Many local authorities now offer a direct electronic searches service for official searches often using their own form of application.

Transfer of LLC1 data to HMLR

Following the **Infrastructure Act 2015**, HMLR is gradually taking over the local land charges registers and local land charges searches from local authorities. Once the changes are complete, HMLR will be the sole registering authority for local land charges and will maintain a single consolidated local land charges register. All local land charges (LLC1) searches will then be made at HMLR rather than being sent to the relevant local authority. This changeover has been taking place on a phased basis however since it is a huge project for all the various local authority registers to be consolidated into a single register.

Activity

Follow the link below and check the current list of local authorities whose data has been transferred to HMLR. it is an on-going process, if you are in practice, you should check whether the local authority in your area has had the data transfer completed.

https://www.gov.uk/government/publications/hm-land-registry-local-land-charges-programme

The key point to grasp is that once the data has been transferred to HMLR, it will be necessary to make the LLC1 application to HMLR and not to the relevant local authority.

Link to practice

It must be stressed that this only affects local land charges (LLC1) searches and that the CON29 enquiries (see below) will continue to be dealt with by local authorities. Where the local authority's local land charges searches have been taken over by HMLR, the two parts of the search will therefore become split between HMLR(LLC1) and local authority (CON29), each with a separate fee.

As a practical point, where searches are made through a provider such as NLIS, this may make little difference to the ordering of the searches as the provider will source them from the relevant place.

Where the Land Registry's new LLC1 service is to be used, this can be accessed through the Portal, Business Gateway or on the Land Registry's website at: https://search-local-land-charges.service.gov.uk/?utm_medium=GOV.UK&utm_source=govuk&utm_campaign=Local_Land_Charges&utm_image=No_image&utm_content=programmedetail

The service contains a screening search of the local authority involved to check whether it is within the new scheme. Official local land charges searches from HMLR are digitally signed and Land Registry guaranteed. Unlimited repeat searches are allowed for a six-month period without further charge so a conveyancer could for instance re-check the register at a later date for any new charges. The service allows users to download an official local land charges search for a standard fee of £15.00.

Even when HMLR has dealt with the LLC1 search and issued the search result, any follow up enquiries or queries about local land charges must be made with the local authority, which must also be approached where related documents are required (e.g. a copy of a tree preservation order revealed by an entry on the LLC1 search result).

8.4.2 Enquiries of the local authority (CON 29 form)

In practice, these are submitted to the local authority with the local land charges search (unless LLC1 searches for that local authority have already been transferred to HMLR). Enquiries of the local authority on the CON29 form are made to discover matters which are not registrable as local land charges under the **Local Land Charges Act 1975**, but are to find out about other matters affecting the property.

There are two standard forms for the enquiries of the local authority:

- CON29 Enquiries of the Local Authority (2016) – these are the standard questions that will be answered in every search result(see **Document 3** of the **Appendix**);
- CON 29O Optional Enquiries of the Local Authority (2016) – these optional enquiries will only be answered if the box is ticked and an additional fee paid (see **Document 4** of the **Appendix**).

(1) **CON 29 Enquiries of the Local Authority (2016)**

This contains the standard questions and covers a wide range of matters, including:

- Q2.1 – whether the roads serving the property are adopted by the local authority (i.e. maintained at the public expense). The CON 29 form allows the conveyancer to specify up to three other roads which they wish to be checked in addition to the road on which the property is situated. For example, a road to the rear of the property which is not mentioned in the property address.

Link to practice

This example highlights the importance of looking at the plan of the property before submitting your search application. All searches will be made by reference to the address of the property, but you will only find out about other features around the property, such as another road or pathway or proximity to a river or railway by looking at the plan before you submit the searches. This information will often mean that you need to do additional searches or make other enquiries.

- Q2.2 – whether certain public rights of way affect the property.
- Q3.4 – whether there are any proposals for highways near the property.
- Q3.5 – whether there are any proposals for a railway, light railway or monorail within the local authority boundary.
- Q3.9 – whether there are any notices or proceedings in respect of various legislation.
- Q3.9 – what planning control affects the property. For example, what provision is made in the planning authority's development plans for the site, whether an **Art 4** direction has been passed to suspend or restrict the operation of the **General Permitted Development Order** in the area, or whether there are any entries in the register of planning applications and the result of any applications (see **Chapter 7**).
- Q3.10 – whether the community infrastructure levy (CIL) will affect the property. CIL may have to be paid in certain cases, and in certain local authority areas, where a person develops land, for instance where a developer builds new homes or a person adds a substantial extension to a property. CIL is a planning charge designed to help local authorities pay for new infrastructure for their areas. Most new development which creates additional net floor space of 100 square metres or more, or creates a new dwelling, is potentially liable for CIL, but there are some reliefs and exemptions. Not all local authorities have decided to charge CIL.
- Q3.13 – whether the local authority is taking action to require the clean-up of environmental contamination at the property.
- Q3.14 – whether the property is in a radon-affected area. Radon is a naturally occurring radioactive gas which comes out of rocks and soil. It normally causes

no problems but can sometimes pose a health risk if above a certain level. In some cases, the levels may need to be measured and remedial action taken, such as installing specific ventilation equipment.

Link to practice

Follow the link below to advice which Public Health England has published for conveyancers:

http://www.ukradon.org/information/conveyancing

- Q3.15 – whether the property being purchased has been designated as an asset of community value (ACV). ACVs are properties such as pubs and village halls which have been designated by a prescribed process as being of value to a particular community. This gives the community a right to bid to buy the asset when it is sold (e.g. so that the pub can be run by the villagers) and this can delay a sale.

Link to practice

Note that the number of properties that have been identified by local authorities as being contaminated is very small. This means that a negative reply does not mean that there is no contamination, it could simply mean that the site has not been inspected or that even if pollution has been identified, it is not at sufficient levels to reach the threshold required under statute.

A number of local authorities add a disclaimer in relation to this question along the following lines:

Informative

Negative answers do not imply that the property or any adjoining or adjacent land is free from contamination or from the risk of it, and the reply may not disclose steps taken by another Council in whose area adjoining or adjacent land is situated.

It is for this reason that most conveyancers will consider an environmental search (see below) as an essential search to carry out in every conveyancing matter.

A full list of the matters covered is set out on the back of the form.

(2) **CON 29O Enquiries of the Local Authority (2016)**

This contains optional enquiries that may be relevant to certain transactions. Replies to any or all of the questions on the form can be requested. It can be carried out independently of CON 29.

The enquiries cover a wide-ranging of matters including:

- Q4 – road proposals by private bodies;
- Q8 – pipelines;
- Q9 – houses in multiple occupation;
- Q12 – whether the property is in an enterprise zone;
- Q22 – whether the property, or any land which abuts the property is registered as common land or a town or village green (TVG). This optional enquiry will be carried out more frequently than the others.

Link to practice

Optional enquiry 22 is another reminder of the importance of considering the plan of the property prior to submitting the search application. You will not know the general location or surroundings of the property until you consider the plan.

This enquiry should be made where the buyer is buying land:

- which is rural in character and may be adjoining a village green or common;
- not yet built on;
- newly built on;
- that was once manorial; or
- where it is suspected that the access is over a village green or common land (e.g. where the property is separated from the road by a grass verge).

In ***Bakewell Management Ltd v Brandwood*** **[2004]** it was held that, provided driving across common land or a village green would have been lawful had the owner given his consent, a prescriptive easement was capable of being acquired even though consent was not obtained. The practical effect is that property owners will no longer have to pay significant sums to the owner of the village green or common land in order to acquire rights of access relying on **s68 Countryside and Rights of Way Act 2000**.

Members of the public can use town and village greens for "lawful sports and pastimes" such as playing football or walking a dog. Registered common land is owned by someone (e.g. a council, a private individual or the National Trust), but members of the public usually have a right to roam and can use the land in specific ways such as for walking, bird watching, running and picnicking. It is also possible for people to have rights of common such as rights to graze animals or to fish on the land.

The commons register contains registrations of common land, village greens and rights of common. These would prevent a landowner from building on the land. It would also be relevant for someone buying property to know about the use of any affected land.

This enquiry on CON29O may not be conclusive in relation to the existence of a town or village green (TVG) because certain TVGs are acquired by qualifying user. If it can be demonstrated that lawful sports and pastimes have been enjoyed as of right for a period of 20 years, then the land may obtain village green status. The use must either be continuing at the time of the application for registration or have ceased to do so, but the application is made within one year (in England) or two years (in Wales) of the date the qualifying use ceased. This effectively stops development (even where planning permission has been obtained). As the enquiry in CON 29O cannot be relied on, the buyer should raise enquiries of the seller in relation to the current and past uses of the site.

Recent case law has demonstrated that the land does not necessarily have to be what would normally be thought of as a village "green". The Court of Appeal has held that a tidal beach was capable of being registered as a village green on proof that the local inhabitants had enjoyed 20 years' recreational use of it as of right.

(3) **Local search results**

For the most part, the CON29 and CON29O enquiries are phrased so that the applicant will be hoping to receive replies in the negative, but the replies should be checked carefully. Usually, if there is a reply which the applicant has not expected, further investigations will have to be made. For example, particular attention will need to be paid if the replies reveal the issues outlined below.

Roads/access

If the roads are not adopted, the buyer's conveyancers will have to check whether frontagers (the owners of the land adjoining the road) are likely to be liable for any charges for adoption. In the case of the purchase of a new house, the developers may have entered into an agreement under **s38 Highways Act 1980** with the highway authority to build the road to their specifications subject to the authority adopting it thereafter, and the developers should have provided a financial bond to ensure that the cost of the works would be covered if they failed to carry out the agreement. If so, this will be revealed by the replies.

Enquiries should also be made as to the ownership of any unadopted roads: is the buyer to acquire the necessary easements to be able to reach (and to run service pipes and wires to) a public highway from the property?

Where the road adjoining the property is unadopted, the buyer should be aware of whether they are liable for the cost of maintaining it and, if so, what those costs are likely to be. The seller should be able to inform them of any costs incurred to date. Details of any payments should have been included in the Property Information Form completed by the seller. It may also be sensible to look at the existing state of the road to see whether it needs work done on it.

Drainage/sewers

If the property drains to a private sewer, the buyer should ensure that they will be acquiring the necessary rights or easements to use the drains. Again, the buyer will wish to know whether they will be liable for the cost of maintaining or repairing any private drains.

If the buyer is buying a new house, the builders may have entered into an agreement under **s104 Water Industry Act 1991** to construct the sewers and drains to the specifications of the water authority and have provided a financial bond to cover the cost of the works. If so, these will need to be checked. Again, these matters will be revealed by the replies.

Planning notices

If any planning notices have been served in respect of the property or if there have been any planning applications, further details should be obtained, as the buyer will want to know of any enforcement proceedings commenced (see **Chapter 7**). Copies of planning permissions should also be examined to see that they correspond with the numbers given in the replies from the authority. It is not sufficient simply to note that there has been a permission for development at the property; the conditions imposed upon that permission should also be examined to check they have been complied with and that they are not unduly onerous.

If planning permission has been granted, the search result should also reveal the existence of building regulations consent and a building regulations completion certificate. In some cases of minor development, planning permission is not required. This may be covered under the **General Permitted Development Order**. However, for any building work, building regulations approval must have been obtained. Whilst it is possible to insure against the absence of such consent, as building regulations concern the safety of the structure, it is better to ensure that retrospective consent is obtained by the seller before the buyer proceeds. This is done by applying for a Regularisation Certificate. If the seller is unwilling to do so, insurance can be obtained to insure against enforcement by the local authority, but the buyer's surveyor should be asked to comment upon the safety of the structure.

(4) **Local search liability**

From the disclaimer on the standard form, liability for incorrect answers to enquiries appears to be limited to cases of negligence on behalf of the local authority. This may, however, include negligence not only in tort but also in contract as there will have been a fee paid, which would mean that the disclaimer on the standard form will be valid only in so far as it is reasonable in excluding liability.

Also, as with the local land charges search, there is no guarantee that the replies will not be out of date immediately after they are returned, so care should be taken when relying on replies which are not recent.

As with the local land charges search, a buyer may rely on the results of enquiries obtained by the seller's conveyancers or by a previous prospective buyer, provided that the buyer is aware of the results before exchange of contracts.

(5) **Limitations of the local search**

The local land charges search is specific to the property to which it relates, and only a few of the enquiries of local authorities ask about the locality in which the property is situated.

Link to practice

If a buyer requires further information, for example, regarding proposals for new roads outside the limits stated in the enquiry or regarding neighbours' planning proposals, then further enquiries must be made because the standard search and enquiries do not cover this. It is possible to obtain further searches from commercial search companies which will reveal planning applications and other important information relating to a wider area and it is important to consider with a client whether such additional searches should be carried out.

The key point is to be sensitive to your client's requirements and to ensure that they understand clearly the limitations of the search and enquiries. They may wish to consider visiting the relevant department of the local authority to discuss specific concerns, proposals and problems.

(6) Official vs personal local search

There are two different types of local search:

- an official search; and
- a personal search.

As the name implies, an **official search** is one which is produced by the staff at the local authority. The search is signed on behalf of the local authority and the local authority will be liable if the result of an official search is incorrect. Note that official searches can also be made via NLIS or other commercial search companies.

A **personal search** is one which is carried out by a person or organisation which is independent of the local authority. Unsurprisingly, in this case, the local authority will not be held responsible for any incorrect replies.

If there is no time to obtain an official search, it is possible to do a personal search of the local land charge registers, usually via a search agent. Compensation, however, will not be payable by the local authority – the buyer would have to establish that the person who carried out the search was negligent.

A problem with commercial search companies which offered personal searches is that the answers were not as comprehensive as those produced by the local authority and important issues may thus not be revealed. However, in recent years, the quality of personal searches has increased substantially which is largely due to the Council of Property Search Organisations (CoPSO), which has a Search Code. This Code is enforced by the Property Codes Compliance Board (PCCB) and it provides protection for homebuyers, estate agents, conveyancers and lenders who rely on information in a search report undertaken by subscribers. It sets out minimum standards for organisations selling searches and also ensures, for instance, that there is adequate insurance if there are problems arising from the results.

Link to practice

It is highly likely that any conveyancing firm using a search provider will use one that is a member of CoPSO. However, it is always important for the conveyancer to check Part 2 of the UK Finance Mortgage Lenders' Handbook because some mortgage lenders will not accept personal searches; others state that they will only accept them at the risk of the conveyancing firm.

The conveyancer should ensure that they use a reputable commercial search provider that is a member of CoPSO.

Activity

Follow the link below to the CoPSO website where you can read more about the organisation and, crucially, the organisations which subscribe:

https://www.copso.org.uk/

Look in the membership section – is your search provider on the list?

8.5 Environmental matters and search

As we have seen above, Question 3.13 of the CON29 asks the local authority whether the land being searched against is contaminated. These are asked as part of the local search process because **Part IIA Environmental Protection Act 1990** (**EPA 1990**) requires local authorities to maintain a register of information relating to contaminated land.

Question 3.13 covers:

- any contaminated land notices that have been served in relation to the property;
- whether any entry or decision to make an entry has been made in relation to the **s78R(1)** register. These include remediation notices, remediation statements, appeals and certain convictions;
- whether any consultations are taking place with the current owner of the land being searched against, with regard to clean-up operations on nearby land.

The enquiries also cover nearby land that is so contaminated that it may harm the property being searched against.

It should be remembered that these enquiries can disclose relevant information only where the local authority **knows of it and is taking action.** Since 1 April 2000, councils have been required to take steps to identify and arrange the clean-up of contaminated land, but this is a continuing process. Contamination of land will affect many properties which receive a clear result to the local authority search and enquiries, so only by carrying out further investigations can appropriate information be received. Although the basic principle is that "the polluter pays", subsequent owners of land can also be held responsible for the costs of clean-up, which may often be very considerable. It is therefore prudent to undertake a separate environmental search, especially as many new developments are sited on land formerly used for light industry.

Activity

The Law Society has issued guidance to the profession about contaminated land considerations. The current guidance is contained in its Practice Note on Contaminated Land – follow the link below to read more:

www.lawsociety.org.uk/support-services/advice/practice-notes/contaminated-land/

Full details of contaminated land are outside the scope of this course book, but the Practice Note stresses that conveyancers must be aware of the issue of land contamination and should consider whether it is an issue in the conveyancing transaction. It states that conveyancers should check from local search results whether the land has been designated by the local authority as contaminated and, if so, make all necessary further searches and enquiries. Where the land has not been designated as contaminated (the usual case), if it appears that contamination may be an issue (e.g. the property has been built on former industrial land), the conveyancer should make all necessary further enquiries (including searches).

8.5.1 Environmental search

As we have seen although the enquiries of the local authority may disclose information on contamination of land, they can do so only where the council knows of the problem and is taking action. To provide warning of possible liability, it is now usual practice for many firms of conveyancers to conduct environmental searches. Many firms now regard an environmental search as a standard search to be made in all transactions.

A number of commercial search providers offer such searches. The results are based on published information regarding the past uses of land. For example, the Envirosearch Residential report is a method by which buyers of houses can carry out various checks to reduce the risk of buying contaminated land. More extensive investigations can, of course, be carried out, ranging from standard-form investigations of information on past uses of land, to specialised scientific investigations.

Another approach to the contaminated land problem is to insure against the risk of land being possibly contaminated. Various products are available. Homecheck Professional Land Insurance Policy, for example, provides cover against the risk of land contamination for a single insurance premium, and the cover can transfer to successors in title during the period of cover. Some new build warranties (including NHBC) cover for new residential properties also provides some protection.

The insurance will not, of course, establish whether the land is possibly contaminated. It can cover only the possible expenses of rectifying the problem and is unlikely to be available where there is a clear danger of contamination.

Environmental searches can also look into other issues, depending on the product, including such matters as flood risk, mining, radon gas, old oil and gas tanks and historical land use data.

If an environmental search adequately covers flood issues, there will be no need for a separate flood search. The scope of the environmental search product being used is therefore important as the conveyancer must ensure that no issues have been missed.

Some commercial providers include information about subsidence risk to its environmental search reports. The risk rating will determine the level of threat which subsidence poses to a specific postcode. It is reported that subsidence, which is caused by soil shrinkage and movement, is becoming an increasing risk to property owners due to long dry spells of weather and climate change. The search provider indicated that subsidence affects as many properties in the UK on an annual basis as flooding and can result in a similar number of insurance claims per year. Subsidence can of course have an impact on the value of the property and affect its saleability as well as insurance premiums.

The conveyancer may also want to carry out a Groundsure Energy and Transportation Report (this is an all-in-one infrastructure report). It will look at, if relevant to the transaction, all energy and infrastructure issues which could affect the property such as:

- existing or proposed oil, gas and shale gas sites;
- existing or proposed large-scale energy infrastructure projects and power stations;
- existing or proposed wind and solar farms;
- HS2 data including routes, stations, noise and visual impact assessment data;
- Crossrail data;
- underground railway data, including stations and proposed tube extensions.

These may have an impact on the monetary value of the property, either at the time of purchase or on future re-sale. They may also have an impact on amenity value of the property – a high speed train might be noisy for example.

Link to practice

There is a wide range of environmental searches available from the commercial search providers. It is important to ensure that the search product is appropriate for the property being purchased. For example, if you are acting in relation to the purchase of a piece of land for development, it would be appropriate to carry out a commercial environmental search.

You may need to consider notifying a lender of any adverse matter revealed on an environmental search result.

Linked to the issue of environmental searches is the much wider issue of climate change. Note that the Law Society has issued a Practice Note: "The Impact of Climate Change on Solicitors". You can read the guidance here:

https://www.lawsociety.org.uk/topics/climate-change/impact-of-climate-change-on-solicitors

Note also that a number of the search providers have products flagging certain types of climate change risk available. This is a controversial area for conveyancing practitioners. Many feel that extending the responsibility to conveyancing practitioners to advise on climate change risks is a step too far in terms of risk.

8.6 Water and drainage search (CON 29DW)

Local authorities have handed over responsibility for the maintenance of sewers and drains to statutory undertakers, generally known as the "water companies". CON 29DW (Residential) (see **Document 5** of the **Appendix**) should be submitted (together with the appropriate fee) to the relevant water company at the same time as submitting CON 29 to the relevant local authority to establish that the property has mains drainage and water supply, whether this is directly to the public sewer and other information which may be of importance to the buyer. The matters covered can be seen by reading the questions on the back of the form. The fee varies between the different water companies. Some companies have direct online search facilities and the search can also be made via NLIS or other online search providers. Alternatively, the form can be sent to the water company by post.

Responsibility for sewers

The replies to the water and drainage search must be read in the light of changes to sewer arrangements over the last few years. There are now far fewer private sewers and drains in existence, as the water companies took over responsibility for most of them in October 2011. The transfer arrangements will be reflected in the CON 29DW search results and can be summarised very briefly as follows.

From 1 October 2011, the responsibility for maintaining most private sewers and shared drains passed from private land owners to the relevant water companies. There was an automatic transfer of ownership on that date, unless the existing sewer or drain owner objected. The idea was that this would relieve landowners of having to pay for repairs (the cost is often shared between owners of the shared drains and sewers) and prevent disputes between landowners as to who was responsible for clearing or replacing them, or whether appropriate rights existed for use of the shared facilities. These sorts of issues often arise where there are disputes following blocked or leaking pipes. Repairs will now be the responsibility of the water company.

Some drains and sewers did not transfer to the water companies in 2011, for example:

- private owners retain responsibility for any part of a drain that **only serves their own property** and is located **within the boundary** (e.g. a drain leading from a detached house to the property boundary). This means that the pipe-work within a property boundary connecting drains from the property to the sewer or drain will remain the responsibility of the property owner unless other properties also drain through it (in which case it will be the water company's responsibility);
- systems that drain to private facilities such as septic tanks;
- certain centrally managed self-contained drainage systems (e.g. for airports, railway stations and shopping malls).

Full details of drains and sewers are beyond the scope of this course book, but it is important to appreciate that these changes will be relevant in practice when a conveyancer advises upon responsibility for drains and sewers, or checks the replies to CON 29DW.

Private pumping stations transferred in October 2016. There will be a supplementary transfer phase at a future date to catch some sewers and shared drains that did not transfer in October 2011, due to their date of construction. New legislation will take effect to ensure that new sewers built in the future will be constructed to minimum build standards and that they will be adopted by the water companies (i.e. there will be mandatory build standards and adoption). The option of retaining the sewer in private ownership will no longer exist.

8.7 Enquiries of the seller

Some of the matters a buyer wishes to discover will be within the seller's knowledge, but will not be apparent from the title documentation. The result of the local land charges search and additional enquiries received from the local authority may well indicate that further enquiries are necessary.

The 4th edition of the of the Property Information Form, contains questions including:

- ownership and maintenance of boundaries;
- disputes and complaints;
- notices affecting the property;

- alterations and planning matters;
- guarantees and warranties;
- insurance arrangements;
- flooding;
- septic tanks;
- radon gas;
- the EPC and whether the Green Deal scheme affects the property;
- Japanese knotweed;
- rights and informal arrangements;
- services;
- parking;
- charges affecting the property;
- occupiers;
- utilities;
- information about linked transactions and moving dates.

Form TA6 asks about new home warranties, such as the one given under the National House Building Council (NHBC) scheme.

Raising additional enquiries

The content of the Property Information Form is standard, so any additional enquiries should be raised which are relevant to the particular property.

Care should be taken, when raising enquiries, not to ask unnecessary questions or ones to which the answers will be forthcoming from other enquiries.

The Protocol contains provisions about raising additional enquiries. It encourages the use of standard forms, and discourages additional enquiries unless they are necessary in the circumstances. It also states that the seller's conveyancer does not need to obtain the seller's answers to any enquiry seeking opinion rather than fact.

The Protocol further provides that the buyer should raise only those additional enquiries required to clarify issues arising from the documents submitted and which are of relevance to the particular transaction. It also contains a provision that the buyer's conveyancer should not raise additional enquiries about the state and condition of the building unless arising out of the conveyancing search results, the buyer's own enquiries/inspection or from the surveyor's report. It states that indiscriminate use of standard additional enquiries may constitute a breach of the Protocol and, if such enquiries are submitted, the seller's conveyancer is under no obligation to answer them. This is an attempt to stop a practice adopted by some firms of sending a long list of standard additional enquiries, without consideration of whether they are applicable or not.

The replies to these enquiries should be worded so as to emanate from the seller's knowledge rather than that of their conveyancers. Often, the replies are too vague to be of any use, mainly because of the seller's reluctance to make any misrepresentations (i.e. misstatements of fact inducing the buyer to enter into the contract). Where answers are so phrased, the buyer should be warned of the limited value of the replies. Nevertheless, the seller may not be fully protected by vaguely worded replies as illustrated by the following two cases.

William Sindall plc v Cambridgeshire County Council **[1994]** concerned a reply to enquiries before contract which stated: "not so far as the vendor is aware". According to the Court of Appeal, this reply meant that the seller had made reasonable investigations and had taken legal advice in coming to this conclusion and, therefore, a seller-client should check the accuracy of replies given to enquiries before these are sent to the buyer's solicitor.

First National Commercial Bank v Loxleys **[1996]** confirms that where incorrect replies are given to standard enquiries before contract, a disclaimer on the form is subject to the test of reasonableness in the **Unfair Contract Terms Act 1977**. The disclaimer is effective if reasonable in the circumstances, but void if not. Similar provisions are contained in the **Consumer Rights Act 2015** which now regulates contract terms in transactions between businesses and consumers. Under this legislation there is a fairness assessment and unfair terms are not binding on a consumer.

Most firms will use the Property Information Form (TA6) for pre-contract enquiries, and this form can be used irrespective of whether the Protocol is adopted. Additional questions can then be asked separately if necessary (see above).

Page 2 of the Property Information Form contains important advice for sellers and buyers. In particular, it warns the seller of the need for accurate replies to the questions, and warns the seller that incomplete or inaccurate information could result in a claim for compensation or a refusal to complete the purchase. In practice, where clients are unsure about any answers, they should ask their conveyancer for advice.

If form TA6 is not used, pre-contract enquiries can be made using alternative forms, which cover similar matters. In this case the buyer's conveyancer will send the pre-contract enquiries form to the seller's solicitor, who will then answer the enquiries. **Document 6** of the **Appendix** (form CON 29 (Long)) is an example of a non-Protocol form of pre-contract enquiries.

Finally, replies to enquiries should be checked carefully. If unhappy with a reply given, further enquiries should be made of the seller.

Link to practice

When drafting any necessary additional pre-contract enquiries, it is important to be as specific as possible and to say what information or documentation is required to resolve the query.

For example, imagine that the seller has indicated in the replies to the Property Information Form that there has been flooding at the property but has merely stated that this was "many years ago" and that it "affected only part of the house". You would want to raise an additional enquiry along these lines:

Please specify the precise dates of each and every incidence of flooding at the property, and specify which parts of the buildings, surrounding land or gardens were affected in each case. Please additionally specify the type of flooding that occurred and the damage caused in each case by the flooding incident.

8.8 Inspection of the property

The buyer should inspect the property to look for the following.

(1) **Physical defects/survey**

The general rule remains *caveat emptor* (buyer beware). Where the SCs are being used, SC 3.2.1 states that the buyer accepts the property in the physical state it is in at the date of the contract, unless the seller is building or converting the property.

The majority of buyers acquire the property with the aid of a mortgage from a bank or building society and may wish to rely on the valuation which the lender undertakes (to check that the property is good security for the loan) as assurance that the property is in a sound condition. Although the valuation is carried out on behalf of the lender, the valuer may be liable to the buyer for negligence in the light of the House of Lords cases ***Smith v Eric S Bush (a Firm)*** **[1989]** and ***Harris v Wyre Forest Borough Council*** **[1989]**. It appears from these cases that, due to the inequality of the bargaining position of the parties, disclaimers excluding liability will fail the test of reasonableness in most cases where the property involved is a home of relatively modest value.

Care should be taken, however, to advise the buyer on the importance of an independent survey and of the dangers of relying on the lender's valuation, particularly in cases of expensive property or where the mortgage advance is a small amount in relation to the purchase price. The valuer's duty will not extend to defects in areas which are not easy to inspect.

The buyer's conveyancer should always draw their client's attention to the limited nature of a lender's valuation, which is carried out primarily for the lender's own purposes, pointing out which aspects of the property were not surveyed (e.g. as most valuations undertaken on behalf of a lender will be looking purely at the value of the property, the inspection will usually exclude investigation of the condition of the parts not readily accessible, such as floorboards or wall ties).

A surveyor takes professional responsibility for their survey report – this means that if they are negligent or breach their contractual duty they could be sued for damages.

There are several types of independent survey which a buyer may choose to obtain. The Royal Institution of Chartered Surveyors (RICS) is the professional body for surveyors and has recently set out new standards for surveys of residential property. The RICS states as follows:

"**Home Survey Level 1** – The level one survey is designed for clients (buyers, vendors and owners) seeking a professional and objective report on the condition of the property at an economic price. It includes a visual inspection that is less extensive than survey level two and survey level three. No tests of the building fabric or services are undertaken.

This level of survey is designed as a very basic overview of the condition of the property. It will not contain any detailed advice on repairs. This level of service is better suited to conventionally built, modern dwellings in satisfactory condition.

If more detailed advice and guidance are required, the client should consider upgrading to a survey level two or three and should discuss this with their surveyor ahead of the service being undertaken.

It is important that clients fully understand the key differences in the levels of inspection and report provided and discuss any concerns with their surveyor.

Home Survey Level 2 – The level two survey is designed for clients (buyers, vendors and owners) seeking a professional and objective report on the condition of the main elements of a property. It will not contain any detailed advice on repairs.

This intermediate level of service includes a more extensive visual inspection of the building, its services, and grounds. This level of service suits a broader range of conventionally built properties, although the age and type will depend on the knowledge and experience of the RICS member.

It is important that clients fully understand the key differences in the levels of inspection and report provided and discuss any concerns with their surveyor.

Home Survey Level 3 – A level three survey is more thorough and detailed than then others and will address matters such as the materials used for each part of the building, defects and remedial options as well as issues related to the future maintenance of the property. Concealed areas normally opened or used by the occupiers are inspected if it is safe to do so.

Although services are not tested, they are observed in normal operation. This level of service is for clients who are seeking a professional opinion based on a detailed assessment of the property.

It is important that clients fully understand the key differences in the levels of inspection and report provided and discuss any concerns with their surveyor."

Note that the level 2 survey can comprise just a survey or a survey and valuation.

Link to practice

Note that the new survey standards have replaced the:

- Condition Report;
- HomeBuyer Report;
- Full structural survey (often known as a "Building Survey").

Activity

For more information about the RICS Home surveys, follow the link below:

https://www.rics.org/uk/upholding-professional-standards/sector-standards/building-surveying/home-surveys/home-survey-standards/

(2) **Patent defects in title**

This relates to the seller's duty of disclosure, which extends to latent, but not patent, defects in the title. Patent defects in title (i.e. those defects which can be discovered by inspecting the property) do not have to be disclosed by the seller under an open contract, nor must they be disclosed where the SCs apply (SC 3.1.2(b)).

A typical patent defect may be an easement, evidence of which is apparent upon inspection, for example, a paved pathway leading across the property to an entrance in the boundary with the neighbouring property. A legal right of way may be binding upon the buyer whether they knew of it or not, so it is important for the buyer to inspect so that they know of the existence of any such right.

(3) Actual occupation

Another particular problem is the evidence of occupation by someone with an interest in the property.

(a) In unregistered title

The buyer is deemed to have notice of the rights of occupiers which are not registrable as land charges, in so far as they would have been revealed by the making of reasonable enquiries. To take an extreme example, if a buyer sees belongings at the property which are obviously not those of the seller, that may amount to notice of the occupation of the owner of the belongings and therefore of that owner's rights in the property. Since 13 October 2003, when **LRA 2002** came into force, the property concerned is also, when registration is completed, subject to unregistered interests which override first registration (**Sch 1 LRA 2002**).

(b) In registered title

The buyer can potentially be bound by the rights of those persons in actual occupation at the time of completion. If those rights are not overreached upon completion (if they fall into the category of rights which are capable of being overreached), the buyer would normally take free of them only if enquiries were made of the owner of them and that person failed to disclose their rights.

Since 13 October 2003, the test of whether the interest of a person in actual occupation will bind the buyer has been set out in **para 2 Sch 3 LRA 2002**. The interests that **para 2** excludes from being overriding are:

- an interest of a person of whom enquiry was made before the disposition and who failed to disclose the right when they could reasonably have been expected to do so; and
- an interest which belongs to a person whose occupation would not have been obvious on a reasonably careful inspection of the land at the time of the disposition and of which the person to whom the disposition is made does not have actual knowledge at that time.

If the Property Information Form has been completed by the seller, the answer to Question 21 will disclose the existence of any occupiers.

Ideally, in registered and unregistered title, the property should be inspected both before exchange and immediately before completion, in the latter case so that any rights which may have been created or occupation which has become apparent after exchange may be discovered. In practice, many clients do not inspect the property before completion except, perhaps, to confirm that it is vacant.

8.9 Non-standard searches

We will now move on to look at searches which are not carried out in every residential conveyancing transaction. These will only be done if the location, title or property demand it.

Buyers' conveyancers should always consider the purchase property itself, together with the exact location of the property, and make any necessary searches so they are aware of all potential matters and risks which might affect the particular property. As well as the standard searches, more specialist ones may be required and the conveyancer will need to identify which ones are relevant.

The main non-standard searches are:

- bankruptcy search – if the buyer has a mortgage;
- central land charges search – unregistered land only;
- Search of the Index Map (SIM);
- coal mining search;
- other mining searches and Cheshire brine search;
- flood search;
- chancel repair liability search;
- company search;
- canal /rivers search.

8.10 Bankruptcy search – if the buyer has a mortgage

If the buyer is getting a mortgage to assist with the purchase, the buyer's conveyancer will usually carry out a bankruptcy only land charges search against the full name of the buyer prior to exchange of contracts. This can be done by using form K16 (see https://www.gov.uk/government/publications/bankruptcy-official-search-application-k16) and submitting it to HMLR but more usually, the conveyancer will use the HMLR portal.

The purpose of the bankruptcy search is to reveal whether there are any pending or concluded bankruptcy orders or writs against the buyer. This would need to be reported to the lender and, invariably, any mortgage offer would be withdrawn. A search revealed a bankruptcy entry against the buyer would be very rare. Less rare, is a result against the same name as the conveyancer's buyer client. The conveyancer would need to take steps to be satisfied that the bankruptcy entry did not relate to their client.

Link to practice

It is important to point out that a bankruptcy search would be repeated as part of the pre-completion searches. However, you can see the importance of discovering whether your buyer client is bankrupt prior to exchange contracts.

8.11 Central land charges search – unregistered land only

This applies to unregistered title only. Such a search is not theoretically necessary at this stage. The seller is bound to disclose a land charge (the effect of SC 3 is to require its disclosure), so if the buyer discovers an undisclosed charge when searching the register before completion, they may be able to claim damages and possibly rescind.

The search is made against the full name of the seller and all parties in the epitome of title from the root of title to the seller for the full years of their ownership. This can be done by using form K15 (see https://www.gov.uk/government/publications/land-charges-official-search-application-k15 (also in **Appendix**) and submitting it to HMLR but more usually, the conveyancer will use the HMLR portal.

While registration of land charges is deemed to be actual notice by **s198 LPA 1925, s24 Law of Property Act 1969** (**LPA 1969**) provides that the knowledge of the buyer at the date of the contract shall be determined by their actual knowledge without regard to the provisions of **s198 LPA 1925**. The effect is that a search is not strictly necessary before exchange (but it must be made before completion). It may still be desirable to make a search at this stage if the buyer wishes to avoid becoming embroiled in litigation when they try to recover the deposit and rescind after exchange. Rescission is far from an ideal remedy if the buyer is by then contractually bound to sell their existing home.

8.12 Search of the Index Map (SIM)

The Index Map is maintained at HMLR, and reveals whether an estate in the land has been registered. If so, it will give the relevant title number.

A search will also reveal whether there are any cautions against first registration lodged in respect of the land. These are lodged at HMLR by someone who wishes to assert a prior claim over that of the first registered proprietor. For example, in the case of a boundary dispute where one of the neighbours wants to sell their land, the other may lodge a caution against first registration. The burden of a prescriptive easement can also be protected by a caution against first registration for instance.

Since 13 October 2003, it has been possible to lodge a caution against first registration in relation only to particular interests in land. Cautions against registration existing before 13 October 2003 remain unaffected, so a search of the Index Map must still be made.

Activity

For more information about cautions against first registration, follow the link below to HMLR's "Practice guide 3: cautions against first registration":

https://www.gov.uk/government/publications/caution-against-first-registration/practice-guide-3-cautions-against-first-registration

The SIM should be carried out in every case where it is believed that the title to the land concerned has not been registered. Accordingly, it must be done on every purchase of unregistered land. Note that the Protocol requires the seller's conveyancer to include an index map search result with the epitome.

However, another important circumstance where an index map search should be carried out is on the purchase of a new build property where plan approval has not been granted.

This can be done by using form SIM (see https://www.gov.uk/government/publications/index-map-application-for-an-official-search-sim and submitting it to HMLR but more usually, the conveyancer will use the HMLR portal.

MapSearch

HMLR has introduced a free digital service called MapSearch which can be used by e-Business customers through the Portal to find out whether land is registered or not, and to obtain title numbers if so. This is a self-service facility with instant results so an application is not required. Conveyancers may prefer to carry on making SIM searches for buyers as MapSearch results do not carry the benefit of HMLR's indemnity provisions in the event of information errors leading to loss.

Activity

Follow the link below to find out more about the MapSearch service. Note in particular the comment regarding the indemnity provisions:

https://www.gov.uk/guidance/mapsearch

8.13 Coal mining search

A coal mining search is only carried out when necessary in the circumstances of the individual transaction. Essentially a coal mining search is required where a property is in an "affected area" (i.e. a coal mining area where there may be current or past coal workings). The Mining Remediation Authority (formerly the Coal Authority) holds and maintains the national coal mining database and also licenses its data to approved coal mining search providers.

The search is made on a standard form, CON 29M (for domestic property). The form can be sent by post or DX to the Mining Remediation Authority or reports can be ordered from the Authority by telephone or via its online reports service at groundstability.com. CON 29M searches can also be ordered through NLIS or from commercial search providers who have been licensed to provide the CON 29M information.

The search will reveal, amongst other things, whether there are any past, current or future underground or surface coal mining activities affecting the property, whether there are any mine shafts which may endanger the property, whether there are any mine gas emissions, whether there is any coal mining subsidence and whether there have been any claims for subsidence.

Document 7 of the **Appendix** is an example of form CON 29M.

One commercial provider states in its literature that around one quarter of all residential transactions require a CON 29M report.

If there is evidence of a claim for subsidence having been made, enquiry should be made of the seller as to how any claim for damage was resolved. Provisions for compensation for subsidence are complex, and in some cases once compensation has been paid no further claim can be made despite further subsidence to the land. Any evidence of a subsidence claim should be comprehensively reported to the buyer and lender, if any. It is likely that a positive result will cause the transaction to fail. Many lenders are very risk averse and are unlikely to lend on an affected property.

Link to practice

The conveyancer will need to ascertain whether the property the client intends to purchase is located in an affected area. The Law Society's Guidance Notes 2018 contain a list of relevant areas in England and Wales.

Search providers will also provide a screening process to check whether a report is required.

There is an online checker and interactive map, which give guidance as to whether a coal mining search is required. These facilities can be accessed at:

www.gov.uk/check-if-property-is-affected-by-coal-mining

8.14 Other mining searches and Cheshire brine search

Other types of mining may affect a property apart from coal mining. This will depend on the location of the property. Such searches may include those for **tin mining** (e.g. in Cornwall, Devon and Somerset). Tin mining reports can be ordered through various search providers. In the past, tin mining was a major industry in Cornwall, South West Devon and some areas of Somerset. Although most of the mining activity has now ceased, there is still a risk that old mine workings could cause subsidence issues to properties in affected areas. Information revealed by a tin mining search would typically include whether there are any mine shafts under the property, whether any such shafts pose a danger to the property or whether they might restrict development at the property (e.g. if an extension was proposed) or whether the tin mining might have caused any land contamination.

Clay mining searches may be required in Dorset, West Devon or Cornwall. In some areas, **chalk mining** may have taken place.

The headline and photograph from the *Daily Mail* overleaf provides an interesting example of how a property in Cornwall was affected by an old mine shaft:

It may also be necessary to make a **Cheshire brine search** which relates to salt mining.

Where a Cheshire brine search is relevant to a transaction, it must be obtained from the Cheshire Brine Subsidence Compensation Board's supplier which is Groundsure.

The search is known as the Cheshire Salt Search. It provides information about whether brine extraction workings affect a property being purchased in Cheshire. Some areas of Cheshire are at an increased risk of subsidence due to the presence of brine and previous mining activities. Additionally, some previous compensation pay-outs mean that some properties are not eligible for compensation in the event of further damage being identified. The salt search provides information on how these matters affect a given property in Cheshire.

News

Wasn't there a nice patio in the garden yesterday?

300 -foot mine shaft opens up right outside kitchen door

Don't look down: The mine shaft has water 300ft below ground level, meaning the true depth remains unknown

8.15 Flood search

The Environment Agency predict that flooding will continue to be a growing risk to British property as a result of climate change. Aside from the physical damage of floods to a property, it may also be difficult to obtain a mortgage, arrange suitable insurance or sell a property which is in a flood risk area. This also affects the value of the property. Conveyancers are not qualified to give advice on flood risk or interpret technical flood reports. Some firms make flood searches as standard in all transactions. These can be obtained from a variety of commercial search providers, and can cover various different types of flood risk – the precise parameters of the search should be checked to ensure it is adequate. Some environmental searches cover flooding issues, but specific flood searches may be more detailed especially in cases where potential flooding is thought likely to be an issue.

Link to practice

The Law Society has issued a Practice Note on Flood Risk, which gives important guidance on this issue. It states that conveyancers should liaise with clients in relation to any flood searches or investigations which may be appropriate. These may have to be assessed in conjunction with the client's surveyor.

The latest edition of the Practice Note can be viewed on the Law Society's website at:

https://www.lawsociety.org.uk/topics/property/flood-risk

This Practice Note provides you with information to help your clients investigate the terms on which buildings insurance cover, including flood risk, is available prior to entering their purchase contracts. It also points out that if a property is at risk of flooding, it may be difficult to obtain a mortgage and the value of the property may be affected. It may also make the property more difficult to resell.

Other sources of flood information may complement a flood search. The government's website offers information about flood risk for locations in England for example, together with other information about flooding. This can be viewed at:

https://www.gov.uk/check-flood-risk

This should not however be used as the sole means of assessing flood risk for a property.

HMLR has a Flood Risk Indicator for registered properties, which owners can use, for a fee, through Land Registry online services. This Indicator combines Land Registry address data with Environment Agency and Natural Resources Wales data to identify flood risk for registered land within England and Wales. Again, this has limitations and should not be used as the sole means of assessing flood risk for a property.

Conveyancers will also ask about flooding as part of the pre-contract enquiry process (e.g. form TA6 contains a specific question about flooding at the property at Question 7).

As mentioned above, flood risk may also have important implications in relation to property insurance and these should be fully considered where this is a current or potential future issue.

8.16 Chancel repair liability (CRL) search

In view of the decision in ***Aston Cantlow and Wilmcote with Billesley Parochial Church Council v Wallbank* [2003]**, in which owners of property were held liable to meet chancel repair liability (CRL) levied by the local parochial church council, many practitioners carry out a CRL search provided by various providers, which gives some indication as to whether the land is tithe land and therefore potentially subject to such a charge. This is certainly advisable where the property is in the vicinity of an old parish church or where there is an indication from other sources (e.g. old deeds) that the property may be tithe land. One product on offer is a Chancelcheck search which can be followed up with Chancelsure insurance to cover the risk where an issue is identified. The search is not conclusive; however, therefore insurance should be considered.

Until 13 October 2013, CRL was an overriding interest, which meant that it bound land with registered title despite the fact there was no register entry. However, CRL ceased to be an overriding interest with effect from midnight on 12 October 2013. This means that a buyer for valuable consideration will not be bound by an obligation to pay CRL unless it has been protected by way of a notice on the register of title in registered land or by way of a caution against first registration in unregistered land.

However, many conveyancers are continuing to make CRL searches where it is the first time the property has been sold since 13 October 2013, that is, it is the first sale for value after 13 October 2013. This is because of the danger that the church authorities might actually apply to register a notice or enter a caution against first registration during the transaction.

The point is that CRL did not cease to exist on 13 October 2013 – for instance, it lasts indefinitely where a notice has been put on the register. It exists against property owners (even without registration of a notice) who remain the same after 13 October 2013. The church authorities have until a subsequent purchaser comes along to register a protective notice. This could be years away where the current owners do not move after 13 October 2013. So, in registered land, where no notice has been registered, the liability will continue until the first transaction for value after 13 October 2013. It is only when the property has been sold to the new buyer, without any CRL notice on the register, that the property will be free of the liability. As the church authorities can apply to register a notice regarding CRL until the first transaction for value has taken place after 13 October 2013, CRL is still an issue for a first purchaser for value after 13 October 2013 since a binding notice could be registered at any point up until the OS search is made (it is only at this point that the register is frozen). If a notice was applied for within the priority period, it could still be binding if the buyer's registration application was not delivered before the expiry of the OS priority period.

In the case of unregistered land, a buyer for value will only be bound if the CRL is referred to in the deeds or if the church authorities have entered a caution against first registration before the first registration takes place. If a caution has been registered and the CRL can be established by the church authorities, HMLR will then enter a notice on the new register on first registration and the buyer will again be bound. Again, there is a risk of a late application for a caution against first registration during the sale to the buyer.

It is also relevant to note that where there is a transfer of the land which is not for value (e.g. on inheritance or by way of gift), any CRL will remain with the land. Liability will only fall away (where unprotected) where there is a sale for valuable consideration.

There is one further reason, which has more recently been highlighted, as to why firms may still wish to carry on making CRL searches and/or insuring against potential CRL. This is a legal reason based on the interpretation of **LRA 2002**. The Law Commission published its 13th programme for Law Reform in September 2017. The Commission stated that it wishes to ensure "that chancel repair liability does not bind purchasers of land, unless registered – and therefore visible – to purchasers". Following the removal of CRL from the categories of overriding interests as from 13 October 2013 (see above), most observers assumed that this was the case. However, a number of commentators, including the Law Society, have expressed doubts as the effect of **LRA 2002** provisions to render an unprotected CRL liability void as against a buyer and successors in title. The doubts centre on the interpretation of **s29(1) LRA 2002**, which states:

If a registrable disposition of a registered estate is made for valuable consideration, completion of the disposition by registration has the effect of postponing to the interest under the disposition any interest affecting the estate immediately before the disposition whose priority is not protected at the time of the registration.

The concerns centre on what is meant by "interest" and whether such an "interest" includes CRL. A claim against the owner for chancel repairs is not of the same nature as a transaction or charge that must be registered or satisfied in a specific order. If priority of competing interests is viewed following this strict interpretation, failure to register a notice to protect CRL would not appear to have any effect on the enforcement of a chancel repair claim. The net result of all this is that many conveyancers are still making CRL searches.

Attempts have been made to abolish CRL, as many see this liability as old-fashioned and unfair.

The Law Commission's latest project on CRL has not yet started and will start "as soon as resources allow". The project, once started, is expected to last between six and nine months and the outcome will either take the form of advice to government, or recommendations and a draft Bill. The overall aim of the project is to "ensure that [CRL] does not bind purchasers of land unless it is registered, and therefore visible, to purchasers". The Law Commission states that "it will also help to avoid the need for purchasers to undertake [CRL] searches or to pay for insurance". This work remains a future development and CRL searches will continue to be made where relevant as described above.

8.17 Company search

If the seller is a company, a company search may be made before exchange of contracts to identify any problematic issues before exchange. An example of where this search would be necessary would be where the client was buying a house from a developer which was a company (e.g. Smart Homes Limited). The search may be carried out at this stage to check the company:

- exists;
- has the power to sell and buy land;
- has no undisclosed charges which affect the land; and
- is not insolvent.

This search is traditionally undertaken at a later stage, pre-completion. It is nevertheless sensible to make this search before exchange so that any problems which do emerge can be addressed as soon as possible. The results of the search should however be updated before completion.

8.18 Canal/rivers search

If the property is located near a canal for instance, a search can be made with the Canal and River Trust which holds details of all canals in the country. The search application must be accompanied by a colour plan of the land being purchased plus the search fee.

Activity

The Canal and River Trust website contains guidance regarding conveyancers' searches at:

https://canalrivertrust.org.uk/business-and-trade/estates

The search will provide details of such matters as whether the Trust has any rights which may affect the property such as access rights, whether the Trust intends to carry out future works which will affect the property, whether the property boundaries shown on the applicant's plan match the details of the land and its boundaries owned by the Trust and whether the property has any repair and maintenance obligations in respect of the canal banks or towpaths.

8.19 Should searches be repeated?

If there is any delay in the conveyancing process, it may be necessary to repeat some of the searches contained within it. Although mortgage lenders require that any search is no more than six months old at completion (this is specified in the UK Finance Mortgage Lenders' Handbook at clause 5.4.3), good practice would dictate that a local search which is over three months old should be repeated. This is due to the nature of the search and the fact that any results are a snapshot of what the local authority has on its records on the date of the search – much could have changed in the three months since then. A prudent buyer will always repeat an old search just to make sure everything is satisfactory.

The above material covers most of the searches which a practitioner would make, but it is always important for the buyer's conveyancer to consider the exact location of the purchase property together with any special features or instructions (e.g. where the property backs on to a railway line or a canal bank).

Link to practice

You need to be alert to the possibility that non-standard searches might be needed in a particular transaction and you should look out for the sign posts.

It is also important to appreciate that specific searches may be indicated by other conveyancing documentation such as the register entries. Let us look at some examples:

(1) A register entry indicates past ownership by an industrial company, this might point to the importance of making an environmental search in addition to the CON 29 enquiries of the local authority.

(2) A reference to past ownership by church authorities might for example indicate the need to consider a CRL search.

(3) A reference to a property in "Riverbank Mews" might indicate the need to consider a flood search.

(4) A register entry stating that mines and minerals were excepted from the effect of the registration, this would alert the conveyancer to the need to consider a mining search. This would arise because the existence of such an entry means that mining has occurred at or near the property in the past and that mining might possibly occur in the future. In relation to this point, the buyer's conveyancer would also want to raise pre-contract enquiries of the seller's conveyancer such as whether any past or current mining has occurred and whether the property has suffered from any subsidence issues.

8.20 Indemnity insurance

We have seen that various problems can arise during a conveyancing transaction which must be resolved prior to the buyer's conveyancer advising their client to proceed. Examples of such problems relating to matters of title are:

- breach of a restrictive covenant – for example, a property has been extended without consent of a landowner;
- a missing deed in the title – perhaps an old conveyance was not produced to HMLR on first registration;
- lack of rights – perhaps a property does not enjoy a right-of-way over adjoining land for access.

Other problems can arise from the searches and enquiries, for example:

- breach of planning obligations;
- failing to obtain a building regulation completion certificate. ***Cottingham v Attey, Bower & Jones (a Firm)*** **[2000]** (see **Chapter 7**) led to a significant increase in the use of lack of building regulations indemnity policies;
- a property being in an area which is at risk of chancel liability.

Generally, it would be possible to put these problems right from a legal perspective. It might be possible to find the landowner who needs to give their consent to the extension of a dwelling or who needs to grant a right-of-way over their land for access. It might be possible to apply to the local authority for retrospective planning permission or for a regularisation certificate. However, the problem with doing this is that any such action is likely to take a long time and could be expensive and the outcome is not certain. For example, it might be straightforward to locate a landowner over whose land a right-of-way is exercised. However, that landowner would not necessarily be obliged to grant the requested easement and if they did, they might want many thousands of pounds for doing so.

Accordingly, the use of indemnity insurance in residential conveyancing transactions is very commonplace. There are a number of companies offering indemnity insurance products. The purpose of an indemnity insurance policy is that, for the payment of a one-off premium, and insurance policy is issued which would meet the costs of dealing with the specified defect.

It is essential to understand that indemnity insurance does not put the legal problem right. It merely gives a convenient solution to the problem to enable a transaction to proceed.

A seller would be expected to pay for the indemnity insurance and the premium would usually be deducted from the sale proceeds by the seller's conveyancer on completion and the policy would be obtained on completion and provided to the buyer's conveyancer. The agreement for the seller to provide indemnity insurance (and any accompanying statutory declaration or statement of truth – see below) should be referred to in the contract. However, it may be that the seller does not agree to pay for the indemnity insurance. In this case, it is a matter for negotiation between the seller and buyer as to who pays for it. If the buyer has a lender involved, the buyer's conveyancer may consider that it is essential to obtain indemnity insurance and the buyer may have to pay for it.

Please note the comments above in **Chapter 7** regarding planning and building regulations enforcement. The extension of the enforcement period to 10 years may affect the availability or cost of indemnity insurance for these particular issues. This is an evolving area and conveyancing practitioners must keep up to date.

8.20.1 Obtaining a policy

There are a number of organisations which offer indemnity insurance products. The commercial search providers can often offer links to two or three companies or the conveyancing firm can contact an indemnity insurance provider directly. Most indemnity insurance providers offer standard, "off-the-shelf" indemnity insurance products for straightforward defects. It is important for the buyer's conveyancer to ensure that the indemnity insurance product on offer covers the defect.

The limitations on any indemnity insurance products should be carefully explained to the buyer and lender clients, if any. For example, a policy which covers lack of rights for access for a property which is going to be developed might be much cheaper if it does not come into force until the development is complete. However, this would mean that the owner/developer would have no indemnity insurance in place if an adjoining landowner objected to lack of rights during the development.

Generally, indemnity insurance should be obtained to protect the buyer and any successors in title together with lenders. The limit of indemnity, that is the maximum amount that could be claimed under the policy, should generally be the purchase price of the property.

If there is a more complex defect or the buyer's conveyancer concludes that a self-issue policy is not appropriate, it is necessary to contact the indemnity insurance company to ask them for a quotation for the provision of an indemnity policy.

The indemnity insurer will require information such as:

- the nature of the defect;
- copies of any relevant documents;
- the date that the defect arose;
- whether any steps have been taken to remedy the defect;

- whether any third parties have attempted to assert any rights;
- the estimate of the amount of cover needed (usually the purchase price).

The more recent the defect, the less likely it will be that indemnity insurance is available or the indemnity insurance premium will be much higher.

8.20.2 The lender's requirements

Indemnity insurance is a sufficiently important and frequently occurring issue that the Lender's Handbook has a section dealing with it which states as follows:

"9. Indemnity Insurance

9.1 You must effect an indemnity insurance policy whenever the Lenders' Handbook identifies that this is an acceptable or required course to us to ensure that the property has a good and marketable title at completion. This paragraph does not relate to mortgage indemnity insurance. The draft policy should not be sent to us unless we ask for it. Check part 2 to see if the policy must be sent to us after completion.

9.2 Where indemnity insurance is effected:

- you must approve the terms of the policy on our behalf; and
- the limit of indemnity must meet our requirements (see part 2); and
- the policy must be effected without cost to us; and
- you must disclose to the insurer all relevant information which you have obtained; and
- the policy must not contain conditions which you know would make it void or prejudice our interests; and
- you must provide a copy of the policy to the borrower and explain to the borrower why the policy was effected and that a further policy may be required if there is further lending against the security of the property; and
- you must explain to the borrower that the borrower will need to comply with any conditions of the policy and that the borrower should notify us of any notice or potential claim in respect of the policy; and
- the policy should always be for our benefit and, if possible, for the benefit of the borrower and any subsequent owner or mortgagee. If the borrower will not be covered by the policy, you must advise the borrower of this."

8.20.3 Statement of truth/statutory declaration

There are some situations where a buyer will request that a seller provides written confirmation of certain circumstances in addition to an indemnity insurance policy.

The buyer's conveyancer might ask the seller to provide a statutory declaration or a statement of truth. As with provision of the policy, the seller cannot be compelled to provide such a document and it is thus a matter of negotiation between the parties. However, if a property does not enjoy any rights of access, the buyer's conveyancer may consider the issue to be a sufficiently serious defect in title that the absence of any supporting evidence from the seller is a reason for the buyer to consider withdrawing from the transaction.

(1) **Statutory declaration**

A statutory declaration is the more traditional document produced in the circumstances and is a formal statement made in a prescribed format affirming that something is true to the best knowledge of the person making the statement (called the "declarant"). The document should be sworn in front of a solicitor or Notary Public. Whilst the declaration must contain standard wording at the beginning and end of the document, the contents must be from within the declarant's own knowledge and it is not necessary to include formal, legal language.

Link to practice

A statutory declaration for access and service might contain the following (note the formal wording at the beginning and end of the document in bold)

I [INSERT] of [INSERT] ("the Property") DO solemnly and sincerely declare as follows: -

1. I am registered proprietor with Title Absolute under Title number [INSERT] of the Property delineated on the Plan ("the Plan") now produced and shown to me and marked [INSERT] and thereon edged red.
2. To the side of the Property there is a track / road / pathway ("the Access") leading from [INSERT] to [INSERT] being shown on the Plan and thereon coloured yellow.
3. I purchased the Property in [INSERT] and the Plan is to my knowledge an accurate plan of the Property and the Access thereon delineated.
4. The Access has been used by me and my agents servants and friends since [INSERT] as of right without the consent of any person and without interruption objection or dispute and without payment of any kind to any person whosoever from the said year [INSERT] until the present time.

5. The said use has been to pass and repass along the Access and to and from the Property by day or by night with or without vehicles of any description and with or without animals for all purposes connected with the Property, including (but not limited to) [INSERT DETAIL EG TO GAIN ACCESS TO PARK].
6. The service pipes wires and cables running to and from the Property and connecting with the mains have been used by me and my agents servants and friends since [INSERT] as of right without the consent of any person and without interruption objection or dispute and without payment of any kind to any person whosoever from the said year [INSERT] until the present time.

I depose as above of my own knowledge as owner of the Property

AND I make this solemn declaration conscientiously believing the same to be true and by virtue of the provisions of the Statutory Declarations Act 1835

Declared at)
in the)
this day of)
20XX)

Before me

Commissioner for Oaths/ Solicitor / Notary

If there are exhibits attached to the statutory declaration, each will be separately numbered and attached with a separate front sheet as follows:

This is the exhibit marked [INSERT] referred to in the declaration of [INSERT NAME OF DECLARANT] made before me this day of 20XX

....

A Commissioner for Oaths/Solicitor/Notary

(2) **Statement of truth**

In a conveyancing context, a statement of truth is a method of providing evidence in support of an application made to HMLR. The major difference between a statement of truth and statutory declaration is that the former does not need to be sworn in front of a solicitor or Notary Public which makes its production and conclusion more straightforward. Common examples of statements of truth are:

- when an application for registration is made based on adverse possession or lost title deeds;
- when an application is made to register a right acquired by prescription (that is, long use);
- when an application is made to cancel a Form A restriction protecting a trust of land that has come to an end.

The following forms provide a framework to supply the information required by HMLR in the most common cases:

- form ST1: statement of truth in support of an application for registration of land based upon adverse possession;
- form ST2: statement of truth in support of an application for registration of a rentcharge based upon adverse possession;
- form ST3: statement of truth in support of an application for registration of land based on lost or destroyed title deeds;
- form ST4: statement of truth in support of an application for registration and/or noting of a prescriptive easement;
- form ST5: statement of truth in respect of an application to cancel a Form A restriction.

In the context of indemnity insurance, the statement of truth that you are most likely to encounter is ST4 (see https://www.gov.uk/government/publications/prescriptive-easements-statement-of-truth-st4 which is used when noting a prescriptive easement. The ST4 is straightforward to complete and requires the party making the statement to provide information including:

- the land which benefits from the easement;
- the land burdened by the easement (that is, the land over which the right is exercised);
- the title number(s) of the above if known;
- plan(s) of the parcels of land;
- details of the freehold owner of the burdened land if known;
- details of the facts relied on to support the claim that an easement has been acquired by prescription. This would include information such as the length of time that the right has been exercised, the nature of the use (such as with a without vehicles) and the frequency of the use;
- confirmation that the exercise of the right has been exercised without force, secrecy or permission.

Activity

Follow the link below to HMLR's "Practice guide 73: statements of truth and note the requirements for a statement of truth":

https://www.gov.uk/government/publications/statements-of-truth/practice-guide-73-statements-of-truth

Link to practice

The statutory declaration or statement of truth will be drafted by the seller's conveyancer. This is because the content of the document must be from within the personal knowledge of the seller. Often, these documents are poorly drafted. The buyer's conveyancer should resist a poorly drafted document and should try to ensure that it is as comprehensive as possible. The buyer's conveyancer cannot put words into the mouth of the seller, but they can suggest amendments/drafts/further improvements to ensure that the document contains as much information as the seller is able to provide.

Unsurprisingly, if the seller is a personal representative, they are unlikely to have as much personal information and knowledge about the property as the original seller.

Link to practice

It is obvious that the provision of a statutory declaration or statement of truth by the seller can be very important to the buyer. Accordingly, the exact terms of the document to be sworn or provided by the seller should be agreed between the conveyancers prior to exchange of contracts. An additional special condition should be added to the contract, for example:

On or before completion the Seller will provide at their own expense the [statutory declaration or statement of truth] in the form annexed hereto.

Then the agreed form of the statutory declaration or statement of truth (together with any properly coloured plans) should be appended to both parts of the contract.

8.20.4 Non-disclosure is essential

Indemnity insurance is generally available provided that no party or organisation has been alerted to the possibility of a problem. Accordingly, if a property lacks rights for access, the landowner over whose land access is obtained should not be contacted. Similarly, if development has taken place without the benefit of planning permission, the local authority should not be contacted. If any such contact is made, it is unlikely that indemnity insurance will be available. This is because a party will have been put on notice of a potential claim.

It is therefore essential for the conveyancers to notify their clients of this to ensure that both seller and buyer do not contact anyone regarding defects for which indemnity insurance might be a solution.

8.20.5 Insurance Distribution Directive

The **EU Insurance Distribution Directive (IDD) (2016/97/EU)** came into force on 1 October 2018 from which date, advice and arrangements relating to the acquisition or disposal of insurance contracts are classified as "regulated activities". Conveyancing firms are caught by the IDD because they arrange indemnity insurance policies for issues such as defective titles and contaminated land.

Firms which carry out insurance distribution services must have an insurance distribution officer in post. Their role is to oversee compliance with the IDD. The firm must also be registered in the Financial Services Register maintained by the FCA. There are various responsibilities imposed on organisations which are caught by the IDD including:

- all communication must be clear, fair and not misleading;
- before a policy is purchased, clients must know:
    - whether the firm provides a personal recommendation about the insurance products offered;
    - the complaints and redress procedures;
    - whether the firm acts for and on behalf of the insurer;
- the firm must provide a demands and needs statement to the client (in a conveyancing context, a standard statement is provided by most indemnity insurance providers);
- any intermediary used by the firm must be registered in the UK.

The above is only some of the key requirements of the IDD. If a firm gives a personal recommendation of a particular product to a client, it must be on the basis of an analysis of a sufficiently large number of insurance contracts available on the market. This is why many conveyancing firms will now obtain two or three indemnity insurance quotations for conveyancing clients.

8.21 Chapter summary

As the seller's duty of disclosure is limited, it is essential that the buyer's conveyancer carries out extensive pre-contract searches and enquiries. Most searches can now be carried out electronically.

The following searches are almost always carried out:

- local land charges search (LLC1);
- standard enquiries of the local authority (CON 29);
- drainage and water search (CON 29DW);
- pre-contract enquiries of the seller unless a Property Information Form (TA6) has been completed by the seller – the buyer's conveyancer will raise both standard enquiries and those specifically relating to the transaction;
- inspection of the property and survey;
- environmental search.

The following searches may also be required, depending on the transaction:

- optional enquiries of the local authority (CON 29O);
- Index Map search;
- central land charges search;
- coal and other mining search;
- chancel repair liability search;
- flood search;
- company search.

Indemnity insurance is often obtained by conveyancers to deal with title or other defects.

CHAPTER 9

Reporting to client and exchange of contracts

9.1 Introduction

Exchange of contracts is the crucial stage when everyone is ready and the client may finally have a binding contract for their sale or purchase. It takes some time to reach this point, as the buyer's conveyancer needs to ensure it is safe to proceed including ensuring that the buyer has the financing in place and that any appropriate co-ownership advice has been given and the content of any declaration of trust has been agreed. The buyer's conveyancer must report fully to their client before they can proceed. This chapter will consider all of these issues along with exchange of contracts. We will also consider the rarer occurrences when things go wrong between exchange and completion.

This chapter will cover:

- financial matters;
- financial services and the declaration of trust;
- advice on co-ownership;
- the declaration of trust;

- reporting to the buyer;
- reviewing the file;
- synchronising sale and purchase;
- methods of exchanging contracts;
- effect of a binding contract;
- problems between exchange of contracts and completion.

9.2 Financial matters

9.2.1 The general financial situation

Whether the client is buying or selling, or both, they will need advice with regard to their general financial situation. The easiest situation is where the client is selling only. Usually, they will simply need to know whether they will realise as much as they had hoped from the sale after all expenses, etc. are paid.

Where the client is buying only, we need to see whether they will have enough money to complete the transaction once they have taken into account conveyancers' fees, SDLT, search fees, HMLR fees, etc.

The matter of ensuring that the client's finances are in order becomes more complicated where the client is both buying and selling property, as it will be part of the conveyancer's role to reconcile the finances of the two transactions and explain to the client the overall picture. You should ensure that your client has been fully advised on costs at the start of the transaction to ensure they can proceed.

There are two different stages of the transaction which need to be considered when advising the client.

(1) The long-term financial situation

Advice here requires knowing what fees and disbursements are likely to be incurred and then doing a calculation based on the net figure to be received by the client on their sale compared with the figure needed from the client to finance the purchase. If money will, at the conclusion of the transaction, be due to the client then – providing it is of an amount they were expecting – there can be little problem. But what about the situation where, when we have done the calculations, there is going to be a shortfall of funds? The solution depends on the particular client's situation but there are usually four possibilities.

(1) The client comes up with more money, perhaps from savings if they have any. Some clients may be able to get help with additional funding from their parents or other family members (this would, of course, raise issues for the conveyancer in relation to gifted deposit concerns).

(2) The client borrows more money. The possible sources of this borrowing will need to be considered (e.g. the building society or bank might make them a bigger advance on their purchase).

(3) The seller is persuaded to reduce the purchase price. The success of this possibility depends entirely on the state of the market and the frame of mind of the seller.

(4) The client does not proceed with the transaction.

(2) The short-term financial situation

At exchange of contracts a buyer is usually required to pay a deposit of 10 per cent of the purchase price. The buyer will have to find this substantial amount before they receive any money from the lender, as the mortgage advance will be paid at completion, not exchange of contracts. Where the buyer is also selling a property, the deposit on the sale may be used towards the deposit on the purchase, as long as the contract allows this, but there may still be a shortfall where the deposit to be received on the sale is less than the deposit required for the purchase. There are various possible solutions where there is a problem with funding the deposit.

(1) The client could provide the deposit or shortfall from their own savings.

(2) The buyer could make use of a deposit guarantee scheme. In essence, an insurance company, for a fee, agrees that if the transaction after exchange of contracts does not go ahead because of the buyer's default it will provide the deposit money. On the strength of this guarantee the seller may agree to take no deposit. If the buyer does not complete the transaction the insurance company pays the seller and will then pursue the buyer to try to recover what it has paid. This is rare in a residential conveyancing transaction.

(3) The seller may be persuaded to accept a reduced deposit. Most contracts in this situation will provide for the whole 10 per cent to become payable if the buyer defaults on completion – see Standard Condition 6.8.3.

(4) The buyer may be able to borrow the money for a short time by means of a bridging loan. Where the conveyancer is able to explain to a bank that, once the transaction is completed, the client will have more than enough money (e.g. from the receipt of sale proceeds and/or the mortgage advance), then banks will usually be prepared to make a short-term loan. A bank will often, in return, require an undertaking from the firm to pay the sale proceeds to it on completion. This is rare in a residential conveyancing transaction.

Example

Here is an example of advising a client about financial arrangements:

John is selling a flat at £100,000 and buying a house at £150,000. His existing mortgage is £45,000 and his new mortgage is to be £95,000.

The following issues would have to be considered:

(1) The need to fund the 10 per cent deposit on the purchase and the methods of resolving this problem.

(2) On completion, the amount forthcoming from the sale, and the amount needed to complete the purchase. In this case, SDLT, the conveyancing costs, HMLR fees and other disbursements also need to be covered. Estate agents' fees may have to be met on the sale, and the cost of a survey (probably already paid) on the purchase.

(3) In conclusion, that a figure of perhaps a further £4,000 or more will be needed to complete this transaction in addition to any deposit which will be required.

9.2.2 Financial services

Do not confuse the situation above where the conveyancer is doing calculations to ensure that the client has sufficient money to fund their transaction with giving "financial advice". The latter is a situation where advice is given on particular financial products and generally, conveyancers are prohibited from giving specific financial advice as to the suitability of financial or mortgage products.

Link to practice

Conveyancers are permitted to give generic advice as to issues such as the difference between a repayment mortgage or an interest only mortgage and the basic terms of a mortgage offer and the consequences of defaulting on mortgage payments. However, unless properly regulated (see below), which most conveyancing firms are not, a conveyancer cannot advise their client as to whether a particular product or mortgage deal is suitable for the client. This makes sense because, of course, conveyancers generally do not have the appropriate qualifications or product knowledge to give this advice.

If a client asks a conveyancer for specific financial advice, the conveyancer should decline to comment and advise the client to obtain independent financial advice from a suitably qualified professional.

The **Financial Services and Markets Act 2000** (**FSMA 2000**) makes the Financial Conduct Authority (FCA) and the Prudential Regulation Authority (PRA) the statutory regulators of financial services business. Under **FSMA 2000**, firms carrying on **regulated activities** need to be regulated by the FCA.

Part XX FSMA 2000 makes special provision for law firms which do not carry on mainstream investment business but which carry on **regulated activities** during other work such as conveyancing. **Part XX** enables firms of conveyancers which meet certain conditions to be treated as carrying on **exempt regulated activities**. These firms will not need to be regulated by the FCA, but will carry on **exempt regulated activities** under the supervision of, and regulation by, the SRA.

It is up to an individual firm to decide whether or not it requires FCA authorisation. To put it in context, however, only about 300 firms in England and Wales are authorised to conduct mainstream investment business.

It is clear that as far as conveyancing is concerned, conveyancers who give generic advice (e.g. advising on the differences between an endowment mortgage and a repayment mortgage) will not be caught by **FSMA 2000**.

Examples

The SRA (Financial Services) Scope Rules, included in the SRA Handbook, define what can and cannot be done without FCA regulation. The majority of advice given to support and assist conveyancing transactions, and which is incidental to the provision of the professional services (for instance, general advice on types of mortgages), will not require such authorisation, though advice on whether a specific investment product is better than another will. Therefore, for example, if a conveyancer was asked to advise a client about a specific investment product such as a particular life insurance policy to be linked to a mortgage, this would be "investment business" and would require FCA authorisation. In this sort of situation, many conveyancers would decide to refer the client to an independent financial adviser or other such qualified and regulated professional for advice.

Another example would be where a conveyancer wished to arrange a title indemnity insurance policy for a client. The conveyancer could arrange this title indemnity insurance policy if they were acting on a purchase for a specific client and required this as a complement to the professional service they were providing to that client. However, in this latter example there would be additional conditions which must be observed if it is to be done without FCA authorisation. One such condition would be that the firm must be included in a register of exempt professional firms maintained by the FCA.

This is a complex area and legal practitioners must always be aware of their obligations and limitations under **FSMA 2000** in order to avoid committing a criminal offence.

9.3 Co-ownership and the declaration of trust

A buyer's conveyancer may be advising joint buyers, meaning that issues of co-ownership will arise at the instructions stage. The conveyancer will check these instructions during the file review pre-exchange to ensure that the correct co-ownership declaration is made in the transfer (or lease). Co-ownership can be either a joint tenancy or a tenancy in common. The word "tenancy" has nothing to do with the word in the context of paying a landlord or renting but means "ownership".

By way of recap, the **Trusts of Land and Appointment of Trustees Act 1996** provides that, whenever there is co-ownership, the land is subject to a **trust of land.** This trust arises automatically and exists even if the co-owners are not themselves aware of it. A trust is a situation where property is held by one or more people upon trust for another person or persons. The persons holding the property on trust are the trustees and the people for whom the property is held are the beneficiaries. The trustees hold the legal estate in the land for the benefit of the beneficiaries in equity.

Example

Usually (e.g. in a situation where a husband and wife buy a house jointly), the trustees are also the beneficiaries. So, if, for example, Jenna and Sam bought a house together, they would be the trustees holding the legal estate. At the same time, they would also be the beneficiaries in equity holding the land on behalf of each other. They would therefore hold a beneficial or equitable interest in the property as well as being the legal owners.

The **legal estate** can only be held by the trustees (legal owners) as joint tenants. There is no choice in this matter. This means that the legal estate always passes by survivorship (see below for an explanation of this concept) to the remaining joint tenants.

The **beneficial interests** can be held either as a beneficial joint tenancy or as a beneficial tenancy in common. The beneficial owners can therefore choose to be joint tenants or tenants in common. They will make this choice when they buy the property, following advice from the conveyancer.

The important difference in practice relates to the doctrine of survivorship, sometimes referred to as the right of survivorship, which exists in the case of a joint tenancy but not in the case of a tenancy in common. The right of survivorship means that if one joint tenant dies, their share automatically passes to the surviving joint tenant(s). This is because in the case of a joint tenancy, each co-owner is regarded as jointly owning the whole of the property rather than a distinct share in it. The right of survivorship does not apply in the case of a beneficial tenancy in common. On the death of a tenant in common, their share does not pass automatically to the other co-owner(s) but instead passes under their will or, where there is no valid will, under the intestacy rules. The intestacy rules govern what happens to a person's property where there is no will.

The following diagrams act as a simple illustration.

Joint tenants

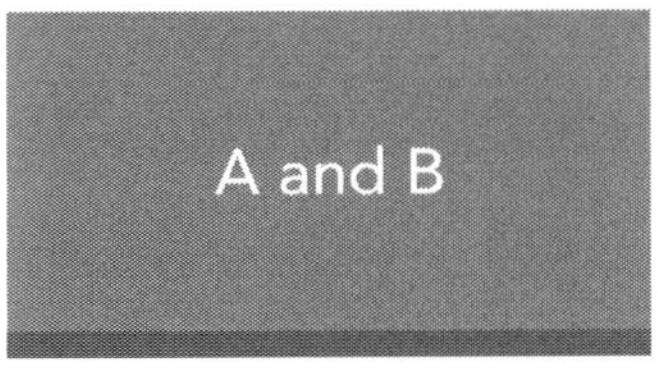

A and B are joint tenants who own the property together. They do not have defined shares.

If A dies, B automatically owns the whole under the survivorship rule. Like this:

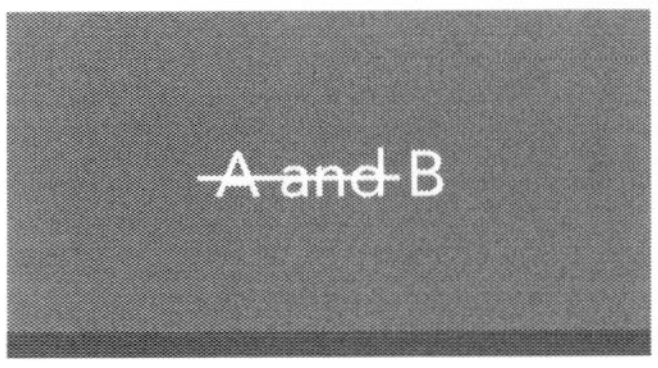

Tenants in common

C and D are beneficial tenants in common. They have decided to hold defined shares of 60:40 as C put more money than D into their purchase.

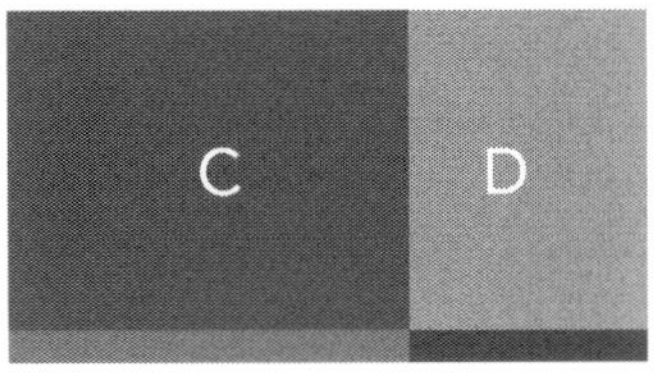

C and D leave their defined shares to each other by will or to someone else, like this.

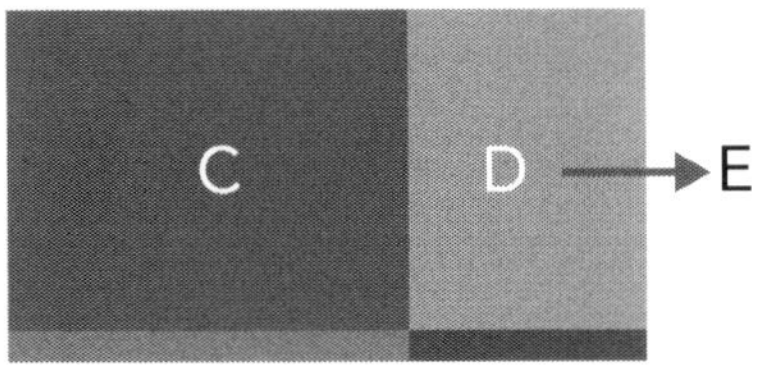

D has died and left her share to E. The beneficial interests in the property are now owned like this.

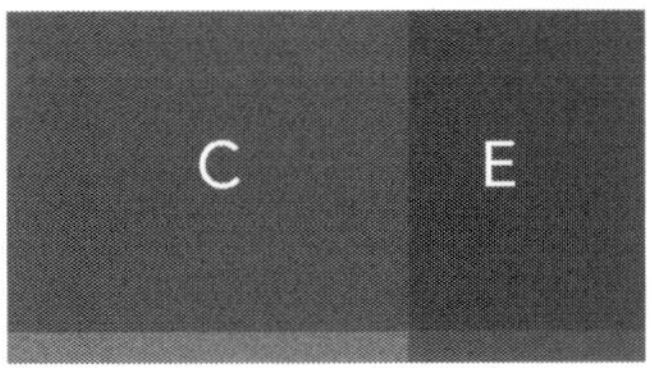

Joint tenancies

In a joint tenancy all the co-owners – joint tenants – together own the whole of the interests in the land. None of them can identify an individual share regardless of their contributions to the purchase price.

Where there is a joint tenancy, the right of survivorship applies. Put simply, this means that, upon the death of one joint tenant, their interest in the property vests in the hands of the remaining joint tenants. It does not pass under their estate.

A beneficial joint tenancy can be turned into a beneficial tenancy in common by **severance**. The legal estate cannot be severed as the legal estate has to be held as a joint tenancy.

Example

So, even if a beneficial joint tenancy is created initially, it may not remain so. It may be severed at a later date. For instance, a husband and wife may initially buy a property as legal and beneficial joint tenants but then experience relationship problems. Imagine that the husband does not want his beneficial interest in the property to pass automatically to his wife if he died (as would happen by survivorship with a joint tenancy). He may therefore wish to sever the beneficial joint tenancy so that he can then leave his separate share as a tenant in common to someone else (e.g. his children) in his will. Conveyancers will usually mention the possibility of future severance when they advise about joint ownership.

A joint tenancy can be severed by the joint tenant giving written notice of severance to the other joint tenants. This is the most common method. Severance can also arise through other actions that suggest that severance has taken place. One example of the latter would be where it could be proved there was a mutual agreement between the joint tenants to hold the equitable interest in separate shares. Another example would be where it could be proved there was a course of dealing (e.g. negotiations) showing that the beneficial interests were being mutually treated as a tenancy in common. In the context of everyday conveyancing practice, a notice of severance would be the most relevant method.

Example

A simple notice of severance is as follows:

NOTICE OF SEVERANCE

To: [INSERT NAME AND ADDRESS OF CO-OWNER]

I [INSERT FULL NAME OF CO-OWNER WHO SERVES THE NOTICE] hereby give you notice of my desire to sever as from this day the joint tenancy in equity of and in the property described in the Schedule hereto now held by you and me as joint tenants both at law and in equity so that the said property shall henceforth belong to you and me in equal shares

Dated day of 20XX

Schedule

[INSERT PROPERTY ADDRESS (AND TITLE NUMBER IF ANY)]

....

[Signature and full name of party serving the notice]

Received a Notice of which the above is a duplicate

Dated day of 20XX

....

[Signature and full name of party receiving the notice]

Tenants in common

Tenants in common have a specific share in the property, even if the shares are equal. The right of survivorship does not apply to tenancies in common: each tenant in common can sell or mortgage their interest or leave it to another in their will.

9.3.1 Advice on co-ownership

It is important that joint buyers are advised appropriately to avoid negligence claims in the future.

When advising joint buyers, the conveyancer should:

- clearly explain the types of co-ownership as above;
- ensure that all clients understand the advice, that they are all in agreement with any decisions, and that there is no conflict of interests between them;
- record the instructions and advice in writing (e.g. as part of the client care letter);
- be aware as to the possibility of a conflict of interest (or a significant risk of a conflict) if the co-owners cannot agree as to the position.

The conveyancer must ensure that instructions are obtained from all co-owners – it is not sufficient to rely on instructions from one co-owner, even if they insist that the other co-owners are in agreement.

Example

Married couples, civil partners or those in stable relationships are more likely to choose to hold as joint tenants (although the specific circumstances may dictate otherwise, as they may wish to hold as tenants in common to reflect unequal contributions, or for tax/estate planning purposes). If they wish to leave their respective shares to others on death (e.g. to children from a previous relationship) a tenancy in common will be necessary. Business partners or friends are more likely to buy as tenants in common.

The choice will be stated in the purchase deed. Typically, this will be in box 10 of form TR1 (https://www.gov.uk/government/publications/registered-titles-whole-transfer-tr1) or box 11 of form TP1 (https://www.gov.uk/government/publications/registered-titles-part-transfer-tp1).

The choices are as follows:

Declaration of trust. The transferee is more than one person and:

- they are to hold the property on trust for themselves as joint tenants
- they are to hold the property on trust for themselves as tenants in common in equal shares
- they are to hold the property on trust:

If the parties are buying as beneficial tenants in common, their respective shares can be set out in the transfer, or, if more complex, in a separate deed of trust. The shares themselves do not appear on the register in registered land – all that the register entries will show is that there are co-owners and that they either hold as joint tenants or tenants in common (indicated by the absence or presence of a Form A restriction on the proprietorship register).

Form JO

Form JO (Trust Information) is an additional method of stating the parties' intentions regarding co-ownership (https://www.gov.uk/government/publications/jointly-owned-property-trust-registration-jo). This form can be used as an alternative method of making a declaration of trust.

There are several situations where form JO can be used to record the clients' interests in the property. In relation to this course, the following have relevance:

- where panel 9 of form FR1 (a first registration application) has not been completed and the applicant is more than one person;
- where form AP1 (an application to change the register) relates to a transfer or assent (in form AS1, TP1, TP2, TR1, TR2 or TR5) or a prescribed clauses lease of registered land to more than one person and the declaration of trust panel in the transfer, assent or lease has not been completed and/or the transfer or assent has not been executed by the joint owners.

If used, form JO must accompany the application to register the transfer, assent or lease, or accompany the form FR1 to which it relates.

In practice, form JO might be useful, for instance, where the joint buyers have not executed the transfer deed (i.e. where it has only been executed by the seller). Joint buyers need to execute the transfer in order to confirm their co-ownership declaration. Where the conveyancer does not want to let the transfer executed by the seller leave the office (perhaps because of a lack of time between exchange and completion or because they do not want to part with the original transfer by posting it out) they could ask the buyers to sign a form JO. This must be sent with the HMLR application with the transfer and all the other relevant documents such as form AP1.

The same would apply if the declaration of trust box in the transfer was not completed. The declaration of trust could be made on form JO instead and sent to HMLR along with the transfer and all other documents (mortgage deed, AP1, etc.) on registration.

It should be stressed that form JO is optional (it is an alternative means of declaring trust interests) and most trust declarations will be made in the transfer and/or by way of a deed of trust.

9.3.2 The declaration of trust

Completing box 10 in the TR1 (or box 11 in the TP1) or form JO to deal with the co-ownership declaration should only be relied upon in the simplest of circumstances. It can be seen that the transfer declaration does not deal with any issues relating to the on-going trust, responsibilities or mortgage payments. In many cases a separate declaration of trust (also referred to as a "deed of trust") should be drafted to cover this detail.

The declaration of trust is a separate document which should set out the parties' respective contributions and shares as tenants in common. The conveyancer will charge an extra fee for the preparation of the trust deed, and clients must be advised about the charges.

Link to practice

Remember that HMLR keeps details of the beneficial interests off the legal title. So, you should not send a copy of the declaration of trust to HMLR.

HMLR will not be concerned as to its contents. Of more importance is the fact that sending it to HMLR places it in the public domain and anyone can apply for a copy of it. The document often contains a lot of personal information that the clients will not want in the public arena.

What should the declaration of trust contain?

The content of the declaration of trust will depend on the client's circumstances and the complexity of their arrangements. However, a basic declaration of trust should contain:

- the parties' names and addresses;
- the address of the property which they have purchased together;
- the purchase price, details of their respective contributions and mortgage, if any; and
- how the parties would like the sale proceeds to be divided.

It can also contain other useful provisions such as details of any mortgage, arrangements for payment of mortgage and outgoings, and procedures for sale where there is a disagreement.

Example

A simple declaration of trust is as follows:

THIS TRUST DEED is made the day of 20XX

BETWEEN [INSERT FULL NAME] of (hereinafter called "[INSERT]") of the first part and and [INSERT FULL NAME] (hereinafter called "[INSERT]") of the second part (together hereinafter called "the Trustees")

WHEREAS

(1) By a transfer of even date but executed before this Deed and made between ("the Transferor") of the one part and the Trustees of the other part and in consideration of the payment of the sum of [INSERT] thousand pounds (£[INSERT]) the property ("the Home") described in the Schedule hereto was transferred to the Trustees in fee simple upon trust as therein stated

(2) The parties have agreed that they are entitled to the beneficial interest in the Home as to [INSERT] per cent (%) to [INSERT FULL NAME] and [INSERT] per cent (%) to [INSERT FULL NAME]

NOW THIS DEED WITNESSES as follows:

1. The Trustees shall hold the Home on trust to sell the same with power to postpone the sale and shall hold the net rents and profits until sale and the net proceeds of sale for themselves as tenants in common as to [INSERT] per cent (%) to [INSERT FULL NAME] and [INSERT] per cent (%) to [INSERT FULL NAME]

2. The Trustees and HEREBY COVENANT with each other: -

   (a) To observe and perform all covenants restrictions conditions and stipulations (if any) at any time affecting the Home

   (b) To keep the Home and Contents insured against all usual comprehensive risks to the full reinstatement or replacement value of the same and to pay the insurance premiums and to apply any moneys received on any policy of insurance effected on the Home and Contents in the replacement or reinstatement thereof

   (c) That neither party shall create or purport to create any charge mortgage lien or other interest in respect of the Home as a whole or their respective shares or to dispose by sale gift or otherwise of the whole or part of their respective shares without the consent in writing of the other party except that this provision shall not restrict the right of either party to dispose of his or her share by Will

3. If either of the Trustees and /or their Personal Representatives) shall wish the Trust for sale to take effect they shall give notice to the other party in writing and if the parties do not reach agreement for one to buy the other's share within Twenty-eight days of such notice the parties shall place the Home to be sold on the open market

4. On completion of the sale of the Home (other than by way of purchase by one party of the other's share) the proceeds after deduction of all expenses of sale shall belong to [INSERT NAME] and [INSERT NAME] in the proportions stated in Clause 1 above

IN WITNESS whereof the parties hereto have executed this deed the day and year first above written

THE SCHEDULE

The [freehold/leasehold] land and dwellinghouse known as [INSERT] registered at H M Land Registry with Title Absolute with title number [INSERT]

SIGNED as a Deed by the said

[INSERT FULL NAME]
In the presence of: -

SIGNED as a Deed by the said
[INSERT FULL NAME]

In the presence of: -

Remember that the case law in this area has tended to develop when unmarried couples who have acquired a property together split up and cannot agree how the proceeds should be divided. A common feature of these cases is often that the co-ownership issues between the parties were not clarified at the outset. This highlights the importance to the conveyancer advising at the time of purchase to ensure that clear, written advice has been given and that the clients' instructions are clearly recorded on the file.

If co-ownership matters are not clearly dealt with in the conveyancing documents, there may be problems later (for instance, if the parties separate and one is disputing the extent of the other's ownership). Disputes may lead to costly and time-consuming court involvement. The court will be forced to come to a conclusion based on what the parties are taken to have intended, which may lead to a different result from that originally envisaged.

In determining what the parties intended, and the extent of their shares, the courts will be guided by case law. The courts now treat the family home in a different way from commercial property.

Where the home is held by both parties, in the absence of any express declaration of a tenancy in common, the courts will presume that the beneficial interests are held on a joint tenancy. This would be the case even where there had been unequal contributions to the purchase of the property. It would then be necessary for the party to prove that this presumption was rebutted and that a tenancy in common was intended.

When trying to ascertain the intentions of the parties and the extent of each party's share, the court must take a holistic approach – taking all factors into account. In ***Stack v Dowden*** **[2007]** the House of Lords set out a guideline list of the factors to be considered. In addition to financial contributions, these include:

- the nature of the parties' relationship;
- advice or discussions at the time of the transfer;
- the purposes for which the home was purchased;
- the payment of outgoings.

These examples are not exhaustive.

A more recent court case has underlined the importance of sorting out co-ownership in writing at the outset. In ***Jones v Kernott*** **[2011]** an unmarried couple owned a house in joint names but there had been no express declaration of trust saying how it was to be shared. The parties in this case were separated for a number of years before the court was asked to decide their respective shares. The Supreme Court decided that a fair split was 90 per cent to Ms Jones and 10 per cent to Mr Kernott. The court said that if there was no express declaration the court could, where necessary, infer or impute an intention to the parties and that this intention could change over time. On the facts of this case, the court found that their common intention had changed, and that the court was entitled to infer or impute an intention as to the division of the property that could be considered fair.

This case attracted much media attention at the time.

News

In the news...

Unmarried father has half share in house cut to 10%

A controversial ruling which awarded an absent father half the value of the family home he left 18 years ago was yesterday overturned by judges – who awarded him just 10 per cent

. . . Supreme Court judges . . . said . . . it was the duty of the courts to decide what the intentions of a couple were during the course of their relationship and afterwards . . . They decided a "'fair" split of assets in the case of Mr Kernott – whose name was on the deeds along with Miss Jones – would be for him to receive just 10 per cent . . .

Daily Mail, 10 November 2011

It is important to note that ***Stack v Dowden*** will not apply where there is an express trust. In ***Pankhania v Chandegra* [2012]** the Court of Appeal considered the application of the law relating to an express trust detailing the parties' respective beneficial interests in a property.

The transfer to the parties contained an express declaration of trust that it was held by them as tenants in common in equal shares. The appellant sought an order for sale with the proceeds to be divided equally as per the trust. The respondent argued that there was an understanding at the time of purchase that she was to be the beneficial owner and that the appellant's name was on the transfer to enable a mortgage to be obtained.

The court held that reliance on ***Stack v Dowden*** and ***Jones v Kernott*** was misplaced in circumstances where there was an express trust. The express trust was conclusive evidence of equal shares. There was no evidence of a sham trust. The appellant was entitled to a 50 per cent share as per the trust deed.

This case again highlights the importance of expressly declaring co-ownership interests at the outset.

Activity

Follow the link below to the Law Society Practice Note on joint ownership:

https://www.lawsociety.org.uk/topics/property/joint-ownership

The Practice Note states that declaring interests at the outset of a transaction provides clarity about the parties' intentions and may help to avoid disputes in the future. The Practice Note looks at the ways in which the parties may declare their intentions, and HMLR practice and procedure in this context, including the use of form JO. Read the Practice Note carefully and make notes as to the steps which the Law Society advises conveyancers to take in relation to co-ownership advice.

Link to practice

If a conveyancer advises co-owners to hold as tenants in common, the conveyancer will almost invariably advise the parties to enter into a declaration of trust (or trust deed). In addition, the conveyancer will advise the parties to have wills prepared to ensure that their share in the property passes in accordance with the wishes of each co-owner. However, many clients often do not want to incur the additional legal fees that a declaration of trust and wills involves. This can mean that parties whose circumstances suggest that they should hold as tenants in common, end up holding as joint tenants because they want to take advantage of the doctrine of survivorship.

Their conveyancer cannot force them to take the conveyancer's advice. However, in this instance, the conveyancer should ensure that very clear instructions are recorded on the file and that all owners provide written confirmation that they are choosing to decline the co-ownership advice from the conveyancer. A failure to do this could lead to a negligence claim if the co-owners subsequently split up, have a dispute about the division of the property and the conveyancer is unable to clearly demonstrate the advice given at the time of purchase.

9.4 Reporting to the buyer

When all the necessary searches, enquiries, inspections and title investigations have been completed, the buyer's conveyancers must consider the terms of the draft contract in the light of their results. They must be satisfied that the contract includes any rights the buyer wishes to acquire and does not include any adverse matters which are not acceptable to the buyer.

Any Special Conditions must be negotiated between the parties, together with the date for completion of the transaction. If the contract has been amended, it is crucial that both parts remain identical.

Both parties' conveyancers must ensure that all the preliminary matters have been dealt with satisfactorily. For example, that the buyer's finances covering the deposit and mortgage have been arranged.

Once all pre-contract matters have been checked and any queries dealt with, the buyer's conveyancer will normally send the client a report about the title and the property. The buyer can then check that they are happy to proceed to exchange and that there is nothing to cause them to withdraw before exchange. The conveyancer should give the whole picture of the property and the title, and point out any problems, indicating their significance and severity. Most conveyancers send the client a written report, attaching any relevant documents (e.g. a copy of the title plan or the wording of any covenants) and most firms have a standard form for such a title report, adapting it to the individual transaction. Matters commonly covered are:

- a summary of the conveyancer's overall view (e.g. that there are no major problems with the proposed purchase, or that there are problems capable of rectification (e.g. with insurance), or that there are major problems which are not capable of rectification);

- a summary of the property (e.g. current ownership and a copy of the plan);
- a summary of the title and any matters burdening and benefiting it (e.g. easements and covenants), highlighting any problems;
- a summary of the source of funding for the purchase (e.g. details of the new mortgage);
- a summary of the main points arising from the pre-contract searches and enquiries, highlighting any problems (e.g. with planning issues, access rights, private roads, service easements, etc.);
- information about the draft contract (the report may be sent with the contract for signature by the client);
- information about the conveyancing transaction generally (e.g. explaining the work still to be carried out).

When the buyer has given instructions to proceed, their conveyancers will return one copy of the contract approved to the seller's conveyancers. Both parties' conveyancers will obtain their clients' signatures to their respective copies of the contract.

Up to this point, the contract is not binding and so either party will be at liberty to withdraw from the transaction without having to pay compensation to the other. When the parties have completed their negotiations and are in a position to proceed, they will wish to effect a legally binding contract conferring upon each rights against the other.

There is no rule of law that there must be an exchange of contracts for there to be a binding contract. It is quite possible to have a binding contract where both parties sign the same document.

9.5 Reviewing the file

We have seen the importance of these checklists, but as the conveyancer is about to exchange contracts, it is vital to ensure that all matters are resolved. The following are basic checklists for a buyer's conveyancer and a seller's conveyancer.

Checklist for buyers' conveyancers

- Searches – results satisfactory?
- Queries answered satisfactorily?
- Additional queries? Do you have any further questions now you have the answers to the original enquiries?
- Requisitions answered? (These are queries on title issues rather than searches.)

- Survey satisfactory?
- Mortgage offer and mortgage instructions received? Any further conditions?
- Finance arranged?
- Deposit – is it the full 10 per cent or do you need to obtain agreement for a lesser deposit and amend the contract?
- Insurance – is it ready to be put on risk from exchange?
- Contract in agreed form and signed?
- Completion date agreed?
- Report sent to client?
- Authority to exchange? – You should always obtain your client's written authority to exchange. This is especially important if using Formula C, which is described later.

Checklist for sellers' conveyancers

- Finance – is there sufficient money to repay the mortgage upon completion and cover all other incidental costs, for example, legal fees?
- Completion date – has it been agreed by everyone?
- Non-owning occupiers – need to sign a clause in the contract so as to oblige them to vacate upon completion.
- Sign contracts – get clients to sign.
- Anything outstanding?
- Authority to exchange? – Get signed authority from your clients.

You must not exchange until every query has been answered and you are certain that it is safe to proceed.

The Protocol contains provisions relating to this stage of the transaction in:

- Stage B – Pre-exchange – submitting a contract;
- Stage C – Prior to exchange of contracts;
- Stage D – Exchange of contracts.

These provisions reflect good modern practice. Some examples of matters which the Protocol deals with at this stage are:

- sharing information with others (e.g. other parties, lenders and estate agents);
- making all necessary searches before exchange;
- raising any necessary additional pre-contract enquiries;

- reporting to the client about the title and other matters;
- considering mortgage instructions and any conditions imposed by the lender;
- approving the contract, and agreeing any transfer supplied before exchange;
- advising the buyer about survey, insurance and deposit arrangements;
- confirming the completion date;
- asking the buyer to sign the contract;
- checking any mortgage discharge arrangements.

As explained earlier in the course book, it is important for practitioners adopting the Protocol to consult the Protocol documentation itself to see the full details and to ensure compliance, as this material in the coursebook is included for educational purposes and to set the Protocol in context.

9.6 Synchronising sale and purchase

Usually, clients will wish to complete their sale and purchase on the same day (only being able to afford the purchase when in receipt of the proceeds from their sale, but at the same time wishing to move immediately into their new home). Their conveyancers must ensure that the clients become neither the owners of two houses, nor homeless. This is done by checking that the date for completion of the sale and purchase is the same in both contracts and making sure that the final time stipulated for completion on that date provides for the receipt of the sale money before the purchase money needs to be paid over.

Failure to synchronise without clear instructions to the contrary may amount to professional negligence. If the clients do not insist on the transactions being synchronised, the implications must be made clear for they will either have to finance the purchase independently from their sale if they buy before selling, or have available accommodation if they sell before buying.

Riskier advice – proceeding on a sale independently of a purchase

A client may have a related sale and purchase; that is transactions which they would like to exchange and complete on at the same time. However, it is sometimes the case that a client's sale proceeds more swiftly than their purchase. If there is a risk that the buyer on the client's sale might withdraw, the client will then need to consider whether to proceed on their sale independently of their purchase and their conveyancer must give clear, unequivocal advice in this regard.

The client needs to understand that if they authorise their conveyancer to proceed on their sale before the purchase transaction, there is a possibility that their purchase transaction might never take place or their mortgage offer might expire. Once exchange has taken place on the sale, there is no guarantee that the purchase would ever "catch up".

The client must understand that exchange of contracts on their sale commits them to a legally binding contract meaning that the client must move out of the property on the agreed completion date. This could involve the client putting their furniture and belongings in storage and having to arrange alternative accommodation, possibly with relatives or renting another property.

Link to practice

Unfortunately, these risks are sometimes not explained to a client particularly if an estate agent and a chain of parties are keen to proceed. The conveyancer would do all that they could to try to ensure that the purchase "catches up" and happens on the same day as the sale, but once exchange has taken place on the sale transactions are no longer synchronised and this can simply not be guaranteed.

Another implication of proceeding on the sale independently of the purchase is connected with the client's mortgage offer. If a client has early redemption penalties to pay on the completion of the sale, the lender will often waive these penalties if the client stays with that lender and completes on a related transaction using a fresh mortgage offer from the same lender. However, lenders often require the sale and purchase to be synchronised to avoid the early redemption penalties. You should always check this point if the client is staying with the same lender on both transactions.

As ever, all advice to the client and the response from the client should be in writing and placed on the file. Any doubt as to the situation if there is a subsequent problem would be construed against the seller if the position was unclear. This could lead to a negligence claim against the conveyancer if the client suffers loss.

9.7 Methods of exchanging contracts

Where the parties have signed separate copies of the approved contract (as is the usual case with ordinary residential conveyancing cases), the formation of a binding contract is by exchange of those documents. Different methods have been devised. The aim of the most common method (telephone exchange) is to ensure that exchange of contracts in two or more related transactions can be synchronised, thereby avoiding the risk that, between exchanging contracts in one transaction and the next, the parties to the latter will withdraw.

Methods of exchange			
		Chain transaction	**Potential difficulties**
(1) Personal		x (Usually inconvenient)	Lack of time General inconvenience
(2) Postal		x (Timescale makes synchronisation impractical)	1. Time taken 2. When does exchange take place?
(3) Telephone	Formula A Formula B	x x	1. Generally, the need to rely on an oral conversation 2. Importance of memos and undertakings 3. Cannot be used except by conveyancers, chartered legal executives or licensed conveyancers 4. A and B were not designed for chain transactions
	Formula C	✔ (Designed for chain transactions)	As for A and B and also 1. Needs client's authority 2. Potential problems concerning deposit, undertakings

If the Protocol is adopted, the parties must use the appropriate Law Society formula for exchange by telephone, unless a personal exchange is carried out.

The standard form of Contract (Incorporating the Standard Conditions of Sale, Fifth Edition – 2018 Revision) contains a box on the front page, in which the parties can record their identities and the method of exchange used (e.g. the appropriate formula or a personal exchange). The contract form expressly states that this information does not form part of the contract itself, but this is a useful place to record these points (see **Document 1** of the **Appendix**).

(1) **Exchange in person**

This method of conveyancers meeting to swap documents is rare as it is only practicable where the conveyancers' offices are close together and there is no chain of transactions involved.

(2) **Exchange by post**

Normally, the buyer's conveyancers will post the buyer's signed contract and deposit to the seller's conveyancers and it is generally assumed that exchange actually takes place when the second part of the contract (usually the seller's) is placed in the post. This is the position under SC 2.1. Note that:

(a) exchange of contracts by post would be extremely protracted in a chain of transactions, as each of the parties involved would have to wait for exchange to be effected on either their sale or purchase before proceeding to exchange contracts on the other. In the meantime, the clients would be at risk of having either two houses or none;

(b) SC 2.1 also provides for exchange by a document exchange, when exchange is effected at the moment the second part of the contract is deposited at the document exchange.

(3) **Exchange by telephone**

This method was given judicial recognition in ***Domb v Isoz* [1980]**. This is where two conveyancers agree over the telephone that contracts should be treated as exchanged, even though the respective documents have not been physically exchanged. SC 2.1 requires that a telephone exchange is effected by a conveyancer (this includes conveyancers and licensed conveyancers – see SC 1.1.1(f)). This method is within the conveyancers' ostensible authority once they have their client's authority to exchange.

To avoid evidential difficulties, the Law Society has produced three alternative formulae for use in telephonic exchanges.

Formula A is for use where one conveyancer holds both parts of the signed contract – that is, where one party's conveyancer (usually the buyer's) has forwarded their client's signed part of the contract to the other party's conveyancer before exchange.

To exchange by this formula, the parties' conveyancers during the course of their telephone conversation agree a completion date, and the conveyancer holding both parts of the contract confirms that they are signed and identical and undertakes to insert forthwith the agreed completion date. They then agree that exchange shall be effected as from that moment, so from then on the conveyancer holding both parts holds their own client's signed contract to the order of the other conveyancer, undertaking either to post it to them that day by first class post, to deposit it at the document exchange or to deliver it by hand, together with any deposit due, if applicable.

Formula B is similar but is for use when each party's conveyancer is holding their own client's part contract. This is more commonly used in practice than Formula A. During the course of their telephone conversation they agree a completion date, they confirm that they each hold their client's signed part contract (incorporating any amendments) and they agree to insert forthwith the agreed completion date.

Each conveyancer then agrees to hold their client's part contract to the order of the other. Exchange is effected at that moment. Each conveyancer further undertakes to send the part contract in their possession to the other that day by first class post, DX or by hand together with, in the case of the buyer's conveyancer, the deposit.

It is important to recognise that these formulae involve professional undertakings being given and received. These are implied undertakings in that the use of the formulae incorporates them whether or not the conveyancers specify that they are 'undertaking' to send the contract and/or deposit for example.

To avoid the risks involved in both of these formulae, identical attendance notes (memoranda of exchange) have to be made recording:

(a) the date and time of exchange;

(b) the formula used and any variations;

(c) the agreed completion date;

(d) the deposit to be paid;

(e) the identities of the parties to the conversation.

Formulae A and B are not ideal where there is a chain of transactions involved, though, in practice, they are often used in a modified form. The risk is that, having exchanged contracts on a client's sale or purchase by telephone, the parties to the second transaction withdraw. So, a third method has been devised – **Formula C** is in two stages.

Part I: First, each conveyancer confirms that they hold a contract in the agreed form signed by their clients. The completion date is agreed and the seller's conveyancer notifies the buyer's conveyancer to whom the deposit should be paid (this can be either to the seller's conveyancer or to a conveyancer acting for parties higher up the chain).

The buyer's conveyancer undertakes that they will continue to hold the part contract signed by their clients to the seller's conveyancer's order until the latest time agreed for exchange of contracts that day, and, if so required within that time by the seller's conveyancer, to activate Part II of the formula. They also undertake to be available until the time agreed or, if they may not be available, to nominate someone else who will be.

After this stage, the seller's conveyancer can be sure that the buyer will not withdraw before the agreed time, and so can proceed to exchange contracts on their client's own purchase, knowing that they can then exchange on their sale at any time up to the agreed time. Where there is a long chain of transactions, Part I of the formula will be followed up the chain until exchange of contracts on the top transaction takes place (usually, by Formula A or B), and the conveyancer of the buyer of that property can telephone their own client's buyer's conveyancers and activate Part II of the formula.

Part II: Here, the seller's conveyancer, having exchanged contracts on their client's purchase, telephones the buyer's conveyancer by the agreed latest time and requests that Part II be activated. Thereafter, both conveyancers undertake to hold the part contract in their possession to the order of the other so exchange is effected as at this moment. They also undertake to despatch the contract to the other that day, and the buyer's conveyancer also undertakes to despatch the deposit that day to the seller's conveyancer, or to some other conveyancer further up the chain if requested. The formula states that the deposit is to be held by the conveyancer unless it is to be used as a deposit in a related property purchase transaction on the same terms. (Thus, the seller will be able to use the deposit received from their sale for their purchase by requesting the buyer's conveyancer to send it directly to the conveyancer acting for the party they are buying from, or, indeed, someone else further still up the chain if so requested.)

Both stages need to be recorded in memoranda, recording the time and date of the conversations, the details of each stage of the formula with any variations, and the arrangements about the deposit.

It will be appreciated that using Formula C involves a conveyancer in giving a number of professional undertakings, the terms of which must be performed precisely.

Formula C also needs the client's authority, which should be written and irrevocable so as to prevent the client changing their mind after the conveyancer has given an undertaking to exchange.

As explained above, where there is a long chain, Formula C Part 1 will be followed up the chain until exchange of contracts on the top transaction takes place (usually using Formula A or Formula B). Formula C Part 2 can then be activated back down the chain.

Example

The following diagram provides an example of exchange using Formula C on Barry's sale and Formula B on Barry's purchase. Formula B is used on Barry's purchase as there is no onward (forward) chain in this case. This is because Claire is not buying another property.

Example of a Formula C exchange

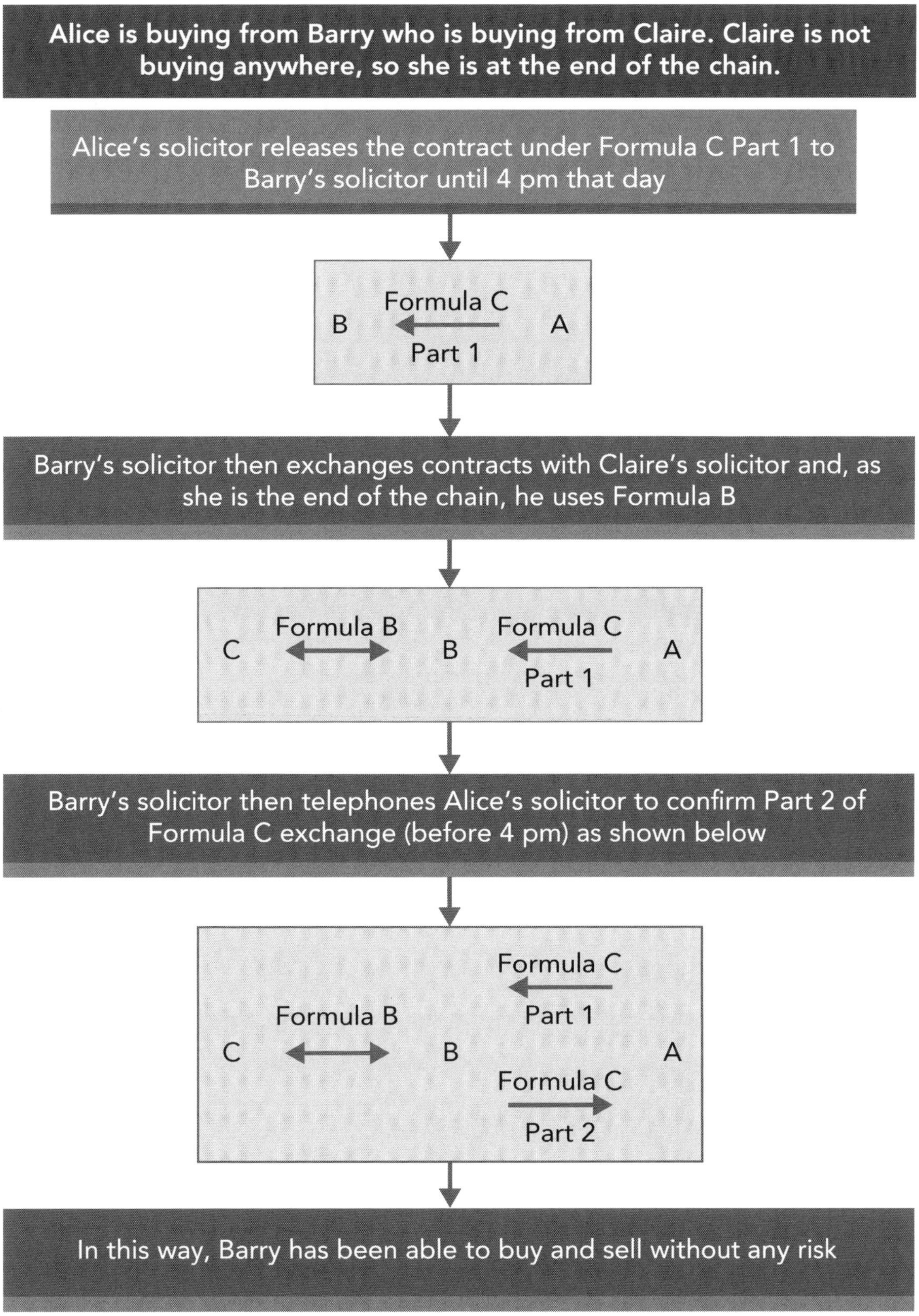

Irrespective of the method of exchange, the deposit will be paid at this stage of the transaction.

Except in the case of a sale by auction, SC 2.2.4 requires payment of the deposit either:

- by electronic means from the buyer's conveyancer's account maintained at a clearing bank to an account in the name of the seller's conveyancer maintained at a clearing bank (or where SC 2.2.5 applies, to a conveyancer higher up the chain); or
- by cheque drawn on the buyer's conveyancer's client account to the seller's conveyancer (or where SC 2.2.5 applies, to a conveyancer higher up the chain).

Both methods are linked to conveyancers' bank accounts. This is to try to minimise opportunities for fraud and money laundering.

Note that we mentioned in **Chapter 1** the possible change to the process of exchanging contracts. In November 2023 the Law Society released the "Code for Signing and Exchanging Property Contracts 2024". There was a short consultation but, as yet, no further information is available as to whether the new Code will be introduced and, if so, when. If the Code is introduced, it will replace the long-standing Formulae for Exchanging Contracts and will represent a significant change in the methods and practice of exchanging contracts.

For more information go to: https://www.lawsociety.org.uk/topics/property/code-for-signing-and-exchanging-property-contracts

This is an area which may evolve, and conveyancing practitioners must keep up to date. For the moment, however, the process of exchange of contracts is as outlined in the coursebook.

9.8 Effect of a binding contract

When a valid contract for sale comes into existence, the seller holds the legal estate being sold on trust for the buyer in equity. The buyer is not yet the legal owner of the property. Legal ownership remains with the seller but the buyer has an estate contract. This is a contract to create a legal estate at a future date, giving the buyer an equitable interest in the property.

Pending completion, the seller has the right to retain possession until payment, the right to a lien on the property for the balance of the price even though they have conveyed the property to the buyer and let them into occupation, the right to take the rents and profits until completion and the right to charge interest on the balance of the purchase money remaining unpaid after the contractual completion date.

After exchange, the seller is liable to maintain the property and is liable to the buyer if they wilfully damage it or even fail to take reasonable care of it (e.g. broken windows or missing slates should be replaced) (***Clarke v Ramuz* [1891]**). The seller's duty lasts so long as they retain possession, even if the date fixed for completion has expired due to the buyer's delay. The seller must bear the cost of maintenance unless the contract provides otherwise. The seller's duty does not extend to making any improvements.

In unregistered title, a contract to buy land is registrable as a Class C(iv) land charge under the **Land Charges Act 1972** (**LCA 1972**), and because of **s4(6)** will be void against the purchaser of a legal estate for money or money's worth if it is not registered. Similarly, in registered land, the contract should be protected by registration of an agreed notice or a unilateral notice under **LRA 2002**. It is, however, comparatively rare for contracts which are likely to be completed within a fairly short time to be so protected. That is not to say that this practice is correct. A conveyancer who failed to protect a contract which subsequently became void for want of registration could be liable in professional negligence to their client. Where there will be a delay between exchange and completion, it will be important to protect the contract by registration. An example of this would be where there is going to be a delay due to the death or bankruptcy of a party.

Since the buyer is an equitable owner from exchange, they may devise by will, mortgage or sell their interest. Under the open contract rules, the buyer must bear any losses occurring after the date of the contract and so should effect insurance against damage to the property. SC 5 deals with insurance risk where the SCs are used. Essentially the risk passes to the buyer on exchange, so normally the buyer must insure from exchange of contracts (this will also be a mortgage lender's requirement).

The buyer may ask to be allowed to go into the property before completion, for example, to decorate or lay carpets. There is a risk to the seller that the buyer may move in and lose the incentive to complete. It is even possible that they might become a tenant and so benefit from statutory protection against eviction. For these reasons, the seller should be advised against allowing the buyer to occupy or to begin works. There is also a risk to the buyer that they will be assumed to have accepted the seller's title.

Under an open contract, the buyer in such situations must pay interest on the outstanding purchase price from the date of occupation and the seller is no longer liable to maintain the property.

The SCs largely follow the general law and provide that where the buyer is let into occupation, the buyer is not a tenant but a licensee under such non-transferable terms as are contained in SC 5.2. This provides for the buyer to pay the seller a fee calculated at the contract rate on a sum equal to the purchase price (less deposit paid) for the period of the licence. There is also provision for the buyer to keep the property in the same state of repair and to vacate the property on five working days' notice. The buyer's right to object to the seller's title is preserved.

Should any variations to the SCs be required, these must be incorporated before exchange.

9.9 Problems between exchange of contracts and completion

Effect of death before completion

Death generally has no effect on the contract, and the PRs of the deceased must complete. There will be a delay pending issue of the grant of representation to the PRs, although an expedited grant can be applied for.

LP(MP)A 1994 includes provisions regarding the service of notices, intended to assist parties to a contract who must serve a notice to complete following the other party's death. If a party serves a notice regarding land without knowing that the intended recipient has died, the notice is still valid (**s17**). If the party serving the notice knows of the death, but a grant has not been issued, **s18** provides a procedure enabling service to take place in the meantime. **s18** service is on "the Personal Representative of . . ." at the deceased's address, with a copy to the Public Trustee.

Before **LP(MP)A 1994** came into force, the death of either party would cause considerable delay while a grant was being obtained. **LP(MP)A 1994** aims to ensure that notices to complete and other notices can be served before the grant has been issued.

The precise position will depend on who has died. The following table provides a summary of the various permutations.

Death of a single seller	The deceased's PR cannot give good title until the grant has been issued and so completion cannot take place until then. It is possible for an expedited grant to be issued by the Probate Registry but there will still be some delay. If completion is delayed beyond the contractual completion date, the deceased's estate will be liable for any compensation and damages (the Probate Registry should be told that the estate is at risk of loss when an expedited grant is applied for). The buyer's conveyancer should be advised, as it may be possible to reach an agreement to postpone completion until an expedited grant has been received. The transfer deed (depending on timing) will have to be redrafted.

Death of a co-seller where there are more than two co-sellers	The sale can proceed as there are at least two remaining trustees. The death certificate will be required to evidence the death. The transfer deed will need to be redrafted to show the change of parties.
Death of a co-seller where there were only two co-sellers	If there were only two co-sellers, another trustee may need to be appointed so that the minimum number of two trustees is satisfied. This will depend on whether the co-owners held the land as beneficial joint tenants or tenants in common. Again, the death certificate will evidence the death and it may be necessary to redraft the transfer deed. If the co-sellers were beneficial tenants in common, the seller must appoint an additional trustee to overreach the beneficial interests under the deceased's estate, which will necessitate an appointment in the transfer deed or a separate deed of appointment of trustee.
Death of a sole buyer	The PRs are bound to complete. They cannot complete until issue of the grant so an expedited grant may need to be applied for. The transfer will have to be redrafted to reflect the change of parties. Problems may arise since any mortgage offer may be withdrawn and the PRs will have to find alternative funding.
Death of co-buyer	The surviving co-buyers must complete the purchase. This may cause problems with any mortgage offer which may cause delay. A new mortgage deed may have to be prepared and again the transfer redrafted.

9.9.1 Insolvency: effect of bankruptcy before completion

(1) **Bankruptcy of the seller** – a bankrupt owner's property will vest in their trustee in bankruptcy. Where the seller becomes bankrupt after exchange of contracts, the trustee in bankruptcy stands in the seller's shoes and can enforce the contract. The trustee in bankruptcy will therefore be appointed and will sell the property in place of the seller. On a practical level this means that completion will be delayed until the trustee in bankruptcy is appointed. The transfer will need to be re-drafted to show the trustee as the seller. The buyer's conveyancers will need to consider protecting the priority of the contract since there will be a delay between exchange and completion (see above concerning protection of the contract). The buyer's mortgage lender will also need to be informed of the situation.

The following points are also relevant where a trustee in bankruptcy is selling:

- The seller's property vests automatically in the trustee in bankruptcy once they have been appointed. If the title is registered, the property vests in the trustee without alteration of the register, so it belongs to them whether or not it is actually registered in their name. The trustee can apply to have the property registered in their name or can sell the property as trustee without being registered as proprietor. The bankrupt cannot be a party to the transfer, so the seller in the transfer will be the trustee.
- The trustee in bankruptcy is obliged to complete if the buyer tenders the balance of the purchase money on the due date. In theory, the trustee in bankruptcy could disclaim an onerous contract, but this is unlikely to be done in practice.
- The buyer should ask for a copy of the bankruptcy order and the documentary proof of the trustee's appointment. The documentation appointing the trustee in bankruptcy will need to be filed as an additional enclosure with the buyer's registration application at HMLR following completion.
- Before the trustee in bankruptcy is appointed, the seller has the power to deal with the legal estate even after presentation of a bankruptcy petition. The disposition may be avoided except against a buyer in good faith and without notice of the petition. The petition will be registrable against the seller and, if registered, will be notice to the buyer.
- Where the sellers are co-owners, the position is slightly different. If one of the co-owners becomes bankrupt, the legal estate in the sale property does not vest in the trustee in bankruptcy. However, a bankruptcy order will sever any beneficial joint tenancy. A bankrupt co-owner's beneficial interest will vest in the trustee in bankruptcy. This does not mean that the legal estate cannot be sold, but it would be necessary to re-draft the transfer so that the trustee joined in the deed to consent to the sale of the beneficial interest.

(2) **Bankruptcy of the buyer** – the buyer's property vests in their trustee in bankruptcy (on appointment) who can compel the seller to complete. The trustee in bankruptcy can disclaim the contract as unprofitable but the seller would then retain the deposit. The seller can serve a notice on the trustee in bankruptcy requesting them to elect to perform or disclaim the contract; if the trustee in bankruptcy has not disclaimed within 28 days, they are deemed to have adopted the contract.

Once the seller has notice of a petition, they should not complete with the buyer or they will be liable to return the money when the statutory vesting operates. If a buyer who has become bankrupt is a co-buyer, their beneficial interest in the property vests in the trustee in bankruptcy. This may cause practical difficulties with any mortgage offer and the ability of the co-owners to complete.

9.10 Chapter summary

(1) A conveyancer should check the financial situation on the sale and purchase of their clients to ensure that the client has sufficient funds to proceed and meet all of the fees and outgoings.

(2) Conveyancers can only give generic advice on financial or mortgage products; they should not give specific financial advice as they are not authorised to do so. The conveyancer should advise their client to take independent financial advice.

(3) The buyer's conveyancer should always give co-ownership advice which is dependent on the client's circumstances.

(4) The legal estate can only be held as joint tenants.

(5) The beneficial interest can be held as joint tenants or tenants in common.

(6) A joint tenancy can be converted into a tenancy in common by severance.

(7) The doctrine of survivorship applies to a joint tenancy but not a tenancy in common.

(8) The declaration of trust between co-owners can be included on the transfer if simple or on form JO.

(9) If the parties are advised to hold as tenants in common, they should be advised to enter into a declaration of trust and to make wills.

(10) The conveyancer should not exchange contracts on the sale and purchase until they have reported to the client on a purchase and check that all issues have been satisfactorily resolved.

(11) The conveyancer should obtain a cleared 10 per cent deposit from their buyer client before exchange of contracts.

(12) The conveyancer should ensure that they hold a signed contract prior to exchange of contracts together with their clients in authority to exchange.

(13) Most clients want to complete their sale and purchase on the same day; this is known as **synchronising** the sale and purchase.

(14) If the client wants to proceed on their sale independently of their purchase, the conveyancer should explain the risks in writing.

(15) It is important to check carefully that there are no outstanding matters which need to be resolved before exchange of contracts as, from that time, the transaction becomes binding. It is useful, therefore, to use checklists to ensure that all matters are covered before exchange.

(16) There are three methods of exchanging contracts:

   (a) in person;

   (b) by post;

   (c) by telephone.

(17) The Law Society has prescribed three methods of exchanging contracts by telephone.

Formula A

Where one conveyancer holds both parts of the contract.

- Usually, the seller's conveyancer will hold both contracts.
- The buyer's conveyancer will have sent signed contract and deposit "to be held to order".
- The exchange will take place by telephone – confirm completion date and insert into the contract.
- The seller's conveyancer undertakes to forward the seller's contract to the buyer's conveyancer that day by DX, first class post or personally.
- Write a memo/attendance note – names of practitioners, date and time, formula used.

Formula B

Both sides have contracts, the buyer's conveyancer has deposit ready in cleared funds.

- Both conveyancers confirm that they hold identical contracts, agree deposit, agree completion date and insert it, then agree they are exchanged.
- As with Formula A, the same requirements for despatch of contracts but applies to both sides.
- Again, must complete memo/attendance note.

Formula C

Both sides have signed contracts and the buyer's conveyancer has the deposit in cleared funds.

- Used for chain transactions.
- Is in two stages – Part I and Part II.
- The parties are bound to exchange if within specified timescale.

(18) Actions to be carried out post-exchange are:

- obligations under Law Society formulae;
- must post contract the same day by first class post or DX – if not, must agree a variation at time of exchange;

- good practice is to write a comprehensive attendance note. Some firms use a standard format for both the letter and to record the exchange;
- retain a photocopy of contract on file.

(19) All formulae rely heavily on undertakings and, therefore, as a matter of professional conduct and good practice, these undertakings should be recorded and great care taken in their use.

(20) Once contracts are exchanged, the seller holds the property on trust for the buyer. The buyer's conveyancer may wish to protect the contract as a Class C(iv) land charge in unregistered land or a notice in registered land.

(21) The death or bankruptcy of either party between exchange and completion may affect both the validity of the contract and, practically, the ability of either party to complete.

CHAPTER 10

Acting on a sale of part and purchase of a new build property

10.1 Introduction

It is not always the case that a seller is selling the whole of the land in their title. They may be selling only part of their land. For instance, a common situation arises if a person with a large garden seeks to sell off part to a neighbour or a developer.

Similarly, it is not always the case that a seller is selling a second-hand property. Newly built properties are often sold. For instance, a developer may buy a large field and obtain planning permission for the development of the field into a housing estate.

We will consider both situations in this chapter. Remember also that where a developer sells houses on a new estate, each plot will be part of the developer's title to the whole estate, so this situation also involves a sale of part.

The same basic conveyancing process is followed with some additions and variations. Some matters such as planning have greater significance both for the seller and the buyer of a new build property.

This chapter will cover:

- third party rights – recap;
- third-party rights in unregistered title;
- third-party rights in registered title;
- sale of part:
    - sale of part – preliminary issues;
    - easements and covenants on a sale of part;
    - drafting new easements and covenants;
    - the draft contract;
    - other issues on a sale of part;
- acting on the purchase of a new build property:
    - taking instructions;
    - Consumer Code for Homebuilders (the Code)/New Homes Quality Board (and Code);
    - key issues to consider when dealing with a new build.

10.2 Acting on a sale of part

10.2.1 Third party rights – recap

A sale of part involves the land owner splitting their existing title and selling part off to someone else. This could involve someone selling part of their garden or a developer selling hundreds of plots on a housing estate. Whatever the nature of the transaction, the principles are the same: land is being sold off which will be subject to existing rights and obligations and the conveyancers acting for seller and buyer must consider what new rights and obligations are required to ensure that both the land being sold and the land being retained by the seller continue to enjoy all appropriate rights. The parties are also likely to consider creating new obligations (that is, covenants) which may bind seller and buyer. Accordingly, a sale of part involves the creation of new third-party rights. We will therefore recap on the basic law and procedure relating to third-party rights – it is important for the conveyancers to ensure that the rights are validly created and protected.

Third party rights

People other than the owners of land may have rights over the land. These third-party rights affect the way in which the freehold or leasehold "owners" use and enjoy their land.

A conveyancer must be able to recognise and determine the effect of any third-party rights which might affect the client's enjoyment of the property. If the client is the seller, will someone else's third party right affect their ability to sell the property? On the other hand, does the seller have any third-party rights over nearby property which might make their own property more saleable? If the client is the buyer, the conveyancer needs to consider whether any third parties might have rights over the property which would spoil the buyer's enjoyment of the property. The conveyancer would also consider whether any rights which the buyer would acquire over adjacent land would be adequate to enable them to enjoy the property as they would wish.

Link to practice

The conveyancer needs to know the relevant law affecting third party rights so that he can apply it to the client's transaction and advise accordingly. For example, the conveyancer might have to advise a client about a right of way (an easement) which a neighbouring landowner has over the property the client is buying. Imagine that the neighbour has a right to walk over a path at the bottom of the garden of the property the client is proposing to buy. The client will want to know whether he is going to be bound by this right after he has bought the property (i.e. whether the easement is binding). This may matter to the client if he does not like the thought of a neighbour being able to walk across his garden! If the easement is not binding, he will be able to stop the neighbour using the path. If the easement is binding, the client will have to allow the neighbour to carry on using the path.

The treatment of third-party rights differs between registered and unregistered titles. It is best to consider each system separately to avoid confusing the two.

LRA 2002 has also changed the rights to which both registered and unregistered land are subject for dispositions which have taken place after 13 October 2003, when **LRA 2002** came into force. The old law under **LRA 1925** will continue to apply in respect of third-party rights in registered land created before **LRA 2002** came into force. The old legislation therefore continues to be of some relevance.

This chapter therefore makes limited reference to the pre-**LRA 2002** law, but the main focus is on third party rights under the current law in **LRA 2002**.

Examples of third-party rights

The following case study will illustrate the scope of third-party rights.

Andrew is selling his bungalow

In 2012, Andrew purchased 12 Southwood Road, which has a large garden. His purchase was partly funded by a mortgage from County Bank plc. Andrew built a small bungalow in the garden and now intends to sell it, splitting the land where shown by the red dotted line on the plan below. The property is subject to a restrictive covenant.

Consider what third party rights benefit or burden Andrew before he sells off the bungalow known as 12A.

Andrew's property is burdened by the mortgage (the third-party being County Bank plc) and by the restrictive covenant (the third party being the owner of the adjacent farm).

The proposed buyer of 12A is Barbara. She would not wish to buy the property by itself, without any accompanying rights, because 12A is a landlocked property. Obviously, she needs to have access to her new house, so she will need to acquire, from Andrew, rights of way to her property (i.e. third party rights). In this case, it will be a right for her to use the driveway shown in yellow on the plan below. This runs from the road to her plot. Perhaps less obviously (but equally importantly), she also needs to acquire similar rights to allow her to run electricity cables, sewers, water pipes, gas pipes and other services over the land being retained by Andrew.

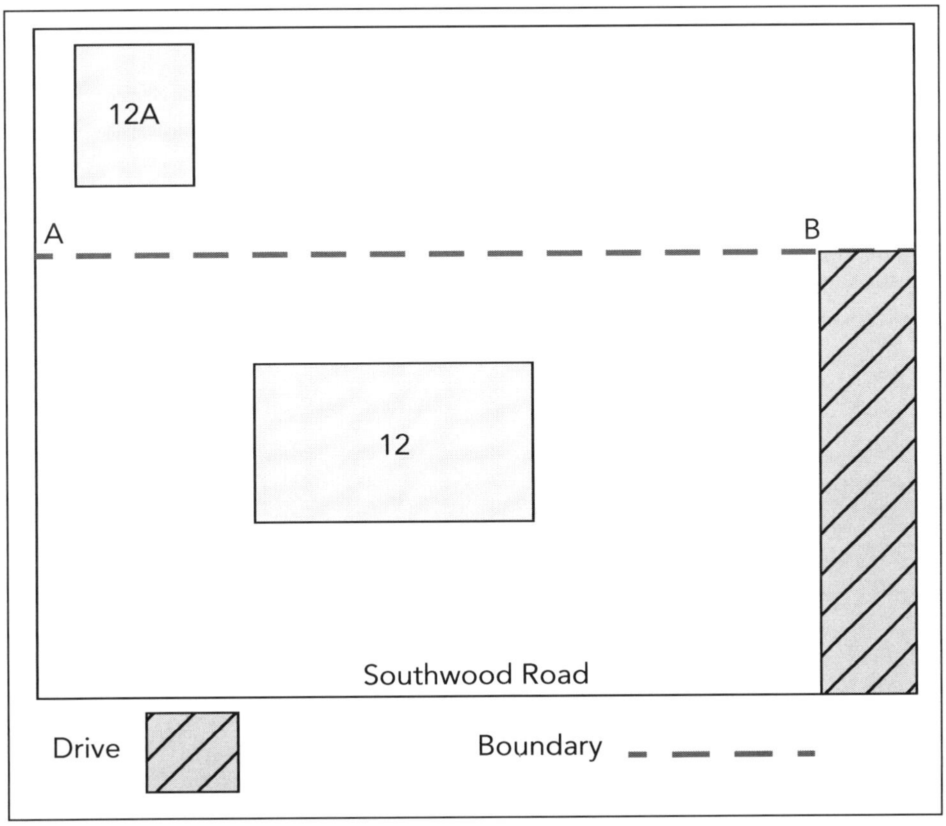

It should be clear that all the rights discussed above are not intended to be personal, but to relate to the land. That is, the person with the benefit of each of the rights intends them to affect the current owners and all the future owners. A future buyer of Andrew's property should normally gain all the benefits and burdens of the third-party rights from which Andrew benefited or to which he was subject – unless, of course, like the mortgage, the third party has agreed to release the right on completion.

The effect of binding successors is achieved by setting up the legal arrangements properly. The third party right has to be created properly and after creating the right, it may be necessary to register it (at HMLR against the title number, for registered land). For some rights, however, it is not necessary (and sometimes not possible) to register the right because a buyer is bound by the right whether registered or not.

Registration of third-party rights

The rules regarding which rights bind successors without registration and which rights need to be registered differ between registered and unregistered land. These rules are very important in practice because a buyer of land needs to know how they can find out about the existing rights which burden the land. It is usually easy to find out about interests which have been registered (you simply carry out a search) – but it may be more difficult to find out about those interests which do not need to be registered.

10.2.2 Third party rights in unregistered title

In unregistered conveyancing, how a third-party interest is discovered or protected is governed by the **Land Charges Act 1972** (**LCA 1972**) and whether the third-party interest is registrable as a land charge under **LCA 1972**.

(1) Land charges

For an interest to be registrable as a land charge it should fit within one of the categories of land charge under **LCA 1972**. The most commonly encountered of these are as follows.

Class C(i): a *puisne* mortgage (i.e. a legal mortgage where the lender does not hold the title deeds). It is usually a second legal mortgage, as the first lender usually takes deposit of the title deeds, an act which, in itself, makes the first mortgage unregistrable as a land charge.

Class C(iii): a general equitable charge. Most interests which are equitable and cannot be found specifically mentioned under another heading may be registered in this class (e.g. an equitable mortgage not protected by deposit of title deeds). The class is important for what it contains, but just as important for the interests which are specifically excluded from it, for example, an equitable interest under a trust cannot be included in this class. All interests under a trust of land, including those under express, implied and resulting trusts of land, are excluded.

Class C(iv): an estate contract, that is, a contract to create or convey a legal estate. It will include not only a typical contract for the purchase of property but also an option to purchase and a right of pre-emption (a right of first refusal).

Class D(ii): a restrictive covenant entered into on or after 1 January 1926 affecting freehold land.

Class D(iii): an equitable easement created on or after 1 January 1926.

Class F: the statutory rights of a spouse or civil partner to occupy the matrimonial or civil partnership home under the **Family Law Act 1996** (**FLA 1996**), as amended by the **Civil Partnership Act 2004** (**CPA 2004**).

The procedure surrounding interests which are registrable as land charges is straightforward. In general terms, so far as a buyer of the property is concerned, they will take subject to the interests if they are registered, even if they do not know about them (**s198 LPA 1925** deems the registration of the land charge to constitute actual notice to the buyer). If the interests are not registered, then a buyer of the freehold estate will take free of the interests. Non-registration of the charges within Classes C(iv) and D renders them void against the buyer of the legal estate for money or money's worth, whereas non-registration of the other classes of land charge renders them void against any buyer. This is true even if the buyer knew of the existence of the interest (***Midland Bank Trust Co v Green*** **[1981]**).

Land charges are registered on the land charges register. This is nothing to do with the register of title which exists for registered land, but is a separate register kept by the Land Charges Department which records third party interests over unregistered land. Land charges are not registered against the legal estate they affect, but against the name of the estate owner at the time the charge was created.

Land charges are registered by applying to the Land Charges Department in Plymouth. Various forms are used, depending on the category of registration.

Activity

You will only come across registering land charges fairly rarely in practice.

If you need more information, follow the link below to HMLR's "Practice guide 63: Land Charges-applications for registration, official search, office copy and cancellation":

https://www.gov.uk/government/publications/land-charges-applications-for-registration-official-search-office-copy-and-cancellation/practice-guide-63-land-charges-applications-for-registration-official-search-office-copy-and-cancellation

(2) Interests which are not registrable as land charges

If the third-party interest does not fall within any of the categories of land charge, then different rules apply, in which case the first thing to do is to decide whether the interest is legal or equitable.

If it is **legal** (e.g. a legal easement or a legal mortgage protected by deposit of title deeds), the maxim "legal rights are good against all the world" applies. Generally, unless the owner of the legal third-party interest has been fraudulent, a party to misrepresentation to the buyer, or grossly negligent, then the legal right will bind a buyer of the freehold property whether or not they knew of the interest.

If the third-party interest is not registrable as a land charge and is **equitable** (e.g. a pre-1926 restrictive covenant), the doctrine of notice applies (**s199 LPA 1925**). The doctrine of notice says that for a buyer to take the property free of the equitable third-party interest they must prove that they are a "*bona fide* buyer for value of the legal estate without notice of the equitable interest". *Bona fide* means that the buyer must be acting in good faith. The question of notice, however, needs some further consideration.

In simple terms, a buyer can have notice of an interest in one of three ways.

(a) **Actual notice**: the buyer may have actual notice in that they knew about the interest.

(b) **Constructive notice**: in order to avoid the situation where a buyer could claim to have no notice of an interest simply by failing to try to find out anything at all about the property, equity developed the rule regarding notice to say that a buyer will be deemed to know about any interests which they could have discovered by making the usual searches and enquiries; this includes not only inspecting the title deeds but also the land itself.

(c) **Imputed notice**: where a buyer employs agents such as valuers or solicitors, they cannot shelter behind the fact that they relied on that agent. If the agent would be fixed with actual or constructive notice, the buyer will have that notice imputed to them as well.

In addition to legal rights, rights protected by registration as a land charge or which are subject to the doctrine of notice, **LRA 2002** introduced a new category of rights. When unregistered land is first registered on or after 13 October 2003, it becomes subject to unregistered interests which override first registration.

(3) Unregistered interests which override first registration

Under **LRA 2002**, any grant or disposition of an estate in land is registrable, except for those such as the grant or assignment of leases of seven years or less and dispositions which take effect by operation of law (e.g. where a deceased's property vests in their personal representative).

On or after 13 October 2003, upon registering an unregistered estate the land becomes subject to unregistered interests which override first registration. These are set out in **Sch 1 LRA 2002** and the most important for conveyancers are:

- a lease granted for seven years or less;
- an interest belonging to a person in actual occupation so far as relating to the land they occupy;
- a legal easement;
- a local land charge.

In addition, **LRA 2002** makes clear that the proprietor will take subject to interests acquired under the **Limitation Acts** of which the proprietor has notice.

In essence, an unregistered title subject to first registration will therefore be subject to:

- legal rights (as they are good against the world);
- rights protected by registration of a land charge;
- equitable interests protected by the doctrine of notice; and
- unregistered interests which override first registration (as set out in **Sch 1 LRA 2002**).

This is intended to reflect the fact that the land will be subject to those interests which were binding on the buyer under the law of unregistered land. The idea is that the register created on first registration will then reflect that position.

10.2.3 Third party rights in registered title

Generally, in registered conveyancing all interests in land, other than those capable of being substantively registered with separate titles, can be divided into:

- registered charges;
- interests which are overriding; or
- interests which must be protected by an entry on the register.

The extent to which these bind a buyer is illustrated in the following diagram.

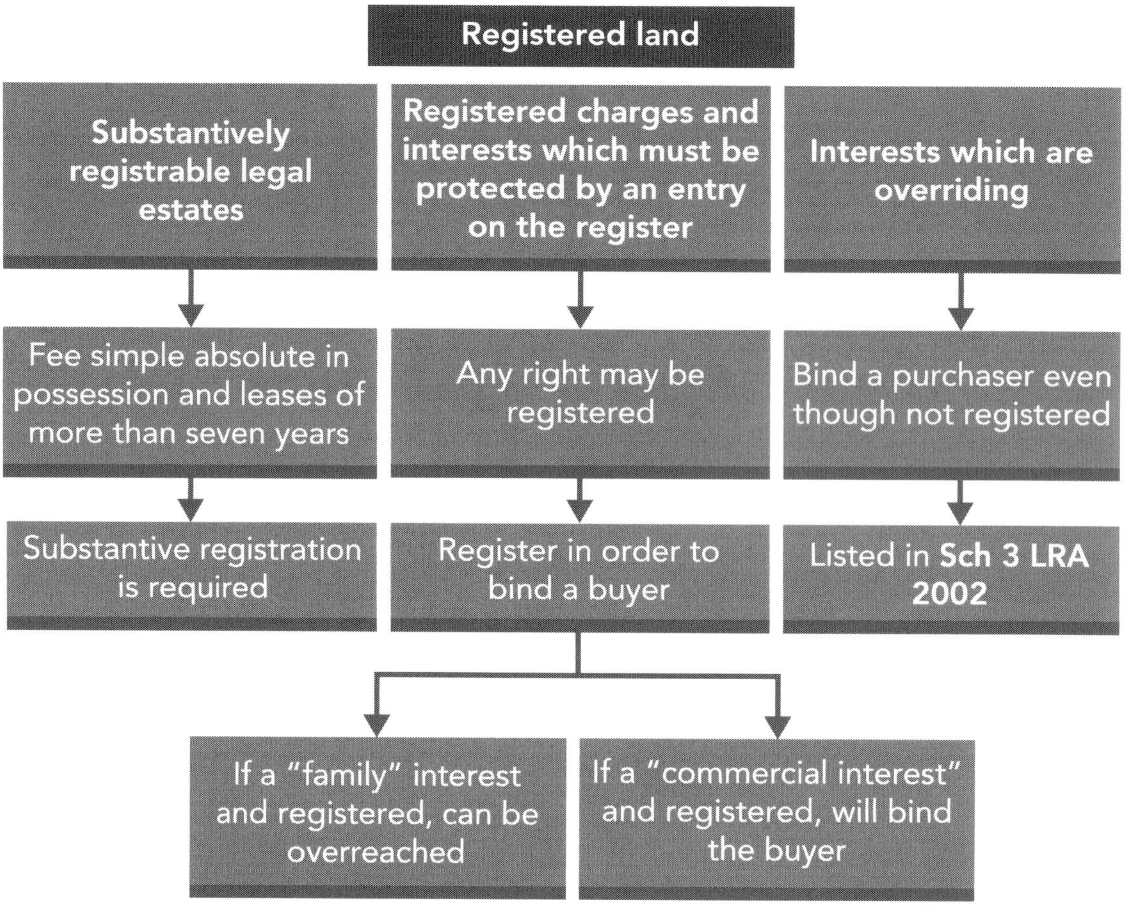

Registered charges

Registered charges (e.g. mortgages) are quite easily identified from obtaining official copies of the entries on the register. To be binding, registered charges must, in all normal circumstances, appear on the register.

10.3 Sale of part

10.3.1 Sale of part – preliminary issues

We will now move on to look at some of the key points that a conveyancer must consider when dealing with a sale of part.

Taking instructions

When taking instructions from a seller or buyer on a sale of part, it is important to ensure that all of the information that you would normally glean from a client is obtained – see Chapter 1. However, in addition, a sale of part requires more thought and the conveyancer acting for the seller will have more complex documentation to draft. We will consider a transfer of part of a freehold title in this chapter.

As we will see, there are various matters upon which the seller's conveyancer will need to take detailed instructions to ensure that the documentation can be accurately drafted, these include:

- obtaining details of the seller's title;
- accurately identifying the land to be sold by reference to a HMLR compliant plan;
- looking at the land to be sold and the land being retained by the seller to consider:
  - the rights to be granted in favour of the land being sold;
  - the rights, if any, to be reserved over the land being sold in favour of the sellers retained land;
  - the covenants which might need to be imposed.
- if the seller's title is mortgaged, the consent of the lender must be obtained to release the land being sold from the mortgage (if it is not intended to redeem the entire mortgage from the sale proceeds on conclusion of the sale). The lender will need to produce a form DS3 (https://www.gov.uk/government/publications/mortgage-release-of-part-of-the-land-for-lenders-ds3 of the land to be released which will be in the plan of the land to be sold. The buyer's conveyancer will require an undertaking from the seller's conveyancer to confirm that the DS3 will be handed over on completion.

Link to practice

In considering the transaction below, we will look at the transfer of part before the contract, this might seem odd but it is the transfer of part which will contain all of the rights and obligations to be created on completion of the sale. In most cases, the contract will be fairly straightforward to draft once the transfer of part is drafted (the contract for the sale of a new build is more detailed which we will consider later in this chapter.).

Every transfer of part will be different because there will be different considerations and requirements in relation to the land to be sold and retained. The conveyancer must of course consider all of the principles and issues contained in this chapter but the conveyancer must also remember to apply common sense. The conveyancer should take instructions and look at the proposed plan of the land to be sold and retained. Initially, this might be no more than a sketch plan but it will give a good idea of the layout of the land. The conveyancer should consider issues such as:

(1) What rights for services do the land to be sold and the retained land need? Remember, it is the rights that a property enjoys which gives it

value. The conveyancer will need to think about access to the nearest public highway and rights for mains services such as foul drainage, gas, electricity and water.

(2) Consider the practicalities – It may be appropriate to restrict the traffic allowed over a right of way – a seller might be quite happy to grant a right of way on foot on a path through their back garden to give the buyer access to the local shops, but would be quite distressed if the buyer used the path for heavy goods vehicles!

(3) What obligations should be imposed on the land being sold? These will be covenants. The conveyancer should consider the reasonableness of the covenants – if they are too onerous, their seller client may have difficulty in selling the land.

(4) Should any obligations be imposed on the land which the seller is retaining? Generally, there will be fewer of these but it might be appropriate, for example, for the owner of the retained land to covenant not to obstruct an access or driveway.

(5) Are the covenants to be imposed restrictive (that is, negative) or positive in nature? You will recall that it is possible for the benefit and burden of restrictive covenants to pass but not positive covenants. This causes a problem if it is necessary to impose obligations to pay money for the upkeep of shared services such as a driveway or private drainage system.

The importance of plans

When selling part of a property we can no longer rely upon reference to the title number and description from the Property Register of the official copies, or the description in the title deeds, as only part of the title is being sold. Instead, we refer to them but have to be more specific. This means that it is important to use a plan to define the exact extent of the property. Whereas some conveyancing plans may refer to property "as illustrated on the plan annexed", with a sale of part the plan should describe the extent of the property "as more particularly delineated" as the area edged red on the plan annexed hereto. HMLR would not usually accept a plan marked "for identification only". If such a plan was supplied by the seller for a sale of part, the buyer should query it as there is a risk it could be rejected by HMLR.

The title plan

When an application is made to HMLR for first registration, in addition to creating the registers of title, the title plan is created. Under **r5 Land Registration Rules 2003**, the property register of a registered estate in land will contain a description of the registered estate which must refer to a plan based on the Ordnance Survey map and known as the title plan.

The purpose of the title plan is to support the property description in the register by providing a graphic representation and identifying the general extent of the land in a registered title. In addition to showing the land in a registered title, a title plan may contain other plan references which identify any parts of the land or adjoining land affected by entries in the register, such as easements, covenants or areas of land removed from the title.

Activity

Follow the link below to HMLR's "Practice guide 40 supplement 5 plans: title plan":

https://www.gov.uk/government/publications/land-registry-plans-title-plan/land-registry-plans-title-plan-practice-guide-40-supplement-5

Read the Practice guide and make notes on what a title plan must always show and colour references. Take particular note of the sample plans in the Practice guide.

All title plans show general boundaries unless the line of boundary is shown as having been determined under **s60 Land Registration Act 2002**. Given the small scale of the title plans, it is not possible for HMLR to accurately indicate on the plan the exact position of the boundary. This is the reason that HMLR works on the "general boundaries rule" under **s60(1) LRA 2002**. Under this rule, HMLR will complete a first registration without making detailed enquiries as to the precise location of legal boundaries. The title plan will reflect what HMLR considers to be a reasonable interpretation of the land in the pre-registration deeds in relation to the detail on Ordnance Survey mapping, taking into account any areas of land that the preregistration deeds showed to have been sold off and any existing adjoining registrations.

There is a procedure available to identify the precise position of a boundary. This is known as the determined boundary procedure.

Activity

If you want to know more about the general boundaries and determined boundaries procedures, go to the following HMLR Practice Guides:

PG 40 – supplement 3 – boundaries:

https://www.gov.uk/government/publications/land-registry-plans-boundaries/land-registry-plans-boundaries-practice-guide-40-supplement-3

PG40 – supplement 4- boundary agreements and determined boundaries:

https://www.gov.uk/government/publications/boundary-agreements-and-determined-boundaries/practice-guide-40-land-registry-plans-supplement-4-boundary-agreements-and-determined-boundaries

Plan for a sale of part

One of the first key steps to be taken by a seller on a sale of part is to produce a HMLR compliant plan of the land to be sold. The seller's title plan will be the starting point but as registration of the sale of part will take place on conclusion of the transaction, it is essential to ensure that the plan accurately identifies the land. The seller may decide to have the plan professionally produced.

As you can see, HMLR has published detailed requirements for plans which are to be lodged with registration applications, such as on the sale of part of the land in a title. These requirements must always be considered when plans are drawn up in practice, as it is important that the plan is not rejected by HMLR.

Link to practice

The main requirements are set out in HMLR Practice Guide 40 Supplement 2 (PG40s2) which contains examples of plans which would be accepted and rejected:

https://www.gov.uk/government/publications/preparing-plans-for-land-registry-applications/guidance-for-preparing-plans-for-land-registry-applications

Some examples of HMLR plans requirements are:

- the plan must be drawn to a stated scale;
- it must show its orientation (e.g. a north point);
- it must contain sufficient detail for the land to be identified on the Ordnance Survey map;
- measurements must be shown in metric units;
- it must ideally not be marked "for identification only" or similar wording;
- it must show the land and property clearly (e.g. by edging, hatching or colouring);

- the plan in the engrossed deed must be signed by the seller (or landlord). If the seller is a company, then it must be signed by the officers of that company who have the necessary authority to sign (i.e. the same officers whose signatures appear in the form of execution at the end of the transfer or lease).

Example

We will now consider, by way of an example, a plan which we are going to draw up for a seller who is selling part of their land. We will call this Plan A.

We will need to use distinct colourings and have marked the land being sold as edged in red (see Plan A below).

There is also the retained land that the seller is keeping and we will edge this in blue on the plan. In this case there is a shared driveway. From Plan A, we can see that that the seller is retaining the driveway on their land. The driveway has been coloured in yellow on the plan. The buyer will need to get to their house once it is built so will need to use the driveway. The seller will need to grant a right of way to the buyer over the driveway. If the seller is willing to do this, they will probably want a contribution from the buyer towards the maintenance of the driveway. They may also want to impose restrictions upon what the buyer can do with their property. For example, you would probably not want your neighbour running a business from their property if you share a drive. You would, as is shown, position the new house away from the boundary so they could not see into your house.

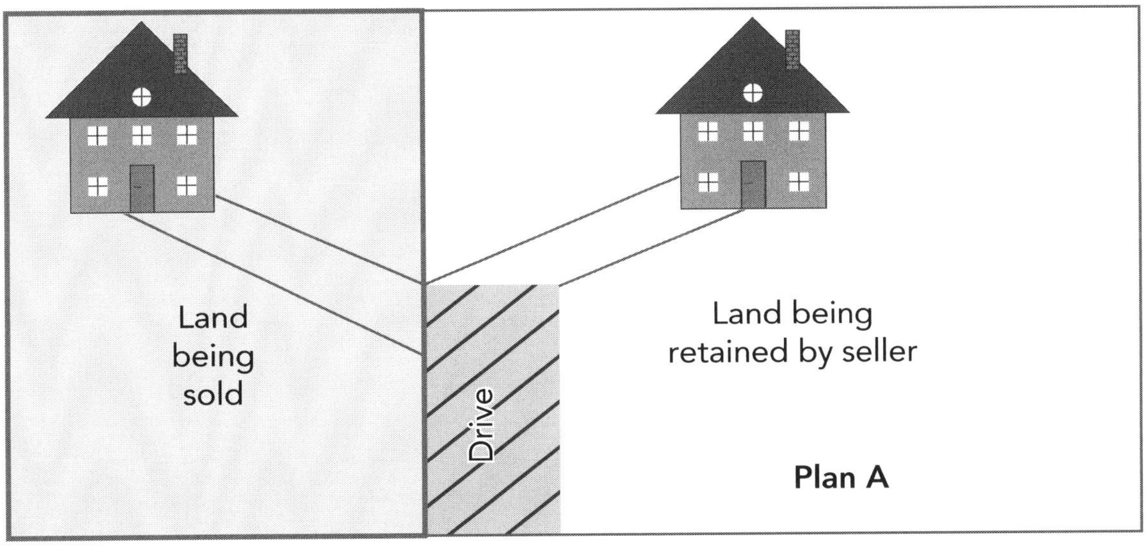

10.3.2 Easements and covenants on a sale of part

On a sale of part of the seller's property there should be express provision for the granting and reserving of easements to the buyer and seller respectively. Consideration when drafting the contract should also be given to the imposing of any appropriate covenants on the buyer to prevent any loss of enjoyment or depreciation in the seller's retained land.

Grant and reservation of easements

Terminology confusion alert!

Before we start, remember the following important distinction:

Grant – the seller will **grant** easements over their retained land for the **benefit of the land being sold**. As we will see, in some circumstances the law will recognise the grant of some easements by implication on a sale if they have not been specifically included/drafted in the transfer. Obviously, it is better to avoid relying on easements arising by implication.

Reservation – the seller might need to **reserve** easements over the land being sold the **benefit of the sellers retained land**. The law will not recognise by implication the creation of easements by reservation. The principle behind this is that the seller controls the drafting and should ensure that all rights which the retained land might require are included in the transfer.

The conveyancer must assess all the circumstances to see what easements are required (e.g. "Where are the mains services?", "Does the property front a public highway?"). They will need to consider all access and service easements (e.g. electricity, gas, water, surface and waste water drainage).

As mentioned above, there should be express provision regarding the grant and reservation of easements on a sale of part, since this is more certain than relying on the general law. The wording and extent of the easements can be controlled by the drafting (e.g. whether an access way is for use on foot or for use by vehicles as well).

Easements arising by implication

If no express provision has been made, easements may arise by implication when part of the land is sold. This may not be satisfactory as explained below.

In the case of easements, the open contract rule would be that the buyer would, on completion, automatically acquire easements over the seller's retained land which are easements of necessity or common intention and those which arise under the rule in ***Wheeldon v Burrows* [1879]**, that is, those quasi-easements which were:

- continuous and apparent;
- in use at the time of the sale;
- reasonably necessary for the enjoyment of the property.

s62 LPA 1925 may also operate to grant easements over retained land in a buyer's favour.

The seller under the open contract rules would have no parallel rights over the land which the buyer bought.

Most contracts will incorporate the Standard Conditions of Sale (Fifth edition – 2018 revision). Standard Condition 3.4 in the Fourth Edition of the Standard Conditions of Sale provided for the exclusion of rights of light and air, and for the mutual grant of easements and reservations on a sale of part. The rights given by this condition were not very clear and were limited in scope. In most cases they would not have been adequate, and essentially, the SC was usually seen as a fallback position only. The Fifth Edition of the Standard Conditions of Sale omitted this condition, and when dealing with a sale of part, it is now important to deal with all such matters expressly. The best way of doing this is to attach an agreed transfer to the contract, setting out all agreed easements, and to add a special condition to the contract to negate the implied easement rules.

In ***Selby District Council v Samuel Smith Old Brewery (Tadcaster) Ltd* [2001]** the contract included the term on a sale of part, that easements were included in favour of both parties, as would be the case if the two plots had been sold to separate buyers. The case concerned a dispute arising from the difference between that term and what the parties actually intended. As a general principle, it is far better for parties expressly to agree regarding easements before exchange, and place a term stating this into the contract and transfer, and excluding the implied grant rules. This would save disputes and possible litigation.

A separate but related point concerns rights of access. If there are no rights of access in the deeds, the **Access to Neighbouring Land Act 1992** may assist. It relates to the situation where X needs access to the land of a neighbour, Y, to effect works, but X does not have Y's consent to enter their land. The court may make an access order to allow X to enter the neighbouring land to carry out the works. It would be far preferable, however, if the parties had the benefit of express rights in order to avoid the expense and difficulty of having to go to court.

Covenants

The benefit of freehold covenants (i.e. the right to enforce the covenant) will pass to successors in title if certain conditions are satisfied. Essentially, these are that:

- the covenant must touch and concern the land; and
- the benefit must be annexed or assigned, or that there is a building scheme.

The second condition is satisfied automatically under **s78 LPA 1925** where the covenant touches and concerns the land, according to ***Federated Homes v Mill Lodge Properties* [1980]**; however, express words indicating annexation (e.g. "for the benefit of the seller and his successors in title . . .") are often used to add greater certainty.

Under ***Elliston v Reacher* [1908]** a building scheme is created where properties are laid out in plots which are to be sold to individual buyers who all enter into the same covenants, intending them to be for the benefit of all plots. The covenants in a building scheme are mutually enforceable like a sort of local law. The effect of a building scheme has been confirmed in more recent cases, notably ***Birdlip Limited v Hunter* [2015]**.

The burden of freehold covenants does **not** run at common law or in equity (with the important exceptions stated below). This means that a subsequent owner of the land does not have to comply with covenants given by predecessors in title.

Under ***Tulk v Moxhay* [1848]** the burden of restrictive (and **only** restrictive) covenants will run where the covenantee retained land and the covenant is not intended to be personal. The covenant must have been registered as a Class D(ii) land charge in unregistered land or a notice in registered land.

Whether or not a covenant is intended to be personal will depend on both the nature of the covenant and the precise wording used in the covenant. ***Morrells of Oxford v Oxford United Football Club* [2000]** related to the running of the burden of a restrictive covenant. It was held that the covenant was personal to the original covenantor (a council). This case was decided on the construction of the wording of the covenant, from such matters as the absence of any reference to successors in title, in spite of the fact that the previous clause did refer to successors in title.

The burden of positive freehold covenants does not run with the land (***Rhone v Stephens* [1994]**). The use of a chain of indemnity covenants made by successive buyers, however, can help to alleviate this problem. Thus, in cases where the seller was the original covenantor, or where the seller gave an indemnity covenant, it is important for the seller to insist on an indemnity covenant from the buyer.

10.3.3 Drafting new easements and covenants

Having taken detailed instructions, the seller's conveyancer will draft a transfer of part using HMLR form TP1 containing all of the rights and obligations which may be required. As we will see, box 12 is the "Additional provisions" section in which the new easements and covenants will be inserted.

It is important to word the easements and covenants as clearly as possible, and to consider the exact aim of the provisions, to ensure that they cover precisely what is required and intended.

Remember that use of the correct terms is important. Easements should be "granted" to the buyer but "reserved" in favour of the seller. The transfer or conveyance contains the actual covenants and easements but the contract states the parties' agreement to enter into those covenants and easements in the future. This is reflected in the wording. Thus, the contract states: "the buyer shall in the transfer covenant . . .", but the transfer states: "the transferee hereby covenants . . .".

When drafting new covenants, the covenants should be framed so as to run (pass) with the land, so that the benefit will run from the seller to the seller's successors in title and the burden will run from the buyer to the buyer's successors in title. If the covenants are merely personal, they will be enforceable only between the present seller and buyer. Covenants are typically joint and several if there is more than one buyer, so that either or both may be sued.

Easements may include rights of way, and use of services such as gas, electricity, water and sewers. Bear in mind that both buyer and seller will need access routes to the mains, and physical (and probably vehicular) access to the property. It is strongly advisable in the interests of certainty that all easements are express easements. Thus, any implied easements (such as those implied under **s62 LPA 1925** or under ***Wheeldon v Burrows* [1879]**) should be excluded in the contract and conveyance.

The TP1

A transfer of part will be used even where the sellers title is unregistered because the sale will trigger first registration within two months of completion.

Every transfer will contain different provisions and there is a wide-ranging of drafting styles. Let's look at some of typical provisions which would be included in the TP1.

HM Land Registry

Transfer of part of registered title(s)

Any parts of the form that are not typed should be completed in black ink and in block capitals.

If you need more room than is provided for in a panel, and your software allows, you can expand any panel in the form. Alternatively use continuation sheet CS and attach it to this form.

For information on how HM Land Registry processes your personal information, see our Personal Information Charter.

Leave blank if not yet registered.	1	Title number(s) out of which the property is transferred: If the seller's title is registered, their title number will be inserted here
When application for registration is made these title number(s) should be entered in panel 2 of Form AP1.	2	Other title number(s) against which matters contained in this transfer are to be registered or noted, if any: If there is additional land in a separate title against which rights or obligations should be noted, this title number will be inserted here
Insert address, including postcode (if any), or other description of the property transferred. Any physical exclusions, such as mines and minerals, should be defined. Place 'X' in the appropriate box and complete the statement. For example 'edged red'. For example 'edged and numbered 1 in blue'. Any plan lodged must be signed by the transferor.	3	Property: The description of the property to be sold will be inserted here. This will be the postal address if available The property is identified • on the attached plan and shown: in most cases, this box should be checked and the HMLR compliant plan that the seller has produced should be attached to the transfer. Convention demands that the land being sold is edged red • on the title plan(s) of the above titles and shown:
Remember to date this deed with the day of completion, but not before it has been signed and witnessed.	4	Date: This will be left blank until completion

Give full name(s) of **all** of the persons transferring the property. Complete as appropriate where the transferor is a company.	5	Transferor: The name of the seller is inserted here <u>For UK incorporated companies/LLPs</u> Registered number of company or limited liability partnership including any prefix: <u>For overseas companies</u> (a) Territory of incorporation: (b) Registered number in the United Kingdom including any prefix:
Give full name(s) of **all** the persons to be shown as registered proprietors. Complete as appropriate where the transferee is a company. Also, for an overseas company, unless an arrangement with HM Land Registry exists, lodge either a certificate in Form 7 in Schedule 3 to the Land Registration Rules 2003 or a certified copy of the constitution in English or Welsh, or other evidence permitted by rule 183 of the Land Registration Rules 2003.	6	Transferee for entry in the register: The name of the buyer is inserted here <u>For UK incorporated companies/LLPs</u> Registered number of company or limited liability partnership including any prefix: <u>For overseas companies</u> (a) Territory of incorporation: (b) Registered number in the United Kingdom including any prefix:
Each transferee may give up to three addresses for service, one of which must be a postal address whether or not in the UK (including the postcode, if any). The others can be any combination of a postal address, a UK DX box number or an electronic address.	7	Transferee's intended address(es) for service for entry in the register: The appropriate address is inserted here

	8	The transferor transfers the property to the transferee
Place 'X' in the appropriate box. State the currency unit if other than sterling. If none of the boxes apply, insert an appropriate memorandum in panel 12.	9	Consideration • The transferor has received from the transferee for the property the following sum (in words and figures): In most cases the land being sold is being transferred for valuable consideration so this box will be checked and the purchase price will be inserted in words and figures • The transfer is not for money or anything that has a monetary value • Insert other receipt as appropriate:
Place 'X' in any box that applies. Add any modifications.	10	The transferor transfers with • full title guarantee • limited title guarantee Unless it is a sale by Personal Representatives (which on a sale of part would be unusual) generally, the seller would be expected to give a full title guarantee and this box will be checked
Where the transferee is more than one person, place 'X' in the appropriate box. Complete as necessary. The registrar will enter a Form A restriction in the register *unless*: • an 'X' is placed: ○ in the first box, or ○ in the third box and the details of the trust or of the trust instrument show that the transferees are to hold the property on trust for themselves alone as joint tenants, *or*	11	Declaration of trust. The transferee is more than one person and • they are to hold the property on trust for themselves as joint tenants • they are to hold the property on trust for themselves as tenants in common in equal shares • they are to hold the property on trust: If there is more than one buyer, their conveyancer will take instructions as to their co-ownership requirements which will be indicated here

- it is clear from completion of a form JO lodged with this application that the transferees are to hold the property on trust for themselves alone as joint tenants.

Please refer to *Joint property ownership* and *practice guide 24: private trusts of land* for further guidance. These are both available on the GOV.UK website.

Use this panel for:

- definitions of terms not defined above
- rights granted or reserved
- restrictive covenants
- other covenants
- agreements and declarations
- any required or permitted statements
- other agreed provisions.

The prescribed subheadings may be added to, amended, repositioned or omitted.

Any other land affected by rights granted or reserved or by restrictive covenants should be defined by reference to a plan.

12 **Additional provisions**

This is the section of the transfer which the seller's conveyancer will draft based on their client's detailed instructions and the plan. The buyer's conveyancer must review this section carefully with their client to ensure that the property will enjoy all of the rights required for the full enjoyment of it

HMLR has added some standard headings which we will indicate in bold to assist the conveyancer with drafting. Not all of these headings will be needed in every case

Definitions

Even the simplest transfer of part would benefit from some definitions for simplicity and clarity of drafting. Some examples are:

"the Driveway" means the driveway coloured brown on the Plan

"the Plan" means the plan attached to this transfer

"the Planning Permission" means planning permission [INSERT REFERENCE] dated [INSERT DATE]

"the Property" means the [INSERT ADDRESS] shown edged red on the Plan

	"Retained Land" means the land comprised in the Title Number [INSERT] (excluding the Property) "Service Channels" means all means for the passage of drainage, water, gas, electricity, fuel and other services
Any other land affected should be defined by reference to a plan and the title numbers referred to in panel 2.	**Rights granted for the benefit of the property** The Transferor grants to the Transferee (in common with other persons also entitled and any person whom the Transferee shall authorise either expressly or impliedly to make use of the rights) the following rights for the benefit of the Property and each and every part of it: The right to use at all times and for all purposes connected with the use of the Property as a private dwellinghouse a right of way with or without vehicles over the Driveway The right of support for the Property and any building on it from support of the Retained Land and any building on the immediate boundary The right to use at all times and for all purposes connected with the use of the Property the Service Channels passing through or over the Retained Land together with rights to enter onto such parts of the Retained Land for the purpose of laying maintaining inspecting cleaning repairing and replacing the Service Channels subject to the Transferee paying a fair proportion (according to user) of the cost of such works The right to use the drains under the Retained Land along the route marked with a blue broken line on the Plan
Any other land affected should be defined by reference to a plan and the title numbers referred to in panel 2.	**Rights reserved for the benefit of other land** The following rights over the Property are reserved for the Transferor and its successors in title and those authorised by it for the benefit of the Retained Land and each and every part: The right of support for the Retained Land and any buildings on thereon from the Property and any buildings on thereon

The right to use at all times and for all purposes connected with the use of the Retained Land the Service Channels passing through or over the Property together with rights to enter onto such parts of the Property for the purpose of laying maintaining inspecting cleaning repairing and replacing the Service Channels subject to the Transferor paying a fair proportion (according to user) of the cost of such works

Include words of covenant.

Restrictive covenants by the transferee

The Transferee covenants with the Transferor so as to benefit the Retained Land and so as to bind the Property and each and every part of it into whosoever hands it may come:

Not to use the Property or any part of it for any purpose other than as a single private residence

Not to keep any animal at the property other than normal domestic pets

Not to use the Property for any illegal or immoral purpose

Not to place any caravan, house on wheels or mobile homes on the Property

Not to use the Property or any part of it for any noxious or offensive activity or for any purposes which is or might be a nuisance or annoyance to the Transferor

Positive covenants by the transferee

This is an additional heading which the seller's conveyancer might need to include depending on the circumstances. An inward T on a plan denotes that the property into which the T mark faces has responsibility for maintaining that boundary

The Transferee covenants with the Transferor:

To maintain the boundaries marked with a T on the Plan

To comply at all times with the Planning Permission

Include words of covenant.	**Restrictive covenants by the transferor** The Transferor so as to bind the Retained Land hereby covenants with the Transferee to observe and perform the following covenants and the following covenants are also for the benefit of all future buyer s of the Property and shall be enforceable against the Transferor who will not be liable personally for any breach after he shall have disposed of his legal interest in the Retained Land: Not to obstruct the Driveway
Insert here any required or permitted statements, certificates or applications and any agreed declarations and so on.	**Other** It might be appropriate to include additional provisions in here such as: An indemnity covenant if the seller's title is burdened with covenants and the seller is entitled to demand an indemnity covenant A clause providing that the provisions of s62 LPA 1925 and Wheeldon v Burrows are not intended to apply to this transaction – this will avoid any implied easements being created in favour of the land being sold A clause excluding the Transferee's right to any light and air and confirming that the Transferor is entitled to develop the retained land as they see fit
The transferor must execute this transfer as a deed using the space opposite. If there is more than one transferor, all must execute. Forms of execution are given in Schedule 9 to the Land Registration Rules 2003. If the transfer contains transferee's covenants or declarations or contains an application by the transferee (such as for a restriction), it must also be executed by the transferee.	**13 Execution** All parties to the transfer must sign and the appropriate execution clauses should be included Remember that the plan must be attached to the transfer. Do not forget to colour the plan to include matters such as the driveway, drain and T mark used in this example.

If there is more than one transferee and panel 11 has been completed, each transferee must also execute this transfer to comply with the requirements in section 53(1)(b) of the Law of Property Act 1925 relating to the declaration of a trust of land. Please refer to *Joint property ownership* and practice guide *24: private trusts of land* for further guidance. Examples of the correct form of execution are set out in practice guide 8: execution of deeds. Execution as a deed usually means that a witness must also sign, and add their name and address. Remember to date this deed in panel 4.

WARNING
If you dishonestly enter information or make a statement that you know is, or might be, untrue or misleading, and intend by doing so to make a gain for yourself or another person, or to cause loss or the risk of loss to another person, you may commit the offence of fraud under section 1 of the Fraud Act 2006, the maximum penalty for which is 10 years' imprisonment or an unlimited fine, or both.

Failure to complete this form with proper care may result in a loss of protection under the Land Registration Act 2002 if, as a result, a mistake is made in the register.

Under section 66 of the Land Registration Act 2002 most documents (including this form) kept by the registrar relating to an application to the registrar or referred to in the register are open to public inspection and copying. If you believe a document contains prejudicial information, you may apply for that part of the document to be made exempt using Form EX1, under rule 136 of the Land Registration Rules 2003.

Example

Consider Plan A – we have already said that rights will be granted to the buyer. Consider Plan B (below) – what will you do in this situation? In this situation the land containing the drive is being sold to the buyer so the seller will need to reserve rights for their benefit but also for the benefit of the people after them, their successors in title. This ensures that the easement continues to benefit their land, not just them.

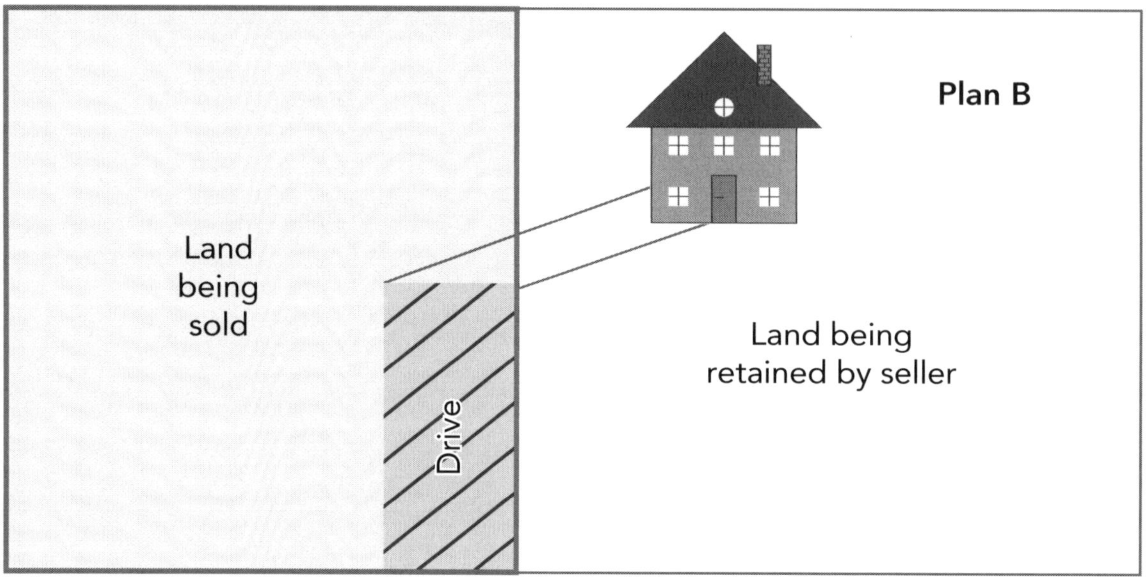

10.3.4 The draft contract

As we have seen, on a sale of part, in practice, it is very common for an agreed draft transfer form (TP1) to be annexed to the contract detailing such rights and any covenants.

The open contract provisions are not ideal. It is far better to decide exactly which rights are needed by the seller and which by the buyer and then set them out clearly and expressly in the Special Conditions in the contract.

There are no rules relating to new covenants under either the open contract rules or the SCs (except regarding indemnity covenants). This means that any covenants which are required by either party must be included in the contract by way of a Special Condition.

When drafting contractual provisions regarding new easements and covenants, it is a common beginner's mistake to attempt to do the granting or covenanting actually in the contract. The contract simply promises what will be done in the future, and the terminology of the draft Special Conditions should reflect this. For example, they might start: "The buyer shall in the transfer covenant . . .", but not "The buyer hereby covenants . . .".

If the transfer of part is appended to the contract, there will be few changes to make to the standard form of contract when drafting. Note however:

In the particulars of sale:

- The **property** will be defined by reference to the address or description of the land to be sold followed by the words "shown edged red on the plan attached hereto".
- The **title number** will be inserted followed by "(part)" to indicate that not all of the land contained in the seller's title number is being sold.
- An additional special condition will be added as follows:

  "The transfer to the buyer will be in the form annexed hereto"
- If, as is often the case, the seller has agreed to do some work, this must be dealt with as an **additional special condition** in the contract. Often a seller will agree to clear a site or, perhaps, construct a driveway on their retained land as part of the overall agreement with the buyer. Note that obligations which will be concluded in a relatively short space of time are more appropriately dealt with in the contract. For example, if the seller agrees to construct a driveway on their retained land within three months of completion of the sale, it is more appropriate for this to appear in the contract rather than a short-term obligation fettering the freehold in the transfer. Standard condition 7.3 contains a non-merger clause meaning that any term contained in the contract which remains to be performed after completion is still valid and enforceable.

10.3.5 Other issues on a sale of part

If the seller's title is registered, the appropriate pre-completion search is the OS2: official search with priority part of the land in a registered title (available at: https://www.gov.uk/government/publications/official-search-with-priority-part-of-the-title-os2.

To obtain priority for a purchase of part of the land in a title, the HMLR search must be against the correct part of the land only. A HMLR search against the whole of the land in the title does not give priority if only part of the land is purchased. It will be necessary to attach a plan to the OS2 application unless the conveyancer can refer to the property on a HMLR approved estate plan or on a HMLR title plan (see box 6 of the OS2 form). Many practitioners now use the HMLR Portal, which enables searches (as well as official copies and other services) to be ordered electronically.

Where the buyer is obtaining a mortgage, the search must be made in the mortgage lender's name instead of in the buyer's name. The lender will be named as the applicant and the search form will state (as the reason for the application) that the lender intends to take a registered charge (boxes 7 and 9 of the OS2 form). There is no need to make another search in the name of the buyer because the search made in the name of the mortgage lender will protect the buyer also.

The search may be made by post, DX or electronically through the Portal, NLIS, Business Gateway or an electronic search provider. The result of the search is forwarded to the applicant in the form of the official search certificate. This affords the buyer the following protection.

- Entries existing at the time of the search but which are not revealed will bind the buyer but they will be entitled to compensation.
- There is a priority period conferred upon the buyer. Providing the buyer's application for registration of the transaction is delivered to HMLR within **30 working days** of the date of the search, the buyer will not be bound by any later registrations after the date of the search. The register is effectively frozen.

It is important that the priority period is diarised to ensure that a prompt application for registration is made.

Where the seller's title is unregistered, the first registration application will be made using form FR1 and HMLR will note any new easements and restrictive covenants on the register of the new title.

Where the land is already registered, the registration application on form AP1 will essentially be as for a transfer of whole, except that the enclosures will vary (e.g. a certified copy of TP1 will be sent instead of TR1 and if there is a mortgage a DS3 will be supplied instead of a DS1). The AP1 form will refer in box 3 to the application affecting part of the title (e.g. "as shown edged red on the plan to the transfer dated . . .").

10.4 Acting on the purchase of a new build property

Clients may not be buying a second-hand dwelling. In many cases they may be buying a brand new home. The new home may have been physically completed or may be an uncompleted property being purchased "off plan" if the development has not been finished.

When a new dwelling is bought, the conveyancing procedure can be rather more complex than in other situations.

The first important point to note is that the basic conveyancing sale and purchase procedure is the same whether a new build property is being purchased or a second-hand property. So, by way of reminder, the basic outline of a conveyancing transaction as oulined in the chart below remains the same – buying a new build property just involves additional steps and considerations.

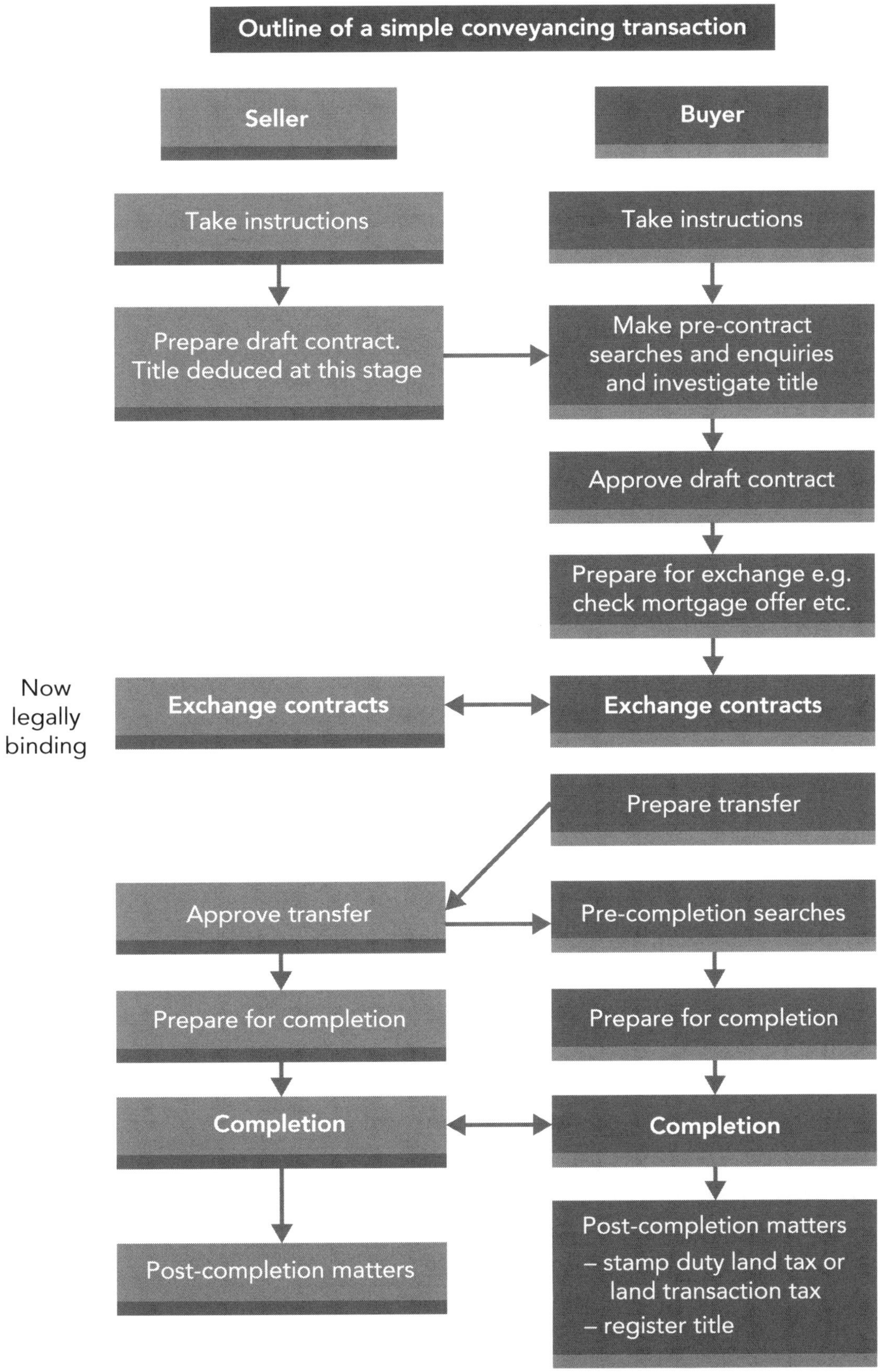

We will now look at some of the key considerations relating to the purchase of a new build property. We will assume that a buyer client is purchasing a new build property on an estate from a developer. The developer will be a limited company. All of the considerations discussed above regarding the transfer of part will be relevant to this transaction. Some new build transactions can be complex and the new build contract is often a substantial document. This chapter will consider some key issues that the conveyancer should consider, though not all of them.

A buyer is often purchasing a new leasehold property in a block of flats. This transaction is outside the scope of this coursebook.

10.4.1 Taking instructions

This course book will consider the position when acting for the buyer as this is a situation which residential conveyancers are more likely to come across. Law firms acting for developers often have specialist teams to take instructions and draft all the necessary documentation together with dealing with the lenders and individual plot sales.

The biggest challenge when acting for a buyer on a new build is often that the developer imposes a deadline for exchange of contracts; this is often 28 days from receipt of the contract pack by the buyer's conveyancer. This imposes a significant pressure on the conveyancer and their client particularly if the buyer has also paid a reservation deposit to the developer. The purpose of the deposit is to secure the property for an agreed period of time. If the matter proceeds to exchange, the reservation deposit will be deducted from the 10 per cent deposit payable on exchange of contracts. However, if the buyer does not exchange within the specified timeframe, they are likely to forfeit their reservation deposit.

When taking instructions on a new build transaction, all of the issues considered in this chapter must be considered when acting for the buyer. In addition, detailed advice as to the new build transaction must be given to the buyer client in sufficient time for them to digest prior to exchange of contracts. This advice might include issues such as:

(1) The risks of exchanging contracts on a property that is not structurally complete at the time of exchange.

(2) The risks of exchanging contracts where completion might not be for many months. The buyer will be contractually obliged to purchase the property in accordance with the contract and must be sure that they can fund the purchase. Most mortgage offers are only valid for a matter of three or four months and therefore many buyers will not have a valid mortgage offer in place at the time of exchange of contracts or will have one that is likely to expire before completion. There is no obligation on a mortgage lender to renew a mortgage offer if it expires.

(3) A clear explanation as to the rights and obligations contained in the transfer of part – developers tend to impose a significant number of covenants.

(4) A clear explanation of the significance of roads and sewers not being adopted at the time of completion.

(5) A clear explanation of the implications of the removal of any General Permitted Development rights in a planning permission.

The conveyancer acting for the developer will produce a contract pack which would typically include the following assuming that the developer's title is registered and mortgaged:

- draft contract with transfer of part annexed;
- the developer's title;
- HMLR compliant plan of the plot. The plot should be clearly identified on a plan annexed to the contract and transfer to avoid possible boundary disputes and this plan must comply with detailed HMLR requirements (e.g. as to dimensions, scale of the plan and other features); see above. Note that HMLR has a service to assist developers which includes simplifying processes from initial registration of the site, through pre-sales services to plot sales. Of particular importance to the buyer's conveyancer is to establish whether the plot plan has estate plan approval. HMLR will give written confirmation that such approval has been obtained meaning that the approved plan can then form the basis of the transfer of part. The significance is that the plot plan has been checked by HMLR and they are essentially confirming that the plot falls within the seller's title and that there are no discrepancies between adjoining plots. The developer is under a continuing duty to notify HMLR of any changes to the plans. The significance for the buyer is that the details of the date of the estate plan approval can be included on the OS2 search.

Activity

Follow the link below to HMLR's "Practice Guide 41 – Supplement 2 – Developing estates: registration services: estate plan approval":

https://www.gov.uk/government/publications/developing-estates-estate-plan-approval/developing-estates-registration-services-estate-plan-approval-practice-guide-41-supplement-2

Read the Practice guide – it is short. Then click to Supplement 5 and look at the examples of the plans to familiarise yourself with HMLR's requirements as to plan specifications.

PG 41 has a number of supporting supplements concerning specific aspects of the developing estates service which is designed to cover the estate development through from its early stages when it is a building site to the point when the plots are sold. These supplements are:

Supplement 1	Estate boundary approval
Supplement 2	Estate plan approval
Supplement 3	Approval of draft transfers and leases
Supplement 4	Plot sales, transfers and leases
Supplement 5	Plans requirements and surveying specifications
Supplement 6	Voluntary applications to note overriding interests

- Energy Performance Certificate – often on a new build, this will not be available until the property is physically complete and the buyer might exchange contracts before the property is constructed. Accordingly, the developer should produce a Predicted Energy Assessment;
- replies to enquiries before contract – the Protocol is not used for new build transactions. The developer will complete standard enquiries before contract as opposed to the Property Information Form and will not provide the Fittings and Contents Form. However, if the seller has agreed to include certain items in the sale price, these should be specified and included in the contract;
- information sheet for the buyer's conveyancer – this can be a helpful document giving general information about the development;
- relevant planning permission(s);
- building regulations for plans approval;
- any relevant agreements and bonds (see below);
- any relevant planning agreements (see below);
- details of the new build warranty (see below);
- HMLR estate plan approval (see below);
- Disclosure of Incentives Form, if relevant (see below).

10.4.2 Consumer Code for Homebuilders (the Code)/New Homes Quality Board

The Code was developed by the homebuilding industry to make the home buying process fairer and more transparent for buyers. It is designed to help buyers understand the expectations and level of service from their homebuilder and to be aware of their consumer rights before and after they moved in. Importantly for buyers, in the event that there is a problem, there is a free dispute resolution scheme in place to deal with complaints about breaches of the Code.

All homebuilders who are registered with the main new build warranty organisations (see below) must comply with the Code and these warranty bodies represent over 95 per cent of the new homes built in the UK. The key requirements of the Code are:

- effective customer service training;
- clear and truthful advertising and marketing materials;
- sufficient pre-purchase information to help you make an informed decision about your purchase;
- contact details for the Home Builder and other relevant bodies;
- home warranty information;
- contract information including termination rights;
- timing of construction, completion and handover;
- after-sales service;
- complaints process.

The New Homes Quality Board (NHQB) has been set up under the **Building Safety Act 2022**. It was set up to develop a new framework to oversee reforms in the build quality of new homes and customer service provided by developers. The NHQB has published its New Homes Quality Code. The NHQB state that the Code:

- Protects vulnerable customers, prohibits high pressure selling; requires any deposits the customer pays to their builder to be protected.
- Requires the developer to provide all relevant information about the home during the sales process – including its tenure and any future management or service charges – which allows them to make an informed decision about their purchase.
- Sets out requirements for a fair reservation agreement, which includes a "cooling off" period, and sales contract requirements.
- Allows customers to have a professional carry out a pre-completion inspection of their home on their behalf.
- Specifies that a home must be "complete", preventing builders from paying customers to move into an incomplete new home early.

- Crucially, and to address the biggest gap in the existing arrangements, the New Homes Quality Code requires builders to have an effective after-care service in place to deal with any issues or "snagging" problems that customers have with their new home; together with a robust complaints process that responds to customers' concerns in a timely manner and to their satisfaction, keeping them informed throughout. A customer who is not satisfied with the way in which any complaint they have made has been dealt with can refer their complaint to the independent New Homes Ombudsman Service.

The Code and the NHQB will run in parallel for some time and conveyancers should check the scheme with which a developer is registered when they take on a new build matter for a buyer client.

Activity

Follow the links below to find out more about the Code and the New Homes Quality Board

https://consumercode.co.uk/

https://www.nhqb.org.uk/

10.4.3 Key issues to consider when dealing with a new build

We will now move on to look at some of the important considerations for conveyancers when acting for a client who is purchasing a new build property.

Planning

This is dealt with in detail in **Chapter 7**. The buyer will need to check:

- planning permissions for the erection of the dwelling (usually outline and full permissions). It is also important to check any conditions attached to the planning permission to ensure that they will be complied with (e.g. landscaping conditions for an estate development). On a new build transaction, there are often a significant number of pre-commencement conditions with which the developer must comply and the buyer's conveyancer should ensure that they have evidence of compliance with these conditions prior to exchange of contracts;
- **Building Regulations** consent – the developer should provide the full plans approval notice with the contract pack. The building regulation completion certificate will only be produced once the dwelling is structurally complete.

This document is not likely to be forthcoming until after completion has taken place. The developer should be under a contractual obligation to produce the completion certificate within a specified timeframe following completion;

- possibly, also planning permission for change of use of the land.

Planning agreements/Community Infrastructure Levy

A developer is often required to enter into a planning agreement with the local authority as a condition of obtaining planning permission. The purpose of planning obligations is to mitigate the impacts of a development proposal and often require the developer to make financial contribution to local infrastructure or projects such as road widening, health centres, education or playgroup facilities. Importantly, the requirements for the provision of affordable housing as part of a development scheme are contained in a planning agreement which is entered into under **s106 Town and Country Planning Act 1990**. It is for this reason that they are often referred to as "**s106** agreements".

s106 agreements can be entered into by a person with an interest in the land and the local planning authority or if the planning obligations are less extensive, a unilateral undertaking might be entered into by a person with an interest in the land without the local planning authority.

Planning obligations run with the land, are legally binding and enforceable. Copies of any **s106** agreements should accompany the developers contract pack and will be revealed by the local search. The buyer's conveyancer should read the terms of the **s106** agreement carefully and advise their client accordingly. Some agreements make it clear that the obligations are not intended to bind individual plot buyers. However, if this provision is not contained in the agreement, the buyer must be advised that they could be called upon to make the contributions under the terms of the **s106** agreement if the developer defaults.

The buyer's conveyancer should seek evidence from the developer's conveyancer that all obligations under the **s106** agreement have been complied with for example, that all payments due have been made. Often, these obligations are extensive and will not be concluded by the time a buyer's transaction completes. This is particularly relevant on a large development which is concluded in different phases. In this case, the buyer's conveyancer should ensure that the developer enters into an indemnity in the contract and transfer of part confirming that they will meet the ongoing planning obligations and it is necessary to report any ongoing obligations to the buyer's lender prior to exchange of contracts (paragraph 5.5.4 of the Lenders Handbook).

The **Community Infrastructure Levy** (**CIL**) is a charge which can be levied by local authorities on new development in their area. This is an additional tool for local authorities to use to help them raise funds to deliver the infrastructure needed to support development in their area. Most new development which creates net additional floorspace of 100 m^2 or more, or creates a new dwelling, is potentially liable for the levy. Some developments may be eligible for relief or exemption from the levy which includes residential annexes and extensions and houses and flats which are built by "self-builders". It is therefore unlikely that a plot purchase from a developer is likely to be excluded from the CIL provisions if it is applicable in the locality.

A key point relating to CIL is that it is not adopted by all local authorities. Accordingly, the buyer's conveyancer must look at the answer to question 3.10 of the CON 29 part of the local search very carefully as this will indicate whether the CIL is payable in the locality where the property is being purchased.

Link to practice

Question 3.10 of the CON29 is below – you can see that it is comprehensive. If CIL is payable, you should check that it has been paid and raise further enquiries if there is any indication of default or non-payment.

"3.10. Community infrastructure levy (CIL)

(a) Is there a CIL charging schedule?

(b) If, yes, do any of the following subsist in relation to the property, or has a local authority decided to issue, serve, make or commence any of the following:

- a liability notice
- a notice of chargeable development
- a demand notice
- a default liability notice
- an assumption of liability notice
- a commencement notice

(c) Has any demand notice been suspended?

(d) Has the local authority received full or part payment of any CIL liability?

(e) Has the local authority received any appeal against any of the above?

(f) Has a decision been taken to apply for a liability order?

(g) Has a liability order been granted?

(h) Have any other enforcement measures been taken?"

There is no written agreement relating to CIL liability as there is with a **s106** agreement. If the CIL is payable, the developer must give the appropriate notice to the local authority when development has commenced to trigger the payment. Liability to pay runs with the land. Accordingly, it is very important for the buyer's conveyancer to seek written evidence from the developer that CIL liability has been paid prior to exchange of contracts. The developer can agree with the local authority to pay by instalments in which case the buyer's conveyancer should ensure that the developer enters into an indemnity in the contract and transfer of part confirming that they will meet the ongoing payments and any ongoing obligations must be reported to the buyer's lender prior to exchange of contracts.

In areas where the CIL is payable, the funds for infrastructure which would have been payable under a **s106** agreement will be payable under the CIL regime. However, it is still possible to have a **s106** agreement and CIL liability because the **s106** agreement will still deal with any affordable housing requirements.

The risks of paying sums due under the **s106** agreement or CIL in the event of default by the developer must be explained very clearly to the buyer.

Infrastructure

Access to the property needs to be considered. Are there rights of way to enter the property, and suitable easements for services (e.g. gas, electricity, sewers)?

The expense is considerable to make up a road to the standards required by the local authority for adoption as a public highway. This expense falls on the frontagers (i.e. the owners of the land adjoining the road). To resolve this problem, a **s38 Highways Act 1980** agreement and bond needs to be completed. The buyer may need to take expert advice to ascertain whether the amount of the financial bond provided is adequate. If the roads are not going to be adopted by the local authority, there must be adequate alternative provisions for their construction and maintenance. If the roads are not going to be adopted, there must also be adequate easements for the buyer to use the roads and footways once constructed.

Similarly, there should be an agreement and bond for the sewers (**s104 Water Industry Act 1991**).

As explained in **Chapter 8**, the water companies took over responsibility for many sewers from October 2011. This has had an impact on **s104** agreements. Where sewers transferred to the water companies, existing **s104** agreements ceased to have effect as they had no ongoing purpose. Where sewers have not transferred, **s104** agreements and any bonds continue in force until the sewers are adopted or until they transfer under supplementary transfer arrangements.

Once the new mandatory build standards and sewer adoption arrangements are implemented, there will no longer be an option to retain sewers in private ownership. Developers will not be permitted to connect sewers unless there is a **s104** agreement in place and they are constructed to the minimum build standards. **s104** agreements will have to contain a commitment from those building the sewers to build to agreed standards, and the agreement must also contain a binding commitment from the water company to adopt the sewer thereafter.

Searches

All the usual searches will need to be made. Note in particular the importance of the local search when dealing with a new build transaction. It will reveal issues such as:

- whether the road fronting the property is adopted by the local authority – if it is not, the developer should produce a **s38** agreement;
- the planning permission(s) relating to construction of the dwelling;
- the building regulations for plans approval notice (and completion certificate if issued);
- whether there are any **s106** agreements;
- whether the development is affected by the CIL;
- whether there are any planning enforcement proceedings.

The drainage search will reveal whether the developer has entered into a drainage agreement and bond regarding the drainage assets.

In addition to the usual searches, it might be necessary to conduct:

- **A commons registration search** (optional enquiry 22 of the CON29). This is to establish whether previously undeveloped land is subject to any rights of common or registration as a TVG.
- **A SIM search**. If there is no estate plan approval of the plot plan, the buyer's conveyancer should carry out a SIM even if the developer's title is registered. This will reveal whether the land edged red on the plot plan falls entirely within the developer's registered title.
- **Environmental matters**. As we have seen in **Chapter 8**, most conveyancers will consider an environmental search to be a standard search on a purchase but it must be considered to be essential on the purchase of a new build. The former use of the land upon which the development being built is important. If it is a brownfield site (for example, the land had former industrial use) the buyer's conveyancer must ensure on behalf of their buyer (and lender, if any) that any contamination has been adequately addressed by the developer.

- **Company search**. A developer is almost invariably going to be a limited company so company search will be required as discussed in **Chapter 8**. It is prudent to conduct research prior to exchange of contracts and to repeat it just before completion.
- **OS2** – on a sale of part, the appropriate pre-completion search is the OS2 as detailed above.

Flooding and insurance

(1) Flooding

New residential developments are increasingly being built on land which has formally been used as a floodplain that is, land which is deliberately kept there and free of dwellings to ensure that run-off and floodwater does not adversely impact a locality. Flooding is a significant concern for buyers and their conveyancers.

The environmental search would reveal whether the property is situated in an area which might be prone to flooding. It might be necessary to carry out an additional flood risk report and the result should be reported to the buyer and lender if there is a heightened risk of flooding.

Activity

Follow the link below and read and make notes on the key points in the Law Society's Practice Note on flooding:

https://www.lawsociety.org.uk/en/topics/property/flood-risk

Developers have increasing responsibility to ensure that they have adequate flood mitigation schemes in place. The local authority may impose planning conditions requiring the developer to assess and mitigate flood risk in the planning permission. One of the methods which the developer can use is a Sustainable Urban Drainage System (SuDS). This is a system which is designed to slow the rate of surface water run-off and improve infiltration by mimicking natural drainage in both rural and urban areas. The idea is to reduce the risk of flash flooding which occurs when rainwater rapidly flows into the public sewerage and drainage systems.

There are various different methods to provide SuDS which can include the use of permeable paving, detention basins, purpose-built ponds and wetlands or underground storage facilities where water can collect quickly and be allowed to dissipate.

Question 3.3 of the CON 29 part of the local search asks the following:

"3.3. Drainage matters

(a) Is the property served by a sustainable urban drainage system (SuDS)?

(b) Are there SuDS features within the boundary of the property? If yes, is the owner responsible for maintenance?

(c) If the property benefits from a SuDS for which there is a charge, who bills the property for the surface water drainage charge?"

The significance of this for the buyer is that the plot could be affected by having part of an underground SuDS system within the boundary of the plot. This could involve disruption due to access or maintenance issues.

In addition, some SuDS systems have pumps and mechanical aspects which require regular maintenance and thus, cost. The transfer should contain appropriate rights and responsibilities to deal with these issues and the cost impact should be clearly explained to the buyer (and lender if relevant).

(2) Insurance and Flood Re

In a new build transaction, the contract should reflect the fact that the developer will retain the risk in the property until completion. This means that the developer will insure the property between exchange of contracts and completion. The buyer will need to ensure that their buildings insurance is ready to go on risk on completion. Buyers of new build properties need to be particularly aware of buildings insurance issues in flood risk areas.

Standard buildings and contents insurance in the UK usually covers against damage from flooding, including other issues such as fire or theft. However, in recent years, homeowners have experienced significant flooding meaning that the cost of flood insurance and policy excesses have increased considerably. Indeed, some homeowners in flood risk areas might not be able to secure buildings insurance at all. The government and the insurance industry had an understanding that buildings insurance would continue to include flood risk and be reasonably priced but this memorandum of understanding expired. In its place the Flood Re scheme was introduced in 2016.

The basic premise of the Flood Re scheme is that a small part of every home owner's buildings insurance premium goes into the scheme and this fund can then be used to pay for flood damage. Homeowners will still buy their insurance from insurers or insurance brokers in the usual way, they will not deal directly with Flood Re. The aim is to keep buildings insurance premiums at a manageable level.

We have seen that as part of the planning process, developers are required to take on greater responsibility for flood mitigation and this is reflected in the availability of buildings insurance covering flooding for new build properties. This is significant in terms of the Flood Re scheme because it only applies to properties built before 2009. The aim of this cut-off point is to discourage developers from building homes in flood risk areas. This means that homes built after 2009 do not have the benefit of being in the Flood Re scheme. There are other properties that do not qualify for the scheme such as holiday lets, properties owned by buy to let landlords, commercial and leasehold properties.

This does not mean that a buyer will not be able to secure buildings insurance for a property that is in a flood prone area, but it does mean that there is no obligation on insurers to offer buildings insurance in these areas and no cap on the buildings insurance premium. Accordingly, conveyancers should alert buyer clients to this issue if the searches reveal that the property is in an area which might be prone to flood risk. The buyer should research the market carefully for buildings insurance.

Activity

Follow the link below to the Flood Re website. Read more about the scheme and make notes about the eligibility criteria:

https://www.floodre.co.uk/can-flood-re-help-me/eligibility-criteria/

(3) Title

Often, a building estate will comprise several different titles. Before land registration became widespread, it was necessary to investigate and convey the title to each part of the plot of land separately. Today, however, the entire estate is likely to be registered, and any differences in the existing covenants or easements marked on the title plan.

As we have seen, before the development is commenced, the developer may have obtained estate plan approval from HMLR, a service which compares the developer's site survey with the developer's registered title to the estate development land. This can assist particularly if the developers title plan is large or complex. We have seen that HMLR uses colour conventions on title plans to denote areas which are affected by different rights and obligations. Developers often acquire development sites in a piecemeal fashion meaning that the final register of title and title plan can be large and complex. This is where buyer's conveyancer could apply for a **certificate of inspection** (**CI**). This is a special procedure, based on the use of an officially approved estate layout plan and simplifies the task of buying, selling or leasing plots on a development title. It involves the use of recognised plot numbers and instead of applying for an official copy of the title plan, it is possible to apply for a certificate of inspection.

The certificate of inspection can be applied for by using panel 7 on form OC1 (https://www.gov.uk/government/publications/official-copies-of-register-or-plan-registration-oc1) or by making an application via the Portal. The certificate will confirm that the plot is within the developer's title and will reveal whether it is affected by any references (such as colouring) on the developer's title plan. Where HMLR has approved an estate plan, it is simply necessary to give the plot number.

Activity

Follow the link to HMLR "Practice Guide 11: Inspection and application for official copies"

https://www.gov.uk/government/publications/inspection-and-application-for-official-copies/practice-guide-11-inspection-and-application-for-official-copies

Go to Section 5, which contains more information on the CI.

(4) New build warranty

A key feature of every new build purchase is that the dwelling is protected for the first 10 years after completion under a new build warranty. The most well-known of these is the National House Building Council (NHBC) but there are a number of other schemes which follow a similar pattern.

Note that under the **Building Safety Act 2022**, the provision of a new build warranty on the sale of a new property will become a statutory requirement. In addition, the of cover will increase from the current 10 years to 15 years. At the moment, neither of these provisions are in force.

Despite the many benefits of buying a brand-new property, there is a possibility that a buyer could be left vulnerable. This vulnerability could arise in several ways. The builder might, for example, have become insolvent or absconded, and the buyer could be left with a partially completed building. Second, completed dwellings might have developed structural faults that were not detectable when the dwelling was first occupied. The new build warranty is designed to protect against these risks and to give consumer confidence when buying a new build property. Most institutional lenders are not prepared to lend on a new build property unless it comes with the benefit of an acceptable new build warranty.

The schemes have similar features which are broadly as follows:

(1) **A deposit protection scheme** – one of the risks of purchasing a new build is that a buyer pays a 10 per cent deposit on exchange of contracts which is generally

paid to the developer as agent (see below). This means that the deposit will be paid to the developer immediately after exchange. Often there is a significant period of time between exchange of contracts and completion. If the developer goes out of business in this time, this could mean that the buyer loses their deposit. All new build warranty providers recognise this as being an inherent risk in the new build procedure. Accordingly, deposit protection as a standard part of the new build warranty has become standard. This means that the buyers deposit will be protected in the event that the developer is registered with a new build warranty provider and goes out of business between exchange of contracts and completion. Developers often place a limit on the maximum deposit that can be recovered. For example, the NHBC provides that they will cover the deposit of 10 per cent of the purchase price up to a maximum of £100,000. This means that if a buyer is purchasing a new build property from more than £1 million, the part of their deposit which exceeds £100,000 will be at risk.

(2) **Years 1 and 2 after completion** – if defects are revealed during this time, the developer is expected to step in and put them right.

(3) **Years 3 to 10 after completion** – if defects are revealed during this time, the new build warranty provider will step in.

The buyer will be expected to provide details of the new build warranty to their buyer if they sell the property within the first 10 years of its construction.

The conveyancer should carefully check the terms of the new build warranty that is on offer and, in particular, that the developer remains registered with the warranty provider at point of exchange of contracts. Some warranty providers carry out physical inspections of the property during the course of construction; others merely offer a financial remedy in the event of a problem.

(5) NHBC

We will look in brief at the NHBC scheme, but others are available. It is essential for the buyer's conveyancer to check Part 2 of the Lender's Handbook to ensure that the new build warranty on offer is acceptable to the buyer's lender.

The NHBC is an independent, non-profit-distributing organisation and the protection provided applies only to dwellings built by builders who are registered with them, though obviously it is in the interest of most builders to register. Around 80 per cent of new homes built in the UK each year are registered with the NHBC. The scheme extends to houses, purpose-built flats and maisonettes, and properties created by the conversion of existing buildings.

The nature of the NHBC scheme

The NHBC has had various schemes over the years. The current scheme for residential housing is Buildmark. Essential to Buildmark is the fact that the builder warrants or undertakes to the buyer that the home is being built or will be built in accordance with the NHBC requirements, that it will be built in an efficient and workmanlike manner with proper materials, and that it will be fit for habitation.

As well as rights under this agreement, the buyer will still have their normal contractual, statutory and common law rights.

The Buildmark scheme

Builders who are registered with the NHBC must offer to enter into an NHBC agreement with buyers of new dwellings. The agreement is made on behalf of the first owner and all subsequent owners within the period of cover. The protection consists of deposit protection, a warranty and insurance cover, which lasts for 10 years and is in three stages.

In practice, there are detailed provisions, with exclusions, conditions and limitations.

If conveyancers have any doubts about the level or type of cover applicable, or whether the builder is registered, etc. the NHBC operates a customer services line, dealing with general enquiries and enquiries about specific builders or plots. It also has a website, with detailed information and contact points.

The buyer's conveyancer must check that the builder is registered with the NHBC and that Buildmark cover will be provided for the property being purchased. Prior to 2012, the NHBC procedure was dealt with using paper documentation. Following completion, the NHBC issued a Buildmark insurance certificate in triplicate. One copy was to be kept with the deeds, another copy kept on the solicitor's file and the third copy passed to the owner along with other supporting documentation and information in a Buildmark pack. When the owner sold the home, the insurance certificate and pack would be passed to the new owner but it was not necessary for the cover to be formally transferred as the benefit of cover transferred automatically to the new owner.

An online Buildmark acceptance process was launched in 2012. This process is now dealt with by developers and conveyancers through the NHBC Conveyancing portal. The online system works as follows:

(1) When the builder or developer registers the plot with the NHBC, the NHBC will send them a Buildmark policy number and an activation code.

(2) The builder forwards the policy number and the activation code to the buyer's conveyancer, although the data may already have been uploaded to the Conveyancing portal by the NHBC.

(3) The conveyancer will have registered to use the online system with the NHBC.

(4) The conveyancer logs on to the firm's NHBC Conveyancing portal account and accesses details of the plot, using the activation code and policy number.

(5) The conveyancer must check that Buildmark cover will be provided for the plot before exchange of contracts.

(6) On exchange, the conveyancer goes back into the system, confirms the date of exchange and updates the buyer's details. This activates the deposit insurance protection under the first stage of the Buildmark cover.

(7) The conveyancer can check via the system that the UK Finance cover note is available (if the buyer is taking out a mortgage, the UK Finance Mortgage Lenders' Handbook states that a cover note must be held by the buyer's conveyancer prior to submission of the report on title and funds request). This will confirm that the property has received its final inspection and that cover will be in place on completion.

(8) The conveyancer will go back into the system and confirm completion once it has taken place. This activates the Buildmark policy.

Link to practice

It is surprisingly common to find that a conveyancer fails to activate the NHBC cover online following completion. This often only comes to light when the property is being sold and can cause delays with a subsequent sale of the property.

(9) The NHBC will validate the completion information and, once approved, the insurance certificate and associated documentation will be available to download.

(10) The conveyancer will then download the insurance certificate and associated documentation to send to the client, to the lender (if the lender wants to receive such documentation) and to keep a copy for the file. The NHBC documentation can then be produced if the home is later sold. The benefit of the Buildmark cover will pass to a later buyer, as a successor in title, without needing to be expressly assigned. In practical terms, it is simply necessary to pass the insurance certificate and policy document to later owners on completion, normally via the conveyancer.

(11) The NHBC offers homeowners with NHBC cover an opportunity to have a free online Home User Guide, which is a portal for storing details and documentation about their home. This may also make it easier to pass on Buildmark details to future buyers.

In some cases, Buildmark also contains insurance against breaches of the **Building Regulations**. This cover will only be included where the NHBC provided the building control service for the home. If it did, this will be stated in the Buildmark certificate. This is not always going to be the case as building control services can be carried out either by local authority or licensed private sector inspectors, who will inspect the home during the build and issue the completion certificate for **Building Regulations** purposes (also see **Chapter 7**). If included, the cover will be provided for the final eight years of the policy and the home owner can make a claim where there is an imminent danger to physical health or safety because the builder has failed to meet specified sections of the **Building Regulations**. These areas include such things as structure, fire safety and fuel storage systems. There are financial limits and exclusions. If the claim is approved, the NHBC will either take on the work necessary to meet the **Building Regulations** standards or will pay for the cost of having the work done. The NHBC will also pay, where necessary, for alternative accommodation and storage of possessions (e.g. where the work requires the home owner to move out or where furniture needs to be put into storage).

Activity

Find out more, follow the link below and locate the "Buildmark for Conveyancers" brochure. Download it and retain it for reference purposes.

https://www.nhbc.co.uk/

There are alternative insurance schemes to Buildmark. A mortgage lender would not normally lend on the security of a new property unless it is covered by NHBC or another suitable scheme. Sometimes, an architect's certificate is used to resolve this problem. Part 2 of the Lenders' Handbook will state which schemes are acceptable to the lender.

The building is inspected a number of times by the local authority and NHBC during construction. Because of this, many buyers are reluctant to pay for a survey too. The most prudent course of action, however, is to have a survey as well.

The draft contract

We have seen that the developer's conveyancer will draft the contract and will usually add the transfer of part to it. The developer's conveyancer often states that no amendments will be accepted to these documents. However, the buyer's conveyancer must check them carefully to ensure that they are satisfactory to the buyer. The developer may be willing to accept amendments to avoid losing the sale. Note that the developer may have had the transfer approved by HMLR.

The buyer's conveyancer should send the draft contract and transfer of part together with the plot plan to their buyer client at the earliest opportunity together with advice as to the content and effect of these documents.

The contract of sale on a new build property can be more complex than a standard residential transaction but some common features to note are:

(1) **Description of the property** – the property must be described by reference to the plot number and the Royal Mail address if one has been allocated and the contract must include the plan of the plot. Some contracts may also include a property specification.

(2) **Reservation deposit** – if the buyer paid a deposit to reserve the property this must be included in the contract and deducted from the deposit payable on exchange.

(3) **Extras** – if the buyer has agreed to pay for extra fittings and contents to be installed at property, ideally, these should be referred to in the contract although some developers will refuse to do so and prefer to keep the supply of these items as a separate contract direct between the developer and buyer.

(4) The developer must **contract to build the dwelling** in accordance with the appropriate planning permission and building regulations requirements.

(5) The developer must contract to provide the **new build warranty cover note** (if relevant) and the building regulation completion certificate.

(6) The property will usually be **at the risk of the developer** until completion and the developer will insure the property until completion.

(7) **Deposit paid on exchange** – typically, a new build contract will provide that the deposit is held as agent for the seller meaning that the deposit will be paid direct to the developer on exchange of contracts. Note the risks above and the fact that most new build warranties tend to mitigate this risk by providing deposit protection.

(8) **Completion** – a developer may be able to offer a fixed completion date on exchange of contracts but in a new build transaction this is unlikely. Generally, the developer will not know when the dwelling will be structurally completed at the point of exchange of contracts. Accordingly, the contract should include a mechanism whereby the developers conveyancer will serve notice on the buyer's conveyancer requiring completion within a specified time (often 14 days) from the point at which the property is structurally complete. This could cause difficulties in a chain of transactions and it is often the case that a buyer of a new build will complete on their sale prior to their new build purchase due to the uncertainty relating to the completion date on the new build. A further issue is that the buyer's conveyancer must ensure that they have sufficient time to drawdown their client's mortgage financing once the completion notice is served by the developer's conveyancer.

(9) **Long stop date** – if completion is going to be on notice, the contract must include a long stop date that is, a date by which if completion has not taken place, both parties can withdraw without penalty. It is essential that at some point in the future, the buyer is entitled to bring the contract to an end and have their deposit returned to them in the event that the developer is unable to complete the construction of the dwelling.

(10) **Snagging** – the contract should provide that within a specified period after completion the buyer is allowed to notify the developer of minor items which the developer agrees to put right without further payment. Typically, the buyer will inspect the property prior to completion and will provide a "snagging" list – these are small items which need to be rectified. The contract will generally provide that the buyer cannot refuse to complete if there are minor items which the developer agrees to rectify after completion.

(11) **Transfer of part** – the contract should include a provision confirming that the transfer will be in the form of the version attached to the contract.

(12) **Extra fee** – a developers contract often includes an additional sum of about £100 plus VAT payable by the buyer on completion for the production of the documents. The buyer's conveyancer must ensure that this is included on their client's completion statement.

(13) **Other provisions** – there will be a host of other provisions in addition to the standard terms that are expected in a contract for the sale of land, including issues such as deducing title, an arbitration clause, governing law and jurisdiction.

Lender's Handbook requirements

In most cases, the buyer of a new build will do so with the aid of a mortgage. The buyer's conveyancer should carefully check Parts 1 and 2 of the Lender's Handbook (or, BSA Handbook) as there are additional issues specific to a new build which must be complied with.

New build warranty (National House Building Council)

New houses and flats should have new build warranty cover, the most common of which is NHBC. Lenders' Handbook 6.7 sets out alternatives, and the documentation that must be filed with the deeds.

Note that this issue may be relevant to a conveyancing transaction not only where the house being bought is brand new (when new warranty cover will be relevant), but also where a buyer is purchasing a home which is less than 10 years old (where the balance – remaining term – of any warranty cover will be relevant).

The Lenders' Handbook contains provisions to govern both new builds and homes which are less than 10 years old. Lenders' Handbook 6.7.1 states that if the property has been built or converted within the last ten years, or is to be occupied for the first time, the conveyancer must ensure that it was built or converted under a scheme acceptable to the lender (which will be detailed in Part 2 of the Handbook). The Handbook contains additional requirements where no acceptable scheme is in place.

It should be noted that alternative building standards indemnity schemes (i.e. other than the NHBC scheme) may be acceptable, depending on the lender. Santander, for instance, currently accepts 17 schemes. These include the NHBC Buildmark scheme, Premier Guarantee and Build Assure. Practitioners should always check Part 2 of the Lenders' Handbook for the requirements and ensure compliance as necessary.

Part 2 also indicates whether any warranty documentation should be sent to the lender after completion. The conveyancer must obtain a copy of a new home warranty provider's cover note from the developer before sending the request for funds and report on title. The cover note must confirm that the property has received a satisfactory final inspection and that the new home warranty will be in place on or before legal completion. It is sensible, before agreeing that the lender can safely lend against the property, that you have evidence that the property has a structural guarantee.

A "one off" new build property or smaller developer might not offer a new build warranty but instead, a Professional Consultants Certificate. This is a document signed off by the architect who is required to oversee the stages of the build. The Handbook sets out the requirements for the Professional Consultants Certificate and, in particular, the indemnity insurance which the professional signing off the certificate must have in place.

Private roads and sewers, etc.

Roads and sewers not yet maintained at public expense are frequently encountered on new building estates, where suitable agreements and bonds should be checked to be in place. If there is no agreement (e.g. a private road) or the bond is inadequate, the lender must be notified (Lenders' Handbook 6.8.1 and 6.8.2). Lenders' Handbook 6.8.4 provides that, where roads and sewers are not adopted but they are to be maintained by local residents or by a management company, this is acceptable as long as there are satisfactory arrangements for maintenance, repairs and costs.

Another aspect to check in these and other cases is that easements exist giving the property the right of access and rights to run service pipes and wires (Lenders' Handbook 6.8 and 6.9).

New easements and covenants

These must be checked to ensure they are satisfactory.

The transfer will typically set out many different covenants relating to the estate. The rules relating to enforcement of these covenants against successors in title are set out above.

For the sake of certainty, it is far better to exclude implied easements by an express clause in the transfer and to rely on easements expressly granted.

Disclosure of incentives

Disclosure of incentives is a relevant issue where a new build property is being sold. This issue is relevant in relation to both buyer and lender.

The issue of incentives arose because lenders had become increasingly concerned that valuations of new property could be distorted if various incentives were included in the package. Examples of such incentives are deposits paid by the seller, payment of SDLT by the seller, cashback schemes, inclusion of white goods and kitchen appliances, free holidays or cars, or free garden landscaping (these examples are not exhaustive). All of these types of incentives mean that the headline purchase price may not be a completely true reflection of the property's true value. One effect is that the borrower might then borrow a sum effectively in excess of the true property value, thus creating a situation of negative equity from the beginning.

In 2008, the CML (as it was then called) introduced a **Disclosure of Incentives form**, to be completed by the developer. This is now called the **UK Finance Disclosure Form**, and a new version was introduced in February 2018. The form captures information about incentives, as well as a wider range of information about the new-build property which might affect a lending decision. Examples of such information in the new form are discounts from the developer's list price, the method of construction of the property, and luxury or non-standard shared facilities on site such as communal gyms or swimming pools.

The form is required for all newly built property including renovations and conversions, where mortgage finance is required. The seller (e.g. developer) must complete the form and it will be given to the valuer and the lender's conveyancer. The lender's conveyancer should be sent the form as early as possible in the conveyancing process and no later than seven working days before exchange of contracts. The lender's conveyancer (who will frequently be acting for both the lender and the buyer) will confirm with the borrower/buyer that the information on the form concerning incentives offered and the agreed sale price is correct. The conveyancer will only be required to report information to the lender where required by the UK Finance Mortgage Lenders' Handbook; for example, some lenders only want to know about incentives where they are in excess of 5 per cent of the purchase price.

Completion of the form should reassure lenders that they have sufficient security for the money secured against the property. The UK Finance Mortgage Lenders' Handbook states that the form must be supplied by the developer's conveyancer in relation to any property which is to be occupied for the first time (i.e. new build) or for the first time in its current form (e.g. a renovation or conversion). The Handbook further says that the certificate of title cannot be submitted to the lender unless the form has been received.

Management companies

Increasingly, freehold developments have shared services such as amenity areas, private roads or assets such as SuDS. We will discuss in **Chapter 12** the mechanics for enforcing the positive obligation to pay for these services in the freehold context but it is often the case that the developer will set up a management company to deal with the ongoing provision of the services.

The developer's conveyancer is likely to set up the management company which will either be limited by shares or limited by guarantee. The contract pack should include the certificate of incorporation of the management company and its Articles of Association (these set the rules that company officers must follow when running the company).

A company limited by shares is a separate legal entity, has shares and shareholders and can keep any profits it makes after paying tax. The buyer may be required to take a share in the management company on completion. The idea is that when the final dwelling on the development is sold, the developer hands over control of the management company to the freeholders on the development.

A company limited by guarantee is usually not for profit. This is also a separate legal entity has guarantors and guaranteed amount and invests any profits that it makes back into the company.

The contract pack should include details of the services which will be shared between the freeholders and a budget for the cost of providing the services in the first year or two. The management company should be a party to the transfer of part to ensure that it takes on the legal responsibility for providing the services.

The sum payable by the buyer to the developer on completion might include an advanced payment for budgeted service charge for the forthcoming six or 12 months. The transfer of part should include detailed definitions as to the services to be provided and a requirement that the management company produces audited accounts.

The buyer's conveyancer should ensure that a company search is carried out against the management company.

The UK Finance Mortgage Lenders' Handbook sets out detailed requirements as to what management arrangements are acceptable for mortgage purposes.

After completion

In addition to ensuring that any new build warranty is activated, the buyer's conveyancer must pay any SDLT (or LTT) due within the appropriate deadline and ensure that the HMLR application is submitted within the 30-working day priority period conferred by the OS2 search. As the majority of newbuild purchases are transfers of part, HMLR will have to register of title and create a title plan of the buyer's plot (see **Chapter 5**). HMLR can take many months to conclude these registrations.

It may also be necessary for the buyer's conveyancer to liaise with the management company to arrange for the transfer of a share in the company to the buyer and to give notice of mortgage to the management company if required by the transfer.

10.5 Chapter summary

There are some variations to the basic conveyancing process, and some additional considerations, where there is a sale of part of the land in a wider title, for example:

- the importance of a plan when defining the property;
- the importance of easements and covenants, in relation to both grant and reservation;
- the use of forms OS2 and TP1.

There are considerations when dealing with the conveyancing of new property, for example:

- the importance of planning and building regulation consents;
- the use of more standardised documentation by the developer;
- the arrangements for roads, sewers, access and other services, together with arrangements for these to be made up and, in many cases, adopted by the local authority;
- HMLR's services for developing estates, such as the pre-approval of transfers;
- the necessity for a new build warranty such as NHBC Buildmark warranty protection or equivalent cover.

CHAPTER 11

Probate sales, buy to let purchases, deeds of easement

11.1 Introduction

We will now move on to look at some more complex transactions that conveyancing practitioners will come across. The basic conveyancing process for a sale and purchase is the same but there are different considerations, for example, if a property is being sold in the context of a probate by personal representatives or if an investor is purchasing a property that is subject to an existing tenancy (commonly called a "buy to let"). Conveyancers are often instructed to deal with one-off matters for clients such as drafting a deed of easement. We will cover some of the key points in relation to all of these conveyancing transactions in this chapter.

This chapter will cover:

Acting on a probate sale and purchase:

- private client recap;
- personal representatives;

- grants of representation;
- chain of representation;
- authority to act;
- issues arising on a probate sale;
- the contract;
- problems if the title is unregistered;
- replying to pre-contract enquiries;
- access to the property between exchange of contracts and completion;
- the transfer.

Acting on the purchase of a buy to let property:

- EPC and contract;
- terms of an assured shorthold tenancy (AST) agreement;
- enquiries before contract;
- notices;
- landlord's position;
- tenancy deposit schemes;
- lenders and buy to lets;
- completion and post completion;
- if the buyer is a limited company;
- Houses in Multiple Occupation (HMOs);
- conveyancer's advice.

Acting on a deed of easement:

- what is an easement?
- acquiring an easement;
- legal and equitable easements;
- the deed of easement.

11.2 Overview of the conveyancing transaction

As you work through the probate and buy to let transactions, it is important to keep the basic structure of a sale and purchase in mind. These transactions have additional points to consider at various intervals and as with any issues, you should ensure that they are resolved prior to exchange of contracts.

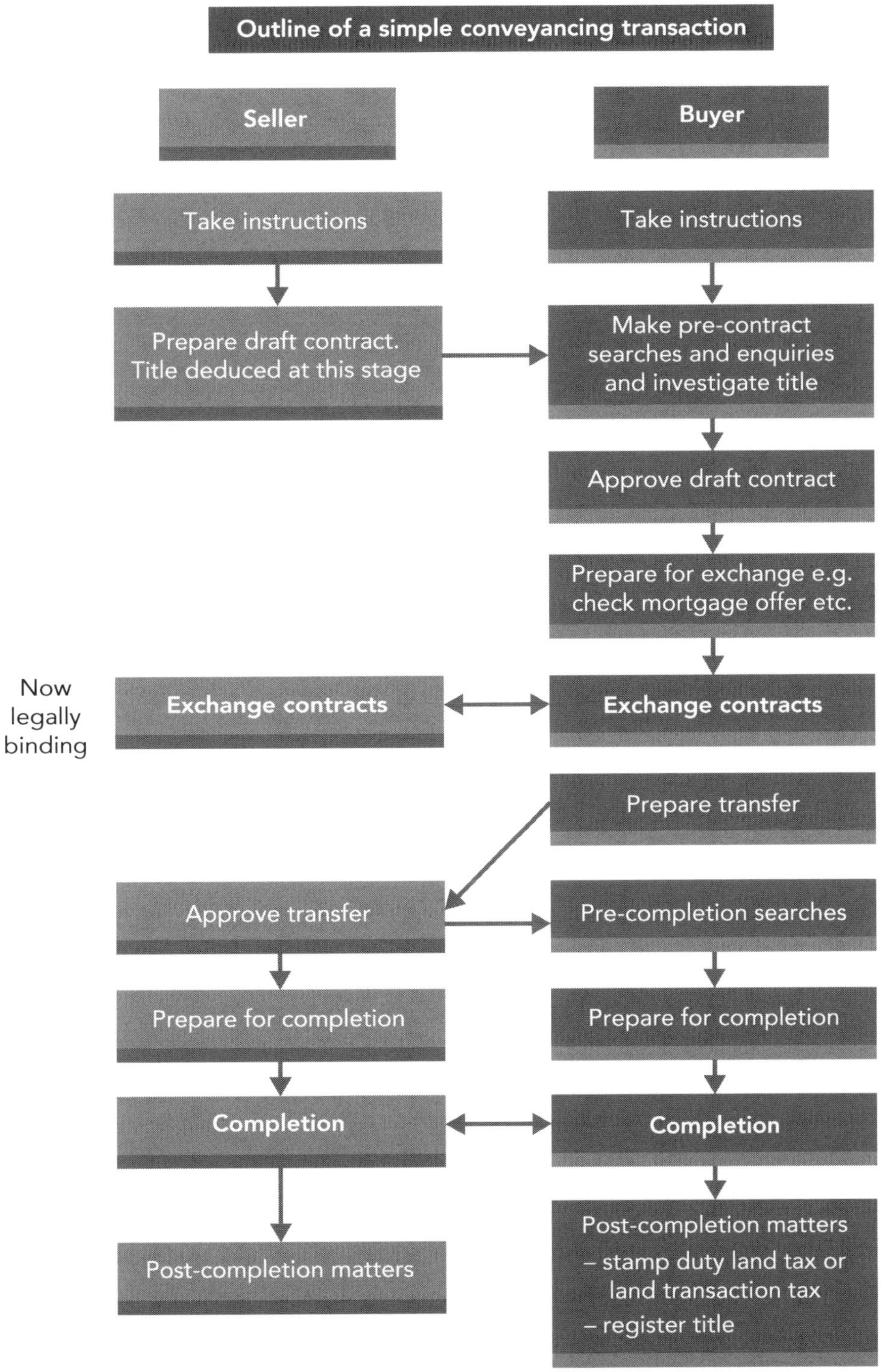

11.3 Acting on a probate sale and purchase

11.3.1 Private client recap

Before we look at some of the issues which are specific to a probate sale, we will recap some key principles and documents arising in a private client context. As we have seen, when acting on a sale or purchase, it is necessary for the conveyancer to be satisfied that the seller has good title to the property being sold. Nowhere is this more important than when personal representatives are selling a property forming part of the estate of someone who has died. The conveyancer must understand the type of grant that has been produced.

We will use the term "personal representative" or the abbreviation "PR" to describe the party entitled to sell the property of a deceased owner. This is the umbrella term for executors and administrators. We will use the term "grant" and "grant of representation" which is the umbrella term for the different types of grant which can be obtained. "**NCPR**" stands for **Non-Contentious Probate Rules**.

11.3.2 Personal representatives

(1) Capacity to be a personal representative

A minor cannot take a grant. If a minor is one of several executors or potential administrators, the appropriate grant is normally made immediately to the adult applicants. If the minor is the only or last surviving PR, then a grant *durante minore aetate* (pronounced "dur-ant-ay min-or-ay ee-tah-tay") is made until the minor attains majority.

Similar rules apply to those suffering from mental disorder such as to render them incapable of managing their own affairs.

s116 Senior Courts Act 1981 (**SCA 1981**) gives the court a discretionary power to appoint someone other than the person who is, *prima facie*, entitled to a grant, if it considers that, by reason of the **special circumstances**, it is necessary or expedient. The application for an order under the section is made without notice to a District Judge or Registrar by an affidavit as to the facts exhibiting any other material documents. The grant may be general, or limited in any way that the court thinks fit. The special circumstances which the court has in the past taken into account in determining to pass over the person entitled include:

- if the person entitled is shown to be unfit to administer the estate (e.g. by reason of bankruptcy, or convicted of murder or manslaughter of the deceased

– ***In the Estate of Crippen* [1911]** – or because they are in prison – ***In the Estate of Hall* [1914]**);

- the fact that beneficiaries are of full age, full capacity and united in their request for an executor to renounce could amount to special circumstances. In ***Khan v Crossland* [2012]** the claimant sought the removal of will writers, appointed as executors of his stepfather's will, and his own appointment as administrator. He said he and his sister were in agreement as to the disposal of the estate and they had lost trust and confidence in the appointed executors. The court found for the claimant; whilst the testator's choice of executors was a relevant factor, it was not a decisive one in this case;
- if the person entitled is missing and their whereabouts are unknown;
- if a grant is required to bring an action under **s1 Law Reform (Miscellaneous Provisions) Act 1934** (where the deceased had a pursuable cause of action at the date of death). The grant will be expressly limited for the purpose of the grantee being a party to that action;
- if someone wishes to bring a claim for financial provision under the **Inheritance (Provision for Family and Dependants) Act 1975** and there is no one entitled or willing to apply for a grant. The Official Solicitor has indicated that, in such circumstances, they will be prepared to consider applying for a grant to themselves so that the proceedings may be brought.

Sometimes, grants are issued to trust corporations, defined by **s128 SCA 1981**. They include the Public Trustee (see https://www.gov.uk/public-trustee-executor-will), banks and trustee companies and some of the larger law firms.

A trust corporation may be appointed executor of a will and so obtain probate. It may also take a grant of administration (with or without will annexed) on behalf of the persons otherwise entitled. In this event, practice requires that any adult executors must renounce probate and the persons entitled to the residue must file their consent. If any are minors, the matter may have to be referred to the District Judge or Registrar. In the case of a grant of administration (with or without will annexed), all adult potential grantees must consent, as must all other persons interested in the residuary estate.

If some of the persons entitled are under age, a grant may be made to a trust corporation limited until one of the minors obtains a grant on attaining full age – provided that all adults renounce their rights to a grant and consent. If all potential grantees are minors, a trust corporation may take the grant on the consent of the persons having parental responsibility for the minors.

Companies, charities, etc. which are not trust corporations cannot take a grant in their corporate capacity, but only through a nominee, who executes all the papers personally. The grant will issue in their name for the use and benefit of the company and until further representation is granted.

Link to practice

If a firm of solicitors has been appointed as an executor, the partners or members of the firm at the date of death should be specified as the executors and a charging clause should appear in the will.

If the executors are partners in the conveyancing firm, it is still very important for the conveyancer to take formal instructions from the executors as if they were arm's-length clients and not to make any assumptions. This is important because the executors may need to delay exchange of contracts on a probate sale for a reason connected with the administration of the estate. Accordingly, always take clear, unequivocal and written instructions from professional executors, even if they work in your firm.

A power conferred by **s50 Administration of Justice Act 1985** enables the High Court to remove an existing PR and appoint a substitute; and where there are two or more existing PRs, it can terminate the appointment of one or more but not all of them.

Link to practice

You can see from the above that it is essential for the conveyancer to check the grant carefully to ensure that:

- If acting on a sale, they are instructed by all personal representatives who are named on the grant.
- If acting on a purchase, all personal representatives named on the grant appear as sellers in the contract.

(2) Several claimants

On an application for a **grant of probate**, all executors appointed by the will or any codicil must be accounted for. Subject to this and to the limit imposed by **s114 SCA 1981**, the grant may issue to any one or more of them.

On an application for a **grant of administration** (with or without will annexed), all persons having a prior right to a grant must be **cleared off**. If there are a number of persons entitled to a grant in the same degree, then (subject, again, to the limits imposed by **s114 SCA 1981**) a grant may be made to any person so entitled without notice to any others entitled in the same degree (**r27 NCPR 1987**).

Unless a Registrar otherwise directs, **r27 NCPR 1987** also provides that the grant shall be made:

- to a living person in preference to the PR of a deceased person who (if living) would have been entitled in the same degree;
- to a person not under a disability in preference to a minor entitled in the same degree.

In the event of a dispute between persons entitled in the same degree as to who shall take the grant, the matter will be resolved by a summons before a District Judge at the Principal Registry or the Registrar of a District Probate Registry.

(3) Number of PRs required

These rules are important, particularly that requiring a minimum of two administrators or a trust corporation.

The maximum

s114 SCA 1981 provides that a grant of probate or letters of administration (with or without will annexed) **cannot issue to more than four persons** in respect of the same part of the deceased's estate.

s114 does not prevent a testator from appointing any number of executors, but only a maximum of four may prove the will. Those who have not predeceased the testator or renounced and who do not wish to act will have power reserved to them. However, **s114** does not prevent a grant of probate to up to four executors in respect of part of the deceased's estate and four different executors in respect of the remainder of the estate. So, for example, separate grants could issue to four literary executors and four other executors to deal with the rest of the deceased's estate.

A sole executor always has full authority to act, even if there is a minority or life interest, and can give a valid receipt for capital money.

The minimum

In the case of **letters of administration (with or without will annexed)**, **s114** lays down a minimum as well as a maximum number of grantees.

If, under a will or intestacy, any beneficiary is a minor, or a life interest arises, the grant of administration (in either form) must normally be made to not fewer than two individuals, or a trust corporation (acting alone or jointly with an individual).

There is a discretion – exercised by a District Judge or Registrar on a without notice application to the Principal or any District Registry – to appoint an individual as sole administrator if *it appears to the court to be expedient in all the circumstances* to do so. An example might be if there is just a relatively small legacy to a minor and the sole applicant for the grant is a parent of the minor. The application is supported by an affidavit of the applicant setting out the reasons for the application.

There may be occasions when two administrators are needed, but there is only one adult beneficiary. For example, if a person dies intestate, a widower, leaving a daughter aged 20 and a son aged 10, the Registrar will allow the daughter to nominate a suitable person, such as a lawyer or another family member, to act as co-administrator. Note the child does not have power reserved, since this is not a grant of probate.

If, because of a minority or life interest, administration was granted to two individuals and one later dies, there is no requirement for the deceased to be replaced; in other words, the survivor has full authority to act alone.

In any situation where there is only one executor or administrator (not being a trust corporation) acting during the minority of a beneficiary or during the subsistence of a life interest, the court has power to appoint one or more **additional** PRs to act, while the minority or life interest subsists and until the estate is fully administered. An application for such appointment is made without notice to the Principal or any District Registry by any person interested (or their guardian or receiver). The application should be supported by an affidavit as to the facts, the consent of the proposed administrator, the original grant and any further evidence as the Registrar may direct (**r26 NCPR 1987**). The original grant is noted with the appointment.

If no minority or life interest arises under the will or intestacy, a grant may issue to a sole administrator.

(4) Renunciation by personal representatives and power reserved

A person entitled to a grant may renounce their right (unless they have lost the right to do so) in writing (not necessarily a deed).

An **executor** may renounce probate on the death of the testator but not before. The executor may lodge their renunciation at any registry provided that it is accompanied by the original will. This is usually done when an executor decides that they do not wish to act in the estate but is unaware who will be applying for a grant. The renunciation and will are retained by the registry pending an application for a grant.

An executor accepts office, and so loses their right to renounce, if they intermeddle in the estate (acts of charity, humanity or necessity, such as paying for a funeral, do not count) or if a grant is made in their favour.

Note that as an alternative to renunciation, one of several executors could instead decide to reserve power if they do not wish to be actively involved in the administration, at least not at the present time.

Link to practice

You might see on a grant the name of a party next to which is written "power reserved". This means that they have not taken up the appointment at the outset of the administration and that the other executor(s) have taken the grant. As a result, on a probate sale, the seller must be the executor(s) named in the grant and not those to whom power has been reserved.

The significance of power reserved is that this party reserves the right to step in and take up the appointment later on if they so wish.

An **administrator** (with or without will annexed) accepts office by taking a grant. Intermeddling will not deprive them of the right to renounce (but they could be personally liable for their actions taken before renunciation).

Usually, the written renunciation is filed when another person makes application for the grant. Although operative from the date made, it does not technically become final until a grant is sealed by the registry. In practice, however, this occurs when the application is made.

r37(2A) NCPR 1987 provides for the renunciation by members of a partnership to be effected by any two of the partners with the authority of the others. The form of renunciation must state that the executing partners renounce on their own behalf and that of the other partners and with their authority.

Retraction of a renunciation is permitted in special circumstances on a without notice application, supported by an affidavit as to the facts, to the Principal Registry or the District Registry in which the renunciation was filed. Only in exceptional circumstances will leave be given to an executor to retract their renunciation of probate once a grant (of administration with will annexed) has been made to someone entitled in a lower degree.

Link to practice

It is often the case that personal representatives "get ahead of the game" and put a property within an estate on the market before the grant is obtained and even instruct conveyancers. It is important that the conveyancer ensures that they are taking instructions from the correct parties. On a surprising number of occasions it turns out that the person instructing the conveyancing firm does not, in fact, have authority to act when the grant is actually obtained.

Unless the conveyancer also carries out private client work, the conveyancer should not be dealing with any aspects of applying for the grant. This will either be done by the conveyancing firm's private client department, a different firm or the client.

The conveyancer should not get involved in giving any advice to the client in relation to obtaining the grant if the firm is not instructed to deal with this.

11.3.3 Grants of representation

Types of grant

There are three main types of grants of representation:

- a grant of probate;
- a grant of letters of administration with the will annexed;
- a grant of letters of administration.

These are summarised as follows:

Grant	A court order issued by the Probate Registry authorising the distribution of the estate to the beneficiaries.
Grant of letters of administration	A court document authorising distribution of the assets of the estate obtained if there is no valid will and the person died intestate.
Grant of letters of administration with will annexed	A court document authorising distribution of the assets of the estate obtained if there is a valid will, but there is no surviving executor, or there is an executor but they are not taking the grant.
Grant of probate	A court document authorising distribution of the assets of the estate obtained when there is a valid will and at least one surviving executor.

In addition, there are limited and special grants. We will look at the key points in relation to each of these but only to the extent that they might be relevant for a conveyancing transaction.

(1) Grant of probate

This grant issues (is made) only to an executor who is appointed by the will or a codicil. Sometimes, the appointment is by description: if the holder of an office is appointed, the person entitled to act is the holder of that office at the date of death (***In the Estate of Jones* [1927]**). If a law firm (has been appointed, *prima facie*, it is the members of the firm at the date of the will (or codicil republishing the will containing the appointment) who are entitled to act.

An appointment of an executor "according to the tenor of the will" may be implied if the will shows an intention that a particular person should perform the functions of an executor though not expressly so described. So, a direction to "pay the testator's debts" has been held to be sufficient, as has the appointment of a trustee "to get in all my property" (though not a bare appointment as trustee.

Link to practice

Most appointments are unlimited, but it is possible for an appointment to be limited as to time (e.g. "until my son X attains his majority") or as to property (e.g. an appointment as "executor of my business"). Any grant issued to such executors will be similarly limited.

Appointments can be made subject to a condition precedent or subsequent and may be substitutional (e.g. "I appoint X but if he is unable or unwilling to act, then I appoint Y"). Y may then prove the will if for example X is dead or has renounced.

This is important for the conveyancer because whether acting on the sale or purchase, they must inspect the grant carefully to ensure that the personal representative has authority to sell the property that is the subject of the conveyancing transaction. A limited grant would be more unusual in practice which is why it represents a greater risk.

Note that there are two forms of grant of probate that you are likely to see in practice. The first is:

COPIES OF THIS GRANT ARE NOT VALID UNLESS
THEY BEAR THE IMPRESSED SEAL OF THE COURT

In the High Court of Justice

The District Probate Registry at WINCHESTER

BE IT KNOWN that **JAMES MATTHEW APPLEBY** of **"Black Gate", 12 Hoole Road, Westbridge, Hampshire, WA8 1BJ**

died on the **22nd** day of **August 2018**

domiciled in **England & Wales**

AND BE IT FURTHER KNOWN that at the date hereunder written the last Will and Testament (a copy whereof is hereunto annexed) of the said deceased was proved and registered in the said Registry of the High Court of Justice and Administration of all the estate which by law devolves to and vests in the personal representative of the said deceased was granted by the aforesaid Court to the Executor

PETER ANDREW STEVENS of **Abbey Chambers, Westbridge, Hampshire WA1 3ES**

It is hereby certified that it appears from information supplied on the application for this grant that the gross value of the said estate in the United Kingdom amounts to **£374,950** *and that the net value of such estate amounts to* **£371, 969**

Dated the **17th** day of **November 2018**

A. Bridge *District Registrar*

Probate *Extracted by* **Montague & Co (A/245) Solicitors Westbridge, Hampshire WA1 3ES**

From 4 March 2019, the above style of grant certificate was replaced with a new style certificate designed to incorporate counter fraud measures including:

- a hologram;
- a digital seal instead of an embossed seal;
- a digital signature instead of a wet signature and a validation telephone number for people processing the document.

Activity

Follow the link below and look carefully at the new style grant to ensure that you recognise it if presented to you in the conveyancing transaction.

https://www.clc-uk.org/wp-content/uploads/2019/03/hmcts-grant-of-probate-changes.pdf

Note that the old-style grant above is still valid but you should check the date on the grant.

Link to practice

You will see that the new style Grant of Probate has a telephone number on it. You should call the number to check that it is valid if the client or a firm other than yours has obtained the grant and you are instructed on the sale and in every case where you receive this style of grant on a purchase. You should do this early in the transaction to be satisfied that the grant is legitimate.

(2) Grant of letters of administration with will annexed

A grant of letters of administration with the will annexed (*cum testamento annexo*) will be made if a will needs to be proved, but for some valid reason a grant of probate cannot be made to an executor. This may occur if:

- the will appoints no executor; or
- the executors appointed are dead or have renounced; or
- where the executors appointed have been cited* but have not applied for a grant.

*Citation is a procedure by which beneficiaries can require an executor to accept or refuse to a grant.

Other situations in which this grant is appropriate include cases where the executors appointed are minors or are otherwise incapable of taking a grant, for example, if the executors have been passed over by order of the court. If anyone other than an executor obtains a grant, either because there is no valid will at all or there is a will but the executor is not taking the grant, the person appointed as a PR is called an **administrator**.

The persons entitled to the grant are listed in **r20 NCPR 1987**. Essentially, the order of entitlement depends on entitlement to the property under the terms of the will. For this purpose, the principal interest is in the residue (i.e. the estate that is not the subject of specific, general or demonstrative gifts), irrespective of its monetary value in relation to the other gifts under the will.

The full order of entitlement to the grant under **r20** is:

- an executor;
- any trustees of residue (most professionally drafted wills appoint the executors as trustees of the residuary estate, but different people might be appointed);
- any other residuary legatee or devisee (including one for life) or, if residue is wholly or partly undisposed of (i.e. partial intestacy), any person entitled to share in the undisposed of residue. Normally, a person with a vested interest is preferred to one with a contingent interest only;
- the PR (i.e. where a beneficiary dies **after** the deceased) of any residuary legatee or devisee (but not of a residuary life tenant or trustee) or of a person entitled under partial intestacy;
- any other legatee or devisee (including one for life or one holding as trustee) or a creditor. Again, normally, a person with a vested interest is preferred to one with a contingent interest only;
- the PR of any other legatee or devisee (but not a life tenant or trustee) or of a creditor.

Any prior interest in a higher category must be accounted for (**cleared off**) before a claimant in a lower category can establish title to the grant.

(3) Letters of administration

A grant of letters of administration is made if there is no will capable of being proved. In most cases this will be because an intestacy has arisen although there are also special cases where this is the appropriate grant even though there is a will.

When a person dies without a will at all, they are described as dying **intestate**. The PRs, who must obtain a **grant of letters of administration** as their authority to be able to act, are known as **administrators** and their entitlement to apply for a grant is set out in **r22 NCPR 1987**.

On the death of an intestate all the property of the deceased (including land and other property) is made subject to a statutory trust under **s33 Administration of Estates Act 1925** (**AEA 1925**) (as amended). If the estate contains land, the trust will be called a trust of land. Under the statutory trust all funeral and administration expenses, debts, etc. are paid before the balance is distributed under the statutory order of entitlement.

Clearly, it is necessary to identify someone who can deal with the administration of the estate. In the event of an intestacy, the PRs are referred to as "administrators". They are appointed by the court and derive their authority to deal with the estate from the grant of letters of administration issued by the Probate Registry.

The order of entitlement to the grant is governed by **r22 NCPR 1987**. This follows the order of entitlement to share in the estate on intestacy. Note that the PRs of a beneficiary who has died **after** the deceased have the same right to a grant as the beneficiary they replace, although any other living members of the category into which the beneficiary falls are preferred. PRs of a spouse/civil partner will not be preferred over categories (2) to (8) below unless the spouse/civil partner was entitled to the whole estate.

The order of priority to the grant under **r22** is:

(1) surviving spouse/civil partner;

(2) children and the issue of any child who has predeceased the intestate;

(3) parents;

(4) brothers and sisters of the whole blood and the issue of any who have predeceased;

(5) brothers and sisters of the half blood and the issue of any who have predeceased;

(6) grandparents;

(7) uncles and aunts of the whole blood and the issue of any who have predeceased;

(8) uncles and aunts of the half blood and the issue of any who have predeceased;

(9) the Treasury Solicitor on behalf of the Crown;

(10) any creditor of the deceased, or any person who (though not having any immediate beneficial interest in the estate) might have an interest in the event of an increase in its value. (The latter would include a child, if the value of the known estate is currently less than the value of the statutory legacy but the existence of further property would take it above that amount so that part of it is then taken by the child as issue of the intestate.)

So, apart from a creditor, the applicant must be someone who either has a current beneficial interest in the estate or, in category (10), would have if the estate were larger. Again, the maximum number of applicants is four and if there are minor beneficiaries (under 18 at the date of the intestate's death) there must normally be at least two administrators.

Again, any prior claimants must be satisfactorily accounted for (cleared off) before a claimant in a later category can establish title to the grant.

Example

A person entitled under the rules does not have to apply, but anyone applying from a lower category has to explain why those higher up the list are not applying. Those higher in the list are "cleared off".

For example, if a child of the deceased is applying, and the deceased had been married, the child will have to clear off the spouse by stating in their statement of truth that the couple had divorced, or that the spouse died before the deceased, or has renounced.

Limited as to purpose

(1) ***Ad colligenda bona* (r52 NCPR 1987)**

This is always a grant of administration (even if there is a will), issued to enable the collection and preservation of the estate assets prior to a general grant being made. Any assets at risk (e.g. because of a perishable nature) may be preserved by this means if, for some reason, the person entitled to a full grant is not able to proceed quickly to obtain that grant. It confers no authority to distribute the estate.

(2) **Pending determination of a probate claim (s117 Senior Courts Act 1981 (SCA 1981))**

Again, this is a grant of administration, issued to protect the estate where a probate claim has commenced because there is a dispute as to the validity of a will or the title to a grant, or if there are proceedings to revoke a grant. The grant is effective until the proceedings are concluded and is usually made to an independent person – though any person who is a party to the proceedings or interested in the estate may apply for the grant to be made.

Limited as to property

(1) **Limited probate**

Where the testator has appointed, for example, a literary executor or an executor to carry on their business, such executor may only take a grant of probate limited to that property.

(2) **s113 grants**

Under **s113 SCA 1981**, the court has a wide power to grant probate or letters of administration to any part of the deceased's estate, limited in any way the court thinks fit (**r51 NCPR 1987**).

Grants limited as to time

(1) **During a minority (*durante minore aetate*)**

A minor cannot take a grant. If the minor is one of several executors or potential administrators, this does not normally present any problem. If, however, the only executors or potential administrators having the highest priority are minors, a grant of letters of administration (with will annexed if there is a will) will be made to some other person until the minor attains their majority. Normally, the grant then automatically ceases to have effect. The grant is for the use and benefit of the minor and, under **r32 NCPR 1987**, is usually made to the parents or guardians of the minor in preference to others interested in the estate. However, if the minor is sole executor and has no interest in the residuary estate, the grant will issue to the persons entitled to the residue.

(2) **During mental incapacity (r35 NCPR 1987)**

A similar situation arises where the only executors or potential administrators are suffering from mental incapacity. In such a case, a grant for the use and benefit of that person will be made for the duration of the incapacity.

(3) **Grants to an attorney (r31 NCPR 1987)**

If someone entitled as executor or administrator so wishes, administration may be granted to their lawfully constituted attorney for the use and benefit of the person entitled. The grant will be limited until further representation is granted, or as further limited as the District Judge or Registrar considers appropriate.

For example, if the appointed executor lives overseas, they could appoint their lawyer as their attorney. In such case, the grant will not be one of probate but letters of administration with the will annexed.

If the person entitled to seek a grant now lacks mental capacity but has previously granted an enduring or lasting power of attorney, then the appointed attorney can apply for the grant provided that the power of attorney has been registered with the Office of the Public Guardian.

Other special grants

(1) ***De bonis non administratis***

This is a grant of letters of administration (with will annexed in appropriate cases) to enable the administration of an estate to be completed after the death or incapacity of the **sole or last surviving proving PR**, or following the revocation of a previous grant. It is therefore a **second grant** to the same estate.

Such a grant is not required just because one of several PRs has died, because the remaining executors or administrators have full power to complete the administration of the estate. If one of several PRs has become incapable, the original grant is revoked and a new grant issued to the remaining PRs. This is not a *de bonis non* grant.

Nor is a *de bonis non* grant necessary where the chain of representation exists.

The order of entitlement to the *de bonis non* grant is governed by either **r20 NCPR 1987** if the original grant was of probate or administration with will annexed, or **r22 NCPR 1987** if the deceased died intestate. It will, therefore, be granted to someone who would have been entitled to the first grant, if still able and willing to apply.

(2) Double probate

An executor who has not renounced, or been cited to take or renounce probate will have **power reserved** to them if they do not wish to join in taking the grant immediately. Such an executor is entitled at any time afterwards to apply for a grant of double probate. This is a general grant conferring full powers on the executor concerned. The only difference between this and the original grant is that the value of the estate shown on it is the value of the unadministered estate at the date of the second grant.

The application for a grant of double probate may be made at any registry and must normally be accompanied by an office copy of the original grant.

(3) Cessate grant

This is another general grant, most commonly issued where a previous grant limited as to time has ceased to be effective (e.g. on a minor attaining majority, or the recovery of capacity to act). The minor or recovered person may then apply for a cessate grant of probate or letters of administration (with will annexed, if appropriate) as the circumstances dictate.

Link to practice

In the conveyancing context, you are unlikely to come across the special types of grant listed above very often. It is therefore important for you to have an awareness as to these different types of grant and their purpose.

From a risk management point of view, it is important to check with a colleague or a member of the private client department if you are presented with a grant which is unfamiliar.

11.3.4 Chain of representation

Establishing who is entitled to sell a property contained within an estate is essential. This can be a complex task if a personal representative was partway through administering an estate and has died. This is where the conveyancer may need to consider the chain of representation. Note that there is a clear distinction between the position of the executor and the position of the administrator.

If a **sole or last surviving executor who has proved** the testator's will (i.e. obtained a grant of probate) dies testate before they have completed the administration of the estate, the estate remaining unadministered is dealt with by the executor's executor. This chain of representation is created as soon as the executor's executor takes probate of the will of the original executor. No further grant is necessary to deal with the unadministered estate, both grants being produced together to complete the administration (see **s7 AEA 1925**).

A chain of representation may continue through several sole or last surviving proving executors, and will not be broken by a temporary/limited grant. The chain of representation is broken if the sole or last surviving proving executor:

- dies intestate;
- fails to appoint an executor in their will; or
- their executor fails to prove their will.

The chain will also be broken if the original grant was taken by one or more of several executors with power reserved to other executors and one or more of those who had power reserved take(s) a grant of double probate.

To sum up: the chain of representation runs through grants of probate only. So, if a **sole or last remaining proving executor** (not administrator) dies having appointed an **executor** who duly proves their will, the latter executor automatically becomes the executor of the original testator – so, they end up completing the administration of the original estate as well as that of the executor who has just died.

If the **chain does not apply**, or is broken, the unadministered estate must be dealt with by a special grant known as a grant *de bonis non administratis*.

Example

This is best explained by way of example:

(1) Tom appoints Raj and Rafael to be the executors of his estate and subsequently dies.

(2) During the administration of Tom's estate, Raj dies.

(3) Rafael continues as the sole executor of Tom's estate.

(4) Rafael has appointed Bill as **his** executor.

(5) Rafael dies before completing the administration of Tom's estate.

(6) Bill is now the executor of Rafael's estate **and** Tom's. Note that Bill does **not** need to obtain a new grant for Tom's estate.

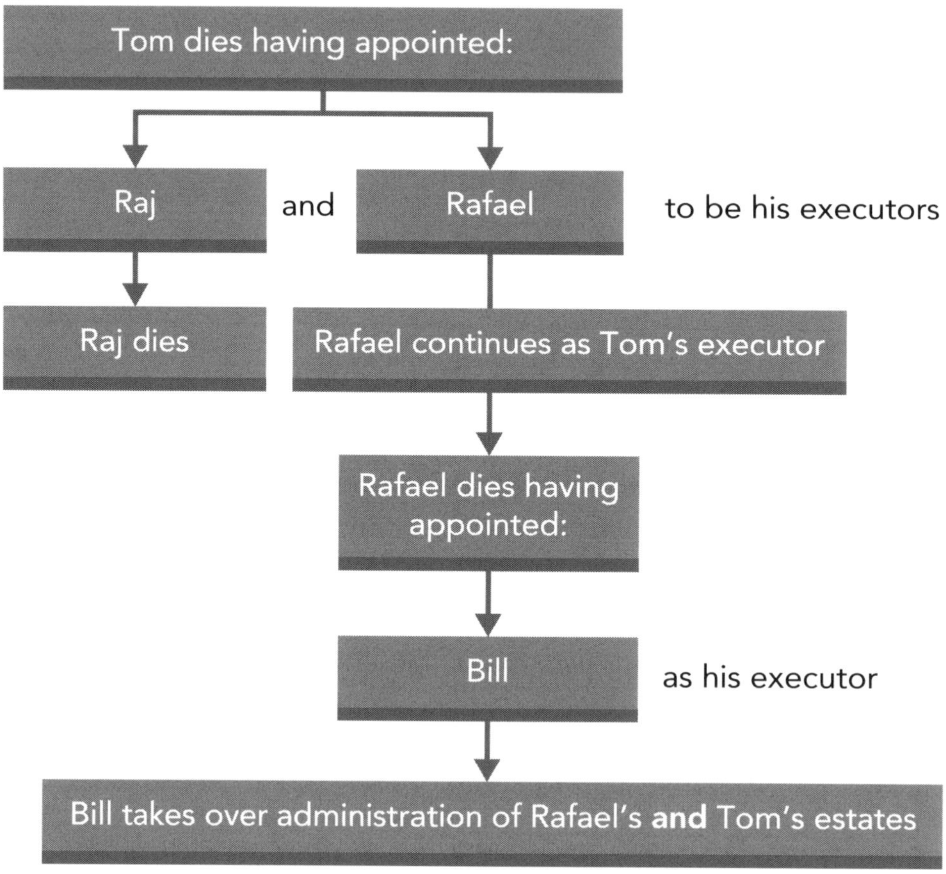

An executor in a chain automatically becomes executor of all preceding testators. Here, Bill must accept the executorship of both Tom's **and** Rafael's estates or neither. He cannot choose one or the other. Bill is in the same position as an original executor.

Remember that there can be no chain of representation of administrators because their authority to act (see below) derives from the grant.

11.3.5 Authority to act

Executors and administrators receive their authority to deal with a deceased person's estate at different times.

An executor's authority is derived from the will itself. This means that when a testator dies, their executor is immediately entitled to deal with the deceased's assets and, in theory, needs no further documentation to appoint them.

Link to practice

Why, then, does the executor need to obtain a grant of probate? The purpose of the grant is to serve as sufficient evidence to relevant parties, such as the deceased's bank, that the deceased has died, that the will under which the executor is appointed was the last will (and was validly executed), and that the person claiming to be the executor **is** the executor. Once the bank has seen the grant, it can pay out the money, confident that it has paid the right person.

However, it could be that all the deceased's assets were in such a form that no grant is needed – they might, for example, have owned only cash (i.e. actual notes and coins), some paintings and a few pieces of domestic furniture. In that case, an executor would be able to deal with the estate without obtaining a grant of probate. In other words, the grant of probate is **proof** of an executor's authority, not the source of it.

You can see that this is very significant for a conveyancing transaction. In practice, a conveyancer instructed on a sale should not draft and send a contract to the buyer's conveyancer until such time as the grant of probate is obtained as the conveyancer is required to ensure that the seller referred to in the contract has capacity to sell.

Conversely, a conveyancer acting for a buyer from a personal representative will want to see the grant of probate to prove that the seller has capacity.

In neither case should the conveyancers exchange contracts until the grant of probate has been obtained.

Since an administrator obtains authority from the grant of letters of administration, they must await the issue of the grant before commencing the administration of the estate.

Activity

Follow the link below to HMLR's "Practice guide 6: devolution of title on the death or a registered proprietor":

https://www.gov.uk/government/publications/devolution-on-the-death-of-a-registered-proprietor/practice-guide-6-devolution-on-the-death-of-a-registered-proprietor

Make notes and ensure that you understand and can apply all of the issues covered.

11.3.6 Issues arising on a probate sale

The contract

We have seen above the importance of ensuring that the seller who is a personal representative is entitled to sell the property in question. The basic contract drafting on a probate sale is the same and, of course, any contract must reflect the particular circumstances of the transaction in hand. However, note the following:

Seller: the holder of the legal estate generally remains the deceased and the personal representatives will generally not either submit an application for first registration if the title is unregistered or apply to have their own names included on the proprietorship register. Generally, this will only be done if the personal representatives intend to hold a property in the estate for some time, for example to rent it out. All proving personal representatives must appear in the contract as sellers. Therefore, the sellers will generally be expressed as follows:

"[insert name and address of personal representatives as appearing on the grant] as personal representatives of [insert name of deceased], deceased"

Note that if there is more than one personal representative, just one of them could sign the contract of sale. However, best practice demands that the conveyancer obtains the signatures of personal representatives or at the very least, their written authority for one of their number to sign the contract on their behalf.

Title guarantee: sale by personal representatives is the classic situation where a limited title guarantee will be given.

Link to practice

Remember that where a full title guarantee is given the seller warrants that:

- they have the right to dispose of the property;
- they will at their own cost do all they reasonably can to give the transferee the purported title;

- they dispose of the whole interest where the interest is registered;
- they dispose of the whole lease where the interest is leasehold;
- they are disposing of it free from all charges and encumbrances (whether monetary or not) and from all other rights exercisable by third parties, not being rights which the transfer does not and could not reasonably be expected to know about.

Where **limited title guarantee** is given, all of the above warranties apply except for the last one which is replaced (that is, limited) with the following:

- that they have not charged or encumbered the property by a charge or encumbrance which still exists, that they have not granted any third-party rights which will still subsist and they are not aware of anyone that has done so since the last disposition for value.

Many conveyancers drafting a contract for the sale of a property falling within an estate will limit the above warranty further by including a provision in the contract along the following lines:

The transfer shall contain the following:

The covenants implied under the LPMPA 1994 are modified so that:

(a) The words "at his own cost" in section 2(1)(b) of the LPMPA 1994 are deleted and substituted by the words "at the cost of the person requiring compliance with this covenant"; and

(b) The covenant implied in this transfer by Section 3(3) of the Law of Property (Miscellaneous Provisions) Act 1994 applies (so far as it relates to the actions or omissions of the Transferor) only to the period since the death of [insert deceased's name]

Physical state: standard condition 3.2 provides that the buyer accepts the property in the physical state it is in at the date of the contract (unless the seller is building or converting it). In addition to dealing with insurance (see below) the personal representatives should take all reasonable steps to ensure that they can comply with this standard condition. They should consider turning off water if the property is going to be vacant during the cold months and ensure that the property is regularly visited/inspected.

Insurance: standard condition 5.1 provides that risk in the property passes to the buyer on exchange and it is unlikely that personal representatives on a probate sale would want to alter or exclude this provision. However, as the personal representatives owe a duty to the estate, they should keep the property insured until completion. Note that any insurer must be notified that the property will be unoccupied if the owner has died. This will alter the terms of the insurance and it might be necessary for the personal representatives to turn to a specialist insurer which often involves payment of a higher insurance premium.

11.3.7 Problems if the title is unregistered

Conveyancers are perhaps more likely to come across an unregistered title when dealing with a probate sale because an elderly party who has died may have acquired their property many years ago when the title was unregistered. This chapter will mention a couple of issues which could cause a problem on a probate sale.

It is likely that even though the transaction is a probate sale, the Protocol will be used. Accordingly, the seller's conveyancer should provide an epitome of title, including full land charges searches against all relevant legal owners and an index map search. Unregistered title is often included in very poor plans. The conveyancer acting for the personal representatives should decline to attach a more up-to-date plan to the contract; the buyer's conveyancer will often download a plan from Map Search and would suggest that it is appended to the contract. This suggestion should be resisted. The personal representatives should only contract to transfer the title comprised in the unregistered title deeds. The addition of a more up-to-date plan of the property could inadvertently impose an obligation on the personal representatives to transfer additional land to which they did not have title.

If it transpires that the deceased occupied more land than is contained in their title, the personal representatives may feel able to offer a statement of truth as to if they have sufficient personal knowledge to comment. However professional executors (for example, partners in law firms) are unlikely to have this information. If additional land falling outside the title is going to be included in the sale, the contract and transfer should separately identify this piece of land, make it clear that no title is being given and that no title guarantee is being given for that particular area of land.

Link to practice

If the buyer's conveyancer requests defective title indemnity insurance, the conveyancer acting for the will needs to advise the personal representatives as to whether such a request is appropriate and they will need to instruct the conveyancer as to whether they are prepared to meet the cost of the insurance out of the estate. In practice, if the price of the indemnity insurance premium is modest and the policy is acceptable to the buyer's conveyancer, it is probably good advice for the personal representatives to agree to meet the cost from the estate to ensure that the sale transaction proceeds.

If the unregistered title appears to have a defect or the extent of the property is unclear from the title documents, the seller's conveyancer should consider advising their personal representative clients as to whether a voluntary application for first registration would be prudent. This will involve additional HMLR (and possibly legal) fees. One of the main reasons for not taking this course of action would be timescale – if the sale transaction is already underway, there may be insufficient time to conclude the first registration application.

11.3.8 Replying to pre-contract enquiries

In a standard residential conveyancing transaction, the buyer on a probate sale will generally expect the personal representatives to complete a Property Information Form and for this to be included as part of the contract package in the usual way. A seller is not obliged to complete the Property Information Form but a failure to include this form with the contract pack might be a red flag for a buyer and their conveyancer as they may think that there is something to hide. Accordingly, it would be standard practice to include the Property Information Form as a matter of course but if the personal representative has little or no personal knowledge of the property, this should be made clear to the buyer's conveyancer. This limitation should be similarly made clear if the personal representative provide replies to any pre-contract enquiries as the transaction progresses.

The conveyancer acting for the personal representatives may be able to assist with any enquiries which relate specifically to the title.

The personal representatives should be advised of the potential liability of giving inaccurate replies to the Property Information Form and/or enquiries. Following ***William Sindall plc v Cambridgeshire County Council* [1993]**, the use of the words "not so far as the seller is aware" will probably not be sufficient to mitigate liability for an inaccurate reply. If the personal representatives have made no enquiry or investigation to answer any questions or enquiries, this should be made clear in their responses.

As we have seen, a seller's duty of disclosure in terms of what should be included in the contract is limited but they should include latent defects which are those defects which cannot be discovered from an inspection of the property. The seller's duty extends to disclosing matters about which they know, or about which they have the means to know, if acting reasonably and diligently. Examples of latent defects include: a restrictive covenant, a tenancy, a right of drainage or right-of-way which would not be apparent from an inspection of the property. Even if the seller is a personal representative, these defects should be included in the contract to ensure compliance with the duty of disclosure.

The seller is not under a duty to disclose patent defects that is, those which are discoverable from a physical inspection of the property.

Note that a personal representative has a more general duty under **s25 AEA 1925** to administer and distribute the deceased's estate. This means that they must act properly in relation to a probate sale.

11.3.9 Access to the property between exchange of contracts and completion

Access to carry out work

Personal representatives frequently receive a request from the buyers for access to the property between exchange of contracts and completion. This is because a probate property is generally empty and often needs a significant amount of work to bring up to today's standards.

If such a request is received, the seller's conveyancer must explain the risks to their personal representative clients and must obtain the written instructions from personal representatives.

If the buyer simply wants access to measure up for work, refurbishments, furnishings, etc. this probably represents fairly little risk to the seller. However, if the buyer wants access to start work, this will often involve removing existing fixtures such as boilers and central heating and could cause significant damage to the property. The risk to the seller is that the buyer does not complete and although the seller would be entitled to retain the buyer's deposit in the event that a notice to complete was not complied with, the question would remain whether in this case the deposit would be sufficient to cover the loss caused by the damage to the property.

Personal representatives should always remember that they owe personal duties to the estate and the beneficiaries and therefore should not agree lightly to access to the property between exchange of contracts and completion. Each case will turn on its own facts but a risk averse view would be that the buyer should not be allowed access to the property.

If the buyer is going to be permitted access to the property for the purpose of carrying out work, best practice demands that a condition is included in the contract to deal with the situation or at the very least that the buyer signs a key undertaking. Most firms will have their own precedent for this but in general terms, a key undertaking is a document which the buyer who is obtaining access to the property signs prior to having access and includes information such as:

- the fact that they take responsibility from exchange for any damage to the property;
- they insure the property from exchange;
- the work that they are permitted to carry out is specified;

- arrangements regarding return of the key – it may be that the sellers require the key to be returned to the estate agent at the end of every day or that it is returned on demand;
- the buyer is not permitted to have any more keys cut nor take-up possession of the property, move in nor move any belongings into the property.

Living in the property between exchange of contracts and completion

A clear distinction should be drawn between a request for access to the property between exchange and completion for measuring up or carrying out work, as opposed to the buyer taking up physical occupation of the property. If this is the request, again the conveyancer should explain the detail and the risks to their personal representative client very carefully. The risk is that the buyer fails to complete and refuses to vacate and/or causes damage to the property as well. A risk averse approach would be to decline such a request.

However, if the buyer is to be permitted to occupy the property between exchange of contracts and completion, standard condition 5.2 makes provision for this. It sets out that the buyer is a licensee and not a tenant and standard condition 5.2.2 sets out the terms of the licence in that the buyer:

- cannot transfer the licence;
- may permit members of their household to occupy the property;
- is to pay or indemnify the seller against all outgoings and other expenses in respect of the property;
- is to pay the seller a fee calculated at the contract rate on a sum equal to the purchase price (less any deposit paid) for the period of the licence;
- is entitled to any rents and profits from any part of the property which they do not occupy;
- is to keep the property in as good a state of repair as it was when they went into occupation (except for fair wear and tear) and is not to alter it;
- if the property is leasehold, is not to do anything which puts the seller in breach of their obligations in the lease; and
- is to quit the property when the licence ends.

Standard condition 5.2.3 makes it clear that the buyer is not in occupation for the purposes of this condition if they merely exercise rights of access given solely to do work agreed by the seller.

Standard condition 5.2.4 provides that the buyer's licence ends on the earliest of: completion date, rescission of the contract or when five working days' notice given by one party to the other takes effect.

Standard condition 5.2.5 provides that if the buyer is in occupation of the property after the licence has come to an end and the contract is subsequently completed, they are to pay the seller compensation for their continued occupation calculated at the same rate as the fee mentioned above. Occupation under a licence does not affect the buyer's right to raise requisitions on title.

Occupation between exchange of contracts and completion under the licence contemplated by standard condition 5.2 will not amount to "exclusive possession" and the creation of a lease under ***Street v Mountford* [1985]**.

Whilst it is less likely with a probate sale, remember that if the property is still in mortgage on exchange of contracts, then any access whether for works or occupation, should be refused unless the lender's consent can be obtained.

11.3.10 The transfer

The transfer must reflect the terms of the contract so any modification of the limited title guarantee warranty must be carried over into the transfer (see above). All personal representatives must appear as transferors and all must sign the transfer (contrast this with the contract – see above).

Remember also that if any additional land beyond that contained in the title (whether registered or unregistered) is to be included in the sale, the transfer must reflect the fact that no title guarantee is given in relation to any land to which the personal representatives cannot be confident that falls within the title (this would appear in panel 9 of the TR1).

Remember that if the deceased owner gave an indemnity covenant when they purchased, an indemnity covenant should be given by the buyer in the transfer to protect the personal representatives.

Activity

Follow the link below to the HMLR blog. There is some very useful information as to the steps to take when a property owner dies – make notes and ensure that you could advise a client on the key points contained in the blog:

https://hmlandregistry.blog.gov.uk/2018/02/13/property-owner-dies/

11.4 Selling a property subject to a tenancy

The purchase of a property which is the subject of a short-term residential tenancy at the time of completion has proved a popular investment for small and large investors alike; this is often referred to as a "buy to let" transaction. There are a number of buy to let mortgage products on the market the distinguishing feature of which is usually that the purchaser does not live in the property and that the property is let to a tenant under the terms of an assured shorthold tenancy agreement.

Many of the issues that we have considered in this chapter will be relevant to a buy to let transaction, in addition to the basic conveyancing procedure for a residential property.

Some of the key differences between the purchase of a property with vacant possession, and the purchase of a property subject to a short-term residential tenancy are outlined below.

Conveyancers must keep up to date with the progress of the **Renters' Rights Bill** (see **Chapter 13**). If enacted, this will have a significant impact on private residential lettings and thus on buy to let transactions. These changes will represent a risk to conveyancing firms acting on these transactions. Th assured shorthold will no longer be the default tenancy type for short-term residential lettings and the regime to regain possession of the property will change.

11.4.1 EPC and contract

A seller must still provide an Energy Performance Certificate if a property is being sold with an existing tenant in situ.

The contract of sale must be amended. Special condition four of the contract incorporating the Standard Conditions of Sale (Fifth edition – 2018 revision) contains two provisions, one of which will be deleted depending on the circumstances of the transaction. These are either:

"4. The property is sold with vacant possession

Or

4. The property is sold subject to the following leases and tenancies:"

The seller's conveyancer must disclose the details of the tenancy subject to which the property is being sold in special condition 4.

The buyer may wish to include provision in the contract prohibiting the seller from agreeing a further tenancy of the property between exchange of contracts and completion.

11.4.2 Terms of an assured shorthold tenancy agreement

The emergence of the tenancy deposit scheme (see below) resulted in many conveyancing firms who would routinely prepare assured shorthold tenancy (AST) agreements not conducting this type of work any more. The additional work and regulation to deal with the deposit scheme requirements means that far fewer conveyancing firms produce ASTs; it tends to be letting agents who will prepare these agreements.

However, the buyer's conveyancer will still need to check the terms of the tenancy agreement subject to which their client is purchasing the property to ensure that it is on standard terms, imposes suitable obligations on the tenant and does not impose onerous obligations on the landlord. The tenancy agreement (and any notices served in relation to it) should form part of the contract pack. However, if they do not, the buyer's conveyancer must raise this as a pre-contract enquiry and request copies of these documents together with confirmation that the originals will be handed over on completion.

If, as is often the case, a letting agent has set up the tenancy agreement and served all appropriate notices, the buyer's conveyancer may consider liaising with them directly to ensure that all documentation is in order or advising their buyer client to do so.

By definition, the agreement will already be subsisting by the time the buyer and their conveyancer are involved. Accordingly, if any terms of the AST agreement are unacceptable to the buyer, they may have to withdraw from the transaction or raise an enquiry with the seller and arrange for the tenant to vacate and a new AST to be entered into.

A basic AST should contain the following information:

- the parties;
- other occupiers (and maximum number if relevant) address and description of the property;
- common parts/shared facilities, if relevant;
- details of mortgage if relevant;
- the term of the tenancy;

- the rent payable;
- specifics as to what is included in the rent (for example, council tax);
- the rent payment date;
- the method of rent payment;
- the deposit payable;
- additional provisions, if relevant;
- contact details for service of notices;
- inventory and/or report of condition.

Follow the link below to the government's model agreement for an AST and accompanying guidance. Download the agreement and the guidance and read them and make notes on them. Treat the agreement and guidance as part of your course notes and ensure that you refer to them when preparing for any assessment.

https://www.gov.uk/government/publications/model-agreement-for-a-shorthold-assured-tenancy

11.4.3 Enquiries before contract

The buyer's conveyancer will carry out the usual searches and enquiries, dependent on the location of the property and must ensure that the conditions of any mortgage offer are met.

In addition, the buyer's conveyancer will need to carry out the following steps:

- inspect a copy of the tenancy agreement together with any inventory;
- request details of any side letters or variations to the tenancy agreement;
- request a copy of any notices served on the tenant prior to or during the tenancy;
- consider the effect of any security of tenure legislation on the tenant's position;
- obtain details of any letting agent;
- seek confirmation as to when the property was last inspected;
- establish whether the tenancy agreement has been breached and whether there have been any difficulties or complaints regarding the tenant;
- request confirmation as to who is in actual occupation of the property;
- seek confirmation that the rent has been paid on time throughout the term of the tenancy and whether there have been any rent increase;

- establish if a deposit has been paid and if so whether it is appropriately protected under a tenant deposit scheme;
- request a copy of the Prescribed Information and Tenancy Deposit Certificate and agree how the seller proposes to deal with the transfer of the deposit to the buyer;
- request evidence that the EPC was provided to the tenant before the tenancy was entered into;
- request evidence that the government's "How to Rent" Guide was provided to the tenant;
- request a copy of the right to rent documents and checks which were made at the outset of the tenancy.

11.4.4 Notices

If a landlord wants to evict a tenant who has an assured shorthold tenancy, they must use one of two notices (or both):

- a notice under **s21 Housing Act 1988** (**s21** notice); and/or
- a notice under **s8 Housing Act 1988** (**s8** notice).

A **s21 notice** can be used either:

- after a fixed term tenancy ends - if there's a written contract;
- during a tenancy with no fixed end date – known as a "periodic" tenancy.

The above enquiries are important because a failure to comply with some of them could mean that the buyer is unable to serve a **s21** notice of seeking possession.

A **s21** notice cannot be used if any of the following apply:

- it is less than four months since the tenancy started, or the fixed term has not ended, unless there's a clause in the contract which allows you to do this;
- the property is categorised as an HMO and does not have an HMO licence from the council;
- the tenancy started after April 2007 and the tenant's deposit is not in a deposit protection scheme;
- the tenancy started after October 2015 and the landlord has not used form 6A (**s21** notice) or a letter with all the same information on it;
- the council has served an improvement notice on the property in the last six months;

- the council has served a notice in the last six months that says it will do emergency works on the property;
- the landlord has not repaid any unlawful fees or deposits that were charged to the tenant (see **Tenant Fees Act 2019**).

A landlord also cannot use a **s21** notice if they have not given the tenants copies of:

- the property's EPC;
- the government's "How to Rent" guide;
- a current gas safety certificate for the property, if gas is installed.

The gas safety certificate and the "How to Rent" guide must be given to the tenant before they moved in.

The tenant must receive the EPC before they rented the property.

A **s8 notice** requires the landlord to complete a "notice seeking possession of a property let on an assured tenancy or an assured agricultural occupancy" and the notice must specify which terms of the tenancy the tenant has broken. If the tenant does not vacate by the specified date, the landlord can apply to court for a possession order.

Link to practice

Note that the above is only an outline of the key provisions in England.

Residential tenancy law is one area where the law and practice between Wales and England is diverging rapidly.

In addition, the government suspended a number of the "usual" eviction procedures in response to the Covid-19 pandemic to try to protect residential tenants from eviction during lockdown. This involves the regular amendment of a number of statutory timeframes and procedures and some tenants might still be affected by these changes. This is particularly relevant in relation to the amount of notice which the tenant must receive to vacate the property. Generally, a **s21** and **s8** notice must give the tenant at least two months' notice to quit but these timeframes changed a number of times between March 2020 and September 2021.

So, the landscape is complex and patchy and clients should be advised to take advice from a residential leasehold specialist if there is any doubt as to the tenant's position.

The notices enabling the landlord to seek possession are relevant to a buyer of a buy to let because the buyer might be keen to obtain possession of the property soon after completion and it will therefore be of significant relevance to the buyer that the seller has complied with the statutory requirements and served the appropriate notices.

Link to practice

Landlord and tenant work has become fairly specialist and there are now significant statutory obligations imposed on landlords in relation to information to be provided to a residential tenant both before and during the tenancy. The buyer's conveyancer should consider the terms of their retainer carefully.

As we have indicated above, the purchase of a buy to let property will mean that the tenant is already in situ and the tenancy agreement has already been entered into. However, it may be that appropriate notices were not served or prescribed information was not given to a tenant at the beginning of the tenancy. These omissions could result in the buyer being unable to gain possession of the premises from the tenant after their purchase completes.

Conveyancers should consider the scope of their retainer carefully. They need to decide whether they are willing to take on the detailed advice regarding the legalities of creation of the tenancy or not. Conveyancers are generally speaking not litigators. Accordingly, a conveyancer will not be involved in possession proceedings. The conveyancer will need to consider whether they are able to give advice as to whether the tenancy was created properly and if not, refer their client to a specialist.

11.4.5 Landlord's position

In addition to considering the position of the tenant, the buyer's conveyancer must also investigate the seller landlord's position including:

- obtain details as to who is responsible for insuring the building;
- consider the landlord's obligations under the tenancy agreement and seek confirmation that the landlord seller has complied with the obligations;
- if there are any breaches, the buyer should require these to be remedied prior to completion and consider an indemnity from the seller in relation to any such breaches;
- ensure that all health and safety responsibilities have been complied with including: smoke alarms;
- request copies of appropriate gas safety certificates.

The above is only an outline of some of the key considerations if a buyer is acquiring a single residential property subject to a short-term residential tenancy. If the buyer is acquiring a freehold reversion subject to tenancies, additional considerations will apply which are outside the scope of this course book.

11.4.6 Tenancy deposit schemes

If a landlord requires a tenant to pay a deposit dated on or after 6 April 2007 under an AST, the landlord must comply with the tenancy deposit requirements. The landlord is not required to take a deposit but if one is taken it must be safeguarded by an authorised scheme. There are two schemes: a single custodial scheme and two insurance backed schemes.

Tenancy deposit schemes Under **s212 HA 2004**, two deposit schemes for tenants' deposits for new tenancies running from **6 April 2007** were introduced. The schemes apply to all deposits required from tenants under new ASTs; they are not retrospective. A landlord is not required to take a deposit, but if one is taken it must be safeguarded by an authorised scheme.

Statutory requirements

When receiving a deposit for an AST **s213 HA 2004** requires a landlord to comply with the initial requirements of an authorised scheme and serve prescribed information upon the tenant within 30 days of receiving the deposit. The prescribed information is set out in the **Housing (Tenancy Deposits) (Prescribed Information) Order 2007** and includes:

- the scheme that is safeguarding the tenant's deposit;
- how the scheme's initial requirements have been met; and
- details of the relevant legislation which protects the tenant's deposit.

There are two types of scheme:

(1) A single custodial scheme. Under this scheme, landlords or letting agents must pay the deposit into the scheme within 30 days of receipt where it will be retained until the end of the tenancy. It will then be paid out by the agreement of the parties or via an alternative dispute resolution process in the event of a dispute.

(2) Two insurance-based schemes whereby the landlord or letting agent retains the deposit but pays a premium to the insurer. The scheme will have insurance to cover any misappropriation of the deposit. The interest from the deposits goes towards paying for the scheme, although a proportion will be repaid to the tenant in respect of the amount returned.

Enforcement

Where a landlord fails to protect a deposit, a tenant may seek a court order requiring the landlord to comply with the legislation. A landlord that fails to comply faces a penalty of up to three times the value of the deposit. A landlord will also be prevented recovering possession of the property under **s21 HA 1988** if it fails to protect a deposit.

A Court of Appeal decision has held that this information must be provided directly to the tenant. Letting the tenant make their own investigations is not sufficient. In ***Ayannuga v Swindells* [2012]** the landlord protected the deposit but only provided the tenant with some general information. The court held that the obligation under the Act was strict and the full prescribed information must be supplied. The landlord was ordered to pay three times the deposit to the tenant.

Pre-2007 tenancies

The rules for pre-2007 tenancies in outline are as follows:

(1) If a deposit is taken before 6 April 2007 and the tenancy became a periodic tenancy **before** 6 April 2007, then the deposit needs to be protected and the prescribed information needs to be served before a claim for possession under **s21 HA 1988** can be issued but no sanctions will apply.

(2) If a deposit is taken before 6 April 2007 and the tenancy became a periodic tenancy **after** 6 April 2007 and if it was protected before, it is deemed to be always protected. If it was not protected before 23 June 2015, the deposit must be returned and a penalty will apply.

11.4.7 Lenders and buy to lets

It is the willingness of institutional lenders to issue mortgages specifically to enable private individuals (or company) to purchase properties for letting purposes that has led to the significant increase in the number of people holding one or two buy to let properties for investment purposes.

Conveyancers cannot give specific financial advice which means that they cannot recommend a buy to let mortgage product to an investor client, nor can they comment on whether a product represents a "good deal". In the event that a buyer client receives a mortgage offer for a buy to let purchase, their conveyancer will prepare a mortgage report in much the same way as they would if their client was purchasing a residential property to live in. The mortgage report is likely to cover such issues as:

- the basic terms of the mortgage offer (for example, type of mortgage product, fixed or variable rate, purchase price and amount borrowed). Note that most borrowers take out an interest only mortgage meaning that they pay off the interest each month but not the capital amount. At the end of the mortgage term, the capital amount will remain outstanding and the borrower must have the facility to pay off the capital amount at the end of the term. The conveyancer must ensure that the significance of this is explained to the borrower otherwise they might have to sell the property to repay the mortgage;

- the meaning of the key mortgage conditions;
- arrangements to sign the mortgage deed;
- the consequences to the client of failing to keep up the repayments on the mortgage.

The buyer will need to source a buy to let mortgage product if they intend to borrow money to purchase a property that they want to rent out. Traditional residential mortgages are only for borrowers who intend to live in the property that they are buying. The fact that it is a buy to let transaction will be declared to the lender on application. The buyer must have a good credit rating and make a full declaration as to their financial circumstances to the lender on application, together with the monthly rental income. The lenders consider that there is a greater risk involved with buy to let lending and will adjust their interest rates accordingly.

The criteria for a buy to let mortgage includes:

- the rental income (rental yield) must usually be at least 125% of the mortgage payment;
- some lenders require the borrower to have a minimum income;
- often the buyer must have a larger deposit to put down (at least 20% in some cases);
- there are often minimum age requirements; some lenders require the borrower to be at least 25 to be eligible for a loan;
- some lenders also require the borrower to have a residential mortgage.

11.4.8 Completion and post completion

Rent

On completion, it may be necessary to deal with apportionment of the rent. If there are any rent arrears due to the seller, this should be resolved on completion. It is important for a buyer to know whether a tenant has persistently delayed paying rent as this may affect the buyer's decision to purchase the property.

The contract should include an obligation for the seller to provide all relevant information and documentation to enable the buyer to access the tenant's deposit under the tenancy deposit scheme and the originals should be handed over on completion.

In addition, the buyer's conveyancer should receive the original tenancy agreement and a rent authority letter signed by the seller and addressed to the tenant authorising the tenant to pay future rent to the buyer.

The terms of the rent authority letter should be agreed and appended to the contract prior to exchange.

Example

A simple rent authority letter might contain the following and be on headed note paper of the seller's conveyancer or managing agent:

For the attention of:

Name and address of tenant

Date:

Reference:

Dear Tenant

Property: [insert address of property that is let]

Tenancy: [insert details of tenancy: date, parties]

Former landlord: [insert name of seller]

New landlord: [insert name of buyer]

We act on behalf of your former landlord under the above tenancy. Please note that your former landlord has today transferred its interest in the Property to the new landlord.

You should pay all future rent (and any other payments due to the landlord under the tenancy) to the new landlord at [insert address for receipt of rents] or in accordance with the instructions given by your new landlord.

This letter does not affect how you should pay rent or other monies due to your former landlord under the tenancy on or before today's date. You should continue to make those payments to your former landlord.

Yours faithfully

....

Duly authorised for and on behalf of at [[insert name of former landlord]

Copied to: [insert name of the landlord] and [insert name of the landlord's solicitor or conveyancer]

SDLT and LTT

On completion, the conveyancer must ensure that the appropriate amount of SDLT (or LTT) is paid within the relevant timeframe. The buyer will be liable to pay more SDLT (or LTT) for a second or subsequent property that is not their main home. Refer to **Chapter 2** for more detail on SDLT and LTT.

Notices

After completion, in accordance with **s3 Landlord and Tenant Act 1985**, the buyer must give written notice of assignment and their name and address to the tenant not later than the next day upon which the rent is payable or if that is within two months of the date of the assignment, the end of the period of two months.

s48 Landlord and Tenant Act 1987 requires the landlord to provide the tenant with an address in England and Wales for service of notices. Importantly, until this notice is given, any rental service charge and the tenancy agreement is treated as not being due and is thus not recoverable by action by the buyer.

11.4.9 If the buyer is a limited company

In addition to considering the work required to deal with the purchase of a buy to let property, the conveyancer will have additional responsibilities if their buyer client is a limited company which is more likely in a transaction of this type.

AML and due diligence

Conveyancers must ensure that they comply with the AML due diligence requirements in relation to their company client. The conveyancer must ensure that they follow their firm's policies regarding identification and due diligence of company clients which must incorporate the Legal Sector Affinity Group (LSAG) guidance(https://www.sra.org.uk/solicitors/resources/money-laundering/guidance-support/). This includes:

(1) Verifying a party who purports to act on behalf of a client, for example a director (para 6.14.9).

(2) A requirement that where the customer's the company, the customer must be identified and the firm must take reasonable measures to understand the ownership and control structure of that company. This requires tracing ownership back

to any ultimate beneficial ownership of the entity by natural persons. Firms must then take reasonable measures to verify the identity of the beneficial owner so that they are satisfied that they know who the beneficial owner is (para 6.14.10).

(3) The requirement to identify and verify the name of the company, the company number or other registration number and the address of its registered office and principal place of business (if different the address). The practice must take reasonable measures to determine and verify the law to which the company is subject and its constitution and the full names of the board of directors and the senior persons responsible for the operations of the body corporate. The firm must collect proof of registration or an excerpt from the relevant read (6.14.11).

There are different due diligence requirements depending on the type of company involved but in most residential conveyancing transactions, the client company is likely to be private and unlisted in the UK. Private companies are generally subject to a lower level of public disclosure than public companies.

The LSAG guidance suggests that sources for verifying corporate identification may include (para 6.14.11.2):

- certificate of incorporation;
- articles of association (or equivalent formation documents);
- details from the relevant company registry, confirming details of the company and the directors and their addresses;
- filed audited accounts; or
- information from a reputable electronic verification service provider.

All investigations should be recorded on the client or matter risk assessment.

As indicated above, the conveyancer must ensure that any director of the company instructing the firm has authority to do so on behalf of the company.

Link to practice

In this situation, the conveyancer must be very wary of the possibility of a conflict of interest between the director and that of the company. The conveyancer must ensure that they do not stray into giving advice to the director as to their own personal circumstances as opposed to issues directly relating to that of the company.

An example of where this is likely to arise is if the company is obtaining a mortgage to fund the purchase and the lender requires the company directors to give personal guarantees for the mortgage loan. In this case, the conveyancing firm should not advise the directors in their personal capacity as to the giving of the guarantee.

Registration of a charge

If a company borrows money to fund the purchase of a property, the conveyancer must ensure that the mortgage is registered with Companies House within 21 days of completion (**s859A Companies Act 2006**). This will be done using form MR01 (see https://www.gov.uk/government/publications/register-particulars-of-a-charge-mr01?msclkid=44a257bbcfa111eca4965a76a6a55c07). This can be done online although the firm will need to sign up for online filing. To complete form MR01 the following information will be required:

- company name;
- company registration number (CRN);
- date on which the charge is created;
- name(s) of person(s) entitled to the charge (i.e. the lender);
- description of the charge;
- answers to questions about the nature of the charge, including whether it is a fixed charge or floating charge.

A certified copy of the mortgage deed must accompany the application which will be shown on the company public record. There is a fee to register the charge (£15 for online filing or £23 for paper filing) which must be added to the client's completion statement. Companies House acknowledge receipt of the form within a couple of days of filing and once accepted, the charge will be registered and Companies House will issue a certificate of Registration of Charge within approximately five days. This certificate must accompany the HMLR application.

The 21-day filing period is strictly applied and starts the day after the charge is created. This is a risk for conveyancers because if the deadline is missed, this could result in a negligence claim because at that point, only the court can allow an extension of time.

Activity

Follow the link below to the Companies House log on registering a company charge:

https://companieshouse.blog.gov.uk/2018/10/10/mortgage-charges-save-time-file-online/

11.5 Houses in Multiple Occupation (HMOs)

If the property is let to several tenants who are not members of the same family, it might be a "House in Multiple Occupation" under the **Housing Act 2004**. The property is an HMO If both of the following apply:

- at least three tenants live there, forming more than one household; and
- toilet, bathroom or kitchen facilities are shared.

A "household" consists of either a single person or members of the same family who live together and includes people who are married or living together and people in same sex relationships.

An HMO must have a licence if it is occupied by five or more people. If the property being sold is an HMO, the buyer's conveyancer must ensure that the property is properly licensed. This is another area which is governed by a number of statutory obligations and a residential conveyancer may find that they need to refer their buyer client for specialist advice. It is also another area where the regulations have been routinely changed due to the pandemic and the conveyancer must ensure that they are referring to the most up-to-date guidance.

Activity

Follow the link below to the Shelter website:

https://england.shelter.org.uk/housing_advice/private_renting/houses_in_multiple_occupation_hmo

Make a note of the responsibilities of HMO landlords and ensure that you understand when and HMO licence is required from the council.

11.5.1 Conveyancer's advice

The buyer's conveyancer must ensure that they are qualified to give any advice which their client might need in relation to the transaction. For example, the buyer might be an individual and seek advice as to whether they should set up a limited company to deal with the acquisition and the subsequent letting. The conveyancer may feel that they must seek input from someone in the commercial department to assist with such advice.

The conveyancing firm is also unlikely to be giving tax advice to their buyer client. There are tax implications for buy to let investors. Tax may be due on the rental income and when the property is sold. The conveyancer should refer their buyer to let client to an accountant prior to exchange of contracts to ensure that the client is fully aware as to their tax liability prior to committing themselves to the transaction.

11.6 Acting on a deed of easement

We will now move on to consider another more complex conveyancing transaction which might be encountered in practice; acting on the creation of a deed of easement. This is a transaction where every situation will be different and the conveyancer will either act for the party granting the easement (grantor) or the party taking the benefit of the easement (grantee). Detailed instructions should be taken from the client in every case and it is essential for the conveyancer to understand the nature of the rights required.

We will cover some of the key considerations in this chapter and will first start with a recap on some of the background law relating to the creation of an easement.

11.6.1 What is an easement?

This question cannot be answered by looking for a definition in a statute. Instead, case law has to provide guidance.

An easement is a right attached to one piece of land which allows the owner of that land either to use the land of another person in a particular manner, or to restrict its use by that other person to a particular extent, but which does not allow them to take any part of its natural produce or soil.

Therefore, easements can be positive or negative. A right of way or right to place things on land would be positive easements, whereas a right of light or air through a defined aperture would be negative. The courts largely oppose negative easements.

With easements, there must always be two parcels of land involved. These are called "tenements". The land which enjoys the benefit of the easement is the "dominant tenement", the one which carries the burden is the "servient tenement".

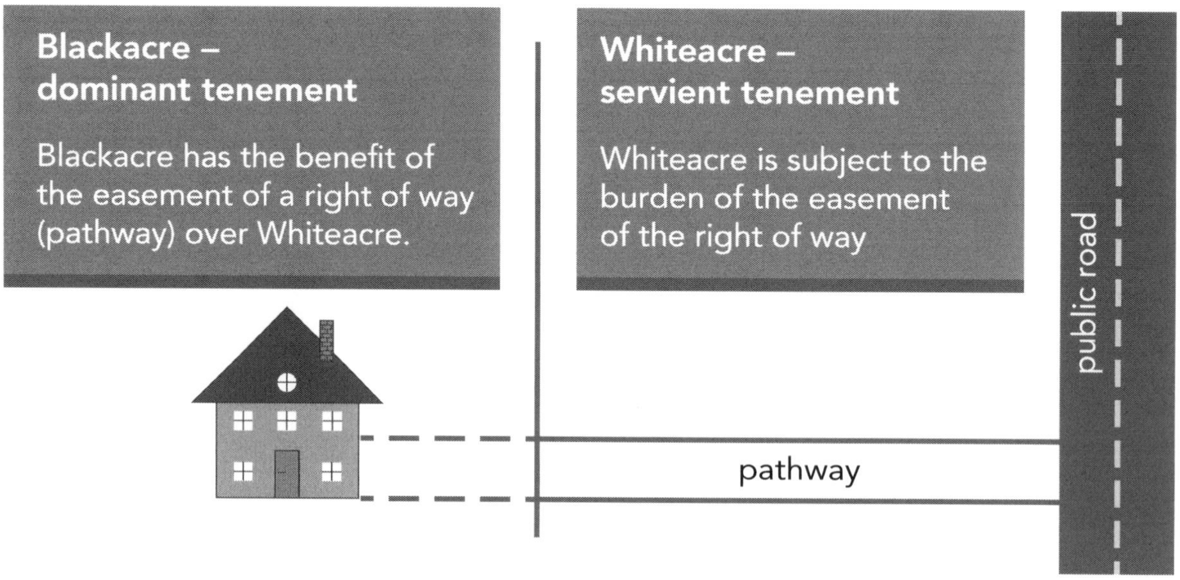

11.6.2 Acquiring an easement

The first question must always be: Is the right claimed capable of being an easement? This question can only be answered by looking at the essential characteristics of an easement and seeing if they have all been met. There is always case law development in the law of easements because, as times and technology change, so do the rights that people would like to claim over another's land.

Assuming that the right claimed is capable of being an easement, the next question is: How, if at all, has it been acquired?

Easements can either be given (granted) by the owner of the land or taken (reserved) by the owner of the land. There are three ways of granting or creating a legal easement.

(1) Express grant

If D owns both Blackacre and Whiteacre, and sells Whiteacre to C together with an easement over the land D retains (Blackacre), this is a grant as in the diagram below. Equally, grants may also arise when the two tenements are already separately owned and occupied. A grants their neighbour B an easement over A's land, usually in return for money or other consideration.

Express grants are usually made by including express words of grant into a conveyance of the legal estate. If created by deed and equivalent to a term of years absolute or a fee simple absolute in possession, the easement will be legal under **s1(2)(a) LPA 1925**. If the easement is created in writing, and such writing meets the requirements of **s2 Law of Property (Miscellaneous Provisions) Act 1989**, the easement will be equitable.

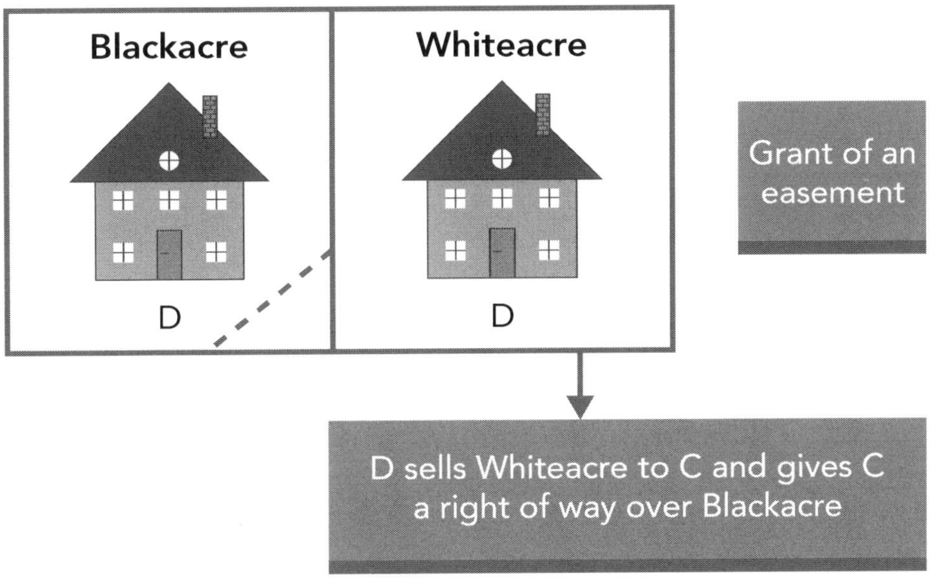

Express grant is the most obvious means of creating an easement. One property holder expressly agrees that another should have an easement over their land. If the easement is to be recognised by law, it must be created by deed under **s52 LPA 1925** and be equivalent to a legal estate. If not created in this way, it will be equitable; such an equitable easement must, at the very least, be in writing (**s53(1) LPA 1925**).

(2) Implied grant

Easements created by implied grant or prescription (long use) are legal easements. Under the rules on implied grant and prescription a claimant has the burden of proving the existence of the easement. If there is sufficient evidence to that effect, the court will declare that the easement exists, and it will be deemed to be a legal easement despite the fact that it is **not** created by deed and is not even in writing.

An easement may be implied into a contract or a conveyance in certain circumstances. The various methods of implied grant are based on what the parties to the agreement are presumed to have intended. These are as follows.

(a) Necessity

An easement will be implied if absolutely necessary. This can arise where land is landlocked and there is no other access without a right of way (***Nickerson v Barraclough* [1981]**). Mere inconvenience is insufficient to create an easement of necessity. In ***Titchmarsh v Royston Water Co Ltd* [1899]** there was no easement of necessity where vehicular access to the highway was possible, albeit down a sheer 20-foot embankment. An easement of necessity may arise where the only alternative would be to destroy a barrier (in this case, a workshop) on part of the retained land (***Sweet and Another v Sommer and Another* [2004]**).

An easement of support will arise by implication where an owner sells one of two adjoining properties.

(b) Common intention

There may be an implied easement if the parties to the transaction must clearly have intended this. In ***Liverpool City Council v Irwin*** **[1977]** there was no express grant of an easement in favour of the tenants to use staircases and lifts to reach their ninth- and tenth-storey flats. Nevertheless, such an easement must obviously be implied.

(c) The rule in *Wheeldon v Burrows* [1879]

A person who divides their land into two and then sells one part always needs to be careful that implied easements are not being created in favour of the buyer. Implication of an easement under ***Wheeldon v Burrows*** requires several conditions to apply.

(i) Unity of ownership and occupation

This means that, originally, one person must own and occupy the whole of a piece of land.

(ii) Exercise of quasi-easements

The original owner must have exercised rights which would be easements but for the fact of common ownership and occupation. As a person cannot have an easement over their own land, this is known as a **quasi-easement**.

(iii) Continuous and apparent

The right must, to some extent, be obvious. For example, a right of way may be obvious to someone inspecting the land, as there may be some defined track. Similarly, a right of drainage would be apparent if drain covers were visible. A right to receive light through windows will be less obvious and may not qualify under ***Wheeldon v Burrows***.

(iv) Necessary to reasonable enjoyment of the land

The right must render use of the land more convenient.

(v) Division of the land

If the above requirements are met, the quasi-easements will become actual easements when the land is divided (unless the seller makes it clear to the contrary).

(d) s62 LPA 1925

s62 is used to create new easements in two different ways.

(i) Where there is diversity of ownership and occupation

This is an important means whereby tenants may acquire an easement over land retained by their landlord. The wording of **s62** has the effect of converting mere permissions into easements.

As well as diversity of ownership and occupation, two additional requirements must also be met for a new easement to arise under **s62**:

- permission must be given to the occupier to use the easement; and
- there must be a conveyance (including a lease), that is, the transfer of legal title to the occupier.

The requirement for diversity of occupation means that **s62** claims have been applied primarily to tenants claiming rights over land retained by the landlord. In ***Wright v Macadam* [1949]** a tenant successfully claimed an easement of storage in a garden shed on land retained by the landlord as a result of **s62**. The landlord had given the tenant permission to use a shed for storage purposes. This was originally a licence (permission) only. When the tenant's lease was renewed, that is, there was a grant or conveyance of a new lease, this conveyance converted the licence into an easement.

(ii) Where there is no diversity of ownership and occupation

Following ***Wood v Waddington* [2015]** there is now a further method of creating an easement under **s62**. In this instance, no diversity of ownership and occupation is required. This case says that an easement can be created under **s62** provided the following conditions are met:

- the right is continuous and apparent; and
- the use must have been for the benefit of the land conveyed.

It is thus easier to establish an easement under ***Wood v Waddington*** than under ***Wheeldon v Burrows*** where the additional condition that the easement is necessary to the reasonable enjoyment of the land must be complied with.

(3) Presumed grant or prescription

Prescription implies that if a person can prove that for a particular period (usually 20 years) they have exercised a right which has the characteristics of an easement, they may be presumed to have an easement by prescription. As explained in (2) above, this will be deemed to be a legal easement despite the lack of deeds.

This is regarded as a legal fiction. If a person can show acquisition of an easement by prescription, it is presumed that some grant of a legal easement occurred in the past.

For prescription to occur, the following criteria must be satisfied:

- there must have been **continuous** user (the legal term for usage): the purported easement must have been used regularly;
- user must have continued for the **prescriptive period** – generally 20 or more years;
- user must be **by, or on behalf of, and against, the fee simple** (i.e. freehold). In other words, one freehold owner must be claiming against another. A tenant cannot acquire an easement by prescription over land adjoining their leasehold land if that neighbouring land is owned by their landlord;
- there must be **user as of right**. This means that it must have been exercised without force, secrecy or permission. Where a person forcibly removes a fence to create a shortcut, or where the servient owner does not appreciate that their land is being used (e.g. where drains are buried under the land), no right of prescription can arise. Also, if permission has been given to use the particular right, then there can be no prescriptive right.

In ***Winterburn v Bennett* [2016]** the erection of a clearly visible sign saying: "Private car park. For the use of [Conservative] Club patrons only" was sufficient to show that the landowners were not acquiescing in the acts of trespass committed by customers and delivery drivers to a fish and chip shop. The claimants were unable to show that they had acquired the easement "as of right". Entering the land was not regarded as peaceable where a sign clearly indicated that parking was not allowed. It was not necessary to show that they used force or committed acts of damage to gain entry. The Court of Appeal thus decided that a landowner can prevent someone acquiring rights over land by clear signage alone.

There are three different methods of prescription.

(a) At common law, for an easement to arise by prescription, it had to have been enjoyed since **time immemorial (1189).** The courts have adopted the rule that, if user as of right for 20 years or more is shown, it will be presumed that user has continued since 1189. If it can be shown that at any time since 1189 the easement could not have existed, for example, the land was owned by one person, an easement cannot be acquired by prescription at common law.

(b) Under the doctrine of **lost modern grant**, where the easement must have been used for 20 years. In such cases, the courts may make a (fictional) presumption that the easement was granted, but that the deeds were lost.

(c) Under the **Prescription Act 1832**, where the easement must have been used for at least 20 years. If 40 years' user can be shown, however, the right is deemed to be absolute and indefeasible (cannot be made void).

To claim an easement under the doctrine of lost modern grant, the 20-year period can be any period, whereas to claim an easement under the **Prescription Act 1832**, the 20-year period must be "next before action", that is, run for the 20 years immediately preceding the action.

11.6.3 Legal and equitable easements

Easements and profits *à prendre* are capable of being legal interests (**s1(2)(a) LPA 1925**) but, equally, they can exist in equity. For instance, an easement or profit for life could not be legal as it does not equate in time to either of the two legal estates, therefore it can only be equitable. Likewise, an easement or profit not created by deed can only be equitable (**s52 LPA 1925**). So, if they are to be legal, easements and profits must be for a term equivalent to a fee simple absolute in possession or a term of years absolute and, if created expressly, be created by deed.

In unregistered land, legal rights, including legal easements, bind the world. In registered land, the express grant or reservation of a legal easement must be registered in order to be legal (**s27 Land Registration Act 2002** (**LRA 2002**)). Legal easements in registered land that are not granted or reserved expressly (i.e. easements created under ***Wheeldon v Burrows*** **[1879]**, by common intention or necessity, under **s62 LPA 1925**, by prescription or implied reservation through necessity or intention) are interests that override under **para 3 Sch 3 LRA 2002**, provided **either**:

- that the transferee of the land knew about the easement; **or**
- the easement would have been obvious to the transferee on a reasonably careful inspection of the land; **or**
- the easement had been used in the year before the disposition; **or**
- the easement is registered under the **Commons Registration Act 1965**.

This means that an implied legal easement in registered land is an interest that overrides only if one of the conditions under **para 3 Sch 3 LRA 2002** is met.

11.6.4 The deed of easement

We will now look at some of the considerations which the conveyancing practitioner will need to take into account when acting on a deed of easement. This is the creation of an easement by express grant and is the only method of creation of an easement that will be considered further in this chapter. We have seen in **Chapter 10**, that easements are often created on a transfer of part and in that case, the detail of the rights will be contained in the TP1. What we are going to consider briefly in this chapter is the situation where two landowners have agreed to the creation of an easement independently of any sale. In this instance, the terms of the easement are contained in the deed of easement.

The starting point is to ensure that the dominant and servient tenements are in separate ownership. Usually, the conveyancer acting for the grantor will draft the deed of easement and the conveyancer will need to obtain the title of both areas of land. In most cases, this will involve downloading the registers of title. However, if the title of the grantee is unregistered, it might be necessary for the grantor's conveyancer to request an epitome of title from the conveyancer on the other side.

The next step is to consider what rights and obligations the parties have agreed to; typically, deeds of easement relate to issues such as rights of way, rights to use pipes, utilities and services or rights of access. It is important to ensure that the rights agreed between the parties are capable of forming the subject matter of an easement. The right must benefit the servient land and must not be a purely personal benefit to the landowner.

The party producing the draft deed must produce a HMLR compliant plan of the dominant and servient tenements which clearly show the subject matter of the deed for example, the route of a right of way or pipes. Ideally, the plan should show dimensions such as distance, length of pipes, width of an access – the more detail is included, the less chance there is for misunderstanding or disagreement. The plan must be HMLR compliant because if either title is registered, it must be perfected by registration to be legal (see above).

The right to be granted might have a value: for example, a right of access to a piece of land which is otherwise landlocked can significantly enhance the value of the dominant land. Accordingly, the grantor might want to be paid for the easement. The conveyancer is not qualified to assess the potential value of such an easement and further should not attempt to quantify this. It might be necessary to take specialist advice from a surveyor in this regard.

On the other hand, the value of the servient tenement might be significantly diminished by the creation of an easement over it. If a large part of the servient tenement is going to be taken up with an accessway, for example, this will effectively preclude the landowner from using or developing the land over which the right-of-way is granted.

Both conveyancers will then need to take careful instructions from their respective clients as to the nature of the rights to be granted and the obligations, if any, which accompany. For example, the grantee might covenant to contribute towards the upkeep of a driveway over which they enjoy a right of access and, conversely, the grantor might covenant not to obstruct or park on the driveway.

If either of the parcels of land are in mortgage, it will be necessary to obtain the consent of the lender(s) to the creation of the deed of easement. The lender might be a party to the deed or might issue a letter consenting to the creation of the easement which must accompany the HMLR application.

Note that the grant of an easement could give rise to the payment of SDLT (or LTT) if there is an acquisition of a chargeable interest for chargeable consideration which is more than the nil rate threshold. The VAT situation must also be considered but the detail of this is outside the scope of this coursebook.

When the deed is completed, if the titles are registered, it will be necessary to register the deed at HMLR. The application will be made using form AP1 (see https://www.gov.uk/government/publications/change-the-register-ap1) and paying the appropriate fee. The easement will be noted on the property register of the title benefitting from the easement and on the charges register of the title burdened by the easement.

If one or both of the titles is unregistered, the original deed of easement must be placed with the title deeds.

Conveyancing practitioners will invariably use a precedent document (often from a software supplier) to assist with drafting a deed of easement. They should ensure that the draft is supplied to their client together with a full letter of advice well in advance of concluding the deed. Accordingly, there is no such thing as a '"typical" deed of easement because, as we have seen, each case turns on its own facts. However, please see below for the suggested framework for a straightforward deed of easement.

H M LAND REGISTRY

LAND REGISTRATION ACT 2002

Administrative Area

Title Number

Property

Date

1. Definitions

In this deed:

1.1 'the Grantor' means of the registered proprietor of the Servient Land

1.2 'the Grantee' means of the owner of the Dominant Land

1.3 'the Servient Land' means the land shown edged with on the Plan being part of the land comprised in the title above referred to

1.4 'the Dominant Land' means the land described in schedule 2 below and

1.5 'the Rights' means the rights set out in schedule 1 below and

1.6 'the Plan' means the plan annexed to this deed

2. Grant
In consideration of £ plus VAT (if any) paid by the Grantee to the Grantor receipt of which is acknowledged the Grantor grants the Rights to the Grantee in fee simple with [full or limited] title guarantee

3. Consent to noting of rights and covenant against the Dominant Land
The Grantor consents to notice of the Rights and the burden of his restrictive covenants in clause 5 being noted against his registered title to the Dominant Land Title Number

4. Consent to noting of covenant against the Servient Land
The Grantee consents to notice of the burden of his restrictive covenants in clause 6 being noted against his registered title to the Servient Land Title Number and requests that the Rights should be entered in the property register of that title as appurtenant rights

5. Grantor's covenants
The Grantor so as to bind the Servient Land into whosesoever hands it may come and for the benefit and protection of the Dominant Land covenants with the Grantee for himself and his successors in title to observe and perform at all times after the date of this deed in relation to the Servient Land and the Rights the following stipulations and restrictions

6. Grantee's covenants
The Grantee so as bind the Dominant Land into whosesoever hands it may come and for the benefit of the Grantor's interest in the Servient Land covenants with the Grantor for himself and his successors in title to observe and

perform at all times after the date of this deed in relation to the Dominant Land the following stipulations and restrictions

7. Indemnity
The Grantee covenants with the Grantor to keep the Grantor and his estate indemnified from and against any act loss damage or liability suffered by the Grantor or his estate in the exercise of the Rights

8. Consent of the Grantor's chargee
I of as proprietor of the charge dated and registered on in the Charges Register of the above Title Number consent to the grant of the Rights and to notice of them being entered in the Charges Register of that title number

9. Agreement as to application
The Grantor agrees *(or)* The Grantor and the Grantee agree to apply to the Registrar for entry of notice of the Rights in the Charges Register of Title Number and for the entry of the Rights in the Property Register of Title Number as appurtenant to the land in that title

IN WITNESS

Schedule 1

The Rights

Grant of a right to lay maintain and use a water pipe
The right for the Grantee and his successors in title as owners or occupiers for the time being of the Grantee's Land within of the date of this deed to lay a water pipe limited to under the Grantor's Land along the route marked with a line between the points marked 'A' and 'B' on the Plan and after wards the right to maintain and use the pipe for with power at any time on giving at least hours' notice except in emergency to enter the Grantor's Land to inspect clean maintain or renew the pipe

Schedule 2

The Dominant Land

The land shown edged with on the Plan being part of the land comprised in title number [INSERT]

SIGNED as a Deed by the said)

)

In the presence of:-)

W Signature ....
I
T Name..
N
E Address ....
S
S Occupation ....

11.7 Chapter summary

Probate sales

(1) The grant:

- confirms the validity of the will or, if there is no will, that the deceased died intestate;
- confirms the authority of executors (whose authority derives from the will itself) or grants authority to the administrators.

(2) Executors may be appointed expressly by the will, but their appointment can also be by implication if the intention is clear.

(3) A chain of representation arises, and so no further grant is needed, if a sole (or last surviving) executor dies before they have finished administering the first estate, and they leave a will appointing their own executor(s), who take(s) a grant to their estate. These executors continue administering the first estate as well as dealing with the second.

(4) The order of entitlement to a grant if there is a will is set out in **r20 NCPR 1987** by reference to those entitled under the will. If there is no will, **r22** sets out the order (effectively reflecting the order of entitlement on intestacy). Any prior interest must be satisfactorily accounted for (cleared off) before a claimant in a later category can establish title to the grant.

(5) Special types of grant include:

- an *ad colligenda bona* grant, which allows the applicant to deal with assets prior to a full grant being issued;
- a *durante minore aetate* grant, issued on behalf of a minor;
- a grant *de bonis non administratis*, which is a second grant to allow completion of the administration if all the original PRs under the first grant have died (and there is no chain of representation).

(6) **s116 SCA 198**1 gives the court power to appoint whomever it wishes as PR of an estate, which it can exercise in appropriate cases.

(7) When an application is for a grant of probate, all named executors must be accounted for. If the application is for a grant of letters of administration (with or without the will), anyone with prior entitlement to the applicants must be cleared off, but those within the same degree of entitlement do not need to be notified of the application.

(8) A grant (of any type) cannot be issued to more than four persons. If a will names more than four executors, those who are not applying for a grant will have power reserved (unless they wish to renounce).

(9) A sole executor has full powers to administer an estate, but under a grant of administration (with or without a will), at least two administrators are needed if a life or minority interest arises under the will or intestacy.

(10) Up until the issue of a grant of probate, and providing that they have not intermeddled, an executor can renounce. If, as is often the case, the will also appoints them as a trustee, they will need to renounce in that capacity as well; in other words, they will have to renounce their right both to probate and to letters of administration with the will annexed.

(11) On a probate sale the personal representatives will generally give a limited title guarantee (that might be further modified).

(12) Personal representatives should be cautious if the title is unregistered and/or if the deceased has occupied more land than falls within the title.

(13) Personal representatives should exercise caution when responding to the Property Information Form and replies to pre-contract enquiries and it should be made clear, if relevant, that the personal representatives have little or no personal knowledge of the property.

(14) If access to a property between exchange of contracts and completion is granted to the buyer for the purpose of carrying out works, this should be agreed in the contract and the buyer should sign an appropriate key undertaking.

(15) If the buyer takes up occupation of the property between exchange of contracts and completion, this will be as a licensee under the condition 5.2. However, the personal representatives should consider the risks of this course of action particularly in light of their duties to the beneficiaries.

Selling a property subject to a tenancy

(16) The seller must provide the Energy Performance Certificate.

(17) The contract must be amended to make it clear in special condition 4 that property is sold subject to a tenancy and a copy of the tenancy and any notices must be sent to the buyer's conveyancer.

(18) The buyer should ensure that the seller has complied with all appropriate statutory requirements regarding the tenancy and should obtain the appropriate gas and electricity certificates.

(19) The tenant deposit should be protected under the tenancy deposit scheme.

(20) On completion any rent apportionments should be resolved and a rent authority letter signed by the seller (or their agent or conveyancer) should be handed over on completion.

(21) If the buyer is a limited company the conveyancer should carry out the appropriate AML and due diligence on their company client.

(22) If the company client takes out a mortgage to assist with the purchase, this must be registered with Companies House within 21 days of completion and the Certificate of Registration must accompany the HMLR application.

Acting on a deed of easement

(23) For an easement to be valid there must be two parcels of land involved which are in separate ownership.

(24) The right must be capable of being an easement and must benefit the land and not be a purely personal right.

(25) There are three ways of creating a legal easement:

- express grant;
- implied grant;
- presumed grant or prescription.

(26) In registered land, the express grant or reservation of a legal easement must be registered in order for it to be legal.

CHAPTER 12

HMLR restrictions and requisitions and securing positive obligations

12.1 Introduction

Conveyancers will encounter restrictions on a register of title every day. A restriction is one of the ways of protecting some form of right or interest over registered land. We have seen that the other method of protecting third-party rights is notices. It is important that the correct method to protect a third-party right is chosen and this chapter will look at some of the most common restrictions that conveyancers will encounter. Dealing with a restriction and all other matters to enable registration to proceed smoothly post completion is important to avoid HMLR requisitions. This chapter will also look at these questions which are raised by HMLR on issues which arise during the registration process. The chapter will conclude by considering in outline an important practical matter which can vex conveyancers, that of securing a positive obligation in a freehold context.

This chapter will cover:

- **Restrictions**
  - why it is important to choose the correct method to protect a third-party interest;
  - the general effect of restrictions;
  - standard and non-standard restrictions;

- entry of restrictions;
- removal of a restriction;
- complying with a restriction;
- Form RXC;
- common restrictions.

- **HMLR requisitions**
  - how HMLR raises requisitions and timeframes;
  - common requisitions and acceptable solutions.

- **Securing a positive obligation**
  - covenants – recap;
  - enforcing the covenant.

12.2 Restrictions

The first point to make is that conveyancers should have a working knowledge of HMLR Practice Guide 19: notices and restrictions (PG19). Most questions which might arise relating to restrictions and how to use them will be answered by considering PG19.

Activity

Follow the link below and, if necessary, refresh your memory as to the protection of third-party rights by way of notice.

Then move on to look at the section on restrictions and make any notes to supplement this chapter as appropriate.

You will need to consult this Practice guide regularly in practice; however always ensure that you refer to an online version because it is regularly updated by HMLR.

https://www.gov.uk/government/publications/notices-restrictions-and-the-protection-of-third-party-interests-in-the-register/practice-guide-19-notices-restrictions-and-the-protection-of-third-party-interests-in-the-register

The **LRA 2002** provides two types of entry for the protection of third-party interests affecting registered estates and charges: notices and restrictions.

- A notice is an entry made in the register in respect of the burden of an interest affecting a registered estate or charge (**s32(1) LRA 2002**).
- A restriction is an entry in the register that prevents or regulates the making of an entry in the register in respect of any disposition or a disposition of a specified kind (**s40(1) LRA 2002**).

This chapter will focus on restrictions.

In PG19, HMLR reminds conveyancers of an important preliminary issue: before making an application to HMLR to protect a third-party interest you should ask yourself the following questions:

- What type of interest is being protected?
- Can the interest be protected by notice, and would this be more appropriate? For example, a notice will give priority (provided the interest is valid) but a restriction does not.
- Is the interest only capable of protection by a restriction? For example, an interest under a trust of land can only be protected by a restriction (**s33 LRA 2002**).

12.2.1 Why is it important to choose the correct method to protect a third-party interest?

The answer is due to the provisions of **s77 LRA 2002** which provides as follows:

77. Duty to act reasonably

(1) A person must not exercise any of the following rights without reasonable cause—

(a) the right to lodge a caution under section 15,

(b) the right to apply for the entry of a notice or restriction, and

(c) the right to object to an application to the registrar.

(2) The duty under this section is owed to any person who suffers damage in consequence of its breach.

The explanatory notes to the section make the following point:

Section 56(3) of the 1925 Act makes anyone who lodges a caution without reasonable cause liable to any person who has suffered damage thereby. Section 77 considerably develops this, by providing that a person must not exercise the right to apply for an entry to be added to the register of someone else's title, or for the entry of a notice or object to someone else's application unreasonably and if they do so, they owe a duty to anyone who suffers damage. The existence of this duty entitles the person adversely affected to bring an action for damages.

The effect of **s77** is that a right of action for breach of statutory duty may exist against anyone who applies for a notice or restriction without reasonable cause. The right is in favour of any person who suffers damage as a consequence. Any breach must be pursued through the courts rather than HMLR. The wide-ranging effect of **s77** is that a conveyancer must always ensure that there is reasonable cause to enter the proposed notice or restriction in favour of their client.

12.2.2 The general effect of restrictions

Restrictions prohibit the making of an entry in respect of a disposition or a disposition of a specified kind. The prohibition may be indefinite or for a specified period of time and it may be absolute or conditional on something happening such as obtaining the consent of a third party. The term "disposition" is not defined in **LRA 2002** but includes:

- a transfer;
- certain types of lease;
- the grant or reservation of an easement;
- a rentcharge/right of entry and to a rentcharge;
- charge by way of legal mortgage.

Thus a restriction which includes the words "No disposition…" will catch the above types of transaction and will result in the registration not being concluded until the restriction has been complied with or removed.

Conveyancers must understand a subtle point regarding restrictions in that the purpose of them is to **regulate registration**, not to regulate dispositions. Thus, where a restriction entered in the register requires consent or has an option requiring consent, the consent given in relation to the restriction should expressly consent to the **registration of the disposition**, not consent to the disposition. This requirement does not apply to a restriction that requires a certificate. In that case, all that is needed is that the certificate complies with the requirements of the restriction. A restriction that is entered to regulate dispositions of a registered estate will appear on the proprietorship register.

A restriction makes it apparent from the register that either the powers of the relevant proprietor are limited, or that a prior condition must be met before a disposition can be registered.

Once entered, a restriction will remain in the register until it is cancelled or withdrawn. Restrictions are not automatically cancelled following a disposition, although HMLR may cancel any restriction that has clearly become superfluous.

12.2.3 Standard and non-standard restrictions

The effect of a restriction must be clear from its wording and HMLR must not be placed under an unreasonable burden in relation to a restriction. Over time, HMLR has developed a significant number of standard form restrictions which are intended to cover the majority of applications made.

Activity

Go to Appendix B of PG19. Read through the wide range of standard restrictions and take particular note of those which you do not recognise.

Also read and make notes on section 3.3 of PG19 which explains the format of the standard restrictions and how to use the words in square and round brackets.

HMLR will accept restrictions that are not in a standard format but only if:

- it is reasonable;
- its application would be straightforward;
- its application would not place HMLR under an unreasonable burden.

Crucially, HMLR must preapprove the wording of any non-standard restriction and a fee must be paid for this service.

12.2.4 Entry of restrictions

PG19 contains the detail as to how a restriction is entered upon a register of title. **s42(1) LRA 2002** sets out the registrar's general power to enter a restriction as follows.

The registrar may enter a restriction in the register if it appears to him that it is necessary or desirable to do so for the purpose of –

(a) *preventing invalidity or unlawfulness in relation to dispositions of a registered estate or charge,*

(b) *securing those interests which are capable of being overreached on a disposition of a registered estate or charge are overreached, or*

(c) *protecting a right or claim in relation to a registered estate or charge.*

The registrar may enter a restriction to fulfil one of these purposes whether or not an application is made to do so. However, the registrar will always notify the relevant proprietor when a restriction is entered without an application having been made to do so. It will usually be clear whether a restriction is necessary or desirable for one of the three permitted purposes, but this will not always be the case. HMLR is obliged to enter a restriction where:

- HMLR enters two or more people as joint proprietors of a registered estate in land and the survivor will not be able to give a valid receipt for capital money (**s44(1) LRA 2002**).

Link to practice

It is important to remember that HMLR will automatically enter a restriction regarding the joint ownership where two or more people apply to be registered as joint owners unless it is clear from the documents that they will be holding the property on trust for themselves alone as joint tenants.

This means that the buyer's conveyancer should always ensure that the co-ownership declaration has been completed in any transfer being submitted for registration where there is more than one co-owner. If the relevant box of the transfer has not been ticked, HMLR will enter the Form A restriction, even if the buyers intend to hold as joint tenants.

- some other statute requires the registrar to enter a restriction (**s44(2) LRA 2002**);
- a bankruptcy order is registered under the **Land Charges Act 1972** and it appears that a registered estate or charge is affected (**s86(4) LRA 2002**). (Practice guide 34 provides further detail about the entry of a bankruptcy restriction);
- the court makes an order that requires the registrar to enter a restriction (**s46 LRA 2002**).

A party can only apply for the entry of a restriction if:

- they are the relevant proprietor;
- they are entitled to be registered as the relevant proprietor;
- they have got the consent of the relevant proprietor (or someone entitled to be registered as such); or
- they otherwise have a sufficient interest in the making of the entry. **r93 LRR 2003** contains a list of standard situations where a party will be regarded as having sufficient interest.

Most applications to register a restriction must be made on form RX1 (see https://www.gov.uk/government/publications/enter-a-restriction-registration-rx1) along with payment of the relevant fee. An application can also be made in various other standard documents including forms TR1 (https://www.gov.uk/government/publications/registered-titles-whole-transfer-tr1), TP1 (https://www.gov.uk/government/publications/registered-titles-part-transfer-tp1) and AS1 (https://www.gov.uk/government/publications/whole-of-registered-title-assent-as1).

12.2.5 Removal of a restriction

Restrictions can be removed from the register by:

- being withdrawn voluntarily by the appropriate people interested in the restriction using form RX4 (see https://www.gov.uk/government/publications/withdraw-a-restriction-registration-rx4?msclkid=f57c801bcfa611eca27e96ad07cf0240).
- an application by anyone to cancel a restriction that is no longer required using form RX3 (see https://www.gov.uk/government/publications/cancel-a-restriction-registration-rx3).
- HMLR cancelling the restriction if it is clear that it is superfluous or in respect of a trust of land where HMLR is satisfied that the affected estate is no longer subject to the trust.

There is a distinction between cancellation and withdrawal. Cancellation is the term used in **r97 LRR 2003** to refer to an application to cancel a restriction that is no longer required. Any person may apply to cancel a restriction. The application must be made in form RX3 and no fee is payable. If the restriction being cancelled is a Form A restriction, the applicant can use form ST5 (https://www.gov.uk/government/publications/cancellation-of-restriction-statement-of-truth-st5) to supply the necessary evidence in support of the application.

Withdrawal of a restriction is the term used in **s47 LRA 2002** and **r98 LRR 2003**. **rr98(1)** and **(2) LRR 2003** requires an application for the withdrawal of a restriction to be accompanied by "the required consent". If HMLR is satisfied the required consent has been given, they will remove the entry without investigating whether the restriction continues to serve any purpose. The application must be made in from RX4; no fee is payable.

There are certain restrictions which cannot be withdrawn and it is possible to apply to disapply or modify a restriction to enable a disposition to be registered but these issues are beyond the scope of this course book. This is only a brief outline, please read PG19 for more detail.

12.2.6 Complying with a restriction

It is particularly important for the conveyancer acting for a buyer to ensure that any restriction certificate or consent will be acceptable to HMLR otherwise the registration will not proceed. Note the following:

(1) Any certificate or consent required by a restriction must be signed in wet ink but note that with the exception of the restriction in Form LL (see below), a certificate or consent by a conveyancer can be signed by an individual conveyancer in their own name or in the name of the firm. The certificate or consent must state the full name of the individual and their status in the firm (for example, partner, solicitor). A certificate or consent given by a conveyancer can be given in an email (other than Form LL).

(2) Where a restriction catches two or more dispositions being lodged at the same time, the consent or certificate of compliance must be to **all** of the dispositions being registered.

Example

If both a transfer and charge are being registered and both are caught by a restriction that requires consent, the consent given must be to the registration of both the transfer and the charge.

---

(3) As indicated above, a consent required by a restriction must state that it is to the registration of the disposition, and not just to the disposition itself.

(4) If an application is being made by post and the certificate or consent is being lodged with that application, the original certificate or consent, or a certified copy of it, must be lodged by post.

(5) If an application is being made via the portal or HMLR Business Gateway, a scanned copy of the certificate or consent should be uploaded and the copy should be certified as a true copy of the original.

12.2.7 Form RXC

Form RXC is designed to assist with the provision of restriction consents and certificates as it contains standardised wording and format. The purpose is to ensure that HMLR requirements are met with the objective of avoiding requisitions Form RXC can be used whenever the wording of a restriction requires a consent or certificate. As a result, it is suitable for use with the vast majority of standard form restrictions and many non-standard form restrictions. Note that HMLR is still refining its practice in relation to the use of this form so always check that the most up-to-date version of the form is being used.

HMLR will still accept consents and certificates described as above which are often provided on headed notepaper but HMLR is encouraging use of form RXC.

Activity

Go to HMLR PG19 and find the section on "Form RXC". Read the form at https://www.gov.uk/government/publications/restriction-consent-or-certificate-rxc and the relevant section of PG19 and make notes on how to complete and use the form. HMLR has specific requirements as to who should give the consent and their status in different situations. Take particular care to ensure that panel 3 is completed correctly.

Note that form RXC must accompany or relate to an application lodged under cover of form AP1. It can be used in all situations where a restriction on the register requires a consent or a certificate to be provided – this includes a certificate to comply with a Form LL restriction. A single form RXC cannot be used to provide consents or certificates in respect of multiple titles.

Activity

Follow the link below to the list of HMLR webinars. Select and watch the following:

Introducing form RXC
Restrictions (included in the section entitled "common reasons for requests for information")

https://www.gov.uk/guidance/hm-land-registry-webinars

12.2.8 Common restrictions

Conveyancing practitioners should be familiar with the most common restrictions that they are likely to encounter in practice. If a register contains a restriction which is not familiar to the conveyancer, they should immediately check PG19 to understand the nature and effect of the restriction.

It is essential that the conveyancer acting for a buyer considers the terms of all restrictions on the seller's proprietorship register prior to exchange of contracts to be satisfied as to the steps required to comply with the restriction. It is not safe to leave compliance with what might look like a fairly run-of-the-mill restriction until after completion. If the buyer's conveyancer is unable to secure compliance with the restriction, they may be unable to complete their registration application which could lead to a negligence claim.

The detailed workings of restrictions are beyond the scope of this course book particularly in relation to identifying a client's interest and applications to register the appropriate form of restriction. Examples of situations where practitioners may need to register a restriction to protect their client's interest apply to matrimonial matters or bankruptcy. We will look at some common restrictions which conveyancers might come across on a register of title and will briefly consider what is required to remove the restriction.

Link to practice

The importance of ensuring that a conveyancer can comply with a restriction prior to exchange of contracts cannot be overstated. Accordingly, in relation to all of the restrictions below, the buyer's conveyancer may need to liaise with the seller's conveyancer to seek confirmation as to the documents or evidence required to comply with the restriction. The buyer's conveyancer may consider it prudent to refer to documents which the seller might need to sign or produce in the contract and to agree the form of any documents prior to exchange to append to the contract.

The buyer's conveyancer may also seek an undertaking from the seller's conveyancer to hand over the required document or evidence on or before completion. Any such request for an undertaking should be treated with care by the seller's conveyancer. Remember that as a matter of professional conduct, an undertaking will bind the party giving the undertaking and potentially the firm. Best practice demands that anyone giving an undertaking must ensure that they can comply with it at the time the undertaking is given.

In any situation where the buyer's conveyancer is unsure as to whether the proposed declaration, statement, certificate or consent will be acceptable to HMLR, they should consider doing the following:

- insisting that the restriction is removed prior to exchange of contracts – in practice this might be difficult to achieve;
- contacting HMLR prior to exchange of contracts for their comments on the proposed document – in practice, HMLR are often helpful but will not give "advice" and in all cases will include a disclaimer that they cannot give a definitive comment on proposed documents until the registration is received;
- seek an undertaking from the seller's conveyancer that they will immediately and at their client's expense provide any assistance required by HMLR to ensure the removal of all compliance with the restriction in question.

Form A (Restriction on dispositions by sole proprietor)

"No disposition by a sole proprietor of the registered estate (except a trust corporation) under which capital money arises is to be registered unless authorised by an order of the court."

An interest under a trust of land can only be protected by a restriction which generally should be restriction in Form A. Any capital money must be paid to two trustees or a trust corporation. If there are two trustees in the transfer submitted for registration, HMLR will remove the Form A restriction automatically.

Form B (Dispositions by trustees of the legal estate – certificates required)

"No {disposition or specify type of disposition} by the proprietors of the registered estate is to be registered unless one or more of them makes a statutory declaration or statement of truth, or their conveyancer gives a certificate, that the {disposition or specify type of disposition} is in accordance with {specify the disposition creating the trust} or some variation thereof referred to in the declaration, statement or certificate."

The buyer's conveyancer should insist on sight of the appropriate statutory declaration, statement or truth or conveyancer certificate prior to exchange of contracts to enable the conveyancer to be satisfied that the proposed document will comply with the terms of the restriction.

Form C (Dispositions by personal representatives – certificate required)

"No disposition by the personal representative of {name} deceased, other than a transfer by way of assent, is to be registered unless such personal representative makes a statutory declaration or statement of truth, or their conveyancer gives a certificate, that the disposition is in accordance with the terms of

{choose whichever bulleted clause is appropriate}

- the will of the deceased [as varied by {specify date of, and parties to, deed of variation or other appropriate details}]
- the law relating to intestacy as varied by {specify date of, and parties to, deed of variation or other appropriate details}

or some [further] variation thereof referred to in the declaration, statement or certificate, or is necessary for the purposes of administration."

The buyer's conveyancer should insist on sight of the appropriate statutory declaration, statement or truth or conveyancer certificate prior to exchange of contracts to enable the conveyancer to be satisfied that the proposed document will comply with the terms of the restriction.

Form J (Trustee in bankruptcy and beneficial interest – certificate required)

"No disposition of the

{choose whichever bulleted clause is appropriate}

- registered estate, other than a disposition by the proprietor of any registered charge registered before the entry of this restriction
- registered charge dated [date] referred to above, other than a disposition by the proprietor of any registered sub-charge of that charge registered before the entry of this restriction

is to be registered without a certificate signed by the applicant for registration or their conveyancer that written notice of the disposition was given to {name of trustee in bankruptcy} (the trustee in bankruptcy of {name of bankrupt person}) at {address for service}."

If a bankruptcy petition is filed against a sole registered proprietor, a bankruptcy notice is entered in the register. Once the bankruptcy order has been made against the sole registered proprietor, a bankruptcy restriction is entered in the register. Where one or more joint registered proprietors is subject to a petition in bankruptcy or bankruptcy order, neither a bankruptcy notice nor a bankruptcy restriction will be entered. The trustee in bankruptcy will apply to enter a Form J restriction once the bankruptcy order has been made.

Compliance with the Form J restriction requires "a certificate signed by the applicant for registration or their conveyancer that written notice of the disposition was given to…". This means that compliance with the restriction is within the control of the buyer's conveyancer because they can give written notice of the disposition to the appropriate beneficiary and will be able to send evidence that this notice was given with their registration application.

However, the Form J restriction might be accompanied by a Form A restriction. The buyer's conveyancer must ensure that they obtain an undertaking from the seller's conveyancer to provide the appropriate document to remove the Form A restriction.

Form K (Charging order affecting beneficial interest – certificate required)

"No disposition of the

{choose whichever bulleted clause is appropriate}

- registered estate, other than a disposition by the proprietor of any registered charge registered before the entry of this restriction
- registered charge dated {date} referred to above, other than a disposition by the proprietor of any registered sub-charge of that charge registered before the entry of this restriction

is to be registered without a certificate signed by the applicant for registration or their conveyancer that written notice of the disposition was given to [name of person with the benefit of the charging order] at [address for service], being the person with the benefit of [an interim or a final] charging order on the beneficial interest of {name of judgment debtor} made by the {name of court} on [date] (Court reference {insert reference})."

Note that this is a different restriction in that compliance merely requires "a certificate signed by the applicant for registration or their conveyancer that written notice of the disposition was given to…". This means that compliance with the restriction is within the control of the buyer's conveyancer because they can give written notice of the disposition to the appropriate beneficiary and will be able to send evidence that this notice was given with their registration application.

Form L (Disposition by registered proprietor of a registered estate or proprietor of charge – certificate required)

"No [disposition {or specify type of disposition}] of the registered estate [(other than a charge)] by the proprietor of the registered estate [, or by the proprietor of any registered charge, not being a charge registered before the entry of this restriction,] is to be registered without a certificate signed by

{choose one of the bulleted clauses}

- a conveyancer
- the applicant for registration [or their conveyancer]
- {name} of {address} [or their personal representatives] [or [their conveyancer {or specify appropriate details}]]
- {name} of {address} [or their personal representatives] and {name} of {address} [or their personal representatives] [or [their conveyancer {or specify appropriate details}]]
- {name} of {address} and {name} of {address} or the survivor of them [or by the personal representatives of the survivor] [or [their conveyancer {or specify appropriate details}]]
- {name} of {address} or [after that person's death] by {name} of {address} [or [their conveyancer {or specify appropriate details}]]

that the provisions of {specify clause, paragraph or other particulars} of {specify details} have been complied with [or that they do not apply to the disposition].

Where the restriction applied for requires compliance with all of the provisions in a deed or document (rather than certain specified clauses) we will treat this as a non-standard form restriction. This must be applied for in form RX1 accompanied by the fixed fee.

Remember: A standard Form L restriction is used when a certificate is required that provisions in a deed have been complied with. If a consent is required, Form NN is an alternative standard restriction which gives the option of either a consent of a named party or a certificate."

This is potentially a wide ranging restriction and the buyer's conveyancer should carefully consider what is required to comply with it. If compliance requires a certificate provided by a third party, the buyer's conveyancer should require the seller's conveyancer to produce a draft of the required certificate together with written confirmation from the appropriate third party that they agree to the terms of the certificate. The seller's conveyancer should be required to give an undertaking to hand over the signed certificate on completion.

Link to practice

Conveyancers may find restrictions in this format on leasehold titles. It may provide that the management company has to give consent or a certificate to the registration. The purpose of this restriction is to protect the collection of service charge because the consent or certificate will only be given if the payments are up-to-date. The buyer's conveyancer may wish to liaise directly with the management company prior to exchange of contracts to ensure that the handing over of the appropriate consent or certificate is within their control.

The essential point for the buyer's conveyancer is to ensure that they attend to this prior to exchange of contracts. Too many conveyancers assume that the restriction consent or certificate will be handed over by the management company as a matter of course following completion and this can cause considerable delays to concluding their registration application.

Form N (Disposition by registered proprietor of registered estate or proprietor of charge - consent required)

"No [disposition {or specify type of disposition}] of the registered estate [(other than a charge)] by the proprietor of the registered estate [, or by the proprietor of any registered charge, not being a charge registered before the entry of this restriction,] is to be registered without a written consent signed by

{choose one of the bulleted clauses}

- {name} of {address} [or their personal representatives] [or [their conveyancer {or specify appropriate details}]]
- {name} of {address} [or their personal representatives] and {name} of {address} [or their personal representatives] [or [their conveyancer {or specify appropriate details}]]
- {name} of {address} and [name] of [address] or the survivor of them [or by the personal representatives of the survivor] [or [their conveyancer {or specify appropriate details}]]
- {name} of {address} or [after that person's death] by {name} of {address} [or [their conveyancer {or specify appropriate details}]]"

The Form N restriction is a specific restriction which will be used in narrow circumstances such as where a beneficiary is entitled to give consent to a disposition contained in a trust deed. This will only arise relatively rarely. A party that merely has an interest under a trust of land will register a Form A restriction. A consent restriction in Form N will not normally be appropriate in the circumstances as this would give the beneficiary a right that they are not entitled to. If the buyer's conveyancer encountered a Form N restriction, they would require an undertaking that form RX4 signed by the beneficiary of the restriction is supplied on completion.

Form P: Disposition by registered proprietor of registered estate or proprietor of charge – consent of proprietor of specified charge or certificate required

"No [disposition {or specify type of disposition}] of the registered estate [(other than a charge)] by the proprietor of the registered estate [, or by the proprietor of any registered charge, not being a charge registered before the entry of this restriction,] is to be registered without a written consent signed by the proprietor for the time being of the charge dated {date} in favour of {chargee} referred to in the charges register [or [their conveyancer {or specify appropriate details}]].

{The text of the restriction may be continued as follows, to allow for the provision of a certificate as an alternative to the consent.}

or without a certificate signed by

{choose one of the bulleted clauses}

- a conveyancer
- the applicant for registration [or their conveyancer]
- {name} of {address} [or [their conveyancer {or specify appropriate details}]]

that the provisions of {specify clause, paragraph or other particulars} of {specify details} have been complied with [or that they do not apply to the disposition].

Where the restriction applied for requires compliance with all of the provisions in a deed or document (rather than certain specified clauses) we will treat this as a non-standard form restriction. This must be applied for in form RX1 accompanied by the fixed."

This is a restriction requiring the consent of a particular lender to the registration of the disposition. The buyer's conveyancer should carefully consider what is required to comply with it. If the charge to which the restriction relates is going to be redeemed on completion, the restriction will be removed on registration. However, if the charge is going to remain on the register, the written consent of the specified lender will be required to register any disposition. Examples of the latter would be a transfer of equity or the registration of a subsequent charge.

Form AA (Freezing order on the registered estate)

"Under an order of the {name of court} made on {date} (Court reference {insert reference}) no disposition by the proprietor of the registered estate is to be registered except with the consent of {name} of {address} or under a further order of the Court."

Once a freezing order is granted, it will be protected by a restriction in Form AA or BB. Such a restriction on the register would alert the buyer's conveyancer to the fact that the seller is in financial difficulty. In general terms, a freezing order is an injunction preventing a defendant (or potential defendant) from disposing of all dissipating assets. The purpose is to preserve assets pending enforcement of a judgement. The buyer's conveyancer should proceed with extreme caution because the seller is unlikely to be permitted to proceed with the transaction.

Form II (Beneficial interest that is a right or claim in relation to a registered estate)

"No disposition of the registered estate, other than a disposition by the proprietor of any registered charge registered before the entry of this restriction, is to be registered without a certificate signed by the applicant for registration or their conveyancer that written notice of the disposition was given to {name} at {address}."

Note that this is a different restriction in that compliance merely requires "a certificate signed by the applicant for registration or their conveyancer that written notice of the disposition was given to…". This means that compliance with the restriction is within the control of the buyer's conveyancer because they can give written notice of the disposition to the appropriate beneficiary and will be able to send evidence that this notice was given with their registration application.

Form JJ (Statutory charge of beneficial interest in favour of the Lord Chancellor)

"No disposition of the

{choose whichever bulleted clause is appropriate}

- registered estate, other than a disposition by the proprietor of any registered charge registered before the entry of this restriction
- registered charge dated {date} referred to above, other than a disposition by the proprietor of any registered sub-charge of that charge registered before the entry of this restriction

is to be registered without a certificate signed by the applicant for registration or their conveyancer that written notice of the disposition was given to the Lord Chancellor, at {address and Lord Chancellor's reference number}."

This is a restriction denoting that the Legal Aid Agency has provided public financing for litigation in the past but has taken the statutory charge over the property to secure the repayment of that financing upon sale of the property. Compliance requires "a certificate signed by the applicant for registration or their conveyancer that written notice of the disposition was given to the Lord Chancellor, at...". This means that compliance with the restriction is within the control of the buyer's conveyancer because they can give written notice of the disposition to the appropriate beneficiary and will be able to send evidence that this notice was given with their registration application.

Form LL (Restriction as to evidence of execution)

"No disposition of the

{choose whichever bulleted clause is appropriate}

- registered estate by the proprietor of the registered estate
- registered charge dated {date} referred to above by the proprietor of that registered charge

is to be registered without a certificate signed by a conveyancer that that conveyancer is satisfied that the person who executed the document submitted for registration as disponor is the same person as the proprietor."

This is the anti-fraud restriction (and is often registered using form RQ (see https://www.gov.uk/government/publications/restriction-by-owner-not-living-at-property-request-registration-rq). The seller's conveyancer should check whether they are required to give the certificate at the time the contract is drafted. The buyer's conveyancer should request sight of the certificate and obtain an undertaking from the seller's conveyancer prior to exchange of contracts that the certificate will be given.

The buyer's conveyancer should check the provisions of PG19 carefully to ensure that all of HMLR's requirements in relation to the certificate of compliance are complied with; but note in particular:

- the certificate must be signed by a conveyancer in their own name and not in the name of the firm or employer;
- certificates signed by a member of the conveyancer's staff are not acceptable even if signed in the name of the individual conveyancer;
- the certificate must state "I certify", not "We certify";

- the conveyancer must sign the certificate personally in "wet ink". Such a certificate will also normally be required on an application to cancel or withdraw this restriction;
- the certificate of compliance must be signed in a conveyancer's own name and not by one of their staff in the firm's name;
- per pro signatures are not acceptable;
- while all chartered legal executives may verify identity, only CILEX Conveyancing Practitioners can provide certificates to comply with Form LL restrictions. Please note that it is not sufficient for the person giving the certificate to describe themselves simply as CILEX Practitioner; this must always be CILEX Conveyancing Practitioner;
- the restriction requires the conveyancer to certify that they are satisfied that the person who has executed the document submitted for registration as disponor is the same person as the proprietor. A certificate which merely states that the person who signed the document is the registered proprietor is therefore not acceptable;
- form RXC can be used (see above).

Example

HMLR states that an acceptable certificate might be as follows:

"I certify that I am satisfied that the person who has executed the ... (description of the document) submitted for registration as disponor is the same person as the proprietor of registered title ... . Signed by ... (name of individual conveyancer & status) ... (Signature in wet ink)"

12.3 HMLR requisitions

If HMLR has a question about a registration application that has been submitted, they will raise a "requisition" of the conveyancing firm that submitted the application. HMLR also calls them "requests for information".

The detail is in HMLR "Practice guide 50: requisition and cancellation procedures".

You should do the following to supplement this chapter:

Read and make notes on the above Practice Guide – here is the link: https://www.gov.uk/government/publications/requisition-and-cancellation-procedures/practice-guide-50-requisition-and-cancellation-procedures

Read and make notes on HMLR's general advice for conveyancers on how to avoid requisitions (and download the checklists and variation in names flowchart) – here is the link: https://www.gov.uk/guidance/hm-land-registry-requisitions

Go to HMLR's webinars page and watch the webinar "How to avoid requisitions; restrictions" and the guidance video on "avoiding requests for information (requisition)" – here is the link: https://www.gov.uk/guidance/hm-land-registry-webinars

Conveyancing firms should seek to minimise the number of requisitions received from HMLR. They should analyse their own registrations and data but note also that HMLR does the same. A failure to comply with a requisition to HMLR's satisfaction could result in the registration application being cancelled.

12.3.1 How HMLR raises requisitions and timeframes

HMLR might raise an informal telephone or email requisition if an issue can be dealt with quickly and easily. These will be held over for a maximum of three working days and if no response is received then a formal requisition will be issued.

Requisitions will be issued either in paper form, by email or by an alternative electronic means of delivery such as via Business Gateway.

For each application lodged using the portal, HMLR will use the email address supplied at the point of submission. This can pose a risk to conveyancing firms if the user who submitted the application is on holiday, leaves the firm or for some other reason is not monitoring their emails.

HMLR is willing to use an alternative or additional email address for raising requisitions if they receive a specific request from the firm to do so. Accordingly, to avoid the risk of requisitions received by email going astray, firms should always consider making a specific request to include an additional address. Note that if the email address supplied at the point of submission differs from the email address in an application form, HMLR will use the email address supplied on submission. If a firm needs to request the use of an alternative email address whilst an application is still pending, they should notify HMLR using the "reply to requisition" function in the portal.

In a formal requisition, HMLR will explain what they need and request a response as soon as possible. The application will be cancelled if HMLR does not receive a full reply but not before 20 working days have passed from the date of the requisition. If a full reply has not been received, they will send a reminder 20 working days before the application is due to be cancelled provided that an email address has been supplied at point of submission or there is an alternative electronic means of delivery, such as Business Gateway.

The specified period within which requisitions must be complied with is 20 working days from the date of requisition, but for most applications, HMLR will allow a longer period of 60 days. A warning of cancellation is normally sent after 40 working days which will explain how the firm can request an extension of time if they are still unable to reply fully in that time. HMLR will cancel the application in its entirety if they do not receive a full reply and a successful application for an extension of time to reply is not made.

12.3.2 Common requisitions and acceptable solutions

Some common requisitions and HMLR's suggested remedy are below.

Plans

Requisition

Extent of plot on plan to deed does not agree with that shown on the approved estate layout plan.

Tip

As approved estate layout plans are subject to revision, ensure the deed plan is based on the current version.

Requisition

Extent shown on plan does not agree with the property description supplied in clause LR4 of a prescribed clauses lease.

Tip

Ensure that clause LR4 of a prescribed clauses lease is completed to account for all the land included in the application to identify any exclusions and to agree with plan.

Requisition

Floor levels are not clear in plans relating to flats and other parts of buildings.

Tip

Ensure floor levels on plans are clearly defined and correspond with verbal references in the deed.

Ensure any edgings are not too thick and do not obscure any other detail on the plan. On a small-scale plan thick lines can be several metres across on the ground.

Requisition

On first registrations where the extent on the plan:

- *cannot be related to the Ordnance Survey map*
- *is not clearly defined, for example by edging, colouring or hatching*
- *includes land already registered*

Tip

Ensure any edgings are not too thick and do not obscure any other detail on the plan. On a small-scale plan thick lines can be several metres across on the ground.

Check the extent against the result of your search of the index map (form SIM).

Requisition

On first registrations plans that bear the following (or similar) statement of disclaimer, for example:

'Note: This plan is for reference only and although believed to be correct, its accuracy is in no way guaranteed and it is expressly excluded from any contract.'

Tip

We will accept a disclaimer that appears on deed plans created by National Grid Gas plc (Co Regn No 2006000) (formerly Transco plc) where the disclaimer relates to the positioning and/or existence of pipes, equipment and so on.

Requisition

On first registrations where a marking or colouring referred to in the text of a deed has been omitted from the plan.

On first registrations where plans have been reduced from their original scale but still bear the original scale endorsement.

Tips

Please prepare any plan for a new deed or application having regard to the following guidelines PG 40:

- *draw and show to its actual scale*
- *show its orientation (such as a north point)*

- *use preferred scales of 1/1250 - 1/500 for urban properties*
- *do not base on a scale of imperial measurement (for example, 16 feet to 1 inch)*
- *do not reduce in scale (see PG40)*
- *do not mark or refer to as being for identification only*
- *do not show statements of disclaimer used under the Property Misdescriptions Act 1991*
- *show sufficient detail to be identified on the Ordnance Survey map*
- *show its general location by showing roads, road junctions or other landmarks*
- *show the land of the property including any garage or garden ground*
- *show buildings in their correct (or intended) position*
- *show access drives or pathways if they form part of the property boundaries*
- *show the land and property clearly (for example by edging, colouring or hatching)*
- *have edgings of a thickness that does not obscure any other detail*
- *show separate parts by suitable plan markings (house, parking space, dustbin space)*
- *identify different floor levels (where appropriate)*
- *show intricate boundaries with a larger scale or inset plan*
- *show measurements in metric units only, to two decimal places*
- *show undefined boundaries accurately and, where necessary, by reference to measurements*
- *show measurements that correspond, so far as possible, to scaled measurements*

Missing deeds

Requisition

Deed omitted from application.

Tip

If you are temporarily unable to lodge a deed, please explain why and supply a certified copy.

Requisition

Deed lost or destroyed.

Tip

If a deed has been lost or destroyed please provide a duplicate, or where this is not feasible, evidence to support its original existence.

Deed incorrectly witnessed

Requisition

Signature not witnessed.

Tip

Each signature needs to be separately witnessed.

Requisition

Authority to execute not supplied.

Tip

Where a deed has been executed on behalf of a party please supply evidence of authority, for example:

- *grant of probate or letters of administration*
- *appointment of Trustee in Bankruptcy*
- *special resolution of the board*
- *deed of incorporation of non-English, Scottish or Welsh company*
- *certified copy of power of attorney*
- *appointment of Public Trustee*
- *copy of an HM Land Registry letter stating that evidence has already been filed with us and need not be produced*

Requisition

Deed has to be executed by donor where they have appointed another joint proprietor as attorney.

Tip

Certain requirements apply where a joint proprietor is acting as an attorney for the other joint proprietor(s).

A failure to indicate co-ownership

Requisition

Application does not state if a tenants in common restriction in Form A (Schedule 4 to the Land Registration Rules 2003) is required.

Application gives conflicting information about whether a Form A restriction is required.

No evidence of receipt of a notice of severance of joint tenancy.

Deed has to be executed by donor where they have appointed another joint proprietor as attorney.

Tips

When applying to register joint tenants, ensure that your application states the nature of the joint tenancy. Panels are provided for this on some forms (for example, panel 10 on form TR1, panel 9 on form FR1, panel 10 on form AS1 or clause LR14 of a prescribed clauses lease).

Ensure that the information in these panels does not conflict with any other information you supply. A restriction may be entered without further consultation if there is a conflict.

Ensure that any notice of severance is endorsed as received by the recipient.

Activity

Follow the link below and read and make notes on the "Application checklist: avoiding requisitions" on other common requisitions not mentioned above:

https://www.gov.uk/government/publications/requisition-and-cancellation-procedures/practice-guide-50-requisition-and-cancellation-procedures#-application-checklist-avoiding-requisitions

This contains a lot of practical information and tips on common requisitions and how to avoid them.

12.3.3 Missing identification information

When making an application for registration, the conveyancer has to confirm on the application form that appropriate evidence of identity for all parties to the transaction has been obtained. "Confirmation of identity" is the evidence required by:

- panels 12 to 14 of form AP1;
- panels 8 to 10 of form DS2;
- panels 14 to 16 of form FR1.

The purpose of this is to prevent registration fraud.

Activity

Follow the link below to HMLR "Practice guide 67: evidence of identity; conveyancers" and consider section 11. Look carefully at examples of how the conveyancer should complete the panels in form AP1:

https://www.gov.uk/government/publications/evidence-of-identity-conveyancers/practice-guide-67-evidence-of-identity-conveyancers

Conveyancers are affected by these identification requirements in two main ways:

- as the conveyancer sending an application to HMLR on behalf of the client; and
- as a conveyancer providing evidence of identity for an unrepresented person involved in a transaction using form ID1 or ID2.

The conveyancer will indicate on the form which has acted for the various parties in the transaction and, in essence, HMLR will rely on the fact that the conveyancing firm has obtained appropriate identification documents for the party involved. However, **r17 LRR 2003** allows HMLR to ask for more documents or evidence to help them complete an application and they may cancel the application if they do not provide what is needed.

There are certain exceptions to the **r17** identity requirement including, for example, the "low value exception'" which states that ID1 or ID2 is not required for an unrepresented party where the value of the land is £6,000 or less. It also might not be practicable to provide ID1 or ID2 such as where the parties exchanged contracts before 10 November 2008 (which is the date on which the requirement for confirmation of identity was introduced). In such situations, the conveyancer making the application should explain in a covering letter why they are not able to provide the identity evidence.

Activity

Follow the link below to HMLR "Practice guide 67: evidence of identity; conveyancer" and consider section 4 which contains a table setting out when confirmation of identity or rule 17 identity evidence is required. Please also note the exceptions:

https://www.gov.uk/government/publications/evidence-of-identity-conveyancers/practice-guide-67-evidence-of-identity-conveyancers

Also consider section 8 and consider how forms ID1 and ID 2 should be completed. Note that HMLR has agreed with CILEX and CILEX Regulation that all chartered legal executives can verify identity even though some may not be conveyancers.

12.4 Securing a positive obligation

We will now move on to consider how a positive obligation in the freehold context can be secured. Most covenants in freehold land are restrictive that is, negative in nature; this means that the party with the burden of the covenant does not need to take active steps to comply with it. Common examples might be:

> "not to use the property as anything other than a private dwellinghouse"
>
> "not to be a nuisance or annoyance to neighbouring property owners"

However, positive obligations arise in the freehold context and it is therefore necessary to consider how they can be enforced. If the positive covenant is something straightforward such as:

> "To maintain the fence between the points marked A and B on the plan",

then a failure to comply with this obligation might be somewhat irritating for the party with the benefit of the covenant but it is unlikely to involve substantial loss or diminution in value of the land with the benefit. Increasingly, however, freehold developments share a number of services which will remain in private ownership. This could include private roadways, park area, flood mitigation, to name but a few. You can see that such facilities will be more expensive to maintain and it is important for the development as a whole that the obligation to make the appropriate contribution to the cost of the services is secured in such a way that the obligation to make the payments can be adequately enforced against the freehold property owners.

Let's recap on why enforceability of positive covenants in the freehold context can be problematic and consider whether there are any sensible solutions. We will only give an outline of the key points and considerations; the detail is outside the scope of this course book.

12.4.1 Covenants – recap

Covenants are a way in which landowners attempt to control the use of land. A covenant is an agreement or a promise within a deed. The covenantor promises the covenantee that they will do, or refrain from doing, certain things on the land. Covenants are very useful because they can regulate relationships between owners of neighbouring land and, with the ability to bind successors in title, the value of land is maintained or increased. Covenants can also ensure that land is used efficiently.

Consider the situation regarding payment of money to maintain routes. If there is a shared driveway, one or possibly both of the parties will require rights of way over the driveway, and the non-owner will covenant to pay an appropriate part of the cost of repairs. Thus, the seller might continue to own the whole driveway to be used by both, but the buyer might receive an easement over it subject to their paying half the maintenance costs. Such covenants are often linked with easements in this way – the related benefit and burden ensures that the burden of the covenant continues to run (pass) at law with the land which has the benefit of the easement.

Positive and restrictive covenants

As we have seen, covenants are either positive or restrictive. Positive covenants impose on the covenantor an obligation to perform some specified act, or activity, in relation to a specified plot of land. Positive covenants tell the covenantor what they must do, though they may be so worded as to read – at first glance – like a negative obligation. For example, a covenant not to allow a party wall to fall into disrepair is, in fact, a positive covenant to keep it in repair.

Restrictive covenants, on the other hand, restrict the use of the covenantor's land. In other words, they tell them what they must not do. A covenant not to use land for any trade or business purposes is a restrictive covenant. Restrictive covenants are used to maintain the character of a property. A common covenant employed in "open plan" developments is that the covenantor shall not erect any boundary wall or fence which is more than one foot high. An example of the drafting of a restrictive covenant would be as follows:

> *"The Transferee, with the intent and so as to bind the land hereby transferred and to benefit and protect the retained land of the Transferor, hereby covenants with the Transferor that no buildings or structures erected on the land or any part thereof shall be used for any purposes whatsoever other than as a single private dwelling-house."*

Under the rule in ***Tulk v Moxhay* [1848]**, successors will generally be bound by such covenants in these situations (a sale of part, where the covenant is not intended to be personal). It may assist the running of the benefit to state that covenants are "for the benefit of the seller and his successors in title".

12.4.2 Enforcing the covenant

We are concerned here with how a positive obligation can be enforced.

Positive covenants require the covenantor to expend money or work in order to comply with them, for example, to paint the house every three years, erect and maintain a fence or pay half the cost of maintaining the shared driveway. Although such covenants are binding between the original covenantor and covenantee (and remain binding after the parties have sold on), it can be difficult to ensure that they continue to benefit and burden future owners of the properties.

The benefit of a positive covenant can pass in law and equity but the problem comes in relation to the burden of the covenant which does not pass.

There are some exceptions to this rule.

(1) s153 LPA 1925

This provides for a lease which is for more than 300 years' duration of which at least 200 years remain unexpired, which does not involve the payment of any rent and for which the landlord does not reserve the right to forfeiture for any breach, to be enlarged into a freehold estate. The enlarged freehold estate will be subject to the same covenants that were in the lease, including positive covenants. Positive covenants can run in leasehold land and it is therefore suggested, although not yet decided, that the covenants can bind a purchaser of the freehold estate. In terms of effectiveness, it is inconvenient to do this using **s153** and the conditions in the section have to be met. This is not widely applicable in practice.

(2) Mutual benefit and burden

The burden of covenants may bind third parties under the doctrine of "mutual benefit and burden" – also known as the rule in ***Halsall v Brizell* [1957]**.

This rule was considered by the Court of Appeal in ***Thamesmead Town v Allotey* [1998]**. It was held that the rule only allowed the enforcement of a burden which was directly related to the benefit being enjoyed. If a conveyance of land on a housing estate gives the purchaser the right to use the estate road, but at the same time imposes on them the liability to contribute to the cost of its upkeep, a successor in title cannot use the road without paying the contributions. The use of the road would not, however, also justify, for instance, a liability to contribute towards the upkeep of other communal facilities on the estate, such as landscaped areas.

In ***Davies v Jones* [2009]** the court emphasised the three requirements for the doctrine to be upheld.

(1) The burden must be conferred in or by the same transaction as the benefit.

(2) The benefit must be conditional on, or reciprocal to, the burden.

(3) The person who has the burden must have had the opportunity of rejecting or disclaiming the benefit, not merely the right to receive the benefit.

In the case the first condition was not met. Although there was an understanding between the parties that there was a benefit and burden, an understanding could not confer benefits nor impose burdens. It needed a transaction having legal effect so, as the benefit and burden related to land, a deed should have been used. The second condition was not met either as the benefit was not made conditional on the performance of the burden.

In ***Wilkinson v Kerdene* [2013]** it was held that the successors in title to owners of holiday bungalows had to comply with a covenant to pay towards the upkeep of the roads and footpaths in return for using them, provided there was a sufficient degree of correlation between the obligation of the positive covenant and the right being exercised. The grant of the right did not have to be expressly stated as conditional on the payment being made. Here, there was sufficient correlation and so payment had to be made. ***Goodman v Elwood* [2013]** stated that the burden of a positive covenant arising under ***Halsall*** does not have to be registered under the **LRA 2002** to bind successors in title to the covenantor because it did not create an estate or interest in land but was a personal right in equity to enforce the covenant.

(3) Chain of indemnity covenants

Another situation where positive covenants will continue to bind is if a chain of indemnity covenants is set up. Successive purchasers from the covenantor of the burdened land undertake to indemnify (compensate) their immediate predecessor in title, that is, the seller from whom they purchased the burdened land. The original covenantor will remain liable upon their initial covenant because of privity of contract but should they be sued, they can sue their immediate successor, who will then sue their successor and so on.

Theoretically, the chain can extend – link by link – indefinitely. In practice, such protection is lost by the disappearance or insolvency of the original covenantor, or the breaking of the chain by a conveyance of the servient land where no indemnity is obtained. Another weakness is that the owner of the dominant tenement can claim damages only. This will not resolve the actual breach of the covenant. These two weaknesses in chains of indemnities undermine their value.

So, on sale of the land with the burden of the covenant, the seller insists that the buyer covenants to observe and perform the existing covenant and to indemnify the seller accordingly. Any prudent seller who gave a positive covenant or an indemnity covenant when they bought should insist on this. It might be possible to set this up by including a covenant in the conveyance that the present buyer must, when they sell, enter into an appropriate covenant with their then buyer.

As we have seen, the weakness with the chain of indemnity covenants is that the further away a transaction is from the date that the original positive covenant was imposed, the more likely it is that the chain of indemnity will be broken. Over time, an incoming buyer may fail to give an indemnity covenant to the seller and the chain of indemnity breaks down.

Link to practice

The conveyancer will know if an indemnity covenant was given by the seller when they purchased the land because the wording will be contained in the conveyance by which the seller acquired the land if the title is unregistered. If the title is registered, the following wording will be included on the proprietorship register to indicate that the registered proprietor gave an indemnity covenant when they purchased:

> *"The transfer to the proprietor contains a covenant to observe and perform the covenants referred to in the Charges Register and of indemnity in respect thereof."*

If this wording is not contained on the proprietorship register, the seller is not entitled to demand an indemnity covenant from the incoming buyer.

Some conveyancers might include a special condition in the contract to provide that the buyer should give an indemnity covenant in the transfer on completion. However, this is not strictly necessary because the Standard Conditions of Sale provide as follows:

> *"4.6.4 If after completion the Seller will remain bound by any obligation affecting the property which was disclosed to the buyer before the contract was made, but the law does not imply any covenant by the buyer to indemnify the seller against liability for future breaches of it:*
>
> *(a) the buyer is to covenant in the transfer to indemnify the seller against liability for any future breach of the obligation and to perform it from then on"*

An important point for the seller is to ensure that if the buyer is giving an indemnity covenant, the buyer (transferee) signs the transfer and a duplicate transfer is provided by the buyer on completion. Alternatively, the buyer could sign the transfer in escrow (that is, in readiness for completion) and the seller's conveyancer could retain a certified copy of the signed transfer on completion. By signing the transfer, the transferee is indicating their willingness to be bound by the indemnity covenant contained in the transfer.

(4) Restriction and deed of covenant

A very common method of securing a positive obligation that conveyancers will frequently encounter is a transfer of part which imposes an obligation requiring an incoming buyer to enter into a deed of covenant with the party for the time being which takes the benefit of the covenant. In this way, the incoming buyer covenants to take the burden of the positive obligations and, of course, privity of contract has been created between the parties for the time being of the land taking the benefit and burden.

On a freehold estate where services are provided for the benefit of property owners, the party with the obligation to provide the services and collect the service charge is often a management company so the incoming buyer of each freehold property enters into a separate deed of covenant with the management company upon completion of their purchase.

It can be seen that this mechanism could still break down if an incoming buyer simply failed to enter into the deed of covenant. Accordingly, this mechanism is reinforced by placing an appropriate restriction on the register of the burdened land which prevents any disposition of the land unless the person to whom it is disposed of enters into a similar covenant.

Link to practice

The deed of covenant backed up by a restriction mechanism is probably the most familiar method of securing a positive obligation and is one which most conveyancers are comfortable with. Assuming that the terms of the covenants are not unduly onerous, this mechanism will be acceptable to buyers and lenders and is favourable to the rentcharge referred to below.

Example

In addition to the positive obligations to contribute to the service charge payments, the transfer of part is likely to contain a covenant by the transferee as follows:

"Not to transfer the Property or any part of it without procuring that the Transferee enters into a Deed of Covenant"

The terms of the deed of covenant might be contained in the transfer. The key terms that should be included are:

- **date** – the deed should be the same date as the transfer;
- **parties** – this should include the rentcharge holder (for example, developer or management company), outgoing seller and incoming buyer;
- **property** – details of the property to which the deed relates;
- **original transfer** – details of the transfer of part containing the rentcharge obligations;
- **new covenant** – the incoming buyer must covenant with the rentcharge holder to comply with the terms of the original transfer from the date of the deed of covenant.

The transfer of part will also contain a provision whereby the parties apply to register a restriction, which is likely to be based on the form L restriction. An example might be:

"Application to register a restriction

The Transferor and the Transferee apply to the Chief Land Registrar at HM Land Registry to enter the following restriction against the title number to be allocated to the Property:

No disposition of the registered estate (other than a charge) by the Proprietor of the registered estate or by the proprietor of any registered charge is to be registered without the certificate signed by [INSERT PARTY] that the provisions of clauses [INSERT RELEVANT CLAUSES] of the Transfer dated [INSERT DATE] between [INSERT PARTIES] have been complied with"

(5) Rentcharges

In recent years, developers have turned to rentcharges as a means of enforcing positive covenants on freehold developments. However, as many conveyancing practitioners will be aware, this mechanism is not without its problems.

s1(2)(b): *A rentcharge in possession issuing out of or charged on land being either perpetual or for a term of years absolute.*

A rentcharge is a right to a periodic payment of money attached to freehold land. It should not be confused with the rent payable by a tenant to a landlord under a lease. This is strictly called rent-service.

There are two types of rentcharge, the first being the rather old-fashioned historic rentcharges which are commonly encountered with old housing stock in certain parts of the country (mainly the North West and the Bristol and Bath areas). On sale, a seller would not just demand a lump sum payment as is usual, but would also reserve the right to a periodic payment of money which, being an interest in land, is capable of passing to the seller's successors. Historically, these are relatively small sums and if they have not been demanded or paid for a number of years, a buyer will often require a seller to provide an indemnity insurance policy to insure against the possibility of a demand for historic rentcharge being made. It is no longer possible to create this type of rentcharge. Under **s2(1) Rentcharges Act 1977** provides that, with exceptions, *no rentcharge may be created whether at law or in equity* after 22 August 1977.

The second type of rentcharge is an estate rentcharge. This a means whereby positive covenants are made to run in housing or industrial estates. An estate rentcharge is a periodical payment in respect of land. The owner of the rentcharge can demand a rent from the owner of the land that is affected. When a rentcharge is granted, the owner of the charge can also require the covenantor to enter into other covenants, such as a covenant to repair. Estate rentcharges are excluded from the prohibition on the creation of new rentcharges under the **Rentcharges Act 1977** meaning that this is the type of rentcharge that developers create to secure the positive obligation to pay service charges on freehold estates.

One of the problems with charges is the remedies available to enforce non-payment. There is an action for debt but the wide-ranging remedies under **s121 Law of Property Act 1925** include: a right of entry into possession and the right to grant a lease of the charged land. This is a very Draconian remedy in that the rentcharge holder could legitimately enter the premises and grant a lease to a trustee. The validity of this remedy was confirmed in ***Roberts v Lawton* [2016]**.

Activity

Follow the link below to the judgement in ***Roberts v Lawton* [2016]**:

https://www.bailii.org/uk/cases/UKUT/TCC/2016/395.html

Read the judgment and make notes on the law relating to rentcharges.

Look at paragraph 33 of the judgment – do you think that the judge approves of the rentcharge lease as a means of enforcement?

The wide-ranging nature of these remedies means that lenders are more wary of these provisions because they might put the lenders' security at risk and as a result, many buyers' conveyancers are trying to find solutions to mitigate the problems caused by **s121**. One solution is for the transfer of part to provide that the remedies contained in **s121** are not applicable, but this is often not acceptable to the developer's conveyancer. An alternative solution is to amend the remedies contained in **s121** to provide that there is no right to grant the lease if the rentcharge remains unpaid.

Link to practice

This area has become complex in practice and only a couple of possible solutions to the problem have been mentioned. Often, in practice, the amendments to the **s121** remedies are negotiated between the conveyancers.

The attitude of the lenders to rentcharges differ wildly. It is essential for the conveyancer acting for the lender and buyer to check the lender's requirements under Part 2 of the Lenders Handbook.

The lenders are frequently changing their requirements regarding what is acceptable in terms of rentcharges to secure positive obligations and the conveyancer must always ensure that they are complying with the most up-to-date requirements.

Note that the **Leasehold and Freehold Reform Act 2024 (LFRA 2024)** is on the statute book, although most of it is not yet in force (see **Chapter 13** update). However, an important provision came into force on 24 July 2024. It abolishes the **s121** remedies for the "historic" rentcharges (which can no longer be created following the **Rentcharges Act 1977**). The result is that this will remove the need to enter into a deed of variation to mitigate the effect of the **s121** provisions for "historic" rentcharges. However, **LFRA 2024** does not abolish the application of **s121** to the more problematic estate rentcharges.

(6) Other possibilities

An alternative way of ensuring that covenants are binding on successors is not to sell the freehold at all. Covenants in a long lease will generally bind successors. By granting a lease rather than a fee simple absolute, the purchaser of leasehold land will generally be bound by both positive and negative covenants. This is a very common method of enforcing positive obligations, particularly when occupiers are in close proximity, for example, in blocks of flats. Typically, a 999-year lease will be granted, the grant including enforceable obligations upon the tenant to maintain, repair, etc. The difficulty is that the leasehold covenant is enforceable only by the landlord, not by other tenants.

Another alternative is that the covenantee requires the covenantor to ask for the covenantee's consent to sell the burdened land. Consent would only be given if the purchaser of the burdened land entered into a new covenant with the covenantee or their successors in title. In registered land a restriction entered on the register of the burdened land would prevent sale in breach of the requirement. However, such a requirement would almost certainly detract from the attraction and value of the property.

It is also possible to ensure that such interests run with the land if a freehold estate in commonhold is granted (see **Chapter 13**). The common law will enforce covenants only within very narrow limits. The **Commonhold and Leasehold Reform Act 2002** (**CLRA 2002**) does, however, address the particular problem of blocks of flats and other multi-occupied properties. The common method of granting long leases with a view to enforcing obligations in such cases can be replaced by the freehold ownership of individual units in such properties. Under the commonhold ownership scheme in **CLRA 2002**, each unit holder is a member of a commonhold association which owns the common parts of the shared property, such as its structure and means of access. The commonhold association is responsible for the repair, maintenance and insurance of these common parts, funded by service charges collected from each unit holder. The rights and obligations of each unit holder are governed by a commonhold community statement in respect of the property and become mutually binding by force of statute, regardless of any subsequent change in the ownership of the individual unit. The disadvantage is that there may be difficulties in, for example, converting existing leasehold into commonhold. Whilst commonhold is a method of avoiding the problem that the burden of a positive covenant does not run with the land; it is rarely used and few commonholds have been created.

Activity

Follow the link below to a House of Commons Library briefing paper (number 8560, 14 December 2020) entitled "Freehold covenants":

https://commonslibrary.parliament.uk/research-briefings/cbp-8560

Download the paper and read it. Make notes as necessary. It contains a very useful overview of the nature of freehold covenants and the challenges relating to enforceability. It also contains some suggestions for possible reform.

12.5 Chapter summary

Restrictions

- (1) The detail regarding restrictions is contained in HMLR Practice Guide 19.
- (2) A restriction is an entry in the register that prevents or regulates the making of an entry in the register in respect of any disposition or a disposition of a specified kind.
- (3) A restriction must not be registered without reasonable cause as **s77 LRA 2002** imposes a duty to act reasonably.
- (4) There is a wide-ranging of standard restrictions at Appendix B of PG19; it should not be necessary to use a non-standard restriction.
- (5) A restriction can be entered on a register because it is included in a document such as a TP1, otherwise form RX1 must be used.
- (6) A restriction can be withdrawn using form RX4.
- (7) A restriction can be cancelled using form RX3.
- (8) HMLR has specific requirements regarding the format of restriction consent and certificates.
- (9) Restriction consent must be to the registration, not the disposition.
- HMLR has introduced Form RXC to assist with the provision of restriction consents and certificates; it contains standardised wording and format.
- (10) Conveyancers must consider the restriction on the register prior to exchange of contracts to ensure that they can comply with it when they make the registration application following completion.

HMLR requisitions

- (1) If HMLR has a question about a registration application that has been submitted, they will raise a requisition; also called a "request for information".
- (2) The detailed requirements are contained in HMLR Practice Guide 50.
- (3) A written requisition will give the firm 20 working days to comply with the requisition; it is possible to apply for an extension.

Securing a positive obligation

- (1) The benefit of a positive covenant can pass in law and equity but the problem comes in relation to the burden of the covenant which does not pass.

- (2) There are some exceptions to this rule:
  - s153 LPA 1925;
  - mutual benefit and burden;
  - chain of indemnity covenants;
  - restriction and deed of covenant;
  - rentcharge.

CHAPTER 13
Proposed reform

13.1 Introduction

Conveyancing is a fast-moving area at the moment in terms of reform. The pandemic and SDLT "holiday" led to considerable delays and pressures for all involved in the home moving process and the government has turned its eye again to possible reform. We will mention a few areas that are on the horizon, but conveyancers should keep abreast of changes in this area.

We have mentioned commonhold in this course book as the third form of land ownership, designed to try to overcome some of the drawbacks of freehold and leasehold. It has been with us for some time, but it proved very unpopular in practice and so has had little prominence; which was reinforced when some standard conditions of sale mentioning commonhold were dropped from the fifth edition of the contract of sale. The Law Society's explanatory notes to the fifth edition stated:

> "Condition 9 of the fourth edition of the SCS has been deleted. Commonhold is not widely used as a firm of tenure. Where relevant, provision for commonhold land should be make by special condition (April 2011)."

However, commonhold is back on the agenda and the Law Commission favour it, so we have included more information about this in case you encounter it in practice.

We will also mention digital changes being introduced by HMLR and on the possible mandating of reservation agreements.

This chapter will cover:

- commonhold;
- HMLR digital developments;
- reservation agreements;
- leasehold reform.

13.2 Commonhold

13.2.1 Introduction

Commonhold ownership has only been available since 2004. This chapter will look at how the commonhold system works and the type of property it can be used for.

Commonhold aims to address some of the failings in the leasehold system and is designed to be an innovative way of holding communal property and governing the arrangements for service charges, etc. in a fairer way, with the unit holders (e.g. individual flat owners) responsible for the decisions about the communal areas instead of the landlord. That said, it has not proved popular so far. It is very difficult to convert an existing leasehold property to commonhold and so in practical terms it is really only available to new developments. The associated costs of setting up a commonhold association and registering the commonhold with the Land Registry has acted as a disincentive for setting up commonhold property developments. Also, some developers do not fully understand why commonhold may be a better way forward, and many lenders are reluctant to lend against commonhold for a variety of reasons. So, although it exists and you should be aware of the advantages of this type of landholding, it is still rare at present and it is unlikely you will come across this very often in practice.

A large proportion of flats in England and Wales are held under long leases. Traditionally, the reason for this has been the difficulty of ensuring that the burden of positive obligations, such as to contribute to the cost of repair or insurance costs, runs with the freehold title to land (see Chapter 12). Thus, a developer selling off a block of flats would, generally speaking, be able to ensure that future owners of the property who were not the original owners could be required to pay for the upkeep of the structure, exterior and common parts of a block only by granting long leases. There are two main disadvantages, however, for owners in receiving a long lease.

(1) Leases are wasting assets, as they are limited in time. Generally speaking, it becomes more difficult to sell and obtain a mortgage to buy a lease of residential property once the unexpired residue of the term of the lease falls below

about 70 years. Though residential lessees have statutory rights to extend their leases and, collectively, to acquire their lessor's freehold, this can be a slow and costly process, so the value of the lessee's interest in the lease diminishes significantly as time passes.

(2) The freehold of the block may be owned by a lessor who has little incentive to manage the block properly. Legislation since 1985 has strengthened the rights of lessees against landlords but lessees can still encounter significant difficulties with landlords charging excessive service charges or failing to maintain buildings properly.

In an attempt to eliminate such problems, proposals were made as long ago as 1987 to introduce a new form of ownership, which would give the occupant and owner of a property an interest equivalent to a freehold but which would also vest the ownership of common parts and the obligation to maintain the property in an association jointly managed by the occupants of a block or estate. This form of ownership would also require subsequent owners of each unit to comply with positive obligations, such as to pay towards the upkeep of the block or estate.

The commonhold provisions are contained in **Part 1 CLRA 2002** and were brought into force in September 2004 by the introduction of:

- the **Commonhold Regulations 2004** (**CR 2004**); and
- the **Commonhold (Land Registration) Rules 2004** (**C(LR)R 2004**).

A great deal of the practical working detail of **CLRA 2002** is contained in the regulations, which have been amended several times since 2004.

As this form of tenure is not often encountered in practice, the following discussion of this part of **CLRA 2002** is only in general terms.

13.2.2 Nature of commonhold

Commonhold is designed to be of use where there are interdependent properties with common facilities, for example, blocks of flats, retirement developments and business parks.

Commonhold is a form of freehold tenure in land. For land to be commonhold, it must first be registered as a freehold estate in land although an application for first registration can be submitted at the same time as a commonhold registration application. The Land Registry will then complete the first registration application before the commonhold one. Therefore, commonhold can only be used for registered land, and does not apply to unregistered land.

Each separate property in a commonhold development, such as a flat, house or business unit, is termed a **commonhold unit** and can comprise more than one separate area of land; so, for instance, a commonhold unit can consist of a flat with a garage, rather than simply being a flat. Though the legislation was primarily aimed at giving the owners of flats a better form of tenure than leasehold, land can be divided into commonhold units either vertically or horizontally, and each commonhold unit can be a free-standing property. Therefore, an estate of detached houses could equally be divided into commonhold units, rather than being sold as separate freehold units. In addition, the use of commonhold is not restricted to residential property and can equally be used for commercial properties, such as an estate of industrial units.

Any part of a commonhold title which is a common part or shared facility will be owned by a **commonhold association** (CA) (effectively a residents' association). The CA will manage the common parts and facilities and will be a company limited by guarantee whose members will be the current commonhold unit-holders. Each CA must consist of at least two unit-holders, and each unit-holder will have a direct interest in their unit and an interest, in common with the other unit-holders, in the association. **CLRA 2002** specifies the principal documents which will govern the operation of the association and the relationships between the members.

(1) The CA must, like any company, have **Articles of Association** which will set out the objects of the company, govern what the association can do and detail procedure and rules for managing the association itself.

(2) In addition, each CA must have a **commonhold community statement** (CCS), which will contain the rules and regulations for operating and managing the property. This operates much like the terms of a lease, except that one document covers all unit-holders in an estate rather than each owner having an individual document for their own unit. The terms of the CCS bind the individual members and are enforceable by the CA against each unit-holder.

It should be noted that a CA can control more than one distinct area of land, so two separate developments may be covered by the same CA.

Much of the content of any commonhold scheme (specifically, the CCS and the Articles of Association of the CA) is prescribed, particularly in the case of a residential scheme. There is, therefore, little discretion for particular schemes to tailor the rules to their own schemes (though, notably, it is possible to give different unit-holders different voting rights in the CA).

Example

Daljit is a first-time buyer and has been looking for a property to purchase. She has decided not to buy a leasehold flat but to purchase a flat on a commonhold development called *Meadowfields*. The way commonhold would work is as follows:

Daljit would own the freehold of her flat. Her flat would be termed a "unit" or a "commonhold unit". She would be called the "unit-holder" of the flat.

Daljit would be a member of the commonhold association for her development. The commonhold association would own the freehold of the common parts, such as the communal gardens, communal stairways and the communal car park. The association would insure, repair and maintain the common parts.

There would be a commonhold community statement, setting out the rules for the commonhold. These might, for instance, say that Daljit cannot use her unit for business purposes, that she must not do anything to cause annoyance to other unit holders or that she must make certain payments (the equivalent of service charges).

13.2.3 Restrictions on commonhold

CLRA 2002 specifies certain land which cannot be commonhold: only registered land can be commonhold, and the following land, even if registered, cannot be commonhold:

- land at first-floor level or above unless the land below it is also commonhold; this prevents "flying freeholds" from being commonhold;
- agricultural land; and
- certain titles which are contingent, meaning titles which may revert to previous owners under certain statutes; such titles are rare and this would essentially apply only to former schools or churches.

In addition, any land which is part of a commonhold unit cannot be above or below any other land which is not part of the same CA. It is therefore not possible to have two or more associations operating directly above or below each other over the same land.

13.2.4 Creation of commonhold and consents

Broadly speaking, there are two types of situation where an application may be made to register land as commonhold:

- where there is an existing development of leaseholders (e.g. a block of flats) where the occupants wish to convert to commonhold (**registration with unit-holders**); and
- where a developer wishes to register a new development as commonhold before selling units to individual unit-holders (**registration without unit-holders**).

In each case, the procedure for registration is slightly different – however, for both, certain basic information and documents need to be provided to the Land Registry to register the land as commonhold. In addition, the CA must be formed before the application takes place and this will involve incorporating the CA using Articles which comply with **CR 2004** and appointing directors.

Applications are made on Land Registry form CM1 (https://www.gov.uk/government/publications/commonhold-land-freehold-registration-cm1). The following documentation must also be included with the application:

- certified copies of the CA's Articles of Association and its certificate of incorporation;
- a certified copy of the CCS;
- a certificate of compliance signed by the directors of the CA that the documentation supplied complies with **CLRA 2002**, that the CA has not traded and not incurred any liability, and that the land is not prohibited from becoming commonhold;
- the fee;
- a plan which shows the location of the common parts and the individual units;
- for a **registration with unit-holders**, form COV must be completed which lists the units and the proposed unit-holders;
- all necessary consents to convert to commonhold as required by **CLRA 2002** and **CR 2004** on form CON1 together with a statement of truth by the directors in a specified form confirming that all necessary consents have been obtained.

Various consents are required to create commonhold over an existing registered freehold.

(1) Consent of all registered proprietors of the freehold of all or part of the land concerned.

(2) Consent of the registered proprietors of all leasehold estates granted for a term of more than 21 years of all or part of the land concerned.

(3) Consent of the registered proprietor of a charge of any estate in (1) or (2) over all or any part of the land.

(4) Consent of cautioners of any of these interests.

(5) Anyone else prescribed by regulations – this includes owners of unregistered interests (e.g. unregistered leases).

So, for example, a developer who is sole owner of a piece of vacant registered freehold land and who wishes to create a development of commonhold units must only obtain the consent of any mortgage lender of the land before applying to convert the land to commonhold. For those who wish to convert existing blocks of leasehold flats to commonhold, however, the process is much more complicated. Though it is possible to convert existing blocks and estates containing existing long leases to commonhold, it is likely that few will attempt to do this in practice as it will be necessary to obtain the consent of all leaseholders in the block or estate, the mortgage lenders of those lessees as well as the consent of the freeholder and the freeholder's mortgagee.

As long as all Land Registry requirements have been satisfied, the land will be registered as commonhold land and, if it is a registration with unit-holders, individual owners will be registered with title to their commonhold units and the CA as proprietor of the common parts.

In addition, **CLRA 2002** provides that the effect of the conversion to commonhold will be to extinguish all existing leases, whether registered or not. Therefore, where some owners in a block of flats have sub-let their properties, whether by assured, assured shorthold or other form of residential tenancy, they may well be unwilling to consent to the creation of a commonhold scheme as this will result in them losing their tenants. Such tenants have the right to have granted a compensation lease from the CA; however, it is likely that this will prevent conversions to commonhold taking place where long lessees have sub-let their properties. It is therefore likely that the majority of commonholds will be registrations without unit-holders (i.e. new developments).

On a registration without unit-holders where a commonhold is being established because land is being redeveloped, **CLRA 2002** provides a transitional period for developers between the time that a commonhold scheme is established and when the first unit is sold. During that period, it may be necessary for the developer to make certain decisions about the land and its management. **CLRA 2002** and **CR 2004** enable the developer to include rights in the CCS to enable them to make decisions about the land up until the time the first unit is sold off, without such decisions being taken by the CA. In addition, until the first unit-holder is registered, the CA will not be registered as proprietor of the common parts, and the rights and duties imposed on it by registration come into effect only when the first unit is disposed of.

Until the first unit is sold, the developer will be registered as proprietor of the freehold of the common parts and the individual units, with the common parts transferring to the CA upon registration of the first unit-holder.

Activity

A more detailed summary of the forms and information required to register land as commonhold can be found in HMLR's Practice guide 60, which is located on the HMLR website at:

www.gov.uk/government/publications/commonhold/practice-guide-60-commonhold

Read it and consider in particular the consents required for registration.

13.2.5 Commonhold units and unit-holders

As stated above, an application to register land as commonhold must also include a plan detailing the extent of the commonhold units. This must be defined by the CCS. The elements of each unit need not be contiguous (so can include, for example, a house and a separate parking space) and each unit need not contain all or part of a building, so can be an area of bare land (e.g. a car park).

Each commonhold unit can be owned jointly, though only one registered owner can be a member of the CA. If joint owners do not nominate one of their number as the member of the association for that unit, the person first named on the register of title becomes the member. It is not possible for someone who is not an owner of a unit to be a CA member.

A unit-holder cannot resign from membership of the association, but will cease to be a member of the association once the interest in the unit is transferred. The CCS cannot restrict or prevent the transfer or charging of the whole of the unit, so unit-holders are free to sell or mortgage the entire unit as they wish. Dispositions of part, however, are restricted. Notably, on the transfer of a unit, the new unit-holder must notify the CA of the transfer.

13.2.6 Effect of a transfer of a unit

The effect of transferring a unit to a new unit-holder will be to pass all rights and responsibilities which the former unit-holder had before that date to the new unit-holder. In this way, all positive obligations contained in the CCS by which the unit-holder is bound will pass with the transfer of the unit. A former unit-holder cannot be responsible for any obligation arising after the date of transfer, and any provision in a contract or transfer which attempts to override this is void.

The CA will be able to seek any arrears of commonhold assessment (service charge) from anyone who is subsequently registered as proprietor of the commonhold unit. **CR 2004**, however, make it clear that an incoming unit-holder can apply to the CA for a certificate which confirms how much the outgoing unit-holder owes and, if provided, this limits the liability of the incoming unit-holder to not more than the figure specified in the certificate.

13.2.7 Restrictions on leasing

The purpose of **Part 1 CLRA 2002** is to ensure that some of the problems inherent in granting long leases are avoided. It would therefore seem odd if, having provided a system such as commonhold which seeks to avoid these problems, owners of commonhold units recreated such problems by granting long leases of their units.

For this reason, the legislation places restrictions on the powers of unit-holders to grant leases, though a distinction is drawn between residential and commercial commonholds.

(1) Residential commonholds

For residential commonholds, **CR 2004** specify restrictions on the length of term, circumstances of letting and any other term of any lease which a unit-holder may grant. Only leases which satisfy the following criteria are permitted:

- leases granted without a premium (i.e. without payment of a capital sum) and at a market (rack) rent;
- for a maximum period of seven years (which would mean that any such lease would not be registrable under **LRA 2002** and that the obligation to maintain the structure and exterior of the property would rest with the unit-holder landlord – **ss11–14 LTA 1985**);
- are used only for residential purposes.

(2) Commercial commonholds

For commercial, non-residential commonholds, **CLRA 2002** envisaged fewer restrictions. In fact, the rights of unit-holders to grant leases can be restricted only by provisions in the CCS. **CR 2004** do not prescribe any restrictions on granting leases of commercial commonhold units, as most commercial unit holders wish to have maximum flexibility to lease their units. Any restrictions on leasing commercial commonhold units should therefore be included within the CCS, if required.

One notable feature of leases of commonhold, which can apply to both residential and commercial units, is that the CCS can require lessees of unit-holders to pay the commonhold assessment (the form of service charge levied by the CA) directly to the association. The tenant of the unit-holder can then offset this against rent which they owe their landlord (the unit-holder).

13.2.8 Disposals of part

Because of the difficulties which would arise in respect of membership and constitution of the CA, **CLRA 2002** prevents the creation of interests in part only of a unit. Though unit-holders may, in some circumstances, create leases of part (subject to the type of restrictions referred to above), freehold dispositions of part will be prohibited. The only exception to this is a disposition of the freehold where the CA consents in writing – this will require a resolution with a 75 per cent majority of those voting. In practice, it would seem that this would occur very rarely.

There is an absolute prohibition on granting mortgages of part, though notably, the CA cannot restrict the granting of mortgages over the entire unit, and the unit-holders' powers of charging the whole of the unit are, therefore, unlimited.

13.2.9 Common parts

The common parts of any commonhold title remain vested in the CA. **CLRA 2002** defines common parts as those parts of the commonhold which are not defined in the CCS as units. Some areas of the development may well be available to specified unit-holders (e.g. a particular area of gardens or a specified access way). **CLRA 2002** allows these areas to be designated as limited use areas and for use and access to such areas to be regulated by the CCS.

The CA has power to deal with parts of the common parts; for example, the association may sell an area of land to a developer if the members decide under the Articles that this will benefit them and the association. The association, however, requires a unanimous resolution of all those voting to change the common parts.

CLRA 2002 allows the CA to add to the common parts by acquiring additional land, though the consent of any mortgage lender will be required. As this will alter the area of land controlled by the CA, the CCS must be altered if additional common parts are acquired or disposed of. In addition, the consent of an existing mortgage lender of the common parts is also required.

13.2.10 Commonhold community statement

The CCS defines the rules and regulations for the operation and management of the development and the rights and duties which the association and the unit-holders owe to each other. It is a very significant document in commonhold developments. **CLRA 2002** requires the CCS to be in a prescribed form, and gives power to make regulations determining the form of the CCS.

CR 2004 set out a prescribed form for the CCS which includes mandatory provisions and certain alternative and optional contents. Mandatory requirements include:

(1) A description of the land and of the commonhold units, together with any details of limited rights areas and plans in specified forms. **CR 2004** prescribe that, where a unit is part of a larger independent structure, the structure and exterior will be common parts, maintainable by the CA.

(2) Details of the type of commonhold (i.e. residential, non-residential or mixed use).

(3) Rules of the CA, such as those concerned with dealings with the units and the common parts, repair, insurance and payment of the commonhold assessment (the term used for service charges within a commonhold development). Note, again, that it is a requirement of **CR 2004** that, where a unit is part of a larger structure, the CA must maintain the structure and exterior, and insure the building).

(4) Rules relating to enforcement of obligations.

The legislation itself lists a number of duties which the CCS may include: to pay money, to undertake or refrain from undertaking works, to grant access, to refrain from entering into certain transactions, and to refrain from causing nuisance or annoyance. Such duties will, if included in the CCS, be binding upon the association and the unit-holders without the requirement for further formalities such as a deed. The only formality required will be for the CCS to be signed by, or on behalf of, the original applicants for registration.

In effect, the CCS will operate in much the same way that a lease operates, regulating the conduct of the occupant and the person responsible for managing the building, with a significant difference being that one statement will apply to all units in a development.

Another particularly significant difference from leases is that a CCS may not provide for the transfer or loss of an interest in land on the occurrence or non-occurrence of a specified event. Effectively, this means that, unlike most leases, there will be no right for an association to forfeit a commonhold unit if the unit-holder fails to comply with the terms of a CCS.

13.2.11 Commonhold association

The CA is a company limited by guarantee, and details of the company will be lodged at Companies House as well as at the Land Registry. In a company limited by guarantee, members are required to guarantee the liability of the company. For CAs, however, their liability is limited to £1. Members have negligible direct liability for the debts of the association, though it is possible that members may be forced to pay the association's debts if a creditor seeks to wind up the association.

CLRA 2002 makes provision as to the constitution of the association, the most important of which is that the Articles of Association of the company must comply with regulations. The Articles give detail as to the procedures to be followed for such things as company general meetings, voting on resolutions, and appointment and removal of directors.

Though there are some elements which are discretionary, the form of the documents is largely prescribed. In fact, though it is possible to give some unit-holders additional voting rights in the association (e.g. to give a greater say in the affairs of the association to a larger unit), there is otherwise little flexibility in the form the documents take.

The running of the CA is the responsibility of the directors of the CA. **CLRA 2002** requires the directors of the association to exercise their powers to permit and facilitate the use and enjoyment of the property by the unit-holders and to take appropriate action in the event of a breach of the CCS. In addition, **CLRA 2002** requires the CCS to contain provisions requiring directors to prepare a commonhold assessment (similar to a service charge statement) which are contained in **CR**

2004. These govern the manner in which the commonhold assessment is collected and are similar in many respects to service charge provisions in leases.

In practice, for most residential schemes, the directors of the CA are likely to be unit-holders themselves, though it is likely that much of the day-to-day management of a commonhold block or estate will be undertaken by managing agents, as with many leasehold properties.

13.2.12 Enforcement against unit-holders and disputes

The CA will not be able to enforce any breach of the CCS against individual unit-holders by exercising a right of forfeiture as most lessors can do against lessees (subject to statutory restrictions). **CR 2004** make provision in the CCS for methods of enforcement against unit-holders and the association. This includes enforcement not just by the association against individual unit-holders but also by unit-holders directly against each other.

CR 2004 include within the CCS requirements to use mediation, conciliation and arbitration rather than court proceedings to settle disputes. It is hoped that this will prevent disputes from being taken to court and enable them to be resolved quickly and cheaply.

13.2.13 Termination of commonhold

A CA may either be wound up voluntarily by its members or be terminated on insolvency by its creditors.

(1) Voluntary winding-up

Under **CLRA 2002**, it is possible for the members voluntarily to wind up the CA. This may occur, for instance, where a building is old and requires redevelopment or where a developer has made an offer to redevelop the land and the members can sell the land at a profit. There are two methods of applying voluntarily to wind up an association.

(1) An application can be made to the Land Registry if all of the association's members vote for the application.

(2) If 80 per cent of members approve, an application can be made to the court for an order winding up the association.

A termination statement will need to be prepared to specify how it is proposed to dispose of the land and how the assets of the association should be distributed amongst its members.

(2) Termination on insolvency

There may be circumstances where, if a CA is unable to pay its debts, creditors may present a petition to the court for the association to be wound up. If this is the case, it is possible for either the association itself, any of its members, or the liquidator to apply for a succession order under **CLRA 2002**. If approved, the court will transfer the freehold estate in the common parts to a successor association which will continue running the commonhold. In some circumstances, it will not be possible to make a succession order and the association will be wound up and its assets sold. In theory, it appears, this could mean that unit-holders could lose their properties if the association is wound up and no succession order is made, and this may be one significant feature which may deter owners from setting up commonhold schemes.

13.2.14 Future for commonhold

Though commonhold as a form of tenure has significant advantages over leasehold as a means of owning land where common parts or structures are shared with others, few commonhold schemes have yet been established. At present, however, little use has been made of the commonhold system since 2004. Since **CLRA 2002** requires the consent of so many different people to create a commonhold, it appears unlikely that this form of tenure will be used to any great extent for existing developments. As has been the case so far, it seems more likely that commonhold will be used for new developments, probably of flats, and, possibly, where developers consider that buyers will be attracted by owning a form of freehold flat rather than a lease. Many developers, however, now offer leases of 999 years (so-called "virtual freeholds") and flat owners become registered as shareholders in the company that retains the common parts, thus controlling the management of these areas. This overcomes many of the disadvantages of leasehold ownership, without resorting to commonhold. Some have gone as far as to argue that, in fact, this form of tenure is unnecessary. It is, however, interesting to note that systems similar to commonhold have been operating successfully in other common law jurisdictions such as Australia and the United States for many years, so there is clearly a precedent for this form of tenure to work well. Only time will tell whether commonhold takes off in England and Wales however.

Activity

The government seems committed to reinvigorating commonhold and has produced a White Paper. If introduced, there will be changes to some of the procedures and documents referred to above, so conveyancers will need to keep up to date in this area.

Follow this link and read the White Paper:

https://www.gov.uk/government/publications/commonhold-white-paper/commonhold-white-paper-the-proposed-new-commonhold-model-for-homeownership-in-england-and-wales

13.3 HMLR digital developments

HMLR is moving swiftly with its digital roadmap, to the extent that even this text may be somewhat out of date by the time it is published. Conveyancers must keep up to date with this area and should subscribe to receive HMLR updates by email.

Link to practice

You should regularly check the HMLR digital roadmap by following the link below:

https://www.gov.uk/government/publications/hm-land-registry-digital-services-roadmap/digital-services-roadmap

Key areas for development include the following.

13.3.1 Digital Registration Service

HMLR is moving away from electronic applications, which are scanned copies currently uploaded and submitted using the HMLR eportal electronic Document Registration Service.

Instead, customers should use the new portal Digital Registration Service or lodge a digital application using software connected to HMLR's Business Gateway Platform. Digital applications are quicker to create and process, and see fewer requisitions due to automatic error checking.

Note that from November 2022 HMLR will no longer accept scanned or PDF copies of AP1s for changes to registered titles using the portal.

13.3.2 Electronic signatures

As a response to the pandemic and lockdown, in the middle of 2020 HMLR announced that it would accept deeds signed electronically for registration.

HMLR updated Practice guide 8 to reflect its requirements, but has now produced a new Practice Guide 82 which deals exclusively with electronic signatures accepted by HM Land Registry (see https://www.gov.uk/government/publications/electronic-signatures-accepted-by-hm-land-registry-pg82).

HMLR will accept deeds signed using the "Mercury signature" process. Mercury signing requires a traditional "wet ink" signature. However, it can be regarded as a form of electronic signature because the process involves scanning and returning the signed witnessed deed to the conveyancer by the client and it is this which "converts" it to an electronic signature.

HMLR will also accept deeds signed electronically using what is now called "conveyancer-certified electronic signatures"; previously these were called "witnessed electronic signatures".

In both cases, HMLR has very specific steps that the conveyancers must take to comply with their requirements.

HMLR has a facility whereby the mortgage deed on a remortgage can be signed by the borrower electronically online. This service is only offered on mortgages by about 12 of the larger lenders including Barclays, HSBC, Nationwide and Santander and at the moment the only conveyancing firms using the service are the larger, volume firms.

Activity

For more information on the background to electronic signatures, follow the link below to the Law Commission's report on Electronic Execution of Documents (Law Com No 386):

https://www.lawcom.gov.uk/project/electronic-execution-of-documents/

In particular, read and make notes on the section entitled: "Statement of the law: execution with an electronic signature".

13.3.3 Local land charges programme

Every local authority in England and Wales, with the exception of county councils, is required to hold a local land charge register that records obligations affecting properties within their administrative area. Under the **Infrastructure Act 2015** responsibility for the 331 registers was transferred to HMLR in a phased approach. The first transfer was in summer 2018 and the data from local authorities is being transferred all of the time.

Local authorities will continue to provide replies to CON29 enquiries, such as nearby road schemes or outstanding notices, which may affect a buyer's decision whether to proceed. Once a local authority's local land charges data has been transferred to HMLR, conveyancers will no longer be able to get local land charge search results from that local authority.

Using the new service, firms will have the option of downloading a personal search for free or an official search for £15. Alternatively, they can use a search provider who will access HMLR's Local Land Charges service directly.

13.4 Reservation agreements

It is regularly reported that a significant proportion of conveyancing transactions do not proceed once a buyer has been found, resulting in the loss of millions of pounds every year, not to mention the stress to the parties involved. Before the pandemic, the government was keen to introduce a pilot scheme to introduce reservation agreements. This is an agreement which is signed by seller and buyer once the purchase has been agreed, and will "tie in" both parties for a specified period during which they are expected to progress the transaction towards exchange of contracts. Crucially neither party can withdraw without penalty – the intention being to try to prevent "gazumping" whereby the seller proceeds with a buyer who has made a higher offer, even though they are progressing with a buyer already.

The government has announced that it intends to resurrect the plan to introduce voluntary reservation agreements and to evaluate their effectiveness.

Activity

For more information on reservation agreements, follow the link below to the Home Owners Alliance website:

https://hoa.org.uk/campaigns/end-home-selling-chaos/

Do you foresee any problems with conveyancers holding a reservation deposit before they have carried out the due diligence on the client?

13.5 Leasehold reform

Leasehold Reform (Ground Rent) Act 2022 (LR(GR)A 2022)

This is the first concrete step in the government's wider residential leasehold reforms. The Act restricts ground rents in residential leases of houses and flats to a token "peppercorn" per year. Landlords are also prohibited from charging an administration fee for the peppercorn ground rent.

It applies to residential leases granted on or after the commencement date (30 June 2022). It applies also to leasehold retirement properties from 1 April 2023. Existing residential leases, including those granted under contracts exchanged before 30 June 2022, and business leases are excluded from this requirement. Statutory lease extensions under the **Leasehold Reform Act 1967** (see **14.5.2.4**) are also excluded from **LR(GR)A 2022**.

The Competition and Markets Authority has been running an investigation into costly ground rents and has obtained formal undertakings from a number of large house builders to remove terms in existing leases which cause ground rents to double in price – see https://www.gov.uk/government/news/thousands-more-leaseholders-freed-from-rising-ground-rents

The **Leasehold and Freehold Reform Act 2024 (LFRA 2024)** gained Royal Assent on 24 May 2024, but most of it is currently not in force. If its provisions are introduced, **LFRA 2024** will have a significant impact on the enfranchisement rights of holders of long leases. The government explains the outline of **LFRA 2024** as follows:

"The Act – which has officially received Royal Assent – strengthens existing, and introduces new, consumer rights for homeowners by:

- Making it cheaper and easier for people to extend their lease or buy their freehold so leaseholders pay less to have more security in their home.
- Increasing the standard lease extension term to 990 years for houses and flats (up from 50 years in houses and 90 years in flats), so leaseholders can enjoy secure ownership without the hassle and expense of future lease extensions.
- Giving leaseholders greater transparency over their service charges by making freeholders or managing agents issue bills in a standardised format that can be more easily scrutinised and challenged.
- Making it easier and cheaper for leaseholders to take over management of their building, allowing them to appoint the managing agent of their choice.

- Making it cheaper for leaseholders to exercise their enfranchisement rights as they will no longer have to pay their freeholder's costs when making a claim.
- Extending access to redress schemes for leaseholders to challenge poor practice. The government will require freeholders, who manage their building directly, to belong to a redress scheme so leaseholders can challenge them if needed – managing agents are already required to belong to a scheme.
- Making buying or selling a leasehold property quicker and easier by setting a maximum time and fee that for home buying and selling information.
- Granting homeowners on private and mixed tenure estates comprehensive rights of redress, so they receive more information about what charges they pay, and the ability to challenge how reasonable they are."

There are also other changes that **LFRA 2024** will introduce. However, some of the provisions are controversial, for example, by removing the requirement for the leaseholder to pay their freeholder for the lease extension. These changes were not debated when **LFRA 2024** received Royal Assent and it may be some time, if ever, before they are brought into force.

Renters Rights Bill

If introduced, the **Renters Rights Bill** will have the greatest impact on the private residential letting sector for a generation. Conveyancers must keep up to date in this area. The government's summary of the Bill includes:

"The Renters' Rights Bill will:

- Abolish section 21 evictions and move to a simpler tenancy structure where all assured tenancies are periodic – providing more security for tenants and empowering them to challenge poor practice and unfair rent increases without fear of eviction. We will implement this new system in one stage, giving all tenants security immediately.
- Ensure possession grounds are fair to both parties, giving tenants more security, while ensuring landlords can recover their property when reasonable. The bill introduces new safeguards for tenants, giving them more time to find a home if landlords evict to move in or sell, and ensuring unscrupulous landlords cannot misuse grounds.
- Provide stronger protections against backdoor eviction by ensuring tenants are able to appeal excessive above-market rents which are purely designed to force them out. As now, landlords will still be able to increase rents to market price for their properties and an independent tribunal will make a judgement on this, if needed.
- Introduce a new Private Rented Sector Landlord Ombudsman that will provide quick, fair, impartial and binding resolution for tenants' complaints about

their landlord. This will bring tenant-landlord complaint resolution on par with established redress practices for tenants in social housing and consumers of property agent services

- Create a Private Rented Sector Database to help landlords understand their legal obligations and demonstrate compliance (giving good landlords confidence in their position), alongside providing better information to tenants to make informed decisions when entering into a tenancy agreement. It will also support local councils – helping them target enforcement activity where it is needed most. Landlords will need to be registered on the database in order to use certain possession grounds.
- Give tenants strengthened rights to request a pet in the property, which the landlord must consider and cannot unreasonably refuse. To support this, landlords will be able to require pet insurance to cover any damage to their property.
- Apply the Decent Homes Standard to the private rented sector to give renters safer, better value homes and remove the blight of poor-quality homes in local communities.
- Apply 'Awaab's Law' to the sector, setting clear legal expectations about the timeframes within which landlords in the private rented sector must take action to make homes safe where they contain serious hazards.
- Make it illegal for landlords and agents to discriminate against prospective tenants in receipt of benefits or with children – helping to ensure everyone is treated fairly when looking for a place to live.
- End the practice of rental bidding by prohibiting landlords and agents from asking for or accepting offers above the advertised rent. Landlords and agents will be required to publish an asking rent for their property and it will be illegal to accept offers made above this rate.
- Strengthen local authority enforcement by expanding civil penalties, introducing a package of investigatory powers and bringing in a new requirement for local authorities to report on enforcement activity.
- Strengthen rent repayment orders by extending them to superior landlords, doubling the maximum penalty and ensuring repeat offenders have to repay the maximum amount."

13.6 Chapter summary

Commonhold

(1) Instead of granting long leases in buildings which are multi-occupied, it is now possible to grant a commonhold title over individual units, and circumvent the problem that a lease is a wasting asset.

(2) Commonhold is a form of freehold title in which a larger area of land is divided into smaller units. Unlike other forms of freehold, it is possible to make positive obligations run with the land in commonhold. Therefore, it is a suitable form of title to use when granting freeholds of flats and other units in buildings which are horizontally divided.

(3) There are restrictions on commonhold. Most importantly, it applies only to registered land.

(4) Any common parts of a commonhold title must be owned by a commonhold association, a company limited by guarantee.

(5) Each commonhold association must have a CCS which governs the rights and obligations of each owner of a commonhold unit, much like a lease. Rather than have separate documents (as with leases), however, one CCS will cover the rights and liabilities of all occupants of a development. This document also describes the extent of each unit.

(6) Each unit must have one owner who is also a member of the commonhold association. Each member will have rights to vote in meetings of the association, but the number of votes granted to each unit can vary.

(7) It is necessary to obtain the consent of all freeholders, mortgage lenders and long lessees of a piece of land to convert it to commonhold. For this reason, commonhold is likely to be more common in new, rather than existing, developments.

(8) It is not possible for the CCS to restrict the right of a unit-holder to transfer the whole of their unit, but it can contain restrictions on lettings and, in the case of residential commonholds, the law prevents the granting of leases of more than seven years.

(9) The association cannot forfeit a unit-holder's title and the law prescribes a detailed procedure for resolving disputes, though it is possible for the association to recover some costs owed by a previous owner from new unit-holders.

HMLR is progressing its digital programme including:

- Digital registration service – from November 2022 HMLR will no longer accept scanned or PDF copies of AP1s for changes to registered titles using the portal.
- (Acceptance of deeds singed electronically (the detail is in Practice guide 82).
- Transfer of local land charges information from local authorities to HMLR; local authorities will still have to complete the Con 29 part of the local search.

The government is aiming to trial **reservation agreements**.

There are significant changes happening in the leasehold arena, and conveyancers must keep up to date with these changes.

APPENDIX – CONTENTS

Document 1: Standard Conditions of Sale (5th Edition – 2018)

For conveyancer's use only

Buyer's conveyancer: ....

Seller's conveyancer: ....

Law Society Formula: [A / B / C / Personal exchange]

The information above does not form part of the Contract

CONTRACT

Incorporating the Standard Conditions of Sale (Fifth Edition - 2018 Revision)

Date :

Seller :

Buyer :

Property (freehold/leasehold) :

Title number / root of title :

Specified incumbrances :

Title guarantee (full/limited) :

Completion date :

Contract rate :

Purchase price :

Deposit :

Contents price (if separate) :

Balance :

The seller will sell and the buyer will buy the property for the purchase price.

WARNING	Signed
This is a formal document, designed to create legal rights and legal obligations. Take advice before using it.	Seller/Buyer

SCS1_2/1

STANDARD CONDITIONS OF SALE (FIFTH EDITION - 2018 REVISION)
(NATIONAL CONDITIONS OF SALE 25TH EDITION, LAW SOCIETY'S CONDITIONS OF SALE 2011)

1. GENERAL

1.1 Definitions

1.1.1 In these conditions:
(a) 'accrued interest' means:
(i) if money has been placed on deposit or in a building society share account, the interest actually earned
(ii) otherwise, the interest which might reasonably have been earned by depositing the money at interest on seven days' notice of withdrawal with a clearing bank less, in either case, any proper charges for handling the money
(b) 'clearing bank' means a bank admitted by the Bank of England as a direct participant in its CHAPS system
(c) 'completion date' has the meaning given in condition 6.1.1
(d) 'contents price' means any separate amount payable for contents included in the contract
(e) 'contract rate' means the Law Society's interest rate from time to time in force
(f) 'conveyancer' means a solicitor, barrister, duly certified notary public, licensed conveyancer or recognised body under sections 9 or 23 of the Administration of Justice Act 1985
(g) 'lease' includes sub-lease, tenancy and agreement for a lease or sub-lease
(h) 'mortgage' means a mortgage or charge securing the repayment of money
(i) 'notice to complete' means a notice requiring completion of the contract in accordance with condition 6.8
(j) 'public requirement' means any notice, order or proposal given or made (whether before or after the date of the contract) by a body acting on statutory authority
(k) 'requisition' includes objection
(l) 'transfer' includes conveyance and assignment
(m) 'working day' means any day from Monday to Friday (inclusive) which is not Christmas Day, Good Friday or a statutory Bank Holiday.

1.1.2 In these conditions the terms 'absolute title' and 'official copies' have the special meanings given to them by the Land Registration Act 2002.

1.1.3 A party is ready, able and willing to complete:
(a) if he could be, but for the default of the other party, and
(b) in the case of the seller, even though the property remains subject to a mortgage, if the amount to be paid on completion enables the property to be transferred freed of all mortgages (except any to which the sale is expressly subject).

1.1.4 These conditions apply except as varied or excluded by the contract.

1.2 Joint parties

If there is more than one seller or more than one buyer, the obligations which they undertake can be enforced against them all jointly or against each individually.

1.3 Notices and documents

1.3.1 A notice required or authorised by the contract must be in writing.

1.3.2 Giving a notice or delivering a document to a party's conveyancer has the same effect as giving or delivering it to that party.

1.3.3 Where delivery of the original document is not essential, a notice or document is validly given or sent if it is sent:
(a) by fax, or
(b) by e-mail to an e-mail address for the intended recipient given in the contract

1.3.4 Subject to conditions 1.3.5 to 1.3.7, a notice is given and a document is delivered when it is received.

1.3.5 (a) A notice or document sent through a document exchange is received when it is available for collection.
(b) A notice or document which is received after 4.00pm on a working day, or on a day which is not a working day, is to be treated as having been received on the next working day.
(c) An automated response to a notice or document sent by e-mail that the intended recipient is out of the office is to be treated as proof that the notice or document was not received.

1.3.6 Condition 1.3.7 applies unless there is proof:
(a) that a notice or document has not been received, or
(b) of when it was received.

1.3.7 A notice or document sent by the following means is treated as having been received as follows:

(a) by first-class post:	before 4.00pm on the second working day after posting
(b) by second-class post:	before 4.00pm on the third working day after posting
(c) through a document exchange:	before 4.00pm on the first working day after the day on which it would normally be available for collection by the addressee
(d) by fax:	one hour after despatch
(e) by e-mail:	before 4.00pm on the first working day after despatch.

1.4 VAT

1.4.1 The purchase price and the contents price are inclusive of any value added tax.

1.4.2 All other sums made payable by the contract are exclusive of any value added tax and where a supply is made which is chargeable to value added tax, the recipient of the supply is to pay the supplier (in addition to any other amounts payable under the contract) a sum equal to the value added tax chargeable on that supply.

1.5 Assignment and sub-sales

1.5.1 The buyer is not entitled to transfer the benefit of the contract.

1.5.2 The seller cannot be required to transfer the property in parts or to any person other than the buyer.

1.6 Third party rights

Unless otherwise expressly stated nothing in this contract will create rights pursuant to the Contracts (Rights of Third Parties) Act 1999 in favour of anyone other than the parties to the contract.

2. FORMATION

2.1 Date

2.1.1 If the parties intend to make a contract by exchanging duplicate copies by post or through a document exchange, the contract is made when the last copy is posted or deposited at the document exchange.

2.1.2 If the parties' conveyancers agree to treat exchange as taking place before duplicate copies are actually exchanged, the contract is made as so agreed.

2.2 Deposit

2.2.1 The buyer is to pay or send a deposit of 10 per cent of the purchase price no later than the date of the contract.

2.2.2 If a cheque tendered in payment of all or part of the deposit is dishonoured when first presented, the seller may, within seven working days of being notified that the cheque has been dishonoured, give notice to the buyer that the contract is discharged by the buyer's breach.

2.2.3 Conditions 2.2.4 to 2.2.6 do not apply on a sale by auction.

2.2.4 The deposit is to be paid:
(a) by electronic means from an account held in the name of a conveyancer at a clearing bank to an account in the name of the seller's conveyancer or (in a case where condition 2.2.5 applies) a conveyancer nominated by him and maintained at a clearing bank or
(b) to the seller's conveyancer or (in a case where condition 2.2.5 applies) a conveyancer nominated by him by cheque drawn on a solicitor's or licensed conveyancer's client account

2.2.5 If before completion date the seller agrees to buy another property in England and Wales for his residence, he may use all or any part of the deposit as a deposit in that transaction to be held on terms to the same effect as this condition and condition 2.2.6.

2.2.6 Any deposit or part of a deposit not being used in accordance with condition 2.2.5 is to be held by the seller's conveyancer as stakeholder on terms that on completion it is paid to the seller with accrued interest.

2.3 Auctions

2.3.1 On a sale by auction the following conditions apply to the property and, if it is sold in lots, to each lot.

2.3.2 The sale is subject to a reserve price.

2.3.3 The seller, or a person on his behalf, may bid up to the reserve price.

2.3.4 The auctioneer may refuse any bid.

2.3.5 If there is a dispute about a bid, the auctioneer may resolve the dispute or restart the auction at the last undisputed bid.

2.3.6 The deposit is to be paid to the auctioneer as agent for the seller.

3. MATTERS AFFECTING THE PROPERTY

3.1 Freedom from incumbrances

3.1.1 The seller is selling the property free from incumbrances, other than those mentioned in condition 3.1.2.

3.1.2 The incumbrances subject to which the property is sold are:
(a) those specified in the contract
(b) those discoverable by inspection of the property before the date of the contract
(c) those the seller does not and could not reasonably know about
(d) those, other than mortgages, which the buyer knows about
(e) entries made before the date of the contract in any public register except those maintained by the Land Registry or its Land Charges Department or by Companies House
(f) public requirements.

3.1.3 After the contract is made, the seller is to give the buyer written details without delay of any new public requirement and of anything in writing which he learns about concerning a matter covered by condition 3.1.2.

3.1.4 The buyer is to bear the cost of complying with any outstanding public requirement and is to indemnify the seller against any liability resulting from a public requirement.

3.2 Physical state

3.2.1 The buyer accepts the property in the physical state it is in at the date of the contract unless the seller is building or converting it.

3.2.2 A leasehold property is sold subject to any subsisting breach of a condition or tenant's obligation relating to the physical state of the property which renders the lease liable to forfeiture.

3.2.3 A sub-lease is granted subject to any subsisting breach of a condition or tenant's obligation relating to the physical state of the property which renders the seller's own lease liable to forfeiture.

3.3 Leases affecting the property

3.3.1 The following provisions apply if any part of the property is sold subject to a lease.

3.3.2 (a) The seller having provided the buyer with full details of each lease or copies of the documents embodying the lease terms, the buyer is treated as entering into the contract knowing and fully accepting those terms.
(b) The seller is to inform the buyer without delay if the lease ends or if the seller learns of any application by the tenant in connection with the lease; the seller is then to act as the buyer reasonably directs, and the buyer is to indemnify him against all consequent loss and expense.
(c) Except with the buyer's consent, the seller is not to agree to any proposal to change the lease terms nor to take any step to end the lease.
(d) The seller is to inform the buyer without delay of any change to the lease terms which may be proposed or agreed.
(e) The buyer is to indemnify the seller against all claims arising from the lease after actual completion; this includes claims which are unenforceable against a buyer for want of registration.
(f) The seller takes no responsibility for what rent is lawfully recoverable, nor for whether or how any legislation affects the lease.
(g) If the let land is not wholly within the property, the seller may apportion the rent.

4. TITLE AND TRANSFER

4.1 Proof of title

4.1.1 Without cost to the buyer, the seller is to provide the buyer with proof of the title to the property and of his ability to transfer it, or to procure its transfer.

4.1.2 Where the property has a registered title the proof is to include official copies of the items referred to in rules 134(1)(a) and (b) and 135(1)(a) of the Land Registration Rules 2003, so far as they are not to be discharged or overridden at or before completion.

4.1.3 Where the property has an unregistered title, the proof is to include:
(a) an abstract of title or an epitome of title with photocopies of the documents, and
(b) production of every document or an abstract, epitome or copy of it with an original marking by a conveyancer either against the original or an examined abstract or an examined copy.

4.2 Requisitions

4.2.1 The buyer may not raise requisitions:
(a) on any title shown by the seller before the contract was made
(b) in relation to the matters covered by condition 3.1.2.

4.2.2 Notwithstanding condition 4.2.1, the buyer may, within six working days of a matter coming to his attention after the contract was made, raise written requisitions on that matter. In that event, steps 3 and 4 in condition 4.3.1 apply.

4.2.3 On the expiry of the relevant time limit under condition 4.2.2 or condition 4.3.1, the buyer loses his right to raise requisitions or to make observations.

4.3 Timetable

4.3.1 Subject to condition 4.2 and to the extent that the seller did not take the steps described in condition 4.1.1 before the contract was made, the following are the steps for deducing and investigating the title to the property to be taken within the following time limits:

Step	Time Limit
1. The seller is to comply with condition 4.1.1	Immediately after making the contract
2. The buyer may raise written requisitions	Six working days after either the date of the contract or the date of delivery of the seller's evidence of title on which the requisitions are raised, whichever is the later
3. The seller is to reply in writing to any requisitions raised	Four working days after receiving the requisitions
4. The buyer may make written observations on the seller's replies	Three working days after receiving the replies

The time limit on the buyer's right to raise requisitions applies even where the seller supplies incomplete evidence of his title, but the buyer may, within six working days from delivery of any further evidence, raise further requisitions resulting from that evidence.

4.3.2 The parties are to take the following steps to prepare and agree the transfer of the property within the following time limits:

Step	Time Limit
A. The buyer is to send the seller a draft transfer	At least twelve working days before completion date
B. The seller is to approve or revise that draft and either return it or retain it for use as the actual transfer	Four working days after delivery of the draft transfer
C. If the draft is returned the buyer is to send an engrossment to the seller	At least five working days before completion date

4.3.3 Periods of time under conditions 4.3.1 and 4.3.2 may run concurrently.

4.3.4 If the period between the date of the contract and completion date is less than 15 working days, the time limits in conditions 4.2.2, 4.3.1 and 4.3.2 are to be reduced by the same proportion as that period bears to the period of 15 working days. Fractions of a working day are to be rounded down except that the time limit to perform any step is not to be less than one working day.

4.4 Defining the property

The seller need not:
(a) prove the exact boundaries of the property
(b) prove who owns fences, ditches, hedges or walls
(c) separately identify parts of the property with different titles further than he may be able to do from information in his possession.

4.5 Rents and rentcharges

The fact that a rent or rentcharge, whether payable or receivable by the owner of the property, has been, or will on completion be, informally apportioned is not to be regarded as a defect in title.

4.6 Transfer

4.6.1 The buyer does not prejudice his right to raise requisitions, or to require replies to any raised, by taking any steps in relation to preparing or agreeing the transfer.

4.6.2 Subject to condition 4.6.3, the seller is to transfer the property with full title guarantee.

SCS1_2/2

4.6.3 The transfer is to have effect as if the disposition is expressly made subject to all matters covered by condition 3.1.2 and, if the property is leasehold, is to contain a statement that the covenants set out in section 4 of the Law of Property (Miscellaneous Provisions) Act 1994 will not extend to any breach of the tenant's covenants in the lease relating to the physical state of the property.

4.6.4 If after completion the seller will remain bound by any obligation affecting the property which was disclosed to the buyer before the contract was made, but the law does not imply any covenant by the buyer to indemnify the seller against liability for future breaches of it:
(a) the buyer is to covenant in the transfer to indemnify the seller against liability for any future breach of the obligation and to perform it from then on, and
(b) if required by the seller, the buyer is to execute and deliver to the seller on completion a duplicate transfer prepared by the buyer.

4.6.5 The seller is to arrange at his expense that, in relation to every document of title which the buyer does not receive on completion, the buyer is to have the benefit of:
(a) a written acknowledgement of his right to its production, and
(b) a written undertaking for its safe custody (except while it is held by a mortgagee or by someone in a fiduciary capacity).

4.7 **Membership of company**
Where the seller is, or is required to be, a member of a company that has an interest in the property or has management responsibilities for the property or the surrounding areas, the seller is, without cost to the buyer, to provide such documents on completion as will enable the buyer to become a member of that company.

5. RISK, INSURANCE AND OCCUPATION PENDING COMPLETION

5.1.1 The property is at the risk of the buyer from the date of the contract.

5.1.2 The seller is under no obligation to the buyer to insure the property unless:
(a) the contract provides that a policy effected by or for the seller and insuring the property or any part of it against liability for loss or damage is to continue in force, or
(b) the property or any part of it is let on terms under which the seller (whether as landlord or as tenant) is obliged to insure against loss or damage.

5.1.3 If the seller is obliged to insure the property under condition 5.1.2, the seller is to:
(a) do everything necessary to maintain the policy
(b) permit the buyer to inspect the policy or evidence of its terms
(c) if before completion the property suffers loss or damage:
(i) pay to the buyer on completion the amount of the policy monies which the seller has received, so far as not applied in repairing or reinstating the property, and
(ii) if no final payment has then been received, assign to the buyer, at the buyer's expense, all rights to claim under the policy in such form as the buyer reasonably requires and pending execution of the assignment hold any policy monies received in trust for the buyer
(d) cancel the policy on completion.

5.1.4 Where the property is leasehold and the property, or any building containing it, is insured by a reversioner or other third party, the seller is to use reasonable efforts to ensure that the insurance is maintained until completion and if, before completion, the property or building suffers loss or damage the seller is to assign to the buyer on completion, at the buyer's expense, such rights as the seller may have in the policy monies, in such form as the buyer reasonably requires.

5.1.5 If payment under a policy effected by or for the buyer is reduced, because the property is covered against loss or damage by an insurance policy effected by or on behalf of the seller, then, unless the seller is obliged to insure the property under condition 5.1.2, the purchase price is to be abated by the amount of that reduction.

5.1.6 Section 47 of the Law of Property Act 1925 does not apply.

5.2 **Occupation by buyer**

5.2.1 If the buyer is not already lawfully in the property, and the seller agrees to let him into occupation, the buyer occupies on the following terms.

5.2.2 The buyer is a licensee and not a tenant. The terms of the licence are that the buyer:
(a) cannot transfer it
(b) may permit members of his household to occupy the property
(c) is to pay or indemnify the seller against all outgoings and other expenses in respect of the property
(d) is to pay the seller a fee calculated at the contract rate on a sum equal to the purchase price (less any deposit paid) for the period of the licence
(e) is entitled to any rents and profits from any part of the property which he does not occupy
(f) is to keep the property in as good a state of repair as it was in when he went into occupation (except for fair wear and tear) and is not to alter it
(g) if the property is leasehold, is not to do anything which puts the seller in breach of his obligations in the lease, and
(h) is to quit the property when the licence ends.

5.2.3 The buyer is not in occupation for the purposes of this condition if he merely exercises rights of access given solely to do work agreed by the seller.

5.2.4 The buyer's licence ends on the earliest of: completion date, rescission of the contract or when five working days' notice given by one party to the other takes effect.

5.2.5 If the buyer is in occupation of the property after his licence has come to an end and the contract is subsequently completed he is to pay the seller compensation for his continued occupation calculated at the same rate as the fee mentioned in condition 5.2.2(d).

5.2.6 The buyer's right to raise requisitions is unaffected.

6. COMPLETION

6.1 **Date**

6.1.1 Completion date is twenty working days after the date of the contract but time is not of the essence of the contract unless a notice to complete has been served.

6.1.2 If the money due on completion is received after 2.00pm, completion is to be treated, for the purposes only of conditions 6.3 and 7.2, as taking place on the next working day as a result of the buyer's default.

6.1.3 Condition 6.1.2 does not apply and the seller is treated as in default if:
(a) the sale is with vacant possession of the property or any part of it, and
(b) the buyer is ready, able and willing to complete but does not pay the money due on completion until after 2.00pm because the seller has not vacated the property or that part by that time.

6.2 **Arrangements and place**

6.2.1 The buyer's conveyancer and the seller's conveyancer are to co-operate in agreeing arrangements for completing the contract.

6.2.2 Completion is to take place in England and Wales, either at the seller's conveyancer's office or at some other place which the seller reasonably specifies.

6.3 **Apportionments**

6.3.1 On evidence of proper payment being made, income and outgoings of the property are to be apportioned between the parties so far as the change of ownership on completion will affect entitlement to receive or liability to pay them.

6.3.2 If the whole property is sold with vacant possession or the seller exercises his option in condition 7.2.4, apportionment is to be made with effect from the date of actual completion; otherwise, it is to be made from completion date.

6.3.3 In apportioning any sum, it is to be assumed that the seller owns the property until the end of the day from which apportionment is made and that the sum accrues from day to day at the rate at which it is payable on that day.

6.3.4 For the purpose of apportioning income and outgoings, it is to be assumed that they accrue at an equal daily rate throughout the year.

6.3.5 When a sum to be apportioned is not known or easily ascertainable at completion, a provisional apportionment is to be made according to the best estimate available. As soon as the amount is known, a final apportionment is to be made and notified to the other party. Any resulting balance is to be paid no more than ten working days later, and if not then paid the balance is to bear interest at the contract rate from then until payment.

6.3.6 Compensation payable under condition 5.2.5 is not to be apportioned.

6.4 **Amount payable**
The amount payable by the buyer on completion is the purchase price and the contents price (less any deposit already paid to the seller or his agent) adjusted to take account of:
(a) apportionments made under condition 6.3
(b) any compensation to be paid or allowed under condition 7.2
(c) any sum payable under condition 5.1.3.

6.5 **Title deeds**

6.5.1 As soon as the buyer has complied with all his obligations under this contract on completion the seller must hand over the documents of title.

6.5.2 Condition 6.5.1 does not apply to any documents of title relating to land being retained by the seller after completion.

6.6 **Rent receipts**
The buyer is to assume that whoever gave any receipt for a payment of rent or service charge which the seller produces was the person or the agent of the person then entitled to that rent or service charge.

6.7 **Means of payment**
The buyer is to pay the money due on completion by a direct transfer of cleared funds from an account held in the name of a conveyancer at a clearing bank and, if appropriate, an unconditional release of a deposit held by a stakeholder.

6.8 **Notice to complete**

6.8.1 At any time after the time applicable under condition 6.1.2 on completion date, a party who is ready, able and willing to complete may give the other a notice to complete.

6.8.2 The parties are to complete the contract within ten working days of giving a notice to complete, excluding the day on which the notice is given. For this purpose, time is of the essence of the contract.

6.8.3 On receipt of a notice to complete:
(a) if the buyer paid no deposit, he is forthwith to pay a deposit of 10 per cent
(b) if the buyer paid a deposit of less than 10 per cent, he is forthwith to pay a further deposit equal to the balance of that 10 per cent.

7. REMEDIES

7.1 **Errors and omissions**

7.1.1 If any plan or statement in the contract, or in the negotiations leading to it, is or was misleading or inaccurate due to an error or omission by the seller, the remedies available to the buyer are as follows.
(a) When there is a material difference between the description or value of the property, or of any of the contents included in the contract, as represented and as it is, the buyer is entitled to damages.
(b) An error or omission only entitles the buyer to rescind the contract:
(i) where it results from fraud or recklessness, or
(ii) where he would be obliged, to his prejudice, to accept property differing substantially (in quantity, quality or tenure) from what the error or omission had led him to expect.

7.1.2 If either party rescinds the contract:
(a) unless the rescission is a result of the buyer's breach of contract the deposit is to be repaid to the buyer with accrued interest
(b) the buyer is to return any documents he received from the seller and is to cancel any registration of the contract.

7.2 **Late completion**

7.2.1 If there is default by either or both of the parties in performing their obligations under the contract and completion is delayed, the party whose total period of default is the greater is to pay compensation to the other party.

7.2.2 Compensation is calculated at the contract rate on an amount equal to the purchase price, less (where the buyer is the paying party) any deposit paid, for the period by which the paying party's default exceeds that of the receiving party, or, if shorter, the period between completion date and actual completion.

7.2.3 Any claim for loss resulting from delayed completion is to be reduced by any compensation paid under this contract.

7.2.4 Where the buyer holds the property as tenant of the seller and completion is delayed, the seller may give notice to the buyer, before the date of actual completion, that he intends to take the net income from the property until completion. If he does so, he cannot claim compensation under condition 7.2.1 as well.

7.3 **After completion**
Completion does not cancel liability to perform any outstanding obligation under this contract.

7.4 **Buyer's failure to comply with notice to complete**

7.4.1 If the buyer fails to complete in accordance with a notice to complete, the following terms apply.

7.4.2 The seller may rescind the contract, and if he does so:
(a) he may:
(i) forfeit and keep any deposit and accrued interest
(ii) resell the property and any contents included in the contract
(iii) claim damages
(b) the buyer is to return any documents he received from the seller and is to cancel any registration of the contract.

7.4.3 The seller retains his other rights and remedies.

7.5 **Seller's failure to comply with notice to complete**

7.5.1 If the seller fails to complete in accordance with a notice to complete, the following terms apply.

7.5.2 The buyer may rescind the contract, and if he does so:
(a) the deposit is to be repaid to the buyer with accrued interest
(b) the buyer is to return any documents he received from the seller and is, at the seller's expense, to cancel any registration of the contract.

7.5.3 The buyer retains his other rights and remedies.

8. LEASEHOLD PROPERTY

8.1 **Existing leases**

8.1.1 The following provisions apply to a sale of leasehold land.

8.1.2 The seller having provided the buyer with copies of the documents embodying the lease terms, the buyer is treated as entering into the contract knowing and fully accepting those terms.

8.2 **New leases**

8.2.1 The following provisions apply to a contract to grant a new lease.

8.2.2 The conditions apply so that:
'seller' means the proposed landlord
'buyer' means the proposed tenant
'purchase price' means the premium to be paid on the grant of a lease.

8.2.3 The lease is to be in the form of the draft attached to the contract.

8.2.4 If the term of the new lease will exceed seven years, the seller is to deduce a title which will enable the buyer to register the lease at the Land Registry with an absolute title.

8.2.5 The seller is to engross the lease and a counterpart of it and is to send the counterpart to the buyer at least five working days before completion date.

8.2.6 The buyer is to execute the counterpart and deliver it to the seller on completion.

8.3 **Consent**

8.3.1 (a) The following provisions apply if a consent to let, assign or sub-let is required to complete the contract
(b) In this condition 'consent' means consent in the form which satisfies the requirement to obtain it.

8.3.2 (a) The seller is to apply for the consent at his expense, and to use all reasonable efforts to obtain it
(b) The buyer is to provide all information and references reasonably required.

8.3.3 Unless he is in breach of his obligation under condition 8.3.2, either party may rescind the contract by notice to the other party if three working days before completion date (or before a later date on which the parties have agreed to complete the contract):
(a) the consent has not been given, or
(b) the consent has been given subject to a condition to which a party reasonably objects. In that case, neither party is to be treated as in breach of contract and condition 7.1.2 applies.

9. CONTENTS

9.1 The following provisions apply to any contents which are included in the contract, whether or not a separate price is to be paid for them.

9.2 The contract takes effect as a contract for sale of goods.

9.3 The buyer takes the contents in the physical state they are in at the date of the contract.

9.4 Ownership of the contents passes to the buyer on actual completion.

SCS1_2/3

SPECIAL CONDITIONS

1 (a) This contract incorporates the Standard Conditions of Sale (Fifth Edition - 2018 Revision).

(b) The terms used in this contract have the same meaning when used in the Conditions.

2 Subject to the terms of this contract and to the Standard Conditions of Sale, the seller is to transfer the property with either full title guarantee or limited title guarantee, as specified on the front page.

3 (a) The sale includes those contents which are indicated on the attached list as included in the sale and the buyer is to pay the contents price for them.

(b) The sale excludes those fixtures which are at the property and are indicated on the attached list as excluded from the sale

4 The property is sold with vacant possession.

(or)

4 The property is sold subject to the following leases or tenancies:

5 Conditions 6.1.2 and 6.1.3 shall take effect as if the time specified in them were rather than 2.00 p.m.

6 **Representations**
Neither party can rely on any representation made by the other, unless made in writing by the other or his conveyancer, but this does not exclude liability for fraud or recklessness.

7 **Occupier's consent**
Each occupier identified below agrees with the seller and the buyer, in consideration of their entering into this contract, that the occupier concurs in the sale of the property on the terms of this contract, undertakes to vacate the property on or before the completion date and releases the property and any included fixtures and contents from any right or interest that the occupier may have.

Note: this condition does not apply to occupiers under leases or tenancies subject to which the property is sold.

Name(s) and signature(s) of the occupier(s) (if any):

Name

Signature

Notices may be sent to:

Seller's conveyancer's name:

E-mail address:*

Buyer's conveyancer's name:

E-mail address:*

*Adding an e-mail address authorises service by e-mail see condition 1.3.3(b)

Document 2: Explanatory Notes - Standard Conditions of Sale (5th Edition – 2018)

EXPLANATORY NOTES ON THE STANDARD CONDITIONS OF SALE (FIFTH EDITION)

(April 2011)

GENERAL

The fifth edition of the Standard Conditions of Sale (the "SCS") takes effect on 1 April 2011 and supersedes the fourth edition of the SCS issued in October 2003.

The revisions to the fourth edition have been made to bring the SCS in line with current law and practice with the aim of reducing the need for special conditions. The changes are intended to achieve a balance between the interests of the buyer and seller.

The main change is that, reflecting the position under the general law, the buyer is now to assume the risk from the date of exchange. Nonetheless, as explained below, there are certain cases in which the seller is obliged to insure.

The SCS are intended primarily for use in residential sales. Although they may be suitable for the sale of small business premises, conveyancers are likely to find that, for most commercial transactions, the Standard Commercial Property Conditions (the "SCPC") are better suited to their needs.

The revisions maintain the policy of using plain English rather than legal terminology where possible.

The fifth edition of the SCS represents the 25th edition of the National Conditions of Sale and the Law Society's Conditions of Sale 2011.

DEFINITIONS

"contents price"
Condition 1.1.1(d) now refers to "contents" rather than "chattels".

"direct credit"
The previous definition of "direct credit" (meaning a "direct transfer of cleared funds to an account nominated by the seller's conveyancer and maintained by a clearing bank") has been deleted, since this concept is now used only in condition 6.7. See also the explanation of the changes to condition 2.2.4.

"mortgage"
A new definition of "mortgage" has been added, which clarifies the meaning of the term in condition 1.1.3(b) and is used in the new paragraph (d) of condition 3.1.2.

VAT

Condition 1.4.1 has been amended to make it clear that the agreed purchase price and contents price for a property are inclusive of VAT. This reflects the fact that the SCS are intended primarily to be used for residential transactions, which are usually exempt for VAT purposes.

If the sale does constitute a chargeable supply for VAT purposes, a special condition should be inserted if the seller requires the buyer to pay a sum equal to the VAT. In commercial or mixed-use transactions, it is likely to be more appropriate to use the SCPC.

By virtue of condition 1.4.2, any other sums payable under the contract (*i.e.* sums other than the purchase price and contents price) will continue to be exclusive of VAT. In these circumstances, the recipient of a taxable supply will be liable to pay to the supplier a sum equal to the VAT chargeable on that supply.

ASSIGNMENT AND SUB-SALES

A new condition 1.5.2 provides that the seller cannot be required to transfer the property, or any part of it, to any person other than the buyer. The amendment is intended to protect the seller from becoming involved in a transaction with an unknown third party. This change clarifies the position and ensures consistency with the SCPC.

THIRD PARTY RIGHTS

Condition 1.6 has been added to exclude the operation of the Contracts (Rights of Third Parties) Act 1999. This ensures that a third party will not have any rights under the contract by virtue of that Act.

DEPOSIT

Condition 2.2.1 has been amended so that the 10% deposit is calculated by reference only to the purchase price and not, as before, the total of the purchase price and any separate contents price. This has been changed in order to provide certainty at an early stage as to the amount of the deposit that will be required. The buyer will not be required to pay 10% of the contents price, which can still be the subject of negotiation up until the point at which contracts are exchanged. If the deposit is also to take account of the contents price, this should be provided for by special condition. This change largely reflects practice.

As noted above, the definition of "direct credit" has been deleted from the SCS. In condition 2.2.4, reference to "direct credit" has been replaced by a reference to the deposit being paid by "electronic means". This has the effect that, unlike payments due on completion, the deposit does not have to be paid in cleared funds. Additional wording has been inserted so that the money transfer must now be made from an account held in the name of a conveyancer at a clearing bank to an account maintained at a clearing bank held in the name of either the seller's conveyancer or, where condition 2.2.5 applies, a conveyancer higher up the chain. It is hoped that limiting payments to those from a conveyancer's account will assist the seller's conveyancer in complying with anti-money laundering obligations. Express provision by way of special condition will be required for any alternative arrangements. Condition 2.2.4(b) continues to make provision for the payment of the deposit by cheque but, where condition 2.2.5 applies, now permits the cheque to be made payable to a conveyancer higher up the chain.

MATTERS AFFECTING THE PROPERTY

Condition 3.1.2(d) has been added to provide that the property is sold subject to any incumbrances (other than mortgages) which the buyer knows about. It is not considered fair for a buyer to be able to take action against a seller in respect of a matter which he knew about, but which was not expressly a matter subject to which the property was sold.

RETAINED LAND

Condition 3.4 in the fourth edition of the SCS has been deleted. It sought to deal with the situation where land is retained by the seller. Issues relating to retained land, such as rights and covenants, should be dealt with by way of special condition and by annexing an agreed form of transfer.

REQUISITIONS

The wording of condition 4.2.1(a) has been slightly amended to make it clear that the buyer cannot raise requisitions on any title shown by the seller before the contract was made. This is consistent with practice where title is deduced in full before exchange.

DEFINING THE PROPERTY

Condition 4.4.2 of the fourth edition has been deleted so that the buyer can no longer require the seller to provide a statutory declaration about facts relevant to matters such as boundaries, hedges, ditches and walls. It is not considered to be reasonable to expect the seller to provide a statutory declaration after exchange of contracts when investigation of title has taken place prior to exchange.

If necessary, this issue should be dealt with by special condition.

TRANSFER

The wording in condition 4.6.3 has been amended. In the case of a transfer of leasehold property, the contract requires the transfer to contain an express statement modifying the title guarantee by excluding the operation of section 4 of the Law of Property (Miscellaneous Provisions) Act 1994 in respect of any breach of the tenant's covenants in the lease relating to the physical state of the property. This has been inserted because similar provisions are widely used in practice and it is consistent with condition 3.2.2.

MEMBERSHIP OF COMPANY

Condition 4.7 has been inserted to enable the buyer to become a member of a management company or any other relevant company that has an interest in the property. This addition will reduce the need for a special condition to deal with this point. The condition stipulates that all relevant documents (which may include membership or share certificates and/or a duly signed stock transfer form) are to be provided to the buyer on completion. The condition has been drafted to apply not only to those companies with responsibilities in relation to leasehold property but also to those which have management obligations in relation to freehold property.

SCS_Notes/2

RISK, INSURANCE AND OCCUPATION PENDING COMPLETION

Significant changes have been made to the conditions relating to risk and insurance. The principal effect is that the risk position is reversed (from that in the fourth edition of the SCS) and the buyer bears the risk from exchange. Previous editions of the SCS left the risk with the seller until completion and, in practice, special conditions were frequently included to make the buyer bear the risk from exchange. This change brings the SCS broadly into line with the SCPC.

Even though the buyer takes the risk from exchange (meaning he still has to complete if the property is destroyed between exchange and completion), the seller may still have an obligation to insure the property between exchange and completion by virtue of condition 5.1.2. Under this condition, the seller is obliged to insure if the contract so provides or if the property is leasehold and the seller (whether as landlord or as tenant) is obliged to insure under the terms of the lease.

Condition 5.1.3 sets out the seller's obligations where he is required to insure.

Under condition 5.1.4, where the property is leasehold and insurance is effected by a landlord or other third party, the seller is to use reasonable efforts to ensure that the insurance is maintained until completion and if, before completion, the building suffers any loss or damage, the seller is to assign to the buyer any rights that the seller may have in the policy monies.

Condition 5.1.5 has been added in an attempt to clarify the position as regards 'double insurance'. This is where both the seller and buyer insure the property between exchange and completion. The new condition provides that where a payment under the buyer's insurance is reduced because the property is covered under an insurance policy taken out by or on behalf of the seller, then, provided the seller is not obliged to insure the property under condition 5.1.2, the purchase price is to be abated by the amount of that reduction. The position in this respect is now similar to that under the SCPC.

OCCUPATION BY BUYER

Condition 5.2.2(d) has been amended in line with condition 2.2.1 so that the licence fee is to be calculated by reference to the purchase price only.

Condition 5.2.2(g) of the fourth edition of the SCS, which dealt with the buyer's duty to insure the property, has been deleted because the risk will have passed to the buyer under the amended condition 5.1. The new condition 5.2.2(g) stipulates that, if the property is leasehold, the buyer is not to do anything which puts the seller in breach of his obligations in the lease.

APPORTIONMENTS

Condition 6.3.1 has been amended to require the party requesting apportionment to provide evidence of payment in relation to the relevant income and outgoings of the property.

TITLE DEEDS

The wording in condition 6.5.1 has been slightly amended so that the reference to the buyer's obligations is expressly limited to those under the SCS.

MEANS OF PAYMENT

The wording in condition 6.7 has been amended and now refers to a "direct transfer" of cleared funds on completion. The previous edition used the defined term "direct credit" which, as noted above, has been deleted in these conditions. This new wording makes it clear that the completion monies should come from and be paid to an account held in the name of a conveyancer. As with conditions 1.5.2 and 2.2.4, this change was made with the aim of combating fraud and assisting compliance with anti-money laundering measures.

NOTICE TO COMPLETE

Condition 6.8.1 has been amended so that notice to complete cannot be given before 2.00 pm on the day of completion. This change is intended to prevent the seller from serving a notice to complete on the morning of completion date.

SCS_Notes/3

LATE COMPLETION
Under condition 7.2.2, and in line with other relevant provisions in the SCS, compensation for late completion is calculated by reference to the purchase price only and not the purchase price and the contents price.

COMMONHOLD LAND
Condition 9 of the fourth edition of the SCS has been deleted. Commonhold is not widely used as a form of tenure. Where relevant, provision for commonhold land should be made by special condition.

CONTENTS
As previously noted, all references to "chattels" in the SCS have been changed to "contents".

FRONT AND BACK PAGES
The general layout of the front page has been changed to allow conveyancers to record on the contract cover sheet details of the exchange of contracts including the names of the respective solicitors acting for the parties, the time of exchange and the relevant formula used.

SPECIAL CONDITIONS

CONTENTS AND FIXTURES
A revised special condition 3 makes clear which contents are included in the sale and which fixtures are excluded.

COMPLETION
Special condition 5 allows the parties to vary condition 6.1.2 by specifying a time other than 2.00 pm in order to identify the day on which completion is to be treated as taking place for the purposes of condition 6.3 (apportionments) and 7.2 (compensation for late completion). This time will also become the earliest time for giving a notice to complete under condition 6.8.1. It is a special condition so that the parties will need to make a conscious decision if they wish to depart from the fallback provision in condition 6.1.2. It may be particularly useful where there is a chain of transactions. For example, the seller under the first contract in a chain might require payment of the purchase price by 1.30 pm to allow sufficient time to receive those funds and transmit them on his own purchase by 2.00 pm.

REPRESENTATIONS
The limitation on liability for representations in special condition 6 aims to exclude liability for oral statements made by or on behalf of the parties. It does not exclude liability for fraud or recklessness. The exclusion is mutual but it is most likely in practice to be relied upon by the seller. Terms similar in effect to special condition 6 are commonly found in contracts. It has been included as a special condition (rather than one of the general conditions) in the light of judicial comments in *Morgan v Pooley* [2010] EWHC 2447 (QB) that the clause in that case should be given effect because it was a special condition printed in large type and easily readable.

OCCUPIERS' CONSENT
Special condition 7 is frequently required and has been inserted for ease of use and reference.

E-MAIL SERVICE OF NOTICE
The general position under the conditions is that service by e-mail is not authorised. If the parties wish to authorise service by e-mail they will need to add an e-mail address in the space indicated at the end of the special conditions.

Document 3: CON 29 – Enquiries of the Local Authority (2016)

Law Society CON 29 Enquiries of the Local Authority (2016)

The Law Society

If you are applying for an electronic search, you need only supply one copy of the form and plan. If you are submitting a paper-based search, the form and plan must be submitted in duplicate. Please type or use BLOCK LETTERS

A.

Local Authority Name and Address

Search No:

Signed:

On behalf of:
Local authority/private search company/member of the public (indicate as applicable)

Dated:

B.

Address of the land/property

UPRN(s):

Secondary name/number:

Primary name/number:

Street:

Locality/Village:

Town:

Postcode:

C.

Other roadways, footways and footpaths in respect of which a reply to enquiries 2.1 and 3.6 is required (maximum 3 roads):

____

____

____

D.

Fees

£__________ is enclosed/is paid by NLIS transfer
(delete as applicable)

Signed:

Dated:

Reference:

Telephone No:

Fax No:

E-mail:

E.

Please reply to:

DX Address:

Notes

A. Enter name and address of appropriate local authority. If the property is near a local authority boundary, consider raising certain enquiries (e.g. road schemes) with the adjoining local authority.

B. Enter address and description of the property. Please give the UPRN(s) (Unique Property Reference Number) where known. **A duplicate plan is required for all searches submitted directly to a local authority**. The search may be returned if land/property cannot easily be identified.

C. Enter name and/or mark on plan any other roadways, footways and footpaths abutting the property (in addition to those entered in Box B) to which a reply at enquiries 2.1 and 3.6 is required (subject to a maximum of 3 roads excluding any Box B road).

D. Details of fees can be obtained from the local authority, your chosen NLIS Channel or search provider.

E. Enter the name and address/DX address of the person or company lodging or conducting this enquiry.

Oyez Peterboat Close, London SE10 0PX
www.oyezforms.co.uk

Conveyancing 29 (Enquiries)

7.2016
CON29/1
5033390

Law Society CON 29 Enquiries of the Local Authority (2016)

The Law Society

PLANNING AND BUILDING REGULATIONS

1.1. Planning and building decisions and pending applications

Which of the following relating to the property have been granted, issued or refused or (where applicable) are the subject of pending applications or agreements?
(a) a planning permission
(b) a listed building consent
(c) a conservation area consent
(d) a certificate of lawfulness of existing use or development
(e) a certificate of lawfulness of proposed use or development
(f) a certificate of lawfulness of proposed works for listed buildings
(g) a heritage partnership agreement
(h) a listed building consent order
(i) a local listed building consent order
(j) building regulations approval
(k) a building regulation completion certificate and
(l) any building regulations certificate or notice issued in respect of work carried out under a competent person self-certification scheme?

1.2. Planning designations and proposals

What designations of land use for the property, or the area, and what specific proposals for the property, are contained in any existing or proposed development plan?

ROADS AND PUBLIC RIGHTS OF WAY

Roadways, footways and footpaths

2.1. Which of the roads, footways and footpaths named in the application for this search (via boxes B and C) are:
(a) highways maintainable at public expense
(b) subject to adoption and, supported by a bond or bond waiver
(c) to be made up by a local authority who will reclaim the cost from the frontagers
(d) to be adopted by a local authority without reclaiming the cost from the frontagers

Public rights of way

2.2. Is any public right of way which abuts on, or crosses the property, shown on a definitive map or revised definitive map?
2.3. Are there any pending applications to record a public right of way that abuts, or crosses the property, on a definitive map or revised definitive map?
2.4. Are there any legal orders to stop up, divert, alter or create a public right of way which abuts, or crosses the property not yet implemented or shown on a definitive map?
2.5. If so, please attach a plan showing the approximate route

OTHER MATTERS

Apart from matters entered on the registers of local land charges, do any of the following matters apply to the property? If so, how can copies of relevant documents be obtained?

3.1. Land required for public purposes
Is the property included in land required for public purposes?

3.2. Land to be acquired for road works
Is the property included in land to be acquired for road works?

3.3. Drainage matters
(a) Is the property served by a sustainable urban drainage system (SuDS)?
(b) Are there SuDS features within the boundary of the property? If yes, is the owner responsible for maintenance?
(c) If the property benefits from a SuDS for which there is a charge, who bills the property for the surface water drainage charge?

3.4. Nearby road schemes
Is the property (or will it be) within 200 metres of any of the following?
(a) the centre line of a new trunk road or special road specified in any order, draft order or scheme
(b) the centre line of a proposed alteration or improvement to an existing road involving construction of a subway, underpass, flyover, footbridge, elevated road or dual carriageway
(c) the outer limits of construction works for a proposed alteration or improvement to an existing road involving:
 (i) construction of a roundabout (other than a mini roundabout), or
 (ii) widening by construction of one or more additional traffic lanes
(d) the outer limits of:
 (i) construction of a new road to be built by a local authority,
 (ii) an approved alteration or improvement to an existing road involving construction of a subway, underpass, flyover, footbridge, elevated road or dual carriageway,
 (iii) construction of a roundabout (other than a mini roundabout) or widening by construction of one or more additional traffic lanes
(e) the centre line of the proposed route of a new road under proposals published for public consultation
(f) the outer limits of:
 (i) construction of a proposed alteration or improvement to an existing road involving construction of a subway, underpass, flyover, footbridge, elevated road or dual carriageway
 (ii) construction of a roundabout (other than a mini roundabout)
 (iii) widening by construction of one or more additional traffic lanes, under proposals published for public consultation

3.5. Nearby railway schemes
(a) Is the property (or will it be) within 200 metres of the centre line of a proposed railway, tramway, light railway or monorail?
(b) Are there any proposals for a railway, tramway, light railway or monorail within the Local Authority's boundary?

3.6. Traffic schemes
Has a local authority approved but not yet implemented any of the following for the roads, footways and footpaths which are named in Boxes B and C and are within 200 metres of the boundaries of the property?
(a) permanent stopping up or diversion
(b) waiting or loading restrictions
(c) one way driving
(d) prohibition of driving
(e) pedestrianisation
(f) vehicle width or weight restriction
(g) traffic calming works including road humps
(h) residents parking controls
(i) minor road widening or improvement
(j) pedestrian crossings
(k) cycle tracks
(l) bridge building

3.7. Outstanding notices
Do any statutory notices which relate to the following matters subsist in relation to the property other than those revealed in a response to any other enquiry in this form?
(a) building works
(b) environment
(c) health and safety
(d) housing
(e) highways
(f) public health
(g) flood and coastal erosion risk management

3.8. Contravention of building regulations
Has a local authority authorised in relation to the property any proceedings for the contravention of any provision contained in building regulations?

3.9. Notices, orders, directions and proceedings under Planning Acts
Do any of the following subsist in relation to the property, or has a local authority decided to issue, serve, make or commence any of the following?
(a) an enforcement notice
(b) a stop notice
(c) a listed building enforcement notice
(d) a breach of condition notice
(e) a planning contravention notice
(f) another notice relating to breach of planning control
(g) a listed building repairs notice
(h) in the case of a listed building deliberately allowed to fall into disrepair, a compulsory purchase order with a direction for minimum compensation
(i) a building preservation notice
(j) a direction restricting permitted development
(k) an order revoking or modifying planning permission
(l) an order requiring discontinuance of use or alteration or removal of building or work
(m) a tree preservation order
(n) proceedings to enforce a planning agreement or planning contribution

3.10. Community infrastructure levy (CIL)
(a) Is there a CIL charging schedule?
(b) If yes, do any of the following subsist in relation to the property, or has a local authority decided to issue, serve, make or commence any of the following:-
 (i) a liability notice?
 (ii) a notice of chargeable development?
 (iii) a demand notice?
 (iv) a default liability notice?
 (v) an assumption of liability notice?
 (vi) a commencement notice?
(c) Has any demand notice been suspended?
(d) Has the Local Authority received full or part payment of any CIL liability?
(e) Has the Local Authority received any appeal against any of the above?
(f) Has a decision been taken to apply for a liability order?
(g) Has a liability order been granted?
(h) Have any other enforcement measures been taken?

3.11. Conservation area
Do the following apply in relation to the property?
(a) the making of the area a conservation area before 31 August 1974
(b) an unimplemented resolution to designate the area a conservation area

3.12. Compulsory purchase
Has any enforceable order or decision been made to compulsorily purchase or acquire the property?

3.13. Contaminated land
Do any of the following apply (including any relating to land adjacent to or adjoining the property which has been identified as contaminated land because it is in such a condition that harm or pollution of controlled waters might be caused on the property)?
(a) a contaminated land notice
(b) in relation to a register maintained under section 78R of the Environmental Protection Act 1990
 (i) a decision to make an entry
 (ii) an entry
(c) consultation with the owner or occupier of the property conducted under section 78G of the Environmental Protection Act 1990 before the service of a remediation notice

3.14. Radon gas
Do records indicate that the property is in a 'Radon Affected Area' as identified by Public Health England or Public Health Wales?

3.15. Assets of Community Value
(a) Has the property been nominated as an asset of community value? If so:-
 (i) Is it listed as an asset of community value?
 (ii) Was it excluded and placed on the 'nominated but not listed' list?
 (iii) Has the listing expired?
 (iv) Is the Local Authority reviewing or proposing to review the listing?
 (v) Are there any subsisting appeals against the listing?
(b) If the property is listed:
 (i) Has the Local Authority decided to apply to the Land Registry for an entry or cancellation of a restriction in respect of listed land affecting the property?
 (ii) Has the Local Authority received a notice of disposal?
 (iii) Has any community interest group requested to be treated as a bidder?

NOTES

1. *References to the provisions of particular Acts of Parliament or Regulations include any provisions which they have replaced and also include existing or future amendments or re-enactments.*
2. *The replies will be given in the belief that they are in accordance with information presently available to the officers of the replying local authority, but none of the local authorities or their officers accepts legal responsibility for an incorrect reply, except for negligence. Any legal responsibility for negligence will be owed to the person who raised the enquiries and the person on whose behalf they were raised. It will also be owed to any other person who has knowledge (personally or through an agent) of the replies before the time when he purchases, takes a tenancy of, or lends money on the security of the property or (if earlier) the time when he becomes contractually bound to do so.*
3. *This Form should be read in conjunction with the guidance notes available separately.*
4. *Area means any area in which the property is located.*
5. *References to the Local Authority include any predecessor Local Authority and also any Local Authority committee, sub-committee or other body or person exercising powers delegated by the Local Authority and their approval includes their decision to proceed. The replies given to certain enquiries cover knowledge and actions of both the District Local Authority and County Local Authority*
6. *Where relevant, the source department for copy documents should be provided.*

CON29/2

Document 4: CON 29O – Optional Enquiries of the Local Authority (2016)

Law Society CON 29O Enquiries of local authority (2016)

The Law Society

If you are applying for an electronic search, you need only supply one copy of the form and plan. If you are submitting a paper-based search, the form and plan must be submitted in duplicate. Please type or use BLOCK LETTERS

A.

Local authority name and address:

Search No:

Signed:

On behalf of:

Local authority/private search company/member of the public:(Indicate as appropriate)

Dated:

B.

Address of the land/property:

UPRN(s):

Secondary name/number:

Primary name/number:

Street:

Locality/Village:

Town:

Postcode:

C.

Optional enquiries (please tick as required)

- ☐ 4. Road proposals by private bodies
- ☐ 5. Advertisements
- ☐ 6. Completion Notices
- ☐ 7. Parks and countryside
- ☐ 8. Pipelines
- ☐ 9. Houses in Multiple Occupation
- ☐ 10. Noise Abatement
- ☐ 11. Urban Development Areas
- ☐ 12. Enterprise Zones, Local Development Orders and BIDs
- ☐ 13. Inner urban improvement areas
- ☐ 14. Simplified planning zones
- ☐ 15. Land maintenance notices
- ☐ 16. Mineral consultation and safeguarding areas
- ☐ 17. Hazardous substance consents
- ☐ 18. Environmental and pollution notices
- ☐ 19. Food safety notices
- ☐ 20. Hedgerow notices
- ☐ 21. Flood Defence and Land Drainage consents
- ☐ 22. Common Land and Town or Village Green

D.

Fees

£ is enclosed/is paid by NLIS transfer
(delete as applicable)

Signed:

Dated:

Reference:

Tel No:

Fax No:

Email:

E.

Please reply to:

DX Address:

Notes

A. Enter name and address of appropriate local authority. If the property is near a local authority boundary, consider raising certain enquiries (e.g. road schemes) with the adjoining local authority.
B. Enter address and description of the property. Please quote the UPRN(s) (Unique Property Reference Number) where known.
A duplicate plan is required for all searches submitted directly to a local authority. The search may be returned if land/property cannot easily be identified.
D. Details of fees can be obtained from the local authority, your chosen NLIS Channel or Search Provider.
E. Enter the name and address /DX address of the person or company lodging or conducting this enquiry

Oyez Peterboat Close, London SE10 0PX. www.oyezforms.co.uk

Conveyancing 29O (Enquiries)

7.2016
CON29O/1
5033384

Law Society CON 29O Enquiries of local authority (2016)

The Law Society

ROAD PROPOSALS BY PRIVATE BODIES

4. What proposals by others have been approved, or are the subject of pending applications, the limits of construction of which are adjoining or adjacent to the property, for-
(a) the construction of a new road, or
(b) the alteration or improvement of an existing road, involving the construction, whether or not within existing highway limits, of a subway, underpass, flyover, footbridge, elevated road, dual carriageway, the construction of a roundabout (other than a mini roundabout) or the widening of an existing road by the construction of one or more additional traffic lanes?

ADVERTISEMENTS

Entries in the register

5.1. Please list any entries in the register of applications, directions and decisions relating to consent for the display of advertisements.

5.2. If there are any entries, where can that register be inspected?

Notices, proceedings and orders

5.3. Except as shown in the official certificate of search:
(a) Has any notice been given by the Secretary of State or served in respect of a direction or proposed direction restricting deemed consent for any class of advertisement?
(b) Has the local authority resolved to serve a notice requiring the display of any advertisement to be discontinued?
(c) If a discontinuance notice has been served, has it been complied with to the satisfaction of the local authority?
(d) Has the local authority resolved to serve any other notice or proceedings relating to a contravention of the control of advertisements?
(e) Has the local authority resolved to make an order for the special control of advertisements for the area?

COMPLETION NOTICES

6. Which of the planning permissions in force has the local authority resolved to terminate by means of a completion notice under s.94 of the Town & Country Planning Act 1990?

PARKS AND COUNTRYSIDE

Areas of Outstanding Natural Beauty

7.1. Has any order under s.82 of the Countryside and Rights of Way Act 2000 been made?

National Parks

7.2. Is the property within a National Park designated under s.7 of the National Parks and Access to the Countryside Act 1949?

PIPELINES

8. Has a map been deposited under s.35 of the Pipelines Act 1962, or Schedule 7 of the Gas Act 1986, showing a pipeline laid through, or within 100 feet (30.48 metres) of the property?

HOUSES IN MULTIPLE OCCUPATION

9. Is the property a house in multiple occupation, or is it designated or proposed to be designated for selective licensing of residential accommodation in accordance with the Housing Act 2004?

NOISE ABATEMENT

Noise Abatement Zone

10.1. Has the local authority made, or resolved to make, any noise abatement zone order under s.63 of the Control of Pollution Act 1974 for the area?

Entries in Register

10.2. Has any entry been recorded in the Noise Level Register kept pursuant to s.64 of the Control of Pollution Act 1974?
10.3. If there is any entry, how can copies be obtained and where can that Register be inspected?

URBAN DEVELOPMENT AREAS

11.1. Is the area an urban development area designated under Part XVI of the Local Government, Planning and Land Act 1980?
11.2. If so, please state the name of the urban development corporation and the address of its principal office.

ENTERPRISE ZONES, LOCAL DEVELOPMENT ORDERS & BIDS

12.1. Is the area designated as an enterprise zone?
12.2. Is the area subject to a local development order?
12.3. Is the area a business improvement district (BID)?

INNER URBAN IMPROVEMENT AREAS

13. Has the local authority resolved to define the area as an improvement area under s.4 of the Inner Urban Areas Act 1978?

SIMPLIFIED PLANNING ZONES

14.1. Is the area a simplified planning zone adopted or approved pursuant to s.83 of the Town & Country Planning Act 1990?
14.2. Has the local authority approved any proposal for designating the area as a simplified planning zone?

LAND MAINTENANCE NOTICES

15. Has the local authority authorised the service of a maintenance notice under s.215 of the Town & Country Planning Act 1990?

MINERAL CONSULTATION AND SAFEGUARDING AREAS

16. Is the area a mineral consultation area or mineral safeguarding area notified by the county planning authority under Schedule 1 para 7 of the Town & Country Planning Act 1990?

HAZARDOUS SUBSTANCE CONSENTS

17.1. Please list any entries in the Register kept pursuant to s.28 of the Planning (Hazardous Substances) Act 1990.
17.2 If there are any entries:
(a) How can copies of the entries be obtained?
(b) Where can the Register be inspected?

ENVIRONMENTAL AND POLLUTION NOTICES

18. What outstanding statutory or informal notices have been issued by the local authority under the Environmental Protection Act 1990 or the Control of Pollution Act 1974?
(This enquiry does not cover notices under Part IIA or Part III of the EPA, to which enquiries 3.7 or 3.13 apply)

FOOD SAFETY NOTICES

19. What outstanding statutory notices or informal notices have been issued by the local authority under the Food Safety Act 1990 or the Food Safety and Hygiene (England) Regulations 2013?

HEDGEROW NOTICES

20.1. Please list any entries in the record maintained under regulation 10 of the Hedgerows Regulations 1997.
20.2. If there are any entries:
(a) How can copies of the matters entered be obtained?
(b) Where can the record be inspected?

FLOOD DEFENCE AND LAND DRAINAGE CONSENTS

21. Has any flood defence or land drainage consent relating to the property been given or refused, or (if applicable) is the subject of a pending application?

COMMON LAND AND TOWN OR VILLAGE GREEN

22.1. Is the property, or any land which abuts the property, registered common land or town or village green under the Commons Registration Act 1965 or the Commons Act 2006?
22.2. Is there any prescribed information about maps and statements, deposited under s.15A of the Commons Act 2006, in the register maintained under s.15B(1) of the Commons Act 2006 or under s.31A of the Highways Act 1980?
22.3. If there are any entries, how can copies of the matters registered be obtained and where can the register be inspected?

Notes:

1. References to the provisions of particular Acts of Parliament or Regulations include any provisions which they have replaced and also include existing or future amendments or re-enactments.
2. The replies will be given in the belief that they are in accordance with information presently available to the officers of the replying local authority, but none of the local authorities or their officers accepts legal responsibility for an incorrect reply, except for negligence. Any legal responsibility for negligence will be owed to the person who raised the enquiries and the person on whose behalf they were raised. It will also be owed to any other person who has knowledge (personally or through an agent) of the replies before the time when he purchases, takes a tenancy of, or lends money on the security of the property or (if earlier) the time when he becomes contractually bound to do so.
3. This form should be read in conjunction with the guidance notes available separately.
4. 'Area' means any area in which the property is located.
5. References to 'the local authority' include any predecessor local authority and also any local authority committee, sub-committee or other body or person exercising powers delegated by the local authority and their "approval" includes their decision to proceed The replies given to certain enquiries cover knowledge and actions of both the district local authority and county local authority.
6. Where relevant, the source department for copy documents should be provided.

CON29O/2

Document 5: CON DW – Drainage and Water Enquiry (2016)

CON 29DW Drainage and Water Enquiry (2016)

This search form must be submitted with the appropriate fee and a copy of the location plan.

A. Name and address of water company

(For use by water company only)

B. Address of the land/property

UPRN(s)

House name/number

Street

Locality

Town

County

Postcode

If the enquiries are made of a plot of land or of a property less than 5 years old:

Name of developer

Plot no.

Site name and phase

C. Your details

Signed ....

Name/contact name

Company name

Date

Your reference

Telephone

Fax

Email

Account no.

D. Fees

Search	Fee
CON 29DW Drainage and Water Enquiry 2016	
Total	

E. Reply to

DX

Notes

The drainage and water enquiries are listed on page 2 of this form.

Completing and submitting this form to a water company indicates an acceptance of that water company's terms and conditions. Terms and conditions may vary between water companies. Request a copy of the terms and conditions from the water company or see its website for details.

A. Ensure that search forms are sent to the correct water company, see www.con29drainagewater.co.uk for details.

B. Enter the address of the property. Please give the Unique Property Reference Number if known. If the enquiries are made of a plot of land or the property is less than 5 years old, please give the developer's details.

C. Sign, date and enter your details. Account customers of water companies may enter their account number.

D. Enter the fee for the enquiries. Fees may differ between water companies. Consult the water company or see www.con29drainagewater.co.uk for the current fees.

E. Enter the name and address/DX address of the person or company conducting this enquiry.

Oyez Peterboat Close, London SE10 0PX www.oyezforms.co.uk
Oyez is an approved Law Society supplier.

Conveyancing 29 DW (2016)

7.2016

5033387

CON29DW/1

CON 29DW Drainage and Water Enquiry (2016)

Question

Maps

1.1	Where relevant, please include a copy of an extract from the public sewer map.
1.2	Where relevant, please include a copy of an extract from the map of waterworks.

Drainage

2.1	Does foul water from the property drain to a public sewer?
2.2	Does surface water from the property drain to a public sewer?
2.3	Is a surface water drainage charge payable?
2.4	Does the public sewer map indicate any public sewer, disposal main or lateral drain within the boundaries of the property?
2.4.1	Does the public sewer map indicate any pumping station or ancillary apparatus within the boundaries of the property?
2.5	Does the public sewer map indicate any public sewer within 30.48 metres (100 feet) of any buildings within the property?
2.5.1	Does the public sewer map indicate any pumping station or any other ancillary apparatus within 50 metres (164.04 feet) of any buildings within the property?
2.6	Are any sewers or lateral drains serving or which are proposed to serve the property the subject of an existing adoption agreement or an application for such an agreement?
2.7	Has any Sewerage Undertaker approved or been consulted about any plans to erect a building or extension on the property over or in the vicinity of a public sewer, disposal main or drain?
2.8	Is any building which is or forms part of the property at risk of internal flooding due to overloaded public sewers?
2.9	Please state the distance from the property to the nearest boundary of the nearest sewage treatment works.

Water

3.1	Is the property connected to mains water supply?
3.2	Are there any water mains, resource mains or discharge pipes within the boundaries of the property?
3.3	Is any water main or service pipe serving or which is proposed to serve the property the subject of an existing adoption agreement or an application for such an agreement?
3.4	Is the property at risk of receiving low water pressure or flow?
3.5	What is the classification of the water supply for the property?
3.6	Please include details of the location of any water meter serving the property.

Charging

4.1.1	Who is responsible for providing the sewerage services for the property?
4.1.2	Who is responsible for providing the water services for the property?
4.2	Who bills the property for sewerage services?
4.3	Who bills the property for water services?
4.4	What is the current basis for charging for sewerage and / or water services at the property?
4.5	Will the basis for charging for sewerage and water services at the property change as a consequence of a change of occupation?

CON29DW/2

Document 6: CON 29 (Long) – Enquiries Before Contract

Short description of the property

re

Parties

to

Oyez

ENQUIRIES

BEFORE CONTRACT

In cases of property subject to a tenancy, forms **Con 291** (general business and residential tenancies) *or* **Con 292** (agricultural tenancies) should also be used.

Please strike out enquiries which are not applicable

Replies are requested to the following enquiries.

Proposed buyer's solicitors.

Date

GENERAL ENQUIRIES

The replies are as follows.

Proposed seller's solicitors.

Date

REPLIES

These replies, except in the case of any enquiry expressly requiring a reply from the Seller's solicitors, are given on behalf of the proposed Seller and without responsibility on the part of his solicitors their partners or employees. They are believed to be correct but the accuracy is not guaranteed and they do not obviate the need to make appropriate searches, enquiries and inspections.

1. Boundaries

(A) To whom do all the boundary walls, fences, hedges and ditches belong?

(B) If no definite indications exist, which has the Seller maintained or regarded as his responsibility?

(C) Is the Seller aware of any divergence between the physical boundaries and those shown on the title deeds?

2. Disputes

(A) Is the Seller aware of any past or current disputes regarding boundaries, easements, covenants or other matters relating to the property or its use?

(B) During the last three years, has the Seller complained or had cause to complain about the state and condition, or the manner of use, of any adjoining or neighbouring property? If so, please give particulars.

3. Notices

Please give particulars of all notices relating to the property, or to matters likely to affect its use or enjoyment, that the Seller (or to his knowledge any predecessor in title) has given or received and confirm whether any such notices have been complied with.

4. Guarantees etc.

(A) Please supply a copy of any of the following of which the Buyer is to have the benefit:

agreement, covenant, guarantee, warranty, bond, report, certificate, indemnity and insurance policy,
relating to any of the following matters:
the construction of the property, or any part of it, or of any building of which it forms part;
any contamination which was, is or may be at or under the property;
any repair or replacement of, or treatment or improvement to the fabric of the property;
the maintenance of any accessway;
the construction costs of any road (including lighting, drainage and crossovers) to which the property fronts, and the charges for adopting any such road as maintainable at the public expense;
a defective title;
breach of any restrictive covenant.

(B) (i) What defects or other matters have become apparent, or adverse claims have been made by third parties, which might give rise to a claim under any document mentioned in (A)?
(ii) Has notice of such defect, matter or adverse claim been given? If so, please give particulars.
(iii) Please give particulars of all such claims already made, whether or not already settled.

(C) Has any document relating to the property been the subject of any application for designation as an exempt information document by you or anyone else to your knowledge?

5. Services

(A) Does the property have mains drainage, water, electricity and gas services? Who supplies the services?

(B) Is the property connected to any telephone, television, internet or other media services?

(C) Is the water supply metered?

(D) Do any of the services (except where part of the mains) pass through or over property not included in the sale?

(E) If so, please give details of route and particulars of any easement, grant, exception, reservation, wayleave, licence or consent authorising this.

(F) Please supply a copy of any licence to abstract water and of any consent or licence relating to drainage, issued in respect of the property or the activities carried on there.

6. Facilities

(A) Except in the case of public rights or where particulars have already been given, what rights are there for the use of the following facilities, whether enjoyed by the owner or occupier of the property, or over the property for the benefit of other property:

- Access for light and air;
- Access for pedestrians and vehicles;
- Emergency escape routes;
- Pipes and wires for services not dealt with in Enquiry 5;
- Access and facilities for repair, maintenance and replacement.

Please supply copies of any relevant documents.

(B) Has any person taken any action to stop (whether immediately or at some future time) the use of any facility? If so, please give particulars.

(C) In respect of maintenance, repair or replacement work on any land or fixtures affording any facility:

(i) What work has been done by the Seller (or, to his knowledge, any predecessor in title), and when?
(ii) What work has the Seller been called upon to do which has not yet been done?
(iii) Is the Seller aware of any circumstances likely to give rise to any expenditure in relation to such work?
(iv) What sums has the Seller contributed to work done by others, and when? Is any demand for such sums still outstanding?
(v) What sums has the Seller called upon others to contribute, and when? Is any demand still outstanding?

7. Adverse Rights

(A) Is the Seller aware of any rights or informal arrangements affecting the property, other than any disclosed in the draft contract or immediately apparent on inspection, which are exercisable by virtue of an easement, grant, wayleave, licence, consent, agreement relating to an ancient monument or land near it, or otherwise or which are in the nature of public or common rights?

(B) (i) Please give the full names, and ages if under 18, of all persons in actual occupation of the property.
(ii) What legal or equitable interest in the property has each of those persons?

(C) Whether or not the title is registered, is the Seller aware of any other interests under Schedules 1, 3 and 12 of the Land Registration Act 2002?

8. Restrictions

(A) Have all restrictions affecting the property or its use been observed up to the date hereof? If not, please give details.

(B) Where such restrictions have in the past required any person's consent or approval of plans, does the Seller have written evidence of that consent or approval?

9. Planning etc.

(A) (i) What is the present use of the property?
(ii) When did the present use of the property commence?
(iii) Has this use been continuous since it commenced?

(B) During the four years immediately prior to receipt of these enquiries:

(i) Were any of the buildings on the property erected, or have any been altered or added to?

(ii) Have any other building, engineering, mining or other operations been carried out in, on, over or under the property?
(iii) Has any condition or limitation on any planning permission not been complied with?

If so, please give details.

(C) Please supply a copy of:

(i) Any planning permission authorising or imposing conditions upon the present use of the property, and the erection or retention of the buildings now on it.
(ii) Any bye-law approval or building regulation consent relating to those buildings.
(iii) Any fire risk assessments and any enforcement, prohibition or alteration notices.

(D) (i) Please confirm that all works carried out in, on, over or under the property were carried out in accordance with the Building Regulations in force at the relevant time.
(ii) Please supply certificates of compliance with Building Regulations relating to such works.

(E) Have all statutes and requirements of local and other competent authorities relating to the occupation and use of the property been complied with? If not, please give details.

10. Fixtures, Fittings etc.

(A) What fixtures, fittings, plant and equipment are included in the sale?

(B) What fixtures, fittings, plant and equipment will be removed prior to completion?

(C) Have any claims for capital or other allowances been made in relation to the plant, machinery or industrial buildings included in the sale?
If so, please give details.

11. Outgoings

(A) What is the rateable value or council tax band (as appropriate) of the property?

(B) What other periodic charges affect the property or its occupier, apart from business rates or council tax (as appropriate) and water service charges?

12. Completion

(A) How long after exchange of contracts will the Seller be able to give vacant possession of the whole of the property?

(B) The Buyer's solicitors wish to complete by adopting the current edition of the Law Society's Code for Completion by Post. Do the Seller's solicitors agree?

13. Environment and Environmental Health

(A) Is the Seller aware of:

(i) the presence of dangerous or polluting substances or materials in any soil, groundwater or body of water at or under the property or at or under any adjoining or neighbouring land?

(ii) any previous use or activities or any current use or activities involving dangerous or polluting substances or materials, at the property or any adjoining or neighbouring land?

(iii) any landfill site, whether closed or in operation, at, or within 250 metres of the property?

If the answer to any of the above questions is "Yes", please give details.

(B) Please supply a copy of all environmental audits, assessments, surveys, energy performance certificates and other such reports in respect of the property.

(C) Is the Seller aware of the presence of any asbestos or other harmful materials or substances in the fabric of the property or in any of the fixtures? If so, please give details.

(D) Is the Seller aware of any matter coming from any adjoining or neighbouring land which interferes, or which the Seller believes could interfere, with the use or enjoyment of the property - for example, odours, noise, fumes, dust, steam, gases or smoke? If so, please give details.

(E) Has the property ever flooded from any source?

14. VAT

(A) Will the Seller charge VAT on the sale?

(B) If so, has the Seller made an option to tax in relation to the property?

For Leasehold Enquiries see over

ADDITIONAL ENQUIRIES

LEASEHOLD ENQUIRIES

I. General

(A) Is the lease under which the property is held a head lease or an underlease?

(B) Please state the names and addresses of
- the lessor;
- any superior lessor;
- the solicitors of all of them;
- the receivers of the rent;
- the managing agents.

(C) Please supply copies of all licences granted by the lessor, other than licences to assign.

(D) What steps have been taken to obtain the lessor's consent to the proposed assignment? Please supply a copy of any licence granted.

II. Covenants

(A) Has the lessor complained of any breach of covenant?

(B) Has any obligation in the lease to paint or do any other work by or at a particular time been strictly fulfilled? If not, please give details.

(C) Has the Seller had cause to complain of any breach of the lessor's covenants?

III. Service Charge

(A) Please give details of service charge payments for the last three years, with any supporting accounts or vouchers that the Seller has.

(B) Has the Seller, or to his knowledge any predecessor in title, exercised a statutory right to obtain information? If so, with what result?

IV. Insurance

Please supply details of the insurance covering the building(s), including policy number, insured's name(s), risks covered, for what amount, premium and date to which insured.

V. Reversionary Title

Please supply a copy of a marked abstract or official copy of the freehold title and of any superior lease.

VI. Stamp Duty Land Tax

Please confirm that no further land transaction return is required in respect of any transaction involving the lease and supply a copy of each land transaction return made and a copy of each stamp duty land tax certificate issued by H.M. Revenue & Customs.

ADDITIONAL ENQUIRIES

Oyez Peterboat Close, London SE10 0PX
www.oyezforms.co.uk

2019 Edition 3.2019

5033010

Document 7: CON 29M – Coal Mining Search

CON 29M (2018) COAL MINING SEARCH

A cheque with the appropriate fee MUST be sent with the printed form unless charged to an appropriate account. A location plan should be included with all search requests to avoid delay. Users should retain a copy of the form and the location plan.

The Coal Authority **Mining Reports** 200 Lichfield Lane Mansfield Nottinghamshire **NG18 4RG** **DX 716176 MANSFIELD 5**	(For Coal Authority Use Only)

Complete each applicable box below. Use type or BLOCK LETTERS.	Notes
Reply to: DX	Enter the name, firm/organisation and DX number to which the report is to be returned. If you are not a member of the DX system please enter your name, firm/organisation and the full address, including postcode, to which the report is to be returned.
Email (if applicable):	Only insert your email address when you wish the report to be returned by email in a secure PDF file.
Telephone number:	Insert your telephone number so that the Authority may contact you if necessary regarding this search.
Account number (if applicable):	See User Guide 2018.
Report type requested (tick box): Residential Property Search ☐ Non-Residential Property or Site Search ☐	Please tick the appropriate box and ensure that the correct fee is enclosed for the report type requested (see Notes overleaf). It is inappropriate to request a Residential Property Search for non-residential property or sites and any such requests will be returned for resubmission and the correct fee. A Residential Property Search includes enquiries 1-12 overleaf. A Non-Residential or Site Search includes enquiries 1-15 overleaf.
Expedited Search required (delete as applicable): **YES/NO** **Fax number:**	Expedited Search Reports can be ordered and returned by fax within 48 hours. The full fee, including the expedite element, is payable in advance (see Notes overleaf). Only insert your fax number when you wish the report to be returned by fax or you are requesting an expedited search.
Request date:	Insert the date on which this search form is sent.
Address of the land/site/property: Address Street Locality Town/Village County Postcode	The Address field may be used for house and flat names and numbers. Include the complete address if possible. Always include the postcode where the property has a postal address. Where the land, site or property does not have a postal address, use any fields provided to include a description sufficient for the property to be identified.
Location plan enclosed (delete as applicable): **YES/NO**	Searches may be returned unanswered or delayed if a plan is not enclosed (see Notes overleaf).
Customer reference:	Insert your own file reference number.

TERMS AND CONDITIONS - These enquiries are made and the replies prepared in accordance with the Terms and Conditions 2018, User Guide 2018, and Law Society's Guidance Notes 2018. These are availabe to view at www.miningreports.co.uk or by contacting the Coal Authority's Mining Reports Helpline on 0845 762 6848 or by email to miningreports@coal.gov.uk. These terms and conditions apply regardless of the method used to order and receive reports.

CON 29M (2018) COAL MINING SEARCH

RESIDENTIAL PROPERTY SEARCH ENQUIRIES

1. Past underground coal mining

Is the property within the zone of likely physical influence on the surface of past underground coal workings? If yes, indicate the number of seams involved, their depth and approximate last date of working.

For the purpose of this enquiry "zone of likely physical influence" will be based on the principle of 0.7 times the depth of the working allowing for seam inclination.

2. Present underground coal mining

Is the property within the zone of likely physical influence on the surface of present underground coal workings? If yes, indicate the seams involved.

3. Future underground coal mining

(a) Is the property within any geographical area for which the Coal Authority is determining whether to grant a licence to remove coal by underground methods?

(b) Is the property within any geographical area for which a licence to remove coal by underground methods has been granted? If yes, when was the licence granted?

(c) Is the property within the zone of likely physical influence on the surface of planned future underground coal workings? If yes, indicate the seams involved and approximate date of working.

(d) Has any notice of proposals relating to underground coal mining operations been given under section 46 of the Coal Mining Subsidence Act 1991? If yes, supply the date and details of the last such notice.

For the purpose of this enquiry "geographical area" means the surface area directly above a licence being determined or granted.

4. Shafts and adits (mine entries)

Are there any shafts and adits or other entries to underground coal mine workings within the property or within 20 metres of the boundary of the property? If yes, supply a plan showing the approximate recorded location and any relevant information, where available, regarding any treatment carried out to such shafts, adits or entries.

5. Coal mining geology

Is there any record of any fault or other line of weakness due to coal mining at the surface within the boundary of the property that has made the property unstable?

6. Past opencast coal mining

Is the property situated within the geographical boundary of an opencast site from which coal has been removed in the past by opencast methods?

7. Present opencast coal mining

Is the property within 200 metres of the boundary of an opencast site from which coal is being removed by opencast methods?

8. Future opencast coal mining

(a) Is the property within 800 metres of the boundary of an opencast site for which the Coal Authority are determining whether to grant a licence to remove coal by opencast methods?

(b) Is the property within 800 metres of the boundary of an opencast site for which a licence to remove coal by opencast methods has been granted? If yes, when was the licence granted?

9. Coal mining subsidence claims

(a) Has any damage notice or claim for alleged coal mining subsidence damage to the property been given, made or pursued since 1st January 1994? If yes, supply the date of such notice or claim.

(b) In respect of any such notice or claim has the responsible person given notice agreeing that there is a remedial obligation or otherwise accepted that a claim would lie against him?

(c) In respect of any such notice or acceptance has the remedial obligation or claim been discharged? If yes, state whether such remedial obligation or claim was discharged by repair or payment, or a combination thereof.

(d) Does any current "Stop Notice" delaying the start of remedial works or repairs affect the property? If yes, supply the date of the notice.

(e) Has any request been made under section 33 of the 1991 Act to execute preventive works before coal is worked, which would prevent the occurrence or reduce the extent of subsidence damage to any buildings, structures or works and, if yes, has any person withheld consent or failed to comply with any such request to execute preventive works?

10. Mine gas emissions

Does the Coal Authority have record of any mine gas emission within the boundary of the property being reported that subsequently required action by the Authority to mitigate the effects of the mine gas emission?

11. Emergency Surface Hazard Call Out incidents

Have the Coal Authority carried out any work on or within the boundaries of the property following a report of an alleged hazard related to coal mining under the Authority's Emergency Surface Hazard Call Out procedures?

ADDITIONAL ENQUIRIES FOR NON-RESIDENTIAL PROPERTY OR SITE SEARCH IN COAL MINING AREAS

12. Withdrawal of support

(a) Does the land lie within a geographical area in respect of which a notice of entitlement to withdraw support has been published? If yes, supply the date of the notice.

(b) Does the land lie within a geographical area in respect of which a revocation notice has been given under section 41 of the Coal Industry Act 1994? If yes, supply the date of the notice.

13. Working facilities orders

Is the property within a geographical area subject to an order in respect of the working of coal under the Mines (Working Facilities and Support) Acts 1923 and 1966 or any statutory modification or amendment thereof? If yes, supply the date and title of the order.

14. Payments to owners of former copyhold land

(c) Has any relevant notice, which may affect the property, been given?

(d) If yes, has any notice of retained interests in coal and coal mines been given?

(e) If yes, has any acceptance notice or rejection notice been served?

(f) If any such acceptance notice has been served, has any compensation been paid to a claimant?

NOTES

(A) Advice and information on coal mining and brine subsidence searches

For information on procedure, turnaround and current fees, account facilities or further to a specific search, contact the Coal Authority Mining Reports Helpline on 0845 762 6848 or by email to miningreports@coal.gov.uk or visit www.miningreports.co.uk. There is a higher fee for the Non-Residential or Site Search and an additional fee for Expedited Searches. Searches having incorrect fees will be returned uncompleted.

(B) Refunds

No refund or transfer of any fee (or part of a fee) will be made once a search has been logged onto the Authority's MRSDS computer systems for report production.

(C) Expedited Searches

Select 'YES' against Expedited Search and add your fax number in full. This service is only available to credit account customers or where the full fee, including the expedite element, is paid in advance by credit/debit card (over the telephone 0845 762 6848) or by cheque (postal enquiries).

(D) Affected Areas

A directory of places where a CON 29M (2018) search is required can be found on the Coal Authority's website at www.miningreports.co.uk together with a useful 'search by postcode' facility.

(E) Ordering CON 29M reports

Reports can be ordered by telephone, and ordered and returned by post, fax or electronically via the internet and email (www.miningreports.co.uk). A fully electronic link to the National Land Information Service (NLIS) provides a further channel for customers to order and receive searches.

(F) Terms and Conditions, User Guide and Law Society's Guidance

These Notes should be read in conjunction with the Terms and Conditions 2018, User Guide 2018, and the Law Society's Guidance Notes 2018, under which all replies to these enquiries are made. These terms apply regardless of the method used to order and receive reports. The Terms and Conditions and User Guide have been approved by the Law Society following consultation with key stakeholders including the CML and RICS, and apply to all searches made including those using the CON 29M enquiry form. Copies of these documents can be found on the Coal Authority's website at www.miningreports.co.uk

(G) Plans

If a plan is not submitted there may be difficulties and delays in identifying the property and its extent, in which case the Coal Authority may request that a plan be supplied before the search can be completed.

 CON29M/2

Document 8: TA13 - Completion Information and Undertakings

www.lawsociety.org.uk

The Law Society

Completion information and undertakings (4th edition) (2023)

WARNING: Replies to questions 3.2, 5.2 and 5.3 are solicitor's undertakings.

Address of the property

Address line 1	
Address line 2	
Address line 3	
Town / City	
Postcode	

Full names of the seller(s)

Please supply full names of the seller(s) of the property.
Individual seller(s) complete (a). If the seller is a company, complete (b)

(a) Name of seller(s) if individual(s)

1	First name	2	First name
	Middle name(s)		Middle name(s)
	Last name		Last name
3	First name	4	First name
	Middle name(s)		Middle name(s)
	Last name		Last name

(b) Name of seller if a company

Company name	
Company number	
Director/authorised person	
Country of incorporation	

Full names of the buyer(s)

Please supply full names of the buyer(s) of the property.
Individual buyer(s) complete (a). If the buyer is a company, complete (b)

(a) Name of buyer(s) if individual(s)

1	First name Middle name(s) Last name	2	First name Middle name(s) Last name
3	First name Middle name(s) Last name	4	First name Middle name(s) Last name

(b) Name of buyer if a company

Company name	
Company number	
Director/authorised person	
Country of incorporation	

1. Vacant possession

1.1 If vacant possession (of whole or part) is to be given on completion, what arrangements will be made to hand over the keys, any equivalent electronic devices, passcodes and alarm codes?

☐ Will be left with agents
☐ Will be left with seller's solicitor
☐ Other

If Other, please give details:

1.2 If vacant possession (of whole or part) is not being given, please confirm:

(a) that an authority to the tenant to pay the rent to the buyer will be handed over or be included with the documents to be remitted to the buyer's solicitors on completion. ☐ Confirmed

(b) that any keys and equivalent electronic devices and passcodes and alarm codes in the hands of the seller (as landlord) will be handed over on completion. ☐ Confirmed

2. Deeds and documents

2.1 If the title is unregistered, do you hold all of the title deeds? ☐ Yes ☐ No

If No, please give details:

2.2 Please attach or confirm that you will supply a copy of the executed transfer before completion. ☐ Attached ☐ To follow

2.3 Please list all deeds and documents to be sent on completion.

3. Completion

3.1 Will completion take place at your office? ☐ Yes ☐ No

If No, where or how will it take place?

3.2 We wish to complete through the post in accordance with the Law Society's Code for Completion by Post 2019 (the Code). Please confirm that:

(a) You undertake to adopt the Code; and ☐ Confirmed

(b) The mortgages and charges that you undertake to redeem or discharge in your replies to 5.1 and 5.2 are those specified for the purpose of paragraph 7 of the Code. ☐ Confirmed

4. Money

WARNING: Be alert to the risks of emailing bank details.

4.1 Please state the exact amount payable on completion. £

If it is not just the balance purchase money, please provide copy receipts for any rent or service charge or other payments being apportioned. ☐ Attached ☐ Not applicable

4.2 Please provide details of your bank and the account to which completion monies are to be sent:

Name of bank:

Address of bank:

Address line 1

Address line 2

Address line 3

Town / City

Postcode

Branch sort code:

Client account name:

Client account number:

Client firm's reference:

5. Mortgages and charges

5.1 Please list the mortgages or charges secured on the property which you undertake to redeem or discharge to the extent that they relate to the property on or before completion (this includes repayment of any discount under the Housing Acts).

5.2 Do you undertake to redeem or discharge the mortgages and charges listed in reply to 5.1 on completion and to send to us Form DS1, DS3, the receipted charge(s) or confirmation that notice of release or discharge in electronic form has been given to HM Land Registry as and when you receive them? ☐ Yes ☐ No

5.3 If you DO NOT agree to adopt the current Law Society's Code for Completion by Post, please confirm that you are the duly authorised agent of the proprietor of every mortgage or charge on the property which you have undertaken, in reply to 5.2, to redeem or discharge. ☐ Confirmed

Buyer's solicitor: ____________________ Dated: ____________

Seller's solicitor: ____________________ Dated: ____________

Document 9: TA6 - Property Information Form 5th edition

www.lawsociety.org.uk

The Law Society

Law Society Property Information Form (5th edition) (2024)

Note: Please read the ***Explanatory Notes for Sellers and Buyers*** before completing this form

Full names of the seller(s)

Please state full names of the seller(s) of the property.
Individual seller(s) complete (a) and (b). If the seller is a company, complete (c)

(a) Name of seller(s) if individual(s)
These are the person or persons named as the owner on the HM Land Registry title or on the deeds by the owner's legal representative(s) if selling under a power of attorney or grant of probate or representation.

1 First name: ☐ Middle name(s): ☐ Last name: ☐	**2** First name: ☐ Middle name(s): ☐ Last name: ☐
3 First name: ☐ Middle name(s): ☐ Last name: ☐	**4** First name: ☐ Middle name(s): ☐ Last name: ☐

(b) Please provide details of the capacity in which you are providing information for the sale.

Please tick one:
- ☐ Seller(s)
- ☐ Seller's personal representative
- ☐ Attorney(s)
- ☐ Trustee(s)

(c) Name of seller if a company

Company name

Company number

Director/authorised person

Country of incorporation

When did you become the owner of, or get authority to sell, the property? (DD/MM/YYYY)

Property being sold

Enter the full address

Address line 1

Address line 2

Address line 3

Town / City

Postcode

What is the UPRN (Unique Property Reference Number) of the property?
To find the UPRN go to: **https://www.findmyaddress.co.uk/search**

Seller's solicitor

Enter the details of your solicitor's firm:

Name of solicitor's firm	
Address line 1	
Address line 2	
Address line 3	
Town / City	
Postcode	
Contact name	
Email	
Reference number	

About this form

This form is completed by the seller to supply the detailed information and documents which may be relied upon for both the marketing of your property and the conveyancing process.

Part 1 provides the material information needed by estate agents to start marketing your property.

Material information is explained in the National Trading Standards Estate and Letting Agency Team's guidance to estate agents, ***Material Information in Property Listings (Sales)***, so that property listings comply with the Consumer Protection from Unfair Trading Regulations 2008.

Some of the information in Part 1 will also be needed by your solicitor for the conveyancing process.

Part 2 asks supplementary questions, providing additional information which may be relevant for your property and is needed for the conveyancing process.

Instructions to the seller

- The answers should be prepared by the person or persons named as owner on the deeds or HM Land Registry title or by the owner's legal representative(s) if selling under a power of attorney or grant of probate or representation. If there is more than one seller, you should prepare the answers together, or if only one seller prepares the form, the other(s) should check the answers given, and all sellers should then sign the form.

- You should answer the questions as accurately as you can from your own knowledge (or, in the case of legal representatives, you or the owner). You are not expected to have expert knowledge of legal or technical matters or matters that occurred prior to your ownership of the property, or information that can only be obtained by carrying out surveys, local authority searches or other enquiries.
- It is very important that your answers are truthful. If you give incorrect or incomplete information to the buyer (on this form or otherwise in writing or in conversation, whether through your estate agent or solicitor or directly to the buyer), a prospective buyer may make a claim for compensation from you or refuse to complete the purchase.
- If you become aware of any information which would alter any replies you have given, you must inform your solicitor immediately. This is as important as giving the right answers in the first place. You should not change any arrangements concerning the property (such as with a tenant or neighbour) and affecting the information you have given without consulting your solicitor first.
- If you do not know the answer to any question, you must say so. If you are unsure of the meaning of any questions or answers, please ask your solicitor. Completing this form is not mandatory, but omissions or delays in providing information may affect the sale.
- Please give your solicitor any letters, agreements, or other papers which help answer the questions. The buyer will want the originals, where you have them, in due course, for example, guarantees. If you are aware of any material or information which you are unable to supply with the answers, tell your solicitor. If some of the documentation is lost, you may need to obtain copies at your own expense. You should also pass on promptly to your solicitor any notices or other information you have received concerning the property, and any that arrive at any time before completion of the sale. If you are not sure if a notice is relevant to the sale, ask your solicitor.

Instructions to the buyer

- If, separately from this form, you receive any information about the property (in writing or in conversation, whether direct from the seller or through an estate agent or solicitor or directly to you) on which you wish to rely when buying the property, you should tell your solicitor.
- The seller will only be able to tell you about matters they know. They may not have knowledge of legal or technical matters or the contents of reports. You should not expect the seller to have knowledge of, or give information about, matters prior to their ownership of the property. To obtain up-to-date information about these matters you must make your own enquiries and investigations or arrange for them to be carried out for you. Your solicitor will help you decide which searches you need when buying the property to provide you with the most up-to-date information.
- If you are obtaining a mortgage, please remember that the inspection carried out on behalf of your lender is not a survey but only a valuation for the lender's purposes. To satisfy yourself as to the physical and structural condition of the property, you should instruct a surveyor to carry out a survey for you. Even if the seller has guarantees or other documents relating to these aspects of the property, the seller is not giving any warranty of the condition of the property, and this is not included in the conveyancing work by your solicitor.

Definitions

'Access roads' means any private road(s) giving access from the property to a public highway.

'Alterations' means work intended to change the function or appearance of a place or property.

'Building work' means any work listed in **Regulation 3(1)** of the **Building Regulations 2010** and as amended in Wales since 2014.

'Buyer' means all buyers together where the property is being bought by more than one person.

'Commonhold' is a form of ownership for multi-occupancy developments. Each unit-holder owns the freehold of their home, and a commonhold or residents' association owns and manages the common parts of the property.

'Commonhold community statement' means a document which makes provision in relation to specified land for (a) the rights and duties of the commonhold association, and (b) the rights and duties of the unit-holders.

'Commonhold unit' means a commonhold unit specified in a commonhold community statement.

'Consent' means approval for matters affecting **freehold** title (for example a restrictive covenant) or leasehold title (such as for alterations).

'Freehold' means you own the property and the land it sits on.

'Flooding' means any case where land not normally covered by water becomes covered by water.

'Leasehold' means you do not own the land the property stands on. A lease is an agreement between you and the owner of the freehold or of another lease. The lease sets out what you can and cannot do as a leaseholder.

'Listed property' means a property of special architectural or historic interest as "listed" in the **National Heritage List for England** and the **National Historic Assets of Wales**.

'Planning documents' means any planning permissions, building regulations approvals and completion certificates or planning orders or documents.

'Property' includes all buildings and land within its boundaries.

'Restrictive covenant' means clause(s) in deed(s) or lease(s) that limits what the owner of the land or lease can do with the property.

'Sale contract' means the legal contract between the buyer and seller for the purchase/sale of the property. It is a legal document and once the contract is exchanged it is legally binding on all parties.

'Searches' includes reports in relation to a variety of matters covering topics such as local, planning and environmental.

'Seller' means all sellers together where the property is owned by more than one person.

'Shared ownership' means you buy a share in a property with an organisation such as a housing association, to whom you will pay rent on the part you don't own. Most homes purchased through shared ownership are leasehold.

'Solicitor' includes, for the purposes of this form, 'conveyancer' as defined by HM Land Registry Practice Guide 67.

TA6 PART 1

PART A MATERIAL INFORMATION

1. Council Tax

What Council Tax band is the property in? Band [ ]

2. Asking price

What is the asking price of the property you are selling? £ [ ]

3. Tenure, ownership and charges

3.1 **Is your property freehold, leasehold, shared ownership or commonhold? Please tick all that apply.**
Note: Some freehold properties may have land or property that is also leased. If you have a combination of tenures, please speak to your solicitor.

☐ Freehold ☐ Leasehold ☐ Shared ownership ☐ Commonhold

If 'Freehold', please go to question 3.17 and do not answer questions 3.2–3.16.
If 'Leasehold', please go to question 3.4 and do not answer questions 3.2–3.3.
If 'Commonhold', please go to question 3.13 and do not answer questions 3.2–3.12.

Shared ownership

Note: Information about shared ownership is available at: **https://www.gov.uk/shared-ownership-scheme**

3.2 **What share of the property do you own?** [ ] %

3.3 **How much rent do you pay each year for the remaining share of the property?** £ [ ] / year

Leasehold / Shared ownership

Note: Information about leasehold property is available at: **https://www.gov.uk/leasehold-property**. You will need a copy of your lease to answer these questions. If you do not have a copy of your lease, ask your solicitor for help.

3.4 What is the end date of your lease? (DD/MM/YYYY) ☐

3.5 Have you applied to the landlord:

(a) for an extension of the lease? ☐ Yes ☐ No

(b) to buy the freehold? ☐ Yes ☐ No

(c) to vary the terms of the lease? ☐ Yes ☐ No

If Yes to any question in 3.5(a)–(c), please provide details of when you applied and whether the application has been accepted:

Ground rent

3.6 How much ground rent is due each year? £ / year

3.7 Does your lease say that the ground rent increases? ☐ Yes ☐ No

If Yes, please give details of the next increase (date, frequency, amount):
If you don't have your lease, then your solicitor will be able to obtain a copy.

(a) Date of next increase: (DD/MM/YYYY)

(b) Frequency of increase:

(c) Amount you will pay after the increase (if known): £

(d) How is the increase calculated?

Service charges

Note: Your lease should set out the way the service charge is organised and what can be charged. Service charges are usually for the maintenance and upkeep of the property, including common areas and gardens. Further information is available at: **https://www.gov.uk/leasehold-property/service-charges-and-other-expenses**

3.8 Does the lease require you to pay service charges? ☐ Yes ☐ No

(a) Have you paid service charges? ☐ Yes ☐ No

If No to both question 3.8 and 3.8(a), please continue to question 3.17 and do not answer questions 3.9–3.16

3.9 Please give the dates of your last annual service charge (DD/MM/YYYY) From: ______ To: ______

3.10 How much was your last annual service charge? £

3.11 Is there a budget or known amount for the service charge this year? ☐ Yes ☐ No

If Yes, please provide any relevant documents, such as a service charge bill. ☐ Attached ☐ To follow

3.12 How frequently are the payments due?
Please tick the appropriate box: ☐ Monthly ☐ Six monthly ☐ Quarterly ☐ Annually

Commonhold

3.13 Please provide a copy of the commonhold community statement. ☐ Attached ☐ To follow

3.14 How many units are there in the commonhold? ______

3.15 How much does your unit pay annually under the commonhold assessment? £

3.16 Does the commonhold have a reserve fund? ☐ Yes ☐ No

How much does your unit pay annually into the reserve fund? £

Other charges

Note: Question 3.17 refers to charges other than those payable under a lease. If the property is freehold, there can be additional charges, for example, payments to a management company or other person for the use of a private drainage system.

3.17 Do you have to pay any additional charges relating to the property (apart from council tax, utility charges, etc.), for example, payments to a management company or other person?

☐ Yes ☐ No

If Yes, please give details:

3.18 How much is due annually for these other charges?

£

Access roads and footpaths

3.19 Do you have to pay anything towards the costs of maintaining access roads or footpaths?

☐ Yes ☐ No

If Yes, please give details of who payments are made to:

3.20 How much is due annually towards these costs?

£

PART B MATERIAL INFORMATION

4. Physical characteristics of the property

4.1 Is the property a house, bungalow, flat or maisonette?

☐ House ☐ Bungalow
☐ Flat ☐ Maisonette

4.2 If a house or bungalow, is it detached, semi-detached, terraced or end of terrace?

☐ Detached ☐ Semi-detached
☐ Terraced ☐ End of terrace

4.3 What construction type or materials have been used in the property?
Note: This list is not exhaustive but may include, for example, brick and block, steel framed, timber framed, thatched, prefabricated. If you are unsure about the construction type or materials used, please say 'not known'.

☐

4.4 How many rooms does the property have?

Bedrooms	☐
Bathrooms	☐
Reception rooms	☐
Other	☐

If Other, please specify: ☐

5. Utilities and services

5.1 Which of the following services are connected to the property?

Electricity: ☐ Mains ☐ Solar panels ☐ Wind turbine ☐ Other

If Other, please specify: ☐

Water: ☐ Mains (metered) ☐ Mains (unmetered) ☐ Private water supply

If private water supply, please give details:

☐

Sewerage: ☐ Mains sewerage ☐ Septic tank ☐ Cesspool
☐ Small sewage treatment plant

Heating: ☐ Mains gas ☐ Electric ☐ Oil ☐ LPG ☐ Biofuel
☐ Ground source heat pump ☐ Air source heat pump ☐ Other

If Other, please specify:

5.2 Which of the following services are available at the property?

Broadband: ☐ Yes ☐ No

Broadband type is available here: **https://www.openreach.com/fibre-checker**
Broadband coverage is available here: **https://checker.ofcom.org.uk/en-gb/broadband-coverage**

Mobile signal: ☐ Yes ☐ No

Mobile signal coverage is available here: **https://checker.ofcom.org.uk/en-gb/mobile-coverage**

Are there any known issues or areas of restricted coverage with the mobile signal? ☐ Yes ☐ No

If Yes, please give details:

6. Parking

6.1 Is off-road parking available? ☐ Yes ☐ No
For example, is there a garage, allocated space or driveway?

Please specify the type of parking available

6.2 Is a permit required for on-road parking? ☐ Yes ☐ No
For example, is the property in a controlled parking zone or within a local authority residents' parking scheme?

6.3 If a permit is required, what is the current annual charge? £

6.4 Does the property have an electric vehicle (EV) charging point? ☐ Yes ☐ No

If Yes, please specify the make and its location:

PART C MATERIAL INFORMATION

7. Building Safety

7.1 Are you aware of any defects or hazards at the property that might lead to a fire or a structural failure? ☐ Yes ☐ No

Note: This could include, for example, integrity of building materials used in construction of the property (e.g. asbestos, cladding), structural hazards (damaged roofs, balconies), or non-operative fire/smoke alarm systems.

If Yes, please give details:

7.2 If Yes, have urgent or essential works been recommended? ☐ Yes ☐ No

(a) Are there any proposals for these works to be carried out? ☐ Yes ☐ No

(b) Have these works been carried out? ☐ Yes ☐ No

If Yes, please provide further details and/or relevant documents. ☐ Attached ☐ To follow

8. Restrictions

Conservation area

8.1 Is the property (or any part of it) in a conservation area? ☐ Yes ☐ No ☐ Not sure

If Yes, please supply a copy of any relevant documents: ☐ Attached ☐ To follow

Listed buildings

8.2 Is the property (or any part of it) listed? ☐ Yes ☐ No
To check the list, go to:
England: **https://historicengland.org.uk/listing/the-list/**
Wales: **https://cadw.gov.wales/advice-support/cof-cymru/search-cadw-records**

8.3 If Yes, what grade is the listing? ☐ Grade I ☐ Grade II* ☐ Grade II

If Yes, please provide a copy of any relevant documents, e.g. notice of listing, letter from local authority confirming listing ☐ Attached ☐ To follow

Restrictive covenants

Note: To answer this question, you will need a copy of your registered title document (if your title is registered at HM Land Registry) or your deeds (if it is not registered). If you don't have them, ask your solicitor.

8.4 Does your title contain any restrictive covenants affecting the use of the property? ☐ Yes ☐ No

Please provide a copy of your title and any other relevant documents ☐ Attached ☐ To follow

Tree preservation orders

8.5 Are any trees on your property subject to a Tree Preservation Order? ☐ Yes ☐ No ☐ Not sure
Information about tree preservation orders is available at:
https://www.gov.uk/guidance/tree-preservation-orders-and-trees-in-conservation-areas

(a) Have the terms of the order been complied with? ☐ Yes ☐ No ☐ Not sure

(b) Please provide a copy of any relevant documents. ☐ Attached ☐ To follow

9. Rights and informal arrangements

Note: Rights and arrangements may relate to access or shared use. They may also include rights to mines and minerals, manorial rights, chancel repair, and similar matters. If you are uncertain about whether a right or arrangement is covered by this question, please ask your solicitor.

9.1 Does the property benefit from any rights or arrangements over any neighbouring property (this includes any rights of way)?

☐ Yes ☐ No ☐ Not known

If Yes, please give details:

9.2 Does ownership of the property carry a responsibility to contribute towards the cost of any jointly used services, such as maintenance of a shared driveway, a boundary or drain?

☐ Yes ☐ No ☐ Not known

If Yes, please give details:

9.3 Has anyone taken steps to prevent access to the property or complained about or demanded payment for access to the property?

☐ Yes ☐ No

If Yes, please give details:

9.4 Do you know if any of the following rights benefit the property:

(a) Rights of light? ☐ Yes ☐ No

(b) Rights of support from adjoining properties? ☐ Yes ☐ No

(c) Customary rights (e.g. rights deriving from local traditions)? ☐ Yes ☐ No

9.5 Do you know if any of the following arrangements affect the property:

(a) Other people's rights to mines and minerals under the land? ☐ Yes ☐ No

(b) Chancel repair liability? ☐ Yes ☐ No

(c) Other people's rights to take things from the land (such as timber, hay or fish)? ☐ Yes ☐ No

If Yes, please give details:

9.6 Do you know if there are any other rights or arrangements affecting the property? This includes any rights of way. ☐ Yes ☐ No

If Yes, please give details:

Services crossing the property or neighbouring property

9.7 Do any drains, pipes or wires serving the property cross any neighbour's property? ☐ Yes ☐ No ☐ Not known

9.8 Do any drains, pipes or wires leading to any neighbour's property cross the property? ☐ Yes ☐ No ☐ Not known

9.9 Is there any agreement or arrangement about drains, pipes or wires? ☐ Yes ☐ No ☐ Not known

If Yes, please supply a copy or give details: ☐ Attached ☐ To follow

10. Flood risk

Note: Flooding may take a variety of forms: it may be seasonal, irregular or simply a one-off event. The property does not need to be near a river or coast for flooding to occur.

10.1 What is the flood risk for the area around the property?
Information about the long-term flood risk for the area around the property is available at: **https://www.gov.uk/check-long-term-flood-risk**

10.2 Has any part of the property (buildings, surrounding garden or land) ever been flooded? ☐ Yes ☐ No

(a) When did the flooding take place? (MM/YYYY)

(b) Which parts flooded?

(c) What type of flooding took place?

Ground Water	☐ Yes	☐ No
Sewer flooding	☐ Yes	☐ No
Surface water	☐ Yes	☐ No
Coastal flooding	☐ Yes	☐ No
River flooding	☐ Yes	☐ No
Other	☐ Yes	☐ No

If Yes, please give details:

10.3 Are there any defences to prevent flooding installed at the property? ☐ Yes ☐ No

If Yes, please give details:

Coastal erosion

Note: Information about how coastal erosion is being managed in an area is available at:
https://www.gov.uk/check-coastal-erosion-management-in-your-area

10.4 If the property is near the coast, is there any known risk of coastal erosion affecting the property?

☐ Yes ☐ No
☐ Not applicable

Please give details:

11. Outstanding building work or approvals

11.1 Are you aware of any breaches of planning permission conditions or building regulations consent conditions, unfinished work or work that does not have all necessary consents?

☐ Yes ☐ No

If Yes, please give details:

11.2 Are there any planning or building control issues to resolve?

☐ Yes ☐ No

If Yes, please give details:

12. Notices and proposals

12.1 Have any notices or correspondence been received or sent (e.g. from or to a neighbour, council or government department), or any negotiations or discussions taken place, which affect the property or a property nearby?

☐ Yes ☐ No

If Yes, please give details:

12.2 Are you aware of any plans or proposals to develop property or land nearby? ☐ Yes ☐ No

If Yes, please give details:

12.3 Are you aware of any proposals to make alterations to or change the use of buildings nearby? ☐ Yes ☐ No

If Yes, please give details:

13. Accessibility

Does the property have:

(a) Step free access from the street to inside the property (e.g. ramps / lifts)? ☐ Yes ☐ No

(b) Wet room / level access shower? ☐ Yes ☐ No

(c) Lateral living (entrance level living accommodation)? ☐ Yes ☐ No

(d) Other accessibility adaptations? ☐ Yes ☐ No

If Yes to 13(a)–(d) please give details:

14. Coalfield or mining area

Note: Information about finding out if a property is affected by coal mining is available at: **https://www.gov.uk/check-if-property-is-affected-by-coal-mining** Your solicitor will also be able to help you with this information.

Are you aware of the property being on a past or present coalfield or directly impacted by the effect of other mining activity? ☐ Yes ☐ No

TA6 PART 2

Note: The *Leasehold Information Form (TA7)* has additional questions for leasehold properties that will need to be completed.

15. Boundaries

Note: If the property is leasehold, section 15 or parts of it (questions 15.1 and 15.2) may not apply.

15.1 Looking towards the property from the road, who owns or accepts responsibility to maintain or repair the boundary features:

(a) on the left?	☐ Seller	☐ Neighbour
______	☐ Shared	☐ Not known
(b) on the right?	☐ Seller	☐ Neighbour
______	☐ Shared	☐ Not known
(c) at the rear?	☐ Seller	☐ Neighbour
______	☐ Shared	☐ Not known
(d) at the front?	☐ Seller	☐ Neighbour
______	☐ Shared	☐ Not known

15.2 If the boundaries are irregular, please indicate ownership by written description or by reference to a plan:

☐ Attached ☐ To follow

15.3 Are you aware of any boundary feature having been moved in the last 10 years or during your period of ownership if longer?

☐ Yes ☐ No

If Yes, please give details:

15.4 During your ownership, has any adjacent land or property been purchased by you?

☐ Yes ☐ No

If Yes, please give details:

15.5 **Does any part of the property or any building on the property overhang or project under the boundary of the neighbouring property or road, for example, cellars under the pavement, overhanging eaves or covered walkways?** ☐ Yes ☐ No

If Yes, please give details:

15.6 **Has any notice been received under the Party Wall etc. Act 1996 in respect of any shared/party boundaries?** ☐ Yes ☐ No

If Yes, please supply a copy and give details of any works carried out or agreed: ☐ Attached ☐ To follow

16. Disputes and complaints

16.1 **Have there been any disputes or complaints about your property or a property nearby?** ☐ Yes ☐ No

If Yes, please give details such as when this took place and who was involved:

16.2 **Are you aware of anything that might lead to a dispute about your property or a property nearby?** ☐ Yes ☐ No

If Yes, please give details:

16.3 **Do any neighbours or members of the public have the right to enter your property?** ☐ Yes ☐ No

If Yes, please give details:

17. Alterations, planning and building work

Note to seller: All relevant approvals and supporting paperwork referred to in this form, such as listed building consents, planning permissions, building regulations consents, and completion certificates, should be provided. If you have had works carried out, you should produce the documentation authorising this. Copies may be obtained from the relevant local authority website. Competent Person Certificates may be obtained from the contractor or the scheme provider (e.g. FENSA or Gas Safe Register). Further information about Competent Person Certificates can be found at: **https://www.gov.uk/guidance/competent-person-scheme-current-schemes-and-how-schemes-are-authorised**

Note to buyer: If any alterations or improvements have been made since the property was last valued for council tax, the sale of the property may trigger a revaluation. This may mean that following completion of the sale, the property will be put into a higher council tax band. Further information about council tax valuation can be found at:
http://www.gov.uk/government/organisations/valuation-office-agency

17.1 Have you made or are you aware that any of the following changes have been or are being made to the property (including the garden)?

Please provide plans and details of any consents that were granted. If you are unsure, please ask or consult your solicitor.

(a) Installing replacement windows, roof windows, roof lights, glazed doors since 1 April 2002	☐ Yes ☐ No
(b) Adding an extension	☐ Yes ☐ No
(c) Adding a conservatory	☐ Yes ☐ No
(d) Loft conversion	☐ Yes ☐ No
(e) Garage conversion	☐ Yes ☐ No
(f) Removal of internal walls	☐ Yes ☐ No
(g) Adding insulation	☐ Yes ☐ No
(h) Other building works or changes to the property	☐ Yes ☐ No

17.2 If Yes to any of the questions in 17.1(a)–(h), please give details of the work and the date it was carried out, or state not known:

(a) Is this work completed?	☐ Yes ☐ No

If No, please give details:

If Yes to any of the questions in 17.1(a)–(h) and if the work was undertaken during your ownership of the property:

(b) Did you get planning permissions, building regulations approvals and completion certificates? ☐ Yes ☐ No

(c) Please supply copies of the planning permissions, building regulations approvals and completion certificates. ☐ Attached ☐ To follow
If you are not sure which documents are relevant, ask your solicitor for help.

(d) If planning permissions, building regulations approvals and completion certificates were not required, explain why:
For instance, if the work was exempt from building regulations or permitted development rights applied.

Information about permitted development is available at:
https://www.gov.uk/guidance/when-is-permission-required

Information about building regulations is available at:
https://www.gov.uk/building-regulations-approval/when-you-dont-need-approval

17.3 **Is any part of the property used exclusively for non-residential purposes?** ☐ Yes ☐ No

If Yes, please give details and supply a copy of any relevant documents: ☐ Attached ☐ To follow

17.4 **Have solar panels been installed at the property?** ☐ Yes ☐ No
Solar panels include any solar photovoltaic (PV) system

If No to question 17.4, please continue to question 18 and do not answer questions 17.4(a)–(l)

(a) Which year were the solar panels installed? (YYYY)

(b) Do you own the solar panels outright? ☐ Yes ☐ No

(c) Has a long lease of the roof / air space been granted to a solar panel provider? A typical long lease may last 20 to 25 years. ☐ Yes ☐ No

If Yes, please supply a copy of the lease agreement. ☐ Attached ☐ To follow

(d) Do you have a maintenance agreement in place for the solar panels? ☐ Yes ☐ No

If Yes, please supply a copy of the agreement. ☐ Attached ☐ To follow

(e) Is there a battery for storing solar power? ☐ Yes ☐ No

If Yes, please provide the make, model and storage capacity in kWh of the battery:

(f) Do the solar photovoltaic (PV) cells feed into the National Grid? ☐ Yes ☐ No

(g) Is there a Feed-in Tariff (FIT) or Smart Export Guarantee (SEG) in place? ☐ Yes ☐ No

If Yes, please supply a copy of the agreement. ☐ Attached ☐ To follow

(h) Please provide a copy of the electricity bill showing the credit paid for the generation ☐ Attached ☐ To follow

(i) Please provide details of the procedure for assigning the benefit of the FIT or SEG agreement on completion of the purchase to the purchaser. ☐ Attached ☐ To follow

(j) Are the panels installed so they are not above the highest part of the roof (excluding the chimney) and project no more than 200mm from the roof slope or wall surface? ☐ Yes ☐ No

(k) Please provide a copy of the building regulations completions certificate or compliance certificate for the installation of the panels and generator. ☐ Attached ☐ To follow

(l) Is the roof of the property sufficient to meet the requirements of the additional weight of the PV cells installed? ☐ Yes ☐ No

If Yes, please provide us with the surveyor's calculations showing the structural adequacy of the roof frame. ☐ Attached ☐ To follow

18. Consent

Do you have consent for any matters that need permission in your deeds?
Check with your solicitor that all necessary consents in your deeds have been received. If you are not sure if permission is needed, ask your solicitor as soon as it is practical. ☐ Yes ☐ No ☐ Not sure

Please give details:

19. Guarantees and warranties

Note to seller: All available guarantees, warranties and supporting paperwork should be supplied before exchange of contracts.

Note to buyer: Some guarantees only operate to protect the person who had the work carried out or may not be valid if their terms have been breached. You may wish to contact the company to establish whether it is still trading and, if so, whether the terms of the guarantee will apply to you.

19.1 Does the property benefit from any of the following guarantees or warranties? If Yes, please supply a copy.

(a) New home warranty (e.g. NHBC or similar)	☐ Yes ☐ No ☐ Attached ☐ To follow
(b) Damp proofing	☐ Yes ☐ No ☐ Attached ☐ To follow
(c) Timber treatment	☐ Yes ☐ No ☐ Attached ☐ To follow
(d) Windows, roof lights, roof windows or glazed doors	☐ Yes ☐ No ☐ Attached ☐ To follow
(e) Electrical work	☐ Yes ☐ No ☐ Attached ☐ To follow
(f) Roofing	☐ Yes ☐ No ☐ Attached ☐ To follow
(g) Heating system	☐ Yes ☐ No ☐ Attached ☐ To follow
(h) Underpinning	☐ Yes ☐ No ☐ Attached ☐ To follow
(i) Insulation	☐ Yes ☐ No ☐ Attached ☐ To follow

(j) Other (please state): ☐ Yes ☐ No ☐ Attached ☐ To follow

19.2 Have any claims been made under any of these guarantees or warranties? ☐ Yes ☐ No

If Yes, please give details:

20. Insurance

20.1 Do you insure the property? ☐ Yes ☐ No

If No, who insures the property?

20.2 Have you ever had difficulty obtaining insurance for the property? ☐ Yes ☐ No

If Yes, please give details:

20.3 Has your property insurance ever been subject to special conditions? ☐ Yes ☐ No

If Yes, please give details:

20.4 Have you made any buildings insurance claims? ☐ Yes ☐ No

If Yes, please give details:

21. Occupiers

21.1 Do you live at the property? ☐ Yes ☐ No

21.2 Does anyone else, aged 17 or over, live at the property? ☐ Yes ☐ No

(a) Please state the full names of any occupiers (other than yourself) aged 17 or over:

1 First name Middle name(s) Last name	2 First name Middle name(s) Last name
3 First name Middle name(s) Last name	4 First name Middle name(s) Last name

(b) Are any of the occupiers who are aged 17 or over (other than yourself) tenants or lodgers? ☐ Yes ☐ No

21.3 Is the property being sold with vacant possession? ☐ Yes ☐ No
When buying or selling a property, 'vacant possession' means it will be empty of all occupiers and emptied of anything not contracted to remain on the day of completion e.g. all possessions, furniture and rubbish.

21.4 Have all the occupiers aged 17 or over agreed to sign the sale contract? ☐ Yes ☐ No

21.5 If the property is not being sold with vacant possession, please provide details of all occupiers and copies of their tenancy agreements. ☐ Attached ☐ To follow

22. Connection to services

22.1 Please give details for each of the services that are connected to the property:

Mains electricity	
Provider's name	
Location of meter	
MPAN number	

Mains gas	
Provider's name	
Location of meter	
MPRN number	

Mains water	
Provider's name	
Location of stopcock	
Location of meter (if any)	

Mains sewerage	
Provider's name	

Small sewage treatment plant	
Provider's name	
Make / model	
Service provider's name	

Telephone	
Provider's name	

Broadband	
Provider's name	

Ground and air source heat pumps

Provider's name	
Make / model	
Service provider's name	

If there are any 'Other' services listed in question 5.1, please give details:

Electricity

Note: If the seller does not have the certificate requested below, this can be obtained from the relevant Competent Person Scheme. Further information about Competent Person Schemes can be found at: **https://www.gov.uk/guidance/competent-person-scheme-current-schemes-and-how-schemes-are-authorised**

22.2 Has the whole or any part of the electrical installation been tested by a qualified and registered electrician? ☐ Yes ☐ No

If Yes, please state the year it was tested and provide a copy of the test certificate. ☐ Year ☐ Attached ☐ To follow

22.3 Has the property been rewired or had any electrical installation work carried out since 1 January 2005? ☐ Yes ☐ No ☐ Not known

If Yes, please supply one of the following:

(a) a copy of the signed BS7671 Electrical Safety Certificate ☐ Attached ☐ To follow

(b) the installer's Building Regulations Compliance Certificate ☐ Attached ☐ To follow

(c) the Building Control Completion Certificate ☐ Attached ☐ To follow

Heating

22.4 How is the property heated?
Please tick all that apply

☐ Mains gas ☐ Oil ☐ Heat pumps
☐ Liquid gas ☐ Electricity ☐ Underfloor
☐ Woodburning / multi-fuel stove ☐ Other

(a) When was the boiler installed? (DD/MM/YYYY) — ☐ Date ☐ Not known

(b) When was the heating system installed? (DD/MM/YYYY) — ☐ Date ☐ Not known

(c) Please supply the installation documentation e.g. Gas Safe Register or CORGI certificates for gas boilers and compliance certificates (e.g. HETAS) for other appliances. — ☐ Attached ☐ To follow

(d) Is the boiler/heating system in good working order? — ☐ Yes ☐ No

(e) In what year was the boiler/heating system last serviced/maintained? — ☐ Year ☐ Not known

(f) Please supply a copy of the inspection report. — ☐ Attached ☐ To follow ☐ Not available

(g) If there is more than one heating system, please attach answers to 22.4(a)–(f) separately — ☐ Attached ☐ To follow

Drainage and sewerage

Note: General information about discharges to surface water and groundwater and environmental permits can be found at: **https://www.gov.uk/guidance/discharges-to-surface-water-and-groundwater-environmental-permits**

Note: Information about planning permission, building regulations, general binding rules, and permits governing septic tanks, sewage treatment plants, and cesspools can be found at: **www.gov.uk/permits-you-need-for-septic-tanks**

22.5 Is the property connected to mains:

(a) foul water drainage? — ☐ Yes ☐ No ☐ Not known

(b) surface water drainage? — ☐ Yes ☐ No ☐ Not known

22.6 Is sewerage for any part of the property provided by:

(a) a septic tank? — ☐ Yes ☐ No

(b) a sewage treatment plant? — ☐ Yes ☐ No

(c) cesspool? — ☐ Yes ☐ No

If your answer is Yes to any question in 22.6(a)–(c), please answer questions 22.7–22.14 below. Otherwise continue to question 23.

22.7 When was the system installed? (MM/YYYY) — ☐ Month/Year

22.8 When was the sewerage system last replaced or upgraded? (MM/YYYY) ☐ Month/Year

22.9 If a cesspool, when was the container last emptied? (MM/YYYY) ☐ Month/Year

22.10 If the property is served by a sewage treatment plant, when was the treatment plant last serviced? (MM/YYYY) ☐ Month/Year

22.11 Does the sewerage system discharge to the ground or to surface water? ☐ Ground ☐ Surface water

22.12 If the sewerage system discharges to the ground, does it have an infiltration system? ☐ Yes ☐ No

22.13 Is the use of the sewerage system shared with other properties? If Yes, how many properties share the system? ☐ Yes ☐ No ☐ Properties share

22.14 Is any part of the sewerage system, or the access to it, outside the boundary of the property? If Yes, please supply a plan showing the location of the system and how access is obtained. ☐ Yes ☐ No ☐ Attached ☐ To follow

23. Environmental matters

Energy efficiency

Note: An Energy Performance Certificate (EPC) is a document that gives information about a property's energy usage. Further information about EPCs can be found at: **https://www.gov.uk/buy-sell-your-home/energy-performance-certificates**

23.1 Please supply a copy of the EPC for the property ☐ Attached ☐ To follow

23.2 Have any installations in the property been financed under the Green Deal scheme? ☐ Yes ☐ No

If Yes, please give details of all installations and supply a copy of your last electricity bill. ☐ Attached ☐ To follow

Japanese knotweed

Note: Please see the ***Explanatory Notes for Sellers and Buyers*** for further information about Japanese knotweed.

23.3 Is the property, or an area adjacent to or abutting the boundary, affected by Japanese knotweed?

☐ Yes ☐ No
☐ Not known

If Yes, please state whether there is a Japanese knotweed management and treatment plan in place and supply a copy with any insurance cover linked to the plan.

☐ Yes ☐ No
☐ Not known
☐ Attached ☐ To follow

Radon

Note: Radon is a naturally occurring inert radioactive gas found in the ground. Some parts of England and Wales are more adversely affected by it than others. Remedial action is advised for properties with a test result above the 'recommended action level'. Further information about Radon can be found at: **https://www.gov.uk/government/collections/radon**

23.4 Has a Radon test been carried out on the property?

☐ Yes ☐ No

If Yes:

(a) please supply a copy of the report

☐ Attached ☐ To follow

(b) was the test result below the 'recommended action level'?

☐ Yes ☐ No

23.5 Were any remedial measures undertaken on construction to reduce Radon gas levels in the property?

☐ Yes ☐ No
☐ Not known

24. Transaction information

24.1 Is this sale dependent on the seller completing the purchase of another property on the same day?

☐ Yes ☐ No

24.2 Does the seller have any special requirements about a moving date? If Yes, please give details:

☐ Yes ☐ No

24.3 Will the sale price be sufficient to repay all mortgages and charges secured on the property?

☐ Yes ☐ No
☐ No mortgage

24.4 Will the seller ensure that:

(a) all rubbish is removed from the property (including from the loft, garden, outbuildings, garages and sheds) and that the property will be left in a clean and tidy condition? ☐ Yes ☐ No

(b) if light fittings are removed, the fittings will be replaced with ceiling rose, flex, bulb holder and bulb? ☐ Yes ☐ No

(c) reasonable care will be taken when removing any other fittings or contents? ☐ Yes ☐ No

(d) keys to all windows and doors and details of alarm codes will be left at the property or with the estate agent? ☐ Yes ☐ No

25. Additional information

If there is any further information about any of your answers on this form, please provide them below and/or supply additional documents. ☐ Attached ☐ To follow

Please tick to confirm:

☐ **I/We have considered the answers given on this form carefully and understand they will be relied upon by the buyer.**

Each seller should sign this form.

Signed: ____________________ Dated: ____________

Signed: ____________________ Dated: ____________

Signed: ____________________ Dated: ____________

Signed: ____________________ Dated: ____________

